Deep Learning with TensorFlow and Keras

Third Edition

Build and deploy supervised, unsupervised, deep, and reinforcement learning models

Amita Kapoor

Antonio Gulli

Sujit Pal

BIRMINGHAM—MUMBAI

Deep Learning with TensorFlow and Keras
Third Edition

Lead Senior Publishing Product Manager: Tushar Gupta
Acquisition Editor – Peer Reviews: Gaurav Gavas
Project Editor: Namrata Katare
Content Development Editor: Bhavesh Amin
Copy Editor: Safis Editing
Technical Editor: Aniket Shetty
Proofreader: Safis Editing
Indexer: Rekha Nair
Presentation Designer: Ganesh Bhadwalkar

First published: April 2017
Second edition: December 2019
Third edition: October 2022

Production reference: 1300922

Published by Packt Publishing Ltd.
Livery Place
35 Livery Street
Birmingham
B3 2PB, UK.

ISBN 978-1-80323-291-1

www.packt.com

Foreword

Approachable, well-written, with a great balance between theory and practice. A very enjoyable introduction to machine learning for software developers.

François Chollet,

Creator of Keras

Contributors

About the authors

Amita Kapoor taught and supervised research in the field of neural networks and artificial intelligence for 20+ years as an Associate Professor at the University of Delhi. At present, she works as an independent AI consultant and provides her expertise to various organizations working in the field of AI and EdTech.

First and foremost, I am thankful to the readers of this book. It is your encouragement via messages and emails that motivate me to give my best. I am extremely thankful to my co-authors, Antonio Gulli and Sujit Pal, for sharing their vast experience with me in writing this book. I am thankful to the entire Packt team for the effort they put in since the inception of this book and the reviewers who painstakingly went through the content and verified the code; their comments and suggestions helped improve the book.

Last but not the least, I am thankful to my teachers for their faith in me, my colleagues at the University of Delhi for their love and support, my friends for continuously motivating me, and my family members for their patience and love.

A part of the royalties of the book are donated.

Antonio Gulli has a passion for establishing and managing global technological talent for innovation and execution. His core expertise is in cloud computing, deep learning, and search engines. Currently, Antonio works for Google in the Cloud Office of the CTO in Zurich, working on Search, Cloud Infra, Sovereignty, and Conversational AI. Previously, he served as a founding member of the Office of the CTO in the EMEA. Earlier on, he served as Google Warsaw Site Director Leader, growing the site to 450+ engineers fully focused on cloud managing teams in GCE, Kubernetes, Serverless, Borg, and Console.

So far, Antonio has been lucky enough to gain professional experience in five countries in Europe and to manage teams in six countries in EMEA and the U.S:

- In Amsterdam, as Vice President for Elsevier, a leading scientific publisher.
- In London, as Principal Engineer for Bing Search, Microsoft.

- In Italy and the U.K, as CTO, Europe for Ask.com.
- In Poland, the U.K, and Switzerland with Google.

Antonio has co-invented a number of technologies for search, smart energy, and AI with 11 patents issued (21 applied) and published several books on coding and machine learning also translated into Japanese and Chinese. He speaks Spanish, English, and Italian and is currently learning Polish and French. Antonio is a proud father of Two boys, Lorenzo, 21 and Leonardo, 16, and a little queen, Aurora, 11.

I want to thank my sons, Lorenzo and Leonardo, and my daughter, Aurora, for being the motivation behind my perseverance. Also, I want to thank my partner, Nina, for being the North Star of my life in recent years.

Sujit Pal is a Technology Research Director at Elsevier Labs, an advanced technology group within the Reed-Elsevier Group of companies. His interests include semantic search, natural language processing, machine learning, and deep learning. At Elsevier, he has worked on several initiatives involving search quality measurement and improvement, image classification and duplicate detection, and annotation and ontology development for medical and scientific corpora.

About the reviewer

Raghav Bali is a seasoned data science professional with over a decade's experience in the research and development of large-scale solutions in finance, digital experience, IT infrastructure, and healthcare for giants such as Intel, American Express, UnitedHealth Group, and Delivery Hero. He is an innovator with 7+ patents, a published author of multiple well-received books (including *Hands-On Transfer Learning with Python*), has peer reviewed papers, and is a regular speaker in leading conferences on topics in the areas of machine learning, deep learning, computer vision, NLP, generative models, and augmented reality.

I would like to take this opportunity to congratulate the authors on yet another amazing book. Thanks to Packt for bringing me on board as a reviewer for this book, particularly Namrata, Saby, and Tushar for all their support and assistance and for being so receptive throughout the review process. And finally, I'd like to thank my wife, family, and colleagues for all the support and patience.

Join our book's Discord space

Join our Discord community to meet like-minded people and learn alongside more than 2000 members at: `https://packt.link/keras`

Table of Contents

Chapter 10: Self-Supervised Learning 361

Chapter 14: The Math Behind Deep Learning   473

Chapter 17: Graph Neural Networks 531

Chapter 18: Machine Learning Best Practices 563

Preface

Deep Learning with TensorFlow and Keras, Third Edition, is a concise yet thorough introduction to modern neural networks, artificial intelligence, and deep learning technologies designed especially for software engineers and data scientists. The book is the natural follow-up of the books *Deep Learning with Keras* [1] and *TensorFlow 1.x Deep Learning Cookbook* [2] previously written by the same authors.

This book provides a very detailed panorama of the evolution of learning technologies over the past six years. The book presents dozens of working deep neural networks coded in Python using TensorFlow 2.x, a modular network library based on Keras-like APIs [1].

Artificial Intelligence (**AI**) lays the ground for everything this book discusses. **Machine Learning** (**ML**) is a branch of AI, and **Deep Learning** (**DL**) is in turn a subset of ML. This section will briefly discuss these three concepts, which you will regularly encounter throughout the rest of this book.

AI denotes any activity where machines mimic intelligent behaviors typically shown by humans. More formally, it is a research field in which machines aim to replicate cognitive capabilities such as learning behaviors, proactive interaction with the environment, inference and deduction, computer vision, speech recognition, problem-solving, knowledge representation, and perception. AI builds on elements of computer science, mathematics, and statistics, as well as psychology and other sciences studying human behaviors. There are multiple strategies for building AI. During the 1970s and 1980s, "expert" systems became extremely popular. The goal of these systems was to solve complex problems by representing the knowledge with a large number of manually defined if-then rules. This approach worked for small problems on very specific domains, but it was not able to scale up for larger problems and multiple domains. Later, AI focused more and more on methods based on statistical methods that are part of ML.

ML is a subdiscipline of AI that focuses on teaching computers how to learn without the need to be programmed for specific tasks. The key idea behind ML is that it is possible to create algorithms that learn from, and make predictions on, data. There are three different broad categories of ML:

- **Supervised learning**, in which the machine is presented with input data and the desired output, and the goal is to learn from those training examples in such a way that meaningful predictions can be made for data that the machine has never observed before.
- **Unsupervised learning**, in which the machine is presented with input data only, and the machine has to subsequently find some meaningful structure by itself, with no external supervision or input.

- **Reinforcement learning**, in which the machine acts as an agent, interacting with the environment. The machine is provided with "rewards" for behaving in a desired manner, and "penalties" for behaving in an undesired manner. The machine attempts to maximize rewards by learning to develop its behavior accordingly.

DL took the world by storm in 2012. During that year, the ImageNet 2012 challenge was launched with the goal of predicting the content of photographs using a subset of a large hand-labeled dataset. A deep learning model named AlexNet achieved a top-5 error rate of 15.3%, a significant improvement with respect to previous state-of-the-art results. According to the Economist, *Suddenly people started to pay attention, not just within the AI community but across the technology industry as a whole.*

That was only the beginning. Today, DL techniques are successfully applied in heterogeneous domains including, but not limited to, healthcare, environment, green energy, computer vision, text analysis, multimedia, finance, retail, gaming, simulation, industry, robotics, and self-driving cars. In each of these domains, DL techniques can solve problems with a level of accuracy that was not possible using previous methods.

Looking back at the past eight years, it is fascinating and exciting to see the extent of the contributions that DL has made to science and industry. There is no reason to believe that the next eight years will see any less contribution; indeed, as the field of DL continues to advance, we anticipate that we'll see even more exciting and fascinating contributions provided by DL.

This book introduces you to the magic of deep learning. We will start with simple models and progressively will introduce increasingly sophisticated models. The approach will always be hands-on, with a healthy dose of code to work with.

Who this book is for

If you are a data scientist with experience in ML or an AI programmer with some exposure to neural networks, you will find this book a useful entry point to DL with TensorFlow. If you are a software engineer with a growing interest in the DL tsunami, you will find this book a foundational platform to broaden your knowledge on the topic. Basic knowledge of Python is required for this book.

What this book covers

Chapter 1, Neural Network Foundations with TF, is where we learn the basics of TensorFlow, an open-source library developed by Google for machine learning and deep learning. In addition, we introduce the basics of neural networks and deep learning, two areas of machine learning that had incredible growth during the last few years. The idea behind this chapter is to provide all the tools needed to do basic but fully hands-on deep learning.

Chapter 2, Regression and Classification, focuses on the fundamental tasks in ML techniques: regression and classification. We will learn how to use TensorFlow to build simple, multiple, and multivariate regression models. We will use logistic regression to solve a multi-class classification problem.

Chapter 3, Convolutional Neural Networks, covers how to use deep learning ConvNets for recognizing MNIST handwritten characters with high accuracy.

We use the CIFAR 10 dataset to build a deep learning classifier with 10 categories, and the ImageNet dataset to build an accurate classifier with 1,000 categories. In addition, we investigate how to use large deep learning networks such as VGG16 and very deep networks such as InceptionV3. We will conclude with a discussion on transfer learning

Chapter 4, Word Embeddings, is where we describe the origins of and theory behind distributed representations and word embeddings and chart the progress of word embeddings from static word-based embeddings more dynamic and expressive embeddings based on sentences and paragraphs. We also explore how the idea of word embeddings can be extended to include non-word sequences as well, such as nodes in a graph or user sessions in a web application. The chapter also contains multiple examples of using word embeddings of various kinds.

Chapter 5, Recurrent Neural Networks, describes an important architectural subclass of neural networks that are optimized for handling sequence data such as natural language or time series. We describe the important architectures in this genre, such as **LSTM (Long Short-Term Memory)** and **GRU (Gated Recurrent Unit)** and show how they can be extended to handle bidirectional states and states across batches. We also provide examples of using RNNs with various topologies for specific tasks, such as generating text, sentiment analysis, and part-of-speech tagging. We also describe the popular seq2seq architecture, which uses a pair of RNNs in an encoder-decoder pipeline to solve a variety of NLP tasks.

Chapter 6, Transformers, covers transformers, a deep learning architecture that has revolutionized the traditional natural language processing field. We start by reviewing the key intuitions behind the architecture and various categories of transformers, together with a deep dive into the most popular models. Then, we focus on implementations both based on the vanilla architecture and on popular libraries, such as Hugging Face and TensorFlow Hub. After that, we briefly discuss evaluation, optimization, and some of the best practices commonly adopted when using transformers. The last section is devoted to reviewing how transformers can be used to perform computer vision tasks, a totally different domain from NLP. That requires a careful definition of the attention mechanism. In the end, attention is all you need! And at the core of attention, there is nothing more than the cosine similarity between vectors.

Chapter 7, Unsupervised Learning, delves into unsupervised learning models. It will cover techniques required for clustering and dimensionality reduction like PCA, k-means, and self-organized maps. It will go into the details of Boltzmann machines and their implementation using TensorFlow. The concepts covered will be extended to build **Restricted Boltzmann Machines (RBMs)**.

Chapter 8, Autoencoders, describes autoencoders, a class of neural networks that attempt to recreate the input as its target. It will cover different varieties of autoencoders like sparse autoencoders, convolutional autoencoders, and denoising autoencoders. The chapter will train a denoising autoencoder to remove noise from input images. It will demonstrate how autoencoders can be used to create MNIST digits. It will also cover the steps involved in building an LSTM autoencoder to generate sentence vectors. Finally, we will learn how to build a variational autoencoder to generate images.

Chapter 9, Generative Models, focuses on **Generative Adversarial Networks (GANs)**. We start with the first proposed GAN model and use it to forge MNIST characters. The chapter shows you how to use deep convolutional GANs to create celebrity images.

The chapter discusses the various GAN architectures like SRGAN, InfoGAN, and CycleGAN. The chapter covers a range of cool GAN applications. Finally, the chapter concludes with a TensorFlow implementation of CycleGAN to convert winter-summer images.

Chapter 10, Self-Supervised Learning, provides an overview of various strategies used for self-supervised learning in computer vision, audio, and natural language processing. It covers self-prediction through strategies such as autoregressive generation, masked generation, relationship prediction, and hybrids of these approaches. It also covers contrastive learning, a popular technique for self-supervised learning, and its application to various pretext tasks in various application domains.

Chapter 11, Reinforcement Learning, focuses on reinforcement learning, covering the Q-learning algorithm and the Bellman equation. The chapter covers discounted rewards, exploration and exploitation, and discount factors. It explains policy-based and model-based reinforcement learning. We will build a **Deep Q-learning Network (DQN)** to play an Atari game. And finally, we learn how to train agents using the policy gradient algorithm.

Chapter 12, Probabilistic TensorFlow, introduces TensorFlow Probability, the library built over TensorFlow to perform probabilistic reasoning and statistical analysis. The chapter demonstrates how to use TensorFlow Probability to generate synthetic data. We will build Bayesian networks and perform inference. The chapter also introduces the concept of uncertainty, aleatory and epistemic, and how to calculate the uncertainty of your trained models.

Chapter 13, An Introduction to AutoML, introduces AutoML, whose goal is to enable domain experts who are unfamiliar with machine learning technologies to use ML techniques easily. We will go through a practical exercise using Google Cloud Platform and do quite a bit of hands-on work after briefly discussing the fundamentals. The chapter covers automatic data preparation, automatic feature engineering, and automatic model generation. Then, we introduce AutoKeras and Google Cloud AutoML with its multiple solutions for table, vision, text, translation, and video processing.

Chapter 14, The Math Behind Deep Learning, covers the math behind deep learning. This topic is quite advanced and not necessarily required for practitioners. However, it is recommended reading to understand what is going on "under the hood" when we play with neural networks. We start with a historical introduction, and then we will review the high school concept of derivatives and gradients and introduce the gradient descent and backpropagation algorithms commonly used to optimize deep learning networks.

Chapter 15, Tensor Processing Unit, discusses TPUs. TPUs are very special ASIC chips developed at Google for executing neural network mathematical operations in an ultra-fast manner. The core of the computation is a systolic multiplier that computes multiple dot products (row * column) in parallel, thus accelerating the computation of basic deep learning operations. Think of a TPU as a special-purpose co-processor for deep learning that is focused on matrix or tensor operations. We will review the four generations of TPUs so far, plus an additional Edge TPU for IoT.

Chapter 16, Other Useful Deep Learning Libraries, introduces other deep learning frameworks. We will explore Hugging Face, OpenAI's GPT3, and DALL-E 2. The chapter introduces another very popular deep learning framework, PyTorch. We also cover H2O.ai and its AutoML module. The chapter also briefly discusses the ONNX open-source format for deep learning models.

Chapter 17, *Graph Neural Networks*, introduces graphs and graph machine learning, with particular emphasis on graph neural networks and the popular **Deep Graph Library** (**DGL**). We describe the theory behind various commonly used graph layers used in GNNs (and available in DGL) and provide examples of GNNs used for node classification, link prediction, and graph classification. We also show how to work with your own graph dataset and customize graph layers to create novel GNN architectures. We then cover more cutting-edge advances in the field of Graph ML, such as heterogeneous graphs and temporal graphs.

Chapter 18, *Machine Learning Best Practices*, focuses on strategies and practices to follow to get the best model in training and production. The chapter discusses the best practices from two different perspectives: the best practices for the data and the best practices with respect to models.

Chapter 19, *TensorFlow 2 Ecosystem*, lays out the different components of the TensorFlow ecosystem. We introduce TensorFlow Hub, a repository for pretrained deep learning models. The chapter talks about TensorFlow Datasets – a collection of ready-to-use datasets. We will also talk about TensorFlow Lite and TensorFlow JS – the framework for mobile and embedded systems and the web. Finally, the chapter talks about federated learning, a decentralized machine learning framework.

Chapter 20, *Advanced Convolutional Neural Networks*, shows more advanced uses for **convolutional neural networks** (**CNNs**). We will explore how CNNs can be applied within the areas of computer vision, video, textual documents, audio, and music. We'll conclude with a section summarizing convolution operations.

Download the example code files

The code bundle for the book is hosted on GitHub at `https://packt.link/dltf`. We also have other code bundles from our rich catalog of books and videos available at `https://github.com/PacktPublishing/`. Check them out!

Download the color images

We also provide a PDF file that has color images of the screenshots/diagrams used in this book. You can download it here: `https://static.packt-cdn.com/downloads/9781803232911_ColorImages.pdf`.

Conventions used

There are a number of text conventions used throughout this book.

`CodeInText`: Indicates code words in the text, database table names, folder names, filenames, file extensions, pathnames, dummy URLs, user input, and Twitter handles. For example: "Each neuron can be initialized with specific weights via the `'kernel_initializer'` parameter."

A block of code is set as follows:

```
# Build the model.
model = tf.keras.models.Sequential()
model.add(keras.layers.Dense(NB_CLASSES,
           input_shape=(RESHAPED,),
```

```
            name='dense_layer',
            activation='softmax'))
```

When we wish to draw your attention to a particular part of a code block, the relevant lines or items are highlighted:

```
# Build the model.
model = tf.keras.models.Sequential()
model.add(keras.layers.Dense(NB_CLASSES,
            input_shape=(RESHAPED,),
            name='dense_layer',
            activation='softmax'))
```

Any command-line input or output is written as follows:

```
pip install gym
```

Bold: Indicates a new term, an important word, or words that you see on the screen. For instance, words in menus or dialog boxes appear in the text like this. For example: "A **Deep Convolutional Neural Network (DCNN)** consists of many neural network layers."

 Warnings or important notes appear like this.

 Tips and tricks appear like this.

Get in touch

Feedback from our readers is always welcome.

General feedback: Email feedback@packtpub.com and mention the book's title in the subject of your message. If you have questions about any aspect of this book, please email us at questions@packtpub.com.

Errata: Although we have taken every care to ensure the accuracy of our content, mistakes do happen. If you have found a mistake in this book, we would be grateful if you reported this to us. Please visit http://www.packtpub.com/submit-errata, click **Submit Errata**, and fill in the form.

Piracy: If you come across any illegal copies of our works in any form on the internet, we would be grateful if you would provide us with the location address or website name. Please contact us at copyright@packtpub.com with a link to the material.

If you are interested in becoming an author: If there is a topic that you have expertise in and you are interested in either writing or contributing to a book, please visit http://authors.packtpub.com.

References

1. *Deep Learning with Keras: Implementing deep learning models and neural networks with the power of Python*, Paperback – 26 Apr 2017, Antonio Gulli, Sujit Pal

2. *TensorFlow 1.x Deep Learning Cookbook*: *Over 90 unique recipes to solve artificial-intelligence driven problems with Python*, Antonio Gulli, Amita Kapoor

Share your thoughts

Once you've read *Deep Learning with TensorFlow and Keras, Third Edition*, we'd love to hear your thoughts! Scan the QR code below to go straight to the Amazon review page for this book and share your feedback.

https://packt.link/r/1803232919

Your review is important to us and the tech community and will help us make sure we're delivering excellent quality content.

1

Neural Network Foundations with TF

In this chapter, we learn the basics of TensorFlow, an open-source library developed by Google for machine learning and deep learning. In addition, we introduce the basics of neural networks and deep learning, two areas of machine learning that have had incredible Cambrian growth during the last few years. The idea behind this chapter is to provide all the tools needed to do basic but fully hands-on deep learning.

We will learn:

- What TensorFlow and Keras are
- An introduction to neural networks
- What the perceptron and multi-layer perceptron are
- A real example: recognizing handwritten digits

 All the code files for this chapter can be found at https://packt.link/dltfchp1.

Let's begin!

What is TensorFlow (TF)?

TensorFlow is a powerful open-source software library developed by the Google Brain Team for deep neural networks, the topic covered in this book. It was first made available under the Apache 2.0 License in November 2015 and has since grown rapidly; as of May 2022, its GitHub repository (https://github.com/tensorflow/tensorflow) has more than 129,000 commits, with roughly 3,100 contributors. This in itself provides a measure of the popularity of TensorFlow.

Let us first learn what exactly TensorFlow is and why it is so popular among deep neural network researchers and engineers. Google calls it "an open-source software library for machine intelligence," but since there are so many other deep learning libraries like PyTorch (https://pytorch.org/), Caffe (https://caffe.berkeleyvision.org/), and MXNet (https://mxnet.apache.org/), what makes TensorFlow special? Most other deep learning libraries, like TensorFlow, have auto-differentiation (a useful mathematical tool used for optimization), many are open-source platforms. Most of them support the CPU/GPU option, have pretrained models, and support commonly used NN architectures like recurrent neural networks, convolutional neural networks, and deep belief networks. So, what else is there in TensorFlow? Let me list the top features:

- It works with all popular languages such as Python, C++, Java, R, and Go. TensorFlow provides stable Python and C++ APIs, as well as a non-guaranteed backward-compatible API for other languages.

- Keras – a high-level neural network API that has been integrated with TensorFlow (in 2.0 Keras became the standard API for interacting with TensorFlow). This API specifies how software components should interact.

- TensorFlow allows model deployment and ease of use in production.

- Most importantly, TensorFlow has very good community support.

The number of stars on GitHub (see *Figure 1.1*) is a measure of popularity for all open-source projects. As of May 2022, TensorFlow, Keras, and PyTorch have 165K, 55K, and 56K stars respectively, which makes TensorFlow the most popular framework for machine learning:

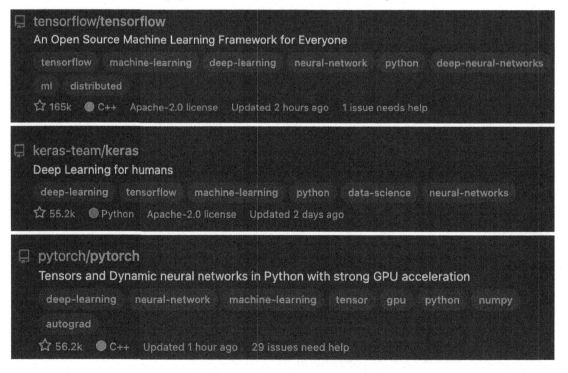

Figure 1.1: Number of stars for various deep learning projects on GitHub

What is Keras?

Keras is a beautiful API for composing building blocks to create and train deep learning models. Keras can be integrated with multiple deep learning engines including Google TensorFlow, Microsoft CNTK, Amazon MXNet, and Theano. Starting with TensorFlow 2.0, Keras, the API developed by François Chollet, has been adopted as the standard high-level API, largely simplifying coding and making programming more intuitive.

Introduction to neural networks

Artificial neural networks (briefly, "nets" or ANNs) represent a class of machine learning models loosely inspired by studies about the central nervous systems of mammals. Each ANN is made up of several interconnected "neurons," organized in "layers." Neurons in one layer pass messages to neurons in the next layer (they "fire," in jargon terms) and this is how the network computes things. Initial studies were started in the early 1950s with the introduction of the "perceptron" [1], a two-layer network used for simple operations, and further expanded in the late 1960s with the introduction of the "back-propagation" algorithm used for efficient multi-layer network training (according to [2] and [3]). Some studies argue that these techniques have roots dating further back than normally cited [4].

Neural networks were a topic of intensive academic studies up until the 1980s, at which point other simpler approaches became more relevant. However, there has been a resurgence of interest since the mid 2000s, mainly thanks to three factors: a breakthrough fast learning algorithm proposed by G. Hinton [3], [5], and [6]; the introduction of GPUs around 2011 for massive numeric computation; and the availability of big collections of data for training.

These improvements opened the route for modern "deep learning," a class of neural networks characterized by a significant number of layers of neurons that are able to learn rather sophisticated models, based on progressive levels of abstraction. People began referring to it as "deep" when it started utilizing 3–5 layers a few years ago. Now, networks with more than 200 layers are commonplace!

This learning via progressive abstraction resembles vision models that have evolved over millions of years within the human brain. Indeed, the human visual system is organized into different layers. First, our eyes are connected to an area of the brain named the visual cortex (V1), which is located in the lower posterior part of our brain. This area is common to many mammals and has the role of discriminating basic properties like small changes in visual orientation, spatial frequencies, and colors.

It has been estimated that V1 consists of about 140 million neurons, with tens of billions of connections between them. V1 is then connected to other areas, V2, V3, V4, V5, and V6 doing progressively more complex image processing and recognition of more sophisticated concepts, such as shapes, faces, animals, and many more. It has been estimated that there are ~16 billion human cortical neurons and about 10–25% of the human cortex is devoted to vision [7]. Deep learning has taken some inspiration from this layer-based organization of the human visual system: early artificial neuron layers learn basic properties of images while deeper layers learn more sophisticated concepts.

This book covers several major aspects of neural networks by providing working nets in TensorFlow. So, let's start!

Perceptron

The "perceptron" is a simple algorithm that, given an input vector x of m values (x_1, x_2,..., and x_m), often called input features or simply features, outputs either a *1* ("yes") or a *0* ("no"). Mathematically, we define a function:

$$f(x) = \begin{cases} 1 & wx + b > 0 \\ 0 & otherwise \end{cases}$$

Where w is a vector of weights, $w \cdot x$ is the dot product $\sum_{j=1}^{m} w_j x_j$, and b is the bias. If you remember elementary geometry, $wx + b$ defines a boundary hyperplane that changes position according to the values assigned to w and b. Note that a hyperplane is a subspace whose dimension is one fewer than that of its ambient space. See (*Figure 1.2*) for an example:

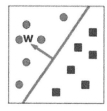

Figure 1.2: An example of a hyperplane

In other words, this is a very simple but effective algorithm! For example, given three input features, the amounts of red, green, and blue in a color, the perceptron could try to decide whether the color is "white" or not.

Note that the perceptron cannot express a "*maybe*" answer. It can answer "yes" (1) or "no" (0) if we understand how to define w and b. This is the "training" process that will be discussed in the following sections.

Our first example of TensorFlow code

There are three ways of creating a model in `tf.keras`: sequential API, functional API, and model subclassing. In this chapter, we will use the simplest one, `Sequential()`, while the other two are discussed in *Chapter 2, Regression and Classification*. A `Sequential()` model is a linear pipeline (a stack) of neural network layers. This code fragment defines a single layer with 10 artificial neurons that expect 784 input variables (also known as features). Note that the net is "dense," meaning that each neuron in a layer is connected to all neurons located in the previous layer, and to all the neurons in the following layer:

```python
import tensorflow as tf
from tensorflow import keras
NB_CLASSES = 10
RESHAPED = 784
model = tf.keras.models.Sequential()
model.add(keras.layers.Dense(NB_CLASSES,
            input_shape=(RESHAPED,), kernel_initializer='zeros',
            name='dense_layer', activation='softmax'))
```

Each neuron can be initialized with specific weights via the `'kernel_initializer'` parameter. There are a few choices, the most common of which are listed below:

- `random_uniform`: Weights are initialized to uniformly random small values in the range (-0.05, 0.05).
- `random_normal`: Weights are initialized according to a Gaussian distribution, with zero mean and a small standard deviation of 0.05. For those of you who are not familiar with a Gaussian distribution, think about a symmetric "bell curve" shape.
- `zero`: All weights are initialized to zero.

A full list is available online (`https://www.tensorflow.org/api_docs/python/tf/keras/initializers`).

Multi-layer perceptron: our first example of a network

In this chapter, we present our first example of a network with multiple dense layers. Historically, "perceptron" was the name given to the model having one single linear layer, and as a consequence, if it has multiple layers, we call it a **Multi-Layer Perceptron** (MLP). Note that the input and the output layers are visible from the outside, while all the other layers in the middle are hidden – hence the name *hidden layers*. In this context, a single layer is simply a linear function and the MLP is therefore obtained by stacking multiple single layers one after the other:

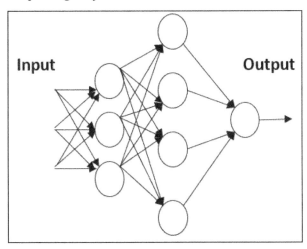

Figure 1.3: An example of multiple layer perceptron

In *Figure 1.3* each node in the first hidden layer receives an input and "fires" (0,1) according to the values of the associated linear function. Then the output of the first hidden layer is passed to the second layer where another linear function is applied, the results of which are passed to the final output layer consisting of one single neuron. It is interesting to note that this layered organization vaguely resembles the organization of the human vision system, as we discussed earlier.

Problems in training the perceptron and solution

Let's consider a single neuron; what are the best choices for the weight w and the bias b? Ideally, we would like to provide a set of training examples and let the computer adjust the weight and the bias in such a way that the errors produced in the output are minimized.

In order to make this a bit more concrete, let's suppose that we have a set of images of cats and another separate set of images not containing cats. Suppose that each neuron receives input from the value of a single pixel in the images. While the computer processes those images, we would like our neuron to adjust its weights and its bias so that we have fewer and fewer images wrongly recognized.

This approach seems very intuitive, but it requires that a small change in the weights (or the bias) causes only a small change in the outputs. Think about it: if we have a big output jump, we cannot learn *progressively*. After all, kids learn little by little. Unfortunately, the perceptron does not show this "little-by-little" behavior. A perceptron is either a 0 or 1, and that's a big jump that will not help in learning (see *Figure 1.4*):

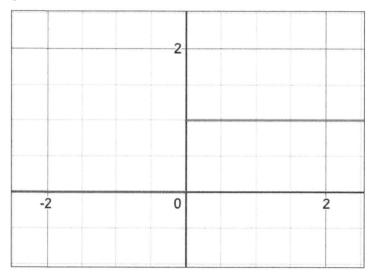

Figure 1.4: Example of a perceptron – either a 0 or 1

We need something different, something smoother. We need a function that progressively changes from 0 to 1 with no discontinuity. Mathematically, this means that we need a continuous function that allows us to compute the derivative. You might remember that in mathematics the derivative is the amount by which a function is changing at a given point. For functions with input given by real numbers, the derivative is the slope of the tangent line at a point on a graph. Later in this chapter we will see why derivatives are important for learning, when we will talk about gradient descent.

Activation function: sigmoid

The sigmoid function, defined as $\sigma(x) = \frac{1}{1+e^{-x}}$ and represented in the image below, has small output changes in the range (0, 1) when the input varies in the range $(-\infty, \infty)$. Mathematically the function is continuous. A typical sigmoid function is represented in *Figure 1.5*:

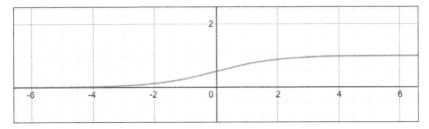

Figure 1.5: A sigmoid function with output in the range (0,1)

A neuron can use the sigmoid for computing the nonlinear function $\sigma(z = wx + b)$. Note that if $z = wx + b$ is very large and positive, then $e^{-z} \to 0$ so $\sigma(z) \to 1$, while if $z = wx + b$ is very large and negative, then $e^{-z} \to \infty$ so $\sigma(z) \to 0$. In other words, a neuron with sigmoid activation has a behavior similar to the perceptron, but the changes are gradual and output values such as 0.5539 or 0.123191 are perfectly legitimate. In this sense a sigmoid neuron can answer "maybe."

Activation function: tanh

Another useful activation function is tanh. It is defined as $\tanh(z) = \frac{e^z - e^{-z}}{e^z + e^{-z}}$ whose shape is shown in *Figure 1.6*. Its outputs range from -1 to 1:

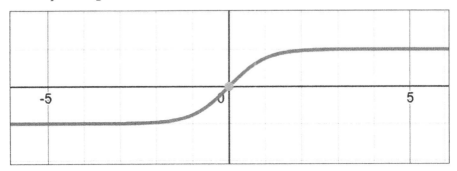

Figure 1.6: Tanh activation function

Activation function: ReLU

The "sigmoid" is not the only kind of smooth activation function used for neural networks. Recently, a very simple function named **ReLU** (**REctified Linear Unit**) became very popular because it helps address some problems of optimizations observed with sigmoids. We will discuss these problems in more detail when we talk about vanishing gradient in *Chapter 5, Recurrent Neural Networks*.

A ReLU is simply defined as $f(x) = max(0, x)$ and the nonlinear function is represented in *Figure 1.7*. As we can see, the function is zero for negative values and it grows linearly for positive values. The ReLU is also very simple to implement (generally three instructions are enough), while the sigmoid is a few orders of magnitude more. This helps to squeeze the neural networks onto an early GPU:

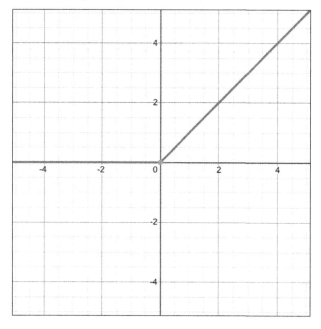

Figure 1.7: A ReLU function

Two additional activation functions: ELU and Leaky ReLU

Sigmoid and ReLU are not the only activation functions used for learning.

Exponential Linear Unit (ELU) is defined as $f(\alpha, x) = \begin{cases} \alpha(e^x - 1) & \text{if } x \leq 0 \\ x & \text{if } x > 0 \end{cases}$ for $\alpha > 0$ and its plot is represented in *Figure 1.8*:

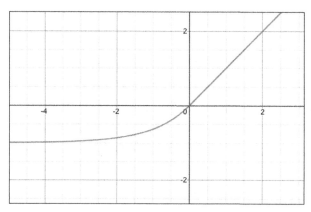

Figure 1.8: An ELU function

LeakyReLU is defined as $f(\alpha, x) = \begin{cases} \alpha x & \text{if } x \leq 0 \\ x & \text{if } x > 0 \end{cases}$ for $\alpha > 0$ and its plot is represented in *Figure 1.9*:

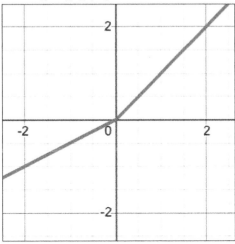

Figure 1.9: A LeakyReLU function

Both the functions allow small updates if x is negative, which might be useful in certain conditions.

Activation functions

Sigmoid, Tanh, ELU, Leaky ReLU, and ReLU are generally called *activation functions* in neural network jargon. In the gradient descent section, we will see that those gradual changes typical of sigmoid and ReLU functions are the basic building blocks to developing a learning algorithm that adapts little by little, by progressively reducing the mistakes made by our nets. An example of using the activation function σ with the $(x_1, x_2,..., x_m)$ input vector, the $(w_1, w_2,..., w_m)$ weight vector, the b bias, and the Σ summation is given in *Figure 1.10* (note that TensorFlow supports many activation functions, a full list of which is available online):

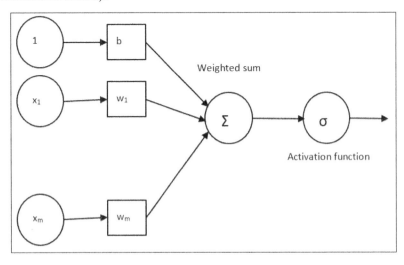

Figure 1.10: An example of an activation function applied after a linear function

In short: what are neural networks after all?

In one sentence, machine learning models are a way to compute a function that maps some inputs to their corresponding outputs. The function is nothing more than a number of addition and multiplication operations. However, when combined with a nonlinear activation and stacked in multiple layers, these functions can learn almost anything [8]. We also need a meaningful metric capturing what we want to optimize (this being the so-called loss function that we will cover later in the book), enough data to learn from, and sufficient computational power.

Now, it might be beneficial to stop one moment and ask ourselves what "learning" really is? Well, we can say for our purposes that learning is essentially a process aimed at generalizing established observations [9] to predict future results. So, in short, this is exactly the goal we want to achieve with neural networks.

A real example: recognizing handwritten digits

In this section we will build a network that can recognize handwritten numbers. To achieve this goal, we use MNIST (http://yann.lecun.com/exdb/mnist/), a database of handwritten digits made up of a training set of 60,000 examples, and a test set of 10,000 examples. The training examples are annotated by humans with the correct answer. For instance, if the handwritten digit is the number "3," then 3 is simply the label associated with that example.

In machine learning, when a dataset with correct answers is available, we say that we can perform a form of *supervised learning*. In this case we can use training examples for improving our net. Testing examples also have the correct answer associated with each digit. In this case, however, the idea is to pretend that the label is unknown, let the network do the prediction, and then later on reconsider the label to evaluate how well our neural network has learned to recognize digits. Unsurprisingly, testing examples are just used to test the performance of our net.

Each MNIST image is in grayscale and consists of 28 x 28 pixels. A subset of these images of numbers is shown in *Figure 1.11*:

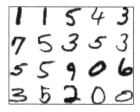

Figure 1.11: A collection of MNIST images

One hot-encoding (OHE)

We will use OHE as a simple tool to encode information used inside neural networks. In many applications, it is convenient to transform categorical (non-numerical) features into numerical variables. For instance, the categorical feature *digit* with value d in [0–9] can be encoded into a binary vector with 10 positions, which has always a 0 value except the d - *th* position where a 1 is present. For example, the digit 3 can be encoded as [0, 0, 0, 1, 0, 0, 0, 0, 0, 0].

This type of representation is called **One-Hot-Encoding (OHE)** or sometimes simply one-hot, and is very common in data mining when the learning algorithm is specialized in dealing with numerical functions.

Defining a simple neural net in TensorFlow

In this section we use TensorFlow to define a network that recognizes MNIST handwritten digits. We start with a very simple neural network and then progressively improve it.

Following Keras' style, TensorFlow provides suitable libraries (https://www.tensorflow.org/api_docs/python/tf/keras/datasets) for loading the dataset and splits it into training sets, X_train, used for fine-tuning our net, and test sets, X_test, used for assessing the performance. Later in the chapter, we are going to formally define what a training set, a validation set, and a test set are. For now, we just need to know that a training set is the dataset used to let our neural network learn from data examples. Data is converted into float32 to use 32-bit precision when training a neural network and normalized to the range [0,1]. In addition, we load the true labels into Y_train and Y_test respectively, and perform one-hot encoding on them. Let's see the code.

For now, do not focus too much on understanding why certain parameters have specific assigned values, as these choices will be discussed throughout the rest of the book. Intuitively, an epoch defines how long the training should last, BATCH_SIZE is the number of samples you feed in your network at a time, and the validation sample is the amount of data reserved for checking or proving the validity of the training process. The reason why we picked EPOCHS = 200, BATCH_SIZE = 128, VALIDATION_SPLIT=0.2, and N_HIDDEN = 128 will be clearer later in this chapter when we will explore different values and discuss hyperparameters optimization. Let's see our first code fragment of a neural network in TensorFlow. Reading is intuitive but you will find a detailed explanation in the upcoming pages:

```
import tensorflow as tf
import numpy as np
from tensorflow import keras


# Network and training parameters.
EPOCHS = 200
BATCH_SIZE = 128
VERBOSE = 1
NB_CLASSES = 10    # number of outputs = number of digits
N_HIDDEN = 128
VALIDATION_SPLIT = 0.2 # how much TRAIN is reserved for VALIDATION


# Loading MNIST dataset.
# verify
# You can verify that the split between train and test is 60,000, and 10,000
respectively.
# Labels have one-hot representation.is automatically applied
mnist = keras.datasets.mnist
```

```
(X_train, Y_train), (X_test, Y_test) = mnist.load_data()

# X_train is 60000 rows of 28x28 values; we  --> reshape it to 60000 x 784.
RESHAPED = 784
#
X_train = X_train.reshape(60000, RESHAPED)
X_test = X_test.reshape(10000, RESHAPED)
X_train = X_train.astype('float32')
X_test = X_test.astype('float32')

# Normalize inputs to be within in [0, 1].
X_train /= 255
X_test /= 255
print(X_train.shape[0], 'train samples')
print(X_test.shape[0], 'test samples')

# One-hot representation of the labels.
Y_train = tf.keras.utils.to_categorical(Y_train, NB_CLASSES)
Y_test = tf.keras.utils.to_categorical(Y_test, NB_CLASSES)
```

You can see from the above code that the input layer has a neuron associated to each pixel in the image for a total of 28 x 28=784 neurons, one for each pixel in the MNIST images.

Typically, the values associated with each pixel are normalized in the range [0,1] (which means that the intensity of each pixel is divided by 255, the maximum intensity value). The output can be one of ten classes, with one class for each digit.

The final layer is a single neuron with the activation function 'softmax', which is a generalization of the sigmoid function. As discussed earlier, a sigmoid function output is in the range (0, 1) when the input varies in the range $(-\infty, \infty)$. Similarly, a softmax "squashes" a K-dimensional vector of arbitrary real values into a K-dimensional vector of real values in the range (0, 1), so that they all add up to 1. In our case, it aggregates ten answers provided by the previous layer with ten neurons. What we have just described is implemented with the following code:

```
# Build the model.
model = tf.keras.models.Sequential()
model.add(keras.layers.Dense(NB_CLASSES,
              input_shape=(RESHAPED,),
              name='dense_layer',
              activation='softmax'))
```

Once we define the model, we have to compile it so that it can be executed by TensorFlow. There are a few choices to be made during compilation. Firstly, we need to select an *optimizer*, which is the specific algorithm used to update weights while we train our model.

A complete list of optimizers is at https://www.tensorflow.org/api_docs/python/tf/keras/optimizers. Second, we need to select an *objective function*, which is used by the optimizer to navigate the space of weights (frequently objective functions are called either *loss functions* or *cost functions* and the process of optimization is defined as a process of loss *minimization*). Third, we need to evaluate the trained model.

Some common choices for objective functions (a complete list of loss functions is at https://www.tensorflow.org/api_docs/python/tf/keras/losses) are:

- mse, which defines the mean squared error between the predictions and the true values. Mathematically if d is a vector of predictions and y is the vector of n observed values, then $MSE = \frac{1}{n}\sum_{i=1}^{n}(d - y)^2$. Note that this objective function is the average of all the mistakes made in each prediction. If a prediction is far off from the true value, then this distance is made more evident by the squaring operation. In addition, the square can add up the error regardless of whether a given value is positive or negative.

- binary_crossentropy, which defines the binary logarithmic loss. Suppose that our model predicts p while the target is c, then the binary cross-entropy is defined as $L(p, c) = -c\ln(p) - (1 - c)\ln(1 - p)$. Note that this objective function is suitable for binary labels prediction.

- categorical_crossentropy, which defines the multiclass logarithmic loss. Categorical cross-entropy compares the distribution of the predictions with the true distribution, with the probability of the true class set to 1 and 0 for the other classes. If the true class is c and the prediction is y, then the categorical cross-entropy is defined as:

$$L(c, p) = -\sum_i c_i \ln(p_i)$$

One way to think about multi-class logarithm loss is to consider the true class represented as a one-hot encoded vector, and the closer the model's outputs are to that vector, the lower the loss. Note that this objective function is suitable for multi-class label predictions. It is also the default choice with softmax activation. A complete list of loss functions is at https://www.tensorflow.org/api_docs/python/tf/keras/losses.

Some common choices for metrics (a complete list of metrics is at https://www.tensorflow.org/api_docs/python/tf/keras/metrics) are:

- Accuracy, defined as the proportion of correct predictions with respect to the total number of predictions.

- Precision, defined as the proportion of correct positive predictions with respect to the number of correct and incorrect positive predictions.

- Recall, defined as the proportion of correct positive predictions with respect to the actual number of positive predictions.

A complete list of metrics is at https://www.tensorflow.org/api_docs/python/tf/keras/metrics. Metrics are similar to objective functions, with the only difference being that they are not used for training a model, only for evaluating the model. However, it is important to understand the difference between metrics and objective functions. As discussed, the loss function is used to optimize your network. This is the function minimized by the selected optimizer. Instead, a metric is used to judge the performance of your network. This is only for you to run an evaluation, and it should be separated from the optimization process. On some occasions, it would be ideal to directly optimize for a specific metric. However, some metrics are not differentiable with respect to their inputs, which precludes them from being used directly.

When compiling a model in TensorFlow, it is possible to select the optimizer, the loss function, and the metric used together with a given model:

```
# Compiling the model.
model.compile(optimizer='SGD',
              loss='categorical_crossentropy',
              metrics=['accuracy'])
```

Stochastic Gradient Descent (SGD) is a particular kind of optimization algorithm used to reduce the mistakes made by neural networks after each training epoch. We will review SGD and other optimization algorithms in the next chapters. Once the model is compiled, it can then be trained with the fit() method, which specifies a few parameters:

- epochs is the number of times the model is exposed to the training set. At each iteration the optimizer tries to adjust the weights so that the objective function is minimized.
- batch_size is the number of training instances observed before the optimizer performs a weight update; there are usually many batches per epoch.

Training a model in TensorFlow is very simple:

```
# Training the model.
model.fit(X_train, Y_train,
          batch_size=BATCH_SIZE, epochs=EPOCHS,
          verbose=VERBOSE, validation_split=VALIDATION_SPLIT)
```

Note that we've reserved part of the training set for validation. The key idea is that we reserve a part of the training data for measuring the performance on the validation while training. This is a good practice to follow for any machine learning task, and one that we will adopt in all of our examples. Please note that we will return to validation later in this chapter when we will talk about overfitting.

Once the model is trained, we can evaluate it on the test set that contains new examples never seen by the model during the training phase.

Note that, of course, the training set and the test set are rigorously separated. There is no point in evaluating a model on an example that was already used for training. In TF we can use the method evaluate(X_test, Y_test) to compute the test_loss and the test_acc:

```
#evaluate the model
test_loss, test_acc = model.evaluate(X_test, Y_test)
print('Test accuracy:', test_acc)
```

Congratulations! You have just defined your first neural network in TensorFlow. A few lines of code and your computer should be able to recognize handwritten numbers. Let's run the code and see what the performance is.

Running a simple TensorFlow net and establishing a baseline

So, let's see what happens when we run the code:

```
Model: "sequential"
_____
Layer (type)                 Output Shape              Param #
=================================================================
dense_layer (Dense)          (None, 10)                7850

=================================================================
Total params: 7,850
Trainable params: 7,850
Non-trainable params: 0
_____
Train on 48000 samples, validate on 12000 samples
Epoch 1/200
48000/48000 [==============================] - 1s 31us/sample - loss: 2.1276 -
accuracy: 0.2322 - val_loss: 1.9508 - val_accuracy: 0.3908
Epoch 2/200
48000/48000 [==============================] - 1s 23us/sample - loss: 1.8251 -
accuracy: 0.5141 - val_loss: 1.6848 - val_accuracy: 0.6277
Epoch 3/200
48000/48000 [==============================] - 1s 25us/sample - loss: 1.5992 -
accuracy: 0.6531 - val_loss: 1.4838 - val_accuracy: 0.7150
Epoch 4/200
48000/48000 [==============================] - 1s 27us/sample - loss: 1.4281 -
accuracy: 0.7115 - val_loss: 1.3304 - val_accuracy: 0.7551
Epoch 5/200
```

First the net architecture is dumped and we can see the different types of layers used, their output shape, how many parameters (i.e., how many weights) they need to optimize, and how they are connected. Then, the network is trained on 48K samples, and 12K are reserved for validation. Once the neural model is built, it is then tested on 10K samples. For now we won't go into the internals of how the training happens, but we can see that the program runs for 200 iterations and each time accuracy improves. When the training ends, we test our model on the test set and we achieve about 89.96% accuracy on the training dataset, 90.70% on validation, and 90.71% on test:

```
Epoch 199/200
48000/48000 [==============================] - 1s 22us/sample - loss: 0.3684 -
accuracy: 0.8995 - val_loss: 0.3464 - val_accuracy: 0.9071
Epoch 200/200
48000/48000 [==============================] - 1s 23us/sample - loss: 0.3680 -
accuracy: 0.8996 - val_loss: 0.3461 - val_accuracy: 0.9070
10000/10000 [==============================] - 1s 54us/sample - loss: 0.3465 -
accuracy: 0.9071
Test accuracy: 0.9071
```

This means that nearly 1 in 10 images are incorrectly classified. We can certainly do better than that.

Improving the simple net in TensorFlow with hidden layers

Okay, we have a baseline of accuracy of 89.96% on the training dataset, 90.70% on validation, and 90.71% on test. It is a good starting point, but we can improve it. Let's see how.

An initial improvement is to add additional layers to our network because these additional neurons might intuitively help to learn more complex patterns in the training data. In other words, additional layers add more parameters, potentially allowing a model to memorize more complex patterns. So, after the input layer, we have a first dense layer with N_HIDDEN neurons and an activation function 'relu'. This additional layer is considered *hidden* because it is not directly connected either with the input or with the output. After the first hidden layer we have a second hidden layer, again with N_HIDDEN neurons, followed by an output layer with ten neurons, each one of which will fire when the relative digit is recognized. The following code defines this new network:

```python
import tensorflow as tf
from tensorflow import keras

# Network and training.
EPOCHS = 50
BATCH_SIZE = 128
VERBOSE = 1
NB_CLASSES = 10    # number of outputs = number of digits
N_HIDDEN = 128
VALIDATION_SPLIT = 0.2 # how much TRAIN is reserved for VALIDATION
```

```python
# Loading MNIST dataset.
# Labels have one-hot representation.
mnist = keras.datasets.mnist
(X_train, Y_train), (X_test, Y_test) = mnist.load_data()


# X_train is 60000 rows of 28x28 values; we reshape it to 60000 x 784.
RESHAPED = 784
#
X_train = X_train.reshape(60000, RESHAPED)
X_test = X_test.reshape(10000, RESHAPED)
X_train = X_train.astype('float32')
X_test = X_test.astype('float32')


# Normalize inputs to be within in [0, 1].
X_train, X_test = X_train / 255.0, X_test / 255.0
print(X_train.shape[0], 'train samples')
print(X_test.shape[0], 'test samples')


# Labels have one-hot representation.
Y_train = tf.keras.utils.to_categorical(Y_train, NB_CLASSES)
Y_test = tf.keras.utils.to_categorical(Y_test, NB_CLASSES)


# Build the model.
model = tf.keras.models.Sequential()
model.add(keras.layers.Dense(N_HIDDEN,
            input_shape=(RESHAPED,),
            name='dense_layer', activation='relu'))
model.add(keras.layers.Dense(N_HIDDEN,
            name='dense_layer_2', activation='relu'))
model.add(keras.layers.Dense(NB_CLASSES,
            name='dense_layer_3', activation='softmax'))


# Summary of the model.
model.summary()


# Compiling the model.
model.compile(optimizer='SGD',
            loss='categorical_crossentropy',
            metrics=['accuracy'])


# Training the model.
```

```
model.fit(X_train, Y_train,
          batch_size=BATCH_SIZE, epochs=EPOCHS,
          verbose=VERBOSE, validation_split=VALIDATION_SPLIT)

# Evaluating the model.
test_loss, test_acc = model.evaluate(X_test, Y_test)
print('Test accuracy:', test_acc)
```

Note that to_categorical(Y_train, NB_CLASSES) converts the array Y_train into a matrix with as many columns as there are classes. The number of rows stays the same. So, for instance, if we have:

```
> labels
array([0, 2, 1, 2, 0])
```

then:

```
to_categorical(labels)
array([[ 1.,   0.,   0.],
       [ 0.,   0.,   1.],
       [ 0.,   1.,   0.],
       [ 0.,   0.,   1.],
       [ 1.,   0.,   0.]], dtype=float32)
```

Let's run the code and see what results we get with this multi-layer network:

```
Layer (type)                 Output Shape              Param #
=================================================================
dense_layer (Dense)          (None, 128)               100480

dense_layer_2 (Dense)        (None, 128)               16512

dense_layer_3 (Dense)        (None, 10)                1290


=================================================================
Total params: 118,282
Trainable params: 118,282
Non-trainable params: 0

_____
Train on 48000 samples, validate on 12000 samples
Epoch 1/50
48000/48000 [==============================] - 3s 63us/sample - loss: 2.2507 -
accuracy: 0.2086 - val_loss: 2.1592 - val_accuracy: 0.3266
```

The previous output shows the initial steps of the run while the following output shows the conclusion. Not bad. As seen in the following output, by adding two hidden layers we reached 90.81% on the training dataset, 91.40% on validation, and 91.18% on test. This means that we have increased accuracy on the test dataset with respect to the previous network, and we have reduced the number of iterations from 200 to 50. That's good, but we want more.

If you want, you can play by yourself and see what happens if you add only one hidden layer instead of two or if you add more than two layers. I leave this experiment as an exercise:

```
Epoch 49/50
48000/48000 [==============================] - 1s 30us/sample - loss: 0.3347 -
accuracy: 0.9075 - val_loss: 0.3126 - val_accuracy: 0.9136
Epoch 50/50
48000/48000 [==============================] - 1s 28us/sample - loss: 0.3326 -
accuracy: 0.9081 - val_loss: 0.3107 - val_accuracy: 0.9140
10000/10000 [==============================] - 0s 40us/sample - loss: 0.3164 -
accuracy: 0.9118
Test accuracy: 0.9118
```

Note that improvement stops (or it become almost imperceptible) after a certain number of epochs. In machine learning this is a phenomenon called *convergence*.

Further improving the simple net in TensorFlow with dropout

Now our baseline is 90.81% on training set, 91.40% on validation, and 91.18% on test. A second improvement is very simple. We decide to randomly drop – with the DROPOUT probability – some of the values propagated inside our internal dense network of hidden layers during training. In machine learning this is a well-known form of regularization. Surprisingly enough, this idea of randomly dropping a few values can improve our performance. The idea behind this improvement is that random dropouts *force* the network to learn redundant patterns that are useful for better generalization:

```
import tensorflow as tf
import numpy as np
from tensorflow import keras

# Network and training.
EPOCHS = 200
BATCH_SIZE = 128
VERBOSE = 1
NB_CLASSES = 10    # number of outputs = number of digits
N_HIDDEN = 128
VALIDATION_SPLIT = 0.2 # how much TRAIN is reserved for VALIDATION
DROPOUT = 0.3

# Loading MNIST dataset.
```

```
# Labels have one-hot representation.
mnist = keras.datasets.mnist
(X_train, Y_train), (X_test, Y_test) = mnist.load_data()


# X_train is 60000 rows of 28x28 values; we reshape it to 60000 x 784.
RESHAPED = 784
#
X_train = X_train.reshape(60000, RESHAPED)
X_test = X_test.reshape(10000, RESHAPED)
X_train = X_train.astype('float32')
X_test = X_test.astype('float32')


# Normalize inputs within [0, 1].
X_train, X_test = X_train / 255.0, X_test / 255.0
print(X_train.shape[0], 'train samples')
print(X_test.shape[0], 'test samples')


# One-hot representations for labels.
Y_train = tf.keras.utils.to_categorical(Y_train, NB_CLASSES)
Y_test = tf.keras.utils.to_categorical(Y_test, NB_CLASSES)


# Building the model.
model = tf.keras.models.Sequential()
model.add(keras.layers.Dense(N_HIDDEN,
            input_shape=(RESHAPED,),
            name='dense_layer', activation='relu'))
model.add(keras.layers.Dropout(DROPOUT))
model.add(keras.layers.Dense(N_HIDDEN,
            name='dense_layer_2', activation='relu'))
model.add(keras.layers.Dropout(DROPOUT))
model.add(keras.layers.Dense(NB_CLASSES,
            name='dense_layer_3', activation='softmax'))


# Summary of the model.
model.summary()
```

```
# Compiling the model.
model.compile(optimizer='SGD',
              loss='categorical_crossentropy',
              metrics=['accuracy'])

# Training the model.
model.fit(X_train, Y_train,
          batch_size=BATCH_SIZE, epochs=EPOCHS,
          verbose=VERBOSE, validation_split=VALIDATION_SPLIT)

# Evaluating the model.
test_loss, test_acc = model.evaluate(X_test, Y_test)
print('Test accuracy:', test_acc)
```

Let's run the code for 200 iterations as before and we see that this net achieves an accuracy of 91.70% on training, 94.42% on validation, and 94.15% on testing:

```
Epoch 199/200
48000/48000 [==============================] - 2s 45us/sample - loss: 0.2850 -
accuracy: 0.9177 - val_loss: 0.1922 - val_accuracy: 0.9442
Epoch 200/200
48000/48000 [==============================] - 2s 42us/sample - loss: 0.2845 -
accuracy: 0.9170 - val_loss: 0.1917 - val_accuracy: 0.9442
10000/10000 [==============================] - 1s 61us/sample - loss: 0.1927 -
accuracy: 0.9415
Test accuracy: 0.9415
```

Note that it has been frequently observed that networks with random dropouts in internal hidden layers can "generalize" better on unseen examples contained in test sets. Intuitively we can consider this phenomenon as each neuron becoming more capable because it knows it cannot depend on its neighbors. Also, it forces information to be stored in a redundant way. During testing there is no dropout, so we are now using all our highly tuned neurons. In short, it is generally a good approach to test how a net performs when some dropout function is adopted.

Besides that, note that training accuracy should still be above test accuracy; otherwise, we might be not training for long enough. This is the case in our example and therefore we should increase the number of epochs. However, before performing this attempt we need to introduce a few other concepts that allow the training to converge faster. Let's talk about optimizers.

Testing different optimizers in TensorFlow

Now that we have defined and used a network, it is useful to start developing some intuition about how networks are trained, using an analogy. Let us focus on one popular training technique known as **gradient descent (GD)**. Imagine a generic cost function $C(w)$ in one single variable w like in *Figure 1.12*:

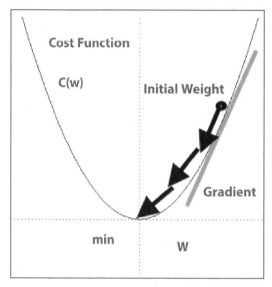

Figure 1.12: An example of GD optimization

GD can be seen as a hiker who needs to navigate down a steep slope and aims to enter a ditch. The slope represents the function C while the ditch represents the minimum C_{min}. The hiker has a starting point w_0. The hiker moves little by little; imagine that there is almost zero visibility, so the hiker cannot see where to go automatically, and they proceed in a zigzag. At each step r, the gradient is the direction of maximum increase.

Mathematically this direction is the value of the partial derivative $\frac{\partial C}{\partial w}$ evaluated at point w_r, reached at step r. Therefore, by taking the opposite direction $-\frac{\partial C}{\partial w}(w_r)$ the hiker can move toward the ditch.

At each step the hiker can decide how big a stride to take before the next stop. This is the so-called "learning rate" $\eta \geq 0$ in GD jargon. Note that if η is too small, then the hiker will move slowly. However, if η is too high, then the hiker will possibly miss the ditch by stepping over it.

Now you should remember that a sigmoid is a continuous function and it is possible to compute the derivative. It can be proven that the sigmoid $\sigma(x) = \frac{1}{1+e^{-x}}$ has the derivative $\frac{d\sigma(x)}{d(x)} = \sigma(x)(1 - \sigma(x))$.

ReLU is not differentiable at 0. We can however extend the first derivative at 0 to a function over the whole domain by defining it to be either a 0 or 1.

The piecewise derivative of ReLU $y = \max(0, x)$ is $\frac{dy}{dx} = \begin{cases} 0 & x \leq 0 \\ 1 & x > 0 \end{cases}$.

Once we have the derivative, it is possible to optimize the nets with a GD technique. TensorFlow computes the derivative on our behalf so we don't need to worry about implementing or computing it.

A neural network is essentially a composition of multiple derivable functions with thousands and sometimes millions of parameters. Each network layer computes a function, the error of which should be minimized in order to improve the accuracy observed during the learning phase. When we discuss backpropagation, we will discover that the minimization game is a bit more complex than our toy example. However, it is still based on the same intuition of descending a slope to reach a ditch.

TensorFlow implements a fast variant of GD known as **Stochastic Gradient Descent (SGD)** and many more advanced optimization techniques such as RMSProp and Adam. RMSProp and Adam include the concept of momentum (a velocity component) in addition to the acceleration component that SGD has. This allows faster convergence at the cost of more computation. Think about a hiker who starts to move in one direction and then decides to change direction but remembers previous choices. It can be proven that momentum helps accelerate SGD in the relevant direction and dampens oscillations [10].

SGD was our default choice so far. So now let's try the other two. It is very simple; we just need to change a few lines:

```
# Compiling the model.
model.compile(optimizer='RMSProp',
              loss='categorical_crossentropy', metrics=['accuracy'])
```

That's it. Let's test it.

```
Layer (type)                 Output Shape              Param #
=================================================================
dense_layer (Dense)          (None, 128)               100480

dropout_2 (Dropout)          (None, 128)               0

dense_layer_2 (Dense)        (None, 128)               16512

dropout_3 (Dropout)          (None, 128)               0

dense_layer_3 (Dense)        (None, 10)                1290

=================================================================
Total params: 118,282
Trainable params: 118,282
Non-trainable params: 0


Train on 48000 samples, validate on 12000 samples
Epoch 1/10
48000/48000 [==============================] - 2s 48us/sample - loss: 0.4715 -
accuracy: 0.8575 - val_loss: 0.1820 - val_accuracy: 0.9471
```

```
Epoch 2/10
48000/48000 [==============================] - 2s 36us/sample - loss: 0.2215 -
accuracy: 0.9341 - val_loss: 0.1268 - val_accuracy: 0.9361
Epoch 3/10
48000/48000 [==============================] - 2s 39us/sample - loss: 0.1684 -
accuracy: 0.9497 - val_loss: 0.1198 - val_accuracy: 0.9651
Epoch 4/10
48000/48000 [==============================] - 2s 43us/sample - loss: 0.1459 -
accuracy: 0.9569 - val_loss: 0.1059 - val_accuracy: 0.9710
Epoch 5/10
48000/48000 [==============================] - 2s 39us/sample - loss: 0.1273 -
accuracy: 0.9623 - val_loss: 0.1059 - val_accuracy: 0.9696
Epoch 6/10
48000/48000 [==============================] - 2s 36us/sample - loss: 0.1177 -
accuracy: 0.9659 - val_loss: 0.0941 - val_accuracy: 0.9731
Epoch 7/10
48000/48000 [==============================] - 2s 35us/sample - loss: 0.1083 -
accuracy: 0.9671 - val_loss: 0.1009 - val_accuracy: 0.9715
Epoch 8/10
48000/48000 [==============================] - 2s 35us/sample - loss: 0.0971 -
accuracy: 0.9706 - val_loss: 0.0950 - val_accuracy: 0.9758
Epoch 9/10
48000/48000 [==============================] - 2s 35us/sample - loss: 0.0969 -
accuracy: 0.9718 - val_loss: 0.0985 - val_accuracy: 0.9745
Epoch 10/10
48000/48000 [==============================] - 2s 35us/sample - loss: 0.0873 -
accuracy: 0.9743 - val_loss: 0.0966 - val_accuracy: 0.9762
10000/10000 [==============================] - 1s 2ms/sample - loss: 0.0922 -
accuracy: 0.9764
Test accuracy: 0.9764
```

As you can see, RMSProp is faster than SDG since we are able to achieve in only 10 epochs an accuracy of 97.43% on the training dataset, 97.62% on validation, and 97.64% on test. That's a significant improvement on SDG. Now that we have a very fast optimizer, let us try to increase significantly the number of epochs up to 250, and we get 98.99% accuracy on the training dataset, 97.66% on validation, and 97.77% on test:

```
Epoch 248/250
48000/48000 [==============================] - 2s 40us/sample - loss: 0.0506 -
accuracy: 0.9904 - val_loss: 0.3465 - val_accuracy: 0.9762
Epoch 249/250
48000/48000 [==============================] - 2s 40us/sample - loss: 0.0490 -
accuracy: 0.9905 - val_loss: 0.3645 - val_accuracy: 0.9765
Epoch 250/250
```

```
48000/48000 [==============================] - 2s 39us/sample - loss: 0.0547 -
accuracy: 0.9899 - val_loss: 0.3353 - val_accuracy: 0.9766
10000/10000 [==============================] - 1s 58us/sample - loss: 0.3184 -
accuracy: 0.9779
Test accuracy: 0.9779
```

It is useful to observe how accuracy increases on training and test sets when the number of epochs increases (see *Figure 1.13*). As you can see, these two curves touch at about 15 epochs and therefore there is no need to train further after that point:

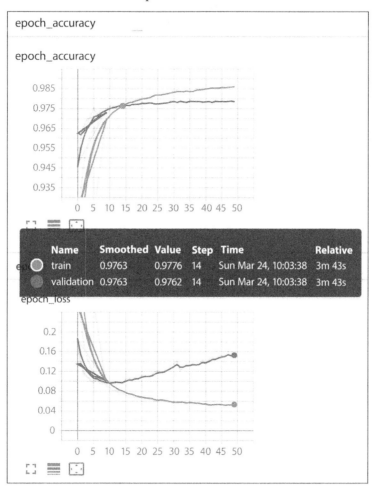

Figure 1.13: An example of accuracy and loss with RMSProp

Okay, let's try the other optimizer, `Adam()`. It's pretty simple to implement:

```python
# Compiling the model.
model.compile(optimizer='Adam',
              loss='categorical_crossentropy',
              metrics=['accuracy'])
```

As we see, `Adam()` is slightly better. With Adam we achieve 98.94% accuracy on the training dataset, 97.89% on validation, and 97.82% on test with 50 iterations:

```
Epoch 49/50
48000/48000 [==============================] - 3s 55us/sample - loss: 0.0313 -
accuracy: 0.9894 - val_loss: 0.0868 - val_accuracy: 0.9808
Epoch 50/50
48000/48000 [==============================] - 2s 51s/sample - loss: 0.0321 -
accuracy: 0.9894 - val_loss: 0.0983 - val_accuracy: 0.9789
10000/10000 [==============================] - 1s 66us/step - loss: 0.0964 -
accuracy: 0.9782
Test accuracy: 0.9782
```

One more time, let's plot how accuracy increases on training and test sets when the number of epochs increases (see *Figure 1.14*). You'll notice that by choosing Adam as an optimizer we are able to stop after just about 12 epochs or steps:

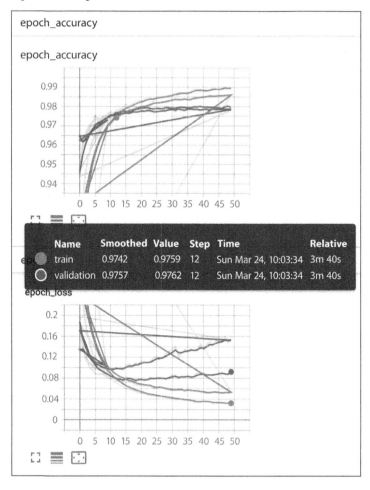

Figure 1.14: An example of accuracy and loss with Adam

Note that this is our fifth variant and remember that our initial baseline was at 90.71% on the test dataset. So far, we've made progressive improvements. However, gains are now more and more difficult to obtain. Note that we are optimizing with a dropout of 30%. For the sake of completeness, it could be useful to report the accuracy of the test dataset for different dropout values (see *Figure 1.15*). In this example, we selected Adam as the optimizer. Note that the choice of optimizer isn't a rule of thumb and we can get different performance depending on the problem-optimizer combination:

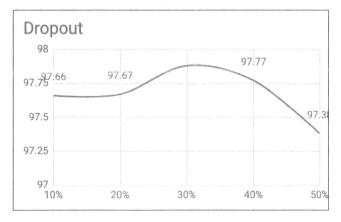

Figure 1.15: An example of changes in accuracy for different dropout values

Increasing the number of epochs

Let's make another attempt and increase the number of epochs used for training from 20 to 200. Unfortunately, this choice increases our computation time tenfold, yet gives us no gain. The experiment is unsuccessful, but we have learned that if we spend more time learning, we will not necessarily improve the result. Learning is more about adopting smart techniques and not necessarily about the time spent in computations. Let's keep track of our five variants in the following graph:

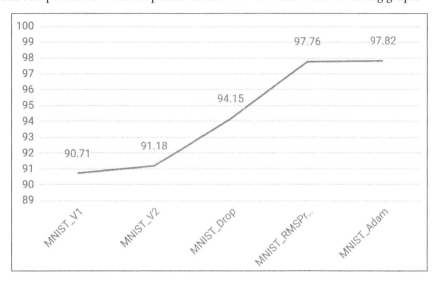

Figure 1.16: Accuracy for different models and optimizers

Controlling the optimizer learning rate

There is another approach we can take that involves changing the learning parameter for our optimizer. As you can see in *Figure 1.17*, the best value reached by our three experiments [lr=0.1, lr=0.01, and lr=0.001] is 0.1, which is the default learning rate for the optimizer. Good! Adam works well out of the box:

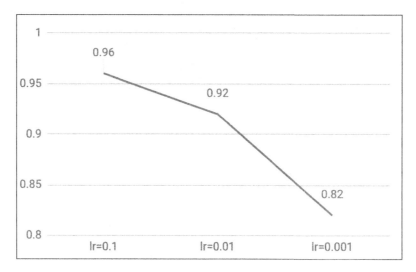

Figure 1.17: Accuracy for different learning rates

Increasing the number of internal hidden neurons

Yet another approach involves changing the number of internal hidden neurons. We report the results of the experiments with an increasing number of hidden neurons. We see that by increasing the complexity of the model, the runtime increases significantly because there are more and more parameters to optimize. However, the gains that we are getting by increasing the size of the network decrease more and more as the network grows (see *Figure 1.18*, *Figure 1.19*, and *Figure 1.20*):

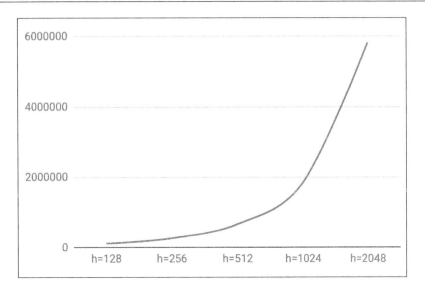

Figure 1.18: Number of parameters for the increasing values of internal hidden neurons

On the other hand, the time needed increases as the size of the internal network increases (see *Figure 1.19*):

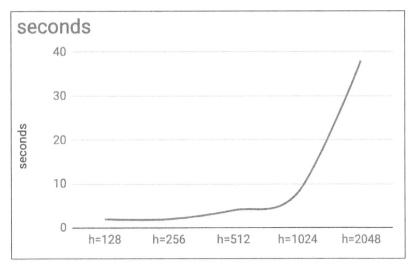

Figure 1.19: Seconds of computation time for the increasing values of internal hidden neurons

Note that increasing the number of hidden neurons after a certain value can reduce the accuracy because the network might not be able to generalize well (as shown in *Figure 1.20*):

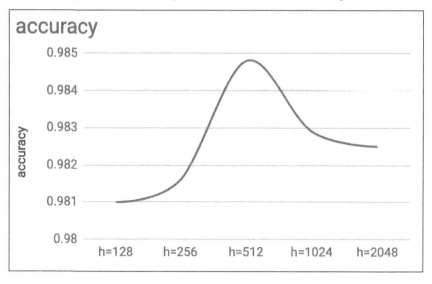

Figure 1.20: Test accuracy for the increasing values of internal hidden neurons

Increasing the size of batch computation

GD tries to minimize the cost function on all the examples provided in the training sets and, at the same time, for all the features provided as input. SGD is a much less expensive variant that considers only BATCH_SIZE examples. So, let us see how it behaves when we change this parameter. As you can see, the best accuracy value is reached for a BATCH_SIZE=64 in our four experiments (see *Figure 1.21*):

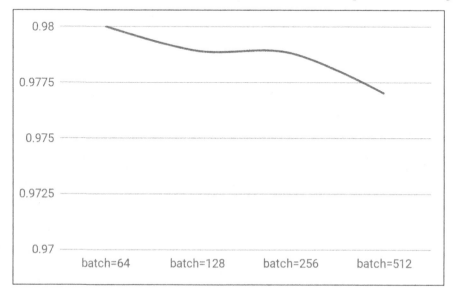

Figure 1.21: Test accuracy for different batch values

Summarizing experiments run to recognizing handwritten digits

So, let's summarize: with five different variants, we were able to improve our performance from 90.71% to 97.82%. First, we defined a simple layer network in TensorFlow. Then, we improved the performance by adding some hidden layers. After that, we improved the performance on the test set by adding a few random dropouts in our network, and then by experimenting with different types of optimizers:

	Accuracy		
Model	**Training**	**Validation**	**Test**
Simple	89.96%	90.70%	90.71%
Two hidden layers (128)	90.81%	91.40%	91.18%
Dropout (30%)	91.70%	94.42%	94.15% (200 epochs)
RMSProp	97.43%	97.62%	97.64% (10 epochs)
Adam	98.94%	97.89%	97.82% (10 epochs)

Table 1.1: Summary of experiments with various levels of accuracy

However, the next two experiments (not shown in *Table 1.1*) were not providing significant improvements. Increasing the number of internal neurons creates more complex models and requires more expensive computations, but it provides only marginal gains. We have the same experience if we increase the number of training epochs. A final experiment consisted of changing the BATCH_SIZE for our optimizer. This also provided marginal results.

Regularization

In this section we will review a few best practices for improving the training phase. In particular, regularization and batch normalization will be discussed.

Adopting regularization to avoid overfitting

Intuitively, a good machine learning model should achieve low error on training data. Mathematically this is equivalent to minimizing the loss function on the training data given the model:

$$min : \{loss(Training\ Data | Model)\}$$

However, this might not be enough. A model can become excessively complex in order to capture all the relations inherently expressed by the training data. This increase in complexity might have two negative consequences. First, a complex model might require a significant amount of time to be executed. Second, a complex model might achieve very good performance on training data but perform quite badly on validation data. This is because the model is able to contrive relationships between many parameters in the specific training context, but these relationships in fact do not exist within a more generalized context. Causing a model to lose its ability to generalize in this manner is termed "overfitting. " Again, learning is more about generalization than memorization. Another phenomenon to consider is "underfitting."

This happens when a data model cannot capture the relationship between the input and output variables accurately, with a high error rate on both the training set and new unseen data:

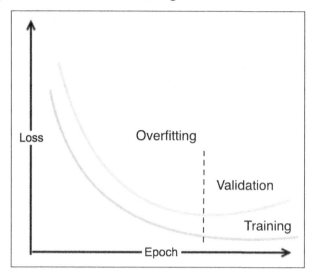

Figure 1.22: Loss function and overfitting

As a rule of thumb, if during the training we see that the loss increases on validation, after an initial decrease, then we have a problem of model complexity that overfits the training data.

In order to solve the overfitting problem, we need a way to capture the complexity of a model, i.e. how complex a model can be. What could the solution be? Well, a model is nothing more than a vector of weights. Each weight affects the output, except for those which are zero, or very close to it. Therefore, the complexity of a model can be conveniently represented as the number of non-zero weights. In other words, if we have two models M1 and M2 achieving pretty much the same performance in terms of a loss function, then we should choose the simplest model, the one which has the minimum number of non-zero weights. We can use a hyperparameter $\lambda >= 0$ for controlling the importance of having a simple model, as in this formula:

$$\min : \{loss(Training\ Data|Model)\} + \lambda * complexity\ (Model)$$

There are three different types of regularization used in machine learning:

- L1 regularization (also known as LASSO). The complexity of the model is expressed as the sum of the absolute values of the weights.
- L2 regularization (also known as Ridge). The complexity of the model is expressed as the sum of the squares of the weights.
- ElasticNet regularization. The complexity of the model is captured by a combination of the two techniques above.

Note that playing with regularization can be a good way to increase the generalization performance of a network, particularly when there is an evident situation of overfitting. This set of experiments is left as an exercise to the interested reader.

Also note that TensorFlow supports L1, L2, and ElasticNet regularization. A complete list of regularizers is at `https://www.tensorflow.org/api_docs/python/tf/keras/regularizers`. Adding regularization is easy:

```
from tf.keras.regularizers import l2, activity_l2
model.add(Dense(64, input_dim=64, W_regularizer=l2(0.01),
    activity_regularizer=activity_l2(0.01)))
```

Understanding batch normalization

Batch normalization is another form of regularization and one of the most effective improvements proposed during the last few years. Batch normalization enables us to accelerate training, in some cases by halving the training epochs, and it offers some regularization. During training, the weights in early layers naturally change and therefore the inputs of later layers can significantly change. In other words, each layer must continuously re-adjust its weights to the different distribution for every batch. This may slow down the model's training greatly. The key idea is to make layer inputs more similar in distribution, batch after batch and epoch after epoch.

Another issue is that the sigmoid activation function works very well close to zero but tends to "get stuck" when values get sufficiently far away from zero. If, occasionally, neuron outputs fluctuate far away from the sigmoid zero, then said neuron becomes unable to update its own weights.

The other key idea is therefore to transform the layer outputs into a Gaussian distribution unit close to zero. This way, layers will have significantly less variation from batch to batch. Mathematically, the formula is very simple. The activation input x is centered around zero by subtracting the batch mean μ from it. Then the result is divided by $\sigma + \epsilon$, the sum of batch variance σ, and a small number ϵ to prevent division by zero. Then, we use a linear transformation $y = \lambda x + \beta$ to make sure that the normalizing effect is applied during training.

In this way, λ and β are parameters that get optimized during the training phase in a way similar to any other layer. Batch normalization has been proven to be a very effective way to increase both the speed of training and accuracy, because it helps to prevent activations becoming either too small and vanishing or too big and exploding.

Playing with Google Colab: CPUs, GPUs, and TPUs

Google offers a truly intuitive tool for training neural networks and for playing with TensorFlow at no cost. You can find an actual Colab, which can be freely accessed, at `https://colab.research.google.com/` and if you are familiar with Jupyter notebooks you will find a very familiar web-based environment here. **Colab** stands for **Colaboratory** and is a Google research project created to help disseminate machine learning education and research. We will see the difference between CPUs, GPUs, and TPUs in *Chapter 15, Tensor Processing Unit*.

For now, it's important to know that CPUs are generic processing units, while GPUs and TPUs are accelerators, specific processing units suitable for deep learning. Let's see how it works, starting with the screenshot shown in *Figure 1.23*:

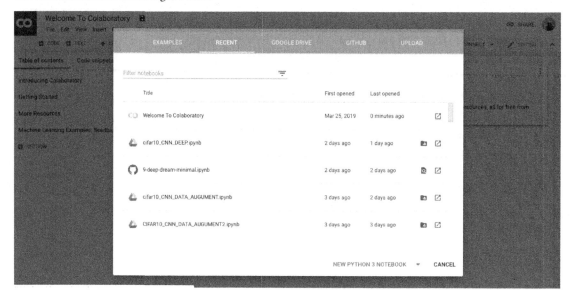

Figure 1.23: An example of notebooks in Colab

By accessing Colab, we can either check a listing of notebooks generated in the past or we can create a new notebook. Different versions of Python are supported.

When we create a new notebook, we can also select if we want to run it on CPUs, GPUs, or in Google's TPUs as shown in *Figure 1.24*:

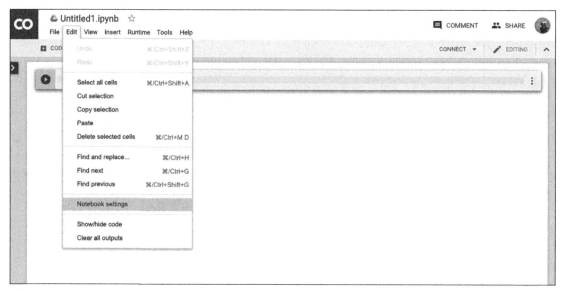

Figure 1.24: Selecting the desired hardware accelerator (None, GPUs, or TPUs) – the first step

By accessing the **Notebook settings** option contained in the **Edit** menu (see *Figure 1.24* and *Figure 1.25*), we can select the desired hardware accelerator (**None, GPUs,** or **TPUs**). Google will allocate the resources at no cost, although they can be withdrawn at any time, for example during periods of a particularly heavy load. In my experience, this is a very rare event, and you can access Colab pretty much any time. However, be polite and do not do something like start mining bitcoins at no cost – you will almost certainly get evicted!

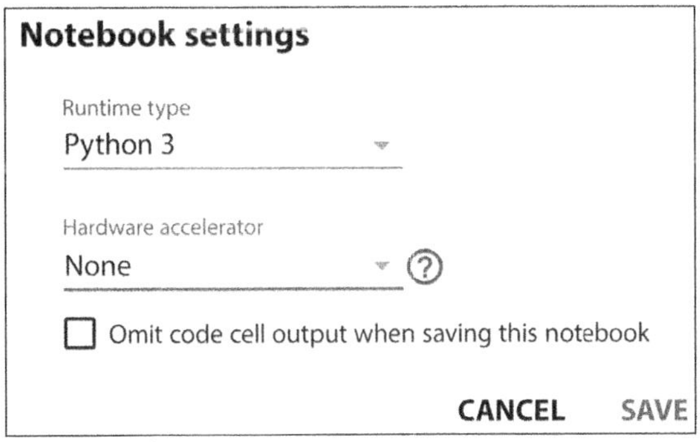

Figure 1.25: Selecting the desired hardware accelerator (None, GPUs, or TPUs) – the second step

The next step is to insert your code (see *Figure 1.26*) in the appropriate Colab notebook cells and *voila!* You are good to go. Execute the code and happy deep learning without the hassle of buying very expensive hardware to start your experiments! *Figure 1.26* contains an example of code in a Google notebook:

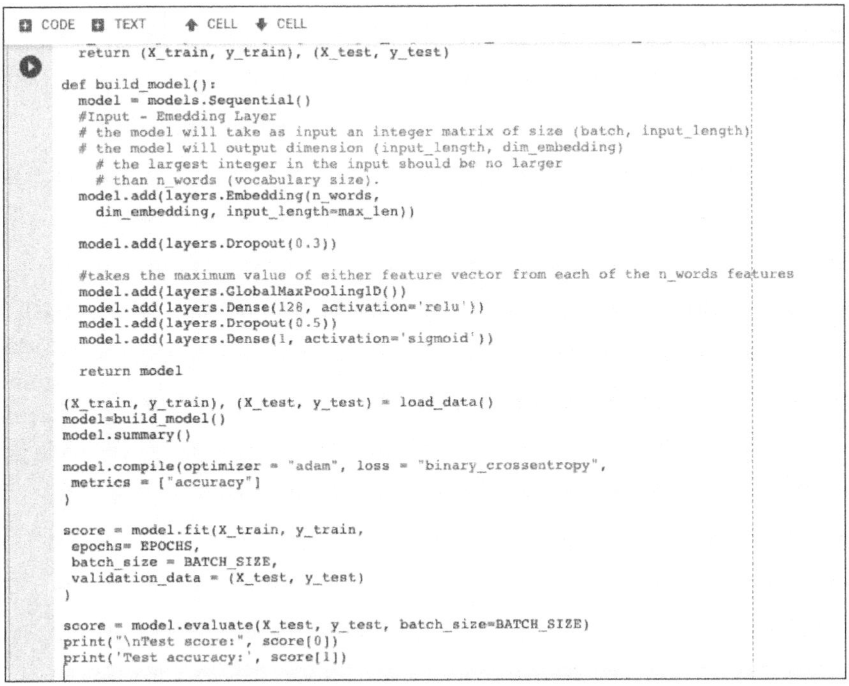

Figure 1.26: An example of code in a notebook

Sentiment analysis

What is the code we used to test Colab? It is an example of sentiment analysis developed on top of the IMDB dataset. The IMDB dataset contains the text of 50,000 movie reviews from the Internet Movie Database. Each review is either positive or negative (for example, thumbs up or thumbs down). The dataset is split into 25,000 reviews for training and 25,000 reviews for testing. Our goal is to build a classifier that can predict the binary judgment given the text. We can easily load IMDB via `tf.keras` and the sequences of words in the reviews have been converted to sequences of integers, where each integer represents a specific word in a dictionary. We also have a convenient way of padding sentences to `max_len`, so that we can use all sentences, whether short or long, as inputs to a neural network with an input vector of fixed size:

```python
import tensorflow as tf
from tensorflow.keras import datasets, layers, models, preprocessing
import tensorflow_datasets as tfds


max_len = 200
n_words = 10000
dim_embedding = 256
EPOCHS = 20
BATCH_SIZE = 500


def load_data():
    # Load data.
    (X_train, y_train), (X_test, y_test) = datasets.imdb.load_data(num_words=n_
words)
    # Pad sequences with max_Len.
    X_train = preprocessing.sequence.pad_sequences(X_train, maxlen=max_len)
    X_test = preprocessing.sequence.pad_sequences(X_test, maxlen=max_len)
    return (X_train, y_train), (X_test, y_test)
```

Now let's build a model. We are going to use a few layers that will be explained in detail in *Chapter 4, Word Embeddings*. For now, let's assume that the `embedding()` layer will map the sparse space of words contained in the reviews into a denser space. This will make computation easier. In addition, we will use a `GlobalMaxPooling1D()` layer, which takes the maximum value of either feature vector from each of the `n_words` features. In addition, we have two `Dense()` layers. The last one is made up of a single neuron with a sigmoid activation function for making the final binary estimation:

```python
def build_model():
    model = models.Sequential()
    # Input: - eEmbedding Layer.
```

```
    # The model will take as input an integer matrix of size (batch, input_
Length).
    # The model will output dimension (input_length, dim_embedding).
    # The largest integer in the input should be no larger
    # than n_words (vocabulary size).
    model.add(layers.Embedding(n_words,
        dim_embedding, input_length=max_len))

    model.add(layers.Dropout(0.3))

    # Takes the maximum value of either feature vector from each of the n_words
features.
    model.add(layers.GlobalMaxPooling1D())
    model.add(layers.Dense(128, activation='relu'))
    model.add(layers.Dropout(0.5))
    model.add(layers.Dense(1, activation='sigmoid'))

    return model
```

Now we need to train our model and this piece of code is very similar to what we have done with MNIST. Let's see:

```
(X_train, y_train), (X_test, y_test) = load_data()
model = build_model()
model.summary()

model.compile(optimizer = "adam", loss = "binary_crossentropy",
 metrics = ["accuracy"]
)

score = model.fit(X_train, y_train,
 epochs = EPOCHS,
 batch_size = BATCH_SIZE,
 validation_data = (X_test, y_test)
)

score = model.evaluate(X_test, y_test, batch_size=BATCH_SIZE)
print("\nTest score:", score[0])
print('Test accuracy:', score[1])
```

Let's see the network and then run a few iterations:

```
Layer (type)                    Output Shape             Param #
=================================================================
embedding (Embedding)           (None, 200, 256)         2560000

dropout (Dropout)               (None, 200, 256)         0

global_max_pooling1d (Global    (None, 256)              0

dense (Dense)                   (None, 128)              32896

dropout_1 (Dropout)             (None, 128)              0

dense_1 (Dense)                 (None, 1)                129

=================================================================
Total params: 2,593,025
Trainable params: 2,593,025
Non-trainable params: 0
```

As shown in the following output, we reach accuracy of 85%, which is not bad at all for a simple network:

```
Epoch 20/20
25000/25000 [==============================] - 23s 925ms/sample - loss: 0.0053
- accuracy: 0.9991 - val_loss: 0.4993 - val_accuracy: 0.8503
25000/25000 [==============================] - 2s 74us/sample - loss: 0.4993 -
accuracy: 0.88503

Test score: 0.4992710727453232
Test accuracy: 0.85028
```

The next section is devoted to tuning hyperparameters and AutoML.

Hyperparameter tuning and AutoML

The experiments defined above give some opportunities for fine-tuning a net. However, what works for this example will not necessarily work for other examples. For a given neural network, there are indeed multiple parameters that can be optimized (such as the number of hidden neurons, batch size, number of epochs, and many more according to the complexity of the net itself). These parameters are called "hyperparameters" to distinguish them from the parameters of the network itself, i.e. the values of the weights and biases.

Hyperparameter tuning is the process of finding the optimal combination of those hyperparameters that minimize cost functions. The key idea is that if we have n hyperparameters, then we can imagine that they define a space with n dimensions, and the goal is to find the point in this space that corresponds to an optimal value for the cost function. One way to achieve this goal is to create a grid in this space and systematically check the value assumed by the cost function for each grid vertex. In other words, the hyperparameters are divided into buckets and different combinations of values are checked via a brute-force approach.

If you think that this process of fine-tuning the hyperparameters is manual and expensive then you are absolutely right! However, during the last few years, we have seen significant results in AutoML, a set of research techniques aimed at both automatically tuning hyperparameters and searching automatically for optimal network architecture. We will discuss more about this in *Chapter 13, An Introduction to AutoML*.

Predicting output

Once a net is trained, it can of course be used for making predictions. In TensorFlow, this is very simple. We can use this method:

```
# Making predictions.
predictions = model.predict(X)
```

For a given input, several types of output can be computed including a method `model.evaluate()` used to compute the loss values, a method `model.predict_classes()` used to compute category outputs, and a method `model.predict_proba()` used to compute class probabilities.

A practical overview of backpropagation

Multi-layer perceptrons learn from training data through a process called backpropagation. In this paragraph we will give an intuition while more details are in *Chapter 14, The Math Behind Deep Learning*. The process can be described as a way of progressively correcting mistakes as soon as they are detected. Let's see how this works.

Remember that each neural network layer has an associated set of weights that determine the output values for a given set of inputs. Additionally, remember that a neural network can have multiple hidden layers.

At the beginning, all the weights have some random assignment. Then the neural network is activated for each input in the training set: values are propagated *forward* from the input stage through the hidden stages to the output stage where a prediction is made.

Note that we keep *Figure 1.27* below simple by only representing a few values with green dotted lines but in reality, all the values are propagated forward through the network:

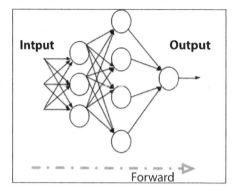

Figure 1.27: Forward step in backpropagation

Since we know the true observed value in the training set, it is possible to calculate the error made in the prediction. The key intuition for backtracking is to propagate the error back (see *Figure 1.28*), using an appropriate optimizer algorithm such as a GD to adjust the neural network weights with the goal of reducing the error (again for the sake of simplicity only a few error values are represented here):

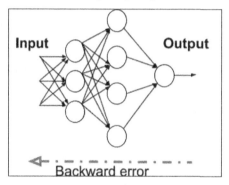

Figure 1.28: Backward step in backpropagation

The process of forward propagation from input to output and backward propagation of errors is repeated several times until the error gets below a predefined threshold. The whole process is represented in *Figure 1.29*:

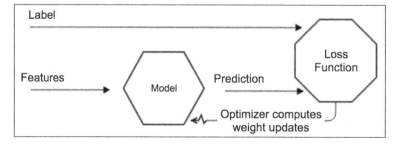

Figure 1.29: Forward propagation and backward propagation

The features represent the input, and the labels are used here to drive the learning process. The model is updated in such a way that the loss function is progressively minimized. In a neural network, what really matters is not the output of a single neuron but the collective weights adjusted in each layer. Therefore, the network progressively adjusts its internal weights in such a way that the prediction increases the number of correctly forecasted labels. Of course, using the right set of features and having quality labeled data is fundamental to minimizing the bias during the learning process.

What have we learned so far?

In this chapter, we have learned the basics of neural networks. More specifically, we have learned what a perceptron is and what a multi-layer perceptron is, how to define neural networks in TensorFlow, how to progressively improve metrics once a good baseline is established, and how to fine-tune the hyperparameter space. In addition to that, we also have a good idea of useful activation functions (sigmoid and ReLU) available, and how to train a network with backpropagation algorithms based on either GD, SGD, or more sophisticated approaches, such as Adam and RMSProp.

Toward a deep learning approach

While playing with handwritten digit recognition, we came to the conclusion that the closer we get to an accuracy of 99%, the more difficult it is to improve. If we want more improvement, we definitely need a new idea. What are we missing? Think about it.

The fundamental intuition is that in our examples so far, we are not making use of the local spatial structure of images, which means we will use the fact that an image can be described as a matrix with data locality. In particular, this piece of code transforms the bitmap representing each written digit into a flat vector where the local spatial structure (the fact that some pixels are closer to each other) is gone:

```
# X_train is 60000 rows of 28x28 values; we  --> reshape it as in 60000 x 784.
X_train = X_train.reshape(60000, 784)
X_test = X_test.reshape(10000, 784)
```

However, this is not how our brain works. Remember that our vision is based on multiple cortex levels, each one recognizing more and more structured information while still preserving the locality. First, we see single pixels, then from that, we recognize simple geometric forms and then more and more sophisticated elements such as objects, faces, human bodies, animals, and so on.

In *Chapter 3*, we will see that a particular type of deep learning network known as the **Convolutional Neural Network** (**CNN**) has been developed by taking into account both the idea of preserving the local spatial structure in images (and more generally in any type of information that has a spatial structure) and the idea of learning via progressive levels of abstraction: with one layer you can only learn simple patterns; with more than one layer you can learn multiple patterns. Before discussing CNN, we need to discuss some aspects of TensorFlow architecture and have a practical introduction to a few additional machine learning concepts.

Summary

In this chapter we learned what TensorFlow and Keras are and introduced neural networks with the perceptron and the multi-layer perceptron. Then, we saw a real example of recognizing handwritten digits with several optimizations.

The next chapter is devoted to regression and classification.

References

1. Rosenblatt, F. (1958). *The perceptron: a probabilistic model for information storage and organization in the brain*. Psychol. Rev, vol. 65, pp. 386–408.

2. Werbos, P. J. (1990). *Backpropagation through time: what it does and how to do it*. Proc. IEEE, vol. 78, pp. 1550–1560.

3. Hinton, G. E., Osindero, S., and Teh, Y. W. (2006). *A fast learning algorithm for deep belief nets*. Neural Comput, vol. 18, pp. 1527–1554.

4. Schmidhuber, J. (2015). *Deep learning in neural networks: an overview*. Neural Networks: Off. J. Int. Neural Netw. Soc., vol. 61, pp. 85–117.

5. Leven, S. (1996). *The roots of backpropagation: From ordered derivatives to neural networks and political forecasting*. Neural Networks, vol. 9.

6. Rumelhart, D. E., Hinton, G. E., and Williams, R. J. (1986). *Learning representations by back-propagating errors*. Nature, vol. 323.

7. Herculano-Houzel, S. (2009). *The human brain in numbers: a linearly scaled-up primate brain*. Front. Hum. Neurosci., vol. 3.

8. Hornick, K., Stinchcombe, M., and White, H. (1989). *Multilayer feedforward networks are universal approximators*. Neural Networks Volume 2, Issue 5. Pages 359–366.

9. Vapnik, V. N. (2013). *The nature of statistical learning theory*.

10. Sutskever, I., Martens, J., Dahl, G., Hinton, G., (2013). *On the importance of initialization and momentum in deep learning*. 30th International Conference on Machine Learning, ICML.

Join our book's Discord space

Join our Discord community to meet like-minded people and learn alongside more than 2000 members at: `https://packt.link/keras`

2

Regression and Classification

Regression and classification are two fundamental tasks ubiquitously present in almost all machine learning applications. They find application in varied fields ranging from engineering, physical science, biology, and the financial market, to the social sciences. They are the fundamental tools in the hands of statisticians and data scientists. In this chapter, we will cover the following topics:

- Regression
- Classification
- Difference between classification and regression
- Linear regression
- Different types of linear regression
- Classification using the TensorFlow Keras API
- Applying linear regression to estimate the price of a house
- Applying logistic regression to identify handwritten digits

 All the code files for this chapter can be found at `https://packt.link/dltfchp2`

Let us first start with understanding what regression really is.

What is regression?

Regression is normally the first algorithm that people in machine learning work with. It allows us to make predictions from data by learning about the relationship between a given set of dependent and independent variables. It has its use in almost every field; anywhere that has an interest in drawing relationships between two or more things will find a use for regression.

Consider the case of house price estimation. There are many factors that can have an impact on the house price: the number of rooms, the floor area, the locality, the availability of amenities, the parking space, and so on. Regression analysis can help us in finding the mathematical relationship between these factors and the house price.

Let us imagine a simpler world where only the area of the house determines its price. Using regression, we could determine the relationship between the area of the house (**independent variable:** these are the variables that do not depend upon any other variables) and its price (**dependent variable:** these variables depend upon one or more independent variables). Later, we could use this relationship to predict the price of any house, given its area. To learn more about dependent and independent variables and how to identify them, you can refer to this post: `https://medium.com/deeplearning-concepts-and-implementation/independent-and-dependent-variables-in-machine-learning-210b82f891db`. In machine learning, the independent variables are normally input into the model and the dependent variables are output from our model.

Depending upon the number of independent variables, the number of dependent variables, and the relationship type, we have many different types of regression. There are two important components of regression: the *relationship* between independent and dependent variables, and the *strength of impact* of different independent variables on dependent variables. In the following section, we will learn in detail about the widely used linear regression technique.

Prediction using linear regression

Linear regression is one of the most widely known modeling techniques. Existing for more than 200 years, it has been explored from almost all possible angles. Linear regression assumes a linear relationship between the input variable (X) and the output variable (Y). The basic idea of linear regression is building a model, using training data that can predict the output given the input, such that the predicted output $\hat{Y}$ is as near the observed training output Y for the input X. It involves finding a linear equation for the predicted value $\hat{Y}$ of the form:

$$\hat{Y} = W^T X + b$$

where $X = \{x_1, x_2, \ldots, x_n\}$ are the n input variables, and $W = \{w_1, w_2, \ldots, w_n\}$ are the linear coefficients, with b as the bias term. We can also expand the preceding equation to:

$$\hat{Y} = \sum_{i=1}^{n} x_i w_i + b$$

The bias term allows our regression model to provide an output even in the absence of any input; it provides us with an option to shift our data for a better fit. The error between the observed values (Y) and predicted values ($\hat{Y}$) for an input sample i is:

$$e_i = Y_i - \hat{Y}_i$$

The goal is to find the best estimates for the coefficients W and bias b, such that the error between the observed values Y and the predicted values $\hat{Y}$ is minimized. Let's go through some examples to better understand this.

Simple linear regression

If we consider only one independent variable and one dependent variable, what we get is a simple linear regression. Consider the case of house price prediction, defined in the preceding section; the area of the house (A) is the independent variable, and the price (Y) of the house is the dependent variable. We want to find a linear relationship between predicted price $\hat{Y}$ and A, of the form:

$$\hat{Y} = A.W + b$$

where b is the bias term. Thus, we need to determine W and b, such that the error between the price Y and the predicted price $\hat{Y}$ is minimized. The standard method used to estimate W and b is called the method of least squares, that is, we try to minimize the sum of the square of errors (S). For the preceding case, the expression becomes:

$$S(W,b) = \sum_{i=1}^{N}\left(Y_i - \hat{Y}_i\right)^2 = \sum_{i=1}^{N}(Y_i - A_iW - b)^2$$

We want to estimate the regression coefficients, W and b, such that S is minimized. We use the fact that the derivative of a function is 0 at its minima to get these two equations:

$$\frac{\partial S}{\partial W} = -2\sum_{i=1}^{N}(Y_i - A_iW - b)A_i = 0$$

$$\frac{\partial S}{\partial b} = -2\sum_{i=1}^{N}(Y_i - A_iW - b) = 0$$

These two equations can be solved to find the two unknowns. To do so, we first expand the summation in the second equation:

$$\sum_{i=1}^{N}Y_i - \sum_{i=1}^{N}A_iW - \sum_{i=1}^{N}b = 0$$

Take a look at the last term on the left-hand side; it just sums up a constant N time. Thus, we can rewrite it as:

$$\sum_{i=1}^{N}Y_i - W\sum_{i=1}^{N}A_i - Nb = 0$$

Reordering the terms, we get:

$$b = \frac{1}{N}\sum_{i=1}^{N}Y_i - \frac{W}{N}\sum_{i=1}^{N}A_i$$

The two terms on the right-hand side can be replaced by $\bar{Y}$, the average price (output), and $\bar{A}$, the average area (input), respectively, and thus we get:

$$b = \bar{Y} - W\bar{A}$$

In a similar fashion, we expand the partial differential equation of S with respect to weight W:

$$\sum_{i=1}^{N}(Y_i A_i - W A_i^2 - b A_i) = 0$$

Substitute the expression for the bias term b:

$$\sum_{i=1}^{N}(Y_i A_i - W A_i^2 - (\bar{Y} - W\bar{A})A_i) = 0$$

Reordering the equation:

$$\sum_{i=1}^{N}(Y_i A_i - \bar{Y}A_i) - W\sum_{i=1}^{N}(A_i^2 - \bar{A}A_i) = 0$$

Playing around with the mean definition, we can get from this the value of weight W as:

$$W = \frac{\sum_{i=1}^{N} Y_i(A_i - \bar{A})}{\sum_{i=1}^{N}(A_i - \bar{A})^2}$$

where $\bar{Y}$ and $\bar{A}$ are the average price and area, respectively. Let us try this on some simple sample data:

1. We import the necessary modules. It is a simple example, so we'll be using only NumPy, pandas, and Matplotlib:

```
import tensorflow as tf
import numpy as np
import matplotlib.pyplot as plt
import pandas as pd
```

2. Next, we generate random data with a linear relationship. To make it more realistic, we also add a random noise element. You can see the two variables (the cause, area, and the effect, price) follow a positive linear dependence:

```
#Generate a random data
np.random.seed(0)
area = 2.5 * np.random.randn(100) + 25
price = 25 * area + 5 + np.random.randint(20,50, size = len(area))
data = np.array([area, price])
data = pd.DataFrame(data = data.T, columns=['area','price'])
plt.scatter(data['area'], data['price'])
plt.show()
```

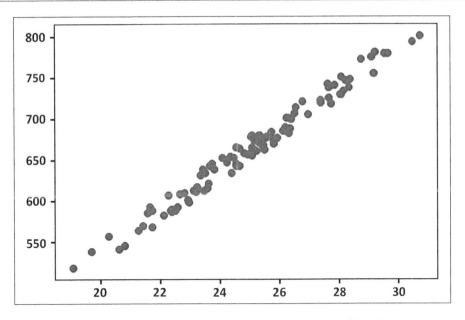

Figure 2.1: Scatter plot between the area of the house and its price

3. Now, we calculate the two regression coefficients using the equations we defined. You can see that the result is very much near the linear relationship we have simulated:

```
W = sum(price*(area-np.mean(area))) / sum((area-np.mean(area))**2)
b = np.mean(price) - W*np.mean(area)
print("The regression coefficients are", W,b)
```

```
The regression coefficients are 24.815544052284988 43.4989785533412
```

4. Let us now try predicting the new prices using the obtained weight and bias values:

```
y_pred = W * area + b
```

5. Next, we plot the predicted prices along with the actual price. You can see that predicted prices follow a linear relationship with the area:

```
plt.plot(area, y_pred, color='red',label="Predicted Price")
plt.scatter(data['area'], data['price'], label="Training Data")
plt.xlabel("Area")
plt.ylabel("Price")
plt.legend()
```

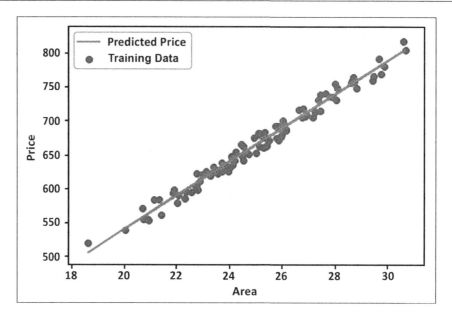

Figure 2.2: Predicted values vs the actual price

From *Figure 2.2*, we can see that the predicted values follow the same trend as the actual house prices.

Multiple linear regression

The preceding example was simple, but that is rarely the case. In most problems, the dependent variables depend upon multiple independent variables. Multiple linear regression finds a linear relationship between the many independent input variables (X) and the dependent output variable (Y), such that they satisfy the predicted Y value of the form:

$$\hat{Y} = W^T X + b$$

where $X = \{x_1, x_2, \ldots, x_n\}$ are the n independent input variables, and $W = \{w_1, w_2, \ldots, w_n\}$ are the linear coefficients, with b as the bias term.

As before, the linear coefficients W_s are estimated using the method of least squares, that is, minimizing the sum of squared differences between predicted values ($\hat{Y}$) and observed values (Y). Thus, we try to minimize the loss function (also called squared error, and if we divide by n, it is the mean squared error):

$$loss = \sum_i \left(Y_i - \hat{Y}_i\right)^2$$

where the sum is over all the training samples.

As you might have guessed, now, instead of two, we will have *n+1* equations, which we will need to simultaneously solve. An easier alternative will be to use the TensorFlow Keras API. We will learn shortly how to use the TensorFlow Keras API to perform the task of regression.

Multivariate linear regression

There can be cases where the independent variables affect more than one dependent variable. For example, consider the case where we want to predict a rocket's speed and its carbon dioxide emission – these two will now be our dependent variables, and both will be affected by the sensors reading the fuel amount, engine type, rocket body, and so on. This is a case of multivariate linear regression. Mathematically, a multivariate regression model can be represented as:

$$\hat{Y}_{ij} = w_{0j} + \sum_{k=1}^{p} w_{kj} x_{ik}$$

where $i \in [1, \dots, n]$ and $j \in [1, \dots, m]$. The term $\hat{Y}_{ij}$ represents the jth predicted output value corresponding to the ith input sample, w represents the regression coefficients, and x_{ik} is the kth feature of the ith input sample. The number of equations needed to solve in this case will now be $n \times m$. While we can solve these equations using matrices, the process will be computationally expensive as it will involve calculating the inverse and determinants. An easier way would be to use the gradient descent with the sum of least square error as the loss function and to use one of the many optimizers that the TensorFlow API includes.

In the next section, we will delve deeper into the TensorFlow Keras API, a versatile higher-level API to develop your model with ease.

Neural networks for linear regression

In the preceding sections, we used mathematical expressions for calculating the coefficients of a linear regression equation. In this section, we will see how we can use the neural networks to perform the task of regression and build a neural network model using the TensorFlow Keras API.

Before performing regression using neural networks, let us first review what a neural network is. Simply speaking, a neural network is a network of many artificial neurons. From *Chapter 1, Neural Network Foundations with TF*, we know that the simplest neural network, the (simple) perceptron, can be mathematically represented as:

$$y = f(W^T x + b)$$

where f is the activation function. Consider, if we have f as a linear function, then the above expression is similar to the expression of linear regression that we learned in the previous section. In other words, we can say that a neural network, which is also called a function approximator, is a generalized regressor. Let us try to build a neural network simple regressor next using the TensorFlow Keras API.

Simple linear regression using TensorFlow Keras

In the first chapter, we learned about how to build a model in TensorFlow Keras. Here, we will use the same `Sequential` API to build a single-layered perceptron (fully connected neural network) using the `Dense` class. We will continue with the same problem, that is, predicting the price of a house given its area:

1. We start with importing the packages we will need. Notice the addition of the Keras module and the Dense layer in importing packages:

```
import tensorflow as tf
import numpy as np
import matplotlib.pyplot as plt
import pandas as pd
import tensorflow.keras as K
from tensorflow.keras.layers import Dense
```

2. Next, we generate the data, as in the previous case:

```
#Generate a random data
np.random.seed(0)
area = 2.5 * np.random.randn(100) + 25
price = 25 * area + 5 + np.random.randint(20,50, size = len(area))
data = np.array([area, price])
data = pd.DataFrame(data = data.T, columns=['area','price'])
plt.scatter(data['area'], data['price'])
plt.show()
```

3. The input to neural networks should be normalized; this is because input gets multiplied with weights, and if we have very large numbers, the result of multiplication will be large, and soon our metrics may cross infinity (the largest number your computer can handle):

```
data = (data - data.min()) / (data.max() - data.min())  #Normalize
```

4. Let us now build the model; since it is a simple linear regressor, we use a Dense layer with only one unit:

```
model = K.Sequential([
                      Dense(1, input_shape = [1,], activation=None)
])
model.summary()
```

```
Model: "sequential"
_____
 Layer (type)            Output Shape              Param #
=================================================================
 dense (Dense)           (None, 1)                 2


=================================================================
Total params: 2
Trainable params: 2
Non-trainable params: 0
_____
```

5. To train a model, we will need to define the loss function and optimizer. The loss function defines the quantity that our model tries to minimize, and the optimizer decides the minimization algorithm we are using. Additionally, we can also define metrics, which is the quantity we want to log as the model is trained. We define the loss function, optimizer (see *Chapter 1*, *Neural Network Foundations with TF*), and metrics using the compile function:

```
model.compile(loss='mean_squared_error', optimizer='sgd')
```

6. Now that model is defined, we just need to train it using the fit function. Observe that we are using a batch_size of 32 and splitting the data into training and validation datasets using the validation_spilt argument of the fit function:

```
model.fit(x=data['area'],y=data['price'], epochs=100, batch_size=32,
verbose=1, validation_split=0.2)
```

```
model.fit(x=data['area'],y=data['price'], epochs=100, batch_size=32,
verbose=1, validation_split=0.2)
Epoch 1/100
3/3 [==============================] - 0s 78ms/step - loss: 1.2643 - val_
loss: 1.4828
Epoch 2/100
3/3 [==============================] - 0s 13ms/step - loss: 1.0987 - val_
loss: 1.3029
Epoch 3/100
3/3 [==============================] - 0s 13ms/step - loss: 0.9576 - val_
loss: 1.1494
Epoch 4/100
3/3 [==============================] - 0s 16ms/step - loss: 0.8376 - val_
loss: 1.0156
Epoch 5/100
3/3 [==============================] - 0s 15ms/step - loss: 0.7339 - val_
loss: 0.8971
Epoch 6/100
3/3 [==============================] - 0s 16ms/step - loss: 0.6444 - val_
loss: 0.7989
Epoch 7/100
3/3 [==============================] - 0s 14ms/step - loss: 0.5689 - val_
loss: 0.7082
   .
   .
   .
Epoch 96/100
3/3 [==============================] - 0s 22ms/step - loss: 0.0827 - val_
loss: 0.0755
```

```
Epoch 97/100
3/3 [==============================] - 0s 17ms/step - loss: 0.0824 - val_
loss: 0.0750
Epoch 98/100
3/3 [==============================] - 0s 14ms/step - loss: 0.0821 - val_
loss: 0.0747
Epoch 99/100
3/3 [==============================] - 0s 21ms/step - loss: 0.0818 - val_
loss: 0.0740
Epoch 100/100
3/3 [==============================] - 0s 15ms/step - loss: 0.0815 - val_
loss: 0.0740
<keras.callbacks.History at 0x7f7228d6a790>
```

7. Well, you have successfully trained a neural network to perform the task of linear regression. The mean squared error after training for 100 epochs is 0.0815 on training data and 0.074 on validation data. We can get the predicted value for a given input using the `predict` function:

    ```
    y_pred = model.predict(data['area'])
    ```

8. Next, we plot a graph of the predicted and the actual data:

    ```
    plt.plot(data['area'], y_pred, color='red',label="Predicted Price")
    plt.scatter(data['area'], data['price'], label="Training Data")
    plt.xlabel("Area")
    plt.ylabel("Price")
    plt.legend()
    ```

9. *Figure 2.3* shows the plot between the predicted data and the actual data. You can see that, just like the linear regressor, we have got a nice linear fit:

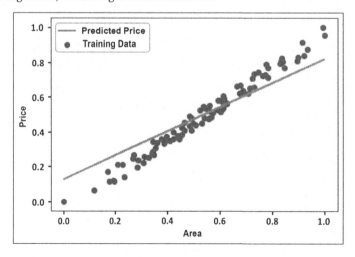

Figure 2.3: Predicted price vs actual price

10. In case you are interested in knowing the coefficients W and b, we can do it by printing the weights of the model using `model.weights`:

```
[<tf.Variable 'dense/kernel:0' shape=(1, 1) dtype=float32,
numpy=array([[-0.33806288]], dtype=float32)>,
<tf.Variable 'dense/bias:0' shape=(1,) dtype=float32,
numpy=array([0.68142694], dtype=float32)>]
```

We can see from the result above that our coefficients are W= 0.69 and bias b= 0.127. Thus, using linear regression, we can find a linear relationship between the house price and its area. In the next section, we explore multiple and multivariate linear regression using the TensorFlow Keras API.

Multiple and multivariate linear regression using the TensorFlow Keras API

The example in the previous section had only one independent variable, the *area* of the house, and one dependent variable, the *price* of the house. However, problems in real life are not that simple; we may have more than one independent variable, and we may need to predict more than one dependent variable. As you must have realized from the discussion on multiple and multivariate regression, they involve solving multiple equations. We can make our tasks easier by using the Keras API for both tasks.

Additionally, we can have more than one neural network layer, that is, we can build a **deep neural network**. A deep neural network is like applying multiple function approximators:

$$f(x) = f_L\big(f_{L-1}(\ldots f_1(x)\ldots)\big)$$

with f_L being the function at layer L. From the expression above, we can see that if f was a linear function, adding multiple layers of a neural network was not useful; however, using a non-linear activation function (see *Chapter 1, Neural Network Foundations with TF*, for more details) allows us to apply neural networks to the regression problems where dependent and independent variables are related in some non-linear fashion. In this section, we will use a deep neural network, built using TensorFlow Keras, to predict the fuel efficiency of a car, given its number of cylinders, displacement, acceleration, and so on. The data we use is available from the UCI ML repository (Blake, C., & Merz, C. (1998), the UCI repository of machine learning databases (`http://www.ics.uci.edu/~mlearn/MLRepository.html`):

1. We start by importing the modules that we will need. In the previous example, we normalized our data using the DataFrame operations. In this example, we will make use of the Keras `Normalization` layer. The `Normalization` layer shifts the data to a zero mean and one standard deviation. Also, since we have more than one independent variable, we will use Seaborn to visualize the relationship between different variables:

```
import tensorflow as tf
import numpy as np
import matplotlib.pyplot as plt
import pandas as pd
import tensorflow.keras as K
from tensorflow.keras.layers import Dense, Normalization
```

```
import seaborn as sns
```

2. Let us first download the data from the UCI ML repo.

```
url = 'https://archive.ics.uci.edu/ml/machine-learning-databases/auto-
mpg/auto-mpg.data'
column_names = ['mpg', 'cylinders', 'displacement', 'horsepower',
'weight', 'acceleration', 'model_year', 'origin']


data = pd.read_csv(url, names=column_names, na_values='?', comment='\t',
sep=' ', skipinitialspace=True)
```

3. The data consists of eight features: mpg, cylinders, displacement, horsepower, weight, acceleration, model year, and origin. Though the origin of the vehicle can also affect the fuel efficiency "mpg" (*miles per gallon*), we use only seven features to predict the mpg value. Also, we drop any rows with NaN values:

```
data = data.drop('origin', 1)
print(data.isna().sum())
data = data.dropna()
```

4. We divide the dataset into training and test datasets. Here, we are keeping 80% of the 392 datapoints as training data and 20% as test dataset:

```
train_dataset = data.sample(frac=0.8, random_state=0)
test_dataset = data.drop(train_dataset.index)
```

5. Next, we use Seaborn's `pairplot` to visualize the relationship between the different variables:

```
sns.pairplot(train_dataset[['mpg', 'cylinders',
'displacement','horsepower', 'weight', 'acceleration', 'model_year']],
diag_kind='kde')
```

6. We can see that mpg (fuel efficiency) has dependencies on all the other variables, and the dependency relationship is non-linear, as none of the curves are linear:

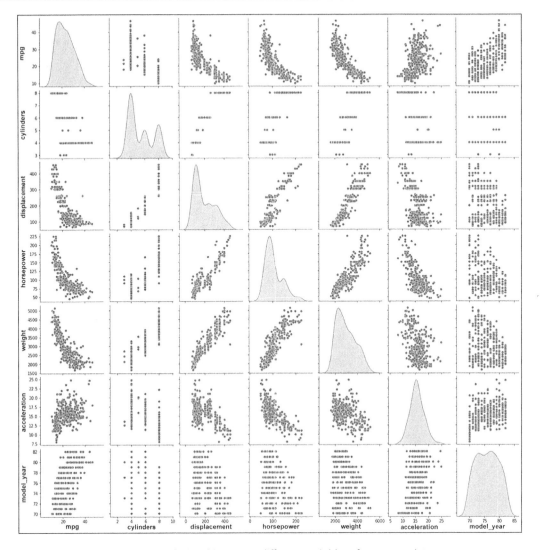

Figure 2.4: Relationship among different variables of auto-mpg data

7. For convenience, we also separate the variables into input variables and the label that we want to predict:

```
train_features = train_dataset.copy()
test_features = test_dataset.copy()


train_labels = train_features.pop('mpg')
test_labels = test_features.pop('mpg')
```

8. Now, we use the Normalization layer of Keras to normalize our data. Note that while we normalized our inputs to a value with mean 0 and standard deviation 1, the output prediction `'mpg'` remains as it is:

```
#Normalize
data_normalizer = Normalization(axis=1)
data_normalizer.adapt(np.array(train_features))
```

9. We build our model. The model has two hidden layers, with 64 and 32 neurons, respectively. For the hidden layers, we have used **Rectified Linear Unit (ReLU)** as our activation function; this should help in approximating the non-linear relation between fuel efficiency and the rest of the variables:

```
model = K.Sequential([
    data_normalizer,
    Dense(64, activation='relu'),
    Dense(32, activation='relu'),
    Dense(1, activation=None)
])
model.summary()
```

10. Earlier, we used stochastic gradient as the optimizer; this time, we try the Adam optimizer (see *Chapter 1, Neural Network Foundations with TF*, for more details). The loss function for the regression we chose is the mean squared error again:

```
model.compile(optimizer='adam', loss='mean_squared_error')
```

11. Next, we train the model for 100 epochs:

```
history = model.fit(x=train_features,y=train_labels, epochs=100,
verbose=1, validation_split=0.2)
```

12. Cool, now that the model is trained, we can check if our model is overfitted, underfitted, or properly fitted by plotting the loss curve. Both validation loss and training loss are near each other as we increase the training epochs; this suggests that our model is properly trained:

```
plt.plot(history.history['loss'], label='loss')
plt.plot(history.history['val_loss'], label='val_loss')
plt.xlabel('Epoch')
plt.ylabel('Error [MPG]')
plt.legend()
plt.grid(True)
```

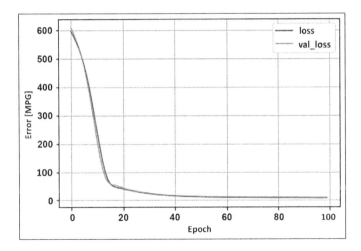

Figure 2.5: Model error

13. Let us finally compare the predicted fuel efficiency and the true fuel efficiency on the test dataset. Remember that the model has not seen a test dataset ever, thus this prediction is from the model's ability to generalize the relationship between inputs and fuel efficiency. If the model has learned the relationship well, the two should form a linear relationship:

```
y_pred = model.predict(test_features).flatten()
a = plt.axes(aspect='equal')
plt.scatter(test_labels, y_pred)
plt.xlabel('True Values [MPG]')
plt.ylabel('Predictions [MPG]')
lims = [0, 50]
plt.xlim(lims)
plt.ylim(lims)
plt.plot(lims, lims)
```

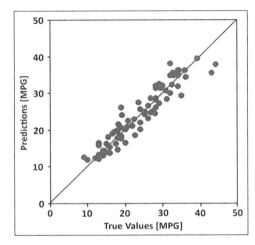

Figure 2.6: Plot between predicted fuel efficiency and actual values

14. Additionally, we can also plot the error between the predicted and true fuel efficiency:

```
error = y_pred - test_labels
plt.hist(error, bins=30)
plt.xlabel('Prediction Error [MPG]')
plt.ylabel('Count')
```

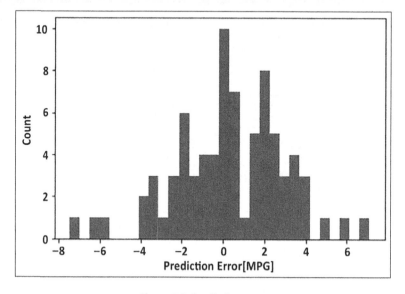

Figure 2.7: Prediction error

In case we want to make more than one prediction, that is, dealing with a multivariate regression problem, the only change would be that instead of one unit in the last dense layer, we will have as many units as the number of variables to be predicted. Consider, for example, we want to build a model which takes into account a student's SAT score, attendance, and some family parameters, and wants to predict the GPA score for all four undergraduate years; then we will have the output layer with four units. Now that you are familiar with regression, let us move toward the classification tasks.

Classification tasks and decision boundaries

Till now, the focus of the chapter was on regression. In this section, we will talk about another important task: the task of classification. Let us first understand the difference between regression (also sometimes referred to as prediction) and classification:

- In classification, the data is grouped into classes/categories, while in regression, the aim is to get a continuous numerical value for given data. For example, identifying the number of handwritten digits is a classification task; all handwritten digits will belong to one of the ten numbers lying between 0-9. The task of predicting the price of the house depending upon different input variables is a regression task.

- In a classification task, the model finds the decision boundaries separating one class from another. In the regression task, the model approximates a function that fits the input-output relationship.

- Classification is a subset of regression; here, we are predicting classes. Regression is much more general.

Figure 2.8 shows how classification and regression tasks differ. In classification, we need to find a line (or a plane or hyperplane in multidimensional space) separating the classes. In regression, the aim is to find a line (or plane or hyperplane) that fits the given input points:

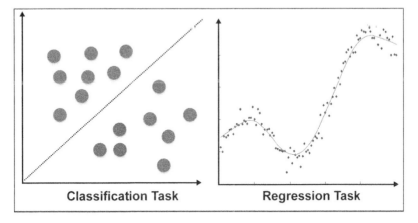

Figure 2.8: Classification vs regression

In the following section, we will explain logistic regression, which is a very common and useful classification technique.

Logistic regression

Logistic regression is used to determine the probability of an event. Conventionally, the event is represented as a categorical dependent variable. The probability of the event is expressed using the sigmoid (or "logit") function:

$$P(\hat{Y} = 1 | X = x) = \frac{1}{1 + e^{-(b + w^T x)}}$$

The goal now is to estimate weights $W = \{w_1, w_2, \ldots, w_n\}$ and bias term b. In logistic regression, the coefficients are estimated using either the maximum likelihood estimator or stochastic gradient descent. If p is the total number of input data points, the loss is conventionally defined as a cross-entropy term given by:

$$loss = \sum_{1=1}^{p} Y_i \log(\hat{Y}_i) + (1 - Y_i) \log(1 - \hat{Y}_i)$$

Logistic regression is used in classification problems. For example, when looking at medical data, we can use logistic regression to classify whether a person has cancer or not. If the output categorical variable has two or more levels, we can use multinomial logistic regression. Another common technique used for two or more output variables is one versus all.

For multiclass logistic regression, the cross-entropy loss function is modified as:

$$loss = \sum_{i=1}^{p} \sum_{j=1}^{k} Y_{ij} \log \hat{Y}_{ij}$$

where K is the total number of classes. You can read more about logistic regression at `https://en.wikipedia.org/wiki/Logistic_regression`.

Now that you have some idea about logistic regression, let us see how we can apply it to any dataset.

Logistic regression on the MNIST dataset

Next, we will use TensorFlow Keras to classify handwritten digits using logistic regression. We will be using the **MNIST (Modified National Institute of Standards and Technology)** dataset. For those working in the field of deep learning, MNIST is not new, it is like the ABC of machine learning. It contains images of handwritten digits and a label for each image, indicating which digit it is. The label contains a value lying between 0-9 depending on the handwritten digit. Thus, it is a multiclass classification.

To implement the logistic regression, we will make a model with only one dense layer. Each class will be represented by a unit in the output, so since we have 10 classes, the number of units in the output would be 10. The probability function used in the logistic regression is similar to the sigmoid activation function; therefore, we use sigmoid activation.

Let us build our model:

1. The first step is, as always, importing the modules needed. Notice that here we are using another useful layer from the Keras API, the `Flatten` layer. The `Flatten` layer helps us to resize the 28 x 28 two-dimensional input images of the MNIST dataset into a 784 flattened array:

    ```
    import tensorflow as tf
    import numpy as np
    import matplotlib.pyplot as plt
    import pandas as pd
    import tensorflow.keras as K
    from tensorflow.keras.layers import Dense, Flatten
    ```

2. We take the input data of MNIST from the `tensorflow.keras` dataset:

    ```
    ((train_data, train_labels),(test_data, test_labels)) = tf.keras.
    datasets.mnist.load_data()
    ```

3. Next, we preprocess the data. We normalize the images; the MNIST dataset images are black and white images with the intensity value of each pixel lying between 0-255. We divide it by 255, so that now the values lie between 0-1:

    ```
    train_data = train_data/np.float32(255)
    train_labels = train_labels.astype(np.int32)
    ```

```
test_data = test_data/np.float32(255)
test_labels = test_labels.astype(np.int32)
```

4. Now, we define a very simple model; it has only one Dense layer with 10 units, and it takes an input of size 784. You can see from the output of the model summary that only the Dense layer has trainable parameters:

```
model = K.Sequential([
    Flatten(input_shape=(28, 28)),
    Dense(10, activation='sigmoid')
])
model.summary()
```

```
Model: "sequential"

_____
 Layer (type)              Output Shape            Param #
=================================================================
 flatten (Flatten)         (None, 784)             0

 dense (Dense)             (None, 10)              7850

=================================================================
Total params: 7,850
Trainable params: 7,850
Non-trainable params: 0
_____
```

5. Since the test labels are integral values, we will use SparseCategoricalCrossentropy loss with logits set to True. The optimizer selected is Adam. Additionally, we also define accuracy as metrics to be logged as the model is trained. We train our model for 50 epochs, with a train-validation split of 80:20:

```
model.compile(optimizer='adam', loss=tf.keras.losses.
SparseCategoricalCrossentropy(from_logits=True), metrics=['accuracy'])

history = model.fit(x=train_data,y=train_labels, epochs=50, verbose=1,
validation_split=0.2)
```

6. Let us see how our simple model has fared by plotting the loss plot. You can see that since the validation loss and training loss are diverging, as the training loss is decreasing, the validation loss increases, thus the model is overfitting. You can improve the model performance by adding hidden layers:

```
plt.plot(history.history['loss'], label='loss')
plt.plot(history.history['val_loss'], label='val_loss')
```

```
plt.xlabel('Epoch')
plt.ylabel('Loss')
plt.legend()
plt.grid(True)
```

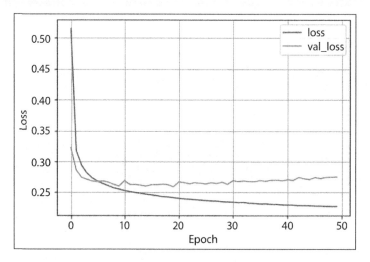

Figure 2.9: Loss plot

7. To better understand the result, we build two utility functions; these functions help us in visualizing the handwritten digits and the probability of the 10 units in the output:

```
def plot_image(i, predictions_array, true_label, img):
    true_label, img = true_label[i], img[i]
    plt.grid(False)
    plt.xticks([])
    plt.yticks([])

    plt.imshow(img, cmap=plt.cm.binary)

    predicted_label = np.argmax(predictions_array)
    if predicted_label == true_label:
        color ='blue'
    else:
        color ='red'

    plt.xlabel("Pred {} Conf: {:2.0f}% True ({})".format(predicted_label,
                           100*np.max(predictions_array),
                           true_label),
                           color=color)
```

```
def plot_value_array(i, predictions_array, true_label):
    true_label = true_label[i]
    plt.grid(False)
    plt.xticks(range(10))
    plt.yticks([])
    thisplot = plt.bar(range(10), predictions_array,
    color"#777777")
    plt.ylim([0, 1])
    predicted_label = np.argmax(predictions_array)
    thisplot[predicted_label].set_color('red')
    thisplot[true_label].set_color('blue')
```

8. Using these utility functions, we plot the predictions:

```
predictions = model.predict(test_data)
i = 56
plt.figure(figsize=(10,5))
plt.subplot(1,2,1)
plot_image(i, predictions[i], test_labels, test_data)
plt.subplot(1,2,2)
plot_value_array(i, predictions[i],  test_labels)
plt.show()
```

9. The plot on the left is the image of the handwritten digit, with the predicted label, the confidence in the prediction, and the true label. The image on the right shows the probability (logistic) output of the 10 units; we can see that the unit which represents the number 4 has the highest probability:

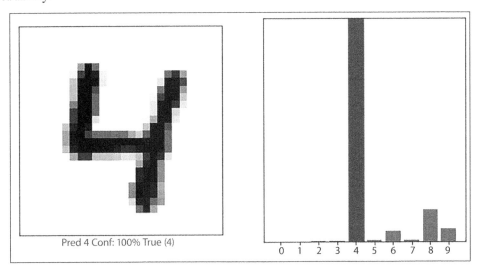

Pred 4 Conf: 100% True (4)

Figure 2.10: Predicted digit and confidence value of the prediction

10. In this code, to stay true to logistic regression, we used a sigmoid activation function and only one `Dense` layer. For better performance, adding dense layers and using softmax as the final activation function will be helpful. For example, the following model gives 97% accuracy on the validation dataset:

```
better_model = K.Sequential([
    Flatten(input_shape=(28, 28)),
    Dense(128,  activation='relu'),
    Dense(10, activation='softmax')
])
better_model.summary()
```

You can experiment by adding more layers, or by changing the number of neurons in each layer, and even changing the optimizer. This will give you a better understanding of how these parameters influence the model performance.

Summary

This chapter dealt with different types of regression algorithms. We started with linear regression and used it to predict house prices for a simple one-input variable case. We built simple and multiple linear regression models using the TensorFlow Keras API. The chapter then moved toward logistic regression, which is a very important and useful technique for classifying tasks. The chapter explained the TensorFlow Keras API and used it to implement both linear and logistic regression for some classical datasets. The next chapter will introduce you to convolutional neural networks, the most commercially successful neural network models for image data.

References

Here are some good resources if you are interested in knowing more about the concepts we've covered in this chapter:

1. TensorFlow website: `https://www.tensorflow.org/`
2. *Exploring bivariate numerical data*: `https://www.khanacademy.org/math/statistics-probability/describing-relationships-quantitative-data`
3. Murphy, K. P. (2022). *Probabilistic Machine Learning: An introduction*, MIT Press.
4. Blake, C., & Merz, C. (1998). UCI repository of machine learning databases: `http://www.ics.uci.edu/~mlearn/MLRepository.html`

Join our book's Discord space

Join our Discord community to meet like-minded people and learn alongside more than 2000 members at: `https://packt.link/keras`

3

Convolutional Neural Networks

In *Chapter 1, Neural Network Foundations with TF*, we discussed dense networks, in which each layer is fully connected to the adjacent layers. We looked at one application of those dense networks in classifying the MNIST handwritten characters dataset. In that context, each pixel in the input image has been assigned to a neuron for a total of 784 (28 x 28 pixels) input neurons. However, this strategy does not leverage the spatial structure and relationships between each image. In particular, this piece of code is a dense network that transforms the bitmap representing each written digit into a flat vector where the local spatial structure is removed. Removing the spatial structure is a problem because important information is lost:

```
#X_train is 60000 rows of 28x28 values --> reshaped in 60000 x 784
X_train = X_train.reshape(60000, 784)
X_test = X_test.reshape(10000, 784)
```

Convolutional neural networks leverage spatial information, and they are therefore very well-suited for classifying images. These nets use an ad hoc architecture inspired by biological data taken from physiological experiments performed on the visual cortex. Biological studies show that our vision is based on multiple cortex levels, each one recognizing more and more structured information. First, we see single pixels, then from that, we recognize simple geometric forms and then more and more sophisticated elements such as objects, faces, human bodies, animals, and so on.

Convolutional neural networks are a fascinating subject. Over a short period of time, they have shown themselves to be a disruptive technology, breaking performance records in multiple domains from text, to video, to speech, going well beyond the initial image processing domain where they were originally conceived. In this chapter, we will introduce the idea of convolutional neural networks (also known as CNNs, DCNNs, and ConvNets), a particular type of neural network that has large importance for deep learning.

This chapter covers the following topics:

- Deep convolutional neural networks
- An example of a deep convolutional neural network
- Recognizing CIFAR-10 images with deep learning

- Very deep convolutional networks for large-scale image recognition
- Deep Inception V3 networks for transfer learning
- Other CNN architectures
- Style transfer

 All the code files for this chapter can be found at `https://packt.link/dltfchp3`.

Let's begin with deep convolutional neural networks.

Deep convolutional neural networks

A **Deep Convolutional Neural Network (DCNN)** consists of many neural network layers. Two different types of layers, convolutional and pooling (i.e., subsampling), are typically alternated. The depth of each filter increases from left to right in the network. The last stage is typically made of one or more fully connected layers.

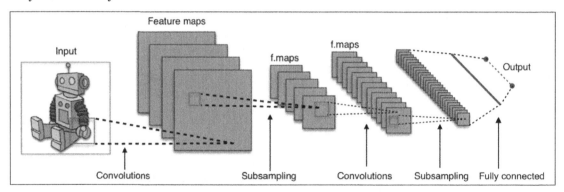

Figure 3.1: An example of a DCNN

There are three key underlying concepts for ConvNets: local receptive fields, shared weights, and pooling. Let's review them together.

Local receptive fields

If we want to preserve the spatial information of an image or other form of data, then it is convenient to represent each image with a matrix of pixels. Given this, a simple way to encode the local structure is to connect a submatrix of adjacent input neurons into one single hidden neuron belonging to the next layer. That single hidden neuron represents one local receptive field. Note that this operation is named convolution, and this is where the name for this type of network is derived. You can think about convolution as the treatment of a matrix by another matrix, referred to as a kernel.

Of course, we can encode more information by having overlapping submatrices. For instance, let's suppose that the size of every single submatrix is 5 x 5 and that those submatrices are used with MNIST images of 28 x 28 pixels. Then we will be able to generate 24 x 24 local receptive field neurons in the hidden layer. In fact, it is possible to slide the submatrices by only 23 positions before touching the borders of the images. In TensorFlow, the number of pixels along one edge of the kernel, or submatrix, is the kernel size, and the stride length is the number of pixels by which the kernel is moved at each step in the convolution.

Let's define the feature map from one layer to another. Of course, we can have multiple feature maps that learn independently from each hidden layer. For example, we can start with 28 x 28 input neurons for processing MNIST images, and then define *k* feature maps of size 24 x 24 neurons each (again with shape of 5 x 5) in the next hidden layer.

Shared weights and bias

Let's suppose that we want to move away from the pixel representation in a raw image, by gaining the ability to detect the same feature independently from the location where it is placed in the input image. A simple approach is to use the same set of weights and biases for all the neurons in the hidden layers. In this way, each layer will learn a set of position-independent latent features derived from the image, bearing in mind that a layer consists of a set of kernels in parallel, and each kernel only learns one feature.

A mathematical example

One simple way to understand convolution is to think about a sliding window function applied to a matrix. In the following example, given the input matrix **I** and the kernel **K**, we get the convolved output. The 3 x 3 kernel **K** (sometimes called the filter or feature detector) is multiplied elementwise with the input matrix to get one cell in the output matrix. All the other cells are obtained by sliding the window over **I**:

J

1	1	1	0	0
0	1	1	1	0
0	0	1	1	1
0	0	1	1	0
0	1	1	0	0

K

1	0	1
0	1	0
1	0	1

Convolved

4	3	4
2	4	3
2	3	4

In this example, we decided to stop the sliding window as soon as we touch the borders of **I** (so the output is 3 x 3). Alternatively, we could have chosen to pad the input with zeros (so that the output would have been 5 x 5). This decision relates to the padding choice adopted. Note that kernel depth is equal to input depth (channel).

Another choice is about how far along we slide our sliding windows with each step. This is called the stride and it can be one or more. A larger stride generates fewer applications of the kernel and a smaller output size, while a smaller stride generates more output and retains more information.

The size of the filter, the stride, and the type of padding are hyperparameters that can be fine-tuned during the training of the network.

ConvNets in TensorFlow

In TensorFlow, if we want to add a convolutional layer with 32 parallel features and a filter size of 3x3, we write:

```
import tensorflow as tf
from tensorflow.keras import datasets, layers, models
model = models.Sequential()
model.add(layers.Conv2D(32, (3, 3), activation='relu', input_shape=(28, 28,
1)))
```

This means that we are applying a 3x3 convolution on 28x28 images with 1 input channel (or input filters) resulting in 32 output channels (or output filters).

An example of convolution is provided in *Figure 3.2*:

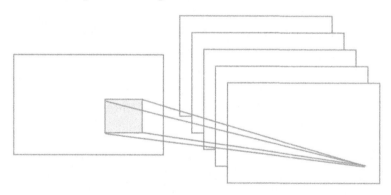

Figure.3.2: An example of convolution

Pooling layers

Let's suppose that we want to summarize the output of a feature map. Again, we can use the spatial contiguity of the output produced from a single feature map and aggregate the values of a sub-matrix into one single output value synthetically describing the "meaning" associated with that physical region.

Max pooling

One easy and common choice is the so-called max pooling operator, which simply outputs the maximum activation as observed in the region. In Keras, if we want to define a max pooling layer of size 2 x 2, we write:

```
model.add(layers.MaxPooling2D((2, 2)))
```

An example of the max-pooling operation is given in *Figure 3.3*:

Figure 3.3: An example of max pooling

Average pooling

Another choice is average pooling, which simply aggregates a region into the average values of the activations observed in that region.

Note that Keras implements a large number of pooling layers, and a complete list is available online (see `https://keras.io/layers/pooling/`). In short, all the pooling operations are nothing more than a summary operation on a given region.

ConvNets summary

So far, we have described the basic concepts of ConvNets. CNNs apply convolution and pooling operations in one dimension for audio and text data along the time dimension, in two dimensions for images along the (height x width) dimensions, and in three dimensions for videos along the (height x width x time) dimensions. For images, sliding the filter over an input volume produces a map that provides the responses of the filter for each spatial position.

In other words, a ConvNet has multiple filters stacked together that learn to recognize specific visual features independently from the location in the image itself. Those visual features are simple in the initial layers of the network and become more and more sophisticated deeper in the network. Training of a CNN requires the identification of the right values for each filter so that an input, when passed through multiple layers, activates certain neurons of the last layer so that it will predict the correct values.

An example of DCNN: LeNet

Yann LeCun, who won the Turing Award, proposed [1] a family of ConvNets named LeNet, trained for recognizing MNIST handwritten characters with robustness to simple geometric transformations and distortion. The core idea of LeNet is to have lower layers alternating convolution operations with max-pooling operations. The convolution operations are based on carefully chosen local receptive fields with shared weights for multiple feature maps. Then, higher levels are fully connected based on a traditional MLP with hidden layers and softmax as the output layer.

LeNet code in TF

To define a LeNet in code, we use a convolutional 2D module (note that `tf.keras.layers.Conv2D` is an alias of `tf.keras.layers.Convolution2D`, so the two can be used in an interchangeable way – see `https://www.tensorflow.org/api_docs/python/tf/keras/layers/Conv2D`):

```
layers.Convolution2D(20, (5, 5), activation='relu', input_shape=input_shape)
```

where the first parameter is the number of output filters in the convolution and the next tuple is the extension of each filter. An interesting optional parameter is padding. There are two options: `padding='valid'` means that the convolution is only computed where the input and the filter fully overlap and therefore the output is smaller than the input, while `padding='same'` means that we have an output that is the same size as the input, for which the area around the input is padded with zeros.

In addition, we use a `MaxPooling2D` module:

```
layers.MaxPooling2D(pool_size=(2, 2), strides=(2, 2))
```

where `pool_size=(2, 2)` is a tuple of 2 integers representing the factors by which the image is vertically and horizontally downscaled. So (2, 2) will halve the image in each dimension, and `strides=(2, 2)` is the stride used for processing.

Now, let us review the code. First, we import a number of modules:

```
import tensorflow as tf
from tensorflow.keras import datasets, layers, models, optimizers
# network and training
EPOCHS = 5
BATCH_SIZE = 128
VERBOSE = 1
OPTIMIZER = tf.keras.optimizers.Adam()
VALIDATION_SPLIT=0.90

IMG_ROWS, IMG_COLS = 28, 28 # input image dimensions
INPUT_SHAPE = (IMG_ROWS, IMG_COLS, 1)
NB_CLASSES = 10  # number of outputs = number of digits
```

Then we define the LeNet network:

```
#define the convnet
def build(input_shape, classes):
    model = models.Sequential()
```

We have a first convolutional stage with ReLU activations followed by max pooling. Our network will learn 20 convolutional filters, each one of which has a size of 5x5. The output dimension is the same as the input shape, so it will be 28 x 28. Note that since `Convolutional2D` is the first stage of our pipeline, we are also required to define its input_shape.

The max pooling operation implements a sliding window which slides over the layer and takes the maximum of each region with a step of two pixels both vertically and horizontally:

```
# CONV => RELU => POOL
model.add(layers.Convolution2D(20, (5, 5), activation='relu',
            input_shape=input_shape))
model.add(layers.MaxPooling2D(pool_size=(2, 2), strides=(2, 2)))
```

Then there is a second convolutional stage with ReLU activations, followed again by a max pooling layer. In this case, we increase the number of convolutional filters learned to 50 from the previous 20. Increasing the number of filters in deeper layers is a common technique in deep learning:

```
# CONV => RELU => POOL
model.add(layers.Convolution2D(50, (5, 5), activation='relu'))
model.add(layers.MaxPooling2D(pool_size=(2, 2), strides=(2, 2)))
```

Then we have a pretty standard flattening and a dense network of 500 neurons, followed by a softmax classifier with 10 classes:

```
# Flatten => RELU layers
model.add(layers.Flatten())
model.add(layers.Dense(500, activation='relu'))
# a softmax classifier
model.add(layers.Dense(classes, activation="softmax"))
return model
```

Congratulations, you have just defined your first deep convolutional learning network! Let's see how it looks visually:

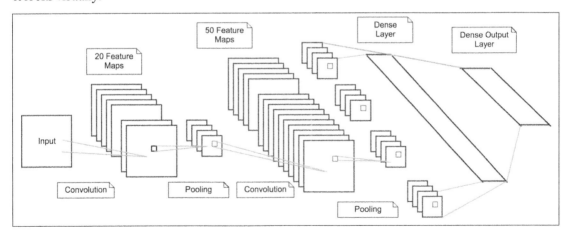

Figure 3.4: Visualization of LeNet

Now we need some additional code for training the network, but this is very similar to what we described in *Chapter 1, Neural Network Foundations with TF*. This time we also show the code for printing the loss:

```python
# data: shuffled and split between train and test sets
(X_train, y_train), (X_test, y_test) = datasets.mnist.load_data()

# reshape
X_train = X_train.reshape((60000, 28, 28, 1))
X_test = X_test.reshape((10000, 28, 28, 1))

# normalize
X_train, X_test = X_train / 255.0, X_test / 255.0

# cast
X_train = X_train.astype('float32')
X_test = X_test.astype('float32')

# convert class vectors to binary class matrices
y_train = tf.keras.utils.to_categorical(y_train, NB_CLASSES)
y_test = tf.keras.utils.to_categorical(y_test, NB_CLASSES)

# initialize the optimizer and model
model = LeNet.build(input_shape=INPUT_SHAPE, classes=NB_CLASSES)
model.compile(loss="categorical_crossentropy", optimizer=OPTIMIZER,
    metrics=["accuracy"])
model.summary()

# use TensorBoard, princess Aurora!
callbacks = [
  # Write TensorBoard logs to './logs' directory
  tf.keras.callbacks.TensorBoard(log_dir='./logs')
]

# fit
history = model.fit(X_train, y_train,
        batch_size=BATCH_SIZE, epochs=EPOCHS,
        verbose=VERBOSE, validation_split=VALIDATION_SPLIT,
        callbacks=callbacks)

score = model.evaluate(X_test, y_test, verbose=VERBOSE)
print("\nTest score:", score[0])
print('Test accuracy:', score[1])
```

Now let's run the code. As you can see in *Figure 3.5*, the time had a significant increase, and each iteration in our deep net now takes ~28 seconds against ~1-2 seconds for the network defined in *Chapter 1, Neural Network Foundations with TF*. However, the accuracy reached a new peak at 99.991% on training, 99.91% on validation, and 99.15% on test!

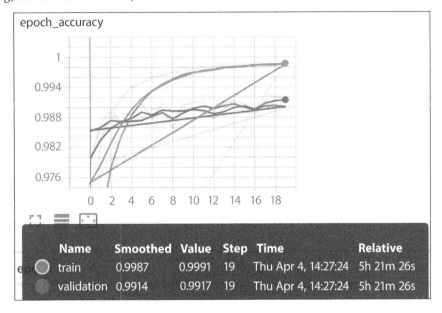

Figure 3.5: LeNet accuracy

Let's see the execution of a full run for 20 epochs:

```
Model: "sequential_1"
_____
Layer (type)                    Output Shape              Param #
=================================================================
conv2d_2 (Conv2D)               (None, 24, 24, 20)        520

max_pooling2d_2 (MaxPooling 2D) (None, 12, 12, 20)        0

conv2d_3 (Conv2D)               (None, 8, 8, 50)          25050

max_pooling2d_3 (MaxPooling 2D) (None, 4, 4, 50)          0

flatten    (Flatten)            (None, 800)               0

dense    (Dense)                (None, 500)               400500

dense_1 (Dense)                 (None, 10)                5010
```

```
====================================================================
Total params: 431,080
Trainable params: 431,080
Non-trainable params: 0
_____

Train on 48000 samples, validate on 12000 samples
Epoch 1/20
[2019-04-04 14:18:28.546158: I tensorflow/core/profiler/lib/profiler_session.
cc:164] Profile Session started.
48000/48000 [==============================] - 28s 594us/sample - loss: 0.2035
- accuracy: 0.9398 - val_loss: 0.0739 - val_accuracy: 0.9783
Epoch 2/20
48000/48000 [==============================] - 26s 534us/sample - loss: 0.0520
- accuracy: 0.9839 - val_loss: 0.0435 - val_accuracy: 0.9868
Epoch 3/20
48000/48000 [==============================] - 27s 564us/sample - loss: 0.0343
- accuracy: 0.9893 - val_loss: 0.0365 - val_accuracy: 0.9895
Epoch 4/20
48000/48000 [==============================] - 27s 562us/sample - loss: 0.0248
- accuracy: 0.9921 - val_loss: 0.0452 - val_accuracy: 0.9868
Epoch 5/20
48000/48000 [==============================] - 27s 562us/sample - loss: 0.0195
- accuracy: 0.9939 - val_loss: 0.0428 - val_accuracy: 0.9873
Epoch 6/20
48000/48000 [==============================] - 28s 548us/sample - loss: 0.0585
- accuracy: 0.9820 - val_loss: 0.1038 - val_accuracy: 0.9685
Epoch 7/20
48000/48000 [==============================] - 26s 537us/sample - loss: 0.0134
- accuracy: 0.9955 - val_loss: 0.0388 - val_accuracy: 0.9896
Epoch 8/20
48000/48000 [==============================] - 29s 589us/sample - loss: 0.0097
- accuracy: 0.9966 - val_loss: 0.0347 - val_accuracy: 0.9899
Epoch 9/20
48000/48000 [==============================] - 29s 607us/sample - loss: 0.0091
- accuracy: 0.9971 - val_loss: 0.0515 - val_accuracy: 0.9859
Epoch 10/20
48000/48000 [==============================] - 27s 565us/sample - loss: 0.0062
- accuracy: 0.9980 - val_loss: 0.0376 - val_accuracy: 0.9904
Epoch 11/20
48000/48000 [==============================] - 30s 627us/sample - loss: 0.0068
```

```
- accuracy: 0.9976 - val_loss: 0.0366 - val_accuracy: 0.9911
Epoch 12/20
48000/48000 [==============================] - 24s 505us/sample - loss: 0.0079
- accuracy: 0.9975 - val_loss: 0.0389 - val_accuracy: 0.9910
Epoch 13/20
48000/48000 [==============================] - 28s 584us/sample - loss: 0.0057
- accuracy: 0.9978 - val_loss: 0.0531 - val_accuracy: 0.9890
Epoch 14/20
48000/48000 [==============================] - 28s 580us/sample - loss: 0.0045
- accuracy: 0.9984 - val_loss: 0.0409 - val_accuracy: 0.9911
Epoch 15/20
48000/48000 [==============================] - 26s 537us/sample - loss: 0.0039
- accuracy: 0.9986 - val_loss: 0.0436 - val_accuracy: 0.9911
Epoch 16/20
48000/48000 [==============================] - 25s 513us/sample - loss: 0.0059
- accuracy: 0.9983 - val_loss: 0.0480 - val_accuracy: 0.9890
Epoch 17/20
48000/48000 [==============================] - 24s 499us/sample - loss: 0.0042
- accuracy: 0.9988 - val_loss: 0.0535 - val_accuracy: 0.9888
Epoch 18/20
48000/48000 [==============================] - 24s 505us/sample - loss: 0.0042
- accuracy: 0.9986 - val_loss: 0.0349 - val_accuracy: 0.9926
Epoch 19/20
48000/48000 [==============================] - 29s 599us/sample - loss: 0.0052
- accuracy: 0.9984 - val_loss: 0.0377 - val_accuracy: 0.9920
Epoch 20/20
48000/48000 [==============================] - 25s 524us/sample - loss: 0.0028
- accuracy: 0.9991 - val_loss: 0.0477 - val_accuracy: 0.9917
10000/10000 [==============================] - 2s 248us/sample - loss: 0.0383 -
accuracy: 0.9915


Test score: 0.03832608199457617
Test accuracy: 0.9915
```

Let's plot the model accuracy and the model loss, and we understand that we can train in only 10 iterations to achieve a similar accuracy of 99.1%:

```
Train on 48000 samples, validate on 12000 samples
Epoch 1/10
[2019-04-04 15:57:17.848186: I tensorflow/core/profiler/lib/profiler_session.
cc:164] Profile Session started.
48000/48000 [==============================] - 26s 544us/sample - loss: 0.2134
- accuracy: 0.9361 - val_loss: 0.0688 - val_accuracy: 0.9783
Epoch 2/10
```

```
48000/48000 [==============================] - 30s 631us/sample - loss: 0.0550
- accuracy: 0.9831 - val_loss: 0.0533 - val_accuracy: 0.9843
Epoch 3/10
48000/48000 [==============================] - 30s 621us/sample - loss: 0.0353
- accuracy: 0.9884 - val_loss: 0.0410 - val_accuracy: 0.9874
Epoch 4/10
48000/48000 [==============================] - 37s 767us/sample - loss: 0.0276
- accuracy: 0.9910 - val_loss: 0.0381 - val_accuracy: 0.9887
Epoch 5/10
48000/48000 [==============================] - 24s 509us/sample - loss: 0.0200
- accuracy: 0.9932 - val_loss: 0.0406 - val_accuracy: 0.9881
Epoch 6/10
48000/48000 [==============================] - 31s 641us/sample - loss: 0.0161
- accuracy: 0.9950 - val_loss: 0.0423 - val_accuracy: 0.9881
Epoch 7/10
48000/48000 [==============================] - 29s 613us/sample - loss: 0.0129
- accuracy: 0.9955 - val_loss: 0.0396 - val_accuracy: 0.9894
Epoch 8/10
48000/48000 [==============================] - 27s 554us/sample - loss: 0.0107
- accuracy: 0.9965 - val_loss: 0.0454 - val_accuracy: 0.9871
Epoch 9/10
48000/48000 [==============================] - 24s 510us/sample - loss: 0.0082
- accuracy: 0.9973 - val_loss: 0.0388 - val_accuracy: 0.9902
Epoch 10/10
48000/48000 [==============================] - 26s 542us/sample - loss: 0.0083
- accuracy: 0.9970 - val_loss: 0.0440 - val_accuracy: 0.99892
10000/10000 [==============================] - 2s 196us/sample - loss: 0.0327 -
accuracy: 0.9910


Test score: 0.03265062951518773
Test accuracy: 0.991
```

Let us see some of the MNIST images just to understand how good the number 99.1% is! For instance, there are many ways in which humans write a 9, one of them being in *Figure 3.6*. The same goes for 3, 7, 4, and 5, and number 1 in this figure is so difficult to recognize that even a human would likely have trouble:

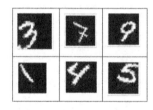

Figure 3.6: An example of MNIST handwritten characters

We can summarize all the progress made so far with our different models in the following graph. Our simple net started with an accuracy of 90.71%, meaning that about 9 handwritten characters out of 100 are not correctly recognized. Then, we gained 8% with the deep learning architecture, reaching an accuracy of 99.2%, which means that less than one handwritten character out of one hundred is incorrectly recognized, as shown in *Figure 3.7*:

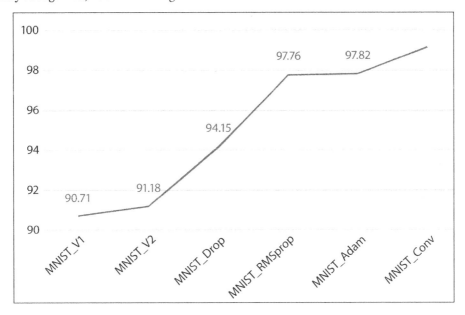

Figure 3.7: Accuracy for different models and optimizers

Understanding the power of deep learning

Another test we can run for a better understanding of the power of deep learning and ConvNets is to reduce the size of the training set and observe the resulting decay in performance. One way to do this is to split the training set of 50,000 examples into two different sets:

- The proper training set used for training our model will progressively reduce in size: 5,900, 3,000, 1,800, 600, and 300 examples.
- The validation set used to estimate how well our model has been trained will consist of the remaining examples. Our test set is always fixed, and it consists of 10,000 examples.

With this setup, we compare the previously defined deep learning ConvNet against the first example neural network defined in *Chapter 1, Neural Network Foundations with TF*. As we can see in the following graph, our deep network always outperforms the simple network when there is more data available. With 5,900 training examples, the deep learning net had an accuracy of 97.23% against an accuracy of 94% for the simple net.

In general, deep networks require more training data available to fully express their power, as shown in *Figure 3.8*:

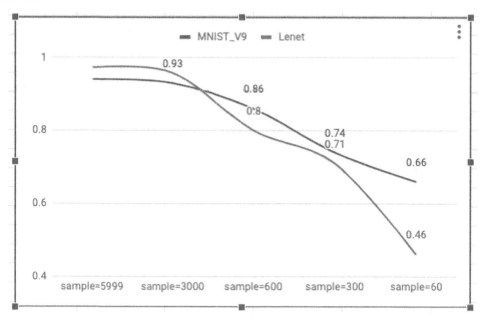

Figure 3.8: Accuracy for different amounts of data

A list of state-of-the-art results (for example, the highest performance available) for MNIST is available online (see `http://rodrigob.github.io/are_we_there_yet/build/classification_datasets_results.html`). As of March 2019, the best result has an error rate of 0.21% [2].

Recognizing CIFAR-10 images with deep learning

The CIFAR-10 dataset contains 60,000 color images of 32 x 32 pixels in three channels, divided into 10 classes. Each class contains 6,000 images. The training set contains 50,000 images, while the test set provides 10,000 images. This image taken from the CIFAR repository (see `https://www.cs.toronto.edu/~kriz/cifar.html`) shows a few random examples from the 10 classes:

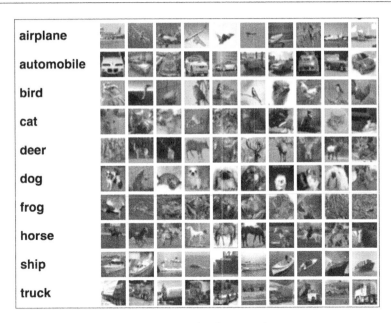

Figure 3.9: An example of CIFAR-10 images

 The images in this section are from *Learning Multiple Layers of Features from Tiny Images*, Alex
Krizhevsky, 2009: https://www.cs.toronto.edu/~kriz/learning-features-2009-TR.
pdf. They are part of the CIFAR-10 dataset (toronto.edu): https://www.cs.toronto.
edu/~kriz/cifar.html.

The goal is to recognize previously unseen images and assign them to one of the ten classes. Let us
define a suitable deep net.

First of all, we import a number of useful modules and define a few constants and load the dataset
(the full code including the load operations is available online):

```
import tensorflow as tf
from tensorflow.keras import datasets, layers, models, optimizers


# CIFAR_10 is a set of 60K images 32x32 pixels on 3 channels
IMG_CHANNELS = 3
IMG_ROWS = 32
IMG_COLS = 32
```

```
#constant
BATCH_SIZE = 128
EPOCHS = 20
CLASSES = 10
VERBOSE = 1
VALIDATION_SPLIT - 0.2
OPTIM = tf.keras.optimizers.RMSprop()
```

Our net will learn 32 convolutional filters, each of which with a 3 x 3 size. The output dimension is the same as the input shape, so it will be 32 x 32 and the activation function used is a ReLU function, which is a simple way of introducing non-linearity. After that, we have a `MaxPooling` operation with a pool size of 2 x 2 and dropout at 25%:

```
#define the convnet
def build(input_shape, classes):
    model = models.Sequential()
    model.add(layers.Convolution2D(32, (3, 3), activation='relu',
                          input_shape=input_shape))
    model.add(layers.MaxPooling2D(pool_size=(2, 2)))
    model.add(layers.Dropout(0.25))
```

The next stage in the deep pipeline is a dense network with 512 units and ReLU activation followed by dropout at 50% and by a softmax layer with 10 classes as output, one for each category:

```
    model.add(layers.Flatten())
    model.add(layers.Dense(512, activation='relu'))
    model.add(layers.Dropout(0.5))
    model.add(layers.Dense(classes, activation='softmax'))
    return model
```

After defining the network, we can train the model. In this case, we split the data and compute a validation set in addition to the training and testing sets. The training is used to build our models, the validation is used to select the best-performing approach, while the test set is used to check the performance of our best models on fresh unseen data:

```
# use TensorBoard, princess Aurora!
callbacks = [
  # Write TensorBoard logs to './logs' directory
  tf.keras.callbacks.TensorBoard(log_dir='./logs')
]

# train
model.compile(loss='categorical_crossentropy', optimizer=OPTIM,
    metrics=['accuracy'])
```

```
model.fit(X_train, y_train, batch_size=BATCH_SIZE,
    epochs=EPOCHS, validation_split=VALIDATION_SPLIT,
    verbose=VERBOSE, callbacks=callbacks)
score = model.evaluate(X_test, y_test,
                    batch_size=BATCH_SIZE, verbose=VERBOSE)
print("\nTest score:", score[0])
print('Test accuracy:', score[1])
```

Let's run the code. Our network reaches a test accuracy of 66.8% with 20 iterations. We also print the accuracy and loss plot and dump the network with model.summary():

```
Epoch 17/20
40000/40000 [==============================] - 112s 3ms/sample - loss: 0.6282 -
accuracy: 0.7841 - val_loss: 1.0296 - val_accuracy: 0.6734
Epoch 18/20
40000/40000 [==============================] - 76s 2ms/sample - loss: 0.6140 -
accuracy: 0.7879 - val_loss: 1.0789 - val_accuracy: 0.6489
Epoch 19/20
40000/40000 [==============================] - 74s 2ms/sample - loss: 0.5931 -
accuracy: 0.7958 - val_loss: 1.0461 - val_accuracy: 0.6811
Epoch 20/20
40000/40000 [==============================] - 71s 2ms/sample - loss: 0.5724 -
accuracy: 0.8042 - val_loss: 0.1.0527 - val_accuracy: 0.6773
10000/10000 [==============================] - 5s 472us/sample - loss: 1.0423 -
accuracy: 0.6686

Test score: 1.0423416819572449
Test accuracy: 0.6686
```

Figure 3.10 shows the accuracy and loss plot:

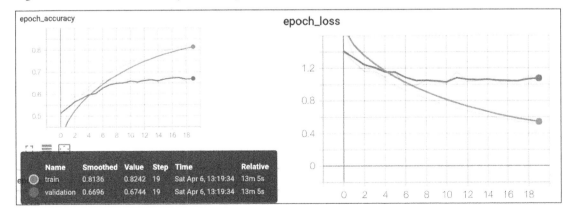

Figure 3.10: Accuracy and loss for the defined network

We have seen how to improve accuracy and how the loss changes for CIFAR-10 datasets. The next section is about improving the current results.

Improving the CIFAR-10 performance with a deeper network

One way to improve the performance is to define a deeper network with multiple convolutional operations. In the following example, we have a sequence of modules:

1st module: (CONV+CONV+MaxPool+DropOut)

2nd module: (CONV+CONV+MaxPool+DropOut)

3rd module: (CONV+CONV+MaxPool+DropOut)

These are followed by a standard dense output layer. All the activation functions used are ReLU functions. There is a new layer that we also discussed in *Chapter 1, Neural Network Foundations with TF,* `BatchNormalization()`, used to introduce a form of regularization between modules:

```python
def build_model():
    model = models.Sequential()

    #1st block
    model.add(layers.Conv2D(32, (3,3), padding='same',
        input_shape=x_train.shape[1:], activation='relu'))
    model.add(layers.BatchNormalization())
    model.add(layers.Conv2D(32, (3,3), padding='same', activation='relu'))
    model.add(layers.BatchNormalization())
    model.add(layers.MaxPooling2D(pool_size=(2,2)))
    model.add(layers.Dropout(0.2))

    #2nd block
    model.add(layers.Conv2D(64, (3,3), padding='same', activation='relu'))
    model.add(layers.BatchNormalization())
    model.add(layers.Conv2D(64, (3,3), padding='same', activation='relu'))
    model.add(layers.BatchNormalization())
    model.add(layers.MaxPooling2D(pool_size=(2,2)))
    model.add(layers.Dropout(0.3))

    #3d block
    model.add(layers.Conv2D(128, (3,3), padding='same', activation='relu'))
    model.add(layers.BatchNormalization())
    model.add(layers.Conv2D(128, (3,3), padding='same', activation='relu'))
    model.add(layers.BatchNormalization())
    model.add(layers.MaxPooling2D(pool_size=(2,2)))
    model.add(layers.Dropout(0.4))
```

```
#dense
model.add(layers.Flatten())
model.add(layers.Dense(NUM_CLASSES, activation='softmax'))
return model


model.summary()
```

Congratulations! You have defined a deeper network. Let us run the code for 40 iterations reaching an accuracy of 82%! Let's add the remaining part of the code for the sake of completeness. The first part is to load and normalize the data:

```
import tensorflow as tf
from tensorflow.keras import datasets, layers, models, regularizers, optimizers
from tensorflow.keras.preprocessing.image import ImageDataGenerator
import numpy as np

EPOCHS=50
NUM_CLASSES = 10

def load_data():
    (x_train, y_train), (x_test, y_test) = datasets.cifar10.load_data()
    x_train = x_train.astype('float32')
    x_test = x_test.astype('float32')

    #normalize
    mean = np.mean(x_train,axis=(0,1,2,3))
    std = np.std(x_train,axis=(0,1,2,3))
    x_train = (x_train-mean)/(std+1e-7)
    x_test = (x_test-mean)/(std+1e-7)

    y_train =  tf.keras.utils.to_categorical(y_train,NUM_CLASSES)
    y_test =  tf.keras.utils.to_categorical(y_test,NUM_CLASSES)

    return x_train, y_train, x_test, y_test
```

Then we need to have a part to train the network:

```
(x_train, y_train, x_test, y_test) = load_data()
model = build_model()
model.compile(loss='categorical_crossentropy',
            optimizer='RMSprop',
            metrics=['accuracy'])
```

```
#train
batch_size = 64
model.fit(x_train, y_train, batch_size=batch_size,
    epochs=EPOCHS, validation_data=(x_test,y_test))
score = model.evaluate(x_test, y_test,
                        batch_size=batch_size)
print("\nTest score:", score[0])
print('Test accuracy:', score[1])
```

So, we have an improvement of 15.14% with respect to the previous simpler deeper network.

Improving the CIFAR-10 performance with data augmentation

Another way to improve the performance is to generate more images for our training. The idea here is that we can take the standard CIFAR training set and augment this set with multiple types of transformation, including rotation, rescaling, horizontal or vertical flip, zooming, channel shift, and many more. Let's see the code applied on the same network defined in the previous section:

```
from tensorflow.keras.preprocessing.image import ImageDataGenerator


#image augmentation
datagen = ImageDataGenerator(
    rotation_range=30,
    width_shift_range=0.2,
    height_shift_range=0.2,
    horizontal_flip=True,
    )
datagen.fit(x_train)
```

rotation_range is a value in degrees (0-180) for randomly rotating pictures; width_shift and height_shift are ranges for randomly translating pictures vertically or horizontally; zoom_range is for randomly zooming pictures; horizontal_flip is for randomly flipping half of the images horizontally; fill_mode is the strategy used for filling in new pixels that can appear after a rotation or a shift.

After augmentation we have generated many more training images starting from the standard CIFAR-10 set, as shown in *Figure 3.11*:

Figure.3.11: An example of image augmentation

Now we can apply this intuition directly for training. Using the same ConvNet defined before, we simply generate more augmented images, and then we train. For efficiency, the generator runs in parallel to the model. This allows an image augmentation on a CPU while training in parallel on a GPU. Here is the code:

```
#train
batch_size = 64
model.fit_generator(datagen.flow(x_train, y_train, batch_size=batch_size),
                    epochs=EPOCHS,
                    verbose=1,validation_data=(x_test,y_test))
#save to disk
model_json = model.to_json()
with open('model.json', 'w') as json_file:
    json_file.write(model_json)
model.save_weights('model.h5')

#test
scores = model.evaluate(x_test, y_test, batch_size=128, verbose=1)
print('\nTest result: %.3f loss: %.3f' % (scores[1]*100,scores[0]))
```

Each iteration is now more expensive because we have more training data. Therefore, let's run for 50 iterations only. We see that by doing this we reach an accuracy of 85.91%:

```
Epoch 46/50
50000/50000 [==============================] - 36s 722us/sample - loss: 0.2440
- accuracy: 0.9183 - val_loss: 0.4918 - val_accuracy: 0.8546
Epoch 47/50
50000/50000 [==============================] - 34s 685us/sample - loss: 0.2338
- accuracy: 0.9208 - val_loss: 0.4884 - val_accuracy: 0.8574
Epoch 48/50
50000/50000 [==============================] - 32s 643us/sample - loss: 0.2383
- accuracy: 0.9189 - val_loss: 0.5106 - val_accuracy: 0.8556
Epoch 49/50
50000/50000 [==============================] - 37s 734us/sample - loss: 0.2285
- accuracy: 0.9212 - val_loss: 0.5017 - val_accuracy: 0.8581
Epoch 49/50
50000/50000 [==============================] - 36s 712us/sample - loss: 0.2263
- accuracy: 0.9228 - val_loss: 0.4911 - val_accuracy: 0.8591
10000/10000 [==============================] - 2s 160us/sample - loss: 0.4911 -
accuracy: 0.8591


Test score: 0.4911323667049408
Test accuracy: 0.8591
```

The results obtained during our experiments are summarized in the following figure:

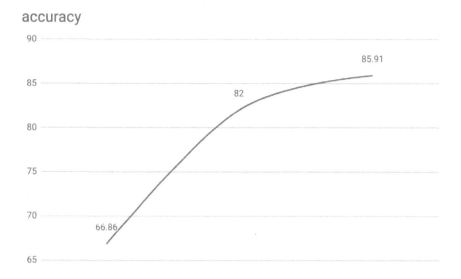

Figure 3.12: Accuracy on CIFAR-10 with different networks. On the x-axis, we have the increasing number of iterations

A list of state-of-the-art results for CIFAR-10 is available online (see `http://rodrigob.github.io/are_we_there_yet/build/classification_datasets_results.html`). As of April 2019, the best result has an accuracy of 96.53% [3].

Predicting with CIFAR-10

Let's suppose that we want to use the deep learning model we just trained for CIFAR-10 for a bulk evaluation of images. Since we saved the model and the weights, we do not need to train each time:

```
import numpy as np
import scipy.misc
from tensorflow.keras.models import model_from_json
from tensorflow.keras.optimizers import SGD

#Load model
model_architecture = 'cifar10_architecture.json'
model_weights = 'cifar10_weights.h5'
model = model_from_json(open(model_architecture).read())
model.load_weights(model_weights)

#Load images
img_names = ['cat-standing.jpg', 'dog.jpg']
imgs = [np.transpose(scipy.misc.imresize(scipy.misc.imread(img_name), (32,
32)),
                     (2, 0, 1)).astype('float32')
        for img_name in img_names]
imgs = np.array(imgs) / 255

# train
optim = SGD()
model.compile(loss='categorical_crossentropy', optimizer=optim,
    metrics=['accuracy'])
# predict
predictions = model.predict_classes(imgs)
print(predictions)
```

Note that we use SciPy's `imread` to load the images and then resize them to 32 × 32 pixels. The resulting image tensor has dimensions of (32, 32, 3). However, we want the color dimension to be first instead of last, so we take the transpose. After that, the list of image tensors is combined into a single tensor and normalized to be between 0 and 1.0.

Now let us get the prediction for a and for a ![dog]. We get categories 3 (cat) and 5 (dog) as output as expected. We successfully created a ConvNet to classify CIFAR-10 images. Next, we will look at VGG16: a breakthrough in deep learning.

Very deep convolutional networks for large-scale image recognition

In 2014, an interesting contribution to image recognition was presented in the paper *Very Deep Convolutional Networks for Large-Scale Image Recognition*, K. Simonyan and A. Zisserman [4]. The paper showed that a *significant improvement on the prior-art configurations can be achieved by pushing the depth to 16-19 weight layers*. One model in the paper denoted as D or VGG16 had 16 deep layers. An implementation in Java Caffe (see `http://caffe.berkeleyvision.org/`) was used for training the model on the ImageNet ILSVRC-2012 (see `http://image-net.org/challenges/LSVRC/2012/`) dataset, which includes images of 1,000 classes, and is split into three sets: training (1.3M images), validation (50K images), and testing (100K images). Each image is (224 x 224) on 3 channels. The model achieves 7.5% top-5 error (the error of the top 5 results) on ILSVRC-2012-val and 7.4% top-5 error on ILSVRC-2012-test.

According to the ImageNet site:

> *The goal of this competition is to estimate the content of photographs for the purpose of retrieval and automatic annotation using a subset of the large hand-labeled ImageNet dataset (10,000,000 labeled images depicting 10,000+ object categories) as training. Test images will be presented with no initial annotation -- no segmentation or labels -- and algorithms will have to produce labelings specifying what objects are present in the images.*

The weights learned by the model implemented in Caffe have been directly converted (`https://gist.github.com/baraldilorenzo/07d7802847aaad0a35d3`) in `tf.Keras` and can be used by preloading them into the `tf.Keras` model, which is implemented below, as described in the paper:

```python
import tensorflow as tf
from tensorflow.keras import layers, models

# define a VGG16 network

def VGG_16(weights_path=None):
    model = models.Sequential()
    model.add(layers.ZeroPadding2D((1,1),input_shape=(224,224, 3)))
    model.add(layers.Convolution2D(64, (3, 3), activation='relu'))
    model.add(layers.ZeroPadding2D((1,1)))
    model.add(layers.Convolution2D(64, (3, 3), activation='relu'))
    model.add(layers.MaxPooling2D((2,2), strides=(2,2)))
```

```python
model.add(layers.ZeroPadding2D((1,1)))
model.add(layers.Convolution2D(128, (3, 3), activation='relu'))
model.add(layers.ZeroPadding2D((1,1)))
model.add(layers.Convolution2D(128, (3, 3), activation='relu'))
model.add(layers.MaxPooling2D((2,2), strides=(2,2)))

model.add(layers.ZeroPadding2D((1,1)))
model.add(layers.Convolution2D(256, (3, 3), activation='relu'))
model.add(layers.ZeroPadding2D((1,1)))
model.add(layers.Convolution2D(256, (3, 3), activation='relu'))
model.add(layers.ZeroPadding2D((1,1)))
model.add(layers.Convolution2D(256, (3, 3), activation='relu'))
model.add(layers.MaxPooling2D((2,2), strides=(2,2)))

model.add(layers.ZeroPadding2D((1,1)))
model.add(layers.Convolution2D(512, (3, 3), activation='relu'))
model.add(layers.ZeroPadding2D((1,1)))
model.add(layers.Convolution2D(512, (3, 3), activation='relu'))
model.add(layers.ZeroPadding2D((1,1)))
model.add(layers.Convolution2D(512, (3, 3), activation='relu'))
model.add(layers.MaxPooling2D((2,2), strides=(2,2)))

model.add(layers.ZeroPadding2D((1,1)))
model.add(layers.Convolution2D(512, (3, 3), activation='relu'))
model.add(layers.ZeroPadding2D((1,1)))
model.add(layers.Convolution2D(512, (3, 3), activation='relu'))
model.add(layers.ZeroPadding2D((1,1)))
model.add(layers.Convolution2D(512, (3, 3), activation='relu'))
model.add(layers.MaxPooling2D((2,2), strides=(2,2)))

model.add(layers.Flatten())

#top layer of the VGG net
model.add(layers.Dense(4096, activation='relu'))
model.add(layers.Dropout(0.5))
model.add(layers.Dense(4096, activation='relu'))
model.add(layers.Dropout(0.5))
model.add(layers.Dense(1000, activation='softmax'))

if weights_path:
    model.load_weights(weights_path)

return model
```

We have implemented a VGG16 network. Note that we could also have used `tf.keras.applications.vgg16.` to get the model and its weights directly. Here, I wanted to show how VGG16 works internally. Next, we are going to utilize it.

Recognizing cats with a VGG16 network

Now let us test the image of a 🐱 .

Note that we are going to use predefined weights:

```
import cv2
im = cv2.resize(cv2.imread('cat.jpg'), (224, 224)).astype(np.float32)
#im = im.transpose((2,0,1))
im = np.expand_dims(im, axis=0)


# Test pretrained model
model = VGG_16('/Users/antonio/.keras/models/vgg16_weights_tf_dim_ordering_tf_
kernels.h5')
model.summary()
model.compile(optimizer='sgd', loss='categorical_crossentropy')
out = model.predict(im)
print(np.argmax(out))
```

When the code is executed, the class 285 is returned, which corresponds (see `https://gist.github.com/yrevar/942d3a0ac09ec9e5eb3a`) to "Egyptian cat":

```
Total params: 138,357,544
Trainable params: 138,357,544
Non-trainable params: 0
-------------------------------------------------------------
285
```

Impressive, isn't it? Our VGG16 network can successfully recognize images of cats! An important step for deep learning. It is only seven years since the paper in [4], but that was a game-changing moment.

Utilizing the tf.Keras built-in VGG16 net module

`tf.Keras` applications are pre-built and pretrained deep learning models. The weights are downloaded automatically when instantiating a model and stored at `~/.keras/models/`. Using built-in code is very easy:

```
import tensorflow as tf
from tensorflow.keras.applications.vgg16 import VGG16
import matplotlib.pyplot as plt
import numpy as np
import cv2
```

```
# pre built model with pre-trained weights on imagenet
model = VGG16(weights='imagenet', include_top=True)
model.compile(optimizer='sgd', loss='categorical_crossentropy')

# resize into VGG16 trained images' format
im = cv2.resize(cv2.imread('steam-locomotive.jpg'), (224, 224))
im = np.expand_dims(im, axis=0)

# predict
out = model.predict(im)
index = np.argmax(out)
print(index)

plt.plot(out.ravel())
plt.show()
#this should print 820 for steaming train
```

Now, let us consider a train, 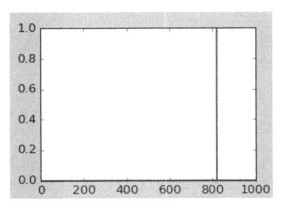. If we run the code, we get 820 as a result, which is the ImageNet code for "steam locomotive." Equally important, all the other classes have very weak support, as shown in *Figure 3.13*:

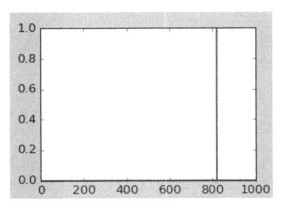

Figure 3.13: A steam train is the most likely outcome

To conclude this section, note that VGG16 is only one of the modules that are pre-built in tf.Keras. A full list of pretrained models is available online (see https://www.tensorflow.org/api_docs/python/tf/keras/applications).

Recycling pre-built deep learning models for extracting features

One very simple idea is to use VGG16, and more generally DCNN, for feature extraction. This code implements the idea by extracting features from a specific layer.

Note that we need to switch to the functional API since the sequential model only accepts layers:

```python
import tensorflow as tf
from tensorflow.keras.applications.vgg16 import VGG16
from tensorflow.keras import models
from tensorflow.keras.preprocessing import image
from tensorflow.keras.applications.vgg16 import preprocess_input
import numpy as np
import cv2


# prebuild model with pre-trained weights on imagenet
base_model = VGG16(weights='imagenet', include_top=True)
print (base_model)
for i, layer in enumerate(base_model.layers):
    print (i, layer.name, layer.output_shape)

# extract features from block4_pool block
model = models.Model(inputs=base_model.input,
    outputs=base_model.get_layer('block4_pool').output)

img_path = 'cat.jpg'
img = image.load_img(img_path, target_size=(224, 224))
x = image.img_to_array(img)
x = np.expand_dims(x, axis=0)
x = preprocess_input(x)

# get the features from this block
features = model.predict(x)
print(features)
```

You might wonder why we want to extract the features from an intermediate layer in a DCNN. The reasoning is that as the network learns to classify images into categories, each layer learns to identify the features that are necessary to perform the final classification. Lower layers identify lower-order features such as color and edges, and higher layers compose these lower-order features into higher-order features such as shapes or objects. Hence, the intermediate layer has the capability to extract important features from an image, and these features are more likely to help in different kinds of classification.

This has multiple advantages. First, we can rely on publicly available large-scale training and transfer this learning to novel domains. Second, we can save time on expensive training. Third, we can provide reasonable solutions even when we don't have a large number of training examples for our domain. We also get a good starting network shape for the task at hand, instead of guessing it.

With this, we will conclude the overview of VGG16 CNNs, the last deep learning model defined in this chapter.

Deep Inception V3 for transfer learning

Transfer learning is a very powerful deep learning technique that has applications in a number of different domains. The idea behind transfer learning is very simple and can be explained with an analogy. Suppose you want to learn a new language, say Spanish. Then it could be useful to start from what you already know in a different language, say English.

Following this line of thinking, computer vision researchers now commonly use pretrained CNNs to generate representations for novel tasks [1], where the dataset may not be large enough to train an entire CNN from scratch. Another common tactic is to take the pretrained ImageNet network and then fine-tune the entire network to the novel task. For instance, we can take a network trained to recognize 10 categories of music and fine-tune it to recognize 20 categories of movies.

Inception V3 is a very deep ConvNet developed by Google [2]. tf.Keras implements the full network, as described in *Figure 3.14*, and it comes pretrained on ImageNet. The default input size for this model is 299x299 on three channels:

Figure 3.14: The Inception V3 deep learning model

This skeleton example is inspired by a scheme available online (see https://keras.io/applications/). Let's suppose we have a training dataset D in a different domain from ImageNet. D has 1,024 features in input and 200 categories in output. Let's look at a code fragment:

```
import tensorflow as tf
from tensorflow.keras.applications.inception_v3 import InceptionV3
from tensorflow.keras.preprocessing import image
from tensorflow.keras import layers, models
# create the base pre-trained model
base_model = InceptionV3(weights='imagenet', include_top=False)
```

We use a trained Inception V3 model: we do not include the fully connected layer – the dense layer with 1,024 inputs – because we want to fine-tune on *D*. The preceding code fragment will download the pretrained weights on our behalf:

```
Downloading data from https://github.com/fchollet/deep-learning-models/
releases/download/v0.5/inception_v3_weights_tf_dim_ordering_tf_kernels_notop.h5
87916544/87910968 [==============================] - 26s 0us/step
```

So, if you look at the last four layers (where `include_top=True`), you see these shapes:

```
# layer.name, layer.input_shape, layer.output_shape
('mixed10', [(None, 8, 8, 320), (None, 8, 8, 768), (None, 8, 8, 768), (None, 8,
8, 192)], (None, 8, 8, 2048))
('avg_pool', (None, 8, 8, 2048), (None, 1, 1, 2048))
('flatten', (None, 1, 1, 2048), (None, 2048))
('predictions', (None, 2048), (None, 1000))
```

When `include_top=False`, you are removing the last three layers and exposing the `mixed_10` layer. The `GlobalAveragePooling2D` layer converts (`None, 8, 8, 2048`) to (`None, 2048`), where each element in the (`None, 2048`) tensor is the average value for each corresponding (8,8) subtensor in the (`None, 8, 8, 2048`) tensor. None means an unspecified dimension, which is useful if you define a placeholder:

```
x = base_model.output
# Let's add a fully-connected layer as first layer
x = layers.Dense(1024, activation='relu')(x)
# and a logistic layer with 200 classes as last layer
predictions = layers.Dense(200, activation='softmax')(x)
# model to train
model = models.Model(inputs=base_model.input, outputs=predictions)
```

All the convolutional levels are pretrained, so we freeze them during the training of the full model:

```
# i.e. freeze all convolutional InceptionV3 layers
for layer in base_model.layers:
    layer.trainable = False
```

The model is then compiled and trained for a few epochs so that the top layers are trained. For the sake of simplicity, here we are omitting the training code itself:

```
# compile the model (should be done *after* setting layers to non-trainable)
model.compile(optimizer='rmsprop', loss='categorical_crossentropy')

# train the model on the new data for a few epochs
model.fit_generator(...)
```

Then, we freeze the top inception layers and fine-tune the other inception layers. In this example, we decide to freeze the first 172 layers (this is a tunable hyperparameter):

```
# we chose to train the top 2 inception blocks, i.e. we will freeze
# the first 172 layers and unfreeze the rest:
for layer in model.layers[:172]:
    layer.trainable = False
for layer in model.layers[172:]:
    layer.trainable = True
```

The model is then recompiled for fine-tuning optimization:

```
# we need to recompile the model for these modifications to take effect
# we use SGD with a low learning rate
from tensorflow.keras.optimizers import SGD
model.compile(optimizer=SGD(lr=0.0001, momentum=0.9), loss='categorical_
crossentropy')

# we train our model again (this time fine-tuning the top 2 inception blocks
# alongside the top Dense layers
model.fit_generator(...)
```

Now we have a new deep network that reuses a standard Inception V3 network, but it is trained on a new domain *D* via transfer learning. Of course, there are many fine-tuning parameters for achieving good accuracy. However, we are now re-using a very large pretrained network as a starting point via transfer learning. In doing so, we can save the need for training on our machines by reusing what is already available in tf.Keras.

Other CNN architectures

In this section, we will discuss many other different CNN architectures, including AlexNet, residual networks, highwayNets, DenseNets, and Xception.

AlexNet

One of the first convolutional networks was AlexNet [4], which consisted of only eight layers; the first five were convolutional ones with max-pooling layers, and the last three were fully connected. AlexNet [4] is an article cited more than 35,000 times, which started the deep learning revolution (for computer vision). Then, networks started to become deeper and deeper. Recently, a new idea has been proposed.

Residual networks

Residual networks are based on the interesting idea of allowing earlier layers to be fed directly into deeper layers. These are the so-called skip connections (or fast-forward connections). The key idea is to minimize the risk of vanishing or exploding gradients for deep networks (see *Chapter 8, Autoencoders*).

The building block of a ResNet is called a "residual block" or "identity block," which includes both forward and fast-forward connections. In this example (*Figure 3.15*), the output of an earlier layer is added to the output of a later layer before being sent into a ReLU activation function:

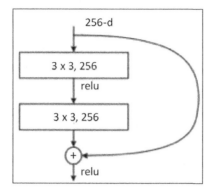

Figure 3.15: An example of image segmentation

HighwayNets and DenseNets

An additional weight matrix may be used to learn the skip weights and these models are frequently denoted as HighwayNets. Instead, models with several parallel skips are known as DenseNets [5]. It has been noticed that the human brain might have similar patterns to residual networks since the cortical layer VI neurons get input from layer I, skipping intermediary layers. In addition, residual networks can be faster to train than traditional CNNs since there are fewer layers to propagate through during each iteration (deeper layers get input sooner due to the skip connection). *Figure 3.16* shows an example of a DenseNet (based on http://arxiv.org/abs/1608.06993):

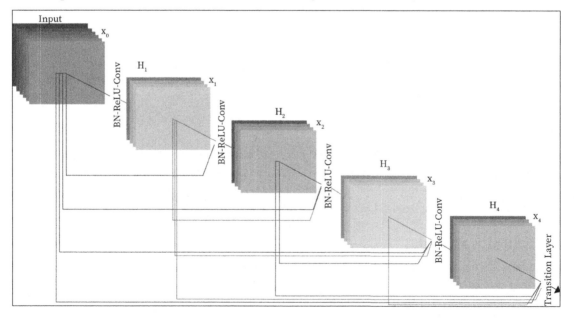

Figure 3.16: An example of a DenseNet

Xception

Xception networks use two basic blocks: a depthwise convolution and a pointwise convolution. A depthwise convolution is the channel-wise n x n spatial convolution. Suppose an image has three channels, then we have three convolutions of n x n. A pointwise convolution is a 1 x 1 convolution. In Xception, an "extreme" version of an Inception module, we first use a 1 x 1 convolution to map cross-channel correlations, and then separately map the spatial correlations of every output channel as shown in *Figure 3.17* (from https://arxiv.org/pdf/1610.02357.pdf):

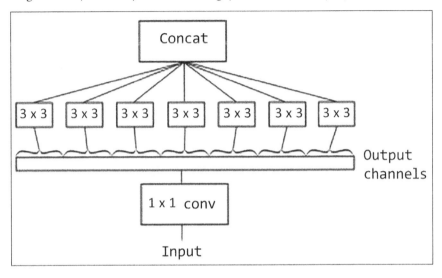

Figure 3.17: An example of an extreme form of an Inception module

Xception (**eXtreme Inception**) is a deep convolutional neural network architecture inspired by Inception, where Inception modules have been replaced with depthwise separable convolutions. Xception uses multiple skip-connections in a similar way to ResNet. The final architecture is rather complex as illustrated in *Figure 3.18* (from `https://arxiv.org/pdf/1610.02357.pdf`). Data first goes through the entry flow, then through the middle flow, which is repeated eight times, and finally through the exit flow:

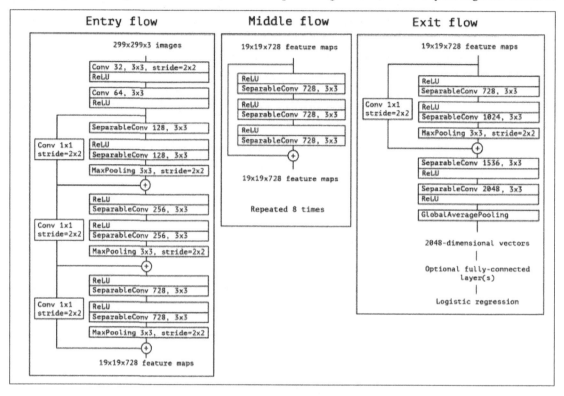

Figure 3.18: The full Xception architecture

Residual networks, HyperNets, DenseNets, Inception, and Xceptions are all available as pretrained nets in both `tf.Keras.application` and `tf.Hub`. The Keras website has a nice summary of the performance achieved on the ImageNet dataset and the depth of each network. The summary is available at `https://keras.io/applications/`:

Model	Size (MB)	Top-1 Accuracy	Top-5 Accuracy	Parameters	Depth	Time (ms) per inference step (CPU)	Time (ms) per inference step (GPU)
Xception	88	79.0%	94.5%	22.9M	81	109.4	8.1
VGG16	528	71.3%	90.1%	138.4M	16	69.5	4.2
VGG19	549	71.3%	90.0%	143.7M	19	84.8	4.4
ResNet50	98	74.9%	92.1%	25.6M	107	58.2	4.6
ResNet50V2	98	76.0%	93.0%	25.6M	103	45.6	4.4
ResNet101	171	76.4%	92.8%	44.7M	209	89.6	5.2
ResNet101V2	171	77.2%	93.8%	44.7M	205	72.7	5.4
ResNet152	232	76.6%	93.1%	60.4M	311	127.4	6.5
ResNet152V2	232	78.0%	94.2%	60.4M	307	107.5	6.6
InceptionV3	92	77.9%	93.7%	23.9M	189	42.2	6.9
InceptionResNetV2	215	80.3%	95.3%	55.9M	449	130.2	10.0
MobileNet	16	70.4%	89.5%	4.3M	55	22.6	3.4
MobileNetV2	14	71.3%	90.1%	3.5M	105	25.9	3.8
DenseNet121	33	75.0%	92.3%	8.1M	242	77.1	5.4
DenseNet169	57	76.2%	93.2%	14.3M	338	96.4	6.3
DenseNet201	80	77.3%	93.6%	20.2M	402	127.2	6.7
NASNetMobile	23	74.4%	91.9%	5.3M	389	27.0	6.7
NASNetLarge	343	82.5%	96.0%	88.9M	533	344.5	20.0

Figure 3.19: Different CNNs and accuracy on top-1 and top-5 results

The top-1 and top-5 accuracy refers to a model's performance on the ImageNet validation dataset.

In this section, we have discussed many CNN architectures. The next section is about style transfer, a deep learning technique used for training neural networks to create art.

Style transfer

Style transfer is a funny neural network application that provides many insights into the power of neural networks. So what exactly is it? Imagine that you observe a painting done by a famous artist. In principle, you are observing two elements: the painting itself (say the face of a woman, or a landscape) and something more intrinsic, the "style" of the artist. What is the style? That is more difficult to define, but humans know that Picasso had his own style, Matisse had his own style, and each artist has his/her own style. Now, imagine taking a famous painting of Matisse, giving it to a neural network, and letting the neural network repaint it in Picasso's style. Or, imagine taking your own photo, giving it to a neural network, and having your photo painted in Matisse's or Picasso's style, or in the style of any other artist that you like. That's what style transfer does.

For instance, go to `https://deepart.io/` and see a cool demo as shown in the image below, where deepart has been applied by taking the "Van Gogh" style as observed in the Sunflowers painting (this is a public domain image: "Sonnenblumen. Arles, 1888 Öl auf Leinwand, 92,5 x 73 cm Vincent van Gogh" `https://commons.wikimedia.org/wiki/Vincent_van_Gogh#/media/File:Vincent_Van_Gogh_0010.jpg`) and applying it to a picture of my daughter Aurora:

Figure 3.20: An example of deepart

Now, how can we define more formally the process of style transfer? Well, style transfer is the task of producing an artificial image x that shares the content of a source content image p and the style of a source style image a. So, intuitively we need two distance functions: one distance function measures how different the content of two images is, $L_{content}$, while the other distance function measures how different the style of two images is, L_{style}. Then, the transfer style can be seen as an optimization problem where we try to minimize these two metrics. As in *A Neural Algorithm of Artistic Style* by Leon A. Gatys, Alexander S. Ecker, and Matthias Bethge (`https://arxiv.org/abs/1508.06576`), we use a pretrained network to achieve style transfer. In particular, we can feed a VGG19 (or any suitable pretrained network) to extract features that represent images in an efficient way. Now we are going to define two functions used for training the network: the content distance and the style distance.

Content distance

Given two images, p content image and x input image, we define the content distance as the distance in the feature space defined by a layer l for a VGG19 network receiving the two images as an input. In other words, the two images are represented by the features extracted by a pretrained VGG19. These features project the images into a feature "content" space where the "content" distance can be conveniently computed as follows:

$$L_{content}^{l}(p,x) = \sum_{i,j} \left(F_{ij}^{l}(x) - P_{ij}^{l}(p) \right)^{2}$$

To generate nice images, we need to ensure that the content of the generated image is similar to (i.e. has a small distance from) that of the input image. The distance is therefore minimized with standard backpropagation. The code is simple:

```
#
#content distance
#
```

```
def get_content_loss(base_content, target):
    return tf.reduce_mean(tf.square(base_content - target))
```

Style distance

As discussed, the features in the higher layers of VGG19 are used as content representations. You can think about these features as filter responses. To represent the style we use in a gram matrix G (defined as the matrix $v^T v$ for a vector v), we consider $G_{i,j}^l$ as the inner matrix for map i and map j at layer l of the VGG19. It is possible to show that the Gram matrix represents the correlation matrix between different filter responses.

The contribution of each layer to the total style loss is defined as:

$$E_l = \frac{1}{4N_l^2 M_l^2} \sum_{i,j} \left(G_{ij}^l - A_{ij}^l \right)^2$$

where $G_{i,j}^l$ is the Gram matrix for input image x and $A_{i,j}^l$ is the gram matrix for the style image a, and N_l is the number of feature maps, each of size $M_{l=height \times width}$. The Gram matrix can project the images into a space where the style is taken into account. In addition, the feature correlations from multiple VGG19 layers are used because we want to consider multi-scale information and a more robust style representation. The total style loss across levels is the weighted sum:

$$L_{style}(a, x) = \sum_{l \in L} w_l E_l \qquad\qquad \left(w_l = \frac{1}{\|L\|} \right)$$

The key idea is therefore to perform gradient descent on the content image to make its style similar to the style image. The code is simple:

```
#style distance
#
def gram_matrix(input_tensor):
    # image channels first
    channels = int(input_tensor.shape[-1])
    a = tf.reshape(input_tensor, [-1, channels])
    n = tf.shape(a)[0]
    gram = tf.matmul(a, a, transpose_a=True)
    return gram / tf.cast(n, tf.float32)


def get_style_loss(base_style, gram_target):
    # height, width, num filters of each layer
    height, width, channels = base_style.get_shape().as_list()
    gram_style = gram_matrix(base_style)

    return tf.reduce_mean(tf.square(gram_style - gram_target))
```

In short, the concepts behind style transfer are simple: first, we use VGG19 as a feature extractor and then we define two suitable function distances, one for style and the other one for contents, which are appropriately minimized. If you want to try this out for yourself, then TensorFlow tutorials are available online. A tutorial is available at `https://colab.research.google.com/github/tensorflow/models/blob/master/research/nst_blogpost/4_Neural_Style_Transfer_with_Eager_Execution.ipynb`. If you are interested in a demo of this technique, you can go to the deepart.io free site where they do style transfer.

Summary

In this chapter, we have learned how to use deep learning ConvNets to recognize MNIST handwritten characters with high accuracy. We used the CIFAR-10 dataset to build a deep learning classifier with 10 categories, and the ImageNet dataset to build an accurate classifier with 1,000 categories. In addition, we investigated how to use large deep learning networks such as VGG16 and very deep networks such as Inception V3. We concluded with a discussion on transfer learning.

In the next chapter, we'll see how to work with word embeddings and why these techniques are important for deep learning.

References

1. LeCun, Y. and Bengio, Y. (1995). *Convolutional networks for images, speech, and time series*. The Handbook of Brain Theory Neural Networks, vol. 3361.

2. Wan. L, Zeiler M., Zhang S., Cun, Y. L., and Fergus R. (2014). *Regularization of neural networks using dropconnect*. Proc. 30th Int. Conf. Mach. Learn., pp. 1058–1066.

3. Graham B. (2014). *Fractional Max-Pooling*. arXiv Prepr. arXiv: 1412.6071.

4. Simonyan K. and Zisserman A. (Sep. 2014). *Very Deep Convolutional Networks for Large-Scale Image Recognition*. arXiv ePrints.

Join our book's Discord space

Join our Discord community to meet like-minded people and learn alongside more than 2000 members at: `https://packt.link/keras`

4

Word Embeddings

In the previous chapter, we talked about convolutional networks, which have been very successful against image data. Over the next few chapters, we will switch tracks to focus on strategies and networks to handle text data.

In this chapter, we will first look at the idea behind word embeddings, and then cover the two earliest implementations – Word2Vec and GloVe. We will learn how to build word embeddings from scratch using the popular library Gensim on our own corpus and navigate the embedding space we create.

We will also learn how to use pretrained third-party embeddings as a starting point for our own NLP tasks, such as spam detection, that is, learning to automatically detect unsolicited and unwanted emails. We will then learn about various ways to leverage the idea of word embeddings for unrelated tasks, such as constructing an embedded space for making item recommendations.

We will then look at extensions to these foundational word embedding techniques that have occurred in the last decade since Word2Vec – adding syntactic similarity with fastText, adding the effect of context using neural networks such as ELMo and Google Universal Sentence Encoder, sentence encodings such as InferSent and skip-thoughts, and the introduction of language models such as ULMFiT and BERT.

In this chapter, we'll learn about the following:

- Word embeddings – origins and fundamentals
- Distributed representations
- Static embeddings
- Creating your own embedding with Gensim
- Exploring the embedding space with Gensim
- Using word embedding for spam detection
- Neural embedding – not just for words
- Character and subword embedding
- Dynamic embeddings
- Sentence and paragraph embeddings
- Language-based model embeddings

All the code files for this chapter can be found at `https://packt.link/dltfchp4`.

Let's begin!

Word embedding – origins and fundamentals

Wikipedia defines word embedding as the collective name for a set of language modeling and feature learning techniques in **natural language processing** (**NLP**) where words or phrases from a vocabulary are mapped to vectors of real numbers.

Deep learning models, like other machine learning models, typically don't work directly with text; the text needs to be converted to numbers instead. The process of converting text to numbers is a process called vectorization. An early technique for vectorizing words was one-hot encoding, which you learned about in *Chapter 1, Neural Network Foundations with TF*. As you will recall, a major problem with one-hot encoding is that it treats each word as completely independent from all the others, since the similarity between any two words (measured by the dot product of the two word vectors) is always zero.

The dot product is an algebraic operation that operates on two vectors $a = [a_1, ..., a_N]$ and $b = [b_1, ..., b_N]$ of equal length and returns a number. It is also known as the inner product or scalar product:

$$a \, b = \sum_{i=1}^{N} a_i b_i = a_1 b_1 + \cdots + a_N b_N$$

Why is the dot product of one-hot vectors of two words always 0? Consider two words w_i and w_j. Assuming a vocabulary size of V, their corresponding one-hot vectors are a zero vector of rank V with positions i and j set to 1. When combined using the dot product operation, the 1 in a[i] is multiplied by 0 in b[i], and 1 in b[j] is multiplied by 0 in a[j], and all other elements in both vectors are 0, so the resulting dot product is also 0.

To overcome the limitations of one-hot encoding, the NLP community has borrowed techniques from **Information Retrieval** (**IR**) to vectorize text using the document as the context. Notable techniques are **Term Frequency-Inverse Document Frequency** (**TF-IDF**) [35], **Latent Semantic Analysis** (**LSA**) [36], and topic modeling [37]. These representations attempt to capture a document-centric idea of semantic similarity between words. Of these, one-hot and TF-IDF are relatively sparse embeddings, since vocabularies are usually quite large, and a word is unlikely to occur in more than a few documents in the corpus.

The development of word embedding techniques began around 2000. These techniques differ from previous IR-based techniques in that they use neighboring words as their context, leading to a more natural semantic similarity from a human understanding perspective. Today, word embedding is a foundational technique for all kinds of NLP tasks, such as text classification, document clustering, part-of-speech tagging, named entity recognition, sentiment analysis, and many more. Word embeddings result in dense, low-dimensional vectors, and along with LSA and topic models can be thought of as a vector of latent features for the word.

Word embeddings are based on the distributional hypothesis, which states that words that occur in similar contexts tend to have similar meanings. Hence the class of word embedding-based encodings is also known as distributed representations, which we will talk about next.

Distributed representations

Distributed representations attempt to capture the meaning of a word by considering its relations with other words in its context. The idea behind the distributed hypothesis is captured in this quote from *J. R. Firth*, a linguist, who first proposed this idea:

> *You shall know a word by the company it keeps.*

How does this work? By way of example, consider the following pair of sentences:

Paris is the capital of France.

Berlin is the capital of Germany.

Even assuming no knowledge of world geography, the sentence pair implies some sort of relationship between the entities Paris, France, Berlin, and Germany that could be represented as:

"Paris" is to "France" as "Berlin" is to "Germany."

Distributed representations are based on the idea that there exists some transformation, as follows:

Paris : France :: Berlin : Germany

In other words, a distributed embedding space is one where words that are used in similar contexts are close to one another. Therefore, the similarity between the word vectors in this space would roughly correspond to the semantic similarity between the words.

Figure 4.1 shows a TensorBoard visualization of word embedding of words around the word "important" in the embedding space. As you can see, the neighbors of the word tend to be closely related, or interchangeable with the original word.

For example, "crucial" is virtually a synonym, and it is easy to see how the words "historical" or "valuable" could be substituted in certain situations:

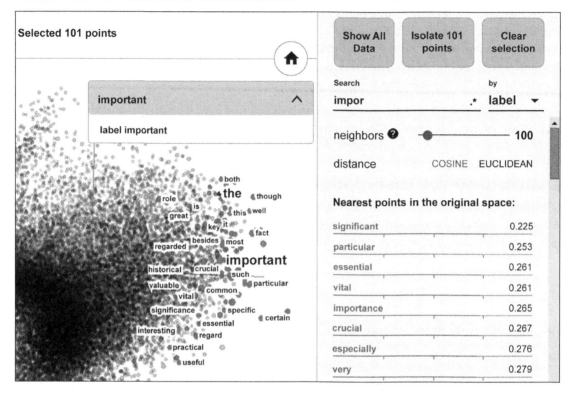

Figure 4.1: Visualization of nearest neighbors of the word "important" in a word embedding dataset, from the TensorFlow Embedding Guide (https://www.tensorflow.org/guide/embedding)

In the next section, we will look at various types of distributed representations (or word embeddings).

Static embeddings

Static embeddings are the oldest type of word embedding. The embeddings are generated against a large corpus but the number of words, though large, is finite. You can think of a static embedding as a dictionary, with words as the keys and their corresponding vector as the value. If you have a word whose embedding needs to be looked up that was not in the original corpus, then you are out of luck. In addition, a word has the same embedding regardless of how it is used, so static embeddings cannot address the problem of polysemy, that is, words with multiple meanings. We will explore this issue further when we cover non-static embeddings later in this chapter.

Word2Vec

The models known as Word2Vec were first created in 2013 by a team of researchers at Google led by *Tomas Mikolov* [1, 2, 3]. The models are self-supervised, that is, they are supervised models that depend on the structure of natural language to provide labeled training data.

The two architectures for Word2Vec are as follows:

- **Continuous Bag of Words (CBOW)**
- Skip-gram

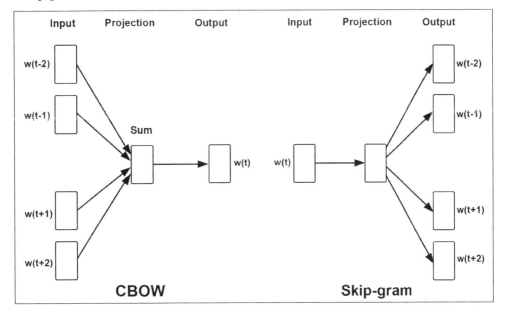

Figure 4.2: Architecture of the CBOW and Skip-gram Word2Vec models

In the CBOW architecture, the model predicts the current word given a window of surrounding words. The order of context words does not influence the prediction (that is, the bag of words assumption, hence the name). In the skip-gram architecture, the model predicts the surrounding words given the context word. According to the Word2Vec website, CBOW is faster, but skip-gram does a better job at predicting infrequent words.

Figure 4.2 summarizes the CBOW and skip-gram architectures. To understand the inputs and outputs, consider the following example sentence:

The Earth travels around the Sun once per year.

Assuming a window size of 5, that is, two context words to the left and right of the content word, the resulting context windows are shown as follows. The word in bold is the word under consideration, and the other words are the context words within the window:

[_, _, **The**, Earth, travels]

[_, The, **Earth**, travels, around]

[The, Earth, **travels**, around, the]

[Earth, travels, **around**, the, Sun]

[travels, around, **the**, Sun, once]

[around, the, **Sun**, once, per]

[the, Sun, **once**, per, year]

[Sun, **once**, per, year, _]

[**once**, per, year, _, _]

For the CBOW model, the input and label tuples for the first three context windows are as follows. In the following first example, the CBOW model would learn to predict the word "The" given the set of words ("Earth," "travels"), and so on. More correctly, the input of sparse vectors for the words "Earth" and "travels." The model will learn to predict a dense vector whose highest value, or probability, corresponds to the word "The":

([Earth, travels], **The**)

([The, travels, around], **Earth**)

([The, Earth, around, the], **travels**)

For the skip-gram model, the first three context windows correspond to the following input and label tuples. We can simplify the skip-gram model objective of predicting a context word given a target word to basically predicting if a pair of words are contextually related. Contextually related means that a pair of words within a context window are somehow related. That is, the input to the skip-gram model for the following first example would be the sparse vectors for the context words "The" and "Earth," and the output would be the value 1:

([**The**, Earth], 1)

([**The**, travels], 1)

([**Earth**, The], 1)

([**Earth**, travels], 1)

([**Earth**, around], 1)

([**travels**, The], 1)

([**travels**, Earth], 1)

([**travels**, around], 1)

([**travels**, the], 1)

We also need negative samples to train a model properly, so we generate additional negative samples by pairing each input word with some random word in the vocabulary. This process is called negative sampling and might result in the following additional inputs:

([**Earth**, aardvark], 0)

([**Earth**, zebra], 0)

A model trained with all of these inputs is called a **Skip-Gram with Negative Sampling (SGNS)** model.

It is important to understand that we are not interested in the ability of these models to classify; rather, we are interested in the side effect of training – the learned weights. These learned weights are what we call the embedding.

While it may be instructive to implement the models on your own as an academic exercise, at this point Word2Vec is so commoditized, you are unlikely to ever need to do this. For the curious, you will find code to implement the CBOW and skip-gram models in the files `tf2_cbow_model.py` and `tf2_cbow_skipgram.py` in the source code accompanying this chapter.

The Word2Vec model was trained in a self-supervised manner by Google on roughly 100 billion words from the Google News dataset and contains a vocabulary of 3 million words. Google then released the pretrained model for anyone to download and use. The pretrained Word2Vec model is available here (`https://drive.google.com/file/d/0B7XkCwpI5KDYNlNUTTlSS21pQmM/edit`). The output vector dimensionality is 300. It is available as a BIN file and can be opened using Gensim by using `gensim.models.Word2Vec.load_word2vec_format()` or using the `gensim()` data downloader.

The other early implementation of word embedding is GloVe, which we will talk about next.

GloVe

The **Global vectors for word representation (GloVe)** embeddings were created by *Jeffrey Pennington, Richard Socher*, and *Christopher Manning* [4]. The authors describe GloVe as an unsupervised learning algorithm for obtaining vector representations for words. Training is performed on aggregated global word-word co-occurrence statistics from a corpus, and the resulting representations show similar clustering behavior between similar words as seen in Word2Vec.

GloVe differs from Word2Vec in that Word2Vec is a predictive model while GloVe is a count-based model. The first step is to construct a large matrix of (word, context) pairs that co-occur in the training corpus. Rows correspond to words and columns correspond to contexts, usually a sequence of one or more words. Each element of the matrix represents how often the word co-occurs in the context.

The GloVe process factorizes this co-occurrence matrix into a pair of (word, feature) and (feature, context) matrices. The process is known as matrix factorization and is done using **Stochastic Gradient Descent (SGD)**, an iterative numerical method. For example, consider that we want to factorize a matrix R into its factors P and Q:

$$R = P * Q \approx R'$$

The SGD process will start with P and Q composed of random values and attempt to reconstruct the matrix R' by multiplying them. The difference between the matrices R and R' represents the loss and is usually computed as the mean-squared error between the two matrices. The loss dictates how much the values of P and Q need to change for R' to move closer to R to minimize the reconstruction loss. This process is repeated multiple times until the loss is within some acceptable threshold. At that point, the (word, feature) matrix P is the GloVe embedding.

The GloVe process is much more resource-intensive than Word2Vec. This is because Word2Vec learns the embedding by training over batches of word vectors, while GloVe factorizes the entire co-occurrence matrix in one shot. In order to make the process scalable, SGD is often used in parallel mode, as outlined in the HOGWILD! paper [5].

Levy and Goldberg have also pointed out equivalences between the Word2Vec and GloVe approaches in their paper [6], showing that the Word2Vec SGNS model implicitly factorizes a word-context matrix.

As with Word2Vec, you are unlikely to ever need to generate your own GloVe embedding, and far more likely to use embeddings pre-generated against large corpora and made available for download. If you are curious, you will find code to implement matrix factorization in tf2_matrix_factorization.py in the source code download accompanying this chapter.

GloVe vectors trained on various large corpora (number of tokens ranging from 6 billion to 840 billion, vocabulary size from 400 thousand to 2.2 million) and of various dimensions (50, 100, 200, 300) are available from the GloVe project download page (https://nlp.stanford.edu/projects/glove/). It can be downloaded directly from the site or using Gensim or spaCy data downloaders.

Creating your own embeddings using Gensim

We will create an embedding using Gensim and a small text corpus, called text8.

Gensim is an open-source Python library designed to extract semantic meaning from text documents. One of its features is an excellent implementation of the Word2Vec algorithm, with an easy-to-use API that allows you to train and query your own Word2Vec model. To learn more about Gensim, see https://radimrehurek.com/gensim/index.html. To install Gensim, please follow the instructions at https://radimrehurek.com/gensim/install.html.

The text8 dataset is the first 10^8 bytes of the Large Text Compression Benchmark, which consists of the first 10^9 bytes of English Wikipedia [7]. The text8 dataset is accessible from within the Gensim API as an iterable of tokens, essentially a list of tokenized sentences. To download the text8 corpus, create a Word2Vec model from it, and save it for later use, run the following few lines of code (available in create_embedding_with_text8.py in the source code for this chapter):

```
import gensim.downloader as api
from gensim.models import Word2Vec
dataset = api.load("text8")
model = Word2Vec(dataset)
model.save("data/text8-word2vec.bin")
```

This will train a Word2Vec model on the text8 dataset and save it as a binary file. The Word2Vec model has many parameters, but we will just use the defaults. In this case, it trains a CBOW model (sg=0) with window size 5 (window=5) and will produce 100 dimensional embeddings (size=100). The full set of parameters is described on the Word2Vec documentation page [8]. To run this code, execute the following commands at the command line:

```
$ mkdir data
$ python create_embedding_with_text8.py
```

The code should run for 5-10 minutes, after which it will write out a trained model into the `data` folder. We will examine this trained model in the next section.

 Word embeddings are central to text processing; however, at the time of writing this book, there is no comparable API within TensorFlow that allows you to work with embeddings at the same level of abstraction. For this reason, we have used Gensim in this chapter to work with Word2Vec models. The online Tensorflow tutorial contains an example of how to train a Word2Vec model from scratch (https://www.tensorflow.org/tutorials/text/word2vec) but that is not our focus here.

Exploring the embedding space with Gensim

Let us reload the Word2Vec model we just built and explore it using the Gensim API. The actual word vectors can be accessed as a custom Gensim class from the model's wv attribute:

```
from gensim.models import KeyedVectors
model = KeyedVectors.load("data/text8-word2vec.bin")
word_vectors = model.wv
```

We can take a look at the first few words in the vocabulary and check to see if specific words are available:

```
words = word_vectors.vocab.keys()
print([x for i, x in enumerate(words) if i < 10])
assert("king" in words)
```

The preceding snippet of code produces the following output:

```
['anarchism', 'originated', 'as', 'a', 'term', 'of', 'abuse', 'first', 'used',
'against']
```

We can look for similar words to a given word ("king"), shown as follows:

```
def print_most_similar(word_conf_pairs, k):
    for i, (word, conf) in enumerate(word_conf_pairs):
        print("{:.3f} {:s}".format(conf, word))
        if i >= k-1:
            break
    if k < len(word_conf_pairs):
        print("...")
print_most_similar(word_vectors.most_similar("king"), 5)
```

The `most_similar()` method with a single parameter produces the following output. Here, the floating-point score is a measure of the similarity, higher values being better than lower values. As you can see, the similar words seem to be mostly accurate:

```
0.760 prince
0.701 queen
0.700 kings
0.698 emperor
0.688 throne
...
```

You can also do vector arithmetic similar to the country-capital example we described earlier. Our objective is to see if the relation Paris : France :: Berlin : Germany holds true. This is equivalent to saying that the distance in embedding space between Paris and France should be the same as that between Berlin and Germany. In other words, France - Paris + Berlin should give us Germany. In code, then, this would translate to:

```
print_most_similar(word_vectors.most_similar(
    positive=["france", "berlin"], negative=["paris"]), 1
)
```

This returns the following result, as expected:

```
0.803 germany
```

The preceding similarity value reported is cosine similarity, but a better measure of similarity was proposed by *Levy* and *Goldberg* [9], which is also implemented in the Gensim API. This measure essentially computes the distance on a log scale thereby amplifying the difference between shorter distances and reducing the difference between longer ones.

```
print_most_similar(word_vectors.most_similar_cosmul(
    positive=["france", "berlin"], negative=["paris"]), 1
)
```

And this also yields the expected result, but with higher similarity:

```
0.984 germany
```

Gensim also provides a `doesnt_match()` function, which can be used to detect the odd one out of a list of words:

```
print(word_vectors.doesnt_match(["hindus", "parsis", "singapore",
"christians"]))
```

This gives us `singapore` as expected, since it is the only country among a set of words identifying religions.

We can also calculate the similarity between two words. Here we demonstrate that the distance between related words is less than that of unrelated words:

```
for word in ["woman", "dog", "whale", "tree"]:
    print("similarity({:s}, {:s}) = {:.3f}".format(
        "man", word,
        word_vectors.similarity("man", word)
    ))
```

This gives the following interesting result:

```
similarity(man, woman) = 0.759
similarity(man, dog) = 0.474
similarity(man, whale) = 0.290
similarity(man, tree) = 0.260
```

The similar_by_word() function is functionally equivalent to similar() except that the latter normalizes the vector before comparing by default. There is also a related similar_by_vector() function, which allows you to find similar words by specifying a vector as input. Here we try to find words that are similar to "singapore":

```
print(print_most_similar(
    word_vectors.similar_by_word("singapore"), 5)
)
```

And we get the following output, which seems to be mostly correct, at least from a geographical point of view:

```
0.882 malaysia
0.837 indonesia
0.826 philippines
0.825 uganda
0.822 thailand
...
```

We can also compute the distance between two words in the embedding space using the distance() function. This is really just 1 - similarity():

```
print("distance(singapore, malaysia) = {:.3f}".format(
    word_vectors.distance("singapore", "malaysia")
))
```

We can also look up vectors for a vocabulary word either directly from the word_vectors object, or by using the word_vec() wrapper, shown as follows:

```
vec_song = word_vectors["song"]
vec_song_2 = word_vectors.word_vec("song", use_norm=True)
```

There are a few other functions that you may find useful depending on your use case. The documentation page for KeyedVectors contains a list of all the available functions [10].

The code shown here can be found in the `explore_text8_embedding.py` file in the code accompanying this book.

Using word embeddings for spam detection

Because of the widespread availability of various robust embeddings generated from large corpora, it has become quite common to use one of these embeddings to convert text input for use with machine learning models. Text is treated as a sequence of tokens. The embedding provides a dense fixed dimension vector for each token. Each token is replaced with its vector, and this converts the sequence of text into a matrix of examples, each of which has a fixed number of features corresponding to the dimensionality of the embedding.

This matrix of examples can be used directly as input to standard (non-neural network based) machine learning programs, but since this book is about deep learning and TensorFlow, we will demonstrate its use with a one-dimensional version of the **Convolutional Neural Network** (**CNN**) that you learned about in *Chapter 3, Convolutional Neural Networks*. Our example is a spam detector that will classify **Short Message Service** (**SMS**) or text messages as either "ham" or "spam." The example is very similar to a sentiment analysis example we'll cover in *Chapter 20, Advanced Convolutional Neural Networks*, that uses a one-dimensional CNN, but our focus here will be on the embedding layer.

Specifically, we will see how the program learns an embedding from scratch that is customized to the spam detection task. Next, we will see how to use an external third-party embedding like the ones we have learned about in this chapter, a process similar to transfer learning in computer vision. Finally, we will learn how to combine the two approaches, starting with a third-party embedding and letting the network use that as a starting point for its custom embedding, a process similar to fine-tuning in computer vision.

As usual, we will start with our imports:

```
import argparse
import gensim.downloader as api
import numpy as np
import os
import shutil
import tensorflow as tf
from sklearn.metrics import accuracy_score, confusion_matrix
```

 Scikit-learn is an open-source Python machine learning toolkit that contains many efficient and easy-to-use tools for data mining and data analysis. In this chapter, we have used two of its predefined metrics, `accuracy_score` and `confusion_matrix`, to evaluate our model after it is trained.

You can learn more about scikit-learn at `https://scikit-learn.org/stable/`.

Getting the data

The data for our model is available publicly and comes from the SMS spam collection dataset from the UCI Machine Learning Repository [11]. The following code will download the file and parse it to produce a list of SMS messages and their corresponding labels:

```
def download_and_read(url):
    local_file = url.split('/')[-1]
    p = tf.keras.utils.get_file(local_file, url,
        extract=True, cache_dir=".")
    labels, texts = [], []
    local_file = os.path.join("datasets", "SMSSpamCollection")
    with open(local_file, "r") as fin:
        for line in fin:
            label, text = line.strip().split('\t')
            labels.append(1 if label == "spam" else 0)
            texts.append(text)
    return texts, labels
DATASET_URL = "https://archive.ics.uci.edu/ml/machine-learning-databases/00228/
smsspamcollection.zip"
texts, labels = download_and_read(DATASET_URL)
```

The dataset contains 5,574 SMS records, 747 of which are marked as "spam" and the other 4,827 are marked as "ham" (not spam). The text of the SMS records is contained in the variable texts, and the corresponding numeric labels (0 = ham, 1 = spam) are contained in the variable labels.

Making the data ready for use

The next step is to process the data so it can be consumed by the network. The SMS text needs to be fed into the network as a sequence of integers, where each word is represented by its corresponding ID in the vocabulary. We will use the Keras tokenizer to convert each SMS text into a sequence of words, and then create the vocabulary using the fit_on_texts() method on the tokenizer.

We then convert the SMS messages to a sequence of integers using texts_to_sequences(). Finally, since the network can only work with fixed-length sequences of integers, we call the pad_sequences() function to pad the shorter SMS messages with zeros.

The longest SMS message in our dataset has 189 tokens (words). In many applications where there may be a few outlier sequences that are very long, we would restrict the length to a smaller number by setting the maxlen flag. In that case, sentences longer than maxlen tokens would be truncated, and sentences shorter than maxlen tokens would be padded:

```
# tokenize and pad text
tokenizer = tf.keras.preprocessing.text.Tokenizer()
tokenizer.fit_on_texts(texts)
text_sequences = tokenizer.texts_to_sequences(texts)
```

```
text_sequences = tf.keras.preprocessing.sequence.pad_sequences(
    text_sequences)
num_records = len(text_sequences)
max_seqlen = len(text_sequences[0])
print("{:d} sentences, max length: {:d}".format(
    num_records, max_seqlen))
```

We will also convert our labels to categorical or one-hot encoding format, because the loss function we would like to choose (categorical cross-entropy) expects to see the labels in that format:

```
# Labels
NUM_CLASSES = 2
cat_labels = tf.keras.utils.to_categorical(
    labels, num_classes=NUM_CLASSES)
```

The tokenizer allows access to the vocabulary created through the word_index attribute, which is basically a dictionary of vocabulary words to their index positions in the vocabulary. We also build the reverse index that enables us to go from index position to the word itself. In addition, we create entries for the PAD character:

```
# vocabulary
word2idx = tokenizer.word_index
idx2word = {v:k for k, v in word2idx.items()}
word2idx["PAD"] = 0
idx2word[0] = "PAD"
vocab_size = len(word2idx)
print("vocab size: {:d}".format(vocab_size))
```

Finally, we create the dataset object that our network will work with. The dataset object allows us to set up some properties, such as the batch size, declaratively. Here, we build up a dataset from our padded sequence of integers and categorical labels, shuffle the data, and split it into training, validation, and test sets. Finally, we set the batch size for each of the three datasets:

```
# dataset
dataset = tf.data.Dataset.from_tensor_slices(
    (text_sequences, cat_labels))
dataset = dataset.shuffle(10000)
test_size = num_records // 4
val_size = (num_records - test_size) // 10
test_dataset = dataset.take(test_size)
val_dataset = dataset.skip(test_size).take(val_size)
train_dataset = dataset.skip(test_size + val_size)
BATCH_SIZE = 128
test_dataset = test_dataset.batch(BATCH_SIZE, drop_remainder=True)
val_dataset = val_dataset.batch(BATCH_SIZE, drop_remainder=True)
train_dataset = train_dataset.batch(BATCH_SIZE, drop_remainder=True)
```

Building the embedding matrix

The Gensim toolkit provides access to various trained embedding models, as you can see from running the following command at the Python prompt:

```
>>> import gensim.downloader as api
>>> api.info("models").keys()
```

This will return (at the time of writing this book) the following trained word embeddings:

- **Word2Vec:** Two flavors, one trained on Google news (3 million word vectors based on 3 billion tokens), and one trained on Russian corpora (word2vec-ruscorpora-300, word2vec-google-news-300).

- **GloVe:** Two flavors, one trained on the Gigawords corpus (400,000 word vectors based on 6 billion tokens), available as 50d, 100d, 200d, and 300d vectors, and one trained on Twitter (1.2 million word vectors based on 27 billion tokens), available as 25d, 50d, 100d, and 200d vectors (glove-wiki-gigaword-50, glove-wiki-gigaword-100, glove-wiki-gigaword-200, glove-wiki-gigaword-300, glove-twitter-25, glove-twitter-50, glove-twitter-100, glove-twitter-200). Smaller embedding sizes would result in greater compression of the input and consequently a greater degree of approximation.

- **fastText:** One million word vectors trained with subword information on Wikipedia 2017, the UMBC web corpus, and statmt.org news dataset (16B tokens) (fastText-wiki-news-subwords-300).

- **ConceptNet Numberbatch:** An ensemble embedding that uses the ConceptNet semantic network, the **paraphrase database** (**PPDB**), Word2Vec, and GloVe as input. Produces 600d vectors [12, 13].

For our example, we chose the 300d GloVe embeddings trained on the Gigaword corpus.

In order to keep our model size small, we want to only consider embeddings for words that exist in our vocabulary. This is done using the following code, which creates a smaller embedding matrix for each word in the vocabulary. Each row in the matrix corresponds to a word, and the row itself is the vector corresponding to the embedding for the word:

```python
def build_embedding_matrix(sequences, word2idx, embedding_dim,
        embedding_file):
    if os.path.exists(embedding_file):
        E = np.load(embedding_file)
    else:
        vocab_size = len(word2idx)
        E = np.zeros((vocab_size, embedding_dim))
        word_vectors = api.load(EMBEDDING_MODEL)
        for word, idx in word2idx.items():
            try:
                E[idx] = word_vectors.word_vec(word)
            except KeyError:    # word not in embedding
                pass
```

```
        np.save(embedding_file, E)
    return E
EMBEDDING_DIM = 300
DATA_DIR = "data"
EMBEDDING_NUMPY_FILE = os.path.join(DATA_DIR, "E.npy")
EMBEDDING_MODEL = "glove-wiki-gigaword-300"
E = build_embedding_matrix(text_sequences, word2idx,
    EMBEDDING_DIM,
    EMBEDDING_NUMPY_FILE)
print("Embedding matrix:", E.shape)
```

The output shape for the embedding matrix is (9010, 300), corresponding to the 9,010 tokens in the vocabulary, and 300 features in the third-party GloVe embeddings.

Defining the spam classifier

We are now ready to define our classifier. We will use a **one-dimensional Convolutional Neural Network** or **ConvNet (1D CNN)**, similar to the network you have seen already in *Chapter 3, Convolutional Neural Networks*.

The input is a sequence of integers. The first layer is an embedding layer, which converts each input integer to a vector of size (embedding_dim). Depending on the run mode, that is, whether we will learn the embeddings from scratch, do transfer learning, or do fine-tuning, the embedding layer in the network would be slightly different. When the network starts with randomly initialized embedding weights (run_mode == "scratch") and learns the weights during the training, we set the trainable parameter to True. In the transfer learning case (run_mode == "vectorizer"), we set the weights from our embedding matrix E but set the trainable parameter to False, so it doesn't train. In the fine-tuning case (run_mode == "finetuning"), we set the embedding weights from our external matrix E, as well as setting the layer to trainable.

The output of the embedding is fed into a convolutional layer. Here, fixed-size 3-token-wide 1D windows (kernel_size=3), also called time steps, are convolved against 256 random filters (num_filters=256) to produce vectors of size 256 for each time step. Thus, the output vector shape is (batch_size, time_steps, num_filters).

The output of the convolutional layer is sent to a 1D spatial dropout layer. Spatial dropout will randomly drop entire feature maps output from the convolutional layer. This is a regularization technique to prevent over-fitting. This is then sent through a global max pool layer, which takes the maximum value from each time step for each filter, resulting in a vector of shape (batch_size, num_filters).

The output of the dropout layer is fed into a pooling layer to flatten it, and then into a dense layer, which converts the vector of shape (batch_size, num_filters) to (batch_size, num_classes). A softmax activation will convert the scores for each of (spam, ham) into a probability distribution, indicating the probability of the input SMS being spam or ham respectively:

```
class SpamClassifierModel(tf.keras.Model):
    def __init__(self, vocab_sz, embed_sz, input_length,
            num_filters, kernel_sz, output_sz,
            run_mode, embedding_weights,
            **kwargs):
        super(SpamClassifierModel, self).__init__(**kwargs)
        if run_mode == "scratch":
            self.embedding = tf.keras.layers.Embedding(vocab_sz,
                embed_sz,
                input_length=input_length,
                trainable=True)
        elif run_mode == "vectorizer":
            self.embedding = tf.keras.layers.Embedding(vocab_sz,
                embed_sz,
                input_length=input_length,
                weights=[embedding_weights],
                trainable=False)
        else:
            self.embedding = tf.keras.layers.Embedding(vocab_sz,
                embed_sz,
                input_length=input_length,
                weights=[embedding_weights],
                trainable=True)
        self.conv = tf.keras.layers.Conv1D(filters=num_filters,
            kernel_size=kernel_sz,
            activation="relu")
        self.dropout = tf.keras.layers.SpatialDropout1D(0.2)
        self.pool = tf.keras.layers.GlobalMaxPooling1D()
        self.dense = tf.keras.layers.Dense(output_sz,
            activation="softmax")
    def call(self, x):
        x = self.embedding(x)
        x = self.conv(x)
        x = self.dropout(x)
        x = self.pool(x)
        x = self.dense(x)
        return x
# model definition
conv_num_filters = 256
conv_kernel_size = 3
model = SpamClassifierModel(
```

```
    vocab_size, EMBEDDING_DIM, max_seqlen,
    conv_num_filters, conv_kernel_size, NUM_CLASSES,
    run_mode, E)
model.build(input_shape=(None, max_seqlen))
```

Finally, we compile the model using the categorical cross entropy loss function and the Adam optimizer:

```
# compile
model.compile(optimizer="adam", loss="categorical_crossentropy",
metrics=["accuracy"])
```

Training and evaluating the model

One thing to notice is that the dataset is somewhat imbalanced; there are only 747 instances of spam compared to 4,827 instances of ham. The network could achieve close to 87% accuracy simply by always predicting the majority class. To alleviate this problem, we set class weights to indicate that an error on a spam SMS is eight times as expensive as an error on a ham SMS. This is indicated by the CLASS_WEIGHTS variable, which is passed into the model.fit() call as an additional parameter.

After training for 3 epochs, we evaluate the model against the test set, and report the accuracy and confusion matrix of the model against the test set. However, for imbalance data, even with the use of class weights, the model may end up learning to always predict the majority class. Therefore, it is generally advisable to report accuracy on a per-class basis to make sure that the model learns to distinguish each class effectively. This can be done quite easily using the confusion matrix by dividing the diagonal element for each row by the sum of elements for that row, where each row corresponds to a labeled class:

```
NUM_EPOCHS = 3
# data distribution is 4827 ham and 747 spam (total 5574), which
# works out to approx 87% ham and 13% spam, so we take reciprocals
# and this works out to being each spam (1) item as being
# approximately 8 times as important as each ham (0) message.
CLASS_WEIGHTS = { 0: 1, 1: 8 }
# train model
model.fit(train_dataset, epochs=NUM_EPOCHS,
    validation_data=val_dataset,
    class_weight=CLASS_WEIGHTS)
# evaluate against test set
labels, predictions = [], []
for Xtest, Ytest in test_dataset:
    Ytest_ = model.predict_on_batch(Xtest)
    ytest = np.argmax(Ytest, axis=1)
    ytest_ = np.argmax(Ytest_, axis=1)
    labels.extend(ytest.tolist())
    predictions.extend(ytest.tolist())
```

```
print("test accuracy: {:.3f}".format(accuracy_score(labels, predictions)))
print("confusion matrix")
print(confusion_matrix(labels, predictions))
```

Running the spam detector

The three scenarios we want to look at are:

- Letting the network learn the embedding for the task.
- Starting with a fixed external third-party embedding where the embedding matrix is treated like a vectorizer to transform the sequence of integers into a sequence of vectors.
- Starting with an external third-party embedding which is further fine-tuned to the task during the training.

Each scenario can be evaluated by setting the value of the mode argument as shown in the following command:

```
$ python spam_classifier --mode [scratch|vectorizer|finetune]
```

The dataset is small, and the model is fairly simple. We were able to achieve very good results (validation set accuracies in the high 90s, and perfect test set accuracy) with only minimal training (3 epochs). In all three cases, the network achieved a perfect score, accurately predicting the 1,111 ham messages, as well as the 169 spam cases.

The change in validation accuracies, shown in *Figure 4.3*, illustrates the differences between the three approaches:

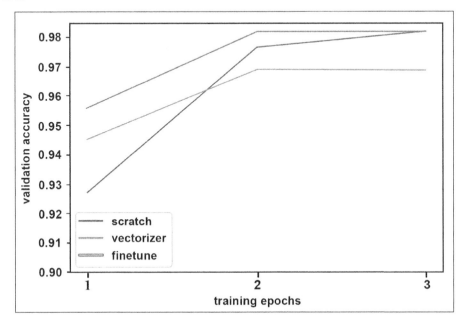

Figure 4.3: Comparison of validation accuracy across training
epochs for different embedding techniques

In the learning from scratch case, at the end of the first epoch, the validation accuracy is 0.93, but over the next two epochs, it rises to 0.98. In the vectorizer case, the network gets something of a head start from the third-party embeddings and ends up with a validation accuracy of almost 0.95 at the end of the first epoch. However, because the embedding weights are not allowed to change, it is not able to customize the embeddings to the spam detection task, and the validation accuracy at the end of the third epoch is the lowest among the three. The fine-tuning case, like the vectorizer, also gets a head start, but can customize the embedding to the task as well, and therefore is able to learn at the most rapid rate among the three cases. The fine-tuning case has the highest validation accuracy at the end of the first epoch and reaches the same validation accuracy at the end of the second epoch that the scratch case achieves at the end of the third.

In the next section, we will see that distributional similarity is not restricted to word embeddings; it applies to other scenarios as well.

Neural embeddings – not just for words

Word embedding technology has evolved in various ways since Word2Vec and GloVe. One such direction is the application of word embeddings to non-word settings, also known as neural embeddings. As you will recall, word embeddings leverage the distributional hypothesis that words occurring in similar contexts tend to have similar meanings, where context is usually a fixed-size (in number of words) window around the target word.

The idea of neural embeddings is very similar; that is, entities that occur in similar contexts tend to be strongly related to each other. The way in which these contexts are constructed is usually situation-dependent. We will describe two techniques here that are foundational and general enough to be applied easily to a variety of use cases.

Item2Vec

The Item2Vec embedding model was originally proposed by Barkan and Koenigstein [14] for the collaborative filtering use case, that is, recommending items to users based on purchases by other users that have similar purchase histories to this user. It uses items in a web-store as the "words" and the itemset (the sequence of items purchased by a user over time) as the "sentence" from which the "word context" is derived.

For example, consider the problem of recommending items to shoppers in a supermarket. Assume that our supermarket sells 5,000 items, so each item can be represented as a sparse one-hot encoded vector of size 5,000. Each user is represented by their shopping cart, which is a sequence of such vectors. Applying a context window similar to the one we saw in the Word2Vec section, we can train a skip-gram model to predict likely item pairs. The learned embedding model maps the items to a dense low-dimensional space where similar items are close together, which can be used to make similar item recommendations.

node2vec

The node2vec embedding model was proposed by Grover and Leskovec [15], as a scalable way to learn features for nodes in a graph. It learns an embedding of the structure of the graph by executing a large number of fixed-length random walks on the graph. The nodes are the "words" and the random walks are the "sentences" from which the "word context" is derived in node2vec.

The **Something2Vec** page [40] provides a comprehensive list of ways in which researchers have tried to apply the distributional hypothesis to entities other than words. Hopefully, this list will spark ideas for your own "Something2Vec" representation.

To illustrate how easy it is to create your own neural embedding, we will generate a node2vec-like model or, more accurately, a predecessor graph-based embedding called DeepWalk, proposed by Perozzi, et al. [42] for papers presented at the NeurIPS conference from 1987-2015, by leveraging word co-occurrence relationships between them.

The dataset is a 11,463 × 5,812 matrix of word counts, where the rows represent words, and columns represent conference papers. We will use this to construct a graph of papers, where an edge between two papers represents a word that occurs in both of them. Both node2vec and DeepWalk assume that the graph is undirected and unweighted. Our graph is undirected, since a relationship between a pair of papers is bidirectional. However, our edges could have weights based on the number of word co-occurrences between the two documents. For our example, we will consider any number of co-occurrences above 0 to be a valid unweighted edge.

As usual, we will start by declaring our imports:

```
import gensim
import logging
import numpy as np
import os
import shutil
import tensorflow as tf
from scipy.sparse import csr_matrix
from sklearn.metrics.pairwise import cosine_similarity
logging.basicConfig(format='%(asctime)s : %(levelname)s : %(message)s',
level=logging.INFO)
```

The next step is to download the data from the UCI repository and convert it to a sparse term-document matrix, TD, then construct a document-document matrix E by multiplying the transpose of the term-document matrix by itself. Our graph is represented as an adjacency or edge matrix by the document-document matrix. Since each element represents a similarity between two documents, we will binarize the matrix E by setting any non-zero elements to 1:

```
DATA_DIR = "./data"
UCI_DATA_URL = "https://archive.ics.uci.edu/ml/machine-learning-
databases/00371/NIPS_1987-2015.csv"
```

```python
def download_and_read(url):
    local_file = url.split('/')[-1]
    p = tf.keras.utils.get_file(local_file, url, cache_dir=".")
    row_ids, col_ids, data = [], [], []
    rid = 0
    f = open(p, "r")
    for line in f:
        line = line.strip()
        if line.startswith("\"\","):
            # header
            continue
        # compute non-zero elements for current row
        counts = np.array([int(x) for x in line.split(',')[1:]])
        nz_col_ids = np.nonzero(counts)[0]
        nz_data = counts[nz_col_ids]
        nz_row_ids = np.repeat(rid, len(nz_col_ids))
        rid += 1
        # add data to big lists
        row_ids.extend(nz_row_ids.tolist())
        col_ids.extend(nz_col_ids.tolist())
        data.extend(nz_data.tolist())
    f.close()
    TD = csr_matrix((
        np.array(data), (
            np.array(row_ids), np.array(col_ids)
            )
        ),
        shape=(rid, counts.shape[0]))
    return TD
# read data and convert to Term-Document matrix
TD = download_and_read(UCI_DATA_URL)
# compute undirected, unweighted edge matrix
E = TD.T * TD
# binarize
E[E > 0] = 1
```

Once we have our sparse binarized adjacency matrix, E, we can then generate random walks from each of the vertices. From each node, we construct 32 random walks of a maximum length of 40 nodes. The walks have a random restart probability of 0.15, which means that for any node, the particular random walk could end with a 15% probability. The following code will construct the random walks and write them out to a file given by RANDOM_WALKS_FILE. To give an idea of the input, we have provided a snapshot of the first 10 lines of this file, showing random walks starting from node 0:

```
0 1405 4845 754 4391 3524 4282 2357 3922 1667
0 1341 456 495 1647 4200 5379 473 2311
0 3422 3455 118 4527 2304 772 3659 2852 4515 5135 3439 1273
0 906 3498 2286 4755 2567 2632
0 5769 638 3574 79 2825 3532 2363 360 1443 4789 229 4515 3014 3683 2967 5206
2288 1615 1166
0 2469 1353 5596 2207 4065 3100
0 2236 1464 1596 2554 4021
0 4688 864 3684 4542 3647 2859
0 4884 4590 5386 621 4947 2784 1309 4958 3314
0 5546 200 3964 1817 845
```

Note that this is a very slow process. A copy of the output is provided along with the source code for this chapter in case you prefer to skip the random walk generation process:

```python
NUM_WALKS_PER_VERTEX = 32
MAX_PATH_LENGTH = 40
RESTART_PROB = 0.15
RANDOM_WALKS_FILE = os.path.join(DATA_DIR, "random-walks.txt")
def construct_random_walks(E, n, alpha, l, ofile):
    if os.path.exists(ofile):
        print("random walks generated already, skipping")
        return
    f = open(ofile, "w")
    for i in range(E.shape[0]):  # for each vertex
        if i % 100 == 0:
            print("{:d} random walks generated from {:d} vertices"
                .format(n * i, i))
        for j in range(n):        # construct n random walks
            curr = i
            walk = [curr]
            target_nodes = np.nonzero(E[curr])[1]
            for k in range(l):    # each of max length l
                # should we restart?
                if np.random.random() < alpha and len(walk) > 5:
                    break
                # choose one outgoing edge and append to walk
                try:
                    curr = np.random.choice(target_nodes)
                    walk.append(curr)
                    target_nodes = np.nonzero(E[curr])[1]
                except ValueError:
```

```
                    continue
            f.write("{:s}\n".format(" ".join([str(x) for x in walk])))
    print("{:d} random walks generated from {:d} vertices, COMPLETE"
        .format(n * i, i))
    f.close()
# construct random walks (caution: very long process!)
construct_random_walks(E, NUM_WALKS_PER_VERTEX, RESTART_PROB, MAX_PATH_LENGTH,
RANDOM_WALKS_FILE)
```

A few lines from the RANDOM_WALKS_FILE are shown below. You could imagine that these look like sentences in a language where the vocabulary of words is all the node IDs in our graph. We have learned that word embeddings exploit the structure of language to generate a distributional representation for words. Graph embedding schemes such as DeepWalk and node2vec do the exact same thing with these "sentences" created out of random walks. Such embeddings can capture similarities between nodes in a graph that go beyond immediate neighbors, as we shall see:

```
0 1405 4845 754 4391 3524 4282 2357 3922 1667
0 1341 456 495 1647 4200 5379 473 2311
0 3422 3455 118 4527 2304 772 3659 2852 4515 5135 3439 1273
0 906 3498 2286 4755 2567 2632
0 5769 638 3574 79 2825 3532 2363 360 1443 4789 229 4515 3014 3683 2967 5206
2288 1615 1166
0 2469 1353 5596 2207 4065 3100
0 2236 1464 1596 2554 4021
0 4688 864 3684 4542 3647 2859
0 4884 4590 5386 621 4947 2784 1309 4958 3314
0 5546 200 3964 1817 845
```

We are now ready to create our word embedding model. The Gensim package offers a simple API that allows us to declaratively create and train a Word2Vec model, using the following code. The trained model will be serialized to the file given by W2V_MODEL_FILE. The Documents class allows us to stream large input files to train the Word2Vec model without running into memory issues. We will train the Word2Vec model in skip-gram mode with a window size of 10, which means we train it to predict up to five neighboring vertices given a central vertex. The resulting embedding for each vertex is a dense vector of size 128:

```
W2V_MODEL_FILE = os.path.join(DATA_DIR, "w2v-neurips-papers.model")


class Documents(object):
    def __init__(self, input_file):
        self.input_file = input_file
    def __iter__(self):
        with open(self.input_file, "r") as f:
            for i, line in enumerate(f):
```

```
                if i % 1000 == 0:
                    logging.info("{:d} random walks extracted".format(i))
                yield line.strip().split()

    def train_word2vec_model(random_walks_file, model_file):
        if os.path.exists(model_file):
            print("Model file {:s} already present, skipping training"
                  .format(model_file))
            return
        docs = Documents(random_walks_file)
        model = gensim.models.Word2Vec(
            docs,
            size=128,      # size of embedding vector
            window=10,     # window size
            sg=1,          # skip-gram model
            min_count=2,
            workers=4
        )
        model.train(
            docs,
            total_examples=model.corpus_count,
            epochs=50)
        model.save(model_file)

    # train model
    train_word2vec_model(RANDOM_WALKS_FILE, W2V_MODEL_FILE)
```

Our resulting DeepWalk model is just a Word2Vec model, so anything you can do with Word2Vec in the context of words, you can do with this model in the context of vertices. Let us use the model to discover similarities between documents:

```
    def evaluate_model(td_matrix, model_file, source_id):
        model = gensim.models.Word2Vec.load(model_file).wv
        most_similar = model.most_similar(str(source_id))
        scores = [x[1] for x in most_similar]
        target_ids = [x[0] for x in most_similar]
        # compare top 10 scores with cosine similarity
        # between source and each target
        X = np.repeat(td_matrix[source_id].todense(), 10, axis=0)
        Y = td_matrix[target_ids].todense()
        cosims = [cosine_similarity(X[i], Y[i])[0, 0] for i in range(10)]
        for i in range(10):
```

```
        print("{:d} {:s} {:.3f} {:.3f}".format(
            source_id, target_ids[i], cosims[i], scores[i]))
source_id = np.random.choice(E.shape[0])
evaluate_model(TD, W2V_MODEL_FILE, source_id)
```

The following output is shown. The first and second columns are the source and target vertex IDs. The third column is the cosine similarity between the term vectors corresponding to the source and target documents, and the fourth is the similarity score reported by the Word2Vec model. As you can see, cosine similarity reports a similarity only between 2 of the 10 document pairs, but the Word2Vec model is able to detect latent similarities in the embedding space. This is similar to the behavior we have noticed between one-hot encoding and dense embeddings:

src_id	dst_id	cosine_sim	w2v_score
1971	5443	0.000	0.348
1971	1377	0.000	0.348
1971	3682	0.017	0.328
1971	51	0.022	0.322
1971	857	0.000	0.318
1971	1161	0.000	0.313
1971	4971	0.000	0.313
1971	5168	0.000	0.312
1971	3099	0.000	0.311
1971	462	0.000	0.310

The code for this embedding strategy is available in `neurips_papers_node2vec.py` in the source code folder accompanying this chapter. Next, we will move on to look at character and subword embeddings.

Character and subword embeddings

Another evolution of the basic word embedding strategy has been to look at character and subword embeddings instead of word embeddings. Character-level embeddings were first proposed by *Xiang* and *LeCun* [17] and have some key advantages over word embeddings.

First, a character vocabulary is finite and small – for example, a vocabulary for English would contain around 70 characters (26 characters, 10 numbers, and the rest special characters), leading to character models that are also small and compact. Second, unlike word embeddings, which provide vectors for a large but finite set of words, there is no concept of out-of-vocabulary for character embeddings, since any word can be represented by the vocabulary. Third, character embeddings tend to be better for rare and misspelled words because there is much less imbalance for character inputs than for word inputs.

Character embeddings tend to work better for applications that require the notion of syntactic rather than semantic similarity. However, unlike word embeddings, character embeddings tend to be task-specific and are usually generated inline within a network to support the task. For this reason, third-party character embeddings are generally not available.

Subword embeddings combine the idea of character and word embeddings by treating a word as a bag of character n-grams, that is, sequences of *n* consecutive words. They were first proposed by Bojanowski, et al. [18] based on research from **Facebook AI Research** (**FAIR**), which they later released as fastText embeddings. fastText embeddings are available for 157 languages, including English. The paper has reported state-of-the-art performance on a number of NLP tasks, especially word analogies and language tasks for languages with rich morphologies.

fastText computes embeddings for character n-grams where n is between 3 and 6 characters (default settings can be changed), as well as for the words themselves. For example, character n-grams for n=3 for the word "green" would be "<gr", "gre", "ree", "een", and "en>". The beginning and end of words are marked with "<" and ">" characters respectively, to distinguish between short words and their n-grams such as "<cat>" and "cat".

During lookup, you can look up a vector from the fastText embedding using the word as the key if the word exists in the embedding. However, unlike traditional word embeddings, you can still construct a fastText vector for a word that does not exist in the embedding. This is done by decomposing the word into its constituent trigram subwords as shown in the preceding example, looking up the vectors for the subwords, and then taking the average of these subword vectors. The fastText Python API [19] will do this automatically, but you will need to do this manually if you use other APIs to access fastText word embeddings, such as Gensim or NumPy.

Next up, we will look at dynamic embeddings.

Dynamic embeddings

So far, all the embeddings we have considered have been static; that is, they are deployed as a dictionary of words (and subwords) mapped to fixed dimensional vectors. The vector corresponding to a word in these embeddings is going to be the same regardless of whether it is being used as a noun or verb in the sentence, for example, the word "ensure" (the name of a health supplement when used as a noun, and to make certain when used as a verb). It also provides the same vector for polysemous words or words with multiple meanings, such as "bank" (which can mean different things depending on whether it co-occurs with the word "money" or "river"). In both cases, the meaning of the word changes depending on clues available in its context, the sentence. Dynamic embeddings attempt to use these signals to provide different vectors for words based on their context.

Dynamic embeddings are deployed as trained networks that convert your input (typically a sequence of one-hot vectors) into a lower-dimensional dense fixed-size embedding by looking at the entire sequence, not just individual words. You can either preprocess your input to this dense embedding and then use this as input to your task-specific network, or wrap the network and treat it similar to the `tf.keras.layers.Embedding` layer for static embeddings. Using a dynamic embedding network in this way is usually much more expensive compared to generating it ahead of time (the first option) or using traditional embeddings.

The earliest dynamic embedding was proposed by McCann, et al. [20], and was called **Contextualized Vectors** (**CoVe**). This involved taking the output of the encoder from the encoder-decoder pair of a machine translation network and concatenating it with word vectors for the same word.

You will learn more about seq2seq networks in the next chapter. The researchers found that this strategy improved the performance of a wide variety of NLP tasks.

Another dynamic embedding proposed by Peters, et al. [21], was **Embeddings from Language Models (ELMo)**. ELMo computes contextualized word representations using character-based word representation and bidirectional **Long Short-Term Memory (LSTM)**. You will learn more about LSTMs in the next chapter. In the meantime, a trained ELMo network is available from TensorFlow's model repository TensorFlow Hub. You can access it and use it for generating ELMo embeddings as follows.

The full set of models available on TensorFlow Hub that are TensorFlow 2.0 compatible can be found on the TensorFlow Hub site for TensorFlow 2.0 [16]. Here I have used an array of sentences, where the model will figure out tokens by using its default strategy of tokenizing on whitespace:

```
import tensorflow as tf
import tensorflow_hub as hub

elmo = hub.load("https://tfhub.dev/google/elmo/3")
embeddings = elmo.signatures["default"](
    tf.constant([
        "i like green eggs and ham",
        "would you eat them in a box"
    ]))["elmo"]
print(embeddings.shape)
```

The output is (2, 7, 1024). The first index tells us that our input contained 2 sentences. The second index refers to the maximum number of words across all sentences, in this case, 7. The model automatically pads the output to the longest sentence. The third index gives us the size of the contextual word embedding created by ELMo; each word is converted to a vector of size (1024).

You can also integrate the ELMo embedding layer into your TF2 model by wrapping it in a tf.keras.KerasLayer adapter. In this simple model, the model will return the embedding for the entire string:

```
embed = hub.KerasLayer("https://tfhub.dev/google/elmo/3",input_shape=[],
dtype=tf.string)
model = tf.keras.Sequential([embed])
embeddings = model.predict([
    "i i like green eggs and ham",
    "would you eat them in a box"
])
print(embeddings.shape)
```

Dynamic embeddings such as ELMo are able to provide different embeddings for the same word when used in different contexts and represent an improvement over static embeddings such as Word2Vec or GloVe. A logical next step is embeddings that represent larger units of text, such as sentences and paragraphs. This is what we will look at in the next section.

Sentence and paragraph embeddings

A simple, yet surprisingly effective solution for generating useful sentence and paragraph embeddings is to average the word vectors of their constituent words. Even though we will describe some popular sentence and paragraph embeddings in this section, it is generally always advisable to try averaging the word vectors as a baseline.

Sentence (and paragraph) embeddings can also be created in a task-optimized way by treating them as a sequence of words and representing each word using some standard word vector. The sequence of word vectors is used as input to train a network for some specific task. Vectors extracted from one of the later layers of the network just before the classification layer generally tend to produce a very good vector representation for the sequence. However, they tend to be very task-specific, and are of limited use as a general vector representation.

An idea for generating general vector representations for sentences that could be used across tasks was proposed by Kiros, et al. [22]. They proposed using the continuity of text from books to construct an encoder-decoder model that is trained to predict surrounding sentences given a sentence. The vector representation of a sequence of words constructed by an encoder-decoder network is typically called a "thought vector." In addition, the proposed model works on a very similar basis to skip-gram, where we try to predict the surrounding words given a word. For these reasons, these sentence vectors were called skip-thought vectors. The project released a Theano-based model that could be used to generate embeddings from sentences. Later, the model was re-implemented with TensorFlow by the Google Research team [23]. The Skip-Thoughts model emits vectors of size (2048) for each sentence. Using the model is not very straightforward, but the README.md file on the repository [23] provides instructions if you would like to use it.

A more convenient source of sentence embeddings is the Google Universal Sentence Encoder, available on TensorFlow Hub. There are two flavors of the encoder in terms of implementation. The first flavor is fast but not so accurate and is based on the **Deep Averaging Network** (**DAN**) proposed by Iyer, et al. [24], which combines embeddings for words and bigrams and sends it through a fully connected network. The second flavor is much more accurate but slower and is based on the encoder component of the transformer network proposed by Vaswani, et al. [25]. We will cover the transformer network in more detail in *Chapter 6, Transformers*.

As with ELMo, the Google Universal Sentence Encoder can also be loaded from TensorFlow Hub into your TF2 code. Here is some code that calls it with two of our example sentences:

```
embed = hub.load("https://tfhub.dev/google/universal-sentence-encoder-large/4")
embeddings = embed([
"i like green eggs and ham",
"would you eat them in a box"
])["outputs"]
print(embeddings.shape)
```

The output is (2, 512); that is, each sentence is represented by a vector of size (512). It is important to note that the Google Universal Sentence Encoder can handle any length of word sequence—so you could legitimately use it to get word embeddings on one end as well as paragraph embeddings on the other. However, as the sequence length gets longer, the quality of the embeddings tends to get "diluted."

A much earlier related line of work in producing embeddings for long sequences such as paragraphs and documents was proposed by Le and Mikolov [26] soon after Word2Vec was proposed. It is now known interchangeably as Doc2Vec or Paragraph2Vec. The Doc2Vec algorithm is an extension of Word2Vec that uses surrounding words to predict a word. In the case of Doc2Vec, an additional parameter, the paragraph ID, is provided during training. At the end of the training, the Doc2Vec network learns an embedding for every word and an embedding for every paragraph. During inference, the network is given a paragraph with some missing words. The network uses the known part of the paragraph to produce a paragraph embedding, then uses this paragraph embedding and the word embeddings to infer the missing words in the paragraph. The Doc2Vec algorithm comes in two flavors—the **Paragraph Vectors - Distributed Memory (PV-DM)** and **Paragraph Vectors - Distributed Bag of Words** (PV-DBOW), roughly analogous to CBOW and skip-gram in Word2Vec. We will not look at Doc2Vec further in this book, except to note that the Gensim toolkit provides prebuilt implementations that you can train with your own corpus.

Having looked at the different forms of static and dynamic embeddings, we will now switch gears a bit and look at language model-based embeddings.

Language model-based embeddings

Language model-based embeddings represent the next step in the evolution of word embeddings. A language model is a probability distribution over sequences of words. Once we have a model, we can ask it to predict the most likely next word given a particular sequence of words. Similar to traditional word embeddings, both static and dynamic, they are trained to predict the next word (or previous word as well, if the language model is bidirectional) given a partial sentence from the corpus. Training does not involve active labeling, since it leverages the natural grammatical structure of large volumes of text, so in a sense, this is a self-supervised learning process.

The main difference between a language model as a word embedding and more traditional embeddings is that traditional embeddings are applied as a single initial transformation on the data and are then fine-tuned for specific tasks. In contrast, language models are trained on large external corpora and represent a model of a particular language, say English. This step is called pretraining. The computing cost to pretrain these language models is usually fairly high; however, the people who pretrain these models generally make them available for use by others so we usually do not need to worry about this step. The next step is to fine-tune these general-purpose language models for your particular application domain. For example, if you are working in the travel or healthcare industry, you would fine-tune the language model with text from your own domain. Fine-tuning involves retraining the last few layers with your own text. Once fine-tuned, you can reuse this model for multiple tasks within your domain. The fine-tuning step is generally much less expensive compared to the pretraining step.

Once you have the fine-tuned language model, you remove the last layer of the language model and replace it with a one-to-two-layer fully connected network that converts the language model embedding for your input into the final categorical or regression output that your task needs. The idea is identical to transfer learning, which you learned about in *Chapter 3, Convolutional Neural Networks*, the only difference here is that you are doing transfer learning on text instead of images. As with transfer learning with images, these language model-based embeddings allow us to get surprisingly good results with very little labeled data. Not surprisingly, language model embeddings have been referred to as the "ImageNet moment" for natural language processing.

The language model-based embedding idea has its roots in the ELMo [21] network, which you have already seen in this chapter. ELMo learns about its language by being trained on a large text corpus to learn to predict the next and previous words given a sequence of words. ELMo is based on a bidirectional LSTM, which you will learn more about in *Chapter 8, Autoencoders*.

The first viable language model embedding was proposed by Howard and Ruder [27] via their **Universal Language Model Fine-Tuning** (**ULMFiT**) model, which was trained on the wikitext-103 dataset consisting of 28,595 Wikipedia articles and 103 million words. ULMFiT provides the same benefits that transfer learning provides for image tasks—better results from supervised learning tasks with comparatively less labeled data.

Meanwhile, the transformer architecture has become the preferred network for machine translation tasks, replacing the LSTM network because it allows for parallel operations and better handling of long-term dependencies. We will learn more about the transformer architecture in *Chapter 6, Transformers*. The OpenAI team of Radford, et al. [29] proposed using the decoder stack from the standard transformer network instead of the LSTM network used in ULMFiT. Using this, they built a language model embedding called **Generative Pretraining** (**GPT**) that achieved state of the art results for many language processing tasks. The paper proposes several configurations for supervised tasks involving single-and multi-sentence tasks such as classification, entailment, similarity, and multiple-choice question answering.

The OpenAI team later followed this up by building even larger language models called GPT-2 and GPT-3 respectively. GPT-2 was initially not released because of fears of misuse of the technology by malicious operators [30].

One problem with the OpenAI transformer architecture is that it is unidirectional whereas its predecessors ELMo and ULMFiT were bidirectional. **Bidirectional Encoder Representations for Transformers** (**BERT**), proposed by the Google AI team [28], uses the encoder stack of the Transformer architecture and achieves bidirectionality safely by masking up to 15% of its input, which it asks the model to predict.

As with the OpenAI paper, BERT proposes configurations for using it for several supervised learning tasks such as single- and multiple-sentence classification, question answering, and tagging.

The BERT model comes in two major flavors—BERT-base and BERT-large. BERT-base has 12 encoder layers, 768 hidden units, and 12 attention heads, with 110 million parameters in all. BERT-large has 24 encoder layers, 1,024 hidden units, and 16 attention heads, with 340 million parameters. More details can be found in the BERT GitHub repository [33].

BERT pretraining is an expensive process and can currently only be achieved using **Tensor Processing Units (TPUs)** or large distributed **Graphics Processing Units (GPUs)** clusters. TPUs are only available from Google via its Colab network [31] or Google Cloud Platform [32]. However, fine-tuning the BERT-base with custom datasets is usually achievable on GPU instances.

Once the BERT model is fine-tuned for your domain, the embeddings from the last four hidden layers usually produce good results for downstream tasks. Which embedding or combination of embeddings (via summing, averaging, max-pooling, or concatenating) to use is usually based on the type of task.

In the following section, we will look at how to extract embeddings from the BERT language model.

Using BERT as a feature extractor

The BERT project [33] provides a set of Python scripts that can be run from the command line to fine-tune BERT:

```
$ git clone https://github.com/google-research/bert.git
$ cd bert
```

We then download the appropriate BERT model we want to fine-tune. As mentioned earlier, BERT comes in two sizes—BERT-base and BERT-large. In addition, each model has a cased and uncased version. The cased version differentiates between upper and lowercase words, while the uncased version does not. For our example, we will use the BERT-base-uncased pretrained model. You can find the download URL for this and the other models further down the README.md page:

```
$ mkdir data
$ cd data
$ wget \
https://storage.googleapis.com/bert_models/2018_10_18/uncased_L-12_H-768_A-12.
zip
$ unzip -a uncased_L-12_H-768_A-12.zip
```

This will create the following folder under the data directory of your local BERT project. The bert_config.json file is the configuration file used to create the original pretrained model, and the vocab.txt is the vocabulary used for the model, consisting of 30,522 words and word pieces:

```
uncased_L-12_H-768_A-12/
├── bert_config.json
├── bert_model.ckpt.data-00000-of-00001
├── bert_model.ckpt.index
├── bert_model.ckpt.meta
└── vocab.txt
```

The pretrained language model can be directly used as a text feature extractor for simple machine learning pipelines. This can be useful for situations where you want to just vectorize your text input, leveraging the distributional property of embeddings to get a denser and richer representation than one-hot encoding.

The input in this case is just a file with one sentence per line. Let us call it `sentences.txt` and put it into our `${CLASSIFIER_DATA}` folder. You can generate the embeddings from the last hidden layers by identifying them as -1 (last hidden layer), -2 (hidden layer before that), and so on. The command to extract BERT embeddings for your input sentences is as follows:

```
$ export BERT_BASE_DIR=./data/uncased_L-12_H-768_A-12
$ export CLASSIFIER_DATA=./data/my_data
$ export TRAINED_CLASSIFIER=./data/my_classifier
$ python extract_features.py \
    --input_file=${CLASSIFIER_DATA}/sentences.txt \
    --output_file=${CLASSIFIER_DATA}/embeddings.jsonl \
    --vocab_file=${BERT_BASE_DIR}/vocab.txt \
    --bert_config_file=${BERT_BASE_DIR}/bert_config.json \
    --init_checkpoint=${BERT_BASE_DIR}/bert_model.ckpt \
    --layers=-1,-2,-3,-4 \
    --max_seq_length=128 \
    --batch_size=8
```

The command will extract the BERT embeddings from the last four hidden layers of the model and write them out into a line-oriented JSON file called `embeddings.jsonl` in the same directory as the input file. These embeddings can then be used as input to downstream models that specialize in some specific task, such as sentiment analysis. Because BERT was pretrained on large quantities of English text, it learns a lot about the nuances of the language, which turn out to be useful for these downstream tasks. The downstream model does not have to be a neural network, it can be a non-neural model such as SVM or XGBoost as well.

There is much more you can do with BERT. The previous use case corresponds to transfer learning in computer vision. As in computer vision, it is also possible to fine-tune BERT (and other transformer models) for specific tasks, where the appropriate "head" network is attached to BERT, and the combined network is fine-tuned for a specific task. You will learn more about these techniques in *Chapter 6, Transformers*.

Summary

In this chapter, we have learned about the concepts behind distributional representations of words and their various implementations, starting from static word embeddings such as Word2Vec and GloVe.

We then looked at improvements to the basic idea, such as subword embeddings, sentence embeddings that capture the context of the word in the sentence, and the use of entire language models for generating embeddings. While language model-based embeddings are achieving state-of-the-art results nowadays, there are still plenty of applications where more traditional approaches yield very good results, so it is important to know them all and understand the tradeoffs.

We also looked briefly at other interesting uses of word embeddings outside the realm of natural language, where the distributional properties of other kinds of sequences are leveraged to make predictions in domains such as information retrieval and recommendation systems.

You are now ready to use embeddings, not only for your text-based neural networks, which we will look at in greater depth in the next chapter, but also in other areas of machine learning.

References

1. Mikolov, T., et al. (2013, Sep 7) *Efficient Estimation of Word Representations in Vector Space.* arXiv:1301.3781v3 [cs.CL].

2. Mikolov, T., et al. (2013, Sep 17). *Exploiting Similarities among Languages for Machine Translation.* arXiv:1309.4168v1 [cs.CL].

3. Mikolov, T., et al. (2013). *Distributed Representations of Words and Phrases and their Compositionality.* Advances in Neural Information Processing Systems 26 (NIPS 2013).

4. Pennington, J., Socher, R., Manning, C. (2014). *GloVe: Global Vectors for Word Representation.* D14-1162, Proceedings of the 2014 Conference on *Empirical Methods in Natural Language Processing (EMNLP)*.

5. Niu, F., et al (2011, 11 Nov). *HOGWILD! A Lock-Free Approach to Parallelizing Stochastic Gradient Descent.* arXiv:1106.5730v2 [math.OC].

6. Levy, O., Goldberg, Y. (2014). *Neural Word Embedding as Implicit Matrix Factorization.* Advances in Neural Information Processing Systems 27 (NIPS 2014).

7. Mahoney, M. (2011, 1 Sep). text8 dataset: `http://mattmahoney.net/dc/textdata.html`

8. Rehurek, R. (2019, 10 Apr). gensim documentation for Word2Vec model: `https://radimrehurek.com/gensim/models/word2vec.html`

9. Levy, O., Goldberg, Y. (2014, 26-27 June). *Linguistic Regularities in Sparse and Explicit Word Representations.* Proceedings of the Eighteenth Conference on Computational Language Learning, pp 171-180 (ACL 2014).

10. Rehurek, R. (2019, 10 Apr). gensim documentation for KeyedVectors: `https://radimrehurek.com/gensim/models/keyedvectors.html`

11. Almeida, T. A., Gamez Hidalgo, J. M., and Yamakami, A. (2011). Contributions to the Study of SMS Spam Filtering: New Collection and Results. Proceedings of the 2011 ACM Symposium on Document Engineering (DOCENG): `https://www.dt.fee.unicamp.br/~tiago/smsspamcollection/doceng11.pdf?ref=https://githubhelp.com`

12. Speer, R., Chin, J. (2016, 6 Apr). *An Ensemble Method to Produce High-Quality Word Embeddings.* arXiv:1604.01692v1 [cs.CL].

13. Speer, R. (2016, 25 May). *ConceptNet Numberbatch: a new name for the best Word Embeddings you can download*: `http://blog.conceptnet.io/posts/2016/conceptnet-numberbatch-a-new-name-for-the-best-word-embeddings-you-can-download/`

14. Barkan, O., Koenigstein, N. (2016, 13-16 Sep). *Item2Vec: Neural Item Embedding for Collaborative Filtering.* IEEE 26th International Workshop on Machine Learning for Signal Processing (MLSP 2016).

15. Grover, A., Leskovec, J. (2016, 13-17 Aug). *node2vec: Scalable Feature Learning for Networks.* Proceedings of the 22nd ACM SIGKDD International Conference on Knowledge Discovery and Data Mining. (KDD 2016).

16. TensorFlow 2.0 Models on TensorFlow Hub: `https://tfhub.dev/s?q=tf2-preview`

17. Zhang, X., LeCun, Y. (2016, 4 Apr). *Text Understanding from Scratch*. arXiv 1502.01710v5 [cs.LG].

18. Bojanowski, P., et al. (2017, 19 Jun). *Enriching Word Vectors with Subword Information*. arXiv: 1607.04606v2 [cs.CL].

19. Facebook AI Research, fastText (2017). GitHub repository: `https://github.com/facebookresearch/fastText`

20. McCann, B., Bradbury, J., Xiong, C., Socher, R. (2017). *Learned in Translation: Contextualized Word Vectors*. Neural Information Processing Systems, 2017.

21. Peters, M., et al. (2018, 22 Mar). *Deep contextualized word representations*. arXiv: 1802.05365v2 [cs.CL].

22. Kiros, R., et al. (2015, 22 June). *Skip-Thought Vectors*. arXiv: 1506.06727v1 [cs.CL].

23. Kiros, R, et al (2017). GitHub repository: `https://github.com/ryankiros/skip-thoughts`

24. Iyer, M., Manjunatha, V., Boyd-Graber, J., Daume, H. (2015, July 26-31). *Deep Unordered Composition Rivals Syntactic Methods for Text Classification*. Proceedings of the 53rd Annual Meeting of the Association for Computational Linguistics and the 7th International Joint Conference on Natural Language Processing (ACL 2015).

25. Vaswani, A., et al. (2017, 6 Dec). *Attention Is All You Need*. arXiv: 1706.03762v5 [cs.CL].

26. Le, Q., Mikolov, T. (2014) *Distributed Representation of Sentences and Documents*. arXiv: 1405.4053v2 [cs.CL].

27. Howard, J., Ruder, S. (2018, 23 May). *Universal Language Model Fine-Tuning for Text Classification*. arXiv: 1801.06146v5 [cs.CL].

28. Devlin, J., Chang, M., Lee, K., Toutanova, K. (2018, 11 Oct). *BERT: Pretraining of Deep Bidirectional Transformers for Language Understanding*. arXiv: 1810.04805v1 [cs.CL]: `https://arxiv.org/pdf/1810.04805.pdf`

29. Radford, A., Narasimhan, K., Salimans, T., Sutskever, I. (2018). *Improving Language Understanding with Unsupervised Learning*: `https://openai.com/blog/language-unsupervised/`

30. Radford, A., et al. (2019). *Language Models are unsupervised Multitask Learners*. OpenAI Blog 2019: `http://www.persagen.com/files/misc/radford2019language.pdf`

31. Google Collaboratory: `https://colab.research.google.com`

32. Google Cloud Platform. `https://cloud.google.com/`

33. Google Research, BERT (2019). GitHub repository: `https://github.com/google-research/bert`

34. Nemeth (2019). Simple BERT using Tensorflow 2.0. *Towards Data Science blog*: `https://towardsdatascience.com/simple-bert-using-tensorflow-2-0-132cb19e9b22`

35. TF-IDF. Wikipedia. Retrieved May 2019: `https://en.wikipedia.org/wiki/Tf%E2%80%93idf`

36. Latent Semantic Analysis. Wikipedia. Retrieved May 2019: `https://en.wikipedia.org/wiki/Latent_semantic_analysis`

37. Topic Model. Wikipedia. Retrieved May 2019: `https://en.wikipedia.org/wiki/Topic_model`

38. Warstadt, A., Singh, A., and Bowman, S. (2018). *Neural Network Acceptability Judgements*. arXiv 1805:12471 [cs.CL]: `https://nyu-mll.github.io/CoLA/`

39. Microsoft Research Paraphrase Corpus. (2018): `https://www.microsoft.com/en-us/download/details.aspx?id=52398`

40. Nozawa, K. (2019). Something2Vec papers: `https://gist.github.com/nzw0301/333afc00bd508501268fa7bf40cafe4e`

41. Perrone, V., et al. (2016). *Poisson Random Fields for Dynamic Feature Models*: `https://archive.ics.uci.edu/ml/datasets/NIPS+Conference+Papers+1987-2015`

42. Perozzi, B., Al-Rfou, R., and Skiena, S. (2014). *DeepWalk: Online Learning of Social Representations.* arXiv 1403.6652v2 [cs.SI].

Join our book's Discord space

Join our Discord community to meet like-minded people and learn alongside more than 2000 members at: `https://packt.link/keras`

5

Recurrent Neural Networks

In *Chapter 3*, we learned about **Convolutional Neural Networks** (**CNNs**) and saw how they exploit the spatial geometry of their inputs. For example, CNNs for images apply convolutions to initially small patches of the image, and progress to larger and larger areas of the image using pooling operations. Convolutions and pooling operations for images are in two dimensions: the width and the height. For audio and text streams, one-dimensional convolution and pooling operations are applied along the time dimension, and for video streams, these operations are applied in three dimensions: along the height, width, and time dimensions.

In this chapter, we will focus on **Recurrent Neural Networks** (**RNNs**), a class of neural networks that is popularly used on text inputs. RNNs are very flexible and have been used to solve problems such as speech recognition, language modeling, machine translation, sentiment analysis, and image captioning, to name a few. RNNs exploit the sequential nature of their input. Sequential inputs could be text, speech, time series, and anything else where the occurrence of an element in a sequence is dependent on the elements that came before it. In this chapter, we will see examples of various RNNs and learn how to implement them with TensorFlow.

We will first look at the internals of a basic RNN cell and how it deals with these sequential dependencies in the input. We will also learn about some limitations of the basic RNN cell (implemented as SimpleRNN in Keras) and see how two popular variants of the SimpleRNN cell – the **Long Short-Term Memory** (**LSTM**) and the **Gated Recurrent Unit** (**GRU**) – overcome this limitation.

We will then zoom out one level and consider the RNN layer itself, which is just the RNN cell applied to every time step. An RNN can be thought of as a graph of RNN cells, where each cell performs the same operation on successive elements of the sequence. We will describe some simple modifications to improve performance, such as making the RNN bidirectional and/or stateful.

Finally, we look at some standard RNN topologies and the kind of applications they can be used to solve. RNNs can be adapted to different types of applications by rearranging the cells in the graph. We will see some examples of these configurations and how they are used to solve specific problems. We will also consider the sequence-to-sequence (or seq2seq) architecture, which has been used with great success in machine translation and various other fields. We will then look at what an attention mechanism is, and how it can be used to improve the performance of sequence-to-sequence architectures.

In this chapter, we will cover the following topics:

- The basic RNN cell
- RNN cell variants
- RNN variants
- RNN topologies
- Encoder-decoder architectures – seq2seq
- Attention mechanism

 All the code files for this chapter can be found at `https://packt.link/dltfchp5`.

It is often said that a journey of a thousand miles starts with a single step, so in that spirit, let's begin our study of RNNs by first considering the RNN cell.

The basic RNN cell

Traditional multilayer perceptron neural networks make the assumption that all inputs are independent of each other. This assumption is not true for many types of sequence data. For example, words in a sentence, musical notes in a composition, stock prices over time, or even molecules in a compound are examples of sequences where an element will display a dependence on previous elements.

RNN cells incorporate this dependence by having a hidden state, or memory, that holds the essence of what has been seen so far. The value of the hidden state at any point in time is a function of the value of the hidden state at the previous time step, and the value of the input at the current time step, that is:

$$h_t = \phi(h_{t-1}, X_t)$$

Here, h_t and h_{t-1} are the values of the hidden states at the time t and $t-1$ respectively, and x_t is the value of the input at time t. Notice that the equation is recursive, that is, h_{t-1} can be represented in terms of h_{t-2} and x_{t-1}, and so on, until the beginning of the sequence. This is how RNNs encode and incorporate information from arbitrarily long sequences.

We can also represent the RNN cell graphically, as shown in *Figure 5.1(a)*. At time t, the cell has an input $x(t)$ and output $y(t)$. Part of the output $y(t)$ (represented by the hidden state h_t) is fed back into the cell for use at a later time step $t+1$.

Just as in a traditional neural network, where the learned parameters are stored as weight matrices, the RNN's parameters are defined by the three weight matrices U, V, and W, corresponding to the weights of the input, output, and hidden states respectively:

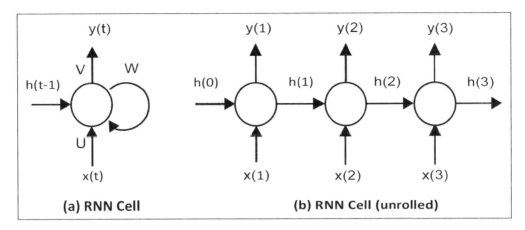

Figure 5.1: (a) Schematic of an RNN cell; (b) the RNN cell unrolled

Figure 5.1(b) shows the same RNN in an "unrolled view." Unrolling just means that we draw the network out for the complete sequence. The network shown here has three time steps, suitable for processing three element sequences. Note that the weight matrices U, V, and W, that we spoke about earlier, are shared between each of the time steps. This is because we are applying the same operation to different inputs at each time step. Being able to share these weights across all the time steps greatly reduces the number of parameters that the RNN needs to learn.

We can also describe the RNN as a computation graph in terms of equations. The internal state of the RNN at a time *t* is given by the value of the hidden vector *h(t)*, which is the sum of the weight matrix W and the hidden state h_{t-1} at time *t-1*, and the product of the weight matrix U and the input x_t at time *t*, passed through a tanh activation function. The choice of tanh over other activation functions such as sigmoid has to do with it being more efficient for learning in practice and helps combat the vanishing gradient problem, which we will learn about later in the chapter.

For notational convenience, in all our equations describing different types of RNN architectures in this chapter, we have omitted explicit reference to the bias terms by incorporating them within the matrix. Consider the following equation of a line in an n-dimensional space. Here, w_1 through w_n refer to the coefficients of the line in each of the *n* dimensions, and the bias *b* refers to the y-intercept along each of these dimensions:

$$y = w_1 x_1 + w_2 x_2 + \cdots + w_n x_n + b$$

We can rewrite the equation in matrix notation as follows:

$$y = WX + b$$

Here, W is a matrix of shape (m, n) and b is a vector of shape $(m, 1)$, where m is the number of rows corresponding to the records in our dataset, and n is the number of columns corresponding to the features for each record. Equivalently, we can eliminate the vector b by folding it into our matrix W by treating the b vector as a feature column corresponding to the "unit" feature of W. Thus:

$$y = w_1 x_1 + w_2 x_2 + \cdots + w_n x_n + w_0(1) = W'X$$

Here, W' is a matrix of shape $(m, n+1)$, where the last column contains the values of b.

The resulting notation ends up being more compact and (we believe) easier to comprehend and retain as well.

The output vector y_t at time t is the product of the weight matrix V and the hidden state h_t, passed through a softmax activation, such that the resulting vector is a set of output probabilities:

$$h_t = \tanh(W h_{t-1} + U x_t)$$

$$y_t = softmax(V h_t)$$

Keras provides the SimpleRNN recurrent layer that incorporates all the logic we have seen so far, as well as the more advanced variants such as LSTM and GRU, which we will learn about later in this chapter. Strictly speaking, it is not necessary to understand how they work to start building with them.

However, an understanding of the structure and equations is helpful when you need to build your own specialized RNN cell to overcome a specific problem.

Now that we understand the flow of data forward through the RNN cell, that is, how it combines its input and hidden states to produce the output and the next hidden state, let us now examine the flow of gradients in the reverse direction. This is a process called **Backpropagation Through Time (BPTT)**.

Backpropagation through time (BPTT)

Just like traditional neural networks, training RNNs also involves the backpropagation of gradients. The difference, in this case, is that since the weights are shared by all time steps, the gradient at each output depends not only on the current time step but also on the previous ones. This process is called backpropagation through time [11]. Because the weights U, V, and W, are shared across the different time steps in the case of RNNs, we need to sum up the gradients across the various time steps in the case of BPTT. This is the key difference between traditional backpropagation and BPTT.

Consider the RNN with five time steps shown in *Figure 5.2*. During the forward pass, the network produces predictions $\hat{y}_t$ at time t that are compared with the label y_t to compute a loss L_t. During backpropagation (shown by the dotted lines), the gradients of the loss with respect to the weights U, V, and W, are computed at each time step and the parameters updated with the sum of the gradients:

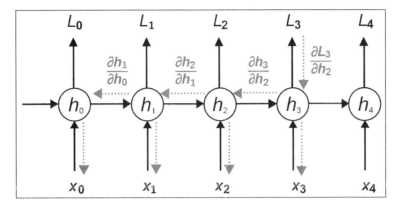

Figure 5.2: Backpropagation through time

The following equation shows the gradient of the loss with respect to W. We focus on this weight because it is the cause of the phenomenon known as the vanishing and exploding gradient problem.

This problem manifests as the gradients of the loss approaching either zero or infinity, making the network hard to train. To understand why this happens, consider the equation of the SimpleRNN we saw earlier; the hidden state h_t is dependent on h_{t-1}, which in turn is dependent on h_{t-2}, and so on:

$$\frac{\partial L}{\partial W} = \sum_t \frac{\partial L_t}{\partial W}$$

Let's now see what happens to this gradient at time step $t=3$. By the chain rule, the gradient of the loss with respect to W can be decomposed to a product of three sub-gradients. The gradient of the hidden state h_2 with respect to W can be further decomposed as the sum of the gradient of each hidden state with respect to the previous one. Finally, each gradient of the hidden state with respect to the previous one can be further decomposed as the product of gradients of the current hidden state against the previous hidden state:

$$\frac{\partial L_3}{\partial W} = \frac{\partial L_3}{\partial \hat{y}_3}\frac{\partial \hat{y}_3}{\partial h_3}\frac{\partial h_3}{\partial W} = \sum_{t=0}^{3}\frac{\partial L_3}{\partial \hat{y}_3}\frac{\partial \hat{y}_3}{\partial h_3}\frac{\partial h_3}{\partial h_t}\frac{\partial h_t}{\partial W} = \sum_{t=0}^{3}\frac{\partial L_3}{\partial \hat{y}_3}\frac{\partial \hat{y}_3}{\partial h_3}(\prod_{j=t+1}^{3}\frac{\partial h_j}{\partial h_{j-1}})\frac{\partial h_t}{\partial W}$$

Similar calculations are done to compute the gradient of the other losses L_0 through L_4 with respect to W, and sum them up into the gradient update for W. We will not explore the math further in this book, but this WildML blog post [12] has a very good explanation of BPTT, including a more detailed derivation of the math behind the process.

Vanishing and exploding gradients

The reason BPTT is particularly sensitive to the problem of vanishing and exploding gradients comes from the product part of the expression representing the final formulation of the gradient of the loss with respect to W. Consider the case where the individual gradients of a hidden state with respect to the previous one are less than 1.

As we backpropagate across multiple time steps, the product of gradients becomes smaller and smaller, ultimately leading to the problem of vanishing gradients. Similarly, if the gradients are larger than 1, the products get larger and larger, and ultimately lead to the problem of exploding gradients.

Of the two, exploding gradients are more easily detectable. The gradients will become very large and turn into **Not a Number** (NaN), and the training process will crash. Exploding gradients can be controlled by clipping them at a predefined threshold [13]. TensorFlow 2.0 allows you to clip gradients using the `clipvalue` or `clipnorm` parameter during optimizer construction, or by explicitly clipping gradients using `tf.clip_by_value`.

The effect of vanishing gradients is that gradients from time steps that are far away do not contribute anything to the learning process, so the RNN ends up not learning any long-range dependencies. While there are a few approaches toward minimizing the problem, such as proper initialization of the W matrix, more aggressive regularization, using ReLU instead of `tanh` activation, and pretraining the layers using unsupervised methods, the most popular solution is to use LSTM or GRU architectures, both of which will be explained shortly. These architectures have been designed to deal with vanishing gradients and learn long-term dependencies more effectively.

RNN cell variants

In this section, we'll look at some cell variants of RNNs. We'll begin by looking at a variant of the SimpleRNN cell: the LSTM RNN.

Long short-term memory (LSTM)

The LSTM is a variant of the SimpleRNN cell that is capable of learning long-term dependencies. LSTMs were first proposed by Hochreiter and SchmidHuber [14] and refined by many other researchers. They work well on a large variety of problems and are the most widely used RNN variant.

We have seen how the SimpleRNN combines the hidden state from the previous time step and the current input through a `tanh` layer to implement recurrence. LSTMs also implement recurrence in a similar way, but instead of a single `tanh` layer, there are four layers interacting in a very specific way. *Figure 5.3* illustrates the transformations that are applied in the hidden state at time step t.

The diagram looks complicated, but let's look at it component by component. The line across the top of the diagram is the cell state c, representing the internal memory of the unit.

The line across the bottom is the hidden state h, and the i, f, o, and g gates are the mechanisms by which the LSTM works around the vanishing gradient problem. During training, the LSTM learns the parameters of these gates:

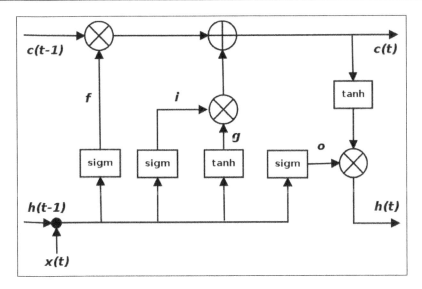

Figure 5.3: An LSTM cell

An alternative way to think about how these gates work inside an LSTM cell is to consider the equations of the cell. These equations describe how the value of the hidden state h_t at time t is calculated from the value of hidden state h_{t-1} at the previous time step. In general, the equation-based description tends to be clearer and more concise and is usually the way a new cell design is presented in academic papers. Diagrams, when provided, may or may not be comparable to the ones you saw earlier. For these reasons, it usually makes sense to learn to read the equations and visualize the cell design. To that end, we will describe the other cell variants in this book using equations only.

The set of equations representing an LSTM is shown as follows:

$$i = \sigma(W_i h_{t-1} + U_i x_t + V_i c_{t-1})$$
$$f = \sigma(W_f h_{t-1} + U_f x_t + V_f c_{t-1})$$
$$o = \sigma(W_o h_{t-1} + U_o x_t + V_o c_{t-1})$$
$$g = \tanh W_g h_{t-1} + U_g x_t$$
$$c_t = (f * c_{t-1}) + (g * i)$$
$$h_t = \tanh(c_t) * o$$

Here, i, f, and o are the input, forget, and output gates. They are computed using the same equations but with different parameter matrices W_i, U_i, W_f, U_f, and W_o, U_o. The sigmoid function modulates the output of these gates between 0 and 1, so the output vectors produced can be multiplied element-wise with another vector to define how much of the second vector can pass through the first one.

The forget gate defines how much of the previous state h_{t-1} you want to allow to pass through. The input gate defines how much of the newly computed state for the current input x_t you want to let through, and the output gate defines how much of the internal state you want to expose to the next layer. The internal hidden state g is computed based on the current input x_t and the previous hidden state h_{t-1}. Notice that the equation for g is identical to that of the SimpleRNN, except that in this case, we will modulate the output by the output of input vector i.

Given i, f, o, and g, we can now calculate the cell state c_t at time t as the cell state c_{t-1} at time $(t-1)$ multiplied by the value of the forget gate g, plus the state g multiplied by the input gate i. This is basically a way to combine the previous memory and the new input – setting the forget gate to 0 ignores the old memory and setting the input gate to 0 ignores the newly computed state. Finally, the hidden state h_t at time t is computed as the memory c_t at time t, with the output gate o.

One thing to realize is that the LSTM is a drop-in replacement for a SimpleRNN cell; the only difference is that LSTMs are resistant to the vanishing gradient problem. You can replace an RNN cell in a network with an LSTM without worrying about any side effects. You should generally see better results along with longer training times.

TensorFlow 2.0 also provides a ConvLSTM2D implementation based on the paper by Shi, et al. [18], where the matrix multiplications are replaced by convolution operators.

If you would like to learn more about LSTMs, please take a look at the WildML RNN tutorial [15] and Christopher Olah's blog post [16]. The first covers LSTMs in somewhat greater detail, and the second takes you step by step through the computations in a very visual way.

Now that we have covered LTSMs, we will cover the other popular RNN cell architecture – GRUs.

Gated recurrent unit (GRU)

The GRU is a variant of the LSTM and was introduced by Cho, et al [17]. It retains the LSTM's resistance to the vanishing gradient problem, but its internal structure is simpler, and is, therefore, faster to train, since fewer computations are needed to make updates to its hidden state.

Instead of the input (i), forgot (f), and output (o) gates in the LSTM cell, the GRU cell has two gates, an update gate z and a reset gate r. The update gate defines how much previous memory to keep around, and the reset gate defines how to combine the new input with the previous memory. There is no persistent cell state distinct from the hidden state as it is in LSTM.

The GRU cell defines the computation of the hidden state h_t at time t from the hidden state h_{t-1} at the previous time step using the following set of equations:

$$z = \sigma(W_z h_{t-1} + U_z x_t)$$
$$r = \sigma(W_r h_{t-1} + U_r x_t)$$
$$c = \tanh(W_c(h_{t-1} * r) + U_c x_t)$$
$$h_t = (z * c) + ((1 - z) * h_{t-1})$$

The outputs of the update gate z and the reset gate r are both computed using a combination of the previous hidden state h_{t-1} and the current input x_t. The sigmoid function modulates the output of these functions between 0 and 1. The cell state c is computed as a function of the output of the reset gate r and input x_t. Finally, the hidden state h_t at time t is computed as a function of the cell state c and the previous hidden state h_{t-1}. The parameters W_z, U_z, W_r, U_r, and W_c, U_c, are learned during training.

Similar to LSTM, TensorFlow 2.0 (tf.keras) provides an implementation for the basic GRU layer as well, which is a drop-in replacement for the RNN cell.

Peephole LSTM

The peephole LSTM is an LSTM variant that was first proposed by Gers and Schmidhuber [19]. It adds "peepholes" to the input, forget, and output gates, so they can see the previous cell state c_{t-1}. The equations for computing the hidden state h_t, at time t, from the hidden state h_{t-1} at the previous time step, in a peephole LSTM are shown next.

Notice that the only difference from the equations for the LSTM is the additional c_{t-1} term for computing outputs of the input (i), forget (f), and output (o) gates:

$$i = \sigma(W_i h_{t-1} + U_i x_t + V_i c_{t-1})$$
$$f = \sigma(W_f h_{t-1} + U_f x_t + V_f c_{t-1})$$
$$o = \sigma(W_o h_{t-1} + U_o x_t + V_o c_{t-1})$$
$$g = \tanh W_g h_{t-1} + U_g x_t$$
$$c_t = (f * c_{t-1}) + (g * i)$$
$$h_t = \tanh(c_t) * o$$

TensorFlow 2.0 provides an experimental implementation of the peephole LSTM cell. To use this in your own RNN layers, you will need to wrap the cell (or list of cells) in the RNN wrapper, as shown in the following code snippet:

```
hidden_dim = 256
peephole_cell = tf.keras.experimental.PeepholeLSTMCell(hidden_dim)
rnn_layer = tf.keras.layers.RNN(peephole_cell)
```

In the previous section, we saw some RNN cell variants that were developed to target specific inadequacies of the basic RNN cell. In the next section, we will look at variations in the architecture of the RNN network itself, which were built to address specific use cases.

RNN variants

In this section, we will look at a couple of variations of the basic RNN architecture that can provide performance improvements in some specific circumstances. Note that these strategies can be applied to different kinds of RNN cells, as well as for different RNN topologies, which we will learn about later.

Bidirectional RNNs

We have seen how, at any given time step t, the output of the RNN is dependent on the outputs at all previous time steps. However, it is entirely possible that the output is also dependent on the future outputs as well. This is especially true for applications such as natural language processing where the attributes of the word or phrase we are trying to predict may be dependent on the context given by the entire enclosing sentence, not just the words that came before it.

This problem can be solved using a bidirectional LSTM (see *Figure 5.4*), also called biLSTM, which is essentially two RNNs stacked on top of each other, one reading the input from left to right, and the other reading the input from the right to the left.

The output at each time step will be based on the hidden state of both RNNs. Bidirectional RNNs allow the network to place equal emphasis on the beginning and end of the sequence, and typically result in performance improvements:

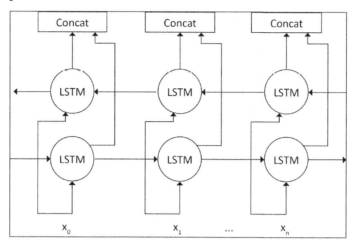

Figure 5.4: Bidirectional LSTM

TensorFlow 2.0 provides support for bidirectional RNNs through a bidirectional wrapper layer. To make an RNN layer bidirectional, all that is needed is to wrap the layer with this wrapper layer, which is shown as follows. Since the output of each pair of cells in the left and right LSTM in the biLSTM pair are concatenated (see *Figure 5.4*), it needs to return output from each cell. Hence, we set return_sequences to True (the default is False meaning that the output is only returned from the last cell in the LSTM):

```
self.lstm = tf.keras.layers.Bidirectional(
    tf.keras.layers.LSTM(10, return_sequences=True,
        input_shape=(5, 10))
)
```

The next major RNN variation we will look at is the Stateful RNN.

Stateful RNNs

RNNs can be stateful, which means that they can maintain state across batches during training. That is, the hidden state computed for a batch of training data will be used as the initial hidden state for the next batch of training data. However, this needs to be explicitly set, since TensorFlow 2.0 (tf.keras) RNNs are stateless by default, and resets the state after each batch. Setting an RNN to be stateful means that it can build state across its training sequence and even maintain that state when doing predictions.

The benefits of using stateful RNNs are smaller network sizes and/or lower training times. The disadvantage is that we are now responsible for training the network with a batch size that reflects the periodicity of the data and resetting the state after each epoch. In addition, data should not be shuffled while training the network since the order in which the data is presented is relevant for stateful networks.

To set an RNN layer as stateful, set the named variable stateful to True. In our example of a one-to-many topology for learning how to generate text, we provide an example of using a stateful RNN. Here, we train using data consisting of contiguous text slices, so setting the LSTM to stateful means that the hidden state generated from the previous text chunk is reused for the current text chunk.

In the next section on RNN topologies, we will look at different ways to set up the RNN network for different use cases.

RNN topologies

We have seen examples of how MLP and CNN architectures can be composed to form more complex networks. RNNs offer yet another degree of freedom, in that they allow sequence input and output. This means that RNN cells can be arranged in different ways to build networks that are adapted to solve different types of problems. *Figure 5.5* shows five different configurations of inputs, hidden layers, and outputs.

Of these, the first one (one-to-one) is not interesting from a sequence processing point of view, as it can be implemented as a simple dense network with one input and one output.

The one-to-many case has a single input and outputs a sequence. An example of such a network might be a network that can generate text tags from images [6], containing short text descriptions of different aspects of the image. Such a network would be trained with image input and labeled sequences of text representing the image tags:

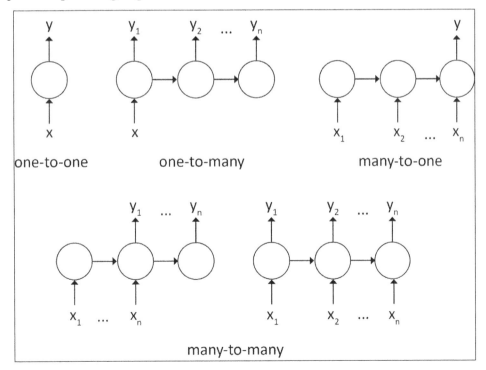

Figure 5.5: Common RNN topologies

The many-to-one case is the reverse; it takes a sequence of tensors as input but outputs a single tensor. Examples of such networks would be a sentiment analysis network [7], which takes as input a block of text such as a movie review and outputs a single sentiment value.

The many-to-many use case comes in two flavors. The first one is more popular and is better known as the seq2seq model. In this model, a sequence is read in and produces a context vector representing the input sequence, which is used to generate the output sequence.

The topology has been used with great success in the field of machine translation, as well as problems that can be reframed as machine translation problems. Real-life examples of the former can be found in [8, 9], and an example of the latter is described in [10].

The second many-to-many type has an output cell corresponding to each input cell. This kind of network is suited for use cases where there is a 1:1 correspondence between the input and output, such as time series. The major difference between this model and the seq2seq model is that the input does not have to be completely encoded before the decoding process begins.

In the next three sections, we provide examples of a one-to-many network that learns to generate text, a many-to-one network that does sentiment analysis, and a many-to-many network of the second type, which predicts **Part-of-Speech** (**POS**) for words in a sentence. Because of the popularity of the seq2seq network, we will cover it in more detail later in this chapter.

Example – One-to-many – Learning to generate text

RNNs have been used extensively by the **Natural Language Processing** (**NLP**) community for various applications. One such application is to build language models. A language model is a model that allows us to predict the probability of a word in a text given previous words. Language models are important for various higher-level tasks such as machine translation, spelling correction, and so on.

The ability of a language model to predict the next word in a sequence makes it a generative model that allows us to generate text by sampling from the output probabilities of different words in the vocabulary. The training data is a sequence of words, and the label is the word appearing at the next time step in the sequence.

For our example, we will train a character-based RNN on the text of the children's stories *Alice in Wonderland* and its sequel *Through the Looking Glass* by Lewis Carroll. We have chosen to build a character-based model because it has a smaller vocabulary and trains quicker. The idea is the same as training and using a word-based language model, except we will use characters instead of words. Once trained, the model can be used to generate some text in the same style.

The data for our example will come from the plain texts of two novels on the Project Gutenberg website [36]. Input to the network are sequences of 100 characters, and the corresponding output is another sequence of 100 characters, offset from the input by 1 position.

That is, if the input is the sequence $[c_1, c_2, ..., c_n]$, the output will be $[c_2, c_3, ..., c_{n+1}]$. We will train the network for 50 epochs, and at the end of every 10 epochs, we will generate a fixed-size sequence of characters starting with a standard prefix. In the following example, we have used the prefix "Alice", the name of the protagonist in our novels.

As always, we will first import the necessary libraries and set up some constants. Here, DATA_DIR points to a data folder under the location where you downloaded the source code for this chapter. CHECKPOINT_DIR is the location, a folder of checkpoints under the data folder, where we will save the weights of the model at the end of every 10 epochs:

```
import os
import numpy as np
import re
import shutil
import tensorflow as tf
DATA_DIR = "./data"
CHECKPOINT_DIR = os.path.join(DATA_DIR, "checkpoints")
```

Next, we download and prepare the data for our network to consume. The texts of both books are publicly available from the Project Gutenberg website. The tf.keras.utils.get_file() function will check to see whether the file has already been downloaded to your local drive, and if not, it will download to a datasets folder under the location of the code. We also preprocess the input a little here, removing newline and byte order mark characters from the text. This step will create the texts variable, a flat list of characters for these two books:

```
def download_and_read(urls):
    texts = []
    for i, url in enumerate(urls):
        p = tf.keras.utils.get_file("ex1-{:d}.txt".format(i), url,
            cache_dir=".")
        text = open(p, "r").read()
        # remove byte order mark
        text = text.replace("\ufeff", "")
        # remove newlines
        text = text.replace('\n', ' ')
        text = re.sub(r'\s+', " ", text)
        # add it to the list
        texts.extend(text)
    return texts
texts = download_and_read([
    "http://www.gutenberg.org/cache/epub/28885/pg28885.txt",
    "https://www.gutenberg.org/files/12/12-0.txt"
])
```

Next, we will create our vocabulary. In our case, our vocabulary contains 90 unique characters, composed of uppercase and lowercase alphabets, numbers, and special characters. We also create some mapping dictionaries to convert each vocabulary character into a unique integer and vice versa. As noted earlier, the input and output of the network is a sequence of characters.

However, the actual input and output of the network are sequences of integers, and we will use these mapping dictionaries to handle this conversion:

```
# create the vocabulary
vocab = sorted(set(texts))
print("vocab size: {:d}".format(len(vocab)))
# create mapping from vocab chars to ints
char2idx = {c:i for i, c in enumerate(vocab)}
idx2char = {i:c for c, i in char2idx.items()}
```

The next step is to use these mapping dictionaries to convert our character sequence input into an integer sequence and then into a TensorFlow dataset. Each of our sequences is going to be 100 characters long, with the output being offset from the input by 1 character position. We first batch the dataset into slices of 101 characters, then apply the split_train_labels() function to every element of the dataset to create our sequences dataset, which is a dataset of tuples of two elements, with each element of the tuple being a vector of size 100 and type tf.int64. We then shuffle these sequences and create batches of 64 tuples for each input to our network. Each element of the dataset is now a tuple consisting of a pair of matrices, each of size (64, 100) and type tf.int64:

```
# numericize the texts
texts_as_ints = np.array([char2idx[c] for c in texts])
data = tf.data.Dataset.from_tensor_slices(texts_as_ints)
# number of characters to show before asking for prediction
# sequences: [None, 100]
seq_length = 100
sequences = data.batch(seq_length + 1, drop_remainder=True)
def split_train_labels(sequence):
    input_seq = sequence[0:-1]
    output_seq = sequence[1:]
    return input_seq, output_seq
sequences = sequences.map(split_train_labels)
# set up for training
# batches: [None, 64, 100]
batch_size = 64
steps_per_epoch = len(texts) // seq_length // batch_size
dataset = sequences.shuffle(10000).batch(
    batch_size, drop_remainder=True)
```

We are now ready to define our network. As before, we define our network as a subclass of tf.keras. Model, as shown next. The network is fairly simple; it takes as input a sequence of integers of size 100 (num_timesteps) and passes them through an embedding layer so that each integer in the sequence is converted into a vector of size 256 (embedding_dim). So, assuming a batch size of 64, for our input sequence of size (64, 100), the output of the embedding layer is a matrix of shape (64, 100, 256).

The next layer is an RNN layer with 100 time steps. The implementation of RNN chosen is a GRU. This GRU layer will take, at each of its time steps, a vector of size (256,) and output a vector of shape (1024,) (rnn_output_dim). Note also that the RNN is stateful, which means that the hidden state output from the previous training epoch will be used as input to the current epoch. The return_sequences=True flag also indicates that the RNN will output at each of the time steps rather than an aggregate output at the last time steps.

Finally, each of the time steps will emit a vector of shape (1024,) into a dense layer that outputs a vector of shape (90,) (vocab_size). The output from this layer will be a tensor of shape (64, 100, 90). Each position in the output vector corresponds to a character in our vocabulary, and the values correspond to the probability of that character occurring at that output position:

```python
class CharGenModel(tf.keras.Model):
    def __init__(self, vocab_size, num_timesteps,
            embedding_dim, **kwargs):
        super(CharGenModel, self).__init__(**kwargs)
        self.embedding_layer = tf.keras.layers.Embedding(
            vocab_size,
            embedding_dim
        )
        self.rnn_layer = tf.keras.layers.GRU(
            num_timesteps,
            recurrent_initializer="glorot_uniform",
            recurrent_activation="sigmoid",
            stateful=True,
            return_sequences=True)
        self.dense_layer = tf.keras.layers.Dense(vocab_size)
    def call(self, x):
        x = self.embedding_layer(x)
        x = self.rnn_layer(x)
        x = self.dense_layer(x)
        return x
vocab_size = len(vocab)
embedding_dim = 256

model = CharGenModel(vocab_size, seq_length, embedding_dim)
model.build(input_shape=(batch_size, seq_length))
```

Next, we define a loss function and compile our model. We will use the sparse categorical cross-entropy as our loss function because that is the standard loss function to use when our inputs and outputs are sequences of integers. For the optimizer, we will choose the Adam optimizer:

```python
def loss(labels, predictions):
    return tf.losses.sparse_categorical_crossentropy(
```

```
            labels,
            predictions,
            from_logits=True
        )
    model.compile(optimizer=tf.optimizers.Adam(), loss=loss)
```

Normally, the character at each position of the output is found by computing the argmax of the vector at that position, that is, the character corresponding to the maximum probability value. This is known as greedy search. In the case of language models where the output of one time step becomes the input to the next time step, this can lead to a repetitive output. The two most common approaches to overcome this problem are either to sample the output randomly or to use beam search, which samples from *k* the most probable values at each time step. Here, we will use the `tf.random.categorical()` function to sample the output randomly. The following function takes a string as a prefix and uses it to generate a string whose length is specified by `num_chars_to_generate`. The temperature parameter is used to control the quality of the predictions. Lower values will create a more predictable output.

The logic follows a predictable pattern. We convert the sequence of characters in our `prefix_string` into a sequence of integers, then `expand_dims` to add a batch dimension so the input can be passed into our model. We then reset the state of the model. This is needed because our model is stateful, and we don't want the hidden state of the first time step in our prediction run to be carried over from the one computed during training. We then run the input through our model and get back a prediction. This is the vector of shape (90,) representing the probabilities of each character in the vocabulary appearing at the next time step. We then reshape the prediction by removing the batch dimension and dividing by the temperature, and then randomly sampling from the vector. We then set our prediction as the input of the next time step. We repeat this for the number of characters we need to generate, converting each prediction back into character form and accumulating them in a list, and returning the list at the end of the loop:

```
def generate_text(model, prefix_string, char2idx, idx2char,
        num_chars_to_generate=1000, temperature=1.0):
    input = [char2idx[s] for s in prefix_string]
    input = tf.expand_dims(input, 0)
    text_generated = []
    model.reset_states()
    for i in range(num_chars_to_generate):
        preds = model(input)
        preds = tf.squeeze(preds, 0) / temperature
        # predict char returned by model
        pred_id = tf.random.categorical(
            preds, num_samples=1)[-1, 0].numpy()
        text_generated.append(idx2char[pred_id])
        # pass the prediction as the next input to the model
        input = tf.expand_dims([pred_id], 0)
    return prefix_string + "".join(text_generated)
```

Finally, we are ready to run our training and evaluation loop. As mentioned earlier, we will train our network for 50 epochs, and at every 10-epoch interval, we will try to generate some text with the model trained so far. Our prefix at each stage is the string "Alice ". Notice that in order to accommodate a single string prefix, we save the weights after every 10 epochs and build a separate generative model with these weights but with an input shape with a batch size of 1. Here is the code to do this:

```
num_epochs = 50
for i in range(num_epochs // 10):
    model.fit(
        dataset.repeat(),
        epochs=10,
        steps_per_epoch=steps_per_epoch
        # callbacks=[checkpoint_callback, tensorboard_callback]
    )
    checkpoint_file = os.path.join(
        CHECKPOINT_DIR, "model_epoch_{:d}".format(i+1))
    model.save_weights(checkpoint_file)
    # create generative model using the trained model so far
    gen_model = CharGenModel(vocab_size, seq_length, embedding_dim)
    gen_model.load_weights(checkpoint_file)
    gen_model.build(input_shape=(1, seq_length))
    print("after epoch: {:d}".format(i+1)*10)
    print(generate_text(gen_model, "Alice ", char2idx, idx2char))
    print("---")
```

The output after the very first epoch of training contains words that are completely undecipherable:

```
Alice nIPJtce otaishein r. henipt il nn tu t hen mlPde hc efa
hdtioDDeteeybeaewI teu"t e9B ce nd ageiw  eai rdoCr ohrSI ey Pmtte:vh ndte
taudhor0-gu s5'ria,tr gn inoo luwomg Omke dee sdoohdn ggtdhiAoyaphotd t- kta e
c t- taLurtn  hiisd tl'lpei od y' tpacoe dnlhr oG mGhod ut hlhoy .i, sseodli.,
ekngnhe idlue'aa'  ndti-rla nt d'eiAier adwe ai'otteniAidee hy-ouasq"plhgs
tuutandhptiw  oohe.Rastnint:e,o odwsir"omGoeuall1*g taetphhitoge ds wr li,raa,
h$jeuorsu  h cidmdg't ku..n,HnbMAsn nsaathaa,' ase woe  ehf re ig"hTr ddloese
eod,aed toe rh k. nalf bte seyr udG n,ug lei hn icuimty"onw Qee ivtsae zdrye
g eut rthrer n sd,Zhqehd' sr caseruhel are fd yse e  kgeiiday odW-ldmkhNw
endeM[harlhroa h Wydrygslsh EnilDnt e "lue "en wHeslhglidrth"ylds rln n iiato
taue flitl nnyg ittlno re 'el yOkao itswnadoli'.dnd Akib-ehn hftwinh yd ee
tosetf tonne.;egren t wf, ota nfsr, t&he desnre e" oo fnrvnse aid na tesd is
ioneetIf ·itrn tttpakihc s nih'bheY ilenf yoh etdrwdplloU ooaeedo,,dre snno'ofh
o epst. lahehrw
```

However, after about 30 epochs of training, we begin to see words that look familiar:

```
Alice Red Queen. He best I had defores it,' glily do flose time it makes the
talking of find a hand mansed in she loweven to the rund not bright prough: the
and she a chill be the sand using that whever sullusn--the dear of asker as
'IS now-- Chich the hood." "Oh!"' '_I'm num about--again was wele after a WAG
LoANDE BITTER OF HSE!0 UUL EXMENN 1*.t, this wouldn't teese to Dumark THEVER
Project Gutenberg-tmy of himid out flowal woulld: 'Nis song, Eftrin in pully be
besoniokinote. "Com, contimemustion--of could you knowfum to hard, she can't
the with talking to alfoeys distrint, for spacemark!' 'You gake to be would
prescladleding readieve other togrore what it mughturied ford of it was sen!"
You squs, _It I hap: But it was minute to the Kind she notion and teem what?"
said Alice, make there some that in at the shills distringulf out to the Froge,
and very mind to it were it?' the King was set telm, what's the old all reads
talking a minuse. "Where ream put find growned his so," _you 'Fust to t
```

After 50 epochs of training, the model still has trouble expressing coherent thought but has learned to spell reasonably well. What is amazing here is that the model is character-based and has no knowledge of words, yet it learns to spell words that look like they might have come from the original text:

```
Alice Vex her," he prope of the very managed by this thill deceed. I will ear
she a much daid. "I sha?' Nets: "Woll, I should shutpelf, and now and then,
cried, How them yetains, a tround her about in a shy time, I pashng round the
sandle, droug" shrees went on what he seting that," said Alice. "Was this
will resant again. Alice stook of in a faid.' 'It's ale. So they wentle shall
kneeltie-and which herfer--the about the heald in pum little each the UKECE P@
TTRUST GITE Ever been my hever pertanced to becristrdphariok, and your pringing
that why the King as I to the King remark, but very only all Project Grizly:
thentiused about doment,' Alice with go ould, are wayings for handsn't replied
as mave about to LISTE!' (If the UULE 'TARY-HAVE BUY DIMADEANGNE'G THING NOOT,'
be this plam round an any bar here! No, you're alard to be a good aftered of
the sam--I canon't?" said Alice. 'It's one eye of the olleations. Which saw do
it just opened hardly deat, we hastowe. 'Of coum, is tried try slowing
```

Generating the next character or next word in the text isn't the only thing you can do with this sort of model. Similar models have been built to make stock price predictions [3] or generate classical music [4]. Andrej Karpathy covers a few other fun examples, such as generating fake Wikipedia pages, algebraic geometry proofs, and Linux source code in his blog post [5].

The full code for this example is available in alice_text_generator.py in the source code folder for this chapter. It can be run from the command line using the following command:

```
$ python alice_text_generator.py
```

Our next example will show an implementation of a many-to-one network for sentiment analysis.

Example – Many-to-one – Sentiment analysis

In this example, we will use a many-to-one network that takes a sentence as input and predicts its sentiment as being either positive or negative. Our dataset is the Sentiment-labeled sentences dataset on the UCI Machine Learning Repository [20], a set of 3,000 sentences from reviews on Amazon, IMDb, and Yelp, each labeled with 0 if it expresses a negative sentiment, or 1 if it expresses a positive sentiment.

As usual, we will start with our imports:

```
import numpy as np
import os
import shutil
import tensorflow as tf
from sklearn.metrics import accuracy_score, confusion_matrix
```

The dataset is provided as a zip file, which expands into a folder containing three files of labeled sentences, one for each provider, with one sentence and label per line and with the sentence and label separated by the tab character. We first download the zip file, then parse the files into a list of (sentence, label) pairs:

```
def download_and_read(url):
    local_file = url.split('/')[-1]
    local_file = local_file.replace("%20", " ")
    p = tf.keras.utils.get_file(local_file, url,
        extract=True, cache_dir=".")
    local_folder = os.path.join("datasets", local_file.split('.')[0])
    labeled_sentences = []
    for labeled_filename in os.listdir(local_folder):
        if labeled_filename.endswith("_labelled.txt"):
            with open(os.path.join(
                    local_folder, labeled_filename), "r") as f:
                for line in f:
                    sentence, label = line.strip().split('\t')
                    labeled_sentences.append((sentence, label))
    return labeled_sentences
labeled_sentences = download_and_read(
    "https://archive.ics.uci.edu/ml/machine-learning-databases/" +
    "00331/sentiment%20labelled%20sentences.zip")
sentences = [s for (s, l) in labeled_sentences]
labels = [int(l) for (s, l) in labeled_sentences]
```

Our objective is to train the model so that, given a sentence as input, it learns to predict the corresponding sentiment provided in the label. Each sentence is a sequence of words. However, to input it into the model, we have to convert it into a sequence of integers.

Each integer in the sequence will point to a word. The mapping of integers to words for our corpus is called a vocabulary. Thus, we need to tokenize the sentences and produce a vocabulary. This is done using the following code:

```
tokenizer = tf.keras.preprocessing.text.Tokenizer()
tokenizer.fit_on_texts(sentences)
vocab_size = len(tokenizer.word_counts)
print("vocabulary size: {:d}".format(vocab_size))
word2idx = tokenizer.word_index
idx2word = {v:k for (k, v) in word2idx.items()}
```

Our vocabulary consists of 5,271 unique words. It is possible to make the size smaller by dropping words that occur fewer than some threshold number of times, which can be found by inspecting the `tokenizer.word_counts` dictionary. In such cases, we need to add 1 to the vocabulary size for the UNK (unknown) entry, which will be used to replace every word that is not found in the vocabulary.

We also construct lookup dictionaries to convert from the word-to-word index and back. The first dictionary is useful during training to construct integer sequences to feed the network. The second dictionary is used to convert from the word index back into words in our prediction code later.

Each sentence can have a different number of words. Our model will require us to provide sequences of integers of identical length for each sentence. To support this requirement, it is common to choose a maximum sequence length that is large enough to accommodate most of the sentences in the training set. Any sentences that are shorter will be padded with zeros, and any sentences that are longer will be truncated. An easy way to choose a good value for the maximum sequence length is to look at the sentence length (as in the number of words) at different percentile positions:

```
seq_lengths = np.array([len(s.split()) for s in sentences])
print([(p, np.percentile(seq_lengths, p)) for p
    in [75, 80, 90, 95, 99, 100]])
```

This gives us the following output:

```
[(75, 16.0), (80, 18.0), (90, 22.0), (95, 26.0), (99, 36.0), (100, 71.0)]
```

As can be seen, the maximum sentence length is 71 words, but 99% of the sentences are under 36 words. If we choose a value of 64, for example, we should be able to get away with not having to truncate most of the sentences.

The preceding blocks of code can be run interactively multiple times to choose good values of vocabulary size and maximum sequence length respectively. In our example, we have chosen to keep all the words (so `vocab_size = 5271`), and we have set our `max_seqlen` to 64.

Our next step is to create a dataset that our model can consume. We first use our trained tokenizer to convert each sentence from a sequence of words (sentences) into a sequence of integers (sentences_as_ints), where each corresponding integer is the index of the word in the `tokenizer.word_index`. It is then truncated and padded with zeros.

The labels are also converted into a NumPy array `labels_as_ints`, and finally, we combine the tensors `sentences_as_ints` and `labels_as_ints` to form a TensorFlow dataset:

```
max_seqlen = 64
# create dataset
sentences_as_ints = tokenizer.texts_to_sequences(sentences)
sentences_as_ints = tf.keras.preprocessing.sequence.pad_sequences(
    sentences_as_ints, maxlen=max_seqlen)
labels_as_ints = np.array(labels)
dataset = tf.data.Dataset.from_tensor_slices(
    (sentences_as_ints, labels_as_ints))
```

We want to set aside 1/3 of the dataset for evaluation. Of the remaining data, we will use 10% as an inline validation dataset, which the model will use to gauge its own progress during training, and the remaining as the training dataset. Finally, we create batches of 64 sentences for each dataset:

```
dataset = dataset.shuffle(10000)
test_size = len(sentences) // 3
val_size = (len(sentences) - test_size) // 10
test_dataset = dataset.take(test_size)
val_dataset = dataset.skip(test_size).take(val_size)
train_dataset = dataset.skip(test_size + val_size)
batch_size = 64
train_dataset = train_dataset.batch(batch_size)
val_dataset = val_dataset.batch(batch_size)
test_dataset = test_dataset.batch(batch_size)
```

Next, we define our model. As you can see, the model is fairly straightforward, each input sentence is a sequence of integers of size `max_seqlen` (64). This is input into an embedding layer that converts each word into a vector given by the size of the vocabulary + 1. The additional word is to account for the padding integer 0 that was introduced during the pad_sequences() call above. The vector at each of the 64 time steps is then fed into a bidirectional LSTM layer, which converts each word into a vector of size (64,). The output of the LSTM at each time step is fed into a dense layer, which produces a vector of size (64,) with ReLU activation. The output of this dense layer is then fed into another dense layer, which outputs a vector of (1,) at each time step, modulated through a sigmoid activation.

The model is compiled with the binary cross-entropy loss function and the Adam optimizer, and then trained over 10 epochs:

```
class SentimentAnalysisModel(tf.keras.Model):
    def __init__(self, vocab_size, max_seqlen, **kwargs):
        super(SentimentAnalysisModel, self).__init__(**kwargs)
        self.embedding = tf.keras.layers.Embedding(
            vocab_size, max_seqlen)
        self.bilstm = tf.keras.layers.Bidirectional(
```

```
            tf.keras.layers.LSTM(max_seqlen)
        )
        self.dense = tf.keras.layers.Dense(64, activation="relu")
        self.out = tf.keras.layers.Dense(1, activation="sigmoid")
    def call(self, x):
        x = self.embedding(x)
        x = self.bilstm(x)
        x = self.dense(x)
        x = self.out(x)
        return x
model = SentimentAnalysisModel(vocab_size+1, max_seqlen)
model.build(input_shape=(batch_size, max_seqlen))
model.summary()
# compile
model.compile(
    loss="binary_crossentropy",
    optimizer="adam",
    metrics=["accuracy"]
)
# train
data_dir = "./data"
logs_dir = os.path.join("./logs")
best_model_file = os.path.join(data_dir, "best_model.h5")
checkpoint = tf.keras.callbacks.ModelCheckpoint(best_model_file,
    save_weights_only=True,
    save_best_only=True)
tensorboard = tf.keras.callbacks.TensorBoard(log_dir=logs_dir)
num_epochs = 10
history = model.fit(train_dataset, epochs=num_epochs,
    validation_data=val_dataset,
    callbacks=[checkpoint, tensorboard])
```

As you can see from the output, the training set accuracy goes to 99.8% and the validation set accuracy goes to about 78.5%. Having a higher accuracy over the training set is expected since the model was trained on this dataset. You can also look at the following loss plot to see exactly where the model starts overfitting on the training set. Notice that the training loss keeps going down, but the validation loss comes down initially and then starts going up. It is at the point where it starts going up that we know that the model overfits on the training set:

```
Epoch 1/10
29/29 [==============================] - 7s 239ms/step - loss: 0.6918 -
accuracy: 0.5148 - val_loss: 0.6940 - val_accuracy: 0.4750
```

```
Epoch 2/10
29/29 [==============================] - 3s 98ms/step - loss: 0.6382 -
accuracy: 0.5928 - val_loss: 0.6311 - val_accuracy: 0.6000
Epoch 3/10
29/29 [==============================] - 3s 100ms/step - loss: 0.3661 -
accuracy: 0.8250 - val_loss: 0.4894 - val_accuracy: 0.7600
Epoch 4/10
29/29 [==============================] - 3s 99ms/step - loss: 0.1567 -
accuracy: 0.9564 - val_loss: 0.5469 - val_accuracy: 0.7750
Epoch 5/10
29/29 [==============================] - 3s 99ms/step - loss: 0.0768 -
accuracy: 0.9875 - val_loss: 0.6197 - val_accuracy: 0.7450
Epoch 6/10
29/29 [==============================] - 3s 100ms/step - loss: 0.0387 -
accuracy: 0.9937 - val_loss: 0.6529 - val_accuracy: 0.7500
Epoch 7/10
29/29 [==============================] - 3s 99ms/step - loss: 0.0215 -
accuracy: 0.9989 - val_loss: 0.7597 - val_accuracy: 0.7550
Epoch 8/10
29/29 [==============================] - 3s 100ms/step - loss: 0.0196 -
accuracy: 0.9987 - val_loss: 0.6745 - val_accuracy: 0.7450
Epoch 9/10
29/29 [==============================] - 3s 99ms/step - loss: 0.0136 -
accuracy: 0.9962 - val_loss: 0.7770 - val_accuracy: 0.7500
Epoch 10/10
29/29 [==============================] - 3s 99ms/step - loss: 0.0062 -
accuracy: 0.9988 - val_loss: 0.8344 - val_accuracy: 0.7450
```

Figure 5.6 shows TensorBoard plots of accuracy and loss for the training and validation datasets:

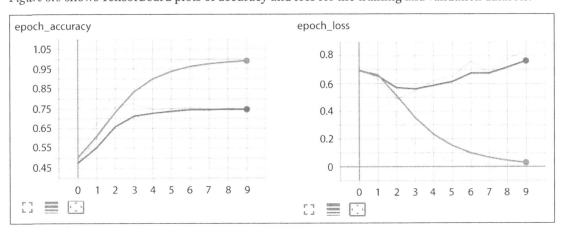

Figure 5.6: Accuracy and loss plots from TensorBoard for sentiment analysis network training

Our checkpoint callback has saved the best model based on the lowest value of validation loss, and we can now reload this for evaluation against our held out test set:

```
best_model = SentimentAnalysisModel(vocab_size+1, max_seqlen)
best_model.build(input_shape=(batch_size, max_seqlen))
best_model.load_weights(best_model_file)
best_model.compile(
    loss="binary_crossentropy",
    optimizer="adam",
    metrics=["accuracy"]
)
```

The easiest high-level way to evaluate a model against a dataset is to use the `model.evaluate()` call:

```
test_loss, test_acc = best_model.evaluate(test_dataset)
print("test loss: {:.3f}, test accuracy: {:.3f}".format(
    test_loss, test_acc))
```

This gives us the following output:

```
test loss: 0.487, test accuracy: 0.782
```

We can also use `model.predict()` to retrieve our predictions and compare them individually to the labels and use external tools (from scikit-learn, for example) to compute our results:

```
labels, predictions = [], []
idx2word[0] = "PAD"
is_first_batch = True
for test_batch in test_dataset:
    inputs_b, labels_b = test_batch
    pred_batch = best_model.predict(inputs_b)
    predictions.extend([(1 if p > 0.5 else 0) for p in pred_batch])
    labels.extend([l for l in labels_b])
    if is_first_batch:
        # print first batch of label, prediction, and sentence
        for rid in range(inputs_b.shape[0]):
            words = [idx2word[idx] for idx in inputs_b[rid].numpy()]
            words = [w for w in words if w != "PAD"]
            sentence = " ".join(words)
            print("{:d}\t{:d}\t{:s}".format(
                labels[rid], predictions[rid], sentence))
        is_first_batch = False
print("accuracy score: {:.3f}".format(accuracy_score(labels, predictions)))
print("confusion matrix")
print(confusion_matrix(labels, predictions))
```

For the first batch of 64 sentences in our test dataset, we reconstruct the sentence and display the label (first column) as well as the prediction from the model (second column). Here, we show the top 10 sentences. As you can see, the model gets it right for most sentences on this list:

```
LBL   PRED   SENT
1     1      one of my favorite purchases ever
1     1      works great
1     1      our waiter was very attentive friendly and informative
0     0      defective crap
0     1      and it was way to expensive
0     0      don't waste your money
0     0      friend's pasta also bad he barely touched it
1     1      it's a sad movie but very good
0     0      we recently witnessed her poor quality of management towards other
guests as well
0     1      there is so much good food in vegas that i feel cheated for wasting
an eating opportunity by going to rice and company
```

We also report the results across all sentences in the test dataset. As you can see, the test accuracy is the same as that reported by the `evaluate` call. We have also generated the confusion matrix, which shows that out of 1,000 test examples, our sentiment analysis network predicted correctly 782 times and incorrectly 218 times:

```
accuracy score: 0.782
confusion matrix
[[391  97]
 [121 391]]
```

The full code for this example is available in `lstm_sentiment_analysis.py` in the source code folder for this chapter. It can be run from the command line using the following command:

```
$ python lstm_sentiment_analysis.py
```

Our next example will describe a many-to-many network trained for POS tagging English text.

Example – Many-to-many – POS tagging

In this example, we will use a GRU layer to build a network that does **Part of Speech** (**POS**) tagging. A POS is a grammatical category of words that are used in the same way across multiple sentences. Examples of POS are nouns, verbs, adjectives, and so on. For example, nouns are typically used to identify things, verbs are typically used to identify what they do, and adjectives are used to describe attributes of these things. POS tagging used to be done manually in the past, but this is now mostly a solved problem, initially through statistical models, and more recently by using deep learning models in an end-to-end manner, as described in Collobert, et al. [21].

For our training data, we will need sentences tagged with POS tags. The Penn Treebank [22] is one such dataset; it is a human-annotated corpus of about 4.5 million words of American English. However, it is a non-free resource. A 10% sample of the Penn Treebank is freely available as part of NLTK [23], which we will use to train our network.

Our model will take a sequence of words in a sentence as input, then will output the corresponding POS tag for each word. Thus, for an input sequence consisting of the words [The, cat, sat. on, the, mat, .], the output sequence should be the POS symbols [DT, NN, VB, IN, DT, NN, .].

In order to get the data, you need to install the NLTK library if it is not already installed (NLTK is included in the Anaconda distribution), as well as the 10% treebank dataset (not installed by default). To install NLTK, follow the steps on the NLTK install page [23]. To install the treebank dataset, perform the following in the Python REPL:

```
>>> import nltk
>>> nltk.download("treebank")
```

Once this is done, we are ready to build our network. As usual, we will start by importing the necessary packages:

```
import numpy as np
import os
import shutil
import tensorflow as tf
```

We will lazily import the NLTK treebank dataset into a pair of parallel flat files, one containing the sentences and the other containing a corresponding **POS** sequence:

```
def download_and_read(dataset_dir, num_pairs=None):
    sent_filename = os.path.join(dataset_dir, "treebank-sents.txt")
    poss_filename = os.path.join(dataset_dir, "treebank-poss.txt")
    if not(os.path.exists(sent_filename) and os.path.exists(poss_filename)):
        import nltk
        if not os.path.exists(dataset_dir):
            os.makedirs(dataset_dir)
        fsents = open(sent_filename, "w")
        fposs = open(poss_filename, "w")
        sentences = nltk.corpus.treebank.tagged_sents()
        for sent in sentences:
            fsents.write(" ".join([w for w, p in sent]) + "\n")
            fposs.write(" ".join([p for w, p in sent]) + "\n")
        fsents.close()
        fposs.close()
    sents, poss = [], []
    with open(sent_filename, "r") as fsent:
```

```
            for idx, line in enumerate(fsent):
                sents.append(line.strip())
                if num_pairs is not None and idx >= num_pairs:
                    break
        with open(poss_filename, "r") as fposs:
            for idx, line in enumerate(fposs):
                poss.append(line.strip())
                if num_pairs is not None and idx >= num_pairs:
                    break
        return sents, poss
    sents, poss = download_and_read("./datasets")
    assert(len(sents) == len(poss))
    print("# of records: {:d}".format(len(sents)))
```

There are 3,194 sentences in our dataset. The preceding code writes the sentences and corresponding tags into parallel files, that is, line 1 in `treebank-sents.txt` contains the first sentence, and line 1 in `treebank-poss.txt` contains the corresponding POS tags for each word in the sentence. *Table 5.1* shows two sentences from this dataset and their corresponding POS tags:

Sentences	POS Tags
Pierre Vinken, 61 years old, will join the board as a nonexecutive director Nov. 29.	NNP NNP , CD NNS JJ , MD VB DT NN IN DT JJ NN NNP CD.
Mr. Vinken is chairman of Elsevier N.V., the Dutch publishing group.	NNP NNP VBZ NN IN NNP NNP , DT NNP VBG NN.

Table 5.1: Sentences and their corresponding POS tags

We will then use the TensorFlow (`tf.keras`) tokenizer to tokenize the sentences and create a list of sentence tokens. We reuse the same infrastructure to tokenize the POS, although we could have simply split on spaces. Each input record to the network is currently a sequence of text tokens, but they need to be a sequence of integers. During the tokenizing process, the Tokenizer also maintains the tokens in the vocabulary, from which we can build mappings from the token to the integer and back.

We have two vocabularies to consider, the vocabulary of word tokens in the sentence collection and the vocabulary of POS tags in the part-of-speech collection. The following code shows how to tokenize both collections and generate the necessary mapping dictionaries:

```
def tokenize_and_build_vocab(texts, vocab_size=None, lower=True):
    if vocab_size is None:
        tokenizer = tf.keras.preprocessing.text.Tokenizer(lower=lower)
    else:
        tokenizer = tf.keras.preprocessing.text.Tokenizer(
            num_words=vocab_size+1, oov_token="UNK", lower=lower)
    tokenizer.fit_on_texts(texts)
```

```
        if vocab_size is not None:
            # additional workaround, see issue 8092
            # https://github.com/keras-team/keras/issues/8092
            tokenizer.word_index = {e:i for e, i in
                tokenizer.word_index.items() if
                i <= vocab_size+1 }
        word2idx = tokenizer.word_index
        idx2word = {v:k for k, v in word2idx.items()}
        return word2idx, idx2word, tokenizer
word2idx_s, idx2word_s, tokenizer_s = tokenize_and_build_vocab(
    sents, vocab_size=9000)
word2idx_t, idx2word_t, tokenizer_t = tokenize_and_build_vocab(
    poss, vocab_size=38, lower=False)
source_vocab_size = len(word2idx_s)
target_vocab_size = len(word2idx_t)
print("vocab sizes (source): {:d}, (target): {:d}".format(
    source_vocab_size, target_vocab_size))
```

Our sentences are going to be of different lengths, although the number of tokens in a sentence and their corresponding POS tag sequence are the same. The network expects the input to have the same length, so we have to decide how much to make our sentence length. The following (throwaway) code computes various percentiles and prints sentence lengths at these percentiles to the console:

```
sequence_lengths = np.array([len(s.split()) for s in sents])
print([(p, np.percentile(sequence_lengths, p))
    for p in [75, 80, 90, 95, 99, 100]])
[(75, 33.0), (80, 35.0), (90, 41.0), (95, 47.0), (99, 58.0), (100, 271.0)]
```

We see that we could probably get away with setting the sentence length to around 100 and have a few truncated sentences as a result. Sentences shorter than our selected length will be padded at the end. Because our dataset is small, we prefer to use as much of it as possible, so we end up choosing the maximum length.

The next step is to create the dataset from our inputs. First, we have to convert our sequence of tokens and POS tags in our input and output sequences into sequences of integers. Second, we have to pad shorter sequences to the maximum length of 271. Notice that we do an additional operation on the POS tag sequences after padding, rather than keep it as a sequence of integers; we convert it into a sequence of one-hot encodings using the to_categorical() function. TensorFlow 2.0 does provide loss functions to handle outputs as a sequence of integers, but we want to keep our code as simple as possible, so we opt to do the conversion ourselves. Finally, we use the from_tensor_slices() function to create our dataset, shuffle it, and split it up into training, validation, and test sets:

```
max_seqlen = 271

# convert sentences to sequence of integers
```

```
    sents_as_ints = tokenizer_s.texts_to_sequences(sents)
    sents_as_ints = tf.keras.preprocessing.sequence.pad_sequences(
        sents_as_ints, maxlen=max_seqlen, padding="post")

    # convert POS tags to sequence of (categorical) integers
    poss_as_ints = tokenizer_t.texts_to_sequences(poss)
    poss_as_ints = tf.keras.preprocessing.sequence.pad_sequences(
        poss_as_ints, maxlen=max_seqlen, padding="post")

    poss_as_catints = []
    for p in poss_as_ints:
        poss_as_catints.append(tf.keras.utils.to_categorical(p,
            num_classes=target_vocab_size+1, dtype="int32"))
    poss_as_catints = tf.keras.preprocessing.sequence.pad_sequences(
        poss_as_catints, maxlen=max_seqlen)

    dataset = tf.data.Dataset.from_tensor_slices(
        (sents_as_ints, poss_as_catints))

    idx2word_s[0], idx2word_t[0] = "PAD", "PAD"

    # split into training, validation, and test datasets
    dataset = dataset.shuffle(10000)
    test_size = len(sents) // 3
    val_size = (len(sents) - test_size) // 10

    test_dataset = dataset.take(test_size)
    val_dataset = dataset.skip(test_size).take(val_size)
    train_dataset = dataset.skip(test_size + val_size)

    # create batches
    batch_size = 128
    train_dataset = train_dataset.batch(batch_size)
    val_dataset = val_dataset.batch(batch_size)
    test_dataset = test_dataset.batch(batch_size)
```

Next, we will define our model and instantiate it. Our model is a sequential model consisting of an embedding layer, a dropout layer, a bidirectional GRU layer, a dense layer, and a softmax activation layer. The input is a batch of integer sequences with shape (batch_size, max_seqlen). When passed through the embedding layer, each integer in the sequence is converted into a vector of size (embedding_dim), so now the shape of our tensor is (batch_size, max_seqlen, embedding_dim). Each of these vectors is passed to corresponding time steps of a bidirectional GRU with an output dimension of 256.

Because the GRU is bidirectional, this is equivalent to stacking one GRU on top of the other, so the tensor that comes out of the bidirectional GRU has the dimension (batch_size, max_seqlen, 2*rnn_output_dimension). Each time step tensor of shape (batch_size, 1, 2*rnn_output_dimension) is fed into a dense layer, which converts each time step into a vector of the same size as the target vocabulary, that is, (batch_size, number_of_timesteps, output_vocab_size). Each time step represents a probability distribution of output tokens, so the final softmax layer is applied to each time step to return a sequence of output POS tokens.

Finally, we declare the model with some parameters, then compile it with the Adam optimizer, the categorical cross-entropy loss function, and accuracy as the metric:

```
class POSTaggingModel(tf.keras.Model):
    def __init__(self, source_vocab_size, target_vocab_size,
            embedding_dim, max_seqlen, rnn_output_dim, **kwargs):
        super(POSTaggingModel, self).__init__(**kwargs)
        self.embed = tf.keras.layers.Embedding(
            source_vocab_size, embedding_dim, input_length=max_seqlen)
        self.dropout = tf.keras.layers.SpatialDropout1D(0.2)
        self.rnn = tf.keras.layers.Bidirectional(
            tf.keras.layers.GRU(rnn_output_dim, return_sequences=True))
        self.dense = tf.keras.layers.TimeDistributed(
            tf.keras.layers.Dense(target_vocab_size))
        self.activation = tf.keras.layers.Activation("softmax")
    def call(self, x):
        x = self.embed(x)
        x = self.dropout(x)
        x = self.rnn(x)
        x = self.dense(x)
        x = self.activation(x)
        return x
embedding_dim = 128
rnn_output_dim = 256
model = POSTaggingModel(source_vocab_size, target_vocab_size,
    embedding_dim, max_seqlen, rnn_output_dim)
model.build(input_shape=(batch_size, max_seqlen))
model.summary()
model.compile(
    loss="categorical_crossentropy",
    optimizer="adam",
    metrics=["accuracy", masked_accuracy()])
```

Observant readers might have noticed an additional masked_accuracy() metric next to the accuracy metric in the preceding code snippet. Because of the padding, there are a lot of zeros on both the label and the prediction, as a result of which the accuracy numbers are very optimistic. In fact, the validation accuracy reported at the end of the very first epoch is 0.9116. However, the quality of POS tags generated is very poor.

Perhaps the best approach is to replace the current loss function with one that ignores any matches where both numbers are zero; however, a simpler approach is to build a stricter metric and use that to judge when to stop the training. Accordingly, we build a new accuracy function masked_accuracy() whose code is shown as follows:

```
def masked_accuracy():
    def masked_accuracy_fn(ytrue, ypred):
        ytrue = tf.keras.backend.argmax(ytrue, axis=-1)
        ypred = tf.keras.backend.argmax(ypred, axis=-1)
        mask = tf.keras.backend.cast(
            tf.keras.backend.not_equal(ypred, 0), tf.int32)
        matches = tf.keras.backend.cast(
            tf.keras.backend.equal(ytrue, ypred), tf.int32) * mask
        numer = tf.keras.backend.sum(matches)
        denom = tf.keras.backend.maximum(tf.keras.backend.sum(mask), 1)
        accuracy =  numer / denom
        return accuracy
    return masked_accuracy_fn
```

We are now ready to train our model. As usual, we set up the model checkpoint and TensorBoard callbacks, and then call the fit() convenience method on the model to train the model with a batch size of 128 for 50 epochs:

```
num_epochs = 50
best_model_file = os.path.join(data_dir, "best_model.h5")
checkpoint = tf.keras.callbacks.ModelCheckpoint(
    best_model_file,
    save_weights_only=True,
    save_best_only=True)
tensorboard = tf.keras.callbacks.TensorBoard(log_dir=logs_dir)
history = model.fit(train_dataset,
    epochs=num_epochs,
    validation_data=val_dataset,
    callbacks=[checkpoint, tensorboard])
```

A truncated output of the training is shown as follows. As you can see, the masked_accuracy and val_ masked_accuracy numbers seem more conservative than the accuracy and val_accuracy numbers. This is because the masked versions do not consider the sequence positions where the input is a PAD character:

```
Epoch 1/50
19/19 [==============================] - 8s 431ms/step - loss: 1.4363 -
accuracy: 0.7511 - masked_accuracy_fn: 0.00
38 - val_loss: 0.3219 - val_accuracy: 0.9116 - val_masked_accuracy_fn: 0.5833
Epoch 2/50
19/19 [==============================] - 6s 291ms/step - loss: 0.3278 -
accuracy: 0.9183 - masked_accuracy_fn: 0.17
12 - val_loss: 0.3289 - val_accuracy: 0.9209 - val_masked_accuracy_fn: 0.1357
Epoch 3/50
19/19 [==============================] - 6s 292ms/step - loss: 0.3187 -
accuracy: 0.9242 - masked_accuracy_fn: 0.1615 - val_loss: 0.3131 - val_
accuracy: 0.9186 - val_masked_accuracy_fn: 0.2236
Epoch 4/50
19/19 [==============================] - 6s 293ms/step - loss: 0.3037 -
accuracy: 0.9186 - masked_accuracy_fn: 0.1831 - val_loss: 0.2933 - val_
accuracy: 0.9129 - val_masked_accuracy_fn: 0.1062
Epoch 5/50
19/19 [==============================] - 6s 294ms/step - loss: 0.2739 -
accuracy: 0.9182 - masked_accuracy_fn: 0.1054 - val_loss: 0.2608 - val_
accuracy: 0.9230 - val_masked_accuracy_fn: 0.1407
...
Epoch 45/50
19/19 [==============================] - 6s 292ms/step - loss: 0.0653 -
accuracy: 0.9810 - masked_accuracy_fn: 0.7872 - val_loss: 0.1545 - val_
accuracy: 0.9611 - val_masked_accuracy_fn: 0.5407
Epoch 46/50
19/19 [==============================] - 6s 291ms/step - loss: 0.0640 -
accuracy: 0.9815 - masked_accuracy_fn: 0.7925 - val_loss: 0.1550 - val_
accuracy: 0.9616 - val_masked_accuracy_fn: 0.5441
Epoch 47/50
19/19 [==============================] - 6s 291ms/step - loss: 0.0619 -
accuracy: 0.9818 - masked_accuracy_fn: 0.7971 - val_loss: 0.1497 - val_
accuracy: 0.9614 - val_masked_accuracy_fn: 0.5535
Epoch 48/50
19/19 [==============================] - 6s 292ms/step - loss: 0.0599 -
accuracy: 0.9825 - masked_accuracy_fn: 0.8033 - val_loss: 0.1524 - val_
accuracy: 0.9616 - val_masked_accuracy_fn: 0.5579
Epoch 49/50
```

```
19/19 [==============================] - 6s 293ms/step - loss: 0.0585 -
accuracy: 0.9830 - masked_accuracy_fn: 0.8092 - val_loss: 0.1544 - val_
accuracy: 0.9617 - val_masked_accuracy_fn: 0.5621
Epoch 50/50
19/19 [==============================] - 6s 291ms/step - loss: 0.0575 -
accuracy: 0.9833 - masked_accuracy_fn: 0.8140 - val_loss: 0.1569 - val_
accuracy: 0.9615 - val_masked_accuracy_fn: 0.5511
11/11 [==============================] - 2s 170ms/step - loss: 0.1436 -
accuracy: 0.9637 - masked_accuracy_fn: 0.5786
test loss: 0.144, test accuracy: 0.963, masked test accuracy: 0.578
```

Here are some examples of POS tags generated for some random sentences in the test set, shown together with the POS tags in the corresponding ground truth sentences. As you can see, while the metric values are not perfect, it seems to have learned to do POS tagging fairly well:

```
labeled  : among/IN segments/NNS that/WDT t/NONE 1/VBP continue/NONE 2/TO to/VB
operate/RB though/DT the/NN company/POS 's/NN steel/NN division/VBD continued/
NONE 3/TO to/VB suffer/IN from/JJ soft/NN demand/IN for/PRP its/JJ tubular/NNS
goods/VBG serving/DT the/NN oil/NN industry/CC and/JJ other/NNS
predicted: among/IN segments/NNS that/WDT t/NONE 1/NONE continue/NONE 2/
TO to/VB operate/IN though/DT the/NN company/NN 's/NN steel/NN division/NONE
continued/NONE 3/TO to/IN suffer/IN from/IN soft/JJ demand/NN for/IN its/JJ
tubular/NNS goods/DT serving/DT the/NNP oil/NN industry/CC and/JJ other/NNS

labeled  : as/IN a/DT result/NN ms/NNP ganes/NNP said/VBD 0/NONE t/NONE 2/PRP
it/VBZ is/VBN believed/IN that/JJ little/CC or/DT no/NN sugar/IN from/DT the/
CD 1989/NN 90/VBZ crop/VBN has/VBN been/NONE shipped/RB 1/RB yet/IN even/DT
though/NN the/NN crop/VBZ year/CD is/NNS six/JJ
predicted: as/IN a/DT result/NN ms/IN ganes/NNP said/VBD 0/NONE t/NONE 2/PRP
it/VBZ is/VBN believed/NONE that/DT little/NN or/DT no/NN sugar/IN from/DT the/
DT 1989/CD 90/NN crop/VBZ has/VBN been/VBN shipped/VBN 1/RB yet/RB even/IN
though/DT the/NN crop/NN year/NN is/JJ

labeled  : in/IN the/DT interview/NN at/IN headquarters/NN yesterday/NN
afternoon/NN both/DT men/NNS exuded/VBD confidence/NN and/CC seemed/VBD 1/NONE
to/TO work/VB well/RB together/RB
predicted: in/IN the/DT interview/NN at/IN headquarters/NN yesterday/NN
afternoon/NN both/DT men/NNS exuded/NNP confidence/NN and/CC seemed/VBD 1/NONE
to/TO work/VB well/RB together/RB

labeled  : all/DT came/VBD from/IN cray/NNP research/NNP
predicted: all/NNP came/VBD from/IN cray/NNP research/NNP

labeled  : primerica/NNP closed/VBD at/IN 28/CD 25/NONE u/RB down/CD 50/NNS
predicted: primerica/NNP closed/VBD at/CD 28/CD 25/CD u/CD down/CD
```

If you would like to run this code yourself, you can find the code in the code folder for this chapter. To run it from the command line, enter the following command. The output is written to the console:

```
$ python gru_pos_tagger.py
```

Now that we have seen some examples of three common RNN network topologies, let's explore the most popular of them all – the seq2seq model, which is also known as the recurrent encoder-decoder architecture.

Encoder-decoder architecture — seq2seq

The example of a many-to-many network we just saw was mostly similar to the many-to-one network. The one important difference was that the RNN returns outputs at each time step instead of a single combined output at the end. One other noticeable feature was that the number of input time steps was equal to the number of output time steps. As you learn about the encoder-decoder architecture, which is the "other," and arguably more popular, style of a many-to-many network, you will notice another difference – the output is in line with the input in a many-to-many network, that is, it is not necessary for the network to wait until all of the input is consumed before generating the output.

The encoder-decoder architecture is also called a seq2seq model. As the name implies, the network is composed of an encoder and a decoder part, both RNN-based and capable of consuming and returning sequences of outputs corresponding to multiple time steps. The biggest application of the seq2seq network has been in neural machine translation, although it is equally applicable for problems that can be roughly structured as translation problems. Some examples are sentence parsing [10] and image captioning [24]. The seq2seq model has also been used for time series analysis [25] and question answering.

In the seq2seq model, the encoder consumes the source sequence, which is a batch of integer sequences. The length of the sequence is the number of input time steps, which corresponds to the maximum input sequence length (padded or truncated as necessary). Thus, the dimensions of the input tensor are (`batch_size, number_of_encoder_timesteps`). This is passed into an embedding layer, which will convert the integer at each time step into an embedding vector. The output of the embedding is a tensor of shape (`batch_size, number_of_encoder_timesteps, encoder_embedding_dim`).

This tensor is fed into an RNN, which converts the vector at each time step into the size corresponding to its encoding dimension. This vector is a combination of the current time step and all previous time steps. Typically, the encoder will return the output at the last time step, representing the context or "thought" vector for the entire sequence. This tensor has the shape (`batch_size, encoder_rnn_dim`).

The decoder network has a similar architecture as the encoder, except there is an additional dense layer at each time step to convert the output. The input to each time step on the decoder side is the hidden state of the previous time step and the input vector that is the token predicted by the decoder of the previous time step. For the very first time step, the hidden state is the context vector from the encoder, and the input vector corresponds to the token that will initiate sequence generation on the target side. For the translation use case, for example, it is a **beginning-of-string (BOS)** pseudo-token. The shape of the hidden signal is (`batch_size, encoder_rnn_dim`) and the shape of the input signal across all time steps is (`batch_size, number_of_decoder_timesteps`).

Once it passes through the embedding layer, the output tensor shape is (`batch_size, number_of_decoder_timesteps, decoder_embedding_dim`). The next step is the decoder RNN layer, the output of which is a tensor of shape (`batch_size, number_of_decoder_timesteps, decoder_rnn_dim`). The output at each time step is then sent through a dense layer, which converts the vector into the size of the target vocabulary, so the output of the dense layer is (`batch_size, number_of_decoder_timesteps, output_vocab_size`). This is basically a probability distribution over tokens at each time step, so if we compute the argmax over the last dimension, we can convert it back into a predicted sequence of tokens in the target language. *Figure 5.7* shows a high-level view of the seq2seq architecture:

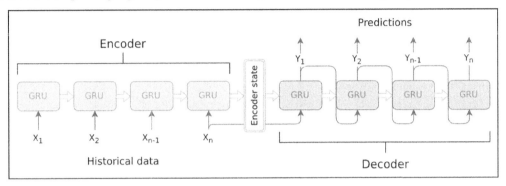

Figure 5.7: Seq2seq network data flow. Image Source: Artur Suilin [25]

In the next section, we will look at an example of a seq2seq network for machine translation.

Example – seq2seq without attention for machine translation

To understand the seq2seq model in greater detail, we will look at an example of one that learns how to translate from English to French using the French-English bilingual dataset from the Tatoeba Project (1997-2019) [26]. The dataset contains approximately 167,000 sentence pairs. To make our training go faster, we will only consider the first 30,000 sentence pairs for our training.

As always, we will start with the imports:

```
import nltk
import numpy as np
import re
import shutil
import tensorflow as tf
import os
import unicodedata
from nltk.translate.bleu_score import sentence_bleu, SmoothingFunction
```

The data is provided as a remote zip file. The easiest way to access the file is to download it from http://www.manythings.org/anki/fra-eng.zip and expand it locally using unzip. The zip file contains a tab-separated file called fra.txt, with French and English sentence pairs separated by a tab, one pair per line. The code expects the fra.txt file in a dataset folder in the same directory as itself. We want to extract three different datasets from it.

If you recall the structure of the seq2seq network, the input to the encoder is a sequence of English words. On the decoder side, the input is a set of French words, and the output is the sequence of French words offset by one time step. The following function will download the zip file, expand it, and create the datasets described before.

The input is preprocessed to *asciify* the characters, separate out specific punctuations from their neighboring word, and remove all characters other than alphabets and these specific punctuation symbols. Finally, the sentences are converted into lowercase. Each English sentence is just converted into a single sequence of words. Each French sentence is converted into two sequences, one preceded by the BOS pseudo-word and the other followed by the **end-of-sentence (EOS)** pseudo-word.

The first sequence starts at position 0 and stops one short of the final word in the sentence, and the second sequence starts at position 1 and goes all the way to the end of the sentence:

```python
def preprocess_sentence(sent):
    sent = "".join([c for c in unicodedata.normalize("NFD", sent)
        if unicodedata.category(c) != "Mn"])
    sent = re.sub(r"([!.?])", r" \1", sent)
    sent = re.sub(r"[^a-zA-Z!.?]+", r" ", sent)
    sent = re.sub(r"\s+", " ", sent)
    sent = sent.lower()
    return sent
def download_and_read():
    en_sents, fr_sents_in, fr_sents_out = [], [], []
    local_file = os.path.join("datasets", "fra.txt")
    with open(local_file, "r") as fin:
        for i, line in enumerate(fin):
            en_sent, fr_sent = line.strip().split('\t')
            en_sent = [w for w in preprocess_sentence(en_sent).split()]
            fr_sent = preprocess_sentence(fr_sent)
            fr_sent_in = [w for w in ("BOS " + fr_sent).split()]
            fr_sent_out = [w for w in (fr_sent + " EOS").split()]
            en_sents.append(en_sent)
            fr_sents_in.append(fr_sent_in)
            fr_sents_out.append(fr_sent_out)
            if i >= num_sent_pairs - 1:
                break
    return en_sents, fr_sents_in, fr_sents_out
sents_en, sents_fr_in, sents_fr_out = download_and_read()
```

Our next step is to tokenize our inputs and create the vocabulary. Since we have sequences in two different languages, we will create two different tokenizers and vocabularies, one for each language.

The tf.keras framework provides a very powerful and versatile tokenizer class – here, we have set filters to an empty string and lower to False because we have already done what was needed for tokenization in our preprocess_sentence() function. The Tokenizer creates various data structures from which we can compute the vocabulary sizes and lookup tables that allow us to go from word to word index and back.

Next, we handle different length sequences of words by padding with zeros at the end, using the pad_sequences() function. Because our strings are fairly short, we do not do any truncation; we just pad to the maximum length of sentence that we have (8 words for English and 16 words for French):

```
tokenizer_en = tf.keras.preprocessing.text.Tokenizer(
    filters="", lower=False)
tokenizer_en.fit_on_texts(sents_en)
data_en = tokenizer_en.texts_to_sequences(sents_en)
data_en = tf.keras.preprocessing.sequence.pad_sequences(
    data_en, padding="post")
tokenizer_fr = tf.keras.preprocessing.text.Tokenizer(
    filters="", lower=False)
tokenizer_fr.fit_on_texts(sents_fr_in)
tokenizer_fr.fit_on_texts(sents_fr_out)
data_fr_in = tokenizer_fr.texts_to_sequences(sents_fr_in)
data_fr_in = tf.keras.preprocessing.sequence.pad_sequences(
    data_fr_in, padding="post")
data_fr_out = tokenizer_fr.texts_to_sequences(sents_fr_out)
data_fr_out = tf.keras.preprocessing.sequence.pad_sequences(
    data_fr_out, padding="post")
vocab_size_en = len(tokenizer_en.word_index)
vocab_size_fr = len(tokenizer_fr.word_index)
word2idx_en = tokenizer_en.word_index
idx2word_en = {v:k for k, v in word2idx_en.items()}
word2idx_fr = tokenizer_fr.word_index
idx2word_fr = {v:k for k, v in word2idx_fr.items()}
print("vocab size (en): {:d}, vocab size (fr): {:d}".format(
    vocab_size_en, vocab_size_fr))
maxlen_en = data_en.shape[1]
maxlen_fr = data_fr_out.shape[1]
print("seqlen (en): {:d}, (fr): {:d}".format(maxlen_en, maxlen_fr))
```

Finally, we convert the data into a TensorFlow dataset, and then split it into a training and test dataset:

```
batch_size = 64
dataset = tf.data.Dataset.from_tensor_slices(
    (data_en, data_fr_in, data_fr_out))
```

```
dataset = dataset.shuffle(10000)
test_size = NUM_SENT_PAIRS // 4
test_dataset = dataset.take(test_size).batch(
    batch_size, drop_remainder=True)
train_dataset = dataset.skip(test_size).batch(
    batch_size, drop_remainder=True)
```

Our data is now ready to be used for training the seq2seq network, which we will define next. Our encoder is an embedding layer followed by a GRU layer. The input to the encoder is a sequence of integers, which is converted into a sequence of embedding vectors of size embedding_dim. This sequence of vectors is sent to an RNN, which converts the input at each of the num_timesteps time steps into a vector of size encoder_dim. Only the output at the last time step is returned, as shown by return_sequences=False.

The decoder has almost the same structure as the encoder, except that it has an additional dense layer that converts the vector of size decoder_dim, which is output from the RNN, into a vector that represents the probability distribution across the target vocabulary. The decoder also returns outputs along with all its time steps.

In our example network, we have chosen our embedding dimension to be 128, followed by an encoder and decoder RNN dimension of 1024 each. Note that we have to add 1 to the vocabulary size for both the English and French vocabularies to account for the PAD character that was added during the pad_sequences() step:

```
class Encoder(tf.keras.Model):
    def __init__(self, vocab_size, num_timesteps,
            embedding_dim, encoder_dim, **kwargs):
        super(Encoder, self).__init__(**kwargs)
        self.encoder_dim = encoder_dim
        self.embedding = tf.keras.layers.Embedding(
            vocab_size, embedding_dim, input_length=num_timesteps)
        self.rnn = tf.keras.layers.GRU(
            encoder_dim, return_sequences=False, return_state=True)
    def call(self, x, state):
        x = self.embedding(x)
        x, state = self.rnn(x, initial_state=state)
        return x, state
    def init_state(self, batch_size):
        return tf.zeros((batch_size, self.encoder_dim))
class Decoder(tf.keras.Model):
    def __init__(self, vocab_size, embedding_dim, num_timesteps,
            decoder_dim, **kwargs):
        super(Decoder, self).__init__(**kwargs)
        self.decoder_dim = decoder_dim
```

```
            self.embedding = tf.keras.layers.Embedding(
                vocab_size, embedding_dim, input_length=num_timesteps)
            self.rnn = tf.keras.layers.GRU(
                decoder_dim, return_sequences=True, return_state=True)
            self.dense = tf.keras.layers.Dense(vocab_size)
        def call(self, x, state):
            x = self.embedding(x)
            x, state = self.rnn(x, state)
            x = self.dense(x)
            return x, state
embedding_dim = 256
encoder_dim, decoder_dim = 1024, 1024
encoder = Encoder(vocab_size_en+1,
    embedding_dim, maxlen_en, encoder_dim)
decoder = Decoder(vocab_size_fr+1,
    embedding_dim, maxlen_fr, decoder_dim)
```

Now that we have defined our `Encoder` and `Decoder` classes, let's revisit the dimensions of their inputs and outputs. The following piece of (throwaway) code can be used to print out the dimensions of the various inputs and outputs of the system. It has been left in for convenience as a commented-out block in the code supplied with this chapter:

```
for encoder_in, decoder_in, decoder_out in train_dataset:
    encoder_state = encoder.init_state(batch_size)
    encoder_out, encoder_state = encoder(encoder_in, encoder_state)
    decoder_state = encoder_state
    decoder_pred, decoder_state = decoder(decoder_in, decoder_state)
    break
print("encoder input            :", encoder_in.shape)
print("encoder output           :", encoder_out.shape, "state:", encoder_state.
shape)
print("decoder output (logits):", decoder_pred.shape, "state:", decoder_state.
shape)
print("decoder output (labels):", decoder_out.shape)
```

This produces the following output, which is in line with our expectations. The encoder input is a batch of a sequence of integers, each sequence being of size 8, which is the maximum number of tokens in our English sentences, so its dimension is (`batch_size, maxlen_en`).

The output of the encoder is a single tensor (`return_sequences=False`) of shape (`batch_size, encoder_dim`) and represents a batch of context vectors representing the input sentences. The encoder state tensor has the same dimensions. The decoder outputs are also a batch of sequences of integers, but the maximum size of a French sentence is 16; therefore, the dimensions are (`batch_size, maxlen_fr`).

The decoder predictions are a batch of probability distributions across all time steps; hence, the dimensions are (`batch_size, maxlen_fr, vocab_size_fr+1`), and the decoder state is the same dimension as the encoder state (`batch_size, decoder_dim`):

```
encoder input          : (64, 8)
encoder output         : (64, 1024) state: (64, 1024)
decoder output (logits): (64, 16, 7658) state: (64, 1024)
decoder output (labels): (64, 16)
```

Next, we define the loss function. Because we padded our sentences, we don't want to bias our results by considering the equality of pad words between the labels and predictions. Our loss function masks our predictions with the labels, so any padded positions on the label are also removed from the predictions, and we only compute our loss using the non-zero elements on both the label and predictions. This is done as follows:

```
def loss_fn(ytrue, ypred):
    scce = tf.keras.losses.SparseCategoricalCrossentropy(
        from_logits=True)
    mask = tf.math.logical_not(tf.math.equal(ytrue, 0))
    mask = tf.cast(mask, dtype=tf.int64)
    loss = scce(ytrue, ypred, sample_weight=mask)
    return loss
```

Because the seq2seq model is not easy to package into a simple Keras model, we have to handle the training loop manually as well. Our `train_step()` function handles the flow of data and computes the loss at each step, applies the gradient of the loss back to the trainable weights, and returns the loss.

Notice that the training code is not quite the same as what was described in our discussion of the seq2seq model earlier. Here, it appears that the entire `decoder_input` is fed in one go into the decoder to produce the output offset by one time step, whereas in the discussion, we said that this happens sequentially, where the token generated in the previous time step is used as the input for the next time step.

This is a common technique used to train seq2seq networks, which is called **Teacher Forcing**, where the input to the decoder is the ground truth output instead of the prediction from the previous time step. This is preferred because it makes training faster but also results in some degradation in prediction quality. To offset this, techniques such as **Scheduled Sampling** can be used, where the input is sampled randomly either from the ground truth or the prediction at the previous time step, based on some threshold (this depends on the problem, but usually varies between 0.1 and 0.4):

```
@tf.function
def train_step(encoder_in, decoder_in, decoder_out, encoder_state):
    with tf.GradientTape() as tape:
        encoder_out, encoder_state = encoder(encoder_in, encoder_state)
        decoder_state = encoder_state
        decoder_pred, decoder_state = decoder(
```

```
                decoder_in, decoder_state)
        loss = loss_fn(decoder_out, decoder_pred)

    variables = (encoder.trainable_variables +
        decoder.trainable_variables)
    gradients = tape.gradient(loss, variables)
    optimizer.apply_gradients(zip(gradients, variables))
    return loss
```

The predict() method is used to randomly sample a single English sentence from the dataset and use the model trained so far to predict the French sentence. For reference, the label French sentence is also displayed. The evaluate() method computes the **BiLingual Evaluation Understudy** (**BLEU**) score [35] between the labels and predictions across all records in the test set. BLEU scores are generally used where multiple ground truth labels exist (we have only one) and compare up to 4-grams (n-grams with *n=4*) in both reference and candidate sentences. Both the predict() and evaluate() methods are called at the end of every epoch:

```
  def predict(encoder, decoder, batch_size,
        sents_en, data_en, sents_fr_out,
        word2idx_fr, idx2word_fr):
    random_id = np.random.choice(len(sents_en))
    print("input    : ",  " ".join(sents_en[random_id]))
    print("label    : ",  " ".join(sents_fr_out[random_id]))
    encoder_in = tf.expand_dims(data_en[random_id], axis=0)
    decoder_out = tf.expand_dims(sents_fr_out[random_id], axis=0)
    encoder_state = encoder.init_state(1)
    encoder_out, encoder_state = encoder(encoder_in, encoder_state)
    decoder_state = encoder_state
    decoder_in = tf.expand_dims(
        tf.constant([word2idx_fr["BOS"]]), axis=0)
    pred_sent_fr = []
    while True:
        decoder_pred, decoder_state = decoder(
            decoder_in, decoder_state)
        decoder_pred = tf.argmax(decoder_pred, axis=-1)
        pred_word = idx2word_fr[decoder_pred.numpy()[0][0]]
        pred_sent_fr.append(pred_word)
        if pred_word == "EOS":
            break
        decoder_in = decoder_pred

    print("predicted: ",  " ".join(pred_sent_fr))
```

```python
def evaluate_bleu_score(encoder, decoder, test_dataset,
        word2idx_fr, idx2word_fr):
    bleu_scores = []
    smooth_fn = SmoothingFunction()
    for encoder_in, decoder_in, decoder_out in test_dataset:
        encoder_state = encoder.init_state(batch_size)
        encoder_out, encoder_state = encoder(encoder_in, encoder_state)
        decoder_state = encoder_state
        decoder_pred, decoder_state = decoder(
            decoder_in, decoder_state)
        # compute argmax
        decoder_out = decoder_out.numpy()
        decoder_pred = tf.argmax(decoder_pred, axis=-1).numpy()
        for i in range(decoder_out.shape[0]):
            ref_sent = [idx2word_fr[j] for j in
                decoder_out[i].tolist() if j > 0]
            hyp_sent = [idx2word_fr[j] for j in
                decoder_pred[i].tolist() if j > 0]
            # remove trailing EOS
            ref_sent = ref_sent[0:-1]
            hyp_sent = hyp_sent[0:-1]
            bleu_score = sentence_bleu([ref_sent], hyp_sent,
                smoothing_function=smooth_fn.method1)
            bleu_scores.append(bleu_score)
    return np.mean(np.array(bleu_scores))
```

The training loop is shown as follows. We will use the Adam optimizer for our model. We also set up a checkpoint so that we can save our model after every 10 epochs. We then train the model for 250 epochs, and print out the loss, an example sentence and its translation, and the BLEU score computed over the entire test set:

```python
optimizer = tf.keras.optimizers.Adam()
checkpoint_prefix = os.path.join(checkpoint_dir, "ckpt")
checkpoint = tf.train.Checkpoint(optimizer=optimizer,
                                 encoder=encoder,
                                 decoder=decoder)
num_epochs = 250
eval_scores = []
for e in range(num_epochs):
    encoder_state = encoder.init_state(batch_size)
    for batch, data in enumerate(train_dataset):
        encoder_in, decoder_in, decoder_out = data
```

```
    # print(encoder_in.shape, decoder_in.shape, decoder_out.shape)
    loss = train_step(
        encoder_in, decoder_in, decoder_out, encoder_state)

print("Epoch: {}, Loss: {:.4f}".format(e + 1, loss.numpy()))
if e % 10 == 0:
    checkpoint.save(file_prefix=checkpoint_prefix)

predict(encoder, decoder, batch_size, sents_en, data_en,
    sents_fr_out, word2idx_fr, idx2word_fr)
eval_score = evaluate_bleu_score(encoder, decoder,
    test_dataset, word2idx_fr, idx2word_fr)
print("Eval Score (BLEU): {:.3e}".format(eval_score))
# eval_scores.append(eval_score)
checkpoint.save(file_prefix=checkpoint_prefix)
```

The results from the first 5 and last 5 epochs of training are shown as follows. Notice that the loss has gone down from about 1.5 to around 0.07 in epoch 247. The BLEU scores have also gone up by around 2.5 times. Most impressive, however, is the difference in translation quality between the first 5 and last 5 epochs:

Epoch-#	Loss (Training)	BLEU Score (Test)	English	French (true)	French (predicted)
1	1.4119	1.957e-02	tom is special.	tom est special.	elle est tres bon.
2	1.1067	2.244e-02	he hates shopping.	il deteste faire les courses.	il est tres mineure.
3	0.9154	2.700e-02	did she say it?	l a t elle dit?	n est ce pas clair?
4	0.7817	2.803e-02	i d rather walk.	je prefererais marcher.	je suis alle a kyoto.
5	0.6632	2.943e-02	i m in the car.	je suis dans la voiture.	je suis toujours inquiet.
...					
245	0.0896	4.991e-02	she sued him.	elle le poursuivit en justice.	elle l a poursuivi en justice.
246	0.0853	5.011e-02	she isn t poor.	elle n est pas pauvre.	elle n est pas pauvre.
247	0.0738	5.022e-02	which one is mine?	lequel est le mien?	lequel est le mien?

248	0.1208	4.931e-02	i m getting old.	je me fais vieux.	je me fais vieux.
249	0.0837	4.856e-02	it was worth a try.	ca valait le coup d essayer.	ca valait le coup d essayer.
250	0.0967	4.869e-02	don t back away.	ne reculez pas!	ne reculez pas!

Table 5.2: Training results by epoch

The full code for this example can be found in the source code accompanying this chapter. You will need a GPU-based machine to run it, although you may be able to run it on the CPU using smaller network dimensions (embedding_dim, encoder_dim, decoder_dim), smaller hyperparameters (batch_size, num_epochs), and a smaller number of sentence pairs. To run the code in its entirety, run the following command. The output will be written to the console:

```
$ python seq2seq_wo_attn.py
```

In the next section, we will look at a mechanism to improve the performance of the seq2seq network, by allowing it to focus on certain parts of the input more than on others in a data-driven way. This mechanism is known as the attention mechanism.

Attention mechanism

In the previous section, we saw how the context or thought vector from the last time step of the encoder is fed into the decoder as the initial hidden state. As the context flows through the time steps on the decoder, the signal gets combined with the decoder output and progressively gets weaker and weaker. The result is that the context does not have much effect on the later time steps in the decoder.

In addition, certain sections of the decoder output may depend more heavily on certain sections of the input. For example, consider an input "thank you very much," and the corresponding output "merci beaucoup" for an English-to-French translation network such as the one we looked at in the previous section. Here, the English phrases "thank you," and "very much," correspond to the French "merci" and "beaucoup" respectively. This information is also not conveyed adequately through the single context vector.

The attention mechanism provides access to all encoder hidden states at every time step on the decoder. The decoder learns which part of the encoder states to pay more attention to. The use of attention has resulted in great improvements to the quality of machine translation, as well as a variety of standard natural language processing tasks.

The use of attention is not limited to seq2seq networks. For example, attention is a key component in the "Embed, Encode, Attend, Predict" formula for creating state-of-the-art deep learning models for NLP [34]. Here, attention has been used to preserve as much information as possible when downsizing from a larger to a more compact representation, for example, when reducing a sequence of word vectors into a single sentence vector.

Essentially, the attention mechanism provides a way to score tokens in the target against all tokens in the source and modify the input signal to the decoder accordingly. Consider an encoder-decoder architecture where the input and output time steps are denoted by indices i and j respectively, and the hidden states on the encoder and decoder at these respective time steps are denoted by h_i and s_j. Inputs to the encoder are denoted by x_i, and outputs from the decoder are denoted by y_j. In an encoder-decoder network without attention, the value of decoder state s_j is given by the hidden state s_{j-1} and output y_{j-1} at the previous time step. The attention mechanism adds a third signal c_j, known as the attention context. With attention, therefore, the decoder's hidden state s_j is a function of y_{j-1}, s_{j-1}, and c_j, which is shown as follows:

$$s_j = f(y_{j-1}, s_{j-1}, c_j)$$

The attention context signal c_j is computed as follows. For every decoder step j, we compute the alignment between the decoder state s_{j-1} and every encoder state h_i. This gives us a set of N similarity values e_{ij} for each decoder state j, which we then convert into a probability distribution by computing their corresponding softmax values b_{ij}. Finally, the attention context c_j is computed as the weighted sum of the encoder states h_i and their corresponding softmax weights b_{ij} over all N encoder time steps. The set of equations shown encapsulates this transformation for each decoder step j:

$$e_{ij} = align(h_i, s_{j-1}) \forall i$$
$$b_{ij} = softmax(e_{ij})$$
$$c_j = \sum_{i=0}^{N} h_i\, b_{ij}$$

Multiple attention mechanisms have been proposed based on how the alignment is done. We will describe a few next. For notational convenience, we will indicate the state vector h_i on the encoder side with h, and the state vector s_{j-1} on the decoder side with s.

The simplest formulation of alignment is **content-based attention**. It was proposed by Graves, Wayne, and Danihelka [27], and is just the cosine similarity between the encoder and decoder states. A precondition for using this formulation is that the hidden state vector on both the encoder and decoder must have the same dimensions:

$$e = cosine(h, s)$$

Another formulation, known as **additive** or **Bahdanau attention**, was proposed by Bahdanau, Cho, and Bengio [28]. This involves combining the state vectors using learnable weights in a small neural network, given by the following equation. Here, the s and h vectors are concatenated and multiplied by the learned weights W, which is equivalent to using two learned weights W_s and W_h to multiply with s and h, and adding the results:

$$e = v^T \tanh(W[s; h])$$

Luong, Pham, and Manning [29] proposed a set of three attention formulations (dot, general, and concat), of which the general formulation is also known as the **multiplicative** or **Luong's attention**.

The dot and concat attention formulations are similar to the content-based and additive attention formulations discussed earlier. The multiplicative attention formulation is given by the following equation:

$$e = h^T W s$$

Finally, Vaswani, et al. [30] proposed a variation on content-based attention, called the **scaled dot-product attention**, which is given by the following equation. Here, N is the dimension of the encoder hidden state h. Scaled dot-product attention is used in transformer architecture, which we will learn about in the next chapter:

$$e = \frac{h^T s}{\sqrt{N}}$$

Attention mechanisms can also be categorized by what they attend to. Using this categorization scheme attention mechanisms can be self-attention, global or soft attention, and local or hard attention.

Self-attention is when the alignment is computed across different sections of the same sequence and has been found to be useful for applications such as machine reading, abstractive text summarization, and image caption generation.

Soft or global attention is when the alignment is computed over the entire input sequence, and hard or local attention is when the alignment is computed over part of the sequence. The advantage of soft attention is that it is differentiable; however, it can be expensive to compute. Conversely, hard attention is cheaper to compute at inference time but is non-differentiable and requires more complicated techniques during training.

In the next section, we will see how to integrate the attention mechanism with a seq2seq network and how it improves performance.

Example – seq2seq with attention for machine translation

Let's look at the same example of machine translation that we saw earlier in this chapter, except that the decoder will now attend to the encoder outputs using the additive attention mechanism proposed by Bahdanau, et al. [28], and the multiplicative one proposed by Luong, et al [29].

The first change is to the encoder. Instead of returning a single context or thought vector, it will return outputs at every time point, because the attention mechanism will need this information. Here is the revised encoder class with the change highlighted:

```
class Encoder(tf.keras.Model):
    def __init__(self, vocab_size, num_timesteps,
            embedding_dim, encoder_dim, **kwargs):
        super(Encoder, self).__init__(**kwargs)
        self.encoder_dim = encoder_dim
        self.embedding = tf.keras.layers.Embedding(
            vocab_size, embedding_dim, input_length=num_timesteps)
        self.rnn = tf.keras.layers.GRU(
```

```
                    encoder_dim, return_sequences=True, return_state=True)
        def call(self, x, state):
            x = self.embedding(x)
            x, state = self.rnn(x, initial_state=state)
            return x, state
        def init_state(self, batch_size):
            return tf.zeros((batch_size, self.encoder_dim))
```

The decoder will have bigger changes. The biggest is the declaration of attention layers, which need to be defined, so let's do that first. Let's first consider the class definition for the additive attention proposed by Bahdanau. Recall that this combines the decoder hidden state at each time step with all the encoder hidden states to produce an input to the decoder at the next time step, which is given by the following equation:

$$e = v^T \tanh(W[s; h])$$

The $W[s;h]$ in the equation is shorthand for two separate linear transformations (of the form $y = Wx + b$), one on s, and the other on h. The two linear transformations are implemented as dense layers, as shown in the following implementation. We subclass a tf.keras Layer object since our end goal is to use this as a layer in our network, but it is also acceptable to subclass a Model object. The call() method takes the query (the decoder state) and values (the encoder states), computes the score, then the alignment as the corresponding softmax, and context vector as given by the equation, and then returns them. The shape of the context vector is given by (batch_size, num_decoder_timesteps), and the alignments have the shape (batch_size, num_encoder_timesteps, 1). The weights for the dense layer's W1, W2, and V tensors are learned during training:

```
    class BahdanauAttention(tf.keras.layers.Layer):
        def __init__(self, num_units):
            super(BahdanauAttention, self).__init__()
            self.W1 = tf.keras.layers.Dense(num_units)
            self.W2 = tf.keras.layers.Dense(num_units)
            self.V = tf.keras.layers.Dense(1)
        def call(self, query, values):
            # query is the decoder state at time step j
            # query.shape: (batch_size, num_units)
            # values are encoder states at every timestep i
            # values.shape: (batch_size, num_timesteps, num_units)
            # add time axis to query: (batch_size, 1, num_units)
            query_with_time_axis = tf.expand_dims(query, axis=1)
            # compute score:
            score = self.V(tf.keras.activations.tanh(
                self.W1(values) + self.W2(query_with_time_axis)))
            # compute softmax
            alignment = tf.nn.softmax(score, axis=1)
```

```
        # compute attended output
        context = tf.reduce_sum(
            tf.linalg.matmul(
                tf.linalg.matrix_transpose(alignment),
                values
            ), axis=1
        )
        context = tf.expand_dims(context, axis=1)
        return context, alignment
```

The Luong attention is multiplicative, but the general implementation is similar. Instead of declaring three linear transformations W1, W2, and V, we only have a single one W. The steps in the call() method follow the same general steps – first, we compute the scores according to the equation for Luong's attention, as described in the last section. Then, we compute the alignments as the corresponding softmax version of the scores and then the context vector as the dot product of the alignment and the values. Like the weights in the Bahdanau attention class, the weight matrices represented by the dense layer W are learned during training:

```
class LuongAttention(tf.keras.layers.Layer):
    def __init__(self, num_units):
        super(LuongAttention, self).__init__()
        self.W = tf.keras.layers.Dense(num_units)
    def call(self, query, values):
        # add time axis to query
        query_with_time_axis = tf.expand_dims(query, axis=1)
        # compute score
        score = tf.linalg.matmul(
            query_with_time_axis, self.W(values), transpose_b=True)
        # compute softmax
        alignment = tf.nn.softmax(score, axis=2)
        # compute attended output
        context = tf.matmul(alignment, values)
        return context, alignment
```

To verify that the two classes are drop-in replacements for each other, we run the following piece of throwaway code (commented out in the source code for this example). We just manufacture some random inputs and send them to both attention classes:

```
batch_size = 64
num_timesteps = 100
num_units = 1024
query = np.random.random(size=(batch_size, num_units))
values = np.random.random(size=(batch_size, num_timesteps, num_units))
# check out dimensions for Bahdanau attention
```

```
b_attn = BahdanauAttention(num_units)
context, alignments = b_attn(query, values)
print("Bahdanau: context.shape:", context.shape,
    "alignments.shape:", alignments.shape)
# check out dimensions for Luong attention
l_attn = LuongAttention(num_units)
context, alignments = l_attn(query, values)
print("Luong: context.shape:", context.shape,
    "alignments.shape:", alignments.shape)
```

The preceding code produces the following output and shows, as expected, that the two classes produce identically shaped outputs when given the same input. Hence, they are drop-in replacements for each other:

```
Bahdanau: context.shape: (64, 1024) alignments.shape: (64, 8, 1)
Luong: context.shape: (64, 1024) alignments.shape: (64, 8, 1)
```

Now that we have our attention classes, let's look at the decoder. The difference in the init() method is the addition of the attention class variable, which we have set to the BahdanauAttention class. In addition, we have two additional transformations, Wc and Ws, that will be applied to the output of the decoder RNN. The first one has a tanh activation to modulate the output between -1 and +1, and the next one is a standard linear transformation. Compared to the seq2seq network without an attention decoder component, this decoder takes an additional parameter encoder_output in its call() method and returns an additional context vector:

```
class Decoder(tf.keras.Model):
    def __init__(self, vocab_size, embedding_dim, num_timesteps,
            decoder_dim, **kwargs):
        super(Decoder, self).__init__(**kwargs)
        self.decoder_dim = decoder_dim
        self.attention = BahdanauAttention(embedding_dim)
        # self.attention = LuongAttention(embedding_dim)

        self.embedding = tf.keras.layers.Embedding(
            vocab_size, embedding_dim, input_length=num_timesteps)
        self.rnn = tf.keras.layers.GRU(
            decoder_dim, return_sequences=True, return_state=True)
        self.Wc = tf.keras.layers.Dense(decoder_dim, activation="tanh")
        self.Ws = tf.keras.layers.Dense(vocab_size)
    def call(self, x, state, encoder_out):
        x = self.embedding(x)
        context, alignment = self.attention(x, encoder_out)
        x = tf.expand_dims(
                tf.concat([
```

```
                    x, tf.squeeze(context, axis=1)
                ], axis=1),
            axis=1)
        x, state = self.rnn(x, state)
        x = self.Wc(x)
        x = self.Ws(x)
        return x, state, alignment
```

The training loop is also a little different. Unlike the seq2seq without attention network, where we used teacher forcing to speed up training, using attention means that we now have to consume the decoder input one by one. This is because the decoder output at the previous step influences more strongly, through attention, the output at the current time step. Our new training loop is described by the train_step function below and is significantly slower than the training loop on the seq2seq network without attention. However, this kind of training loop may be used on the former network as well, especially when we want to implement scheduled sampling strategies:

```
@tf.function
def train_step(encoder_in, decoder_in, decoder_out, encoder_state):
    with tf.GradientTape() as tape:
        encoder_out, encoder_state = encoder(encoder_in, encoder_state)
        decoder_state = encoder_state
        loss = 0
        for t in range(decoder_out.shape[1]):
            decoder_in_t = decoder_in[:, t]
            decoder_pred_t, decoder_state, _ = decoder(decoder_in_t,
                decoder_state, encoder_out)
            loss += loss_fn(decoder_out[:, t], decoder_pred_t)
    variables = (encoder.trainable_variables +
        decoder.trainable_variables)
    gradients = tape.gradient(loss, variables)
    optimizer.apply_gradients(zip(gradients, variables))
    return loss / decoder_out.shape[1]
```

The predict() and evaluate() methods also have similar changes, since they also implement the new data flow on the decoder side that involves an extra encoder_out parameter and an extra context return value.

We trained two versions of the seq2seq network with attention, one with additive (Bahdanau) attention and one with multiplicative (Luong) attention. Both networks were trained for 50 epochs instead of 250. However, in both cases, translations were produced with a quality similar to that obtained from the seq2seq network without attention trained for 250 epochs. The training losses at the end of training for the seq2seq networks with either attention mechanism were marginally lower, and the BLEU scores on the test sets were slightly higher, compared with the seq2seq network without attention:

Network Description	Ending Loss (training set)	Ending BLEU score (test set)
seq2seq without attention, trained for 250 epochs	0.0967	4.869e-02
seq2seq with additive attention, trained for 50 epochs	0.0893	5.508e-02
seq2seq with multiplicative attention, trained for 50 epochs	0.0706	5.563e-02

Table 5.3: BLEU scores for the different methods

Here are some examples of the translations produced by the two networks. Epoch numbers and the type of attention used are mentioned with each example. Notice that even when the translations are not 100% the same as the labels, many of them are valid translations of the original:

Attention Type	Epoch-#	English	French (label)	French (predicted)
Bahdanau	20	your cat is fat.	ton chat est gras.	ton chat est mouille.
	25	i had to go back.	il m a fallu retourner.	il me faut partir.
	30	try to find it.	tentez de le trouver.	tentez de le trouver.
Luong	20	that s peculiar.	c est etrange.	c est deconcertant.
	25	tom is athletic.	thomas est sportif.	tom est sportif.
	30	it s dangerous.	c est dangereux.	c est dangereux.

Table 5.4: Examples of English-to-French translations

The full code for the network described here is in the `seq2seq_with_attn.py` file in the code folder for this chapter. To run the code from the command line, please use the following command. You can switch between Bahdanau (additive) or Luong (multiplicative) attention mechanisms by commenting out one or the other in the `init()` method of the `Decoder` class:

```
$ python seq2seq_with_attn.py
```

Summary

In this chapter, we learned about RNNs, a class of networks that is specialized for dealing with sequences such as natural language, time series, speech, and so on. Just like CNNs exploit the geometry of images, RNNs exploit the sequential structure of their inputs. We learned about the basic RNN cell, how it handles state from previous time steps, and how it suffers from vanishing and exploding gradients because of inherent problems with BPTT. We saw how these problems lead to the development of novel RNN cell architectures such as LSTM, GRU, and peephole LSTMs. We also learned about some simple ways to make your RNN more effective, such as making it bidirectional or stateful.

We then looked at different RNN topologies and how each topology is adapted to a particular set of problems. After a lot of theory, we finally saw examples of three of these topologies. We then focused on one of these topologies, called seq2seq, which first gained popularity in the machine translation community, but has since been used in situations where the use case can be adapted to look like a machine translation problem.

From here, we looked at attention, which started as a way to improve the performance of seq2seq networks but has since been used very effectively in many situations where we want to compress the representation while keeping the data loss to a minimum. We looked at different kinds of attention and an example of using them in a seq2seq network with attention.

In the next chapter, you will learn about transformers, a state-of-the-art encoder-decoder architecture where the recurrent layers have been replaced by attention layers.

References

1. Jozefowicz, R., Zaremba, R. and Sutskever, I. (2015). *An Empirical Exploration of Recurrent Neural Network Architectures*. Journal of Machine Learning

2. Greff, K., et al. (July 2016). *LSTM: A Search Space Odyssey*. IEEE Transactions on Neural Networks and Learning Systems

3. Bernal, A., Fok, S., and Pidaparthi, R. (December 2012). *Financial Markets Time Series Prediction with Recurrent Neural Networks*

4. Hadjeres, G., Pachet, F., and Nielsen, F. (August 2017). *DeepBach: a Steerable Model for Bach Chorales Generation*. Proceedings of the 34th International Conference on Machine Learning (ICML)

5. Karpathy, A. (2015). *The Unreasonable Effectiveness of Recurrent Neural Networks*. URL: http://karpathy.github.io/2015/05/21/rnn-effectiveness/

6. Karpathy, A., Li, F. (2015). *Deep Visual-Semantic Alignments for Generating Image Descriptions*. Conference on Pattern Recognition and Pattern Recognition (CVPR)

7. Socher, et al. (2013). *Recursive Deep Models for Sentiment Compositionality over a Sentiment Treebank*. Proceedings of the 2013 Conference on Empirical Methods in Natural Language Processing (EMNLP)

8. Bahdanau, D., Cho, K., and Bengio, Y. (2015). *Neural Machine Translation by Jointly Learning to Align and Translate*. arXiv: 1409.0473 [cs.CL]

9. Wu, Y., et al. (2016). *Google's Neural Machine Translation System: Bridging the Gap between Human and Machine Translation*. arXiv 1609.08144 [cs.CL]

10. Vinyals, O., et al. (2015). *Grammar as a Foreign Language*. Advances in Neural Information Processing Systems (NIPS)

11. Rumelhart, D. E., Hinton, G. E., and Williams, R. J. (1985). *Learning Internal Representations by Error Propagation*. Parallel Distributed Processing: Explorations in the Microstructure of Cognition

12. Britz, D. (2015). *Recurrent Neural Networks Tutorial, Part 3 - Backpropagation Through Time and Vanishing Gradients*: http://www.wildml.com/2015/10/recurrent-neural-networks-tutorial-part-3-backpropagation-through-time-and-vanishing-gradients/

13. Pascanu, R., Mikolov, T., and Bengio, Y. (2013). *On the difficulty of training Recurrent Neural Networks*. Proceedings of the 30th International Conference on Machine Learning (ICML)

14. Hochreiter, S., and Schmidhuber, J. (1997). *LSTM can solve hard long time lag problems*. Advances in Neural Information Processing Systems (NIPS)

15. Britz, D. (2015). *Recurrent Neural Network Tutorial, Part 4 – Implementing a GRU/LSTM RNN with Python and Theano*: `http://www.wildml.com/2015/10/recurrent-neural-network-tutorial-part-4-implementing-a-grulstm-rnn-with-python-and-theano/`

16. Olah, C. (2015). *Understanding LSTM Networks*: `https://colah.github.io/posts/2015-08-Understanding-LSTMs/`

17. Cho, K., et al. (2014). *Learning Phrase Representations using RNN Encoder-Decoder for Statistical Machine Translation*. arXiv: 1406.1078 [cs.CL]

18. Shi, X., et al. (2015). *Convolutional LSTM Network: A Machine Learning Approach for Precipitation Nowcasting*. arXiv: 1506.04214 [cs.CV]

19. Gers, F.A., and Schmidhuber, J. (2000). *Recurrent Nets that Time and Count*. Proceedings of the IEEE-INNS-ENNS International Joint Conference on Neural Networks (IJCNN)

20. Kotzias, D. (2015). *Sentiment Labeled Sentences Dataset*, provided as part of "From Group to Individual Labels using Deep Features" (KDD 2015): `https://archive.ics.uci.edu/ml/datasets/Sentiment+Labelled+Sentences`

21. Collobert, R., et al (2011). *Natural Language Processing (Almost) from Scratch*. Journal of Machine Learning Research (JMLR)

22. Marcus, M. P., Santorini, B., and Marcinkiewicz, M. A. (1993). *Building a large annotated corpus of English: the Penn Treebank*. Journal of Computational Linguistics

23. Bird, S., Loper, E., and Klein, E. (2009). *Natural Language Processing with Python, O'Reilly Media Inc*. Installation: `https://www.nltk.org/install.html`

24. Liu, C., et al. (2017). *MAT: A Multimodal Attentive Translator for Image Captioning*. arXiv: 1702.05658v3 [cs.CV]

25. Suilin, A. (2017). *Kaggle Web Traffic Time Series Forecasting*. GitHub repository: `https://github.com/Arturus/kaggle-web-traffic`

26. Tatoeba Project. (1997-2019). Tab-delimited Bilingual Sentence Pairs: `http://tatoeba.org` and `http://www.manythings.org/anki`

27. Graves, A., Wayne, G., and Danihelka, I. (2014). *Neural Turing Machines*. arXiv: 1410.5401v2 [cs.NE]

28. Bahdanau, D., Cho, K., and Bengio, Y. (2015). *Neural Machine Translation by jointly learning to Align and Translate*. arXiv: 1409.0473v7 [cs.CL]

29. Luong, M., Pham, H., and Manning, C. (2015). *Effective Approaches to Attention-based Neural Machine Translation*. arXiv: 1508.04025v5 [cs.CL]

30. Vaswani, A., et al. (2017). *Attention Is All You Need*. 31st Conference on Neural Information Processing Systems (NeurIPS)

31. Zhang, A., Lipton, Z. C., Li, M., and Smola, A. J. (2019). *Dive into Deep Learning*: `http://www.d2l.ai`

32. Ba, J. L., Kiros, J. R., and Hinton, G. E. (2016). *Layer Normalization*. arXiv: 1607.06450v1 [stat.ML]

33. Allamar, J. (2018). *The Illustrated Transformer*: `http://jalammar.github.io/illustrated-transformer/`

34. Honnibal, M. (2016). *Embed, encode, attend, predict: The new deep learning formula for state-of-the-art NLP models*: `https://explosion.ai/blog/deep-learning-formula-nlp`

35. Papineni, K., Roukos, S., Ward, T., and Zhu, W. (2002). *BLEU: A Method for Automatic Evaluation of Machine Translation*. Proceedings of the 40th Annual Meeting for the Association of Computational Linguistics (ACL)

36. Project Gutenberg (2019): `https://www.gutenberg.org/`

Join our book's Discord space

Join our Discord community to meet like-minded people and learn alongside more than 2000 members at: `https://packt.link/keras`

6

Transformers

The transformer-based architectures have become almost universal in **Natural Language Processing** (**NLP**) (and beyond) when it comes to solving a wide variety of tasks, such as:

- Neural machine translation
- Text summarization
- Text generation
- Named entity recognition
- Question answering
- Text classification
- Text similarity
- Offensive message/profanity detection
- Query understanding
- Language modeling
- Next-sentence prediction
- Reading comprehension
- Sentiment analysis
- Paraphrasing

and a lot more.

In less than four years, when the *Attention Is All You Need* paper was published by Google Research in 2017, transformers managed to take the NLP community by storm, breaking any record achieved over the previous thirty years.

Transformer-based models use the so-called attention mechanisms that identify complex relationships between words in each input sequence, such as a sentence. Attention helped resolve the challenge of encoding "pairwise correlations"—something that its "predecessors," such as LSTM RNNs and even CNNS, couldn't achieve when modeling sequential data, such as text.

Models—such as BERT, T5, and GPT (covered in more detail later in this chapter)—now constitute the state-of-the-art fundamental building blocks for new applications in almost every field, from computer vision to speech recognition, translation, or protein and coding sequences. Attention has also been applied in reinforcement learning for games: in DeepMind's AlphaStar (`https://rdcu.be/bVI7G` and `https://www.deepmind.com/blog/alphastar-grandmaster-level-in-starcraft-ii-using-multi-agent-reinforcement-learning`), observations of player and opponent StarCraft game units were processed with self-attention, for example. For this reason, Stanford has recently introduced the term "foundation models" to define a set of **Large Language Models (LLMs)** based on giant pretrained transformers.

This progress has been made thanks to a few simple ideas, which we are going to review in the next few sections.

You will learn:

- What transformers are
- How they evolved over time
- Some optimization techniques
- Dos and don'ts
- What the future will look like

Let's start turning our attention to transformers. You will be surprised to discover that attention indeed is all you need!

Architecture

Even though a typical transformer architecture is usually different from that of recurrent networks, it is based on several key ideas that originated in RNNs. At the time of writing this book, the transformer represents the next evolutionary step of deep learning architectures related to texts and any data that can be represented as sequences, and as such, it should be an essential part of your toolbox.

The original transformer architecture is a variant of the encoder-decoder architecture, where the recurrent layers are replaced with (self-)attention layers. The transformer was initially proposed by Google in the seminal paper titled *Attention Is All You Need* by Ashish Vaswani, Noam Shazeer, Niki Parmar, Jakob Uszkoreit, Llion Jones, Aidan N. Gomez, Lukasz Kaiser, and Illia Polosukhin, 2017, `https://arxiv.org/abs/1706.03762`, to which a reference implementation was provided, which we will refer to throughout this discussion.

The architecture is an instance of the encoder-decoder models that have been popular since 2014-2015 (such as *Sequence to Sequence Learning with Neural Networks* by Sutskever et al. (2014), `https://arxiv.org/abs/1409.3215`). Prior to that, attention had been used together with **Long-Short-Term Memory (LSTM)** and other **RNN (Recurrent Neural Network)** models discussed in a previous chapter. Attention was introduced in 2014 in *Neural Machine Translation by Jointly Learning to Align and Translate* by Bahdanau et al., `https://arxiv.org/abs/1409.0473`, and applied to neural machine translation in 2015 in *Effective Approaches to Attention-based Neural Machine Translation* by Luong et al., `https://arxiv.org/abs/1508.04025`, and there have been other combinations of attention with other types of models.

In 2017, the first transformer demonstrated that you could remove LSTMs from **Neural Machine Translation (NMT)** models and use the so-called (self-)attention blocks (hence the paper title *Attention Is All You Need*).

Key intuitions

Let's start by defining some concepts that will be useful later on in this chapter. The innovation introduced with the transformer in 2017 is based on four main key ideas:

- Positional encoding
- Attention
- Self-attention
- Multi-head (self-)attention

In the next sections, we will discuss them in greater detail.

Positional encoding

RNNs keep the word order by processing words sequentially. The advantage of this approach is simplicity, but one of the disadvantages is that this makes parallelization hard (training on multiple hardware accelerators). If we want to effectively leverage highly parallel architectures, such as GPUs and TPUs, we'd need an alternative way to represent ordering.

The transformer uses a simple alternative order representation called positional encoding, which associates each word with a number representing its position in the text. For instance:

```
[("Transformers", 1), ("took", 2), ("NLP", 3), ("by", 4), ("storm", 5)]
```

The key intuition is that enriching transformers with a position allows the model to learn the importance of the position of each token (a word in the text/sentence). Note that positional encoding existed before transformers (as discussed in the chapter on RNNs), but this intuition is particularly important in the context of creating transformer-based models. After (absolute) positional encoding was introduced in the original transformer paper, there have been other variants, such as relative positional encoding (*Self-Attention with Relative Position Representations* by Shaw et al., 2018, https://arxiv.org/abs/1803.02155, and rotary positional encoding (*RoFormer: Enhanced Transformer with Rotary Position Embedding* by Su et al., 2021, https://arxiv.org/abs/2104.09864).

Now that we have defined positional encoding, let's turn our attention to the *attention* mechanism.

Attention

Another crucial ingredient of the transformer recipe is attention. This mechanism was first introduced in the context of machine translation in 2014 by Bahdanou et al. in *Neural Machine Translation by Jointly Learning to Align and Translate* by Dzmitry Bahdanau, KyungHyun Cho, and Yoshua Bengio, https://arxiv.org/pdf/1409.0473.pdf. Some research papers also attribute the idea behind attention to Alex Graves' *Generating Sequences with Recurrent Neural Networks*, which dates back to 2013, https://arxiv.org/pdf/1308.0850.pdf.

This ingredient—this key idea—has since become a part of the title of the first transformer paper, *Attention is All You Need*. To get a high-level overview, let's consider this example from the paper that introduced attention:

The agreement on the European Economic Area was signed in August 1992.

In French, this can be translated as:

L'accord sur la zone économique européenne a été signé en août 1992.

The initial attempts to perform automatic machine translation back in the early 80s were based on the sequential translation of each word. This approach was very limiting because the text structure can change from a source language to a target language in many ways. For instance, some words in the French translation can have a different order: in English, adjectives usually precede nouns, like in "European Economic Area," whereas in French, adjectives can go after nouns—"la zone économique européenne." Moreover, unlike in English, the French language has gendered words. So, for example, the adjectives "économique" and "européenne" must be in their feminine form as they belong to the feminine noun "la zone."

The key intuition behind the attention approach is to build a text model that "looks at" every single word in the source sentence when translating words into the output language. In the original 2017 transformer paper, the authors point out that the cost of doing this is quadratic, but the gain achieved in terms of more accurate translation is considerable. More recent works reduced this initial quadratic complexity, such as the **Fast Attention Via positive Orthogonal Random** (**FAVOR+**) features from the *Rethinking Attention with Performers* paper by Choromanski et al. (2020) from Google, DeepMind, the University of Cambridge, and the Alan Turing Institute.

Let's go over a nice example from that original attention paper by Bahdanou et al. (2014):

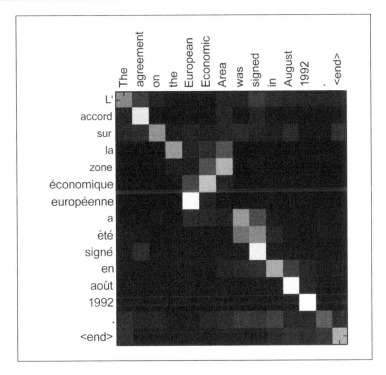

Figure 6.1: An example of attention for the English sentence "The agreement on the European Economic Area was signed in August 1992." The plot visualizes "annotation weights"—the weights associated with the annotations. Source: "Neural Machine Translation by Jointly Learning to Align and Translate" by Bahdanau et al. (2014) (https://arxiv.org/abs/1409.0473)

Using the attention mechanism, the neural network can learn a heatmap of each source English word in relation to each target French word. Note that relationships are not only on the diagonal but might spread across the whole matrix. For instance, when the model outputs the French word "européenne," it will pay a lot of attention to the input words "European" and "Economic." (In *Figure 6.1*, this corresponds to the diagonal and the adjacent cell.) The 2014 attention paper by Bahdanou et al. demonstrated that the model (which used an RNN encoder-decoder framework with attention) can *learn to align and attend* to the input elements without supervision, and, as *Figure 6.1* shows, translate the input English sentences into French. And, of course, the larger the training set is, the greater the number of correlations that the attention-based model can learn.

In short, the attention mechanism can access all previous words and weigh them according to a *learned* measure of relevancy. This way, attention can provide relevant information about tokens located far away in the target sentence.

Now, we can focus on another key ingredient of the transformer—"self-attention."

Self-attention

The third key idea popularized by the original transformer paper is the use of attention within the same sentence in the source language—self-attention. With this mechanism, neural networks can be trained to learn the relationships among all words (or other elements) in each input sequence (such as a sentence) irrespective of their positions before focusing on (machine) translation. Self-attention can be attributed to the idea from the 2016 paper called *Long Short-Term Memory-Networks for Machine Reading* by Cheng et al., `https://arxiv.org/pdf/1601.06733.pdf`.

Let's go through an example with the following two sentences:

"Server, can I have the check?"

"Looks like I just crashed the server."

Clearly, the word "server" has a very different meaning in either sentence and self-attention can understand each word considering the context of the surrounding words. Just to reiterate, the attention mechanism can access all previous words and weigh them according to a learned measure of relevancy. Self-attention provides relevant information about tokens located far away in the source sentence.

Multi-head (self-)attention

The original transformer performs a (self-)attention function multiple times. A single set of the so-called weight matrices (which are covered in detail in the *How to compute Attention* section) is named an attention head. When you have several sets of these matrices, you have multiple attention heads. The multi-head (self-)attention layer usually has several parallel (self-)attention layers. Note that the introduction of multiple heads allows us to have many definitions of which word is "relevant" to each other. Plus, all these definitions of relevance can be computed in parallel by modern hardware accelerators, thus speeding up the computation.

Now that we have gone through the high-level definitions of the key ingredients of the transformers, let's deep dive into how to compute the attention mechanism.

How to compute attention

In the original transformer, the self-attention function is computed by using the so-called scaled dot-product units. The authors of the 2017 paper even called their attention method *Scaled Dot-Product Attention*. You might remember from high school studies that the dot-product between two vectors provides a good sense of how "close" the vectors are.

Each input token sequence (for example, of a sentence) embedding that passes into the transformer (encoder and/or decoder) produces *attention weights* (covered in detail below) that are simultaneously calculated between every sequence element (such as a word). The output results in embeddings produced for every token containing the token itself together with every other relevant token weighted by its relative attention weight.

The attention layer transforms the input vectors into query, key, and value matrices, which are then split into attention heads (hence, multi-head attention):

- The query word can be interpreted as the word *for which* we are calculating the attention function.
- The key and value words are the words *to which* we are paying attention.

The dot-product (explained further below) tells us the similarity between words. If the vectors for two words are more aligned, the *attention score* will be higher. The transformer will learn the weights in such a way that if two words in a sentence are relevant to each other, then their word vectors will be aligned.

Each attention layer learns three weight matrices:

- The query weights W_Q
- The key weights W_K
- The value weights W_V

For each word i, an input word embedding x_i is computed producing:

- A query vector $q_i = x_i W_Q$
- A key vector $k_i = x_i W_K$
- A value vector $v_i = x_i W_V$

Given the query and the corresponding key vectors, the following dot-product formula produces the *attention weight* in the original transformer paper:

$$a_{i,j} = q_i . k_j$$

where:

- $a_{i,j}$ is the attention from word i to a word j.
- . is the dot-product of the query with keys, which will give a sense of how "close" the vectors are.

Note that the attention unit for word i is the weighted sum of the value vectors of all words, weighted by $a_{i,j}$, the attention from word i to a word j.

Now, to stabilize gradients during the training, the attention weights are divided by the square root of the dimension of the key vectors $\sqrt{d_k}$.

Then, the results are passed through a softmax function to normalize the weight. Note that the attention function from a word i to a word j is not the same as the attention from word j to a word i.

Note that since modern deep learning accelerators work well with matrices, we can compute attention for all words using large matrices.

Define q_i, k_i, v_i (where i is the ith row) as matrices Q, K, V, respectively. Then, we can summarize the attention function as an attention matrix:

$$Attention(Q, K, V) = softmax(\frac{QK^T}{\sqrt{d_k}})$$

In this section, we discussed how to compute the attention function introduced in the original transformer paper. Next, let's discuss the encoder-decoder architecture.

Encoder-decoder architecture

Similar to the seq2seq models, (*Sequence to Sequence Learning with Neural Networks* by Ilya Sutskever, Oriol Vinyals, Quoc V. Le (2014)) described in *Chapter 5, Recurrent Neural Networks,* the original transformer model also used an encoder-decoder architecture:

- The encoder takes the input (source) sequence of embeddings and transforms it into a new fixed-length vector of input embeddings.

- The decoder takes the output embeddings vector from the encoder and transforms it into a sequence of output embeddings.

- Both the encoder and the decoder consist of several stacked layers. Each encoder and decoder layer is using the attention mechanism described earlier.

We'll learn about the transformer architecture in much more detail later in this section.

Since the introduction of the transformer architecture, other newer networks have used only the encoder or the decoder components (or both), which are discussed in the *Categories of transformers* section of this chapter.

Next, let's briefly go over the other components of the original transformer—the residual and normalization layers.

Residual and normalization layers

Typically, transformer-based networks reuse other existing state-of-the-art machine learning methodologies, such as attention mechanisms. You shall therefore not be surprised if both encoder and decoder layers combine neural networks with residual connections (*Deep Residual Learning for Image Recognition* by He et al., 2016, https://arxiv.org/abs/1512.03385) and normalization steps (*Layer Normalization* by Ba et al., 2016, https://arxiv.org/abs/1607.06450).

OK, we now have all the key ingredients to deep dive into transformers.

An overview of the transformer architecture

Now that we have covered some of the key concepts behind the original transformer, let's deep dive into the architecture introduced in the seminal 2017 paper. Note that transformer-based models are usually built by leveraging various attention mechanisms without using RNNs. This is also a consequence of the fact that attention mechanisms themselves can match and outperform RNN (encoder-decoder) models with attention. That's why the seminal paper was titled *Attention is all You Need.*

Figure 6.2 shows a seq2seq network with RNNs and attention, and compares it to the original transformer network.

The transformer is similar to seq2seq with an attention model in the following ways:

- Both approaches work with source (inputs) and target (output) *sequences.*
- Both use an encoder-decoder architecture, as mentioned before.
- The output of the last block of the encoder is used as a context—or thought vector—for computing the attention function in the decoder.

- The target (output) sequence embeddings are fed into dense (fully connected) blocks, which convert the output embeddings to the final sequence of an integer form:

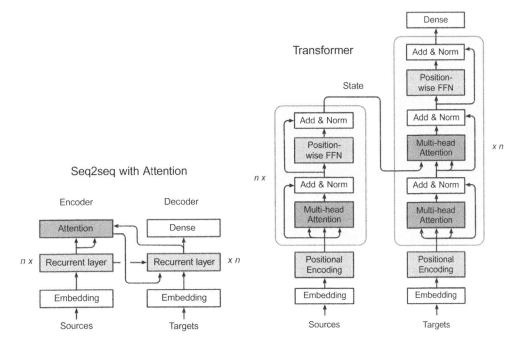

Figure 6.2: Flow of data in (a) seq2seq + Attention, and (b) Transformer architecture. Image Source: Zhang, et al.

And the two architectures differ in the following ways:

- The seq2seq network uses the recurrent and attention layers in the encoder, and the recurrent layer in the decoder.

  The transformer replaced those layers with so-called transformer blocks (a stack of N identical layers), as *Figure 6.2* demonstrates:

  - In the encoder, the transformer block consists of a sequence of sub-layers: a multi-head (self-)attention layer and a position-wise feedforward layer. Each of those two layers has a residual connection, followed by a normalization layer.
  - In the decoder, the transformer block contains a variant of a multi-head (self-)attention layer with *masking*—a masked multi-head self-attention—and a feedforward layer like in the encoder (with identical residual connections and normalization layers). Masking helps prevent positions from attending into the future. Additionally, the decoder contains a second multi-head (self-)attention layer which computes attention over the outputs of the encoder's transformer blockmasking is covered in more detail later in this section.)

- In the seq2seq with attention network, the encoder state is passed to the first recurrent time step as with the seq2seq with attention network.

In the transformer, the encoder state is passed to every transformer block in the decoder. This allows the transformer network to work in parallel across time steps since there is no longer a temporal dependency as with the seq2seq networks.

The last decoder is followed by a final linear transformation (a dense layer) with a softmax function to produce the output (next-token) probabilities.

- Because of the parallelism referred to in the previous point, an encoding layer is added to provide positional information to distinguish the position of each element in the transformer network sequence (positional encoding layer). This way, the first encoder takes the positional information and embeddings of the input sequence as inputs, rather than only encodings, thus allowing taking positional information into account.

Let's walk through the process of data flowing through the transformer network. Later in this chapter, we will use TensorFlow with the Keras API to create and train a transformer model from scratch:

1. As part of data preprocessing, the inputs and the outputs are tokenized and converted to embeddings.

2. Next, positional encoding is applied to the input and output embeddings to have information about the relative position of tokens in the sequences. In the encoder section:

   - As per *Figure 6.2*, the encoder side consists of an embedding and a positional encoding layer, followed by six identical transformer blocks (there were six "layers" in the original transformer). As we learned earlier, each transformer block in the encoder consists of a multi-head (self-)attention layer and a position-wise feedforward layer.

We have already briefly seen that self-attention is the process of attending to parts of the same sequence. When we process a sentence, we might want to know what other words are most aligned with the current one.

   - The multi-head attention layer consists of multiple (eight in the reference implementation contained in the seminal paper) parallel self-attention layers. Self-attention is carried out by constructing three vectors Q (query), K (key), and V (value), out of the input embedding. These vectors are created by multiplying the input embedding with three trainable weight matrices W_Q, W_K, and W_V. The output vector Z is created by combining K, Q, and V at each self-attention layer using the following formula. Here, d_K refers to the dimension of the K, Q, and V vectors (64 in the reference implementation contained in the seminal paper):

$$z = softmax(\frac{QK^T}{\sqrt{d_k}})V$$

   - The multi-head attention layer will create multiple values for Z (based on multiple trainable weight matrices W_Q, W_K, and W_V at each self-attention layer), and then concatenate them for inputs into the position-wise feedforward layer.

- The inputs to the position-wise feedforward layer consist of embeddings for the different elements in the sequence (or words in the sentence), attended via self-attention in the multi-head attention layer. Each token is represented internally by a fixed-length embedding vector (512 in the reference implementation introduced in the seminal paper). Each vector is run through the feedforward layer in parallel. The outputs of the FFN are the inputs to (or fed into) the multi-head attention layer in the following transformer block. In the last transformer block of the encoder, the outputs are the context vector that is passed to the decoder.

- Both the multi-head attention and position-wise FFN layers send out not only the signal from the previous layer but also a residual signal from their inputs to their outputs. The outputs and residual inputs are passed through a layer-normalization step, and this is shown in *Figure 6.2* as the "Add & Norm" layer.

- Since the entire sequence is consumed in parallel on the encoder, the information about the positions of individual elements gets lost. To compensate for this, the input embeddings are augmented with a positional embedding, which is implemented as a sinusoidal function without learned parameters. The positional embedding is added to the input embedding.

3. Next, let's walk through how the data flows through the decoder:

- The output of the encoder results in a pair of attention vectors K and V, which are sent in parallel to all the transformer blocks in the decoder. The transformer block in the decoder is similar to that in the encoder, except that it has an additional multi-head attention layer to handle the attention vectors from the encoder. This additional multi-head attention layer works similarly to the one in the encoder and the one below it, except that it combines the Q vector from the layer below it and the K and Q vectors from the encoder state.

- Similar to the seq2seq network, the output sequence generates one token at a time, using the input from the previous time step. As for the input to the encoder, the input to the decoder is also augmented with a positional embedding. Unlike the encoder, the self-attention process in the decoder is only allowed to attend to tokens at previous time points. This is done by masking out tokens at future time points.

- The output of the last transformer block in the decoder is a sequence of low-dimensional embeddings (512 for reference implementation in the seminal paper as noted earlier). This is passed to the dense layer, which converts it into a sequence of probability distributions across the target vocabulary, from which we generate the most probable word either greedily or by a more sophisticated technique such as beam search.

Figure 6.3 shows the transformer architecture covering everything that's just been described:

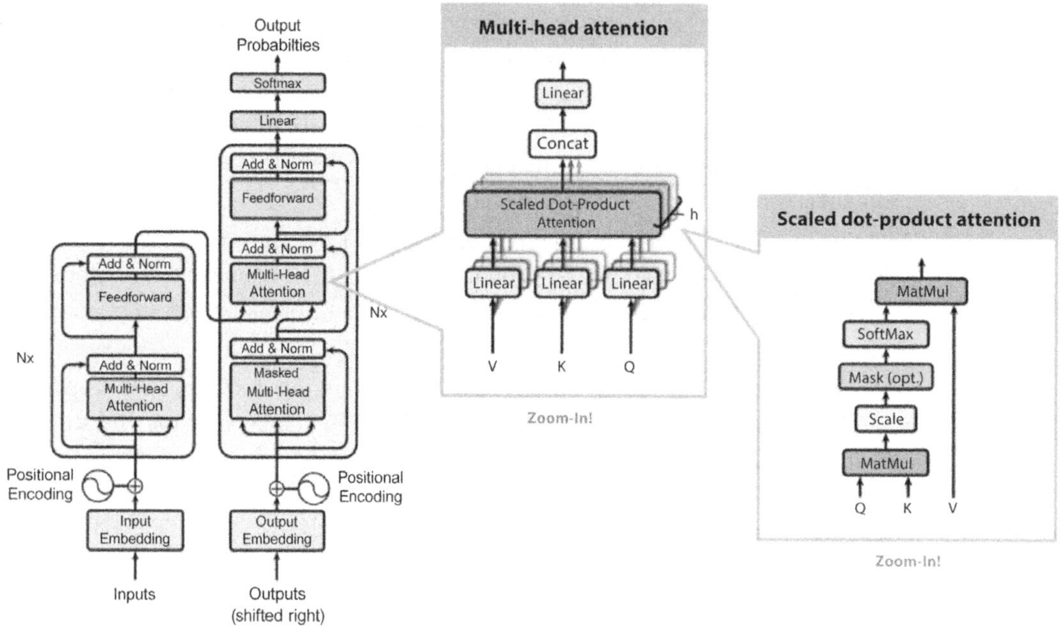

*Figure 6.3: The transformer architecture based on original images from "Attention Is All You Need"
by Vaswani et al. (2017)*

Training

Transformers are typically trained via semi-supervised learning in two steps:

1.   First, an unsupervised pretraining, typically on a very large corpus.
2.   Then, a supervised fine-tuning on a smaller labeled dataset.

Both pretraining and fine-tuning might require significant resources in terms of GPU/TPU, memory, and time. This is especially true, considering that large language models (in short, LLMs) have an increasing number of parameters as we will see in the next section.

Sometimes, the second phase has a very limited set of labeled data. This is the so-called few-shot learning, which considers making predictions based on a limited number of samples.

Transformers' architectures

In this section, we have provided a high-level overview of both the most important architectures used by transformers and of the different ways used to compute attention.

Categories of transformers

In this section, we are going to classify transformers into different categories. The next paragraph will introduce the most common transformers.

Decoder or autoregressive

A typical example is a **GPT** (**Generative Pre-Trained**) model, which you can learn more about in the GPT-2 and GPT-3 sections later in this chapter, or refer to `https://openai.com/blog/language-unsupervised`). Autoregressive models use only the decoder of the original transformer model, with the attention heads that can only see what is before in the text and not after with a masking mechanism used on the full sentence. Autoregressive models use pretraining to guess the next token after observing all the previous ones. Typically, autoregressive models are used for **Natural Language Generation** (**NLG**) text generation tasks. Other examples of autoregressive models include the original GPT, GPT-2, Transformer-XL, Reformer, and XLNet, which are covered later in this chapter.

Encoder or autoencoding

A typical example is **BERT** (**Bidirectional Encoder Representations from Transformers**), which is covered later in this chapter. Autoencoders correspond to the encoder in the original transformer model having access to the full input tokens with no masks. Autoencoding models use pretraining by masking/altering the input tokens and then trying to reconstruct the original sentence. Frequently, the models build a bidirectional representation of the full sentences. Note that the only difference between autoencoders and autoregressive is the pretraining phase, so the same architecture can be used in both ways. Autoencoders can be used for NLG, as well as for classification and many other NLP tasks. Other examples of autoencoding models, apart from BERT, include ALBERT, RoBERTa, and ELECTRA, which you can learn about later in this chapter.

Seq2seq

A typical example is **T5** (**Text-to-Text Transfer Transformer**) and the original transformer. Sequence-to-sequence models use both the encoder and the decoder of the original transformer architecture. Seq2seq can be fine-tuned to many tasks such as translation, summarization, ranking, and question answering. Another example of a seq2seq model, apart from the original transformer and T5, is **Multitask Unified Model** (**MUM**).

Multimodal

A typical example is MUM. Multimodal models mix text inputs with other kinds of content (for example, images, videos, and audio).

Retrieval

A typical example is RETRO. Some models use document retrieval during (pre)training and inference. This is frequently a good strategy to reduce the size of the model and rapidly access memorized information saving on the number of used parameters.

Attention

Now that we have understood how to classify transformers, let's focus on attention!

There is a wide variety of attention mechanisms, such as self-attention, local/hard attention, and global/soft attention, to name a few. Below, we'll focus on some of the examples.

Full versus sparse

As discussed, the (scaled) dot-product attention from the original 2017 transformer paper is typically computed on a full squared matrix $O(L^2)$ where L is the length of the maximal considered sequence (in some configurations $L = 512$). The BigBird type of transformer, proposed by Google Research in 2020 and discussed in more detail later in this chapter, introduced the idea of using sparse attention by leveraging sparse matrices (based on the 2019 work by OpenAI's *Generating long sequences with sparse transformers* by Child et al., https://arxiv.org/abs/1904.10509).

LSH attention

The Reformer introduced the idea of reducing the attention mechanism complexity with hashing—the model's authors called it locality-sensitive hashing attention. The approach is based on the notion of using only the largest elements when $softmax(QK^T)$ is computed. In other words, for each query $q \in Q$ only the keys $k \in K$ that are close to q are computed. For computing closeness, several hash functions are computed according to local sensitive hashing techniques.

Local attention

Some transformers adopted the idea of having only a local window of context (e.g. a few tokens on the right and a few tokens on the left). The idea is that using fewer parameters allows us to consider longer sequences but with a limited degree of attention. For this reason, local attention is less popular.

Pretraining

As you have learned earlier, the original transformer had an encoder-decoder architecture. However, the research community understood that there are situations where it is beneficial to have only the encoder, or only the decoder, or both.

Encoder pretraining

As discussed, these models are also called auto-encoding and they use only the encoder during the pretraining. Pretraining is carried out by masking words in the input sequence and training the model to reconstruct the sequence. Typically, the encoder can access all the input words. Encoder-only models are generally used for classification.

Decoder pretraining

Decoder models are referred to as autoregressive. During pretraining, the decoder is optimized to predict the next word. In particular, the decoder can only access all the words positioned before a given word in the sequence. Decoder-only models are generally used for text generation.

Encoder-decoder pretraining

In this case, the model can use both the encoder and the decoder. Attention in the encoder can use all the words in the sequence, while attention in the decoder can only use the words preceding a given word in the sequence. Encoder-decoder has a large range of applications including text generation, translation, summarization, and generative question answer.

A taxonomy for pretraining tasks

It can be useful to organize pretraining into a taxonomy suggested by *Pre-trained Models for Natural Language Processing: A Survey*, Xipeng Qiu, 2020, `https://arxiv.org/abs/2003.08271`:

- **Language Modeling (LM):** For unidirectional LM, the task is to predict the next token. For bidirectional LM, the task is to predict the previous and next tokens.

- **Masked Language Modeling (MLM):** The key idea is to mask out some tokens from the input sentences. Then, the model is trained to predict the masked tokens given the non-masked tokens.

- **Permuted Language Modeling (PLM):** This is similar to LM, but a random permutation of input sequences is performed. Then, a subset of tokens is chosen as the target, and the model is trained to predict these targets.

- **Denoising Autoencoder (DAE):** Deliberately provide partially corrupted input. For instance, randomly sample input tokens and replace them with special [MASK] elements. Alternatively, randomly delete input tokens. Alternatively, shuffle sentences in random order. The task is to recover the original undistorted input.

- **Contrastive Learning (CTL):** The task is to learn a score function for text pairs by assuming that some observed pairs of text are more semantically similar than randomly sampled text. This class of techniques includes a number of specific techniques such as:

  - **Deep InfoMax (DIM):** Maximize mutual information between an input image representation and various local regions of the same image.

  - **Replaced Token Detection (RTD):** Predict whether an input token is replaced given its surroundings.

  - **Next Sentence Prediction (NSP):** The model is trained to distinguish whether two input sentences are contiguous in the training corpus.

  - **Sentence Order Prediction (SOP):** The same ideas as NSP with some additional signals: two consecutive segments are positive examples, and two swapped segments are negative examples.

In this section, we have briefly reviewed different pretraining techniques. The next section will review a selection of the most used transformers.

An overview of popular and well-known models

After the seminal paper *Attention is All You Need*, a very large number of alternative transformer-based models have been proposed. Let's review some of the most popular and well-known ones.

BERT

BERT, or Bidirectional Encoder Representations from Transformers, is a language representation model developed by the Google AI research team in 2018. Let's go over the main intuition behind that model:

1. BERT considers the context of each word from both the left and the right side using the so-called "bidirectional self-attention."

2. Training happens by randomly masking the input word tokens, and avoiding cycles so that words cannot see themselves indirectly. In NLP jargon, this is called "fill in the blank." In other words, the pretraining task involves masking a small subset of unlabeled inputs and then training the network to recover these original inputs. (This is an example of MLM.)

3. The model uses classification for pretraining to predict whether a sentence sequence S is before a sentence T. This way, BERT can understand relationships among sentences ("Next Sentence Prediction"), such as "does sentence T come after sentence S?" The idea of pretraining became a new standard for LLM.

4. BERT—namely BERT Large—became one of the first large language models with 24 transformer blocks, 1024-hidden layers, 16 self-attention heads, and 340M parameters. The model is trained on a large 3.3 billion words corpus.

BERT produced state-of-the-art results for 11 NLP tasks, including:

- GLUE score of 80.4%, a 7.6% absolute improvement from the previous best result.

- 93.2% accuracy on SQuAD 1.1 and outperforming human performance by 2%.

We will see GLUE and SQuAD metrics later in this chapter. If you want to know more, you can explore the following material:

- The original research paper: *BERT: Pre-training of Deep Bidirectional Transformers for Language Understanding* by Jacob Devlin, Ming-Wei Chang, Kenton Lee, Kristina Toutanova, 2018, `https://arxiv.org/abs/1810.04805`.

- The Google AI blog post: *Open Sourcing BERT: State-of-the-Art Pre-training for Natural Language Processing*, 2018, which discusses the advancement of the (then) state-of-the-art model for 11 NLP tasks (`https://ai.googleblog.com/2018/11/open-sourcing-bert-state-of-art-pre.html`.)

- An open source TensorFlow implementation and the pretrained BERT models are available at `http://goo.gl/language/bert` and from TensorFlow Model Garden at `https://github.com/tensorflow/models/tree/master/official/nlp/modeling/models`.

- A Colab notebook for BERT is available here: `https://colab.research.google.com/github/tensorflow/tpu/blob/master/tools/colab/bert_finetuning_with_cloud_tpus.ipynb`.

- BERT FineTuning with Cloud TPU: A tutorial that shows how to train the BERT model on Cloud TPU for sentence and sentence-pair classification tasks: `https://cloud.google.com/tpu/docs/tutorials/bert`.

- A Google blog post about applying BERT to Google Search to improve language understanding. According to Google, BERT *"will help Search better understand one in 10 searches in the U.S. in English."* Moreover, the post mentions that *"A powerful characteristic of these systems is that they can take learnings from one language and apply them to others. So we can take models that learn from improvements in English (a language where the vast majority of web content exists) and apply them to other languages."* (from *Understanding search better than ever before*): `https://blog.google/products/search/search-language-understanding-bert/`.

GPT-2

GPT-2 is a model introduced by OpenAI in *Language Models Are Unsupervised Multitask Learners* by Alec Radford, Jeffrey Wu, Rewon Child, David Luan, Dario Amodei, and Ilya Sutskever, `https://openai.com/blog/better-language-models/`, `https://openai.com/blog/gpt-2-6-month-follow-up/`, `https://www.openai.com/blog/gpt-2-1-5b-release/`, and `https://github.com/openai/gpt-2.`)

Let's review the key intuitions:

- The largest of four model sizes was a 1.5 billion-parameter transformer with 48 layers trained on a new dataset called Webtext containing text from 45 million webpages.

- GPT-2 used the original 2017 transformer-based architecture and a modified version of the original GPT model (also developed by OpenAI) by Radford et al., 2018, *Improving Language Understanding by Generative Pre-Training*, `https://openai.com/blog/language-unsupervised/`, and `https://cdn.openai.com/research-covers/language-unsupervised/language_understanding_paper.pdf`).

- The research demonstrated that an LLM trained on a large and diverse dataset can perform well on a wide variety of NLP tasks, such as question answering, machine translation, reading comprehension, and summarization. Previously, the tasks had been typically approached with supervised learning on task-specific datasets. GPT-2 was trained in an unsupervised manner and performed well at zero-shot task transfer.

- Initially, OpenAI released only a smaller version of GPT-2 with 117 M parameters, "due to concerns about large language models being used to generate deceptive, biased, or abusive language at scale." Then, the model was released: `https://openai.com/blog/gpt-2-1-5b-release/`.

- Interestingly enough, OpenAI developed an ML-based detection method to test whether an actor is generating synthetic texts for propaganda. The detection rates were ~95% for detecting 1.5B GPT-2-generated text: `https://github.com/openai/gpt-2-output-dataset`.

Similar to the original GPT from 2018, GPT-2 does not require the encoder part of the original transformer model – it uses a multi-layer decoder for language modeling. The decoder can only get information from the prior words in the sentence. It takes word vectors as input and produces estimates for the probability of the next word as output, but it is *autoregressive*, meaning that each token in the sentence relies on the context of the previous words. On the other hand, BERT is not autoregressive, as it uses the entire surrounding context all at once.

GPT-2 was the first LLM showing commonsense reasoning, capable of performing a number of NLP tasks including translation, question answering, and reading comprehension. The model achieved state-of-the-art results on 7 out of 8 tested language modeling datasets.

GPT-3

GPT-3 is an autoregressive language model developed by OpenAI and introduced in 2019 in *Language Models are Few-Shot Learners* by Tom B. Brown, et al., `https://arxiv.org/abs/2005.14165`. Let's look at the key intuitions:

- GPT-3 uses an architecture and model similar to GPT-2 with a major difference consisting of the adoption of a sparse attention mechanism.

- For each task, the model evaluation has three different approaches:

  - **Few-shot learning:** The model receives a few demonstrations of the task (typically, less than one hundred) at inference time. However, no weight updates are allowed.

  - **One-shot learning:** The model receives only one demonstration and a natural language description of the task.

  - **Zero-shot learning:** The model receives no demonstration, but it has access only to a natural language description of the task.

- For all tasks, GPT-3 is applied without any gradient updates, complete with tasks and few-shot demonstrations specified purely via text interaction with the model.

The number of parameters the researchers trained GPT-3 with ranges from 125 million (GPT-3 Small) to 175 billion (GPT-3 175B). With no fine-tuning, the model achieves significant results on many NLP tasks including translation and question answering, sometimes surpassing state-of-the-art models. In particular, GPT-3 showed impressive results in NLG, creating news articles that were hard to distinguish from real ones. The model demonstrated it was able to solve tasks requiring on-the-fly reasoning or domain adaptation, such as unscrambling words, using a novel word in a sentence, or performing 3-digit arithmetic.

GPT-3's underlying model is not publicly available and we can't pretrain the model, but some datasets statistics are available at `https://github.com/openai/gpt-3` and we can run data on and fine-tune GPT-3 engines.

Reformer

The Reformer model was introduced in the 2020 paper *Reformer: The Efficient Transformer* by UC Berkeley and Google AI researchers Nikita Kitaev, Łukasz Kaiser, and Anselm Levskaya, `https://arxiv.org/abs/2001.04451`.

Let's look at the key intuitions:

- The authors demonstrated you can train the Reformer model, which performs on par with transformer models in a more memory-efficient and faster way on long sequences.

- One limitation of transformers is the capacity of dealing with long sequences, due to the quadratic time needed for computing attention.

- Reformer addresses the computations and memory challenges during the training of transformers by using three techniques.

- First, Reformer replaced the (scaled) dot-product attention with an approximation using locality-sensitive hashing attention (described briefly earlier in this chapter). The paper's authors changed the former's $O(L^2)$ factor in attention layers with $O(LlogL)$, where L is the length of the sequence (see *Figure 6.4* where LSH is applied to chunks in sequence). Refer to local sensitive hashing introduced in computer science to learn more: `https://en.wikipedia.org/wiki/Locality-sensitive_hashing`.

- Second, the model combined the attention and feedforward layers with reversible residual layers instead of normal residual layers (based on the idea from *The reversible residual network: Backpropagation without storing activations* by Gomez et al., 2017, `https://proceedings.neurips.cc/paper/2017/hash/f9be311e65d81a9ad8150a60844bb94c-Abstract.html`). Reversible residual layers allow for storage activations once instead of N times, thus reducing the cost in terms of memory and time complexity.

- Third, Reformer used a chunking technique for certain computations, including one for the feedforward layer and for a backward pass.

- You can read the Google AI blog post to learn more about how the Reformer reached efficiency at `https://ai.googleblog.com/2020/01/reformer-efficient-transformer.html`:

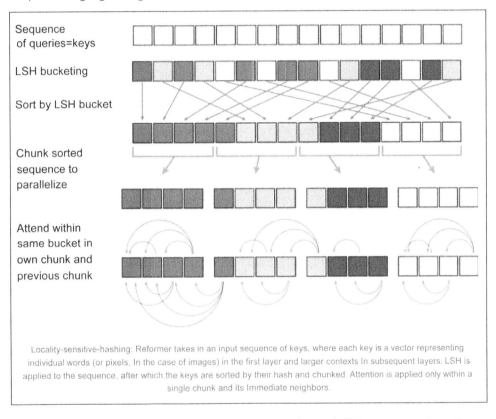

Figure 6.4: Local Sensitive Hashing to improve the transformers' efficiency – source: https://ai.googleblog.com/2020/01/reformer-efficient-transformer.html

BigBird

BigBird is another type of transformer introduced in 2020 by Google Research that uses a sparse attention mechanism for tackling the quadratic complexity needed to compute full attention for long sequences. For a deeper overview, see the paper *Big Bird: Transformers for Longer Sequences* by Manzil Zaheer, Guru Guruganesh, Avinava Dubey, Joshua Ainslie, Chris Alberti, Santiago Ontanon, Philip Pham, Anirudh Ravula, Qifan Wang, Li Yang, and Amr Ahmed, `https://arxiv.org/pdf/2007.14062.pdf`.

Let's look at the key intuitions:

- The authors demonstrated that BigBird was capable of handling longer context—much longer sequences of up to 8x with BERT on similar hardware. Its performance was "drastically" better on certain NLP tasks, such as question answering and document summarization.

- BigBird runs on a sparse attention mechanism for overcoming the quadratic dependency of BERT. Researchers proved that the complexity reduced from $O(L^2)$ to $O(L)$.

- This way, BigBird can process sequences of length up to 8x more than what was possible with BERT. In other words, BERT's limit was 512 tokens and BigBird increased to 4,096 tokens.

Transformer-XL

Transformer-XL is a self-attention-based model introduced in 2019 by Carnegie Mellon University and Google Brain researchers in the paper *Transformer-XL: Attentive Language Models Beyond a Fixed-Length Context* by Zihang Dai, Zhilin Yang, Yiming Yang, Jaime Carbonell, Quoc V. Le, and Ruslan Salakhutdinov, https://aclanthology.org/P19-1285.pdf.

Let's look at the key intuitions:

- Unlike the original transformer and RNNs, Transformer-XL demonstrated it can model longer-term dependency beyond a fixed-length context while generating relatively coherent text.

- Transformer-XL introduced a new segment-level recurrence mechanism and a new type of relative positional encodings (as opposed to absolute ones), allowing the model to learn dependencies that are 80% longer than RNNs and 450% longer than vanilla transformers. Traditionally, transformers split the entire corpus into shorter segments due to computational limits and only train the model within each segment.

- During training, the hidden state sequence computed for the previous segment is fixed and cached to be reused as an extended context when the model processes the following new segment, as shown in *Figure 6.5*. Although the gradient still remains within a segment, this additional input allows the network to exploit information in history, leading to an ability of modeling longer-term dependency and avoiding context fragmentation.

- During evaluation, the representations from the previous segments can be reused instead of being computed from scratch as in the vanilla model case. This way, Transformer-XL proved to be up to 1,800+ times faster than the vanilla model during evaluation:

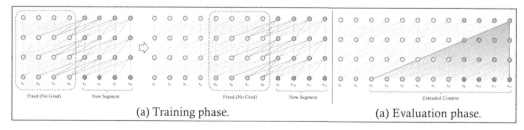

Figure 6.5: Transformer-XL and the input with recurrent caching of previous segments

XLNet

XLNet is an unsupervised language representation learning method developed by Carnegie Mellon University and Google Brain researchers in 2019. It is based on generalized permutation language modeling objectives. XLNet employs Transformer-XL as a backbone model. The reference paper here is *XLNet: Generalized Autoregressive Pre-training for Language Understanding* by Zhilin Yang, Zihang Dai, Yiming Yang, Jaime Carbonell, Ruslan Salakhutdinov, and Quoc V. Le, `https://arxiv.org/abs/1906.08237`.

Let's see the key intuitions:

- Like BERT, XLNet uses a bidirectional context, looking at the words before and after a given token to predict what it should be.
- XLNet maximizes the expected log-likelihood of a sequence with respect to all possible permutations of the factorization order. Thanks to the permutation operation, the context for each position can consist of tokens from both left and right. In other words, XLNet captures bidirectional context.
- XLNet outperforms BERT on 20 tasks and achieves state-of-the-art results on 18 tasks.
- Code and pretrained models are available here: `https://github.com/zihangdai/xlnet`.

XLNet is considered better than BERT in almost all NLP tasks, outperforming BERT on 20 tasks, often by a large margin. When it was introduced, the model achieved state-of-the-art performance on 18 NLP tasks, including sentiment analysis, natural language inference, question answering, and document ranking.

RoBERTa

RoBERTa (a Robustly Optimized BERT) is a model introduced in 2019 by researchers at the University of Washington and Facebook AI (Meta) in *RoBERTa: A Robustly Optimized BERT Pretraining Approach* by Yinhan Liu, Myle Ott, Naman Goyal, Jingfei Du, Mandar Joshi, Danqi Chen, Omer Levy, Mike Lewis, Luke Zettlemoyer, and Veselin Stoyanov, `https://arxiv.org/abs/1907.11692`.

Let's look at the key intuitions:

- When replicating BERT, the researchers discovered that BERT was "significantly undertrained."
- RoBERTa's authors proposed a BERT variant that modifies key hyperparameters (longer training, larger batches, more data), removing the next-sentence pretraining objective, and training on longer sequences. The authors also proposed dynamically changing the masking pattern applied to the training data.
- The researchers collected a new dataset called CC-News of similar size to other privately used datasets.
- The code is available here: `https://github.com/pytorch/fairseq`.

RoBERTa outperformed BERT on GLUE and SQuAD tasks and matched XLNet on some of them.

ALBERT

ALBERT (**A Lite BERT**) is a model introduced in 2019 by researchers at Google Research and Toyota Technological Institute at Chicago in the paper titled *ALBERT: A Lite BERT for Self-supervised Learning of Language Representations* by Zhenzhong Lan, Mingda Chen, Sebastian Goodman, Kevin Gimpel, Piyush Sharma, and Radu Soricut, https://arxiv.org/abs/1909.11942v1.

Let's see the key intuitions:

- Large models typically aim at increasing the model size when pretraining natural language representations in order to get improved performance. However, increasing the model size might become difficult due to GPU/TPU memory limitations, longer training times, and unexpected model degradation.

- ALBERT attempts to address the memory limitation, the communication overhead, and model degradation problems with an architecture that incorporates two parameter-reduction techniques: factorized embedding parameterization and cross-layer parameter sharing. With factorized embedding parameterization, the size of the hidden layers is separated from the size of vocabulary embeddings by decomposing the large vocabulary-embedding matrix into two small matrices. With cross-layer parameter sharing, the model prevents the number of parameters from growing along with the network depth. Both of these techniques improved parameter efficiency without "seriously" affecting the performance.

- ALBERT has 18x fewer parameters and 1.7x faster training compared to the original BERT-Large model and achieves only slightly worse performance.

- The code is available here: https://github.com/brightmart/albert_zh.

ALBERT claimed it established new state-of-the-art results on all of the current state-of-the-art language benchmarks like GLUE, SQuAD, and RACE.

StructBERT

StructBERT is a model introduced in 2019's paper called *StructBERT: Incorporating Language Structures into Pre-training for Deep Language Understanding* by Wei Wang, Bin Bi, Ming Yan, Chen Wu, Zuyi Bao, Jiangnan Xia, Liwei Peng, and Luo Si, https://arxiv.org/abs/1908.04577.

Let's see the key intuitions:

- The Alibaba team suggested extending BERT by leveraging word-level and sentence-level ordering during the pretraining procedure. BERT masking during pretraining is extended by mixing up a number of tokens and then the model has to predict the right order.

- In addition, the model randomly shuffles the sentence order and predicts the next and the previous sentence with a specific prediction task.

- This additional wording and sentence shuffling together with the task of predicting the original order allow StructBERT to learn linguistic structures during the pretraining procedure.

StructBERT from Alibaba claimed to have achieved state-of-the-art results on different NLP tasks, such as sentiment classification, natural language inference, semantic textual similarity, and question answering, outperforming BERT.

T5 and MUM

In 2019, Google researchers introduced a framework dubbed Text-to-Text Transfer Transformer (in short, T5) in *Exploring the Limits of Transfer Learning with a Unified Text-to-Text Transformer* by Colin Raffel, Noam Shazeer, Adam Roberts, Katherine Lee, Sharan Narang, Michael Matena, Yanqi Zhou, Wei Li, and Peter J. Liu, `https://arxiv.org/abs/1910.10683`. This paper is a fundamental one for transformers.

Here are some of the key ideas:

- T5 addresses many NLP tasks as a "text-to-text" problem. T5 is a single model (with different numbers of parameters) that can be trained on a wide number of tasks. The framework is so powerful that it can be applied to summarization, sentiment analysis, question answering, and machine translation.

- Transfer learning, where a model is first pretrained on a data-rich task before being fine-tuned on a downstream task, is extensively analyzed by comparing pretraining objectives, architectures, unlabeled datasets, transfer approaches, and other factors on dozens of language understanding tasks.

- Similar to the original transformer, T5: 1) uses an encoder-decoder structure; 2) maps the input sequences to learned embeddings and positional embeddings, which are passed to the encoder; 3) uses self-attention blocks with self-attention and feedforward layers (each with normalization and skip connections) in both the encoder and the decoder.

- Training happens on a "Colossal Clean Crawled Corpus" (C4) dataset and the number of parameters per each T5 model varies from 60 million (T5 Small) up to 11 billion.

- The computation costs were similar to BERT, but with twice as many parameters.

- The code is available here: `https://github.com/google-research/text-to-text-transfer-transformer`.

- Google also offers T5 with a free TPU in a Colab tutorial at `https://colab.research.google.com/github/google-research/text-to-text-transfer-transformer/blob/main/notebooks/t5-trivia.ipynb`. We will discuss this in more detail later this chapter.

When presented, the T5 model with 11 billion parameters achieved state-of-the-art performances on 17 out of 24 tasks considered and became de-facto one of the best LMs available:

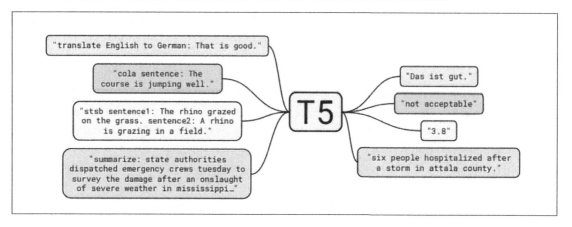

Figure 6.6: T5 uses the same model, loss function, hyperparameters, etc. across our diverse set of tasks —including translation, question answering, and classification

mT5, developed by Xue et al. at Google Research in 2020, extended T5 by using a single transformer to model multiple languages. It was pretrained on a Common Crawl-based dataset covering 101 languages. You can read more about it in *mT5: A Massively Multilingual Pre-trained Text-to-Text Transformer*, https://arxiv.org/pdf/2010.11934.pdf.

MUM (short for **Multitask Unified Model**) is a model using the T5 text-to-text framework and according to Google is 1,000 times more powerful than BERT. Not only does MUM understand language, but it also generates it. It is also multimodal, covering modalities like text and images (expanding to more modalities in the future). The model was trained across 75 different languages and many different tasks at once. MUM is currently used to support Google Search ranking: https://blog.google/products/search/introducing-mum/.

ELECTRA

ELECTRA is a model introduced in 2020 by Stanford University and Google Brain researchers in *ELECTRA: Pre-training Text Encoders as Discriminators Rather Than Generators* by Kevin Clark, Minh-Thang Luong, Quoc V. Le, and Christopher D. Manning, https://arxiv.org/abs/2003.10555.

Let's look at the key intuitions:

- BERT pretraining consists of masking a small subset of unlabeled inputs and then training the network to recover them. Typically only a small fraction of words are used (~15%).

- The ELECTRA authors proposed a new pretraining task named "replaced token detection." The idea is to replace some tokens with alternatives generated by a small language model. Then, the pretrained discriminator is used to predict whether each token is an original or a replacement. This way, the model can learn from all the tokens instead of a subset:

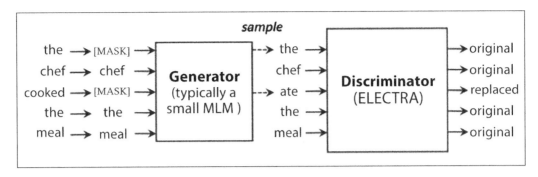

Figure 6.7: ELECTRA replacement strategy. The discriminator's task is to detect whether the word is an original one or a replacement – source: https://arxiv.org/pdf/2003.10555.pdf

ELECTRA outperformed previous state-of-the-art models, requiring at the same time less pretraining efforts. The code is available at https://github.com/google-research/electra.

DeBERTa

DeBERTa is a model introduced by Microsoft's researchers in 2020 in *DeBERTa: Decoding-enhanced BERT with Disentangled Attention* by Pengcheng He, Xiaodong Liu, Jianfeng Gao, and Weizhu Chen, https://arxiv.org/abs/2006.03654.

Let's look at the most important ideas:

- BERT's self-attention is focused on content-to-content and content-to-position, where the content and position embedding are added before self-attention. DeBERTa keeps two separate vectors representing content and position so that self-attention is calculated between content-to-content, content-to-position, position-to-content, and position-to-position.
- DeBERTa keeps absolute position information along with the related position information.

Due to additional structural information used by the model, DeBERTa claimed to have achieved state-of-the-art results with half the training data when compared with other models such as RoBERTa. The code is available at https://github.com/microsoft/DeBERTa.

The Evolved Transformer and MEENA

The Evolved Transformer was introduced in 2019 by Google Brain researchers in the paper *The Evolved Transformer* by David R. So, Chen Liang, and Quoc V. Le, https://arxiv.org/abs/1901.11117.

Let's go over the main ideas:

- Transformers are a class of architectures that are manually drafted. The Evolved Transformers researchers applied **Neural Architecture Search** (**NAS**), a set of automatic optimization techniques that learn how to combine basic architectural building blocks to find models better than the ones manually designed by humans.
- NAS was applied to both the transformer encoder and decoder blocks resulting in a new architecture shown in *Figures 6.8* and *6.9*.

Evolved Transformers demonstrated consistent improvement compared to the original transformer architecture. The model is at the core of MEENA, a multi-turn open-domain chatbot trained end-to-end on data mined and filtered from social media conversations on public domains. MEENA uses Evolved Transformers with 2.6 billion parameters with a single Evolved Transformer encoder block and 13 Evolved Transformer decoder blocks. The objective function used for training focuses on minimizing perplexity, the uncertainty of predicting the next token. MEENA can conduct conversations that are more sensitive and specific than existing state-of-the-art chatbots. Refer to the Google blog post *Towards a Conversational Agent that Can Chat About...Anything*, `https://ai.googleblog.com/2020/01/towards-conversational-agent-that-can.html`:

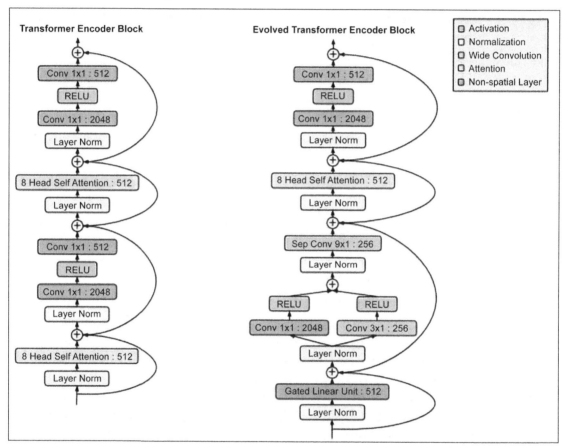

Figure 6.8: The Evolved Transformer encoder block, source: https://arxiv.org/pdf/1901.11117.pdf

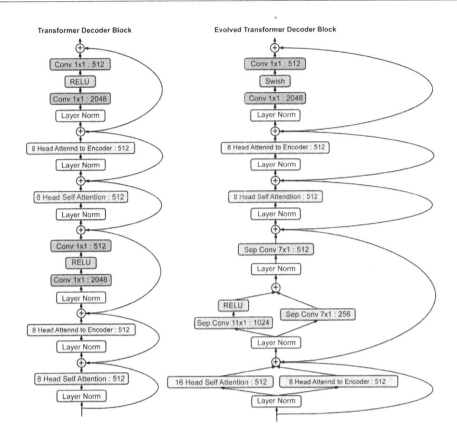

Figure 6.9: The Evolved Transformer decoder block, source: https://arxiv.org/pdf/1901.11117.pdf

LaMDA

LaMDA is a model introduced in 2022 by Google's researchers in *LaMDA: Language Models for Dialog Applications* by Romal Thoppilan, et al., `https://arxiv.org/abs/2201.08239`. It is a family of transformer-based neural language models specialized for dialog. Let's see the key intuitions:

- In the pretraining stage, LaMDA uses a dataset of 1.56 trillion words — nearly 40x more than what was previously used for LLMs — from public dialog data and other public web documents. After tokenizing the dataset into 2.81 trillion SentencePiece tokens, the pretraining predicts every next token in a sentence, given the previous tokens.

- In the fine-tuning stage, LaMDA performs a mix of generative tasks to generate natural-language responses to given contexts, and classification tasks on whether a response is safe and of high quality. The combination of generation and classification provides the final answer (see *Figure 6.10*).

- LaMDA defines a robust set of metrics for quality, safety, and groundedness:

  - Quality: This measure is decomposed into three dimensions, **Sensibleness, Specificity, and Interestingness** (**SSI**). Sensibleness considers whether the model produces responses that make sense in the dialog context. Specificity judges whether the response is specific to the preceding dialog context, and not a generic response that could apply to most contexts. Interestingness measures whether the model produces responses that are also insightful, unexpected, or witty.

  - Safety: Takes into account how to avoid any unintended result that creates risks of harm for the user, and to avoid reinforcing unfair bias.

  - Groundedness: Takes into account plausible information that is, however, contradicting information that can be supported by authoritative external sources.

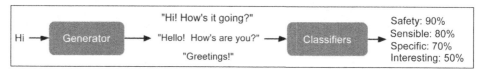

Figure 6.10: LaMDA generates and then scores a response candidate. Source: https://ai.googleblog.com/2022/01/lamda-towards-safe-grounded-and-high.html

LaMDA demonstrated results that were impressively close to the human brain ones. According to Google (`https://ai.googleblog.com/2022/01/lamda-towards-safe-grounded-and-high.html`), LaMDA significantly outperformed the pretrained model in every dimension and across all model sizes. Quality metrics (Sensibleness, Specificity, and Interestingness) generally improved with the number of model parameters, with or without fine-tuning. Safety did not seem to benefit from model scaling alone, but it did improve with fine-tuning. Groundedness improved as model size increased, perhaps because larger models have a greater capacity to memorize uncommon knowledge, but fine-tuning allows the model to access external knowledge sources and to effectively shift some of the load of remembering knowledge to an external knowledge source. With fine-tuning, the quality gap to human levels can be shrunk, though the model performance remains below human levels in safety and groundedness:

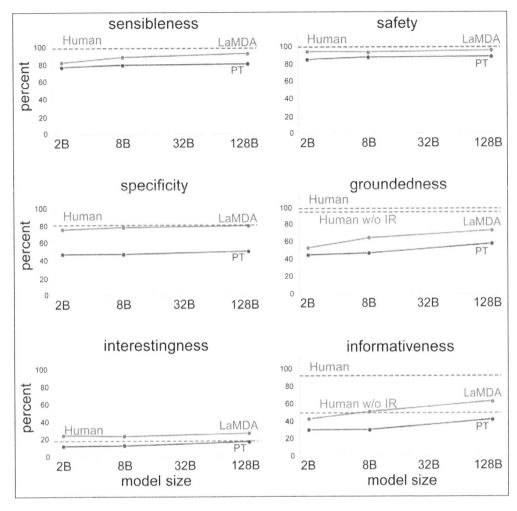

Figure 6.11: LaMDA performance – source: https://ai.googleblog.com/2022/01/lamda-towards-safe-grounded-and-high.html

Switch Transformer

The Switch Transformer is a model introduced in 2021 by Google's researchers in *Switch Transformers: Scaling to Trillion Parameter Models with Simple and Efficient Sparsity* by William Fedus, Barret Zoph, and Noam Shazeer, introduced in `https://arxiv.org/abs/2101.03961`.

Let's look at the key intuitions:

- The Switch Transformer was trained from 7 billion to 1.6 trillion parameters. As discussed, a typical transformer is a deep stack of multi-headed self-attention layers, and at the end of each layer, there's an FFN aggregating the outputs coming from its multiple heads. The Switch Transformer replaces this single FFN with multiple FFNs and calls them "experts." On each forward pass, at each layer, for each token at the input, the model activates exactly one expert:

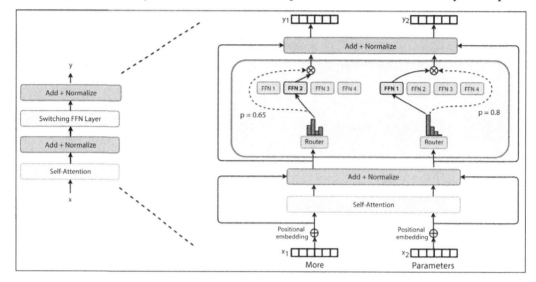

Fig 6.12: The Switch Transformer with multiple routing FFN – The dense FFN layer present in the transformer is replaced with a sparse Switch FFN layer (light blue). Source: https://arxiv.org/pdf/2101.03961.pdf

- Switch-Base (7 billion parameters) and Switch-Large (26 billion parameters) outperformed T5-Base (0.2 billion parameters) and T5-Large (0.7 billion parameters) on tasks such as language modeling, classification, coreference resolution, question answering, and summarization.

An example implementation of Switch Transformer is available at `https://keras.io/examples/nlp/text_classification_with_switch_transformer/`.

RETRO

RETRO (**Retrieval-Enhanced Transformer**) is a retrieval-enhanced autoregressive language model introduced by DeepMind in 2022 in *Improving language models by retrieving from trillions of tokens* by Sebastian Borgeaud et al., `https://arxiv.org/pdf/2112.04426/`. Let's look at the key intuitions:

- Scaling the number of parameters in an LLM has proven to be a way to improve the quality of the results. However, this approach is not sustainable because it is computationally expensive.
- RETRO couples a retrieval **Database** (**DB**) with a transformer in a hybrid architecture. The idea is first to search with the Nearest Neighbors algorithm on pre-computed BERT embeddings stored in a retrieval DB. Then, these embeddings are used as input to a transformer's encoder.

- The combination of retrieval and transformers allows RETRO (scaled from 150 million to 7 billion non-embedding parameters) to save on the number of parameters used by the LLM.

For instance, consider the sample query "The 2021 Women's US Open was won" and *Figure 6.13*, where the cached BERT embeddings are passed to a transformer encoder to get the final result:

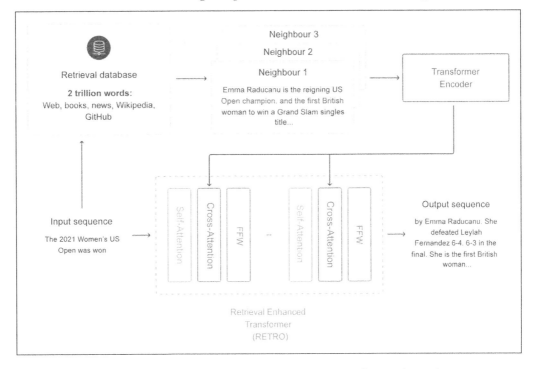

Figure 6.13: A high-level overview of Retrieval Enhanced Transformers (RETRO). Source: https://deepmind.com/research/publications/2021/improving-language-models-by-retrieving-from-trillions-of-tokens

Pathways and PaLM

Google Research announced Pathways (`https://blog.google/technology/ai/introducing-pathways-next-generation-ai-architecture/`), a single model that could generalize across domains and tasks while being highly efficient. Then, Google introduced **Pathways Language Model (PaLM)**, a 540-billion parameter, dense decoder-only transformer model, which enabled us to efficiently train a single model across multiple TPU v4 Pods. Google evaluated PaLM on hundreds of language understanding and generation tasks and found that it achieves state-of-the-art performance across most tasks, by significant margins in many cases (see `https://ai.googleblog.com/2022/04/pathways-language-model-palm-scaling-to.html?m=1`).

Implementation

In this section, we will go through a few tasks using transformers.

Transformer reference implementation: An example of translation

In this section, we will briefly review a transformer reference implementation available at `https://www.tensorflow.org/text/tutorials/transformer` and specifically, we will use the opportunity to run the code in a Google Colab.

Not everyone realizes the number of GPUs it takes to train a transformer. Luckily, you can play with resources available for free at `https://colab.research.google.com/github/tensorflow/text/blob/master/docs/tutorials/transformer.ipynb`.

Note that implementing transformers from scratch is probably not the best choice unless you need to realize some very specific customization or you are interested in core research. If you are not interested in learning the internals, then you can skip to the next section. Our tutorial is licensed under the Creative Commons Attribution 4.0 License, and code samples are licensed under the Apache 2.0 License. The specific task we are going to perform is translating from Portuguese to English. Let's have a look at the code, step by step:

1. First, let's install datasets and import the right libraries. Note that the Colab available online is apparently missing the line `import tensorflow_text`, which is, however, added here:

    ```
    !pip install tensorflow_datasets
    !pip install -U 'tensorflow-text==2.8.*'
    import logging
    import time

    import numpy as np
    import matplotlib.pyplot as plt
    import tensorflow_text

    import tensorflow_datasets as tfds
    import tensorflow as tf
    logging.getLogger('tensorflow').setLevel(logging.ERROR)  # suppress
    warnings
    ```

2. Then, load the Portuguese to English dataset:

    ```
    examples, metadata = tfds.load('ted_hrlr_translate/pt_to_en', with_
    info=True,
                                    as_supervised=True)
    train_examples, val_examples = examples['train'], examples['validation']
    ```

3. Now, let's convert text to sequences of token IDs, which are used as indices into an embedding:

    ```
    model_name = 'ted_hrlr_translate_pt_en_converter'
    tf.keras.utils.get_file(
    ```

```
    f'{model_name}.zip',
    f'https://storage.googleapis.com/download.tensorflow.org/models/
{model_name}.zip',
    cache_dir='.', cache_subdir='', extract=True
)
tokenizers = tf.saved_model.load(model_name)
```

4. Let's see the tokenized IDs and tokenized words:

```
for pt_examples, en_examples in train_examples.batch(3).take(1):

  print('> Examples in Portuguese:')
for en in en_examples.numpy():
  print(en.decode('utf-8'))
```

```
and when you improve searchability , you actually take away the one
advantage of print , which is serendipity .
but what if it were active ?
but they did n't test for curiosity .
```

```
encoded = tokenizers.en.tokenize(en_examples)
for row in encoded.to_list():
  print(row)
```

```
[2, 72, 117, 79, 1259, 1491, 2362, 13, 79, 150, 184, 311, 71, 103, 2308,
74, 2679, 13, 148, 80, 55, 4840, 1434, 2423, 540, 15, 3]
[2, 87, 90, 107, 76, 129, 1852, 30, 3]
[2, 87, 83, 149, 50, 9, 56, 664, 85, 2512, 15, 3]
```

```
round_trip = tokenizers.en.detokenize(encoded)
for line in round_trip.numpy():
  print(line.decode('utf-8'))
```

```
and when you improve searchability , you actually take away the one
advantage of print , which is serendipity .
but what if it were active ?
but they did n ' t test for curiosity .
```

5. Now let's create an input pipeline. First, we define a function to drop the examples longer than MAX_TOKENS. Second, we define a function that tokenizes the batches of raw text. Third, we create the batches:

```python
MAX_TOKENS=128
def filter_max_tokens(pt, en):
  num_tokens = tf.maximum(tf.shape(pt)[1],tf.shape(en)[1])
  return num_tokens < MAX_TOKENS
def tokenize_pairs(pt, en):
    pt = tokenizers.pt.tokenize(pt)
    # Convert from ragged to dense, padding with zeros.
    pt = pt.to_tensor()

    en = tokenizers.en.tokenize(en)
    # Convert from ragged to dense, padding with zeros.
    en = en.to_tensor()
    return pt, en


BUFFER_SIZE = 20000
BATCH_SIZE = 64
def make_batches(ds):
  return (
      ds
      .cache()
      .shuffle(BUFFER_SIZE)
      .batch(BATCH_SIZE)
      .map(tokenize_pairs, num_parallel_calls=tf.data.AUTOTUNE)
      .filter(filter_max_tokens)
      .prefetch(tf.data.AUTOTUNE))


train_batches = make_batches(train_examples)
val_batches = make_batches(val_examples)
```

6. Now we add positional encoding, forcing tokens to be closer to each other based on the similarity of their meaning and their position in the sentence, in the d-dimensional embedding space:

```python
def get_angles(pos, i, d_model):
  angle_rates = 1 / np.power(10000, (2 * (i//2)) / np.float32(d_model))
  return pos * angle_rates


def positional_encoding(position, d_model):
  angle_rads = get_angles(np.arange(position)[:, np.newaxis],
```

```
                          np.arange(d_model)[np.newaxis, :],
                          d_model)


    # apply sin to even indices in the array; 2i
    angle_rads[:, 0::2] = np.sin(angle_rads[:, 0::2])


    # apply cos to odd indices in the array; 2i+1
    angle_rads[:, 1::2] = np.cos(angle_rads[:, 1::2])


    pos_encoding = angle_rads[np.newaxis, ...]


    return tf.cast(pos_encoding, dtype=tf.float32)
```

7. Let's now focus on the masking process. The look-ahead mask is used to mask the future tokens in a sequence, with the mask indicating which entries should not be used. For instance, to predict the third token, only the first and second tokens will be used, and to predict the fourth token, only the first, second, and third tokens will be used, and so on:

```
def create_padding_mask(seq):
    seq = tf.cast(tf.math.equal(seq, 0), tf.float32)


    # add extra dimensions to add the padding
    # to the attention logits.
    return seq[:, tf.newaxis, tf.newaxis, :]  # (batch_size, 1, 1, seq_len)


def create_look_ahead_mask(size):
    mask = 1 - tf.linalg.band_part(tf.ones((size, size)), -1, 0)
    return mask  # (seq_len, seq_len)
```

8. We are getting closer and closer to the essence of transformers. Let's define the attention function as a scaled dot-product:

```
def scaled_dot_product_attention(q, k, v, mask):
    """Calculate the attention weights.
    q, k, v must have matching leading dimensions.
    k, v must have matching penultimate dimension, i.e.: seq_len_k = seq_
len_v.
    The mask has different shapes depending on its type(padding or look
ahead)
    but it must be broadcastable for addition.

    Args:
      q: query shape == (..., seq_len_q, depth)
      k: key shape == (..., seq_len_k, depth)
```

```
    v: value shape == (..., seq_len_v, depth_v)
    mask: Float tensor with shape broadcastable
          to (..., seq_len_q, seq_len_k). Defaults to None.


Returns:
  output, attention_weights
"""


matmul_qk = tf.matmul(q, k, transpose_b=True)  # (..., seq_len_q, seq_
len_k)


# scale matmul_qk
dk = tf.cast(tf.shape(k)[-1], tf.float32)
scaled_attention_logits = matmul_qk / tf.math.sqrt(dk)


# add the mask to the scaled tensor.
if mask is not None:
  scaled_attention_logits += (mask * -1e9)


# softmax is normalized on the last axis (seq_len_k) so that the scores
# add up to 1.
attention_weights = tf.nn.softmax(scaled_attention_logits, axis=-1)  #
(..., seq_len_q, seq_len_k)


output = tf.matmul(attention_weights, v)  # (..., seq_len_q, depth_v)


return output, attention_weights
```

9. Now that the attention is defined, we need to implement the multi-head mechanism. There are three parts: linear layers, scaled dot-product attention, and the final linear layer (see *Figure 6.14*):

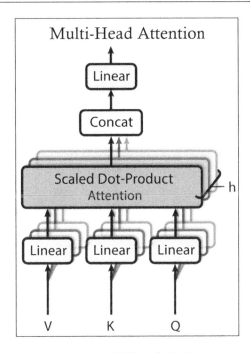

Figure 6.14: Multi-head attention

```
class MultiHeadAttention(tf.keras.layers.Layer):
  def __init__(self,*, d_model, num_heads):
    super(MultiHeadAttention, self).__init__()
    self.num_heads = num_heads
    self.d_model = d_model

    assert d_model % self.num_heads == 0

    self.depth = d_model // self.num_heads

    self.wq = tf.keras.layers.Dense(d_model)
    self.wk = tf.keras.layers.Dense(d_model)
    self.wv = tf.keras.layers.Dense(d_model)

    self.dense = tf.keras.layers.Dense(d_model)

  def split_heads(self, x, batch_size):
    """Split the last dimension into (num_heads, depth).
    Transpose the result such that the shape is (batch_size, num_heads,
seq_len, depth)
```

```
"""
x = tf.reshape(x, (batch_size, -1, self.num_heads, self.depth))
return tf.transpose(x, perm=[0, 2, 1, 3])

def call(self, v, k, q, mask):
    batch_size = tf.shape(q)[0]

    q = self.wq(q)  # (batch_size, seq_len, d_model)
    k = self.wk(k)  # (batch_size, seq_len, d_model)
    v = self.wv(v)  # (batch_size, seq_len, d_model)

    q = self.split_heads(q, batch_size)  # (batch_size, num_heads, seq_
len_q, depth)
    k = self.split_heads(k, batch_size)  # (batch_size, num_heads, seq_
len_k, depth)
    v = self.split_heads(v, batch_size)  # (batch_size, num_heads, seq_
len_v, depth)

    # scaled_attention.shape == (batch_size, num_heads, seq_len_q, depth)
    # attention_weights.shape == (batch_size, num_heads, seq_len_q, seq_
len_k)
    scaled_attention, attention_weights = scaled_dot_product_attention(
        q, k, v, mask)

    scaled_attention = tf.transpose(scaled_attention, perm=[0, 2, 1, 3])
# (batch_size, seq_len_q, num_heads, depth)

    concat_attention = tf.reshape(scaled_attention,
                                  (batch_size, -1, self.d_model))  #
(batch_size, seq_len_q, d_model)

    output = self.dense(concat_attention)  # (batch_size, seq_len_q, d_
model)

    return output, attention_weights
```

10. Now, we can define a point-wise feedforward network that consists of two fully connected layers with a ReLU activation in between:

```
def point_wise_feed_forward_network(d_model, dff):
    return tf.keras.Sequential([
```

```
    tf.keras.layers.Dense(dff, activation='relu'),  # (batch_size, seq_
len, dff)
    tf.keras.layers.Dense(d_model)  # (batch_size, seq_len, d_model)
])
```

11. We can now concentrate on defining the encoder and decoder parts as described in *Figure 6.15*. Remember that the traditional transformer takes the input sentence through *N* encoder layers, while the decoder uses the encoder output and its own input (self-attention) to predict the next word. Each encoder layer has sublayers made by multi-head attention (with a padding mask) and then point-wise feedforward networks. Each sublayer uses a residual connection to contain the problem of vanishing gradient, and a normalization layer:

```
class EncoderLayer(tf.keras.layers.Layer):
  def __init__(self,*, d_model, num_heads, dff, rate=0.1):
    super(EncoderLayer, self).__init__()


    self.mha = MultiHeadAttention(d_model=d_model, num_heads=num_heads)
    self.ffn = point_wise_feed_forward_network(d_model, dff)


    self.layernorm1 = tf.keras.layers.LayerNormalization(epsilon=1e-6)
    self.layernorm2 = tf.keras.layers.LayerNormalization(epsilon=1e-6)


    self.dropout1 = tf.keras.layers.Dropout(rate)
    self.dropout2 = tf.keras.layers.Dropout(rate)

  def call(self, x, training, mask):

    attn_output, _ = self.mha(x, x, x, mask)  # (batch_size, input_seq_
len, d_model)
    attn_output = self.dropout1(attn_output, training=training)
    out1 = self.layernorm1(x + attn_output)  # (batch_size, input_seq_
len, d_model)

    ffn_output = self.ffn(out1)  # (batch_size, input_seq_len, d_model)
    ffn_output = self.dropout2(ffn_output, training=training)
    out2 = self.layernorm2(out1 + ffn_output)  # (batch_size, input_seq_
len, d_model)

    return out2
```

12. Each decoder layer is made of sublayers. First, a masked multi-head attention (with a look-ahead mask and padding mask). Then, a multi-head attention (with a padding mask), V (value), and K (key) receive the encoder output as inputs. Q (query) receives the output from the masked multi-head attention sublayer and, finally, the point-wise feedforward networks:

```python
class DecoderLayer(tf.keras.layers.Layer):
  def __init__(self,*, d_model, num_heads, dff, rate=0.1):
    super(DecoderLayer, self).__init__()

    self.mha1 = MultiHeadAttention(d_model=d_model, num_heads=num_heads)
    self.mha2 = MultiHeadAttention(d_model=d_model, num_heads=num_heads)

    self.ffn = point_wise_feed_forward_network(d_model, dff)

    self.layernorm1 = tf.keras.layers.LayerNormalization(epsilon=1e-6)
    self.layernorm2 = tf.keras.layers.LayerNormalization(epsilon=1e-6)
    self.layernorm3 = tf.keras.layers.LayerNormalization(epsilon=1e-6)

    self.dropout1 = tf.keras.layers.Dropout(rate)
    self.dropout2 = tf.keras.layers.Dropout(rate)
    self.dropout3 = tf.keras.layers.Dropout(rate)

  def call(self, x, enc_output, training,
           look_ahead_mask, padding_mask):
    # enc_output.shape == (batch_size, input_seq_len, d_model)

    attn1, attn_weights_block1 = self.mha1(x, x, x, look_ahead_mask)  #
(batch_size, target_seq_len, d_model)
    attn1 = self.dropout1(attn1, training=training)
    out1 = self.layernorm1(attn1 + x)

    attn2, attn_weights_block2 = self.mha2(
        enc_output, enc_output, out1, padding_mask)  # (batch_size,
target_seq_len, d_model)
    attn2 = self.dropout2(attn2, training=training)
    out2 = self.layernorm2(attn2 + out1)  # (batch_size, target_seq_len,
d_model)

    ffn_output = self.ffn(out2)  # (batch_size, target_seq_len, d_model)
    ffn_output = self.dropout3(ffn_output, training=training)
    out3 = self.layernorm3(ffn_output + out2)  # (batch_size, target_seq_
len, d_model)
```

```
        return out3, attn_weights_block1, attn_weights_block2
```

13. Now that we have defined the encoder layer, we can use it to define the proper encoder. This consists of three stages: input embedding, positional encoding, and *N* encoder layers:

```python
class Encoder(tf.keras.layers.Layer):
  def __init__(self,*, num_layers, d_model, num_heads, dff, input_vocab_
size,
                    rate=0.1):
    super(Encoder, self).__init__()

    self.d_model = d_model
    self.num_layers = num_layers

    self.embedding = tf.keras.layers.Embedding(input_vocab_size, d_model)
    self.pos_encoding = positional_encoding(MAX_TOKENS, self.d_model)

    self.enc_layers = [
        EncoderLayer(d_model=d_model, num_heads=num_heads, dff=dff,
rate=rate)
        for _ in range(num_layers)]

    self.dropout = tf.keras.layers.Dropout(rate)

  def call(self, x, training, mask):

    seq_len = tf.shape(x)[1]

    # adding embedding and position encoding.
    x = self.embedding(x)  # (batch_size, input_seq_len, d_model)
    x *= tf.math.sqrt(tf.cast(self.d_model, tf.float32))
    x += self.pos_encoding[:, :seq_len, :]

    x = self.dropout(x, training=training)

    for i in range(self.num_layers):
      x = self.enc_layers[i](x, training, mask)

    return x  # (batch_size, input_seq_len, d_model)
```

14. We can now focus our attention on the decoder itself. It consists of output embedding, positional
     encoding, and *N* decoder layers:

```python
class Decoder(tf.keras.layers.Layer):
  def __init__(self,*, num_layers, d_model, num_heads, dff, target_vocab_
size,
                    rate=0.1):
    super(Decoder, self).__init__()

    self.d_model = d_model
    self.num_layers = num_layers

    self.embedding = tf.keras.layers.Embedding(target_vocab_size, d_
model)
    self.pos_encoding = positional_encoding(MAX_TOKENS, d_model)

    self.dec_layers = [
        DecoderLayer(d_model=d_model, num_heads=num_heads, dff=dff,
rate=rate)
        for _ in range(num_layers)]
    self.dropout = tf.keras.layers.Dropout(rate)

  def call(self, x, enc_output, training,
           look_ahead_mask, padding_mask):

    seq_len = tf.shape(x)[1]
    attention_weights = {}

    x = self.embedding(x)  # (batch_size, target_seq_len, d_model)
    x *= tf.math.sqrt(tf.cast(self.d_model, tf.float32))
    x += self.pos_encoding[:, :seq_len, :]

    x = self.dropout(x, training=training)

    for i in range(self.num_layers):
      x, block1, block2 = self.dec_layers[i](x, enc_output, training,
                                             look_ahead_mask, padding_
mask)
      attention_weights[f'decoder_layer{i+1}_block1'] = block1
      attention_weights[f'decoder_layer{i+1}_block2'] = block2

    # x.shape == (batch_size, target_seq_len, d_model)
    return x, attention_weights
```

15. Now that we have defined the encoder and decoder, we can now turn our attention to the transformer itself, which is composed of an encoder, a decoder, and a final linear layer (see *Figure 6.15*):

```
class Transformer(tf.keras.Model):
  def __init__(self,*, num_layers, d_model, num_heads, dff, input_vocab_
size,
                 target_vocab_size, rate=0.1):
    super().__init__()
    self.encoder = Encoder(num_layers=num_layers, d_model=d_model,
                           num_heads=num_heads, dff=dff,
                           input_vocab_size=input_vocab_size, rate=rate)

    self.decoder = Decoder(num_layers=num_layers, d_model=d_model,
                           num_heads=num_heads, dff=dff,
                           target_vocab_size=target_vocab_size,
rate=rate)

    self.final_layer = tf.keras.layers.Dense(target_vocab_size)

  def call(self, inputs, training):
    # Keras models prefer if you pass all your inputs in the first
argument
    inp, tar = inputs

    enc_padding_mask, look_ahead_mask, dec_padding_mask = self.create_
masks(inp, tar)

    enc_output = self.encoder(inp, training, enc_padding_mask)  # (batch_
size, inp_seq_len, d_model)

    # dec_output.shape == (batch_size, tar_seq_len, d_model)
    dec_output, attention_weights = self.decoder(
        tar, enc_output, training, look_ahead_mask, dec_padding_mask)

    final_output = self.final_layer(dec_output)  # (batch_size, tar_seq_
len, target_vocab_size)

    return final_output, attention_weights

  def create_masks(self, inp, tar):
    # Encoder padding mask
```

```
enc_padding_mask = create_padding_mask(inp)

# Used in the 2nd attention block in the decoder.
# This padding mask is used to mask the encoder outputs.
dec_padding_mask = create_padding_mask(inp)

# Used in the 1st attention block in the decoder.
# It is used to pad and mask future tokens in the input received by
# the decoder.
look_ahead_mask = create_look_ahead_mask(tf.shape(tar)[1])
dec_target_padding_mask = create_padding_mask(tar)
look_ahead_mask = tf.maximum(dec_target_padding_mask, look_ahead_
mask)
return enc_padding_mask, look_ahead_mask, dec_padding_mask
```

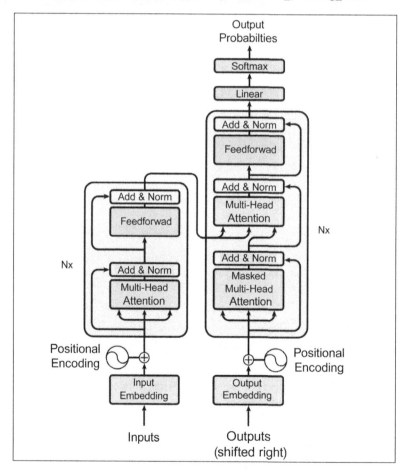

Figure 6.15: The traditional transformer

16. We are almost done. We just need to define hyperparameters and the optimizer, using exactly the same settings as the seminal paper, and the loss function:

```
num_layers = 4
d_model = 128
dff = 512
num_heads = 8
dropout_rate = 0.1


class CustomSchedule(tf.keras.optimizers.schedules.LearningRateSchedule):
  def __init__(self, d_model, warmup_steps=4000):
    super(CustomSchedule, self).__init__()

    self.d_model = d_model
    self.d_model = tf.cast(self.d_model, tf.float32)

    self.warmup_steps = warmup_steps

  def __call__(self, step):
    arg1 = tf.math.rsqrt(step)
    arg2 = step * (self.warmup_steps ** -1.5)

    return tf.math.rsqrt(self.d_model) * tf.math.minimum(arg1, arg2)

learning_rate = CustomSchedule(d_model)

optimizer = tf.keras.optimizers.Adam(learning_rate, beta_1=0.9,
beta_2=0.98,
                                        epsilon=1e-9)

def loss_function(real, pred):
  mask = tf.math.logical_not(tf.math.equal(real, 0))
  loss_ = loss_object(real, pred)

  mask = tf.cast(mask, dtype=loss_.dtype)
  loss_ *= mask

  return tf.reduce_sum(loss_)/tf.reduce_sum(mask)


def accuracy_function(real, pred):
  accuracies = tf.equal(real, tf.argmax(pred, axis=2))
```

```
        mask = tf.math.logical_not(tf.math.equal(real, 0))
        accuracies = tf.math.logical_and(mask, accuracies)

        accuracies = tf.cast(accuracies, dtype=tf.float32)
        mask = tf.cast(mask, dtype=tf.float32)
        return tf.reduce_sum(accuracies)/tf.reduce_sum(mask)

    train_loss = tf.keras.metrics.Mean(name='train_loss')
    train_accuracy = tf.keras.metrics.Mean(name='train_accuracy')
```

17. Time to define the transformer. Let's see the code:

```
    transformer = Transformer(
        num_layers=num_layers,
        d_model=d_model,
        num_heads=num_heads,
        dff=dff,
        input_vocab_size=tokenizers.pt.get_vocab_size().numpy(),
        target_vocab_size=tokenizers.en.get_vocab_size().numpy(),
        rate=dropout_rate)
```

18. Let's also define the checkpoints with the following code:

```
    checkpoint_path = './checkpoints/train'

    ckpt = tf.train.Checkpoint(transformer=transformer,
                               optimizer=optimizer)

    ckpt_manager = tf.train.CheckpointManager(ckpt, checkpoint_path, max_to_
    keep=5)

    # if a checkpoint exists, restore the latest checkpoint.
    if ckpt_manager.latest_checkpoint:
      ckpt.restore(ckpt_manager.latest_checkpoint)
      print('Latest checkpoint restored!!')
```

19. Remember that the transformer is autoregressive. The current output is used to predict what will happen next. We use a look-ahead mask, to prevent the model from peeking at the expected output. We are now ready to define `train_step`:

```
    train_step_signature = [
        tf.TensorSpec(shape=(None, None), dtype=tf.int64),
        tf.TensorSpec(shape=(None, None), dtype=tf.int64),
```

```
]

@tf.function(input_signature=train_step_signature)
def train_step(inp, tar):
  tar_inp = tar[:, :-1]
  tar_real = tar[:, 1:]

  with tf.GradientTape() as tape:
    predictions, _ = transformer([inp, tar_inp],
                                  training = True)
    loss = loss_function(tar_real, predictions)

  gradients = tape.gradient(loss, transformer.trainable_variables)
  optimizer.apply_gradients(zip(gradients, transformer.trainable_
variables))

  train_loss(loss)
  train_accuracy(accuracy_function(tar_real, predictions))


EPOCHS = 20
for epoch in range(EPOCHS):
  start = time.time()

  train_loss.reset_states()
  train_accuracy.reset_states()

  # inp -> portuguese, tar -> english
  for (batch, (inp, tar)) in enumerate(train_batches):
    train_step(inp, tar)

    if batch % 50 == 0:
      print(f'Epoch {epoch + 1} Batch {batch} Loss {train_loss.
result():.4f} Accuracy {train_accuracy.result():.4f}')

  if (epoch + 1) % 5 == 0:
    ckpt_save_path = ckpt_manager.save()
    print(f'Saving checkpoint for epoch {epoch+1} at {ckpt_save_path}')

  print(f'Epoch {epoch + 1} Loss {train_loss.result():.4f} Accuracy
{train_accuracy.result():.4f}')

  print(f'Time taken for 1 epoch: {time.time() - start:.2f} secs\n')
```

After running the training step in Colab, we get the following situation:

```
Epoch 20 Loss 1.5030 Accuracy 0.6720
Time taken for 1 epoch: 169.01 secs
```

20. We are now ready for translation. The following steps are used to translate:

    1. Encode the input sentence using the Portuguese tokenizer (tokenizers.pt).

    2. The decoder input is initialized to the [START] token.

    3. Calculate the padding masks and the look-ahead masks.

    4. The decoder then outputs the predictions by looking at the encoder output and its own output (self-attention).

    5. Concatenate the predicted token to the decoder input and pass it to the decoder:

```python
class Translator(tf.Module):
  def __init__(self, tokenizers, transformer):
    self.tokenizers = tokenizers
    self.transformer = transformer


  def __call__(self, sentence, max_length=MAX_TOKENS):
    # input sentence is portuguese, hence adding the start and end token
    assert isinstance(sentence, tf.Tensor)
    if len(sentence.shape) == 0:
      sentence = sentence[tf.newaxis]

    sentence = self.tokenizers.pt.tokenize(sentence).to_tensor()


    encoder_input = sentence


    # As the output language is english, initialize the output with the
    # english start token.
    start_end = self.tokenizers.en.tokenize([''])[0]
    start = start_end[0][tf.newaxis]
    end = start_end[1][tf.newaxis]


    # 'tf.TensorArray' is required here (instead of a python list) so
that the
    # dynamic-loop can be traced by 'tf.function'.
    output_array = tf.TensorArray(dtype=tf.int64, size=0, dynamic_
size=True)
    output_array = output_array.write(0, start)


    for i in tf.range(max_length):
```

```
        output = tf.transpose(output_array.stack())
        predictions, _ = self.transformer([encoder_input, output],
    training=False)


        # select the last token from the seq_len dimension
        predictions = predictions[:, -1:, :]  # (batch_size, 1, vocab_size)


        predicted_id = tf.argmax(predictions, axis=-1)


        # concatentate the predicted_id to the output which is given to the
    decoder
        # as its input.
        output_array = output_array.write(i+1, predicted_id[0])


        if predicted_id == end:
          break


    output = tf.transpose(output_array.stack())
    # output.shape (1, tokens)
    text = tokenizers.en.detokenize(output)[0]  # shape: ()


    tokens = tokenizers.en.lookup(output)[0]


    # 'tf.function' prevents us from using the attention_weights that
    were
    # calculated on the last iteration of the loop. So recalculate them
    outside
    # the loop.
    _, attention_weights = self.transformer([encoder_input,
    output[:,:-1]], training=False)


    return text, tokens, attention_weights
```

21. Let's call the translator on a sample sentence with this code snippet:

```
translator = Translator(tokenizers, transformer)
def print_translation(sentence, tokens, ground_truth):
  print(f'{"Input:":15s}: {sentence}')
  print(f'{"Prediction":15s}: {tokens.numpy().decode("utf-8")}')
  print(f'{"Ground truth":15s}: {ground_truth}')
sentence = 'os meus vizinhos ouviram sobre esta ideia.'
ground_truth = 'and my neighboring homes heard about this idea .'
```

```
translated_text, translated_tokens, attention_weights = translator(
    tf.constant(sentence))
print_translation(sentence, translated_text, ground_truth)
```

Getting as the result:

```
Input:          : os meus vizinhos ouviram sobre esta ideia.
Prediction      : my neighbors have heard about this idea .
Ground truth    : and my neighboring homes heard about this idea .
```

In this detailed analysis, we have discussed how a traditional transformer is implemented taking positional encoding, multi-head attention, and masking into account. The analyzed code is at `https://www.tensorflow.org/text/tutorials/transformer`.

Next, we will discuss how to use transformers making use of higher-level libraries.

Hugging Face

As discussed, implementing transformers from scratch is probably not the best choice unless you need to realize some very specific customization, or you are interested in core research. This is useful if you want to understand the internal details of a transformer architecture, or perhaps modify the transformer architecture to produce a new variant. Nowadays, there are very good libraries providing high-quality solutions. One of them is Hugging Face, which provides some efficient tools. Hugging Face is built around the idea of commercializing its open source transformers library. Let's see why the library became so popular:

- Hugging Face provides a common API to handle many transformer architectures.
- It not only provides the base model, but models with different types of "head" to handle specific tasks (for example, for the BERT architecture it provides `TFBertModel`, and the `TFBertForSequenceClassification` for tasks like sentiment analysis, `TFBertForTokenClassification` for tasks like named entity recognition, and `TFBertForQuestionAnswering` for Q and A, among others).
- You can also create your own network for a specific task quite easily by using the pretrained weights provided here, for example, by using `TFBertForPreTraining`.
- In addition to the `pipeline()` method in the next subsection, we can also define a model in the regular way and use `fit()` to train it and `predict()` to make inferences against it, just like a normal TF model (PyTorch also has the Trainer interface). We will see an example later on in this chapter.

Now, let's check some examples of how to use Hugging Face.

Generating text

In this section, we are going to use GPT-2 for natural language generation, a software process for producing natural language outputs. Let's start from the beginning by installing the Hugging Face library:

1. The first step is to create a dedicated virtual environment, where we can install the transformer library. In my case, I use the library for TensorFlow 2.0:

```
python -m venv .env
source .env/bin/activate
pip install transformers[tf-cpu]
```

2. Then let's verify that everything is working correctly by downloading a pretrained model used for sentiment analysis:

```
python -c "from transformers import pipeline; print(pipeline('sentiment-
analysis')('we love you'))"
```

Since the expected sentiment should be very positive, we shall see something like the following:

```
[{'label': 'POSITIVE', 'score': 0.9998704791069031}]
```

3. Now let's focus on generating text with GPT-2:

```
from transformers import pipeline
generator = pipeline(task="text-generation")
```

You should see something like the following:

```
No model was supplied, defaulted to gpt2 (https://huggingface.co/gpt2)
Downloading: 100%|                        | 665/665 [00:00<00:00,
167kB/s]
Downloading: 100%|                        | 475M/475M [03:24<00:00,
2.44MB/s
```

4. Let's pass some text to the generator and see what the result is. The first sentence is extracted from Tolkien's work, the second from Einstein's theories, and the third one comes from "Harry Potter":

```
generator("Three Rings for the Elven-kings under the sky, Seven for the
Dwarf-lords in their halls of stone")
```

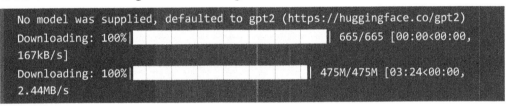

```
Setting 'pad_token_id' to 50256 (first 'eos_token_id') to generate
sequence
[{'generated_text': 'Three Rings for the Elven-kings under the sky, Seven
for the Dwarf-lords in their halls of stone and Eight for the Dwarves in
their halls of rock! Three new Rings of the Elven-kings under the sky,
Seven for'}]
```

```
generator ("The original theory of relativity is based upon the premise
that all coordinate systems in relative uniform translatory motion to
each other are equally valid and equivalent ")
```

```
Setting 'pad_token_id' to 50256 (first 'eos_token_id') to generate
sequence
[{'generated_text': 'The original theory of relativity is based upon
the premise that all coordinate systems in relative uniform translatory
motion to each other are equally valid and equivalent \xa0to one another.
In other words, they can all converge, and therefore all the laws are
valid'}]
```

```
generator ("It takes a great deal of bravery to stand up to our enemies")
```

```
Setting 'pad_token_id' to 50256 (first 'eos_token_id') to generate
sequence
[{'generated_text': 'It takes a great deal of bravery to stand up to
our enemies that day. She still has a lot to learn from it, or it could
take decades to do.\n\nWhile some braver men struggle, many are not as
lucky'}]
```

Pretty easy, isn't it?

Autoselecting a model and autotokenization

Hugging Face does a great job of helping the developer to automate as many steps as possible. Let's see some examples:

1. You can easily import a pretrained model among the several dozen available. A complete list of available models is here: `https://huggingface.co/docs/transformers/model_doc/auto`:

   ```
   from transformers import TFAutoModelForSequenceClassification
   model = TFAutoModelForSequenceClassification.from_pretrained("distilbert-
   base-uncased")
   ```

   ```
   Downloading: 100%|██████████████████████| 483/483 [00:00<00:00,
   68.9kB/s]
   Downloading: 100%|██████████████████████| 347M/347M [01:05<00:00,
   5.59MB/s]
   …
   ```

   You should probably train this model on a downstream task to use it for predictions and inference.

2. You can use `AutoTokenizer` to transform words into tokens used by the models:

   ```
   from transformers import AutoTokenizer
   tokenizer = AutoTokenizer.from_pretrained("bert-base-uncased")
   sequence = "The original theory of relativity is based upon the premise
   ```

```
that all coordinate systems"
print(tokenizer(sequence))
```

```
{'input_ids': [101, 1996, 2434, 3399, 1997, 20805, 2003, 2241, 2588,
1996, 18458, 2008, 2035, 13530, 3001, 102], 'token_type_ids': [0, 0, 0,
0, 0, 0, 0, 0, 0, 0, 0, 0, 0, 0, 0, 0], 'attention_mask': [1, 1, 1, 1, 1,
1, 1, 1, 1, 1, 1, 1, 1, 1, 1, 1]}
```

Named entity recognition

Named Entity Recognition (**NER**) is a classical NLP task. According to Wikipedia, named entity recognition – also known as (named) entity identification, entity chunking, and entity extraction – is a subtask of information extraction that seeks to locate and classify named entities mentioned in unstructured text into predefined categories such as person names, organizations, locations, medical codes, time expressions, quantities, monetary values, and percentages, among others.

Let's see how easily this task can be performed with Hugging Face:

1. First of all, let's create a NER pipeline:

    ```
    from transformers import pipeline
    ner_pipe = pipeline("ner")
    sequence = """Mr. and Mrs. Dursley, of number four, Privet Drive, were
    proud to say that they were perfectly normal, thank you very much."""
    for entity in ner_pipe(sequence):
        print(entity)
    ```

2. You will be able to see something like the following, where the entities are recognized:

    ```
    {'entity': 'I-PER', 'score': 0.99908304, 'index': 6, 'word': 'Du',
    'start': 13, 'end': 15}
    {'entity': 'I-PER', 'score': 0.9869529, 'index': 7, 'word': '##rs',
    'start': 15, 'end': 17}
    {'entity': 'I-PER', 'score': 0.9784202, 'index': 8, 'word': '##ley',
    'start': 17, 'end': 20}
    {'entity': 'I-ORG', 'score': 0.6860208, 'index': 14, 'word': 'P',
    'start': 38, 'end': 39}
    {'entity': 'I-ORG', 'score': 0.7713562, 'index': 15, 'word': '##rive',
    'start': 39, 'end': 43}
    {'entity': 'I-ORG', 'score': 0.76567733, 'index': 16, 'word': '##t',
    'start': 43, 'end': 44}
    {'entity': 'I-ORG', 'score': 0.8087192, 'index': 17, 'word': 'Drive',
    'start': 45, 'end': 50}
    ```

Named entity recognition can understand nine different classes:

*   O: Outside of a named entity.
*   B-MIS: Beginning of a miscellaneous entity right after another miscellaneous entity.

- **I-MIS**: Miscellaneous entity.
- **B-PER**: Beginning of a person's name right after another person's name.
- **I-PER**: A person's name.
- **B-ORG**: Beginning of an organization right after another organization.
- **I-ORG**: Organization.
- **B-LOC**: Beginning of a location right after another location.
- **I-LOC**: Location.

These entities are defined in the CoNLL-2003 dataset typically used for this task and automatically selected by Hugging Face.

Summarization

Let's now turn our attention to summarization, meaning the task of expressing the most important facts or ideas about something or someone in a short and clear form. Hugging Face makes it incredibly easy to use the T5 model as default for this task. Let's see the code:

1. First of all, let's create a summarization pipeline using the default T5 small model:

```
from transformers import pipeline
summarizer = pipeline("summarization")
ARTICLE = """
 Mr.
 and Mrs.
 Dursley, of number four, Privet Drive, were proud to say

 that they were perfectly normal, thank you very much.
 They were the last

 people you'd expect to be involved in anything strange or mysterious,

 because they just didn't hold with such nonsense.


 Mr.
 Dursley was the director of a firm called Grunnings, which made

 drills.
 He was a big, beefy man with hardly any neck, although he did

 have a very large mustache.
 Mrs.
 Dursley was thin and blonde and had
```

```
nearly twice the usual amount of neck, which came in very useful as she

spent so much of her time craning over garden fences, spying on the

neighbors.
The Dursleys had a small son called Dudley and in their

opinion there was no finer boy anywhere"""
print(summarizer(ARTICLE, max_length=130, min_length=30, do_
sample=False))
```

2. As a result, we will see something similar to the following:

```
No model was supplied, defaulted to t5-small (https://huggingface.co/t5-
small)
Downloading: 100%|██████████████████| 1.17k/1.17k [00:00<00:00,
300kB/s]
Downloading: 100%|██████████████████| 231M/231M [01:29<00:00,
2.71MB/s]


[{'summary_text': "Mr. and Mrs. Dursley, of number four, were the last
people you'd expect to be involved in anything strange or mysterious .
the Dursleys had a small son called Dudley and in their opinion there was
no finer boy anywhere ."}]
```

3. Suppose that you want to change to a different model. That's extremely simple as you only need to change one parameter:

```
summarizer = pipeline("summarization", model='t5-base')
```

4. As a result, we can see something like the following:

```
Downloading: 100%|████████████████████████████████
██████| 773k/773k [00:00<00:00, 1.28MB/s]
Downloading: 100%|████████████████████████████████
████| 1.32M/1.32M [00:00<00:00, 1.93MB/s]
[{'summary_text': "bob greene says he and his wife were perfectly normal
. he says they were the last people you'd expect to be involved in
anything strange or mysterious . greene: they were a big, beefy man with
hardly any neck, but had a very large mustache ."}]
```

Fine-tuning

One common usage pattern for transformers is to use a pretrained LLM and then fine-tune the model for specific downstream tasks. Of course, the fine-tuning steps will take place on your own dataset, while pretraining is performed on very large datasets. The advantages of this two-step strategy are in terms of both saving computation costs and in reducing the carbon footprint. Plus, fine-tuning allows you to use state-of-the-art models without having to train one from scratch. Let's see how to fine-tune a model with TF. This example is available at https://huggingface.co/docs/transformers/training, where the pretrained model used is bert-base-cased, which is fine-tuned on the "Yelp Reviews" dataset (available at https://huggingface.co/datasets/yelp_review_full). Let's see the code from https://huggingface.co/docs/transformers/training

1. First, let's load and tokenize the Yelp dataset:

```
from datasets import load_dataset
dataset = load_dataset("yelp_review_full")
from transformers import AutoTokenizer
tokenizer = AutoTokenizer.from_pretrained("bert-base-cased")

def tokenize_function(examples):
    return tokenizer(examples["text"], padding="max_length",
    truncation=True)

tokenized_datasets = dataset.map(tokenize_function, batched=True)

small_train_dataset = tokenized_datasets["train"].shuffle(seed=42).
select(range(1000))
small_eval_dataset = tokenized_datasets["test"].shuffle(seed=42).
select(range(1000))
```

2. Then let's convert them to TF format datasets:

```
from transformers import DefaultDataCollator
data_collator = DefaultDataCollator(return_tensors="tf")

# convert the tokenized datasets to TensorFlow datasets

tf_train_dataset = small_train_dataset.to_tf_dataset(
    columns=["attention_mask", "input_ids", "token_type_ids"],
    label_cols=["labels"],
    shuffle=True,
    collate_fn=data_collator,
    batch_size=8,
)
```

```
tf_validation_dataset = small_eval_dataset.to_tf_dataset(
    columns=["attention_mask", "input_ids", "token_type_ids"],
    label_cols=["labels"],
    shuffle=False,
    collate_fn=data_collator,
    batch size=8,
)
```

3. Now, we can use `TFAutoModelForSequenceClassification`, specifically selecting `bert-base-cased`:

```
import tensorflow as tf
from transformers import TFAutoModelForSequenceClassification

model = TFAutoModelForSequenceClassification.from_pretrained("bert-base-cased", num_labels=5)
```

4. Finally, the fine-tuning is simply using the standard way to train a model used in Keras/TF 2.0 by compiling the model and then using `fit` on it:

```
model.compile(
    optimizer=tf.keras.optimizers.Adam(learning_rate=5e-5),
    loss=tf.keras.losses.SparseCategoricalCrossentropy(from_logits=True),
    metrics=tf.metrics.SparseCategoricalAccuracy(),
)

model.fit(tf_train_dataset, validation_data=tf_validation_dataset,
    epochs=3)
```

If you want, you can test the code on a public Colab notebook (available at https://huggingface.co/docs/transformers/training). If you run the code yourself, you should be able to see something similar to *Figure 6.16*:

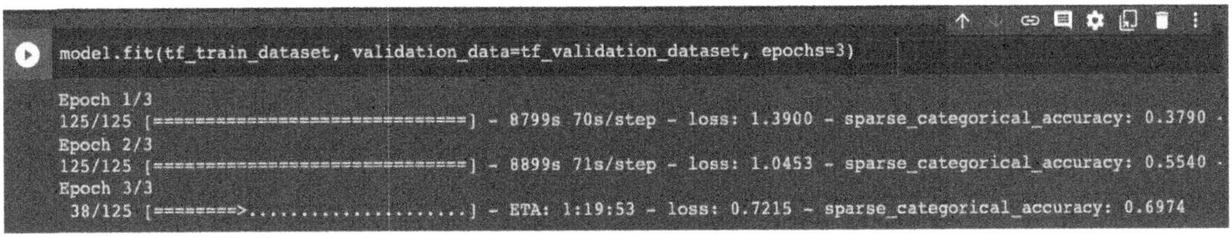

Figure 6.16: Fine-tuning BERT on a Colab notebook

Next, we are going to introduce TFHub.

TFHub

In the previous section, we discussed how to use the Hugging Face Transformer library. Now, we will have a look at another library known as TFHub available at `https://tfhub.dev/`. TensorFlow Hub is a repository of trained machine learning models ready for fine-tuning and deployable anywhere. The key idea is to reuse trained models like BERT and Faster R-CNN with just a few lines of code.

Using TFHub is as easy as writing a few lines of code. Let's see a simple example where we load a pretrained model for computing embeddings. In this case, we use `nnlm-en-dim128`, a token-based text embedding trained on the English Google News 200B corpus:

```
!pip install --upgrade tensorflow_hub

import tensorflow_hub as hub

model = hub.KerasLayer("https://tfhub.dev/google/nnlm-en-dim128/2")
embeddings = model(["The rain in Spain.", "falls",
                    "mainly", "In the plain!"])

print(embeddings.shape)   #(4,128)
```

Now let's see how to use BERT. This code is adapted from `https://www.tensorflow.org/hub/tutorials/bert_experts`, and it is also available on Hugging Face (`https://huggingface.co/docs/transformers/training`):

1. Let's set up the environment and import useful modules:

    ```
    !pip install seaborn
    !pip install sklearn
    !pip install tensorflow_hub
    !pip install tensorflow_text

    import seaborn as sns
    from sklearn.metrics import pairwise

    import tensorflow as tf
    import tensorflow_hub as hub
    import tensorflow_text as text  # Imports TF ops for preprocessing.
    ```

2. Let's define a few sentences used for comparing their similarities:

    ```
    sentences = [
        "Do not pity the dead, Harry. Pity the living, and, above all those
    who live without love.",
        "It is impossible to manufacture or imitate love",
        "Differences of habit and language are nothing at all if our aims are
    ```

```
    identical and our hearts are open.",
        "What do I care how he looks? I am good-looking enough for both of
    us, I theenk! All these scars show is zat my husband is brave!",
        "Love as powerful as your mother's for you leaves it's own mark. To
    have been loved so deeply, even though the person who loved us is gone,
    will give us some protection forever.",
        "Family…Whatever yeh say, blood's important. . . .",
        "I cared more for your happiness than your knowing the truth, more
    for your peace of mind than my plan, more for your life than the lives
    that might be lost if the plan failed."
    ]
```

3. Then, let's use a pretrained BERT model available on TFHub to compute embeddings on the input sentences just defined. BERT's output is the set of embeddings itself:

```
#@title Configure the model { run: "auto" }
BERT_MODEL = "https://tfhub.dev/google/experts/bert/wiki_books/2" # @
param {type: "string"} ["https://tfhub.dev/google/experts/bert/wiki_
books/2", "https://tfhub.dev/google/experts/bert/wiki_books/mnli/2",
"https://tfhub.dev/google/experts/bert/wiki_books/qnli/2", "https://
tfhub.dev/google/experts/bert/wiki_books/qqp/2", "https://tfhub.dev/
google/experts/bert/wiki_books/squad2/2", "https://tfhub.dev/google/
experts/bert/wiki_books/sst2/2",  "https://tfhub.dev/google/experts/bert/
pubmed/2", "https://tfhub.dev/google/experts/bert/pubmed/squad2/2"]
# Preprocessing must match the model, but all the above use the same.
PREPROCESS_MODEL = "https://tfhub.dev/tensorflow/bert_en_uncased_
preprocess/3"

preprocess = hub.load(PREPROCESS_MODEL)
bert = hub.load(BERT_MODEL)
inputs = preprocess(sentences)
outputs = bert(inputs)
```

4. Now let's define some auxiliary functions to show the similarity among embeddings based on `pairwise.cosine_similarity`:

```
def plot_similarity(features, labels):
    """Plot a similarity matrix of the embeddings."""
    cos_sim = pairwise.cosine_similarity(features)
    sns.set(font_scale=1.2)
    cbar_kws=dict(use_gridspec=False, location="left")
    g = sns.heatmap(
        cos_sim, xticklabels=labels, yticklabels=labels,
        vmin=0, vmax=1, cmap="Blues", cbar_kws=cbar_kws)
    g.tick_params(labelright=True, labelleft=False)
```

```
        g.set_yticklabels(labels, rotation=0)
        g.set_title("Semantic Textual Similarity")


    plot_similarity(outputs["pooled_output"], sentences)
```

The interested reader can access the Colab notebook online on the Hugging Face website (available at `https://huggingface.co/docs/transformers/training`) and visualize a heatmap showing similarities among sentences. Overall, using LLMs with TFHub is pretty easy, isn't it?

Evaluation

Evaluating transformers involves considering multiple classes of metrics and understanding the cost tradeoffs among these classes. Let's see the main ones.

Quality

The quality of transformers can be measured against a number of generally available datasets. Let's see the most commonly used ones.

GLUE

The **General Language Understanding Evaluation (GLUE)** benchmark is a collection of resources for training, evaluating, and analyzing natural language understanding systems. GLUE is available at `https://gluebenchmark.com/`.

GLUE consists of:

- A benchmark of nine sentence or sentence-pair language understanding tasks built on established existing datasets and selected to cover a diverse range of dataset sizes, text genres, and degrees of difficulty
- A diagnostic dataset designed to evaluate and analyze model performance with respect to a wide range of linguistic phenomena found in natural language
- A public leaderboard for tracking performance on the benchmark and a dashboard for visualizing the performance of models on the diagnostic set

Figure 6.17 shows the GLUE dashboard from March 2022:

Rank	Name	Model	URL	Score
1	JDExplore d-team	Vega v1		91.3
2	Microsoft Alexander v-team	Turing NLR v5		91.2
3	DIRL Team	DeBERTa + CLEVER		91.1
4	ERNIE Team - Baidu	ERNIE	⬏	91.1
5	AliceMind & DIRL	StructBERT + CLEVER	⬏	91.0
6	DeBERTa Team - Microsoft	DeBERTa / TuringNLRv4	⬏	90.8
7	HFL iFLYTEK	MacALBERT + DKM		90.7
8	PING-AN Omni-Sinitic	ALBERT + DAAF + NAS		90.6
9	T5 Team - Google	T5	⬏	90.3
10	Microsoft D365 AI & MSR AI & GATECH	MT-DNN-SMART	⬏	89.9

Figure 6.17: GLUE dashboard

SuperGLUE

In recent years, new models and methods for pretraining and transfer learning have driven striking performance improvements across a range of language understanding tasks. The GLUE benchmark offers a single-number metric that summarizes progress on a diverse set of such tasks, but performance on the benchmark has recently come close to the level of non-expert humans, suggesting limited headroom for further research.

SuperGLUE is a new benchmark styled after GLUE with a new set of more difficult language understanding tasks, improved resources, and a new public leaderboard. *Figure 6.18* is the SuperGLUE leaderboard from March 2022:

	Rank	Name	Model	Score
+	1	Liam Fedus	ST-MoE-32B	91.2
	2	Microsoft Alexander v-team	Turing NLR v5	90.9
	3	ERNIE Team - Baidu	ERNIE 3.0	90.6
+	4	Zirui Wang	T5 + UDG, Single Model (Google Brain)	90.4
+	5	DeBERTa Team - Microsoft	DeBERTa / TuringNLRv4	90.3
	6	SuperGLUE Human Baselines	SuperGLUE Human Baselines	89.8
+	7	T5 Team - Google	T5	89.3
	8	Descartes Team	frozen T5 1.1 + SPoT	89.2
	9	SPoT Team - Google	Frozen T5 1.1 + SPoT	89.2
+	10	Huawei Noah's Ark Lab	NEZHA-Plus	86.7

Figure 6.18: SuperGLUE leaderboard

SQuAD

SQuAD is a dataset used to evaluate questions and answers, https://rajpurkar.github.io/SQuAD-explorer/. Specifically, the **Stanford Question Answering Dataset (SQuAD)** is a reading comprehension dataset, consisting of questions posed by crowdworkers on a set of Wikipedia articles, where the answer to every question is a segment of text, or span, from the corresponding reading passage, otherwise the question might be unanswerable.

SQuAD2.0 combines the 100,000 questions in SQuAD1.1 with over 50,000 unanswerable questions written adversarially by crowdworkers to look similar to answerable ones. To do well on SQuAD2.0, systems must not only answer questions when possible but also determine when no answer is supported by the paragraph and abstain from answering.

RACE

The **ReAding Comprehension dataset from Examinations (RACE)** dataset is a machine reading comprehension dataset consisting of 27,933 passages and 97,867 questions from English exams, targeting Chinese students aged 12-18. RACE consists of two subsets, RACE-M and RACE-H, from middle school and high school exams, respectively. RACE-M has 28,293 questions and RACE-H has 69,574. Each question is associated with four candidate answers, one of which is correct. The data generation process of RACE differs from most machine reading comprehension datasets. Instead of generating questions and answers by heuristics or crowdsourcing, questions in RACE are specifically designed for testing human reading skills and are created by domain experts. RACE is available at https://www.cs.cmu.edu/~glai1/data/race/. *Figure 6.19* shows the RACE leaderboard:

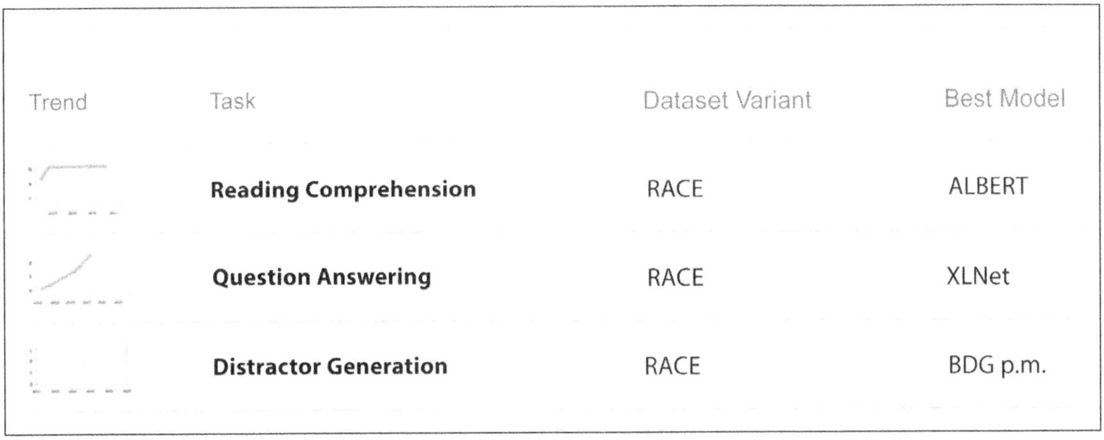

Trend	Task	Dataset Variant	Best Model
	Reading Comprehension	RACE	ALBERT
	Question Answering	RACE	XLNet
	Distractor Generation	RACE	BDG p.m.

Figure 6.19: RACE leaderboard

NLP-progress

NLP-progress is a repository, made to track progress in NLP, including the datasets and the current state-of-the-art models for the most common NLP tasks. The site aims to track the progress in NLP and gives an overview of the state-of-the-art models across the most common NLP tasks and their corresponding datasets. NLP-progress aims to cover both traditional and core NLP tasks such as dependency parsing and part-of-speech tagging as well as more recent ones such as reading comprehension and natural language inference. If you need a good starting point to find quality metrics for your task, then http://nlpprogress.com/ is the place to start with.

Size

The previous section provided an overview of quality metrics. This section focuses on the number of parameters used in various transformer architectures. As shown in *Figure 6.20*, there has been a race to increase transformers' size during the last few years. Back in 2018, BERT's size was about 340 million parameters, then in 2021, T5 reached 11 billion, and Megatron passed 500 billion. The very recent Switch Transformer has more than one trillion parameters and there is an expectation that soon we will see the first model with 100 trillion parameters. Indeed, there is evidence that the larger the model is the merrier, which can memorize information and generalize. However, training such large models requires massive computational resources:

Year	Model	# of Parameters	Dataset Size
2019	BERT [39]	3.4E+08	16GB
2019	DistilBERT [113]	6.60E+07	16GB
2019	ALBERT [70]	2.23E+08	16GB
2019	XLNet (Large) [150]	3.40E+08	126GB
2020	ERNIE-GEN (Large) [145]	3.40E+08	16GB
2019	RoBERTa (Large) [74]	3.55E+08	161GB
2019	MegatronLM [122]	8.30E+09	174GB
2020	T5-11B [107]	1.10E+10	745GB
2020	T-NLG [112]	1.70E+10	174GB
2020	GPT-3 [25]	1.75E+11	570GB
2020	GShard [73]	6.00E+11	–
2021	Switch-C [43]	1.57E+12	745GB

Figure 6.20: Transformers' size in billions of parameters

Trillion parameter transformers are on their way!

In fact, the paper `https://arxiv.org/pdf/1906.02243.pdf` warns about the sustainability impact of training large models (see *Figure 6.21*) in terms of both cloud computing cost and CO2 emissions:

Model	Hardware	Power (W)	Hours	kWh.PUE	CO_2e	Cloud compute cost
Transformer*base*	P100x8	1415.78	12	27	26	$41—$4140
Transformer*big*	P100x8		84	201	192	$289—$981
ELMo	P100x3	517.66	336	275	262	$433—$1472
BERT*base*	V100x64	12,041.51	79	1507	1438	$3751—$12,571
BERT*base*	TPUv2x16	—	96	—	—	$2074—$6912
NAS	P100x8	1515.43	274,120	656,347	626,155	$942,973—$3,201,722
NAS	TPUv2x1	—	32,623	—	—	$44,055—$146,848
GPT-2	TPUv3x32	—	168	—	—	$12,902—$43,008

Figure 6.21: Estimated cost of training a model in terms of CO2 emissions (lbs) and cloud computing cost (USD) - source: https://arxiv.org/pdf/1906.02243.pdf

So, size is not the only factor that enables the quality of transformers to improve, as larger sizes can in reality give only marginal gains and require significant computational resources for training.

Larger doesn't always mean better

At the beginning of 2022, a new trend is emerging consisting of a hybrid approach where large models are used together with a more traditional retrieval mechanism. We discussed this approach earlier in the chapter when we discussed RETRO. The RETRO language model implements a learning scheme based on the use of external memory. DeepMind claimed that RETRO (or "Retrieval Enhanced Transformer") performs like a neural network 25 times its size. GPT-3 has 175 billion parameters and RETRO uses just seven billion of them. Of course, this requires less time, energy, and computing power to train.

Cost of serving

The cost of serving a model depends on many factors and it's difficult to estimate it without making reasonable assumptions. Of course, serving is a function of the number of parameters in the model. In addition, the number of queries submitted to the model for inference is another factor. Then, it's important to consider whether or not a cloud provider manages the model or is served in your on-prem infrastructure. In this context, it might be useful to remember that MLOps (see `https://en.wikipedia.org/wiki/MLOps`) is the process of developing a machine learning model and deploying it as a production system. Of course, MLOps' best practices might be adopted to optimize the costs of serving.

In this section, we have seen some key factors used to evaluate transformers, namely quality, size, and cost of serving. The list is clearly not inclusive, and a proper evaluation will take into account what the optimal tradeoff is among these factors. In the next section, we will discuss optimization.

Optimization

Optimizing a transformer involves building lightweight, responsive, and energy-efficient models. Let's see the most common ideas adopted to optimize a model.

Quantization

The key idea behind quantization is to approximate the weights of a network with a smaller precision. The idea is very simple, but it works quite well in practice. If you are interested in knowing more, we recommend the paper *A Survey of Quantization Methods for Efficient Neural Network Inference*, by Amir Gholami et al., `https://arxiv.org/pdf/2103.13630.pdf`.

Weight pruning

The key idea behind weight pruning is to remove some connections in the network. Magnitude-based weight pruning tends to zero out of model weights during training to increase model sparsity. This simple technique has benefits both in terms of model size and in cost of serving, as magnitude-based weight pruning gradually zeroes out of model weights during the training process to achieve model sparsity. Sparse models are easier to compress, and we can skip the zeroes during inference for latency improvements.

One more time, weight pruning is about tradeoffs as it might generate some quality losses although normally, they are rather small. If you are interested to know more, please have a look at the TensorFlow guide about pruning: `https://www.tensorflow.org/model_optimization/guide/pruning/comprehensive_guide`.

Distillation

The key idea behind knowledge distillation is to have a small model trained to reproduce the behavior of a larger model. This compression technique is sometimes referred to as teacher-student learning. The seminal paper you should check is *Distilling the Knowledge in a Neural Network* by Geoffrey Hinton, Oriol Vinyals, and Jeff Dean, `https://arxiv.org/abs/1503.02531`.

During the last few years, we have seen a number of distilled transformers. For instance, DistilBERT is a small, fast, cheap, and light transformer model based on the BERT architecture. Knowledge distillation is performed during the pretraining phase to reduce the size of a BERT model by 40%. Hugging Face has some ready-to-use Python scripts for distilling seq2seq T5 models available online at `https://github.com/huggingface/transformers/tree/master/examples/research_projects/seq2seq-distillation`. Using the script is quite intuitive:

```
python distillation.py --teacher t5-small --data_dir cnn_dm \
--student_decoder_layers 3 --student_encoder_layers 6 --tokenizer_name t5-small \
--learning_rate=3e-4 --freeze_encoder --no_teacher --freeze_embeds \
--do_train --train_batch_size 32 \
--do_predict \
--model_name_or_path t5-small --eval_beams 2 --eval_max_gen_length 142 \
--val_check_interval 0.25 --n_val 1000 \
--output_dir distilt5 --gpus 1 --logger_name wandb
```

In this section, we have discussed a few techniques used to optimize transformers, namely quantization, weight pruning, and distillation. In the next section, we will discuss common pitfalls for transformers.

Common pitfalls: dos and don'ts

In this section, we will give five dos and a few don'ts that are typically recommended when dealing with transformers.

Dos

Let's start with recommended best practices:

- **Do use pretrained large models.** Today, it is almost always convenient to start from an already available pretrained model such as T5, instead of training your transformer from scratch. If you use a pretrained model, you for sure stand on the giant's shoulders; think about it!
- **Do start with few-shot learning.** When you start working with transformers, it's always a good idea to start with a pretrained model and then perform a lightweight few-shot learning step. Generally, this would improve the quality of results without high computational costs.

- **Do use fine-tuning on your domain data and on your customer data.** After playing with pretraining models and few-shot learning, you might consider doing a proper fine-tuning on your own proprietary data or on publicly available data for your domain of interest

- **Get yourself familiar with transformers' libraries.** Hugging Face or TFHub provide already available state-of-the-art implementations of almost all the known transformers. It might be useful to start from there unless you either have some very peculiar needs or are doing some innovative research work.

- **Get yourself familiar with the most commonly used evaluation metrics.** When you use transformers, it is ideal to take into account the tradeoff faced in terms of quality, size, cost of serving, and many other factors.

Don'ts

Now let's have a look at some of the pitfalls that you should avoid!

- **Do not use very large models as a starting point.** Large models come with a cost in terms of training and serving. You will need significant resources to fine-tune, and you might pay high costs for serving each query. It might be better to start with smaller models and understand whether they are useful for your quality needs.

- **Do not use unoptimized models.** Nowadays, quantization, pruning, and distillation are standard techniques that need to be used by any transformer system that is put into production.

In this section, we have seen some of the best practices for transformers. In the next section, we will talk about future solutions for these architectures.

The future of transformers

Transformers found their initial applications in NLP tasks, while CNNs are typically used for image processing systems. Recently, transformers have started to be successfully used for vision processing tasks. Vision transformers compute relationships among pixels in various small sections of an image (for example, 16 x 16 pixels). This approach has been proposed in the seminar paper *An Image is Worth 16x16 Words: Transformers for Image Recognition at Scale* by Alexey Dosovitskiy et al., `https://arxiv.org/abs/2010.11929`, to make the attention computation feasible.

Vision transformers (ViTs) are today used for complex applications such as autonomous driving. Tesla's engineers showed that their Tesla Autopilot uses a transformer on the multi-camera system in cars. Of course, ViTs are also used for more traditional computer vision tasks, including but not limited to image classification, object detection, video deepfake detection, image segmentation, anomaly detection, image synthesis, and cluster analysis. The results are frequently better than CNNs.

Another direction to consider is few-shot learning. Few-shot learning refers to the practice of feeding a machine learning model with a very small amount of training data to guide its predictions, like a few examples at inference time, as opposed to standard fine-tuning techniques that require a relatively large amount of training data for the pretrained model to adapt to the desired task with accuracy.

So, a model trained for a specific task can be reused for completely new tasks with very marginal costs. For instance, suppose we train a text model to generate text. Then, we want to perform new tasks such as translation or summarization. What we do is give a few examples of translations (say with pairs of text manually translated), or a few examples of summarization (again a few pairs). That's it, no need for retraining or fine-tuning training.

Since FSL is proven to work well in a number of increasing domains, don't be surprised that the training phase will be less and less relevant for future AI. More information can be found in this paper, *Code Generation Tools (Almost) for Free? A Study of Few-Shot, Pre-Trained Language Models on Code* by Patrick Bareiß, Beatriz Souza, Marcelo d'Amorim, and Michael Pradel. The authors propose to use FSL to generate programming code with CodeGen, an open source mode for program synthesis (see `https://github.com/salesforce/CodeGen`).

Summary

In this chapter, we discussed transformers, a deep learning architecture that has revolutionized the traditional natural language processing field. We started reviewing the key intuitions behind the architecture, and various categories of transformers together with a deep dive into the most popular models. Then, we focused on implementations both based on vanilla architecture and on popular libraries such as Hugging Face and TFHub. After that, we briefly discussed evaluation, optimization, and some of the best practices commonly adopted when using transformers. The last section was devoted to reviewing how transformers can be used to perform computer vision tasks, a totally different domain from NLP. That requires a careful definition of the attention mechanism. In the end, attention is all you need! And at the core of attention is nothing more than the cosine similarity between vectors.

The next chapter is devoted to unsupervised learning.

Join our book's Discord space

Join our Discord community to meet like-minded people and learn alongside more than 2000 members at: `https://packt.link/keras`

7

Unsupervised Learning

The book till now has focused on supervised learning and the models that learn via supervised learning. Starting from this chapter we will explore a less explored and more challenging area of unsupervised learning, self-supervised learning, and contrastive learning. In this chapter, we will delve deeper into some popular and useful unsupervised learning models. In contrast to supervised learning, where the training dataset consists of both the input and the desired labels, unsupervised learning deals with a case where the model is provided with only the input. The model learns the inherent input distribution by itself without any desired label guiding it. Clustering and dimensionality reduction are the two most commonly used unsupervised learning techniques. In this chapter, we will learn about different machine learning and neural network techniques for both. We will cover techniques required for clustering and dimensionality reduction, and go into the detail about Boltzmann machines, and finally, cover the implementation of the aforementioned techniques using TensorFlow. The concepts covered will be extended to build **Restricted Boltzmann Machines (RBMs)**. The chapter will include:

- Principal component analysis
- K-means clustering
- Self-organizing maps
- Boltzmann machines
- RBMs

 All the code files for this chapter can be found at `https://packt.link/dltfchp7`.

Let us start with the most common and frequently used technique for dimensionality reduction, the principal component analysis method.

Principal component analysis

Principal component analysis (**PCA**) is the most popular multivariate statistical technique for dimensionality reduction. It analyzes the training data consisting of several dependent variables, which are, in general, intercorrelated, and extracts important information from the training data in the form of a set of new orthogonal variables called principal components.

We can perform PCA using two methods, either **eigen decomposition** or **singular value decomposition (SVD)**.

PCA reduces the n-dimensional input data to r-dimensional input data, where $r<n$. In simple terms, PCA involves translating the origin and performing rotation of the axis such that one of the axes (principal axis) has the highest variance with data points. A reduced-dimensions dataset is obtained from the original dataset by performing this transformation and then dropping (removing) the orthogonal axes with low variance. Here, we employ the SVD method for PCA dimensionality reduction. Consider X, the n-dimensional data with p points, that is, X is a matrix of size $p \times n$. From linear algebra we know that any real matrix can be decomposed using singular value decomposition:

$$X = U\textstyle\sum V^T$$

Where U and V are orthonormal matrices (that is, $U.U^T = V.V^T = 1$) of size $p \times p$ and $n \times n$ respectively. $\sum$ is a diagonal matrix of size $p \times n$. The U matrix is called the **left singular matrix**, and V the **right singular matrix**, and $\sum$, the diagonal matrix, contains the singular values of X as its diagonal elements. Here we assume that the X matrix is centered. The columns of the V matrix are the principal components, and columns of $U\sum$ are the data transformed by principal components.

Now to reduce the dimensions of the data from n to k (where $k < n$), we will select the first k columns of U and the upper-left $k \times k$ part of $\sum$. The product of the two gives us our reduced-dimensions matrix:

$$Y_k = U\textstyle\sum_k$$

The data Y obtained will be of reduced dimensions. Next, we implement PCA in TensorFlow 2.0.

PCA on the MNIST dataset

Let us now implement PCA in TensorFlow 2.0. We will be definitely using TensorFlow; we will also need NumPy for some elementary matrix calculation, and Matplotlib, Matplotlib toolkits, and Seaborn for plotting:

```
import tensorflow as tf
import numpy as np
import matplotlib.pyplot as plt
from mpl_toolkits.mplot3d import Axes3D
import seaborn as sns
```

Next we load the MNIST dataset. Since we are doing dimension reduction using PCA, we do not need a test dataset or even labels; however, we are loading labels so that after reduction we can verify the PCA performance. PCA should cluster similar data points in one cluster; hence, if we see that the clusters formed using PCA are similar to our labels, it would indicate that our PCA works:

```
((x_train, y_train), (_, _)) = tf.keras.datasets.mnist.load_data()
```

Before we do PCA, we should preprocess the data. We first normalize it so that all data has values between 0 and 1, and then reshape the image from being a 28 × 28 matrix to a 784-dimensional vector, and finally, center it by subtracting the mean:

```
x_train = x_train / 255.
x_train = x_train.astype(np.float32)
x_train = np.reshape(x_train, (x_train.shape[0], 784))
mean = x_train.mean(axis = 1)
x_train = x_train - mean[:,None]
```

Now that our data is in the right format, we make use of TensorFlow's powerful linear algebra (linalg) module to calculate the SVD of our training dataset. TensorFlow provides the function svd() defined in tf.linalg to perform this task. And then use the diag function to convert the sigma array (s, a list of singular values) to a diagonal matrix:

```
s, u, v = tf.linalg.svd(x_train)
s = tf.linalg.diag(s)
```

This provides us with a diagonal matrix *s* of size 784 × 784; a left singular matrix *u* of size 60,000 × 784; and a right singular matrix *v* of size 784 × 784. This is so because the argument full_matrices of the function svd() is by default set to False. As a result it does not generate the full *U* matrix (in this case, of size 60,000 × 60,000); instead, if input *X* is of size $m \times n$, it generates *U* of size $p = min(m,n)$.

The reduced-dimension data can now be generated by multiplying respective slices of *u* and *s*. We reduce our data from 784 to 3 dimensions; we can choose to reduce to any dimension less than 784, but we chose 3 here so that it is easier for us to visualize later. We make use of tf.Tensor.getitem to slice our matrices in the Pythonic way:

```
k = 3
pca = tf.matmul(u[:,0:k], s[0:k,0:k])
```

A comparison of the original and reduced data shape is done in the following code:

```
print('original data shape',x_train.shape)
print('reduced data shape', pca.shape)
```

```
original data shape (60000, 784)
reduced data shape (60000, 3)
```

Finally, let us plot the data points in the three-dimensional space:

```
Set = sns.color_palette("Set2", 10)
color_mapping = {key:value for (key,value) in enumerate(Set)}
colors = list(map(lambda x: color_mapping[x], y_train))
fig = plt.figure()
ax = Axes3D(fig)
ax.scatter(pca[:, 0], pca[:, 1],pca[:, 2], c=colors)
```

Figure 7.1: Scatter plot of MNIST dataset after dimensionality reduction using PCA

You can see that the points corresponding to the same color and, hence, the same label are clustered together. We have therefore successfully used PCA to reduce the dimensions of MNIST images. Each original image was of size 28 × 28. Using the PCA method we can reduce it to a smaller size. Normally for image data, dimensionality reduction is necessary. This is because images are large in size and contain a significant amount of redundant data.

TensorFlow Embedding API

TensorFlow also offers an Embedding API where one can find and visualize PCA and tSNE [1] clusters using TensorBoard. You can see the live PCA on MNIST images here: http://projector.tensorflow. org. The following image is reproduced for reference:

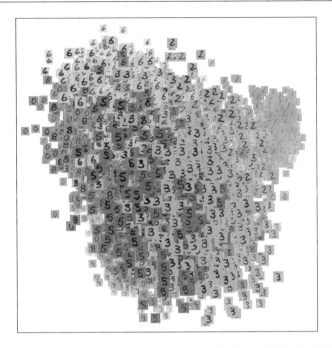

Figure 7.2: A visualization of a principal component analysis, applied to the MNIST dataset

You can process your data using TensorBoard. It contains a tool called **Embedding Projector** that allows one to interactively visualize embedding. The Embedding Projector tool has three panels:

- **Data Panel:** It is located at the top left, and you can choose the data, labels, and so on in this panel.
- **Projections Panel:** Available at the bottom left, you can choose the type of projections you want here. It offers three choices: PCA, t-SNE, and custom.

- **Inspector Panel:** On the right-hand side, here you can search for particular points and see a list of nearest neighbors.

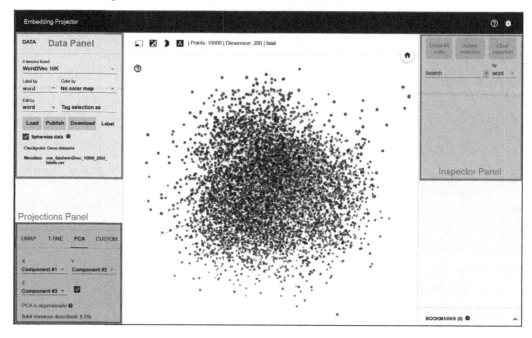

Figure 7.3: Screenshot of the Embedding Projector tool

PCA is a useful tool for visualizing datasets and for finding linear relationships between variables. It can also be used for clustering, outlier detection, and feature selection. Next, we will learn about the k-means algorithm, a method for clustering data.

K-means clustering

K-means clustering, as the name suggests, is a technique to cluster data, that is, to partition data into a specified number of data points. It is an unsupervised learning technique. It works by identifying patterns in the given data. Remember the sorting hat of Harry Potter fame? What it is doing in the book is clustering—dividing new (unlabelled) students into four different clusters: Gryffindor, Ravenclaw, Hufflepuff, and Slytherin.

Humans are very good at grouping objects together; clustering algorithms try to give a similar capability to computers. There are many clustering techniques available, such as hierarchical, Bayesian, or partitional. K-means clustering belongs to partitional clustering; it partitions data into k clusters. Each cluster has a center, called the centroid. The number of clusters k has to be specified by the user. The k-means algorithm works in the following manner:

1. Randomly choose k data points as the initial centroids (cluster centers).

2. Assign each data point to the closest centroid; there can be different measures to find closeness, the most common being the Euclidean distance.

3. Recompute the centroids using current cluster membership, such that the sum of squared distances decreases.

4. Repeat the last two steps until convergence is met.

In the previous TensorFlow versions, the KMeans class was implemented in the Contrib module; however, the class is no longer available in TensorFlow 2.0. Here we will instead use the advanced mathematical functions provided in TensorFlow 2.0 to implement k-means clustering.

K-means in TensorFlow

To demonstrate k-means in TensorFlow, we will use randomly generated data in the code that follows. Our randomly generated data will contain 200 samples, and we will divide them into three clusters. We start by importing all the required modules, defining the variables, and determining the number of sample points (points_n), the number of clusters to be formed (clusters_n), and the number of iterations we will be doing (iteration_n). We also set the seed for a random number to ensure that our work is reproducible:

```
import matplotlib.pyplot as plt
import numpy as np
import tensorflow as tf
points_n = 200
clusters_n = 3
iteration_n = 100
seed = 123
np.random.seed(seed)
tf.random.set_seed(seed)
```

Now we randomly generate data and from the data select three centroids randomly:

```
points = np.random.uniform(0, 10, (points_n, 2))
centroids = tf.slice(tf.random.shuffle(points), [0, 0], [clusters_n, -1])
```

Let us now plot the points:

```
plt.scatter(points[:, 0], points[:, 1], s=50, alpha=0.5)
plt.plot(centroids[:, 0], centroids[:, 1], 'kx', markersize=15)
plt.show()
```

You can see the scatter plot of all the points and the randomly selected three centroids in the following graph:

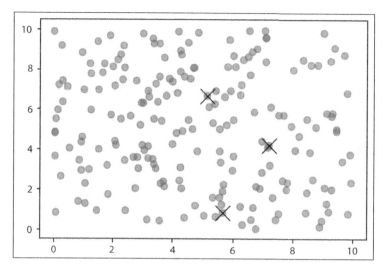

Figure 7.4: Randomly generated data, from three randomly selected centroids, plotted

We define the function `closest_centroids()` to assign each point to the centroid it is closest to:

```
def closest_centroids(points, centroids):
    distances = tf.reduce_sum(tf.square(tf.subtract(points,
centroids[:,None])), 2)
    assignments = tf.argmin(distances, 0)
    return assignments
```

We create another function `move_centroids()`. It recalculates the centroids such that the sum of squared distances decreases:

```
def move_centroids(points, closest, centroids):
    return np.array([points[closest==k].mean(axis=0) for k in range(centroids.
shape[0])])
```

Now we call these two functions iteratively for 100 iterations. We have chosen the number of iterations arbitrarily; you can increase and decrease it to see the effect:

```
for step in range(iteration_n):
    closest = closest_centroids(points, centroids)
    centroids = move_centroids(points, closest, centroids)
```

Let us now visualize how the centroids have changed after 100 iterations:

```
plt.scatter(points[:, 0], points[:, 1], c=closest, s=50, alpha=0.5)
plt.plot(centroids[:, 0], centroids[:, 1], 'kx', markersize=15)
plt.show()
```

In *Figure 7.5*, you can see the final centroids after 100 iterations. We have also colored the points based on which centroid they are closest to. The yellow points correspond to one cluster (nearest the cross in its center), and the same is true for the purple and green cluster points:

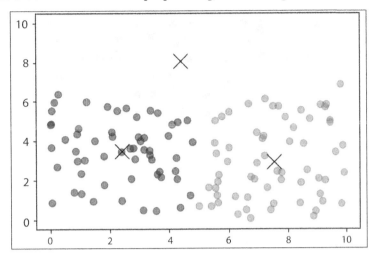

Figure 7.5: Plot of the final centroids after 100 iterations

  Please note that the `plot` command works in `Matplotlib 3.1.1` or higher versions.

In the preceding code, we decided to limit the number of clusters to three, but in most cases with unlabelled data, one is never sure how many clusters exist. One can determine the optimal number of clusters using the elbow method. The method is based on the principle that we should choose the cluster number that reduces the **sum of squared error (SSE)** distance. If k is the number of clusters, then as k increases, the SSE decreases, with SSE = 0; when k is equal to the number of data points, each point is its own cluster. It is clear we do not want this as our number of clusters, so when we plot the graph between SSE and the number of clusters, we should see a kink in the graph, like the elbow of the hand, which is how the method gets its name – the elbow method. The following code calculates the sum of squared errors for our data:

```
def sse(points, centroids):
    sse1 = tf.reduce_sum(tf.square(tf.subtract(points, centroids[:,None]))),
2).numpy()
    s = np.argmin(sse1, 0)
    distance = 0
    for i in range(len(points)):
        distance += sse1[s[i], i]

    return distance/len(points)
```

Let us use the elbow method now for finding the optimum number of clusters for our dataset. To do that we will start with one cluster, that is, all points belonging to a single cluster, and increase the number of clusters sequentially. In the code, we increase the clusters by one, with eleven being the maximum number of clusters. For each cluster number value, we use the code above to find the centroids (and hence the clusters) and find the SSE:

```
w_sse = []
for n in range(1, 11):
  centroids = tf.slice(tf.random.shuffle(points), [0, 0], [n, -1])
  for step in range(iteration_n):
    closest = closest_centroids(points, centroids)
    centroids = move_centroids(points, closest, centroids)
   #print(sse(points, centroids))
  w_sse.append(sse(points, centroids))
plt.plot(range(1, 11),w_sse)
plt.xlabel('Number of clusters')
```

Figure 7.6 shows the different cluster values for the dataset. The kink is clearly visible when the number of clusters is four:

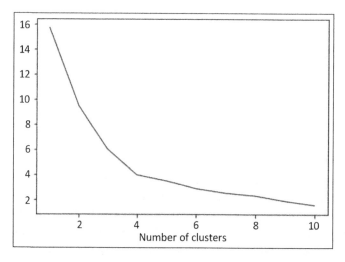

Figure 7.6: Plotting SSE against the number of clusters

K-means clustering is very popular because it is fast, simple, and robust. It also has some disadvantages, the biggest being that the user has to specify the number of clusters. Second, the algorithm does not guarantee global optima; the results can change if the initial randomly chosen centroids change. Third, it is very sensitive to outliers.

Variations in k-means

In the original k-means algorithm each point belongs to a specific cluster (centroid); this is called **hard clustering**. However, we can have one point belong to all the clusters, with a membership function defining how much it belongs to a particular cluster (centroid). This is called *fuzzy clustering* or *soft clustering*.

This variation was proposed in 1973 by J. C. Dunn and later improved upon by J. C. Bezdek in 1981. Though soft clustering takes longer to converge, it can be useful when a point is in multiple classes, or when we want to know how similar a given point is to different clusters.

The accelerated k-means algorithm was created in 2003 by Charles Elkan. He exploited the triangle inequality relationship (that is, a straight line is the shortest distance between two points). Instead of just doing all distance calculations at each iteration, he also kept track of the lower and upper bounds for distances between points and centroids.

In 2006, David Arthur and Sergei Vassilvitskii proposed the k-means++ algorithm. The major change they proposed was in the initialization of centroids. They showed that if we choose centroids that are distant from each other, then the k-means algorithm is less likely to converge on a suboptimal solution.

Another alternative can be that at each iteration we do not use the entire dataset, instead using mini-batches. This modification was proposed by David Sculey in 2010. Now, that we have covered PCA and k-means, we move toward an interesting network called self-organized network or winner-take-all units.

Self-organizing maps

Both k-means and PCA can cluster the input data; however, they do not maintain a topological relationship. In this section, we will consider **Self-Organizing Maps (SOMs)**, sometimes known as **Kohonen networks** or **Winner-Take-All Units (WTUs)**. They maintain the topological relation. SOMs are a very special kind of neural network, inspired by a distinctive feature of the human brain. In our brain, different sensory inputs are represented in a topologically ordered manner. Unlike other neural networks, neurons are not all connected to each other via weights; instead, they influence each other's learning. The most important aspect of SOM is that neurons represent the learned inputs in a topographic manner. They were proposed by Teuvo Kohonen [7] in 1982.

In SOMs, neurons are usually placed on the nodes of a (1D or 2D) lattice. Higher dimensions are also possible but are rarely used in practice. Each neuron in the lattice is connected to all the input units via a weight matrix. *Figure 7.7* shows a SOM with 6 × 8 (48 neurons) and 5 inputs. For clarity, only the weight vectors connecting all inputs to one neuron are shown. In this case, each neuron will have seven elements, resulting in a combined weight matrix of size 40 × 5:

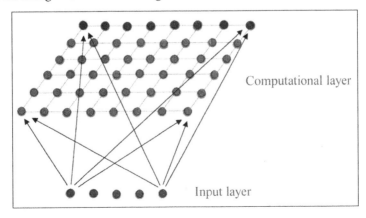

Figure 7.7: A self-organized map with 5 inputs and 48 neurons

A SOM learns via competitive learning. It can be considered as a nonlinear generalization of PCA and, thus, like PCA, can be employed for dimensionality reduction.

In order to implement SOM, let's first understand how it works. As a first step, the weights of the network are initialized either to some random value or by taking random samples from the input. Each neuron occupying a space in the lattice will be assigned specific locations. Now as an input is presented, the neuron with the least distance from the input is declared the winner (WTU). This is done by measuring the distance between the weight vectors (W) and input vectors (X) of all neurons:

$$d_j = \sqrt{\sum_{i=1}^{N}(W_{ji} - X_i)^2}$$

Here, d_j is the distance of the weights of neuron j from input X. The neuron with the lowest d value is the winner.

Next, the weights of the winning neuron and its neighboring neurons are adjusted in a manner to ensure that the same neuron is the winner if the same input is presented next time.

To decide which neighboring neurons need to be modified, the network uses a neighborhood function $\wedge(r)$; normally, the Gaussian Mexican hat function is chosen as a neighborhood function. The neighborhood function is mathematically represented as follows:

$$\wedge(r) = e^{-\frac{d^2}{2\sigma^2}}$$

Here, σ is a time-dependent radius of the influence of a neuron and d is its distance from the winning neuron. Graphically, the function looks like a hat (hence its name), as you can see in *Figure 7.8*:

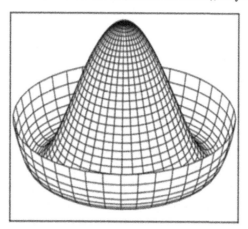

Figure 7.8: The "Gaussian Mexican hat" function, visualized in graph form

Another important property of the neighborhood function is that its radius reduces with time. As a result, in the beginning, many neighboring neurons' weights are modified, but as the network learns, eventually a few neurons' weights (at times, only one or none) are modified in the learning process.

The change in weight is given by the following equation:

$$dW = \eta \wedge (X - W)$$

The process is repeated for all the inputs for a given number of iterations. As the iterations progress, we reduce the learning rate and the radius by a factor dependent on the iteration number.

SOMs are computationally expensive and thus are not really useful for very large datasets. Still, they are easy to understand, and they can very nicely find the similarity between input data. Thus, they have been employed for image segmentation and to determine word similarity maps in NLP.

Colour mapping using a SOM

Some of the interesting properties of the feature map of the input space generated by a SOM are:

- The feature map provides a good representation of the input space. This property can be used to perform vector quantization so that we may have a continuous input space, and using a SOM we can represent it in a discrete output space.
- The feature map is topologically ordered, that is, the spatial location of a neuron in the output lattice corresponds to a particular feature of the input.
- The feature map also reflects the statistical distribution of the input space; the domain that has the largest number of input samples gets a wider area in the feature map.

These features of SOM make them the natural choice for many interesting applications. Here we use SOM for clustering a range of given R, G, and B pixel values to a corresponding color map. We start with the importing of modules:

```
import tensorflow as tf
import numpy as np
import matplotlib.pyplot as plt
```

The main component of the code is our class WTU. The class __init__ function initializes various hyperparameters of our SOM, the dimensions of our 2D lattice (m, n), the number of features in the input (dim), the neighborhood radius (sigma), the initial weights, and the topographic information:

```
# Define the Winner Take All units
class WTU(object):
  #_learned = False
  def __init__(self, m, n, dim, num_iterations, eta = 0.5, sigma = None):
    """
    m x n : The dimension of 2D lattice in which neurons are arranged
    dim : Dimension of input training data
    num_iterations: Total number of training iterations
    eta : Learning rate
    sigma: The radius of neighbourhood function.
    """
    self._m = m
```

```
    self._n = n
    self._neighbourhood = []
    self._topography = []
    self._num_iterations = int(num_iterations)
    self._learned = False
    self.dim = dim
    self.eta = float(eta)

    if sigma is None:
        sigma = max(m,n)/2.0 # Constant radius
    else:
        sigma = float(sigma)
    self.sigma = sigma

    print('Network created with dimensions',m,n)

    # Weight Matrix and the topography of neurons
    self._W = tf.random.normal([m*n, dim], seed = 0)
    self._topography = np.array(list(self._neuron_location(m, n)))
```

The most important function of the class is the `training()` function, where we use the Kohonen algorithm as discussed before to find the winner units and then update the weights based on the neighborhood function:

```
def training(self,x, i):
    m = self._m
    n= self._n

    # Finding the Winner and its Location
    d = tf.sqrt(tf.reduce_sum(tf.pow(self._W - tf.stack([x for i in
range(m*n)]),2),1))
    self.WTU_idx = tf.argmin(d,0)

    slice_start = tf.pad(tf.reshape(self.WTU_idx, [1]),np.array([[0,1]]))
    self.WTU_loc = tf.reshape(tf.slice(self._topography, slice_start,[1,2]),
[2])


    # Change learning rate and radius as a function of iterations
    learning_rate = 1 - i/self._num_iterations
    _eta_new = self.eta * learning_rate
```

```
    _sigma_new = self.sigma * learning_rate



    # Calculating Neighbourhood function
    distance_square = tf.reduce_sum(tf.pow(tf.subtract(
        self._topography, tf.stack([self.WTU_loc for i in range(m * n)])), 2),
1)
    neighbourhood_func = tf.exp(tf.negative(tf.math.divide(tf.cast(
distance_square, "float32"), tf.pow(_sigma_new, 2))))


    # multiply learning rate with neighbourhood func
    eta_into_Gamma = tf.multiply(_eta_new, neighbourhood_func)


    # Shape it so that it can be multiplied to calculate dW
    weight_multiplier = tf.stack([tf.tile(tf.slice(
        eta_into_Gamma, np.array([i]), np.array([1])), [self.dim])
        for i in range(m * n)])
    delta_W = tf.multiply(weight_multiplier,
        tf.subtract(tf.stack([x for i in range(m * n)]),self._W))
    new_W = self._W + delta_W
    self._W = new_W
```

The `fit()` function is a helper function that calls the `training()` function and stores the centroid grid for easy retrieval:

```
def fit(self, X):
    """
    Function to carry out training
    """
    for i in range(self._num_iterations):
        for x in X:
            self.training(x,i)
    # Store a centroid grid for easy retrieval
    centroid_grid = [[] for i in range(self._m)]
    self._Wts = list(self._W)
    self._locations = list(self._topography)
    for i, loc in enumerate(self._locations):
        centroid_grid[loc[0]].append(self._Wts[i])
    self._centroid_grid = centroid_grid
    self._learned = True
```

Then there are some more helper functions to find the winner and generate a 2D lattice of neurons, and a function to map input vectors to the corresponding neurons in the 2D lattice:

```python
def winner(self, x):
    idx = self.WTU_idx,self.WTU_loc
    return idx


def _neuron_location(self,m,n):
    """
    Function to generate the 2D lattice of neurons
    """
    for i in range(m):
        for j in range(n):
            yield np.array([i,j])
def get_centroids(self):
    """
    Function to return a list of 'm' lists, with each inner list containing the
'n' corresponding centroid locations as 1-D NumPy arrays.
    """
    if not self._learned:
        raise ValueError("SOM not trained yet")
    return self._centroid_grid
def map_vects(self, X):
    """
    Function to map each input vector to the relevant neuron in the lattice
    """
    if not self._learned:
        raise ValueError("SOM not trained yet")
    to_return = []
    for vect in X:
        min_index = min([i for i in range(len(self._Wts))],
                        key=lambda x: np.linalg.norm(vect -
                        self._Wts[x]))
        to_return.append(self._locations[min_index])
    return to_return
```

We will also need to normalize the input data, so we create a function to do so:

```python
def normalize(df):
    result = df.copy()
    for feature_name in df.columns:
```

```
        max_value = df[feature_name].max()
        min_value = df[feature_name].min()
        result[feature_name] = (df[feature_name] - min_value) / (max_value -
    min_value)
      return result.astype(np.float32)
```

Let us read the data. The data contains red, green, and blue channel values for different colors. Let us normalize them:

```
## Reading input data from file
import pandas as pd
df = pd.read_csv('colors.csv')  # The last column of data file is a label
data = normalize(df[['R', 'G', 'B']]).values
name = df['Color-Name'].values
n_dim = len(df.columns) - 1
# Data for Training
colors = data
color_names = name
```

Let us create our SOM and fit it:

```
som = WTU(30, 30, n_dim, 400, sigma=10.0)
som.fit(colors)
```

The fit function takes slightly longer to run, since our code is not optimized for performance but for explaining the concept. Now, let's look at the result of the trained model. Let us run the following code:

```
# Get output grid
image_grid = som.get_centroids()
# Map colours to their closest neurons
mapped = som.map_vects(colors)
# Plot
plt.imshow(image_grid)
plt.title('Color Grid SOM')
for i, m in enumerate(mapped):
    plt.text(m[1], m[0], color_names[i], ha='center', va='center',
            bbox=dict(facecolor='white', alpha=0.5, lw=0))
```

You can see the color map in the 2D neuron lattice:

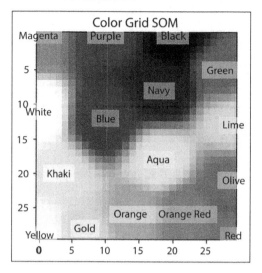

Figure 7.9: A plotted color map of the 2D neuron lattice

You can see that neurons that win for similar colors are closely placed. Next, we move to an interesting architecture, the restricted Boltzmann machines.

Restricted Boltzmann machines

The RBM is a two-layered neural network—the first layer is called the **visible layer** and the second layer is called the **hidden layer.** They are called **shallow neural networks** because they are only two layers deep. They were first proposed in 1986 by Paul Smolensky (he called them Harmony Networks [1]) and later by Geoffrey Hinton who in 2006 proposed **Contrastive Divergence (CD)** as a method to train them. All neurons in the visible layer are connected to all the neurons in the hidden layer, but there is a **restriction**—no neuron in the same layer can be connected. All neurons in the RBM are binary by nature; they will either fire or not fire.

RBMs can be used for dimensionality reduction, feature extraction, and collaborative filtering. The training of RBMs can be divided into three parts: forward pass, backward pass, and then a comparison.

Let us delve deeper into the math. We can divide the operation of RBMs into two passes:

Forward pass: The information at visible units (V) is passed via weights (W) and biases (c) to the hidden units (h_0). The hidden unit may fire or not depending on the stochastic probability (σ is the stochastic probability), which is basically the sigmoid function:

$$\rho(v_0|h_0) = \sigma(V^T W + c)$$

Backward pass: The hidden unit representation (h_0) is then passed back to the visible units through the same weights, W, but a different bias, c, where the model reconstructs the input. Again, the input is sampled:

$$\rho(v_i|h_0) = \sigma(V^T h_0 + c)$$

These two passes are repeated for k steps or until the convergence [4] is reached. According to researchers, $k=1$ gives good results, so we will keep $k = 1$.

The joint configuration of the visible vector V and the hidden vector h has energy given as follows:

$$E(v, h) = -b^T V - c^T h - V^T W h$$

Also associated with each visible vector V is free energy, the energy that a single configuration would need to have in order to have the same probability as all of the configurations that contain V:

$$F(v) = -b^T V - \sum_{j \,\in\, hidden} \log\left(1 + \exp\left(c_j + V^T W\right)\right)$$

Using the contrastive divergence objective function, that is, $Mean(F(V_{original})) - Mean(F(V_{reconstructed}))$, the change in weights is given by:

$$dW = \eta\left[(V^T h)_{input} - (V^T h)_{reconstructed}\right]$$

Here, η is the learning rate. Similar expressions exist for the biases b and c.

Reconstructing images using an RBM

Let us build an RBM in TensorFlow. The RBM will be designed to reconstruct handwritten digits. This is the first generative model that you are learning; in the upcoming chapters, we will learn a few more. We import the TensorFlow, NumPy, and Matplotlib libraries:

```
import tensorflow as tf
import numpy as np
import matplotlib.pyplot as plt
```

We define a class RBM. The class __init_() function initializes the number of neurons in the visible layer (input_size) and the number of neurons in the hidden layer (output_size). The function initializes the weights and biases for both hidden and visible layers. In the following code, we have initialized them to zero. You can try with random initialization as well:

```
#Class that defines the behavior of the RBM
class RBM(object):

    def __init__(self, input_size, output_size, lr=1.0, batchsize=100):
        """
        m: Number of neurons in visible layer
        n: number of neurons in hidden layer
        """

        # Defining the hyperparameters
        self._input_size = input_size # Size of Visible
        self._output_size = output_size # Size of outp
        self.learning_rate = lr # The step used in gradient descent
```

```
        self.batchsize = batchsize              # The size of how much data will be
used for training per sub iteration


        # Initializing weights and biases as matrices full of zeroes
        self.w = tf.zeros([input_size, output_size], np.float32) # Creates and
initializes the weights with 0
        self.hb = tf.zeros([output_size], np.float32) # Creates and initializes
the hidden biases with 0
        self.vb = tf.zeros([input_size], np.float32) # Creates and initializes
the visible biases with 0
```

We define methods to provide the forward and backward passes:

```
    # Forward Pass
    def prob_h_given_v(self, visible, w, hb):
        # Sigmoid
        return tf.nn.sigmoid(tf.matmul(visible, w) + hb)
    # Backward Pass
    def prob_v_given_h(self, hidden, w, vb):
        return tf.nn.sigmoid(tf.matmul(hidden, tf.transpose(w)) + vb)
```

We create a function to generate random binary values. This is because both hidden and visible units are updated using stochastic probability, depending upon the input to each unit in the case of the hidden layer (and the top-down input to visible layers):

```
    # Generate the sample probability
    def sample_prob(self, probs):
        return tf.nn.relu(tf.sign(probs - tf.random.uniform(tf.shape(probs))))
```

We will need functions to reconstruct the input:

```
def rbm_reconstruct(self,X):
    h = tf.nn.sigmoid(tf.matmul(X, self.w) + self.hb)
    reconstruct = tf.nn.sigmoid(tf.matmul(h, tf.transpose(self.w)) + self.vb)
    return reconstruct
```

To train the RBM created we define the train() function. The function calculates the positive and negative gradient terms of contrastive divergence and uses the weight update equation to update the weights and biases:

```
# Training method for the model
def train(self, X, epochs=10):

    loss = []
    for epoch in range(epochs):
```

```
        #For each step/batch
        for start, end in zip(range(0, len(X), self.batchsize),range(self.
batchsize,len(X), self.batchsize)):
            batch = X[start:end]

            #Initialize with sample probabilities

            h0 = self.sample_prob(self.prob_h_given_v(batch, self.w, self.hb))
            v1 = self.sample_prob(self.prob_v_given_h(h0, self.w, self.vb))
            h1 = self.prob_h_given_v(v1, self.w, self.hb)

            #Create the Gradients
            positive_grad = tf.matmul(tf.transpose(batch), h0)
            negative_grad = tf.matmul(tf.transpose(v1), h1)

            #Update learning rates
            self.w = self.w + self.learning_rate *(positive_grad - negative_
grad) / tf.dtypes.cast(tf.shape(batch)[0],tf.float32)
            self.vb = self.vb +  self.learning_rate * tf.reduce_mean(batch -
v1, 0)
            self.hb = self.hb +  self.learning_rate * tf.reduce_mean(h0 - h1,
0)

        #Find the error rate
        err = tf.reduce_mean(tf.square(batch - v1))
        print ('Epoch: %d' % epoch,'reconstruction error: %f' % err)
        loss.append(err)

    return loss
```

Now that our class is ready, we instantiate an object of RBM and train it on the MNIST dataset:

```
(train_data, _), (test_data, _) =  tf.keras.datasets.mnist.load_data()
train_data = train_data/np.float32(255)
train_data = np.reshape(train_data, (train_data.shape[0], 784))
test_data = test_data/np.float32(255)
test_data = np.reshape(test_data, (test_data.shape[0], 784))
#Size of inputs is the number of inputs in the training set
input_size = train_data.shape[1]
rbm = RBM(input_size, 200)
err = rbm.train(train_data,50)
```

Let us plot the learning curve:

```
plt.plot(err)
plt.xlabel('epochs')
plt.ylabel('cost')
```

In the figure below, you can see the learning curve of our RBM:

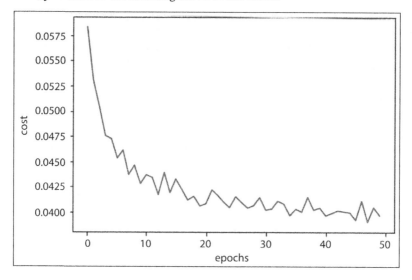

Figure 7.10: Learning curve for the RBM model

Now, we present the code to visualize the reconstructed images:

```
out = rbm.rbm_reconstruct(test_data)
# Plotting original and reconstructed images
row, col = 2, 8
idx = np.random.randint(0, 100, row * col // 2)
f, axarr = plt.subplots(row, col, sharex=True, sharey=True, figsize=(20,4))
for fig, row in zip([test_data,out], axarr):
    for i,ax in zip(idx,row):
        ax.imshow(tf.reshape(fig[i],[28, 28]), cmap='Greys_r')
        ax.get_xaxis().set_visible(False)
        ax.get_yaxis().set_visible(False)
```

And the reconstructed images:

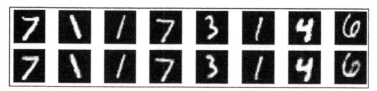

Figure 7.11: Image reconstruction using an RBM

The top row is the input handwritten image, and the bottom row is the reconstructed image. You can see that the images look remarkably similar to the human handwritten digits. In the upcoming chapters, you will learn about models that can generate even more complex images such as artificial human faces.

Deep belief networks

Now that we have a good understanding of RBMs and know how to train them using contrastive divergence, we can move toward the first successful deep neural network architecture, the **deep belief networks** (DBNs), proposed in 2006 by Hinton and his team in the paper *A fast learning algorithm for deep belief nets*. Before this model it was very difficult to train deep architectures, not just because of the limited computing resources, but also, as will be discussed in *Chapter 8, Autoencoders*, because of the vanishing gradient problem. In DBNs it was first demonstrated how deep architectures can be trained via greedy layer-wise training.

In the simplest terms, DBNs are just stacked RBMs. Each RBM is trained separately using the contrastive divergence. We start with the training of the first RBM layer. Once it is trained, we train the second RBM layer. The visible units of the second RBM are now fed the output of the hidden units of the first RBM, when it is fed the input data. The procedure is repeated with each RBM layer addition.

Let us try stacking our RBM class. To make the DBN, we will need to define one more function in the RBM class; the output of the hidden unit of one RBM needs to feed into the next RBM:

```
#Create expected output for our DBN
def rbm_output(self, X):
    out = tf.nn.sigmoid(tf.matmul(X, self.w) + self.hb)
    return out
```

Now we can just use the RBM class to create a stacked RBM structure. In the following code we create an RBM stack: the first RBM will have 500 hidden units, the second will have 200 hidden units, and the third will have 50 hidden units:

```
RBM_hidden_sizes = [500, 200 , 50 ] #create 2 layers of RBM with size 400 and
100
#Since we are training, set input as training data
inpX = train_data
#Create list to hold our RBMs
rbm_list = []
#Size of inputs is the number of inputs in the training set
input_size = train_data.shape[1]
#For each RBM we want to generate
for i, size in enumerate(RBM_hidden_sizes):
    print ('RBM: ',i,' ',input_size,'->', size)
    rbm_list.append(RBM(input_size, size))
    input_size = size
```

```
RBM:   0    784 -> 500
RBM:   1    500 -> 200
RBM:   2    200 -> 50
```

For the first RBM, the MNIST data is the input. The output of the first RBM is then fed as input to the second RBM, and so on through the consecutive RBM layers:

```
#For each RBM in our list
for rbm in rbm_list:
    print ('Next RBM:')
    #Train a new one
    rbm.train(tf.cast(inpX,tf.float32))
    #Return the output layer
    inpX = rbm.rbm_output(inpX)
```

Our DBN is ready. The three stacked RBMs are now trained using unsupervised learning. DBNs can also be trained using supervised training. To do so we need to fine-tune the weights of the trained RBMs and add a fully connected layer at the end. In their publication *Classification with Deep Belief Networks*, Hebbo and Kim show how they used a DBN for MNIST classification; it is a good introduction to the subject.

Summary

In this chapter, we covered the major unsupervised learning algorithms. We went through algorithms best suited for dimension reduction, clustering, and image reconstruction. We started with the dimension reduction algorithm PCA, then we performed clustering using k-means and self-organized maps. After this we studied the restricted Boltzmann machine and saw how we can use it for both dimension reduction and image reconstruction. Next, we delved into stacked RBMs, that is, deep belief networks, and we trained a DBN consisting of three RBM layers on the MNIST dataset.

In the next chapter, we will explore another model using an unsupervised learning paradigm – autoencoders.

References

1. Smith, Lindsay. (2006). *A tutorial on Principal Component Analysis*: http://www.cs.otago.ac.nz/cosc453/student_tutorials/principal_components.pdf

2. Movellan, J. R. *Tutorial on Principal component Analysis*: http://mplab.ucsd.edu/tutorials/pca.pdf

3. TensorFlow Projector: http://projector.tensorflow.org/

4. **Singular Value Decomposition (SVD)** tutorial. MIT: https://web.mit.edu/be.400/www/SVD/Singular_Value_Decomposition.htm

5. Shlens, Jonathon. (2014). *A tutorial on principal component analysis*. arXiv preprint arXiv:1404.1100: https://arxiv.org/abs/1404.1100

6. Goodfellow, I., Bengio, Y., and Courville, A. (2016). *Deep learning*. MIT press: `https://www.deeplearningbook.org`

7. Kohonen, T. (1982). *Self-organized formation of topologically correct feature maps*. Biological cybernetics 43, no. 1: 59-69.

8. Kanungo, Tapas, et al. (2002). *An Efficient k-Means Clustering Algorithm: Analysis and Implementation*. IEEE transactions on pattern analysis and machine intelligence 24.7: 881-892.

9. Ortega, Joaquín Pérez, et al. *Research issues on K-means Algorithm: An Experimental Trial Using Matlab*. CEUR Workshop Proceedings: Semantic Web and New Technologies.

10. Chen, K. (2009). *On Coresets for k-Median and k-Means Clustering in Metric and Euclidean Spaces and Their Applications*. SIAM Journal on Computing 39.3: 923-947.

11. *Determining the number of clusters in a data set*: `https://en.wikipedia.org/wiki/Determining_the_number_of_clusters_in_a_data_set`

12. Lloyd, S. P. (1982). *Least Squares Quantization in PCM*: `http://mlsp.cs.cmu.edu/courses/fall2010/class14/lloyd.pdf`

13. Dunn, J. C. (1973-01-01). *A Fuzzy Relative of the ISODATA Process and Its Use in Detecting Compact Well-Separated Clusters*. Journal of Cybernetics. 3(3): 32–57.

14. Bezdek, James C. (1981). *Pattern Recognition with Fuzzy Objective Function Algorithms*.

15. Peters, G., Crespo, F., Lingras, P., and Weber, R. (2013). *Soft clustering–Fuzzy and rough approaches and their extensions and derivatives*. International Journal of Approximate Reasoning 54, no. 2: 307-322.

16. Sculley, D. (2010). *Web-scale k-means clustering*. In Proceedings of the 19th international conference on World wide web, pp. 1177-1178. ACM.

17. Smolensky, P. (1986). *Information Processing in Dynamical Systems: Foundations of Harmony Theory*. No. CU-CS-321-86. COLORADO UNIV AT BOULDER DEPT OF COMPUTER SCIENCE.

18. Salakhutdinov, R., Mnih, A., and Hinton, G. (2007). *Restricted Boltzmann Machines for Collaborative Filtering*. Proceedings of the 24th international conference on Machine learning. ACM.

19. Hinton, G. (2010). *A Practical Guide to Training Restricted Boltzmann Machines*. Momentum 9.1: 926.

Join our book's Discord space

Join our Discord community to meet like-minded people and learn alongside more than 2000 members at: `https://packt.link/keras`

8

Autoencoders

Autoencoders are neural networks that learn by unsupervised learning, also sometimes called semi-supervised learning, since the input is treated as the target too. In this chapter, you will learn about and implement different variants of autoencoders and eventually learn how to stack autoencoders. We will also see how autoencoders can be used to create MNIST digits, and finally, also cover the steps involved in building a long short-term memory autoencoder to generate sentence vectors. This chapter includes the following topics:

- Vanilla autoencoders
- Sparse autoencoders
- Denoising autoencoders
- Convolutional autoencoders
- Stacked autoencoders
- Generating sentences using LSTM autoencoders
- Variational autoencoders for generating images

 All the code files for this chapter can be found at `https://packt.link/dltfchp8`

Let's begin!

Introduction to autoencoders

Autoencoders are a class of neural networks that attempt to recreate input as their target using backpropagation. An autoencoder consists of two parts: an encoder and a decoder. The encoder will read the input and compress it to a compact representation, and the decoder will read the compact representation and recreate the input from it. In other words, the autoencoder tries to learn the identity function by minimizing the reconstruction error.

They have an inherent capability to learn a compact representation of data. They are at the center of deep belief networks and find applications in image reconstruction, clustering, machine translation, and much more.

You might think that implementing an identity function using deep neural networks is boring; however, the way in which this is done makes it interesting. The number of hidden units in the autoencoder is typically fewer than the number of input (and output) units. This forces the encoder to learn a compressed representation of the input, which the decoder reconstructs. If there is a structure in the input data in the form of correlations between input features, then the autoencoder will discover some of these correlations, and end up learning a low-dimensional representation of the data similar to that learned using **principal component analysis (PCA)**.

While PCA uses linear transformations, autoencoders on the other hand use non-linear transformations.

Once the autoencoder is trained, we would typically just discard the decoder component and use the encoder component to generate compact representations of the input. Alternatively, we could use the encoder as a feature detector that generates a compact, semantically rich representation of our input and build a classifier by attaching a softmax classifier to the hidden layer.

The encoder and decoder components of an autoencoder can be implemented using either dense, convolutional, or recurrent networks, depending on the kind of data that is being modeled. For example, dense networks might be a good choice for autoencoders used to build **collaborative filtering (CF)** models, where we learn a compressed model of user preferences based on actual sparse user ratings. Similarly, convolutional neural networks may be appropriate for the use case described in the article *iSee: Using Deep Learning to Remove Eyeglasses from Faces*, by M. Runfeldt. Recurrent networks, on the other hand, are a good choice for autoencoders working on sequential or text data, such as Deep Patient (*Deep Patient: An Unsupervised Representation to Predict the Future of Patients from the Electronic Health Records*, Miotto et al.) and skip-thought vectors.

We can think of autoencoders as consisting of two cascaded networks. The first network is an encoder; it takes the input x, and encodes it using a transformation h to an encoded signal y, that is:

$$y = h(x)$$

The second network uses the encoded signal y as its input and performs another transformation f to get a reconstructed signal r, that is:

$$r = f(y) = f(h(x))$$

We define error, e, as the difference between the original input x and the reconstructed signal r, $e = x - r$. The network then learns by reducing the loss function (for example, **mean squared error (MSE)**), and the error is propagated backward to the hidden layers as in the case of **multilayer perceptrons (MLPs)**.

Depending upon the actual dimensions of the encoded layer with respect to the input, the loss function, and constraints, there are various types of autoencoders: variational autoencoders, sparse autoencoders, denoising autoencoders, and convolution autoencoders.

Autoencoders can also be stacked by successively stacking encoders that compress their input to smaller and smaller representations, then stacking decoders in the opposite sequence. Stacked autoencoders have greater expressive power and the successive layers of representations capture a hierarchical grouping of the input, similar to the convolution and pooling operations in convolutional neural networks.

Stacked autoencoders used to be trained layer by layer. For example, in the network in *Figure 8.1*, we would first train layer X to reconstruct layer X' using the hidden layer H1 (ignoring H2). We would then train layer H1 to reconstruct layer H1' using the hidden layer H2. Finally, we would stack all the layers together in the configuration shown and fine-tune it to reconstruct X' from X. With better activation and regularization functions nowadays, however, it is quite common to train these networks in totality:

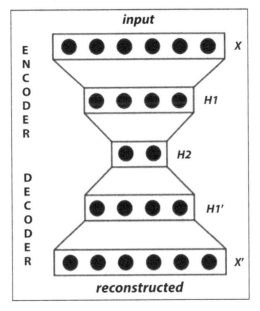

Figure 8.1: Visualization of stacked autoencoders

In this chapter, we will learn about these variations in autoencoders and implement them using TensorFlow.

Vanilla autoencoders

The vanilla autoencoder, as proposed by Hinton in his 2006 paper *Reducing the Dimensionality of Data with Neural Networks*, consists of one hidden layer only. The number of neurons in the hidden layer is fewer than the number of neurons in the input (or output) layer.

This results in producing a bottleneck effect in the flow of information in the network. The hidden layer (y) between the encoder input and decoder output is also called the "bottleneck layer." Learning in the autoencoder consists of developing a compact representation of the input signal at the hidden layer so that the output layer can faithfully reproduce the original input.

In *Figure 8.2*, you can see the architecture of a vanilla autoencoder:

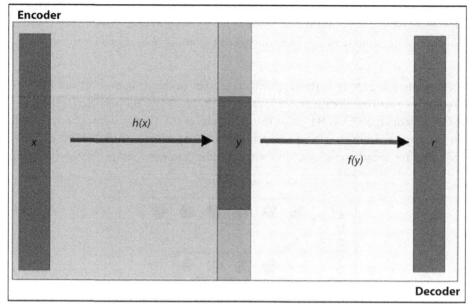

Figure 8.2: Architecture of the vanilla autoencoder

Let's try to build a vanilla autoencoder. While in the paper Hinton used it for dimension reduction, in the code to follow, we will use autoencoders for image reconstruction. We will train the autoencoder on the MNIST database and will use it to reconstruct the test images. In the code, we will use the TensorFlow Keras Layers class to build our own encoder and decoder layers, so firstly let's learn a little about the Layers class.

TensorFlow Keras layers – defining custom layers

TensorFlow provides an easy way to define your own custom layer both from scratch or as a composition of existing layers. The TensorFlow Keras layers package defines a Layers object. We can make our own layer by simply making it a subclass of the Layers class. It is necessary to define the dimensions of the output while defining the layer. Though input dimensions are optional, if you do not define them, it will infer them automatically from the data. To build our own layer we will need to implement three methods:

- __init__(): Here, you define all input-independent initializations.
- build(): Here, we define the shapes of input tensors and can perform rest initializations if required. In our example, since we are not explicitly defining input shapes, we need not define the build() method.
- call(): This is where the forward computation is performed.

Using the tensorflow.keras.layers.Layer class, we now define the encoder and decoder layers. First let's start with the encoder layer. We import tensorflow.keras as K, and create an Encoder class. The Encoder takes in the input and generates the hidden or the bottleneck layer as the output:

```
class Encoder(K.layers.Layer):
    def __init__(self, hidden_dim):
        super(Encoder, self).__init__()
        self.hidden_layer = K.layers.Dense(units=hidden_dim, activation=tf.
nn.relu)
    def call(self, input_features):
        activation = self.hidden_layer(input_features)
        return activation
```

Next, we define the Decoder class; this class takes in the output from the Encoder and then passes it through a fully connected neural network. The aim is to be able to reconstruct the input to the Encoder:

```
class Decoder(K.layers.Layer):
    def __init__(self, hidden_dim, original_dim):
        super(Decoder, self).__init__()
        self.output_layer = K.layers.Dense(units=original_dim, activation=tf.
nn.relu)
    def call(self, encoded):
        activation = self.output_layer(encoded)
        return activation
```

Now that we have both the encoder and decoder defined we use the tensorflow.keras.Model object to build the autoencoder model. You can see in the following code that in the __init__() function we instantiate the encoder and decoder objects, and in the call() method we define the signal flow. Also notice the member list self.loss initialized in the _init_():

```
class Autoencoder(K.Model):
    def __init__(self, hidden_dim, original_dim):
        super(Autoencoder, self).__init__()
        self.loss = []
        self.encoder = Encoder(hidden_dim=hidden_dim)
        self.decoder = Decoder(hidden_dim=hidden_dim, original_dim=original_
dim)
    def call(self, input_features):
        encoded = self.encoder(input_features)
        reconstructed = self.decoder(encoded)
        return reconstructed
```

In the next section, we will use the autoencoder that we defined here to reconstruct handwritten digits.

Reconstructing handwritten digits using an autoencoder

Now that we have our model autoencoder with its layer encoder and decoder ready, let us try to reconstruct handwritten digits. The complete code is available in the GitHub repo of the chapter in the notebook `VanillaAutoencoder.ipynb`. The code will require the NumPy, TensorFlow, and Matplotlib modules:

```python
import numpy as np
import tensorflow as tf
import tensorflow.keras as K
import matplotlib.pyplot as plt
```

Before starting with the actual implementation, let's also define some hyperparameters. If you play around with them, you will notice that even though the architecture of your model remains the same, there is a significant change in model performance. Hyperparameter tuning (refer to *Chapter 1*, *Neural Network Foundations with TF*, for more details) is one of the important steps in deep learning. For reproducibility, we set the seeds for random calculation:

```python
np.random.seed(11)
tf.random.set_seed(11)
batch_size = 256
max_epochs = 50
learning_rate = 1e-3
momentum = 8e-1
hidden_dim = 128
original_dim = 784
```

For training data, we are using the MNIST dataset available in the TensorFlow datasets. We normalize the data so that pixel values lie between [0,1]; this is achieved by simply dividing each pixel element by 255.

We reshape the tensors from 2D to 1D. We employ the `from_tensor_slices` function to generate a batched dataset with the training dataset sliced along its first dimension (slices of tensors). Also note that we are not using one-hot encoded labels; this is because we are not using labels to train the network since autoencoders learn via unsupervised learning:

```python
(x_train, _), (x_test, _) = K.datasets.mnist.load_data()
x_train = x_train / 255.
x_test = x_test / 255.
x_train = x_train.astype(np.float32)
x_test = x_test.astype(np.float32)
x_train = np.reshape(x_train, (x_train.shape[0], 784))
x_test = np.reshape(x_test, (x_test.shape[0], 784))
training_dataset = tf.data.Dataset.from_tensor_slices(x_train).batch(batch_size)
```

Now we instantiate our autoencoder model object and define the loss and optimizers to be used for training. Observe the formulation of the loss function carefully; it is simply the difference between the original image and the reconstructed image. You may find that the term *reconstruction loss* is also used to describe it in many books and papers:

```
autoencoder = Autoencoder(hidden_dim=hidden_dim, original_dim=original_dim)
opt = tf.keras.optimizers.Adam(learning_rate=1e-2)
def loss(preds, real):
    return tf.reduce_mean(tf.square(tf.subtract(preds, real)))
```

Instead of using the auto-training loop, for our custom autoencoder model, we will define a custom training. We use `tf.GradientTape` to record the gradients as they are calculated and implicitly apply the gradients to all the trainable variables of our model:

```
def train(loss, model, opt, original):
    with tf.GradientTape() as tape:
        preds = model(original)
        reconstruction_error = loss(preds, original)
        gradients = tape.gradient(reconstruction_error, model.trainable_
variables)
        gradient_variables = zip(gradients, model.trainable_variables)
    opt.apply_gradients(gradient_variables)
    return reconstruction_error
```

The preceding `train()` function will be invoked in a training loop, with the dataset fed to the model in batches:

```
def train_loop(model, opt, loss, dataset, epochs=20):
    for epoch in range(epochs):
        epoch_loss = 0
        for step, batch_features in enumerate(dataset):
            loss_values = train(loss, model, opt, batch_features)
            epoch_loss += loss_values
        model.loss.append(epoch_loss)
        print('Epoch {}/{}. Loss: {}'.format(epoch + 1, epochs, epoch_loss.
numpy()))
```

Let's now train our autoencoder:

```
train_loop(autoencoder, opt, loss, training_dataset, epochs=max_epochs)
```

And plot our training graph:

```
plt.plot(range(max_epochs), autoencoder.loss)
plt.xlabel('Epochs')
plt.ylabel('Loss')
plt.show()
```

The training graph is shown as follows. We can see that loss/cost is decreasing as the network learns and after 50 epochs it is almost constant about a line. This means that further increasing the number of epochs will not be useful. If we want to improve our training further, we should change the hyperparameters like learning rate and batch_size:

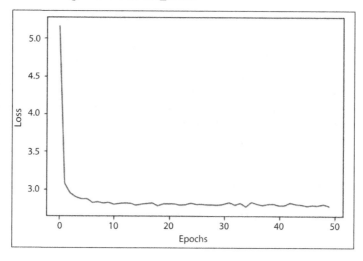

Figure 8.3: Loss plot of the vanilla autoencoder

In *Figure 8.4*, you can see the original (top) and reconstructed (bottom) images; they are slightly blurred, but accurate:

```python
number = 10  # how many digits we will display
plt.figure(figsize=(20, 4))
for index in range(number):
    # display original
    ax = plt.subplot(2, number, index + 1)
    plt.imshow(x_test[index].reshape(28, 28), cmap='gray')
    ax.get_xaxis().set_visible(False)
    ax.get_yaxis().set_visible(False)
    # display reconstruction
    ax = plt.subplot(2, number, index + 1 + number)
    plt.imshow(autoencoder(x_test)[index].numpy().reshape(28, 28), cmap='gray')
    ax.get_xaxis().set_visible(False)
    ax.get_yaxis().set_visible(False)
plt.show()
```

Figure 8.4: Original and reconstructed images using vanilla autoencoder

It is interesting to note that in the preceding code we reduced the dimensions of the input from 784 to 128 and our network could still reconstruct the original image. This should give you an idea of the power of the autoencoder for dimensionality reduction. One advantage of autoencoders over PCA for dimensionality reduction is that while PCA can only represent linear transformations, we can use non-linear activation functions in autoencoders, thus introducing non-linearities in our encodings:

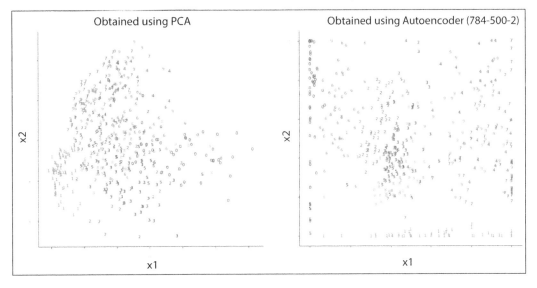

Figure 8.5: LHS image: The two-dimensional code for 500 digits of each class produced by taking the first two principal components of all 60,000 training samples. RHS image: The two-dimensional code found by a 784-500-2 autoencoder

Figure 8.5 compares the result of a PCA with that of stacked autoencoders with architecture consisting of 784-500-2 (here the numbers represent the size of the encoder layers in each autoencoder; the autoencoders had a symmetric decoder).

You can see that the colored dots on the right are nicely separated, thus stacked autoencoders give much better results compared to PCA. Now that you are familiar with vanilla autoencoders, let us see different variants of autoencoders and their implementation details.

Sparse autoencoder

The autoencoder we covered in the previous section works more like an identity network; it simply reconstructs the input. The emphasis is on reconstructing the image at the pixel level, and the only constraint is the number of units in the bottleneck layer. While it is interesting, pixel-level reconstruction is primarily a compression mechanism and does not necessarily ensure that the network will learn abstract features from the dataset. We can ensure that a network learns abstract features from the dataset by adding further constraints.

In sparse autoencoders, a sparse penalty term is added to the reconstruction error. This tries to ensure that fewer units in the bottleneck layer will fire at any given time. We can include the sparse penalty within the encoder layer itself.

In the following code, you can see that the dense layer of `Encoder` now has an additional parameter, `activity_regularizer`:

```
class SparseEncoder(K.layers.Layer):
    def __init__(self, hidden_dim):
        # encoder initializer
        super(SparseEncoder, self).__init__()
        self.hidden_layer = K.layers.Dense(units=hidden_dim, activation=tf.
nn.relu, activity_regularizer=regularizers.l1(10e-5))
    def call(self, input_features):
        # forward function
        activation = self.hidden_layer(input_features)
        return activation
```

The activity regularizer tries to reduce the layer output (refer to *Chapter 1, Neural Network Foundations with TF*). It will reduce both the weights and bias of the fully connected layer to ensure that the output is as small as it can be. TensorFlow supports three types of `activity_regularizer`:

- l1: Here the activity is computed as the sum of absolute values
- l2: The activity here is calculated as the sum of the squared values
- l1_l2: This includes both L1 and L2 terms

Keeping the rest of the code the same, and just changing the encoder, you can get the sparse autoencoder from the vanilla autoencoder. The complete code for the sparse autoencoder is in the Jupyter notebook `SparseAutoencoder.ipynb`.

Alternatively, you can explicitly add a regularization term for sparsity in the loss function. To do so you will need to implement the regularization for the sparsity term as a function. If *m* is the total number of input patterns, then we can define a quantity *p_hat* (you can check the mathematical details in Andrew Ng's lecture here: https://web.stanford.edu/class/cs294a/sparseAutoencoder_2011new.pdf), which measures the net activity (how many times on average it fires) for each hidden layer unit. The basic idea is to put a constraint *p_hat*, such that it is equal to the sparsity parameter *ρ*. This results in adding a regularization term for sparsity in the loss function so that now the loss function becomes:

loss = Mean squared error + Regularization for sparsity parameter

This regularization term will penalize the network if *p_hat* deviates from *ρ*. One standard way to do this is to use **Kullback-Leiber (KL)** divergence (you can learn more about KL divergence from this interesting lecture: https://www.stat.cmu.edu/~cshalizi/754/2006/notes/lecture-28.pdf) between *ρ* and *p_hat*.

Let's explore the KL divergence, D_{KL}, a little more. It is a non-symmetric measure of the difference between the two distributions, in our case, *ρ* and *p_hat*. When *ρ* and *p_hat* are equal then the difference is zero; otherwise, it increases monotonically as *p_hat* diverges from *ρ*. Mathematically, it is expressed as:

$$D_{KL}\left(\rho\|\hat{\rho}_j\right) = \rho \, log\frac{\rho}{\hat{\rho}_j} + (1-\rho)log\frac{1-\rho}{1-\hat{\rho}_j}$$

We add this to the loss to implicitly include the sparse term. We will need to fix a constant value for the sparsity term ρ and compute ρ_hat using the encoder output.

The compact representation of the inputs is stored in weights. Let us visualize the weights learned by the network. The following are the weights of the encoder layer for the standard and sparse autoencoders respectively.

We can see that in the standard autoencoder (a) many hidden units have very large weights (brighter), suggesting that they are overworked, while all the hidden units of the sparse autoencoder (b) learn the input representation almost equally, and we see a more even color distribution:

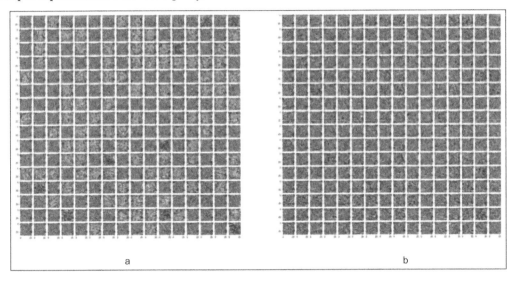

a   b

Figure 8.6: Encoder weight matrix for (a) standard autoencoder and (b) sparse autoencoder

Now that we have learned about sparse autoencoders, we next move to a case where autoencoders can learn to remove noise from the image.

Denoising autoencoders

The two autoencoders that we have covered in the previous sections are examples of undercomplete autoencoders, because the hidden layer in them has lower dimensionality compared to the input (output) layer. Denoising autoencoders belong to the class of overcomplete autoencoders because they work better when the dimensions of the hidden layer are more than the input layer.

A denoising autoencoder learns from a corrupted (noisy) input; it feeds its encoder network the noisy input, and then the reconstructed image from the decoder is compared with the original input. The idea is that this will help the network learn how to denoise an input. It will no longer just make pixel-wise comparisons, but in order to denoise, it will learn the information of neighboring pixels as well.

A denoising autoencoder has two main differences from other autoencoders: first, n_hidden, the number of hidden units in the bottleneck layer is greater than the number of units in the input layer, m, that is, n_hidden > m. Second, the input to the encoder is corrupted input.

To do this, we add a noise term in both the test and training images:

```
noise = np.random.normal(loc=0.5, scale=0.5, size=x_train.shape)
x_train_noisy = x_train + noise
noise = np.random.normal(loc=0.5, scale=0.5, size=x_test.shape)
x_test_noisy = x_test + noise
x_train_noisy = np.clip(x_train_noisy, 0., 1.)
x_test_noisy = np.clip(x_test_noisy, 0., 1.)
```

Let us see the denoising autoencoder in action next.

Clearing images using a denoising autoencoder

Let us use the denoising autoencoder to clear the handwritten MNIST digits:

1. We start by importing the required modules:

   ```
   import numpy as np
   import tensorflow as tf
   import tensorflow.keras as K
   import matplotlib.pyplot as plt
   ```

2. Next, we define the hyperparameters for our model:

   ```
   np.random.seed(11)
   tf.random.set_seed(11)
   batch_size = 256
   max_epochs = 50
   learning_rate = 1e-3
   momentum = 8e-1
   hidden_dim = 128
   original_dim = 784
   ```

3. We read in the MNIST dataset, normalize it, and introduce noise to it:

   ```
   (x_train, _), (x_test, _) = K.datasets.mnist.load_data()
   x_train = x_train / 255.
   x_test = x_test / 255.
   x_train = x_train.astype(np.float32)
   x_test = x_test.astype(np.float32)
   x_train = np.reshape(x_train, (x_train.shape[0], 784))
   x_test = np.reshape(x_test, (x_test.shape[0], 784))
   # Generate corrupted MNIST images by adding noise with normal dist
   # centered at 0.5 and std=0.5
   noise = np.random.normal(loc=0.5, scale=0.5, size=x_train.shape)
   ```

```
x_train_noisy = x_train + noise
noise = np.random.normal(loc=0.5, scale=0.5, size=x_test.shape)
x_test_noisy = x_test + noise
```

4. We use the same encoder, decoder, and autoencoder classes as defined in the *Vanilla autoencoders* section:

```
# Encoder
class Encoder(K.layers.Layer):
    def __init__(self, hidden_dim):
        super(Encoder, self).__init__()
        self.hidden_layer = K.layers.Dense(units=hidden_dim,
activation=tf.nn.relu)
    def call(self, input_features):
        activation = self.hidden_layer(input_features)
        return activation
# Decoder
class Decoder(K.layers.Layer):
    def __init__(self, hidden_dim, original_dim):
        super(Decoder, self).__init__()
        self.output_layer = K.layers.Dense(units=original_dim,
activation=tf.nn.relu)
    def call(self, encoded):
        activation = self.output_layer(encoded)
        return activation
class Autoencoder(K.Model):
    def __init__(self, hidden_dim, original_dim):
        super(Autoencoder, self).__init__()
        self.loss = []
        self.encoder = Encoder(hidden_dim=hidden_dim)
        self.decoder = Decoder(hidden_dim=hidden_dim, original_
dim=original_dim)
    def call(self, input_features):
        encoded = self.encoder(input_features)
        reconstructed = self.decoder(encoded)
        return reconstructed
```

5. Next, we create the model and define the loss and optimizers to be used. Notice that this time, instead of writing the custom training loop, we are using the easier Keras inbuilt `compile()` and `fit()` methods:

```
model = Autoencoder(hidden_dim=hidden_dim, original_dim=original_dim)
model.compile(loss='mse', optimizer='adam')
```

```
loss = model.fit(x_train_noisy,
                 x_train,
                 validation_data=(x_test_noisy, x_test),
                 epochs=max_epochs,
                 batch_size=batch_size)
```

6. Now let's plot the training loss:

```
plt.plot(range(max_epochs), loss.history['loss'])
plt.xlabel('Epochs')
plt.ylabel('Loss')
plt.show()
```

Figure 8.7 shows the loss over epochs:

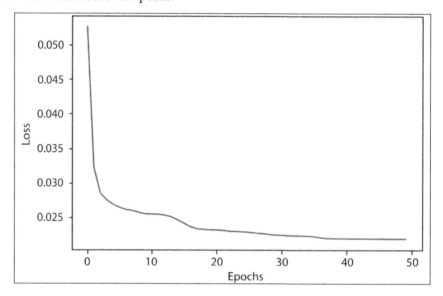

Figure 8.7: Loss plot of a denoising autoencoder

And finally, let's see our model in action:

```
number = 10  # how many digits we will display
plt.figure(figsize=(20, 4))
for index in range(number):
    # display original
    ax = plt.subplot(2, number, index + 1)
    plt.imshow(x_test_noisy[index].reshape(28, 28), cmap='gray')
    ax.get_xaxis().set_visible(False)
    ax.get_yaxis().set_visible(False)
    # display reconstruction
```

```
        ax = plt.subplot(2, number, index + 1 + number)
        plt.imshow(model(x_test_noisy)[index].numpy().reshape(28, 28),
    cmap='gray')
        ax.get_xaxis().set_visible(False)
        ax.get_yaxis().set_visible(False)
    plt.show()
```

The top row shows the input noisy image, and the bottom row shows cleaned images produced from our trained denoising autoencoder:

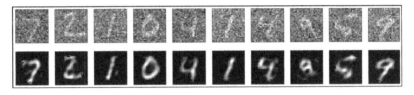

Figure 8.8: The noisy input images and corresponding denoised reconstructed images

An impressive reconstruction of images from noisy images, I'm sure you'll agree. You can access the code in the notebook DenoisingAutoencoder.ipynb if you want to play around with it.

Stacked autoencoder

Until now, we have restricted ourselves to autoencoders with only one hidden layer. We can build deep autoencoders by stacking many layers of both encoders and decoders; such an autoencoder is called a stacked autoencoder. The features extracted by one encoder are passed on to the next encoder as input. The stacked autoencoder can be trained as a whole network with the aim of minimizing the reconstruction error. Alternatively, each individual encoder/decoder network can first be pretrained using the unsupervised method you learned earlier, and then the complete network can be fine-tuned. When the deep autoencoder network is a convolutional network, we call it a **convolutional autoencoder**. Let us implement a convolutional autoencoder in TensorFlow next.

Convolutional autoencoder for removing noise from images

In the previous section, we reconstructed handwritten digits from noisy input images. We used a fully connected network as the encoder and decoder for the work. However, we know that for images, a convolutional network can give better results, so in this section, we will use a convolution network for both the encoder and decoder. To get better results we will use multiple convolution layers in both the encoder and decoder networks; that is, we will make stacks of convolutional layers (along with max pooling or upsampling layers). We will also be training the entire autoencoder as a single entity:

1. We import all the required modules and the specific layers from tensorflow.keras.layers:

    ```
    import numpy as np
    import tensorflow as tf
    ```

```
import tensorflow.keras as K
import matplotlib.pyplot as plt
from tensorflow.keras.layers import Dense, Conv2D, MaxPooling2D,
UpSampling2D
```

2. We specify our hyperparameters. If you look carefully, the list is slightly different compared to earlier autoencoder implementations; instead of learning rate and momentum, this time we are concerned with filters of the convolutional layer:

```
np.random.seed(11)
tf.random.set_seed(11)
batch_size = 128
max_epochs = 50
filters = [32,32,16]
```

3. In the next step, we read in the data and preprocess it. Again, you may observe a slight variation from the previous code, especially in the way we are adding noise and then limiting the range between [0-1]. We are doing so because in this case, instead of the mean squared error loss, we will be using binary cross-entropy loss and the final output of the decoder will pass through sigmoid activation, restricting it between [0-1]:

```
(x_train, _), (x_test, _) = K.datasets.mnist.load_data()
x_train = x_train / 255.
x_test = x_test / 255.
x_train = np.reshape(x_train, (len(x_train),28, 28, 1))
x_test = np.reshape(x_test, (len(x_test), 28, 28, 1))
noise = 0.5
x_train_noisy = x_train + noise * np.random.normal(loc=0.0, scale=1.0,
size=x_train.shape)
x_test_noisy = x_test + noise * np.random.normal(loc=0.0, scale=1.0,
size=x_test.shape)
x_train_noisy = np.clip(x_train_noisy, 0, 1)
x_test_noisy = np.clip(x_test_noisy, 0, 1)
x_train_noisy = x_train_noisy.astype('float32')
x_test_noisy = x_test_noisy.astype('float32')
#print(x_test_noisy[1].dtype)
```

4. Let us now define our encoder. The encoder consists of three convolutional layers, each followed by a max pooling layer. Since we are using the MNIST dataset the shape of the input image is 28 × 28 (single channel) and the output image is of size 4 × 4 (and since the last convolutional layer has 16 filters, the image has 16 channels):

```
class Encoder(K.layers.Layer):
    def __init__(self, filters):
```

```
        super(Encoder, self).__init__()
        self.conv1 = Conv2D(filters=filters[0], kernel_size=3, strides=1,
    activation='relu', padding='same')
        self.conv2 = Conv2D(filters=filters[1], kernel_size=3, strides=1,
    activation='relu', padding='same')
        self.conv3 = Conv2D(filters=filters[2], kernel_size=3, strides=1,
    activation='relu', padding='same')
        self.pool = MaxPooling2D((2, 2), padding='same')


    def call(self, input_features):
        x = self.conv1(input_features)
        x = self.pool(x)
        x = self.conv2(x)
        x = self.pool(x)
        x = self.conv3(x)
        x = self.pool(x)
        return x
```

5. Next comes the decoder. It is the exact opposite of the encoder in design, and instead of max pooling, we are using upsampling to increase the size back. Notice the commented print statements; you can use them to understand how the shape gets modified after each step. (Alternatively, you can also use the model.summary function to get the complete model summary.) Also notice that both the encoder and decoder are still classes based on the TensorFlow Keras Layers class, but now they have multiple layers inside them. So now you know how to build a complex custom layer:

```
class Decoder(K.layers.Layer):
    def __init__(self, filters):
        super(Decoder, self).__init__()
        self.conv1 = Conv2D(filters=filters[2], kernel_size=3, strides=1,
    activation='relu', padding='same')
        self.conv2 = Conv2D(filters=filters[1], kernel_size=3, strides=1,
    activation='relu', padding='same')
        self.conv3 = Conv2D(filters=filters[0], kernel_size=3, strides=1,
    activation='relu', padding='valid')
        self.conv4 = Conv2D(1, 3, 1, activation='sigmoid',
    padding='same')
        self.upsample = UpSampling2D((2, 2))
    def call(self, encoded):
        x = self.conv1(encoded)
        #print("dx1", x.shape)
```

```
        x = self.upsample(x)
        #print("dx2", x.shape)
        x = self.conv2(x)
        x = self.upsample(x)
        x = self.conv3(x)
        x = self.upsample(x)
        return self.conv4(x)
```

6. We combine the encoder and decoder to make an autoencoder model. This remains exactly the same as before:

```
class Autoencoder(K.Model):
    def __init__(self, filters):
        super(Autoencoder, self).__init__()
        self.encoder = Encoder(filters)
        self.decoder = Decoder(filters)
    def call(self, input_features):
        #print(input_features.shape)
        encoded = self.encoder(input_features)
        #print(encoded.shape)
        reconstructed = self.decoder(encoded)
        #print(reconstructed.shape)
        return reconstructed
```

7. Now we instantiate our model, then specify the binary cross-entropy as the loss function and Adam as the optimizer in the compile() method. Then, fit the model to the training dataset:

```
model = Autoencoder(filters)
model.compile(loss='binary_crossentropy', optimizer='adam')
loss = model.fit(x_train_noisy,
            x_train,
            validation_data=(x_test_noisy, x_test),
            epochs=max_epochs,
            batch_size=batch_size)
```

8. Plot the loss curve:

```
plt.plot(range(max_epochs), loss.history['loss'])
plt.xlabel('Epochs')
plt.ylabel('Loss')
plt.show()
```

You can see the loss curve as the model is trained; in 50 epochs the loss was reduced to 0.0988:

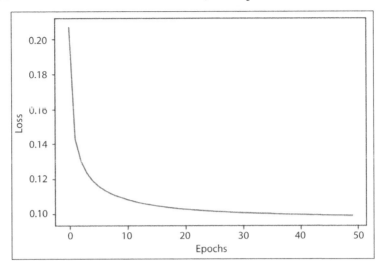

Figure 8.9: Loss plot for the convolutional autoencoder

9. And finally, you can see the wonderful reconstructed images from the noisy input images:

```
number = 10  # how many digits we will display
plt.figure(figsize=(20, 4))
for index in range(number):
    # display original
    ax = plt.subplot(2, number, index + 1)
    plt.imshow(x_test_noisy[index].reshape(28, 28), cmap='gray')
    ax.get_xaxis().set_visible(False)
    ax.get_yaxis().set_visible(False)
    # display reconstruction
    ax = plt.subplot(2, number, index + 1 + number)
    plt.imshow(tf.reshape(model(x_test_noisy)[index], (28, 28)),
cmap='gray')
    ax.get_xaxis().set_visible(False)
    ax.get_yaxis().set_visible(False)
plt.show()
```

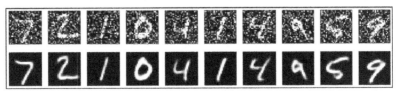

Figure 8.10: The inputted noisy images and reconstructed denoised images

You can see that the images are much clearer and sharper relative to the previous autoencoders we have covered in this chapter. The magic lies in the stacking of convolutional layers. The code for this section is available in the Jupyter notebook ConvolutionAutoencoder.ipynb.

A TensorFlow Keras autoencoder example – sentence vectors

In this example, we will build and train an LSTM-based autoencoder to generate sentence vectors for documents in the Reuters-21578 corpus (https://archive.ics.uci.edu/ml/datasets/reuters-21578+text+categorization+collection). We have already seen in *Chapter 4, Word Embeddings*, how to represent a word using word embeddings to create vectors that represent the word's meaning in the context of other words it appears with. Here, we will see how to build similar vectors for sentences. Sentences are sequences of words, so a sentence vector represents the meaning of a sentence.

The easiest way to build a sentence vector is to just add up the word vectors and divide them by the number of words. However, this treats the sentence as a bag of words, and does not take the order of words into account. Thus, the sentences *The dog bit the man* and *The man bit the dog* would be treated as identical in this scenario. LSTMs are designed to work with sequence input and do take the order of words into consideration, thus providing a better and more natural representation of the sentence.

First, we import the necessary libraries:

```python
from sklearn.model_selection import train_test_split
from tensorflow.keras.callbacks import ModelCheckpoint
from tensorflow.keras.layers import Input
from tensorflow.keras.layers import RepeatVector
from tensorflow.keras.layers import LSTM
from tensorflow.keras.layers import Bidirectional
from tensorflow.keras.models import Model
from tensorflow.keras.preprocessing import sequence
from scipy.stats import describe
import collections
import matplotlib.pyplot as plt
import nltk
import numpy as np
import os
from time import gmtime, strftime
from tensorflow.keras.callbacks import TensorBoard
import re
# Needed to run only once
nltk.download('punkt')
nltk.download('reuters')

from nltk.corpus import reuters
```

In case you are using Google's Colab to run the code, you will also need to unzip the Reuters corpus by adding the following to the code:

```
%%capture
!unzip /root/nltk_data/corpora/reuters.zip -d /root/nltk_data/corpora
```

Next, we will be using the GloVe embeddings, so let us download them as well:

```
!wget http://nlp.stanford.edu/data/glove.6B.zip
!unzip glove*.zip
```

Now that all our tools are in our workspace, we will first convert each block of text (documents) into a list of sentences, one sentence per line. Also, each word in the sentence is normalized as it is added. The normalization involves removing all numbers and replacing them with the number 9, then converting the word to lowercase. Simultaneously we also calculate the word frequencies in the same code. The result is the word frequency table, word_freqs:

```
def is_number(n):
    temp = re.sub("[.,-/]", "",n)
    return temp.isdigit()


# parsing sentences and building vocabulary
word_freqs = collections.Counter()
documents = reuters.fileids()
#ftext = open("text.tsv", "r")
sents = []
sent_lens = []
num_read = 0
for i in range(len(documents)):
    # periodic heartbeat report
    if num_read % 100 == 0:
        print("building features from {:d} docs".format(num_read))
    # skip docs without specified topic
    title_body = reuters.raw(documents[i]).lower()
    if len(title_body) == 0:
        continue
    num_read += 1
    # convert to list of word indexes
    title_body = re.sub("\n", "", title_body)
    for sent in nltk.sent_tokenize(title_body):
        for word in nltk.word_tokenize(sent):
            if is_number(word):
                word = "9"
```

```
                word = word.lower()
                word_freqs[word] += 1
            sents.append(sent)
            sent_lens.append(len(sent))
```

Let us use the preceding generated arrays to get some information about the corpus that will help us figure out good values for the constants for our LSTM network:

```
print("Total number of sentences are: {:d} ".format(len(sents)))
print ("Sentence distribution min {:d}, max {:d} , mean {:3f}, median
{:3f}".format(np.min(sent_lens), np.max(sent_lens), np.mean(sent_lens),
np.median(sent_lens)))
print("Vocab size (full) {:d}".format(len(word_freqs)))
```

This gives us the following information about the corpus:

```
Total number of sentences are: 50470
Sentence distribution min 1, max 3688 , mean 167.072657, median 155.000000
Vocab size (full) 33748
```

Based on this information, we set the following constants for our LSTM model. We choose our VOCAB_SIZE as 5000; that is, our vocabulary covers the most frequent 5,000 words, which covers over 93% of the words used in the corpus. The remaining words are treated as **out of vocabulary** (OOV) and replaced with the token UNK. At prediction time, any word that the model hasn't seen will also be assigned the token UNK. SEQUENCE_LEN is set to approximately half the median length of sentences in the training set. Sentences that are shorter than SEQUENCE_LEN will be padded by a special PAD character, and those that are longer will be truncated to fit the limit:

```
VOCAB_SIZE = 5000
SEQUENCE_LEN = 50
```

Since the input to our LSTM will be numeric, we need to build lookup tables that go back and forth between words and word IDs. Since we limit our vocabulary size to 5,000 and we have to add the two pseudo-words PAD and UNK, our lookup table contains entries for the most frequently occurring 4,998 words plus PAD and UNK:

```
word2id = {}
word2id["PAD"] = 0
word2id["UNK"] = 1
for v, (k, _) in enumerate(word_freqs.most_common(VOCAB_SIZE - 2)):
    word2id[k] = v + 2
id2word = {v:k for k, v in word2id.items()}
```

The input to our network is a sequence of words, where each word is represented by a vector. Simplistically, we could just use one-hot encoding for each word, but that makes the input data very large. So, we encode each word using its 50-dimensional GloVe embeddings.

The embedding is generated into a matrix of shape (VOCAB_SIZE and EMBED_SIZE) where each row represents the GloVe embedding for a word in our vocabulary. The PAD and UNK rows (0 and 1 respectively) are populated with zeros and random uniform values respectively:

```python
EMBED_SIZE = 50
def lookup_word2id(word):
    try:
        return word2id[word]
    except KeyError:
        return word2id["UNK"]
def load_glove_vectors(glove_file, word2id, embed_size):
    embedding = np.zeros((len(word2id), embed_size))
    fglove = open(glove_file, "rb")
    for line in fglove:
        cols = line.strip().split()
        word = cols[0].decode('utf-8')
        if embed_size == 0:
            embed_size = len(cols) - 1
        if word in word2id:
            vec = np.array([float(v) for v in cols[1:]])
        embedding[lookup_word2id(word)] = vec
    embedding[word2id["PAD"]] = np.zeros((embed_size))
    embedding[word2id["UNK"]] = np.random.uniform(-1, 1, embed_size)
    return embedding
```

Next, we use these functions to generate embeddings:

```python
sent_wids = [[lookup_word2id(w) for w in s.split()] for s in sents]
sent_wids = sequence.pad_sequences(sent_wids, SEQUENCE_LEN)
# load glove vectors into weight matrix
embeddings = load_glove_vectors("glove.6B.{:d}d.txt".format(EMBED_SIZE),
word2id, EMBED_SIZE)
```

Our autoencoder model takes a sequence of GloVe word vectors and learns to produce another sequence that is similar to the input sequence. The encoder LSTM compresses the sequence into a fixed-size context vector, which the decoder LSTM uses to reconstruct the original sequence.

A schematic of the network is shown here:

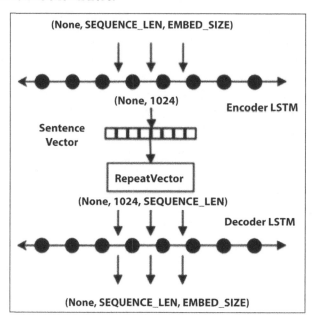

Figure 8.11: Visualization of the LSTM network

Because the input is quite large, we will use a generator to produce each batch of input. Our generator produces batches of tensors of shape (BATCH_SIZE, SEQUENCE_LEN, EMBED_SIZE). Here BATCH_SIZE is 64, and since we are using 50-dimensional GloVe vectors, EMBED_SIZE is 50. We shuffle the sentences at the beginning of each epoch and return batches of 64 sentences. Each sentence is represented as a vector of GloVe word vectors. If a word in the vocabulary does not have a corresponding GloVe embedding, it is represented by a zero vector. We construct two instances of the generator, one for training data and one for test data, consisting of 70% and 30% of the original dataset respectively:

```
BATCH_SIZE = 64
def sentence_generator(X, embeddings, batch_size):
    while True:
        # Loop once per epoch
        num_recs = X.shape[0]
        indices = np.random.permutation(np.arange(num_recs))
        num_batches = num_recs // batch_size
        for bid in range(num_batches):
            sids = indices[bid * batch_size : (bid + 1) * batch_size]
            Xbatch = embeddings[X[sids, :]]
            yield Xbatch, Xbatch
train_size = 0.7
Xtrain, Xtest = train_test_split(sent_wids, train_size=train_size)
train_gen = sentence_generator(Xtrain, embeddings, BATCH_SIZE)
test_gen = sentence_generator(Xtest, embeddings, BATCH_SIZE)
```

Now we are ready to define the autoencoder. As we have shown in the diagram, it is composed of an encoder LSTM and a decoder LSTM. The encoder LSTM reads a tensor of shape (BATCH_SIZE, SEQUENCE_LEN, EMBED_SIZE) representing a batch of sentences. Each sentence is represented as a padded fixed-length sequence of words of size SEQUENCE_LEN. Each word is represented as a 300-dimensional GloVe vector. The output dimension of the encoder LSTM is a hyperparameter, LATENT_SIZE, which is the size of the sentence vector that will come from the encoder part of the trained autoencoder later. The vector space of dimensionality LATENT_SIZE represents the latent space that encodes the meaning of the sentence. The output of the LSTM is a vector of size (LATENT_SIZE) for each sentence, so for the batch, the shape of the output tensor is (BATCH_SIZE, LATENT_SIZE). This is now fed to a RepeatVector layer, which replicates this across the entire sequence; that is, the output tensor from this layer has the shape (BATCH_SIZE, SEQUENCE_LEN, LATENT_SIZE). This tensor is now fed into the decoder LSTM, whose output dimension is the EMBED_SIZE, so the output tensor has shape (BATCH_SIZE, SEQUENCE_LEN, EMBED_SIZE), that is, the same shape as the input tensor.

We compile this model with the Adam optimizer and the MSE loss function. The reason we use MSE is that we want to reconstruct a sentence that has a similar meaning, that is, something that is close to the original sentence in the embedded space of dimension LATENT_SIZE:

```
LATENT_SIZE = 512
EMBED_SIZE = 50
BATCH_SIZE = 64
NUM_EPOCHS = 20
inputs = Input(shape=(SEQUENCE_LEN, EMBED_SIZE), name="input")
encoded = Bidirectional(LSTM(LATENT_SIZE), merge_mode="sum", name="encoder_
lstm")(inputs)
decoded = RepeatVector(SEQUENCE_LEN, name="repeater")(encoded)
decoded = Bidirectional(LSTM(EMBED_SIZE, return_sequences=True), merge_
mode="sum", name="decoder_lstm")(decoded)
autoencoder = Model(inputs, decoded)
```

We define the loss function as mean squared error and choose the Adam optimizer:

```
autoencoder.compile(optimizer="adam", loss="mse")
```

We train the autoencoder for 20 epochs using the following code. 20 epochs was chosen because the MSE loss converges within this time:

```
num_train_steps = len(Xtrain) // BATCH_SIZE
num_test_steps = len(Xtest) // BATCH_SIZE
steps_per_epoch=num_train_steps,
epochs=NUM_EPOCHS,
validation_data=test_gen,
validation_steps=num_test_steps,
history = autoencoder.fit_generator(train_gen,
```

```
                                            steps_per_epoch=num_train_steps,
                                            epochs=NUM_EPOCHS,
                                            validation_data=test_gen,
                                            validation_steps=num_test_steps)
```

The results of the training are shown as follows. The plot below shows the loss plot for both training and validation data; we can see that as our model learns, the losses decrease as expected:

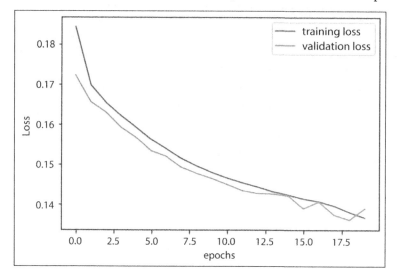

Figure 8.12: Loss plot of the LSTM autoencoder

Since we are feeding in a matrix of embeddings, the output will also be a matrix of word embeddings. Since the embedding space is continuous and our vocabulary is discrete, not every output embedding will correspond to a word. The best we can do is to find a word that is closest to the output embedding in order to reconstruct the original text. This is a bit cumbersome, so we will evaluate our autoencoder in a different way.

Since the objective of the autoencoder is to produce a good latent representation, we compare the latent vectors produced from the encoder using the original input versus the output of the autoencoder.

First, we extract the encoder component into its own network:

```
encoder = Model(autoencoder.input, autoencoder.get_layer("encoder_lstm").output)
```

Then we run the autoencoder on the test set to return the predicted embeddings. We then send both the input embedding and the predicted embedding through the encoder to produce sentence vectors from each and compare the two vectors using *cosine* similarity. Cosine similarities close to "one" indicate high similarity and those close to "zero" indicate low similarity.

The following code runs against a random subset of 500 test sentences and produces some sample values of cosine similarities, between the sentence vectors generated from the source embedding and the corresponding target embedding produced by the autoencoder:

```python
def compute_cosine_similarity(x, y):
    return np.dot(x, y) / (np.linalg.norm(x, 2) * np.linalg.norm(y, 2))
k = 500
cosims = np.zeros((k))
i= 0
for bid in range(num_test_steps):
    xtest, ytest = next(test_gen)
    ytest_ = autoencoder.predict(xtest)
    Xvec = encoder.predict(xtest)
    Yvec = encoder.predict(ytest_)
    for rid in range(Xvec.shape[0]):
        if i >= k:
            break
        cosims[i] = compute_cosine_similarity(Xvec[rid], Yvec[rid])
        if i <= 10:
            print(cosims[i])
        i += 1
    if i >= k:
        break
```

The first 10 values of cosine similarities are shown as follows. As we can see, the vectors seem to be quite similar:

```
0.9765363335609436
0.9862152338027954
0.9831727743148804
0.977733314037323
0.9851642847061157
0.9849132895469666
0.9831638932228088
0.9843543767929077
0.9825796484947205
0.9877195954322815
0.9820773601531982
```

Figure 8.13 shows a histogram of the distribution of values of cosine similarities for the sentence vectors from the first 500 sentences.

As previously mentioned, it confirms that the sentence vectors generated from the input and output of the autoencoder are very similar, showing that the resulting sentence vector is a good representation of the sentence:

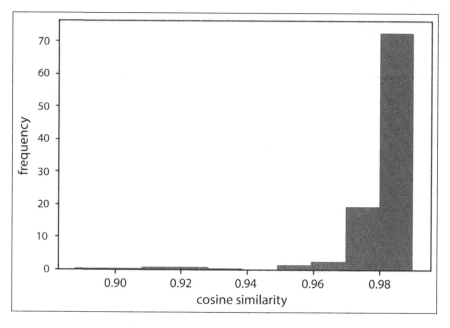

Figure 8.13: Cosine similarity distribution

Till now we have focused on autoencoders that can reconstruct data; in the next section, we will go through a slightly different variant of the autoencoder – the variational autoencoder, which is used to generate data.

Variational autoencoders

Like DBNs (*Chapter 7, Unsupervised Learning*) and GANs (see *Chapter 9, Generative Models*, for more details), variational autoencoders are also generative models. **Variational autoencoders (VAEs)** are a mix of the best neural networks and Bayesian inference. They are one of the most interesting neural networks and have emerged as one of the most popular approaches to unsupervised learning. They are autoencoders with a twist. Along with the conventional encoder and decoder network of autoencoders, they have additional stochastic layers. The stochastic layer, after the encoder network, samples the data using a Gaussian distribution, and the one after the decoder network samples the data using Bernoulli's distribution. Like GANs, VAEs can be used to generate images and figures based on the distribution they have been trained on.

VAEs allow one to set complex priors in the latent space and thus learn powerful latent representations. *Figure 8.14* describes a VAE:

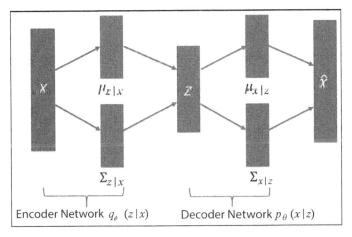

Figure 8.14: Architecture of a variational autoencoder

The encoder network $q_\phi(z|x)$ approximates the true but intractable posterior distribution $p(z|x)$, where x is the input to the VAE and z is the latent representation. The decoder network $p_\theta(x|z)$ takes the d-dimensional latent variables (also called latent space) as its input and generates new images following the same distribution as $P(x)$. As you can see from the preceding diagram, the latent representation z is sampled from $z|x \sim N(\mu_{x|z}, \Sigma_{x|z})$, and the output of the decoder network samples $x|z$ from $x|z \sim N(\mu_{x|z}, \Sigma_{x|z})$. Here N represents a normal distribution with mean μ and variance Σ.

Now that we have the basic architecture of VAEs, the question arises of how they can be trained, since the maximum likelihood of the training data and posterior density are intractable. The network is trained by maximizing the lower bound of the log data likelihood. Thus, the loss term consists of two components: generation loss, which is obtained from the decoder network through sampling, and the Kullback–Leibler divergence term, also called the latent loss.

Generation loss ensures that the image generated by the decoder and the image used to train the network are similar, and latent loss ensures that the posterior distribution $q(z|x)$ is close to the prior $p_\theta(z)$. Since the encoder uses Gaussian distribution for sampling, the latent loss measures how closely the latent variables match this distribution.

Once the VAE is trained, we can use only the decoder network to generate new images. Let us try coding a VAE. This time we are using the Fashion-MNIST dataset; the dataset contains Zalando's (https://github.com/zalandoresearch/fashion-mnist) article images. The test-train split is exactly the same as for MNIST, that is, 60,000 train images and 10,000 test images. The size of each image is also 28 × 28, so we can easily replace the code running on the MNIST dataset with the Fashion-MNIST dataset.

The code in this section has been adapted from `https://github.com/dragen1860/TensorFlow-2.x-Tutorials`. As the first step we, as usual, import all the necessary libraries:

```
import tensorflow as tf
import numpy as np
from matplotlib import pyplot as plt
```

Let us fix the seeds for a random number, so that the results are reproducible. We can also add an `assert` statement to ensure that our code runs on TensorFlow 2.0 or above:

```
np.random.seed(333)
tf.random.set_seed(333)
assert tf.__version__.startswith('2.'), "TensorFlow Version Below 2.0"
```

Before going ahead with making the VAE, let us also explore the Fashion-MNIST dataset a little. The dataset is available in the TensorFlow Keras API:

```
(x_train, y_train), (x_test, y_test) = tf.keras.datasets.fashion_mnist.load_
data()
x_train, x_test = x_train.astype(np.float32)/255., x_test.astype(np.
float32)/255.
print(x_train.shape, y_train.shape)
print(x_test.shape, y_test.shape)
```

```
--------------------------------------------------
(60000, 28, 28) (60000,)
(10000, 28, 28) (10000,)
```

We see some sample images:

```
number = 10   # how many digits we will display
plt.figure(figsize=(20, 4))
for index in range(number):
    # display original
    ax = plt.subplot(2, number, index + 1)
    plt.imshow(x_train[index], cmap='gray')
    ax.get_xaxis().set_visible(False)
    ax.get_yaxis().set_visible(False)
plt.show()
```

Figure 8.15: Sample images from the Fashion-MNIST dataset

Before we start, let us declare some hyperparameters like learning rate, dimensions of the hidden layer and the latent space, batch size, epochs, and so on:

```
image_size = x_train.shape[1]*x_train.shape[2]
hidden_dim = 512
latent_dim = 10
num_epochs = 80
batch_size = 100
learning_rate = 0.001
```

We use the TensorFlow Keras Model API to build a VAE model. The __init__() function defines all the layers that we will be using:

```
class VAE(tf.keras.Model):
    def __init__(self,dim,**kwargs):
        h_dim = dim[0]
        z_dim = dim[1]
        super(VAE, self).__init__(**kwargs)
        self.fc1 = tf.keras.layers.Dense(h_dim)
        self.fc2 = tf.keras.layers.Dense(z_dim)
        self.fc3 = tf.keras.layers.Dense(z_dim)
        self.fc4 = tf.keras.layers.Dense(h_dim)
        self.fc5 = tf.keras.layers.Dense(image_size)
```

We define the functions to give us the encoder output and decoder output and reparametrize. The implementation of the encoder and decoder functions are straightforward; however, we need to delve a little deeper into the reparametrize function. As you know, VAEs sample from a random node z, which is approximated by $q(z\,|\theta)$ of the true posterior. Now, to get parameters we need to use backpropagation. However, backpropagation cannot work on random nodes. Using reparameterization, we can use a new parameter, eps, which allows us to reparametrize z in a way that will allow backpropagation through the deterministic random node (https://arxiv.org/pdf/1312.6114v10.pdf):

```
def encode(self, x):
    h = tf.nn.relu(self.fc1(x))
    return self.fc2(h), self.fc3(h)
def reparameterize(self, mu, log_var):
    std = tf.exp(log_var * 0.5)
    eps = tf.random.normal(std.shape)
    return mu + eps * std
def decode_logits(self, z):
    h = tf.nn.relu(self.fc4(z))
    return self.fc5(h)
def decode(self, z):
    return tf.nn.sigmoid(self.decode_logits(z))
```

Lastly, we define the `call()` function, which will control how signals move through different layers of the VAE:

```
def call(self, inputs, training=None, mask=None):
    mu, log_var = self.encode(inputs)
    z = self.reparameterize(mu, log_var)
    x_reconstructed_logits = self.decode_logits(z)
    return x_reconstructed_logits, mu, log_var
```

Now, we create the VAE model and declare the optimizer for it. You can see the summary of the model:

```
model = VAE([hidden_dim, latent_dim])
model.build(input_shape=(4, image_size))
model.summary()
optimizer = tf.keras.optimizers.Adam(learning_rate)
```

```
Model: "vae"
_____
 Layer (type)                Output Shape              Param #
=================================================================
 dense (Dense)               multiple                  401920

 dense_1 (Dense)             multiple                  5130

 dense_2 (Dense)             multiple                  5130

 dense_3 (Dense)             multiple                  5632

 dense_4 (Dense)             multiple                  402192

=================================================================
Total params: 820,004
Trainable params: 820,004
Non-trainable params: 0
_____
```

Now, we train the model. We define our loss function, which is the sum of the reconstruction loss and KL divergence loss:

```
dataset = tf.data.Dataset.from_tensor_slices(x_train)
dataset = dataset.shuffle(batch_size * 5).batch(batch_size)
num_batches = x_train.shape[0] // batch_size
for epoch in range(num_epochs):
    for step, x in enumerate(dataset):
```

```
            x = tf.reshape(x, [-1, image_size])
            with tf.GradientTape() as tape:
                # Forward pass
                x_reconstruction_logits, mu, log_var = model(x)
                # Compute reconstruction loss and kl divergence
                # Scaled by 'image_size' for each individual pixel.
                reconstruction_loss = tf.nn.sigmoid_cross_entropy_with_
logits(labels=x, logits=x_reconstruction_logits)
                reconstruction_loss = tf.reduce_sum(reconstruction_loss) / batch_
size

                kl_div = - 0.5 * tf.reduce_sum(1. + log_var - tf.square(mu) -
tf.exp(log_var), axis=-1)
                kl_div = tf.reduce_mean(kl_div)
                # Backprop and optimize
                loss = tf.reduce_mean(reconstruction_loss) + kl_div
            gradients = tape.gradient(loss, model.trainable_variables)
            for g in gradients:
                tf.clip_by_norm(g, 15)
            optimizer.apply_gradients(zip(gradients, model.trainable_variables))
            if (step + 1) % 50 == 0:
                print("Epoch[{}/{}], Step [{}/{}], Reconst Loss: {:.4f}, KL Div:
{:.4f}"
                    .format(epoch + 1, num_epochs, step + 1, num_batches,
float(reconstruction_loss), float(kl_div)))
```

Once the model is trained it should be able to generate images similar to the original Fashion-MNIST images. To do so we need to use only the decoder network, and we will pass to it a randomly generated z input:

```
z = tf.random.normal((batch_size, latent_dim))
out = model.decode(z)   # decode with sigmoid
out = tf.reshape(out, [-1, 28, 28]).numpy() * 255
out = out.astype(np.uint8)
```

Figure 8.16 shows the results after 80 epochs:

Figure 8.16: Results after 80 epochs

The generated images resemble the input space. The generated images are similar to the original Fashion-MNIST images as desired.

Summary

In this chapter, we've had an extensive look at a new generation of deep learning models: autoencoders. We started with the vanilla autoencoder, and then moved on to its variants: sparse autoencoders, denoising autoencoders, stacked autoencoders, and convolutional autoencoders. We used the autoencoders to reconstruct images, and we also demonstrated how they can be used to clean noise from an image. Finally, the chapter demonstrated how autoencoders can be used to generate sentence vectors and images. The autoencoders learned through unsupervised learning.

In the next chapter, we will delve deeper into generative adversarial networks, another interesting deep learning model that learns via an unsupervised learning paradigm.

References

1. Rumelhart, D. E., Hinton, G. E., and Williams, R. J. (1985). *Learning Internal Representations by Error Propagation.* No. ICS-8506. University of California, San Diego. La Jolla Institute for Cognitive Science: http://www.cs.toronto.edu/~fritz/absps/pdp8.pdf

2. Hinton, G. E. and Salakhutdinov, R. R. (2016). *Reducing the dimensionality of data with neural networks.* science 313.5786: 504–507: https://www.cs.toronto.edu/~hinton/science.pdf

3. Masci, J. et al. (2011). *Stacked convolutional auto-encoders for hierarchical feature extraction.* Artificial Neural Networks and Machine Learning–ICANN 2011: 52–59: https://www.semanticscholar.org/paper/Reducing-the-dimensionality-of-data-with-neural-Hinton-Salakhutdinov/46eb79e5eec8a4e2b2f5652b66441e8a4c921c3e

4. Japkowicz, N., Myers, C., and Gluck, M. (1995). *A novelty detection approach to classification.* IJCAI. Vol: https://www.ijcai.org/Proceedings/95-1/Papers/068.pdf

5. Sedhain, S. (2015). *AutoRec: Autoencoders Meet Collaborative Filtering.* Proceedings of the 24th International Conference on World Wide Web, ACM.

6. Cheng, H. (2016). *Wide & Deep Learning for Recommender Systems.* Proceedings of the 1st Workshop on Deep Learning for Recommender Systems, ACM.

7. Runfeldt, M. *Using Deep Learning to Remove Eyeglasses from Faces.*

8. Miotto, R. (2016). *Deep Patient: An Unsupervised Representation to Predict the Future of Patients from the Electronic Health Records.* Scientific Reports.

9. Kiros, R. (2015). *Skip-Thought Vectors,* Advances in Neural Information Processing Systems.

10. Kullback-Leibler divergence: http://hanj.cs.illinois.edu/cs412/bk3/KL-divergence.pdf

11. Denoising autoencoders: https://cs.stanford.edu/people/karpathy/convnetjs/demo/autoencoder.html

Join our book's Discord space

Join our Discord community to meet like-minded people and learn alongside more than 2000 members at: https://packt.link/keras

9

Generative Models

Generative models are a type of machine learning algorithm that is used to create data. They are used to generate new data that is similar to the data that was used to train the model. They can be used to create new data for testing or to fill in missing data. Generative models are used in many applications, such as density estimation, image synthesis, and natural language processing. The VAE discussed in *Chapter 8, Autoencoders,* was one type of generative model; in this chapter, we will discuss a wide range of generative models, **Generative Adversarial Networks** (GANs) and their variants, flow-based models, and diffusion models.

GANs have been defined as *the most interesting idea in the last 10 years in ML* (https://www.quora.com/What-are-some-recent-and-potentially-upcoming-breakthroughs-in-deep-learning) by Yann LeCun, one of the fathers of deep learning. GANs are able to learn how to reproduce synthetic data that looks real. For instance, computers can learn how to paint and create realistic images. The idea was originally proposed by Ian Goodfellow (for more information, refer to *NIPS 2016 Tutorial: Generative Adversarial Networks,* by I. Goodfellow, 2016); he has worked with the University of Montreal, Google Brain, and OpenAI, and is presently working in Apple Inc. as the Director of Machine Learning.

In this chapter, we will cover different types of GANs; the chapter will introduce you to flow-based models and diffusion models, and additionally, you will see some of their implementation in TensorFlow. Broadly, we will cover the following topics:

- What is a GAN?
- Deep convolutional GANs
- InfoGAN
- SRGAN
- CycleGAN
- Applications of GANs
- Flow-based generative models
- Diffusion models for data generation

All the code files for this chapter can be found at `https://packt.link/dltfchp9`

Let's begin!

What is a GAN?

The ability of GANs to learn high-dimensional, complex data distributions has made them very popular with researchers in recent years. Between 2016, when they were first proposed by Ian Goodfellow, to March 2022, we have more than 100,000 research papers related to GANs, just in the space of 6 years!

The applications of GANs include creating images, videos, music, and even natural languages. They have been employed in tasks like image-to-image translation, image super-resolution, drug discovery, and even next-frame prediction in video. They have been especially successful in the task of synthetic data generation – both for training the deep learning models and assessing the adversarial attacks.

The key idea of GAN can be easily understood by considering it analogous to "art forgery," which is the process of creating works of art that are falsely credited to other usually more famous artists. GANs train two neural nets simultaneously. The generator *G(Z)* is the one that makes the forgery, and the discriminator *D(Y)* is the one that can judge how realistic the reproductions are, based on its observations of authentic pieces of art and copies. *D(Y)* takes an input *Y* (for instance, an image), and expresses a vote to judge how real the input is. In general, a value close to 1 denotes "real," while a value close to 0 denotes "forgery." *G(Z)* takes an input from random noise *Z* and it trains itself to fool *D* into thinking that whatever *G(Z)* produces is real.

The goal of training the discriminator *D(Y)* is to maximize *D(Y)* for every image from the true data distribution and to minimize *D(Y)* for every image not from the true data distribution. So, *G* and *D* play opposite games, hence the name **adversarial training**. Note that we train *G* and *D* in an alternating manner, where each one of their objectives is expressed as a loss function optimized via a gradient descent. The generative model continues to improve its forgery capabilities, and the discriminative model continues to improve its forgery recognition capabilities. The discriminator network (usually a standard convolutional neural network) tries to classify if an input image is real or generated. The important new idea is to backpropagate through both the discriminator and the generator to adjust the generator's parameters in such a way that the generator can learn how to fool the discriminator more often. In the end, the generator will learn how to produce images that are indistinguishable from the real ones:

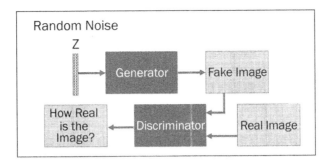

Figure 9.1: Basic architecture of a GAN

Of course, GANs involve working towards equilibrium in a game involving two players. Let us first understand what we mean by equilibrium here. When we start, one of the two players is hopefully better than the other. This pushes the other to improve and this way, both the generator and discriminator push each other towards improvement.

Eventually, we reach a state where the improvement is not significant in either player. We check this by plotting the loss function, to see when the two losses (gradient loss and discriminator loss) reach a plateau. We don't want the game to be skewed too heavily one way; if the forger were to immediately learn how to fool the judge on every occasion, then the forger has *nothing more to learn*. Practically training GANs is really hard, and a lot of research is being done in analyzing GAN convergence; check this site: `https://avg.is.tuebingen.mpg.de/projects/convergence-and-stability-of-gan-training` for details on convergence and stability of different types of GANs. In generative applications of GAN, we want the generator to learn a little better than the discriminator.

Let's now delve deep into how GANs learn. Both the discriminator and generator take turns to learn. The learning can be divided into two steps:

1. Here the discriminator, $D(x)$, learns. The generator, $G(z)$, is used to generate fake images from random noise z (which follows some prior distribution $P(z)$). The fake images from the generator and the real images from the training dataset are both fed to the discriminator, and it performs supervised learning trying to separate fake from real. If $P_{data}(x)$ is the training dataset distribution, then the discriminator network tries to maximize its objective so that $D(x)$ is close to 1 when the input data is real and close to zero when the input data is fake.

2. In the next step, the generator network learns. Its goal is to fool the discriminator network into thinking that generated $G(z)$ is real, that is, force $D(G(z))$ close to 1.

The two steps are repeated sequentially. Once the training ends, the discriminator is no longer able to discriminate between real and fake data and the generator becomes a pro in creating data very similar to the training data. The stability between discriminator and generator is an actively researched problem.

Now that you have got an idea of what GANs are, let's look at a practical application of a GAN in which "handwritten" digits are generated.

MNIST using GAN in TensorFlow

Let us build a simple GAN capable of generating handwritten digits. We will use the MNIST handwritten digits to train the network. We will need to import TensorFlow modules; to keep the code clean, we export all the classes that we will require from the TensorFlow framework:

```
from tensorflow.keras.datasets import mnist
from tensorflow.keras.layers import Input, Dense, Reshape, Flatten, Dropout
from tensorflow.keras.layers import BatchNormalization, Activation,
ZeroPadding2D
from tensorflow.keras.layers import LeakyReLU
from tensorflow.keras.layers import UpSampling2D, Conv2D
from tensorflow.keras.models import Sequential, Model
from tensorflow.keras.optimizers import Adam
from tensorflow.keras import initializers


import matplotlib.pyplot as plt


import numpy as np
```

We use the TensorFlow Keras dataset to access the MNIST data. The data contains 60,000 training images of handwritten digits each of size 28 × 28. The pixel value of the digits lies between 0-255; we normalize the input values such that each pixel has a value in the range [-1, 1]:

```
randomDim = 10
(X_train, _), (_, _) = mnist.load_data()
X_train = (X_train.astype(np.float32) - 127.5)/127.5
```

We will use a simple **multi-layered perceptron** (**MLP**) and we will feed it an image as a flat vector of size 784, so we reshape the training data:

```
X_train = X_train.reshape(60000, 784)
```

Now we will need to build a generator and discriminator. The purpose of the generator is to take in a noisy input and generate an image similar to the training dataset. The size of the noisy input is decided by the variable randomDim; you can initialize it to any integral value. Conventionally, people set it to 100. For our implementation, we tried a value of 10. This input is fed to a dense layer with 256 neurons with LeakyReLU activation. We next add another dense layer with 512 hidden neurons, followed by the third hidden layer with 1024 neurons, and finally the output layer with 784 neurons. You can change the number of neurons in the hidden layers and see how the performance changes; however, the number of neurons in the output unit has to match the number of pixels in the training images. The corresponding generator is then:

```
generator = Sequential()
generator.add(Dense(256, input_dim=randomDim))
generator.add(LeakyReLU(0.2))
```

```
generator.add(Dense(512))
generator.add(LeakyReLU(0.2))
generator.add(Dense(1024))
generator.add(LeakyReLU(0.2))
generator.add(Dense(784, activation='tanh'))
```

Similarly, we build a discriminator. Notice now (*Figure 9.1*) that the discriminator takes in the images, either from the training set or images generated by the generator, thus its input size is 784. Additionally, here we are using a TensorFlow initializer to initialize the weights of the dense layer, we are using a normal distribution with a standard deviation of 0.02 and a mean of 0. As mentioned in *Chapter 1*, *Neural Network Foundations with TF*, there are many initializers available in the TensorFlow framework. The output of the discriminator is a single bit, with 0 signifying a fake image (generated by generator) and 1 signifying that the image is from the training dataset:

```
discriminator = Sequential()
discriminator.add(Dense(1024, input_dim=784, kernel_initializer=initializers.
RandomNormal(stddev=0.02))
)
discriminator.add(LeakyReLU(0.2))
discriminator.add(Dropout(0.3))
discriminator.add(Dense(512))
discriminator.add(LeakyReLU(0.2))
discriminator.add(Dropout(0.3))
discriminator.add(Dense(256))
discriminator.add(LeakyReLU(0.2))
discriminator.add(Dropout(0.3))
discriminator.add(Dense(1, activation='sigmoid'))
```

Next, we combine the generator and discriminator together to form a GAN. In the GAN, we ensure that the discriminator weights are fixed by setting the `trainable` argument to `False`:

```
discriminator.trainable = False
ganInput = Input(shape=(randomDim,))
x = generator(ganInput)
ganOutput = discriminator(x)
gan = Model(inputs=ganInput, outputs=ganOutput)
```

The trick to training the two is that we first train the discriminator separately; we use binary cross-entropy loss for the discriminator. Later, we freeze the weights of the discriminator and train the combined GAN; this results in the training of the generator. The loss this time is also binary cross-entropy:

```
discriminator.compile(loss='binary_crossentropy', optimizer='adam')
gan.compile(loss='binary_crossentropy', optimizer='adam')
```

Let us now perform the training. For each epoch, we take a sample of random noise first, feed it to the generator, and the generator produces a fake image. We combine the generated fake images and the actual training images in a batch with their specific labels and use them to train the discriminator first on the given batch:

```python
def train(epochs=1, batchSize=128):
    batchCount = int(X_train.shape[0] / batchSize)
    print ('Epochs:', epochs)
    print ('Batch size:', batchSize)
    print ('Batches per epoch:', batchCount)
    for e in range(1, epochs+1):
        print ('-'*15, 'Epoch %d' % e, '-'*15)
        for _ in range(batchCount):
            # Get a random set of input noise and images
            noise = np.random.normal(0, 1, size=[batchSize,
            randomDim])
            imageBatch = X_train[np.random.randint(0,
            X_train.shape[0], size=batchSize)]
            # Generate fake MNIST images
            generatedImages = generator.predict(noise)
            # print np.shape(imageBatch), np.shape(generatedImages)
            X = np.concatenate([imageBatch, generatedImages])
            # Labels for generated and real data
            yDis = np.zeros(2*batchSize)
            # One-sided label smoothing
            yDis[:batchSize] = 0.9
            # Train discriminator
            discriminator.trainable = True
            dloss = discriminator.train_on_batch(X, yDis)
```

If you notice, while assigning labels, instead of 0/1 we used 0/0.9 – this is called label smoothing. It has been found that keeping a soft target improves both generalization and learning speed (*When does label smoothing help?*, Muller et al. NeurIPS 2019).

Now, in the same for loop, we will train the generator. We want the images generated by the generator to be detected as real by the discriminator, so we use a random vector (noise) as input to the generator; this generates a fake image and then trains the GAN such that the discriminator perceives the image as real (the output is 1):

```python
            # Train generator
            noise = np.random.normal(0, 1, size=[batchSize,
            randomDim])
            yGen = np.ones(batchSize)
            discriminator.trainable = False
            gloss = gan.train_on_batch(noise, yGen)
```

Cool trick, right? If you wish to, you can save the generator and discriminator loss as well as the generated images. Next, we are saving the losses for each epoch and generating images after every 20 epochs:

```
# Store loss of most recent batch from this epoch
dLosses.append(dloss)
gLosses.append(gloss)
if e == 1 or e % 20 == 0:
        saveGeneratedImages(e)
```

We can now train the GAN by calling the `train` function. In the following graph, you can see the plot of both generative and discriminative loss as the GAN is learning:

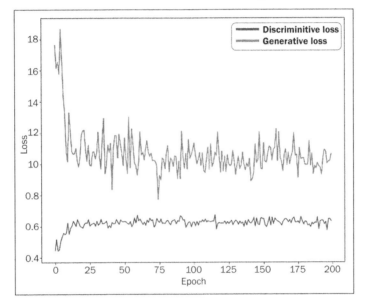

Figure 9.2: Discriminator and generator loss plots

And handwritten digits generated by our GAN:

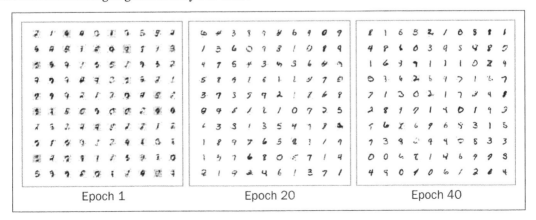

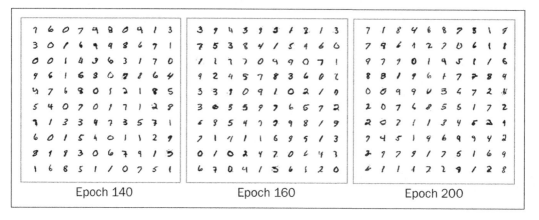

Epoch 140 Epoch 160 Epoch 200

Figure 9.3: Generated handwritten digits

You can see from the preceding figures that as the epochs increase, the handwritten digits generated by the GAN become more and more realistic.

To plot the loss and the generated images of the handwritten digits, we define two helper functions, `plotLoss()` and `saveGeneratedImages()`. Their code is given as follows:

```
# Plot the loss from each batch
def plotLoss(epoch):
    plt.figure(figsize=(10, 8))
    plt.plot(dLosses, label='Discriminitive loss')
    plt.plot(gLosses, label='Generative loss')
    plt.xlabel('Epoch')
    plt.ylabel('Loss')
    plt.legend()
    plt.savefig('images/gan_loss_epoch_%d.png' % epoch)
# Create a wall of generated MNIST images
def saveGeneratedImages(epoch, examples=100, dim=(10, 10), figsize=(10, 10)):
    noise = np.random.normal(0, 1, size=[examples, randomDim])
    generatedImages = generator.predict(noise)
    generatedImages = generatedImages.reshape(examples, 28, 28)
    plt.figure(figsize=figsize)
    for i in range(generatedImages.shape[0]):
        plt.subplot(dim[0], dim[1], i+1)
        plt.imshow(generatedImages[i], interpolation='nearest',
        cmap='gray_r')
        plt.axis('off')
    plt.tight_layout()
    plt.savefig('images/gan_generated_image_epoch_%d.png' % epoch)
```

The `saveGeneratedImages` function saves images in the `images` folder, so make sure you have created the folder in your current working directory. The complete code for this can be found in the notebook `VanillaGAN.ipynb` at the GitHub repo for this chapter. In the coming sections, we will cover some recent GAN architectures and implement them in TensorFlow.

Deep convolutional GAN (DCGAN)

Proposed in 2016, DCGANs have become one of the most popular and successful GAN architectures. The main idea of the design was using convolutional layers without the use of pooling layers or the end classifier layers. The convolutional strides and transposed convolutions are employed for the downsampling (the reduction of dimensions) and upsampling (the increase of dimensions. In GANs, we do this with the help of a transposed convolution layer. To know more about transposed convolution layers, refer to the paper *A guide to convolution arithmetic for deep learning* by Dumoulin and Visin) of images.

Before going into the details of the DCGAN architecture and its capabilities, let us point out the major changes that were introduced in the paper:

- The network consisted of all convolutional layers. The pooling layers were replaced by strided convolutions (i.e., instead of one single stride while using the convolutional layer, we increased the number of strides to two) in the discriminator and transposed convolutions in the generator.
- The fully connected classifying layers after the convolutions are removed.
- To help with the gradient flow, batch normalization is done after every convolutional layer.

The basic idea of DCGANs is the same as the vanilla GAN: we have a generator that takes in noise of 100 dimensions; the noise is projected and reshaped, and is then passed through convolutional layers. *Figure 9.4* shows the generator architecture:

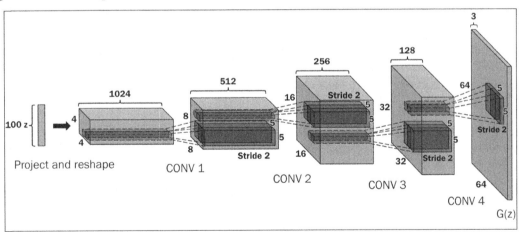

Figure 9.4: Visualizing the architecture of a generator

The discriminator network takes in the images (either generated by the generator or from the real dataset), and the images undergo convolution followed by batch normalization. At each convolution step, the images get downsampled using strides. The final output of the convolutional layer is flattened and feeds a one-neuron classifier layer.

In *Figure 9.5*, you can see the discriminator:

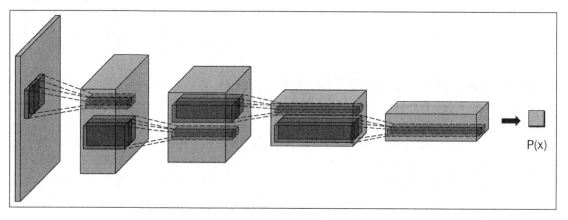

Figure 9.5: Visualizing the architecture of a discriminator

The generator and the discriminator are combined together to form the DCGAN. The training follows in the same manner as before; that is, we first train the discriminator on a mini-batch, then freeze the discriminator and train the generator. The process is repeated iteratively for a few thousand epochs. The authors found that we get more stable results with the Adam optimizer and a learning rate of 0.002.

Next, we'll implement a DCGAN for generating handwritten digits.

DCGAN for MNIST digits

Let us now build a DCGAN for generating handwritten digits. We first see the code for the generator. The generator is built by adding the layers sequentially. The first layer is a dense layer that takes the noise of 100 dimensions as an input. The 100-dimensional input is expanded to a flat vector of size $128 \times 7 \times 7$. This is done so that finally, we get an output of size 28×28, the standard size of MNIST handwritten digits. The vector is reshaped to a tensor of size $7 \times 7 \times 128$. This vector is then upsampled using the TensorFlow Keras UpSampling2D layer. Please note that this layer simply scales up the image by doubling rows and columns. The layer has no weights, so it is computationally cheap.

The Upsampling2D layer will now double the rows and columns of the $7 \times 7 \times 128$ (rows × columns × channels) image, yielding an output of size $14 \times 14 \times 128$. The upsampled image is passed to a convolutional layer. This convolutional layer learns to fill in the details in the upsampled image. The output of a convolution is passed to batch normalization for better gradient flow. The batch normalized output then undergoes ReLU activation in all the intermediate layers. We repeat the structure, that is, upsampling | convolution | batch normalization | ReLU. In the following generator, we have two such structures, the first with 128 filters, and the second with 64 filters in the convolution operation. The final output is obtained from a pure convolutional layer with 3 filters and tan hyperbolic activation, yielding an image of size $28 \times 28 \times 1$:

```
def build_generator(self):
    model = Sequential()
    model.add(Dense(128 * 7 * 7, activation="relu",
```

```
        input_dim=self.latent_dim))
    model.add(Reshape((7, 7, 128)))
    model.add(UpSampling2D())
    model.add(Conv2D(128, kernel_size=3, padding="same"))
    model.add(BatchNormalization(momentum=0.8))
    model.add(Activation("relu"))
    model.add(UpSampling2D())
    model.add(Conv2D(64, kernel_size=3, padding="same"))
    model.add(BatchNormalization(momentum=0.8))
    model.add(Activation("relu"))
    model.add(Conv2D(self.channels, kernel_size=3, padding="same"))
    model.add(Activation("tanh"))
    model.summary()
    noise = Input(shape=(self.latent_dim,))
    img = model(noise)
    return Model(noise, img)
```

The resultant generator model is as follows:

```
Model: "sequential_1"
_____
 Layer (type)                Output Shape              Param #
=================================================================
 conv2d_3 (Conv2D)           (None, 14, 14, 32)        320

 leaky_re_lu (LeakyReLU)     (None, 14, 14, 32)        0

 dropout (Dropout)           (None, 14, 14, 32)        0

 conv2d_4 (Conv2D)           (None, 7, 7, 64)          18496

 zero_padding2d (ZeroPadding (None, 8, 8, 64)          0
 2D)

 batch_normalization_2 (Batc (None, 8, 8, 64)          256
 hNormalization)

 leaky_re_lu_1 (LeakyReLU)   (None, 8, 8, 64)          0

 dropout_1 (Dropout)         (None, 8, 8, 64)          0

 conv2d_5 (Conv2D)           (None, 4, 4, 128)         73856
```

```
batch_normalization_3 (Batc    (None, 4, 4, 128)    512
hNormalization)

leaky_re_lu_2 (LeakyReLU)      (None, 4, 4, 128)    0

dropout_2 (Dropout)            (None, 4, 4, 128)    0

conv2d_6 (Conv2D)              (None, 4, 4, 256)    295168

batch_normalization_4 (Batc    (None, 4, 4, 256)    1024
hNormalization)

leaky_re_lu_3 (LeakyReLU)      (None, 4, 4, 256)    0

dropout_3 (Dropout)            (None, 4, 4, 256)    0

flatten (Flatten)              (None, 4096)         0

dense_1 (Dense)                (None, 1)            4097

=================================================================
Total params: 393,729
Trainable params: 392,833
Non-trainable params: 896
```

You can also experiment with the transposed convolution layer. This layer not only upsamples the input image but also learns how to fill in details during the training. Thus, you can replace upsampling and convolution layers with a single transposed convolution layer. The transpose convolutional layer performs an inverse convolution operation. You can read about it in more detail in the paper: *A guide to convolution arithmetic for deep learning* (https://arxiv.org/abs/1603.07285).

Now that we have a generator, let us see the code to build the discriminator. The discriminator is similar to a standard convolutional neural network but with one major change: instead of max pooling, we use convolutional layers with strides of 2. We also add dropout layers to avoid overfitting, and batch normalization for better accuracy and fast convergence. The activation layer is leaky ReLU. In the following network, we use three such convolutional layers, with filters of 32, 64, and 128 respectively. The output of the third convolutional layer is flattened and fed to a dense layer with a single unit.

The output of this unit classifies the image as fake or real:

```
def build_discriminator(self):
    model = Sequential()
    model.add(Conv2D(32, kernel_size=3, strides=2,
```

```
                    input_shape=self.img_shape, padding="same"))
        model.add(LeakyReLU(alpha=0.2))
        model.add(Dropout(0.25))
        model.add(Conv2D(64, kernel_size=3, strides=2, padding="same"))
        model.add(ZeroPadding2D(padding=((0,1),(0,1))))
        model.add(BatchNormalization(momentum=0.8))
        model.add(LeakyReLU(alpha=0.2))
        model.add(Dropout(0.25))
        model.add(Conv2D(128, kernel_size=3, strides=2, padding="same"))
        model.add(BatchNormalization(momentum=0.8))
        model.add(LeakyReLU(alpha=0.2))
        model.add(Dropout(0.25))
        model.add(Conv2D(256, kernel_size=3, strides=1, padding="same"))
        model.add(BatchNormalization(momentum=0.8))
        model.add(LeakyReLU(alpha=0.2))
        model.add(Dropout(0.25))
        model.add(Flatten())
        model.add(Dense(1, activation='sigmoid'))
        model.summary()
        img = Input(shape=self.img_shape)
        validity = model(img)
        return Model(img, validity)
```

The resultant discriminator network is:

```
Model: "sequential"
_____
 Layer (type)                Output Shape              Param #
=================================================================
 dense (Dense)               (None, 6272)              633472

 reshape (Reshape)           (None, 7, 7, 128)         0

 up_sampling2d (UpSampling2D  (None, 14, 14, 128)      0
 )

 conv2d (Conv2D)             (None, 14, 14, 128)       147584

 batch_normalization (BatchN  (None, 14, 14, 128)      512
 ormalization)

 activation (Activation)     (None, 14, 14, 128)       0
```

```
up_sampling2d_1 (UpSampling   (None, 28, 28, 128)      0
2D)

conv2d_1 (Conv2D)             (None, 28, 28, 64)       73792

batch_normalization_1 (Batc   (None, 28, 28, 64)       256
hNormalization)

activation_1 (Activation)     (None, 28, 28, 64)       0

conv2d_2 (Conv2D)             (None, 28, 28, 1)        577

activation_2 (Activation)     (None, 28, 28, 1)        0

=================================================================
Total params: 856,193
Trainable params: 855,809
Non-trainable params: 384
```

The complete GAN is made by combining the two:

```
class DCGAN():
    def __init__(self, rows, cols, channels, z = 10):
        # Input shape
        self.img_rows = rows
        self.img_cols = cols
        self.channels = channels
        self.img_shape = (self.img_rows, self.img_cols, self.channels)
        self.latent_dim = z

        optimizer = Adam(0.0002, 0.5)

        # Build and compile the discriminator
        self.discriminator = self.build_discriminator()
        self.discriminator.compile(loss='binary_crossentropy',
            optimizer=optimizer,
            metrics=['accuracy'])

        # Build the generator
        self.generator = self.build_generator()
```

```
        # The generator takes noise as input and generates imgs
        z = Input(shape=(self.latent_dim,))
        img = self.generator(z)

        # For the combined model we will only train the generator
        self.discriminator.trainable = False

        # The discriminator takes generated images as input and determines
  validity
        valid = self.discriminator(img)

        # The combined model  (stacked generator and discriminator)
        # Trains the generator to fool the discriminator
        self.combined = Model(z, valid)
        self.combined.compile(loss='binary_crossentropy', optimizer=optimizer)
```

As you might have noticed, we are defining here the binary_crossentropy loss object, which we will use later to define the generator and discriminator losses. Optimizers for both the generator and discriminator is defined in this init method. And finally, we define a TensorFlow checkpoint that we will use to save the two models (generator and discriminator) as the model trains.

The GAN is trained in the same manner as before; at each step, first, random noise is fed to the generator. The output of the generator is added with real images to initially train the discriminator, and then the generator is trained to give an image that can fool the discriminator.

The process is repeated for the next batch of images. The GAN takes between a few hundred to thousands of epochs to train:

```
    def train(self, epochs, batch_size=256, save_interval=50):

        # Load the dataset
        (X_train, _), (_, _) = mnist.load_data()

        # Rescale -1 to 1
        X_train = X_train / 127.5 - 1.
        X_train = np.expand_dims(X_train, axis=3)

        # Adversarial ground truths
        valid = np.ones((batch_size, 1))
        fake = np.zeros((batch_size, 1))

        for epoch in range(epochs):
```

```
                # --------------------
                #  Train Discriminator
                # --------------------

                # Select a random half of images
                idx = np.random.randint(0, X_train.shape[0], batch_size)
                imgs = X_train[idx]

                # Sample noise and generate a batch of new images
                noise = np.random.normal(0, 1, (batch_size, self.latent_dim))
                gen_imgs = self.generator.predict(noise)

                # Train the discriminator (real classified as ones and generated as
        zeros)
                d_loss_real = self.discriminator.train_on_batch(imgs, valid)
                d_loss_fake = self.discriminator.train_on_batch(gen_imgs, fake)
                d_loss = 0.5 * np.add(d_loss_real, d_loss_fake)


                # --------------------
                #  Train Generator
                # --------------------

                # Train the generator (wants discriminator to mistake images as
        real)
                g_loss = self.combined.train_on_batch(noise, valid)

                # Plot the progress
                print ("%d [D loss: %f, acc.: %.2f%%] [G loss: %f]" % (epoch, d_
        loss[0], 100*d_loss[1], g_loss))

                # If at save interval => save generated image samples
                if epoch % save_interval == 0:
                    self.save_imgs(epoch)
```

Lastly, we need a helper function to save images:

```
        def save_imgs(self, epoch):
            r, c = 5, 5
            noise = np.random.normal(0, 1, (r * c, self.latent_dim))
            gen_imgs = self.generator.predict(noise)
```

```python
# Rescale images 0 - 1
gen_imgs = 0.5 * gen_imgs + 0.5
fig, axs = plt.subplots(r, c)
cnt = 0
for i in range(r):
    for j in range(c):
        axs[i,j].imshow(gen_imgs[cnt, :,:,0], cmap='gray')
        axs[i,j].axis('off')
        cnt += 1
fig.savefig("images/dcgan_mnist_%d.png" % epoch)
plt.close()
```

Let us now train our GAN:

```python
dcgan = DCGAN(28,28,1)
dcgan.train(epochs=5000, batch_size=256, save_interval=50)
```

The images generated by our GAN as it learned to fake handwritten digits are:

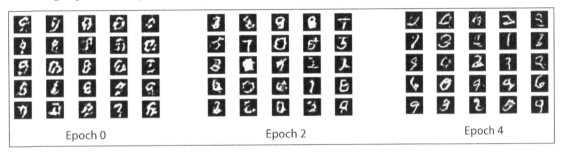

Figure 9.6: Images generated by GAN – initial attempt

The preceding images were the initial attempts by the GAN. As it learned through the following 10 epochs, the quality of digits generated improved manyfold:

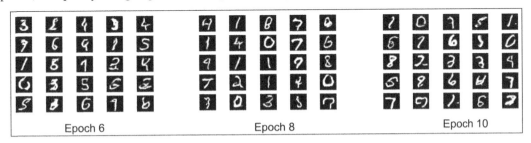

Figure 9.7: Images generated by GAN after 6, 8, and 10 epochs

The complete code is available in DCGAN.ipynb in the GitHub repo. We can take the concepts discussed here and apply them to images in other domains. One of the interesting works on images was reported in the paper, *Unsupervised Representation Learning with Deep Convolutional Generative Adversarial Networks*, Alec Radford, Luke Metz, Soumith Chintala, 2015. Quoting the abstract:

In recent years, supervised learning with convolutional networks (CNNs) has seen huge adoption in computer vision applications. Comparatively, unsupervised learning with CNNs has received less attention. In this work we hope to help bridge the gap between the success of CNNs for supervised learning and unsupervised learning. We introduce a class of CNNs called deep convolutional generative adversarial networks (DCGANs), that have certain architectural constraints, and demonstrate that they are a strong candidate for unsupervised learning. Training on various image datasets, we show convincing evidence that our deep convolutional adversarial pair learns a hierarchy of representations from object parts to scenes in both the generator and discriminator. Additionally, we use the learned features for novel tasks - demonstrating their applicability as general image representations.

—Radford et al., 2015

Following are some of the interesting results of applying DCGANs to a celebrity image dataset:

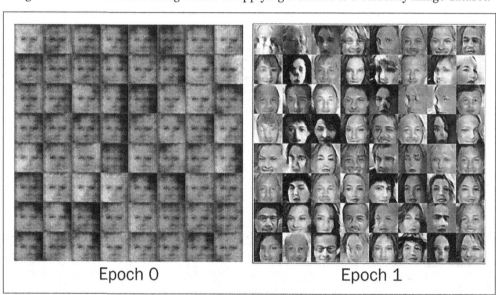

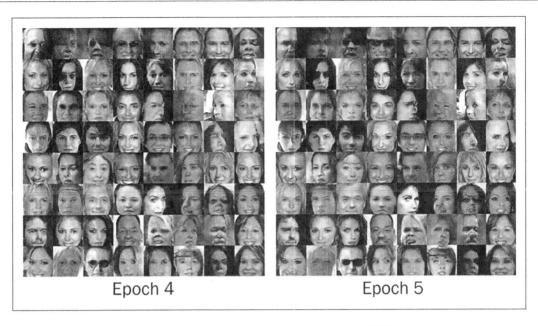

Epoch 4   Epoch 5

Figure 9.8: Generated celebrity images using DCGAN

Another interesting paper is *Semantic Image Inpainting with Perceptual and Contextual Losses*, by Raymond A. Yeh et al. in 2016. Just as content-aware fill is a tool used by photographers to fill in unwanted or missing parts of images, in this paper they used a DCGAN for image completion.

As mentioned earlier, a lot of research is happening around GANs. In the next section, we will explore some of the interesting GAN architectures proposed in recent years.

Some interesting GAN architectures

Since their inception, a lot of interest has been generated in GANs, and as a result, we are seeing a lot of modifications and experimentation with GAN training, architecture, and applications. In this section, we will explore some interesting GANs proposed in recent years.

SRGAN

Remember seeing a crime thriller where our hero asks the computer guy to magnify the faded image of the crime scene? With the zoom, we can see the criminal's face in detail, including the weapon used and anything engraved upon it! Well, **Super Resolution GANs (SRGANs)** can perform similar magic. Magic in the sense that because GANs show that it is possible to get high-resolution images, the final results depend on the camera resolution used. Here, a GAN is trained in such a way that it can generate a photorealistic high-resolution image when given a low-resolution image. The SRGAN architecture consists of three neural networks: a very deep generator network (which uses Residual modules; see ResNets in *Chapter 20, Advanced Convolutional Neural Networks*), a discriminator network, and a pretrained VGG-16 network.

SRGANs use the perceptual loss function (developed by Johnson et al; you can find the link to the paper in the *References* section). In SRGAN, the authors first downsampled a high-resolution image and used the generator to get its "high-resolution" version. The discriminator was trained to differentiate between the real high-resolution image and the generated high-resolution image. The difference in the feature map activations in high layers of a VGG network between the network output and the high-resolution parts comprises the perceptual loss function. Besides perceptual loss, the authors further added content loss and an adversarial loss so that images generated look more natural and the finer details more artistic. The perceptual loss is defined as the weighted sum of the content loss and adversarial loss:

$$l^{SR} = l_X^{SR} + 10^{-3} \times l_{Gen}^{SR}$$

The first term on the right-hand side is the content loss, obtained using the feature maps generated by pretrained VGG 19. Mathematically, it is the Euclidean distance between the feature map of the reconstructed image (that is, the one generated by the generator) and the original high-resolution reference image. The second term on the RHS is the adversarial loss. It is the standard generative loss term, designed to ensure that images generated by the generator can fool the discriminator. You can see in the following figure that the image generated by the SRGAN is much closer to the original high-resolution image with a PSNR value of 37.61:

Figure 9.9: An example following the paper Photo-Realistic Single Image Super-Resolution Using a Generative Adversarial Network, Ledig et al.

Another noteworthy architecture is CycleGAN; proposed in 2017, it can perform the task of image translation. Once trained you can translate an image from one domain to another domain. For example, when trained on a horse and zebra dataset, if you give it an image with horses in the foreground, the CycleGAN can convert the horses to zebras with the same background. We will explore it next.

CycleGAN

Have you ever imagined how some scenery would look if Van Gogh or Manet had painted it? We have many scenes and landscapes painted by Van Gogh/Manet, but we do not have any collection of input-output pairs. A CycleGAN performs the image translation, that is, transfers an image given in one domain (scenery, for example) to another domain (a Van Gogh painting of the same scene, for instance) in the absence of training examples. The CycleGAN's ability to perform image translation in the absence of training pairs is what makes it unique.

To achieve image translation, the authors used a very simple yet effective procedure. They made use of two GANs, the generator of each GAN performing the image translation from one domain to another.

To elaborate, let us say the input is X, then the generator of the first GAN performs a mapping $G: X \rightarrow Y$; thus, its output would be $Y = G(X)$. The generator of the second GAN performs an inverse mapping $F: Y \rightarrow X$, resulting in $X = F(Y)$. Each discriminator is trained to distinguish between real images and synthesized images. The idea is shown as follows:

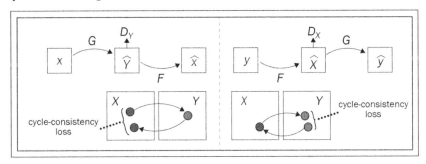

Figure 9.10: Cycle-consistency loss

To train the combined GANs, the authors added, besides the conventional GAN adversarial loss, a forward cycle-consistency loss (left figure) and a backward cycle-consistency loss (right figure). This ensures that if an image X is given as input, then after the two translations $F(G(X)) \sim X$ the obtained image is the same, X (similarly the backward cycle-consistency loss ensures that $G(F(Y)) \sim Y$).

Following are some of the successful image translations by CycleGANs [7]:

Figure 9.11: Examples of some successful CycleGAN image translations

Following are a few more examples; you can see the translation of seasons (summer → winter), photo → painting and vice versa, and horses → zebras and vice versa [7]:

Figure 9.12: Further examples of CycleGAN translations

Later in the chapter, we will also explore a TensorFlow implementation of CycleGANs. Next, we talk about the InfoGAN, a conditional GAN where the GAN not only generates an image, but you also have a control variable to control the images generated.

InfoGAN

The GAN architectures that we have considered up to now provide us with little or no control over the generated images. The InfoGAN changes this; it provides control over various attributes of the images generated. The InfoGAN uses the concepts from information theory such that the noise term is transformed into latent code that provides predictable and systematic control over the output.

The generator in an InfoGAN takes two inputs: the latent space Z and a latent code c, thus the output of the generator is $G(Z,c)$. The GAN is trained such that it maximizes the mutual information between the latent code c and the generated image $G(Z,c)$. The following figure shows the architecture of the InfoGAN:

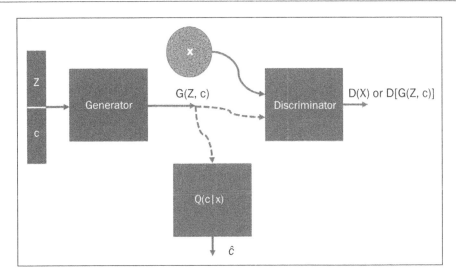

Figure 9.13: The architecture of the InfoGAN, visualized

The concatenated vector *(Z,c)* is fed to the generator. $Q(c|X)$ is also a neural network. Combined with the generator, it works to form a mapping between random noise Z and its latent code *c_hat*. It aims to estimate c given X. This is achieved by adding a regularization term to the objective function of the conventional GAN:

$$min_D max_G V_1(D, G) = V_G(D, G) - \lambda I(c; G(Z, c))$$

The term $V_G(D,G)$ is the loss function of the conventional GAN, and the second term is the regularization term, where λ is a constant. Its value was set to 1 in the paper, and $I(c;G(Z,c))$ is the mutual information between the latent code c and the generator-generated image $G(Z,c)$.

Following are the exciting results of the InfoGAN on the MNIST dataset:

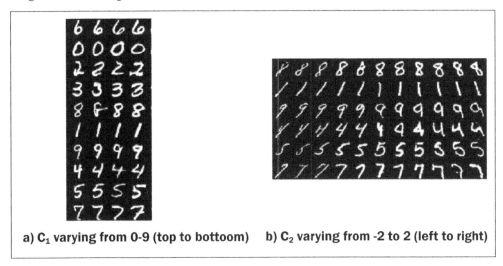

a) C_1 varying from 0-9 (top to bottom)   b) C_2 varying from -2 to 2 (left to right)

Figure 9.14: Results of using the InfoGAN on the MNIST dataset. Here, different rows correspond to different random samples of fixed latent codes and noise

Now, that we have seen some exciting GAN architectures, let us explore some cool applications of GAN.

Cool applications of GANs

We have seen that the generator can learn how to forge data. This means that it learns how to create new synthetic data that is created by the network that appears to be authentic and human-made. Before going into the details of some GAN code, we would like to share the results of the paper [6] (code is available online at https://github.com/hanzhanggit/StackGAN) where a GAN has been used to synthesize forged images starting from a text description. The results are impressive: the first column is the real image in the test set and all the rest of the columns are the images generated from the same text description by Stage-I and Stage-II of StackGAN. More examples are available on YouTube (https://www.youtube.com/watch?v=SuRyL5vhCIM&feature=youtu.be):

Figure 9.15: Image generation of birds, using GANs

Figure 9.16: Image generation of flowers, using GANs

Now let us see how a GAN can learn to "forge" the MNIST dataset. In this case, it is a combination of GAN and CNNs used for the generator and discriminator networks. In the beginning, the generator creates nothing understandable, but after a few iterations, synthetic forged numbers are progressively clearer and clearer. In this image, the panels are ordered by increasing training epochs and you can see the quality improving among the panels:

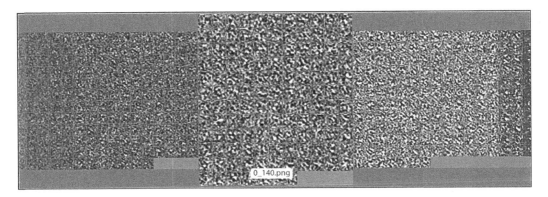

Figure 9.17: Illegible initial outputs of the GAN

As the training progresses, you can see in *Figure 9.17* that the digits start taking a more recognizable form:

Figure 9.18: Improved outputs of the GAN, following further iterations

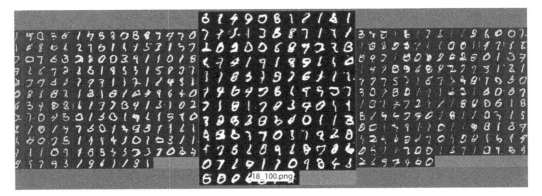

Figure 9.19: Final outputs of the GAN, showing significant improvement from previous iterations

After 10,000 epochs, you can see that the handwritten digits are even more realistic.

One of the coolest uses of GANs is doing arithmetic on faces in the generator's vector Z. In other words, if we stay in the space of synthetic forged images, it is possible to see things like this: *[smiling woman] - [neutral woman] + [neutral man] = [smiling man]*, or like this: *[man with glasses] - [man without glasses] + [woman without glasses] = [woman with glasses]*. This was shown in the paper *Unsupervised Representation Learning with Deep Convolutional Generative Adversarial Networks* by Alec Radford and his colleagues in 2015. All images in this work are generated by a version of GAN. They are NOT REAL. The full paper is available here: `http://arxiv.org/abs/1511.06434`. Following are some examples from the paper. The authors also share their code in this GitHub repo: `https://github.com/Newmu/dcgan_code`:

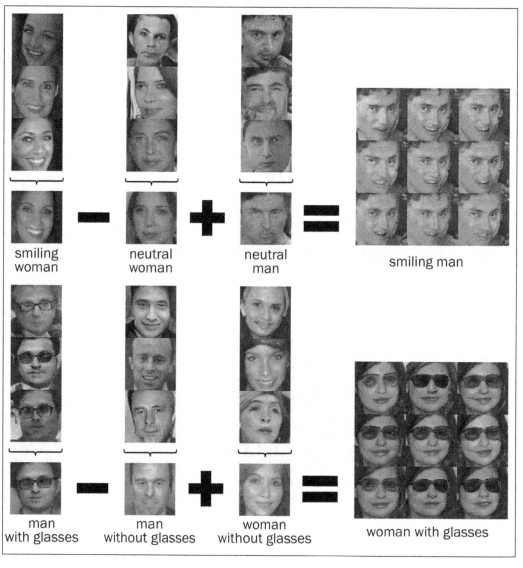

Figure 9.20: Image arithmetic using GANs

Bedrooms: Generated bedrooms after five epochs of training:

Figure 9.21: Generated bedrooms using GAN after 5 epochs of training

Album covers: These images are generated by the GAN, but look like authentic album covers:

Figure 9.22: Album covers generated using DCGAN

Another cool application of GANs is the generation of artificial faces. NVIDIA introduced a model in 2018, which it named StyleGAN (the second version, StyleGAN2, was released in February 2020, and the third version in 2021), which it showed can be used to generate realistic-looking images of people. Below you can see some of the realistic-looking fake people's faces generated by StyleGAN obtained after training of 1,000 epochs; for better results, you will need to train more:

Figure 9.23: Fake faces generated by StyleGAN

Not only does it generate fake images but like InfoGAN, you can control the features from coarse to grain. This is the official video released by NVIDIA showing how features affect the results: `https://www.youtube.com/watch?v=kSLJriaOumA`. They were able to do this by adding a non-linear mapping network after the Latent variable Z. The mapping network transformed the latent variable to a mapping of the same size; the output of the mapping vector is fed to different layers of the generator network, and this allows the StyleGAN to control different visual features. To know more about StyleGAN, you should read the paper *A style-based generator architecture for Generative Adversarial Networks* from NVIDIA Labs [10].

CycleGAN in TensorFlow

In this section, we will implement a CycleGAN in TensorFlow. The CycleGAN requires a special dataset, a paired dataset, from one domain of images to another domain. So, besides the necessary modules, we will use `tensorflow_datasets` as well. Also, we will make use of the library `tensorflow_examples`, we will directly use the generator and the discriminator from the `pix2pix` model defined in `tensorflow_examples`. The code here is adapted from the code here `https://github.com/tensorflow/docs/blob/master/site/en/tutorials/generative/cyclegan.ipynb`:

```
import tensorflow_datasets as tfds
from tensorflow_examples.models.pix2pix import pix2pix

import os
import time
import matplotlib.pyplot as plt
from IPython.display import clear_output
import tensorflow as tf
```

TensorFlow's `Dataset` API contains a list of datasets. It has many paired datasets for CycleGANs, such as horse to zebra, apples to oranges, and so on. You can access the complete list here: `https://www.tensorflow.org/datasets/catalog/cycle_gan`. For our code, we will be using `summer2winter_yosemite`, which contains images of Yosemite (USA) in summer (Dataset A) and winter (Dataset B). We will train the CycleGAN to convert an input image of summer to winter and vice versa.

Let us load the data and get train and test images:

```
dataset, metadata = tfds.load('cycle_gan/summer2winter_yosemite',
                                with_info=True, as_supervised=True)


train_summer, train_winter = dataset['trainA'], dataset['trainB']
test_summer, test_winter = dataset['testA'], dataset['testB']
```

We need to set some hyperparameters:

```
BUFFER_SIZE = 1000
BATCH_SIZE = 1
IMG_WIDTH = 256
IMG_HEIGHT = 256
EPOCHS = 100
LAMBDA = 10
AUTOTUNE = tf.data.AUTOTUNE
```

The images need to be normalized before we train the network. For better performance, we also add random jittering to the train images; the images are first resized to size 286x286, then we randomly crop them back to the size 256x256, and finally apply the random jitter:

```
def normalize(input_image, label):
    input_image = tf.cast(input_image, tf.float32)
    input_image = (input_image / 127.5) - 1
    return input_image


def random_crop(image):
    cropped_image = tf.image.random_crop(image, size=[IMG_HEIGHT,
    IMG_WIDTH, 3])

    return cropped_image


def random_jitter(image):
    # resizing to 286 x 286 x 3
    image = tf.image.resize(image, [286, 286],
    method=tf.image.ResizeMethod.NEAREST_NEIGHBOR)

    # randomly cropping to 256 x 256 x 3
    image = random_crop(image)

    # random mirroring
    image = tf.image.random_flip_left_right(image)

    return image
```

The augmentation (random crop and jitter) is done only to the train images; therefore, we will need to separate functions for preprocessing the images, one for train data, and the other for test data:

```python
def preprocess_image_train(image, label):
    image = random_jitter(image)
    image = normalize(image)
    return image

def preprocess_image_test(image, label):
    image = normalize(image)
    return image
```

The preceding functions, when applied to images, will normalize them in the range [-1,1] and apply augmentation to train images. Let us apply this to our train and test datasets and create a data generator that will provide images for training in batches:

```python
train_summer = train_summer.cache().map(
    preprocess_image_train, num_parallel_calls=AUTOTUNE).shuffle(
    BUFFER_SIZE).batch(BATCH_SIZE)

train_winter = train_winter.cache().map(
    preprocess_image_train, num_parallel_calls=AUTOTUNE).shuffle(
    BUFFER_SIZE).batch(BATCH_SIZE)

test_summer = test_summer.map(
    preprocess_image_test,
    num_parallel_calls=AUTOTUNE).cache().shuffle(
    BUFFER_SIZE).batch(BATCH_SIZE)

test_winter = test_winter.map(
    preprocess_image_test,
    num_parallel_calls=AUTOTUNE).cache().shuffle(
    BUFFER_SIZE).batch(BATCH_SIZE)
```

In the preceding code, the argument num_parallel_calls allows one to take benefit from multiple CPU cores in the system; one should set its value to the number of CPU cores in your system. If you are not sure, use the AUTOTUNE = tf.data.AUTOTUNE value so that TensorFlow dynamically determines the right number for you.

As mentioned in the beginning, we use a generator and discriminator from the `pix2pix` model defined in the `tensorflow_examples` module. We will have two generators and two discriminators:

```
OUTPUT_CHANNELS = 3

generator_g = pix2pix.unet_generator(OUTPUT_CHANNELS, norm_type='instancenorm')
generator_f = pix2pix.unet_generator(OUTPUT_CHANNELS, norm_type='instancenorm')

discriminator_x = pix2pix.discriminator(norm_type='instancenorm', target=False)
discriminator_y = pix2pix.discriminator(norm_type='instancenorm', target=False)
```

Before moving ahead with the model definition, let us see the images. Each image is processed before plotting so that its intensity is normal:

```
to_winter = generator_g(sample_summer)
to_summer = generator_f(sample_winter)
plt.figure(figsize=(8, 8))
contrast = 8

imgs = [sample_summer, to_winter, sample_winter, to_summer]
title = ['Summer', 'To Winter', 'Winter', 'To Summer']

for i in range(len(imgs)):
  plt.subplot(2, 2, i+1)
  plt.title(title[i])
  if i % 2 == 0:
    plt.imshow(imgs[i][0] * 0.5 + 0.5)
  else:
    plt.imshow(imgs[i][0] * 0.5 * contrast + 0.5)
plt.show()
```

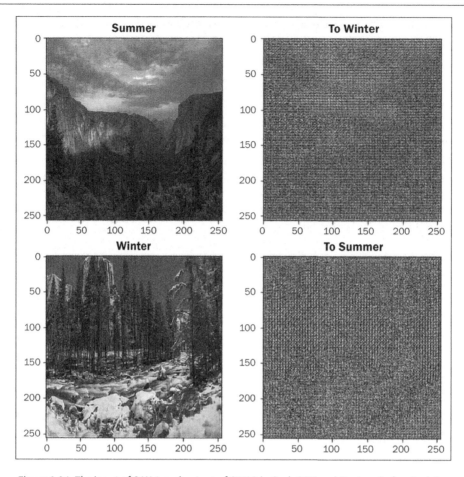

Figure 9.24: The input of GAN 1 and output of GAN 2 in CycleGAN architecture before training

We next define the loss and optimizers. We retain the same loss functions for generator and discriminator as we did in DCGAN:

```
loss_obj = tf.keras.losses.BinaryCrossentropy(from_logits=True)

def discriminator_loss(real, generated):
    real_loss = loss_obj(tf.ones_like(real), real)
    generated_loss = loss_obj(tf.zeros_like(generated), generated)
    total_disc_loss = real_loss + generated_loss
    return total_disc_loss * 0.5

def generator_loss(generated):
    return loss_obj(tf.ones_like(generated), generated)
```

Since there are now four models, two generators and two discriminators, we need to define four optimizers:

```
generator_g_optimizer = tf.keras.optimizers.Adam(2e-4, beta_1=0.5)
generator_f_optimizer = tf.keras.optimizers.Adam(2e-4, beta_1=0.5)


discriminator_x_optimizer = tf.keras.optimizers.Adam(2e-4, beta_1=0.5)
discriminator_y_optimizer = tf.keras.optimizers.Adam(2e-4, beta_1=0.5)
```

Additionally, in the CycleGAN, we require to define two more loss functions, first the cycle-consistency loss; we can use the same function for forward and backward cycle-consistency loss calculation. The cycle-consistency loss ensures that the result is close to the original input:

```
def calc_cycle_loss(real_image, cycled_image):
    loss1 = tf.reduce_mean(tf.abs(real_image - cycled_image))
    return LAMBDA * loss1
```

We also need to define an identity loss, which ensures that if an image *Y* is fed to the generator, it would yield the real image *Y* or an image similar to *Y*. Thus, if we give our summer image generator an image of summer as input, it should not change it much:

```
def identity_loss(real_image, same_image):
    loss = tf.reduce_mean(tf.abs(real_image - same_image))
    return LAMBDA * 0.5 * loss
```

Now we define the function that trains the generator and discriminator in a batch, a pair of images at a time. The two discriminators and the two generators are trained via this function with the help of the tape gradient. The training step can be divided into four parts:

1. Get the output images from the two generators.
2. Calculate the losses.
3. Calculate the gradients.
4. And finally, apply the gradients:

```
@tf.function
def train_step(real_x, real_y):
    # persistent is set to True because the tape is used
    # more than once to calculate the gradients.
    with tf.GradientTape(persistent=True) as tape:
        # Generator G translates X -> Y
        # Generator F translates Y -> X.

        fake_y = generator_g(real_x, training=True)
        cycled_x = generator_f(fake_y, training=True)
```

```python
fake_x = generator_f(real_y, training=True)
cycled_y = generator_g(fake_x, training=True)

# same_x and same_y are used for identity loss.
same_x = generator_f(real_x, training=True)
same_y = generator_g(real_y, training=True)

disc_real_x = discriminator_x(real_x, training=True)
disc_real_y = discriminator_y(real_y, training=True)

disc_fake_x = discriminator_x(fake_x, training=True)
disc_fake_y = discriminator_y(fake_y, training=True)

# calculate the loss
gen_g_loss = generator_loss(disc_fake_y)
gen_f_loss = generator_loss(disc_fake_x)

total_cycle_loss = calc_cycle_loss(real_x, cycled_x) + \
calc_cycle_loss(real_y, cycled_y)

# Total generator loss = adversarial loss + cycle loss
total_gen_g_loss = gen_g_loss + total_cycle_loss + \
identity_loss(real_y, same_y)
total_gen_f_loss = gen_f_loss + total_cycle_loss + \
identity_loss(real_x, same_x)

disc_x_loss = discriminator_loss(disc_real_x,
disc_fake_x)
disc_y_loss = discriminator_loss(disc_real_y,
disc_fake_y)

# Calculate the gradients for generator and discriminator
generator_g_gradients = tape.gradient(total_gen_g_loss,
generator_g.trainable_variables)
generator_f_gradients = tape.gradient(total_gen_f_loss,
generator_f.trainable_variables)

discriminator_x_gradients = tape.gradient(disc_x_loss,
discriminator_x.trainable_variables)
discriminator_y_gradients = tape.gradient(disc_y_loss,
discriminator_y.trainable_variables)
```

```
     # Apply the gradients to the optimizer
     generator_g_optimizer.apply_gradients(zip(generator_g_gradients,
 generator_g.trainable_variables))

     generator_f_optimizer.apply_gradients(zip(generator_f_gradients,
 generator_f.trainable_variables))
     discriminator_x_optimizer.apply_gradients(zip(discriminator_x_
 gradients, discriminator_x.trainable_variables))
     discriminator_y_optimizer.apply_gradients(zip(discriminator_y_
 gradients, discriminator_y.trainable_variables))
```

We define checkpoints to save the model weights. Since it can take a while to train a sufficiently good CycleGAN, we save the checkpoints, and if we start next, we can start with loading the existing checkpoints – this will ensure that model starts learning from where it left:

```
checkpoint_path = "./checkpoints/train"

ckpt = tf.train.Checkpoint(generator_g=generator_g,
                           generator_f=generator_f,
                           discriminator_x=discriminator_x,
                           discriminator_y=discriminator_y,
                           generator_g_optimizer=generator_g_optimizer,
generator_f_optimizer=generator_f_optimizer,
discriminator_x_optimizer=discriminator_x_optimizer,
discriminator_y_optimizer=discriminator_y_optimizer)

ckpt_manager = tf.train.CheckpointManager(ckpt, checkpoint_path, max_to_keep=5)

# if a checkpoint exists, restore the latest checkpoint.
if ckpt_manager.latest_checkpoint:
    ckpt.restore(ckpt_manager.latest_checkpoint)
    print ('Latest checkpoint restored!!')
```

Let us now combine it all and train the network for 100 epochs. Please remember that in the paper, the test network was trained for 200 epochs, so our results will not be that good:

```
for epoch in range(EPOCHS):
    start = time.time()

    n = 0
    for image_x, image_y in tf.data.Dataset.zip((train_summer, train_winter)):
        train_step(image_x, image_y)
        if n % 10 == 0:
```

```
        print ('.', end='')
    n += 1

clear_output(wait=True)
# Using a consistent image (sample_summer) so that the progress of
# the model is clearly visible.
generate_images(generator_g, sample_summer)

if (epoch + 1) % 5 == 0:
    ckpt_save_path = ckpt_manager.save()
    print ('Saving checkpoint for epoch {} at {}'.format(epoch+1,
                                                ckpt_save_path))

print ('Time taken for epoch {} is {} sec\n'.format(epoch + 1,
                                        time.time()-start))
```

You can see some of the images generated by our CycleGAN. Generator *A* takes in summer photos and converts them to winter, while generator *B* takes in winter photos and converts them to summer:

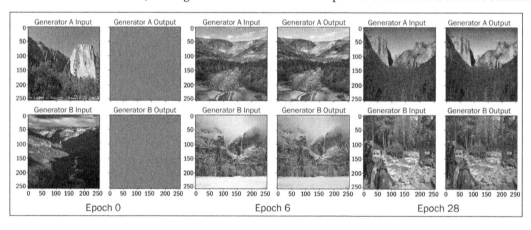

Figure 9.25: Images using CycleGAN after training

We suggest you experiment with other datasets in the TensorFlow CycleGAN datasets. Some will be easy like apples and oranges, but some will require much more training. The authors also maintain a GitHub repository where they have shared their own implementation in PyTorch along with the links to implementations in other frameworks including TensorFlow: https://github.com/junyanz/CycleGAN.

Flow-based models for data generation

While both VAEs (*Chapter 8, Autoencoders*) and GANs do a good job of data generation, they do not explicitly learn the probability density function of the input data. GANs learn by converting the unsupervised problem to a supervised learning problem.

VAEs try to learn by optimizing the maximum log-likelihood of the data by maximizing the **Evidence Lower Bound** (**ELBO**). Flow-based models differ from the two in that they explicitly learn data distribution $p(x)$. This offers an advantage over VAEs and GANs, because this makes it possible to use flow-based models for tasks like filling incomplete data, sampling data, and even identifying bias in data distributions. Flow-based models accomplish this by maximizing the log-likelihood estimation. To understand how, let us delve a little into its math.

Let $p_D(x)$ be the probability density of data D, and let $p_M(x)$ be the probability density approximated by our model M. The goal of a flow-based model is to find the model parameters θ^* such that the distance between two is minimum, i.e.:

$$\theta^* = arg \min_{\theta \in M} distance \ (p_D(x), p_\theta(x))$$

If we use the KL divergence as our distance metrics, the expression above reduces to:

$$\theta^* = \arg \min_{\theta \in M} \ E_{x \sim p_D}[\log p_\theta(x)]$$

This equation represents minimizing the **Negative Log-Likelihood** (**NLL**) (equivalent to maximizing log-likelihood estimation.)

The basic architecture of flow-based models consists of a series of invertible functions, as shown in the figure below. The challenge is to find the function $f(x)$, such that its inverse $f^1(x)$ generates x', the reconstructed version of the input x:

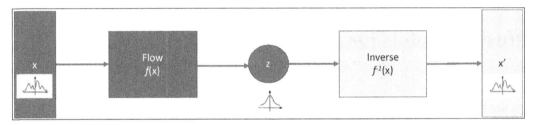

Figure 9.26: Architecture of flow-based model

There are mainly two ways flow-based models are implemented:

- Normalized Flow: Here, the basic idea is to use a series of simple invertible functions to transform the complex input. As we flow through the sequence of transformations, we repeatedly substitute the variable with a new one, as per the change of variables theorem (https://archive.lib.msu.edu/crcmath/math/math/c/c210.htm), and finally, we obtain a probability distribution of the target variable. The path that the variables z_i traverse is the flow and the complete chain formed by the successive distributions is called the normalizing flow.

The **RealNVP (Real-valued Non-Volume Preserving)** model proposed by Dinh et al., 2017, **NICE (Non-linear Independent Components Estimation)** by Dinh et al., 2015, and Glow by Knigma and Dhariwal, 2018, use the normalized flow trick:

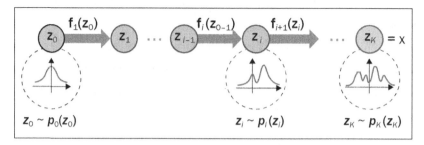

Figure 9.27: Normalizing flow model: https://lilianweng.github.io/posts/2018-10-13-flow-models/

- Autoregressive Flow: Models like **MADE (Masked Autoencoder for Distribution Estimation)**, PixelRNN, and wavenet are based on autoregressive models. Here, each dimension in a vector variable is dependent on the previous dimensions. Thus, the probability of observing z_i depends only on $z_1, z_2, …, z_{i-1}$, and therefore, the product of these conditional probabilities gives us the probability of the entire sequence.

Lilian Weng's blog (`https://lilianweng.github.io/posts/2018-10-13-flow-models/`) provides a very good description of flow-based models.

Diffusion models for data generation

The 2021 paper *Diffusion Models Beat GANs on Image synthesis* by two OpenAI research scientists Prafulla Dhariwal and Alex Nichol garnered a lot of interest in diffusion models for data generation.

Using the **Frechet Inception Distance (FID)** as the metrics for evaluation of generated images, they were able to achieve an FID score of 3.85 on a diffusion model trained on ImageNet data:

Figure 9.28: Selected samples of images generated from ImageNet (FID 3.85). Image Source: Dhariwal, Prafulla, and Alexander Nichol. "Diffusion models beat GANs on image synthesis." Advances in Neural Information Processing Systems 34 (2021)

The idea behind diffusion models is very simple. We take our input image x_0, and at each time step (forward step), we add a Gaussian noise to it (diffusion of noise) such that after T time steps, the original image is no longer decipherable. And then find a model that can, starting from a noisy input, perform the reverse diffusion and generate a clear image:

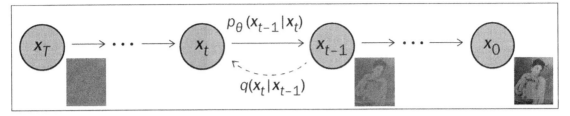

Figure 9.29: Graphical model as a Markov chain for the forward and reverse diffusion process

The only problem is that while the conditional probabilities $p(x_{t-1}|x_t)$ can be obtained using the reparameterization trick, the reverse conditional probability $q(x_t|x_{t-1})$ is unknown. We train a neural network model p_θ to approximate these conditional probabilities. Below is the training and the sampling algorithm used by Ho et al., 2020, in their *Denoising Diffusion Probabilistic Models* paper:

Algorithm 1 Training	Algorithm 2 Sampling
1. **repeat**	1. $x_T \sim \mathcal{N}(0, \mathbf{I})$
2. $x_0 \sim q(x_0)$	2. **for** $t = T, ..., 1$ **do**
3. $t \sim \text{Uniform}(\{1, ..., T\})$	3. $z \sim \mathcal{N}(0, \mathbf{I})$ if $t > 1$, else $\mathbf{z} = \mathbf{0}$
4. $\epsilon \sim \mathcal{N}(0, \mathbf{I})$	4. $x_{t-1} = \frac{1}{\sqrt{\alpha_t}}\left(x_t - \frac{1-\alpha_t}{\sqrt{1-\bar{\alpha}_t}}\epsilon_\theta(x_t, t)\right) + \sigma_t \mathbf{z}$
5. Take gradient descent step on $\nabla_\theta \|\epsilon - \epsilon_\theta(\sqrt{\bar{\alpha}_t}x_0 + \sqrt{1-\bar{\alpha}_t}\epsilon, t)\|^2$	5. **end for**
6. **until** converged	6. **return** x_0

Table 9.1: Training and sampling steps used by Ho et al., 2020

Diffusion models offer both tractability and flexibility – two conflicting objectives in generative models. However, they rely on a long Markov chain of diffusion steps and thus are computationally expensive. There is a lot of traction in diffusion models, and we hope that in the near future there will be algorithms that can give as fast sampling as GANs.

Summary

This chapter explored one of the most exciting deep neural networks of our times: GANs. Unlike discriminative networks, GANs have the ability to generate images based on the probability distribution of the input space. We started with the first GAN model proposed by Ian Goodfellow and used it to generate handwritten digits. We next moved to DCGANs where convolutional neural networks were used to generate images and we saw the remarkable pictures of celebrities, bedrooms, and even album artwork generated by DCGANs. Finally, the chapter delved into some awesome GAN architectures: the SRGAN, CycleGAN, InfoGAN, and StyleGAN. The chapter also included an implementation of the CycleGAN in TensorFlow 2.0.

In this chapter and the ones before it, we have been continuing with different unsupervised learning models, with both autoencoders and GANs examples of self-supervised learning; the next chapter will further detail the difference between self-supervised, joint, and contrastive learning.

References

1. Goodfellow, Ian J. (2014). *On Distinguishability Criteria for Estimating Generative Models*. arXiv preprint arXiv:1412.6515: https://arxiv.org/pdf/1412.6515.pdf

2. Dumoulin, Vincent, and Visin, Francesco. (2016). *A guide to convolution arithmetic for deep learning*. arXiv preprint arXiv:1603.07285: https://arxiv.org/abs/1603.07285

3. Salimans, Tim, et al. (2016). *Improved Techniques for Training GANs*. Advances in neural information processing systems: http://papers.nips.cc/paper/6125-improved-techniques-for-training-gans.pdf

4. Johnson, Justin, Alahi, Alexandre, and Fei-Fei, Li. (2016). *Perceptual Losses for Real-Time Style Transfer and Super-Resolution*. European conference on computer vision. Springer, Cham: https://arxiv.org/abs/1603.08155

5. Radford, Alec, Metz, Luke., and Chintala, Soumith. (2015). *Unsupervised Representation Learning with Deep Convolutional Generative Adversarial Networks*. arXiv preprint arXiv:1511.06434: https://arxiv.org/abs/1511.06434

6. Ledig, Christian, et al. (2017). *Photo-Realistic Single Image Super-Resolution Using a Generative Adversarial Network*. Proceedings of the IEEE conference on computer vision and pattern recognition: http://openaccess.thecvf.com/content_cvpr_2017/papers/Ledig_Photo-Realistic_Single_Image_CVPR_2017_paper.pdf

7. Zhu, Jun-Yan, et al. (2017). *Unpaired Image-to-Image Translation using Cycle-Consistent Adversarial Networks*. Proceedings of the IEEE international conference on computer vision: http://openaccess.thecvf.com/content_ICCV_2017/papers/Zhu_Unpaired_Image-To-Image_Translation_ICCV_2017_paper.pdf

8. Karras, Tero, Laine, Samuli, and Aila, Timo. (2019). *A style-based generator architecture for generative adversarial networks*. In Proceedings of the IEEE/CVF conference on computer vision and pattern recognition, pp. 4401-4410.

9. Chen, Xi, et al. (2016). *InfoGAN: Interpretable Representation Learning by Information Maximizing Generative Adversarial Nets*. Advances in neural information processing systems: https://arxiv.org/abs/1606.03657

10. TensorFlow implementation of the StyleGAN: https://github.com/NVlabs/stylegan

Join our book's Discord space

Join our Discord community to meet like-minded people and learn alongside more than 2000 members at: https://packt.link/keras

10
Self-Supervised Learning

Imagine that you are in the middle of the ocean, and you are thirsty. There is water all around you, but you cannot drink any of it. But what if you had the resources to boil the salt out of the water and thereby make it drinkable? Of course, the energy costs associated with the process can be quite high, so you will likely use the process in moderation. However, if your energy costs effectively became free, for example, if you were harnessing the power of the sun, the process might be more attractive for you to do on a larger scale.

In our somewhat simplistic situation described above, the first scenario is roughly analogous to supervised learning, and the second to the class of unsupervised / semi-supervised learning techniques we will cover in this chapter. The biggest problem with supervised learning techniques is the time and expense associated with the collection of labeled training data. As a result, labeled datasets are often relatively small.

Deep learning trades off computation against manual feature engineering, and while this can be very effective, deep learning models typically need more data to train than traditional (non-deep learning) models. Deep learning models tend to be more complex and have more learnable parameters, which results in them performing better at various tasks. However, more complex models also require more data to train. Because the creation of training data is expensive, this effectively limits us from scaling up Deep learning models using supervised learning.

Unfortunately, completely unsupervised learning techniques that do not need labeled data have had limited success so far. Self-supervised techniques that leverage the structure of data in the wild to create labeled data to feed supervised learning models offer a middle ground. In this chapter, we will learn about various self-supervised techniques and some of their applications in the areas of natural language processing, computer vision, and audio signal processing.

The chapter covers the following topics:

- Previous work
- Self-supervised learning
- Self-prediction

- Contrastive learning
- Pretext tasks

 All the code files for this chapter can be found at https://packt.link/dltfchp10

Self-supervised learning is the process of imaginatively reusing labels that already exist implicitly in your data. In this chapter, we will learn about some common strategies for self-supervised learning and examples of their use to solve real-life problems. Let's begin.

Previous work

Self-supervised learning is not a new concept. However, the term became popular with the advent of transformer-based models such as BERT and GPT-2, which were trained in a semi-supervised manner on large quantities of unlabeled text. In the past, self-supervised learning was often labeled as unsupervised learning. However, there were many earlier models that attempted to leverage regularities in the input data to produce results comparable to that using supervised learning. You have encountered some of them in previous chapters already, but we will briefly cover them again in this section.

The **Restricted Boltzmann Machine** (**RBM**) is a generative neural model that can learn a probability distribution over its inputs. It was invented in 1986 and subsequently improved in the mid-2000s. It can be trained in either supervised or unsupervised mode and can be applied to many downstream tasks, such as dimensionality reduction, classification, etc.

Autoencoders (**AEs**) are unsupervised learning models that attempt to learn an efficient latent representation of input data by learning to reconstruct its input. The latent representation can be used to encode the input for downstream tasks. There are several variants of the model. Sparse, denoising, and contrastive AEs are effective in learning representations for downstream classification tasks, whereas variational AEs are more useful as generative models.

The Word2Vec model is another great example of what we would now call self-supervised learning. The CBOW and skip-gram models used to build the latent representation of words in a corpus, attempt to learn mappings of neighbors to words and words to neighbors respectively. However, the latent representation can now be used as word embeddings for a variety of downstream tasks. Similarly, the GloVe model is also a self-supervised model, which uses word co-occurrences and matrix factorization to generate word embeddings useful for downstream tasks.

Autoregressive (**AR**) models predict future behavior based on past behavior. We cover them in this chapter in the *Self-prediction* section. However, AR models have their roots in time series analysis in statistics, hidden Markov models in pre-neural natural language processing, **Recurrent Neural Networks** (**RNNs**) in neural (but pre-transformer) NLP.

Contrastive Learning (**CL**) models try to learn representations whereby similar pairs of items cluster together and dissimilar pairs are pushed far apart.

CL models are also covered in this chapter in the *Contrastive learning* section. However, **Self Organizing Maps (SOMs)** and Siamese networks use very similar ideas and may have been a precursor of current CL models.

Self-supervised learning

In self-supervised learning, the network is trained using supervised learning, but the labels are obtained in an automated manner by leveraging some property of the data and without human labelling effort. Usually, this automation is achieved by leveraging how parts of the data sample interact with each other and learning to predict that. In other words, the data itself provides the supervision for the learning process.

One class of techniques involves leveraging co-occurrences within parts of the same data sample or co-occurrences between the same data sample at different points in time. These techniques are discussed in more detail in the *Self-prediction* section.

Another class of techniques involves leveraging co-occurring modality for a given data sample, for example, between a piece of text and its associated audio stream, or an image and its caption. Examples of this technique are discussed in the sections on joint learning.

Yet another class of self-supervised learning techniques involves exploiting relationships between pairs of data samples. These pairs are selected from the dataset based on some domain-level heuristic. Examples of these techniques are covered in the *Contrastive learning* section.

These techniques can either be used to train a model to learn to solve a business task (such as sentiment analysis, classification, etc.) directly or to learn a latent (embedding) representation of the data that can then be used to generate features to learn to solve a downstream business task. The latter class of tasks that are used to indirectly learn the latent representation of the data are called pretext tasks. The *Pretext tasks* section will cover this subject, with examples, in more detail.

The advantages of self-supervised learning are twofold. First, as noted already, supervised learning involves the manual labeling of data, which is very expensive to create, and therefore it is difficult to get high-quality labeled data. Second, self-supervised tasks may not address a business task directly but can be used to learn a good representation of the data, which can then be applied to transfer this information to actual business tasks downstream.

Self-prediction

The idea behind self-prediction is to predict one part of a data sample given another part. For the purposes of prediction, we pretend that the part to be predicted is hidden or missing and learn to predict it. Obviously, both parts are known, and the part to be predicted serves as the data label. The model is trained in a supervised manner, using the non-hidden part as the input and the hidden part as the label, learning to predict the hidden part accurately. Essentially, it is to pretend that there is a part of the input that you don't know and predict that.

The idea can also be extended to reversing the pipeline, for example, deliberately adding noise to an image and using the original image as the label and the corrupted image as the input.

Autoregressive generation

Autoregressive (**AR**) models attempt to predict a future event, behavior, or property based on past events, behavior, or properties. Any data that comes with some innate sequential order can be modeled using AR generation. Unlike latent variable models such as VAEs or GANs, AR models make no assumptions of independence.

PixelRNN

The PixelRNN [1] AR model uses two-dimensional **Recurrent Neural Networks** (**RNNs**) to model images on a large scale. The idea is to learn to generate a pixel by conditioning on all pixels to the left and above it. A convolution operation is used to compute all the states along each dimension at once. The LSTM layers used in PixelRNN are one of two types – the Row LSTM and the Diagonal BiLSTM. In the row LSTM, the convolution is applied along each row, and in the Diagonal BiLSTM, the convolutions are applied along the diagonals of the image:

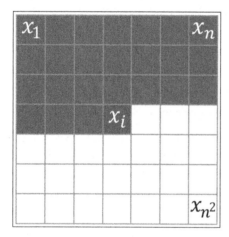

$$p(x) = \prod_{i=1}^{n^2} p(x_i | x_1, \ldots, x_{i-1})$$

Figure 10.1: PixelRNN tries to predict a pixel by conditioning on all pixels to the left and above it. From the paper Pixel Recurrent Neural Networks [1]

Image GPT (IPT)

Image GPT (IPT) [14] is similar to PixelRNN except it works on patches, and each patch is treated as a word. The Image GPT is based on the Transformer model and is trained on images from the ImageNet dataset. The images are corrupted in multiple different ways (super-resolution, bicubic interpolation, adding noise, etc.) and pretrained to predict the original image. The core of the IPT model consisted of a transformer encoder decoder pair but had multiple heads and tails to extract features from the corrupted input image and format the decoder output into the output image respectively. The multiple heads and tails were specialized for each of the different tasks IPT is trained to do (denoising, deraining, x2 and x4 super-resolution, etc.):

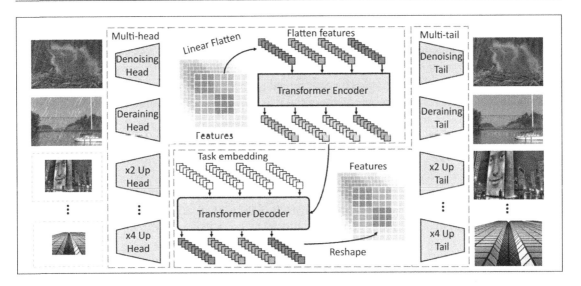

Figure 10.2: Architecture of the Image GPT (IPT) AR model. From the paper Pre-trained Image Processing Transformer [14]

GPT-3

The GPT-3, or Generative Pre-trained Transformer [9] model from OpenAI is an AR language model that can generate human-like text. It generates sequences of words, code, and other data, starting from a human-provided prompt. The first version of GPT used 110 million learning parameters, GPT-2 used 1.5 billion, and GPT-3 used 175 billion parameters. The model is trained on unlabeled text such as Wikipedia that is readily available on the internet, initially in English but later in other languages as well. The GPT-3 model has a wide variety of use cases, including summarization, translation, grammar correction, question answering, chatbots, and email composition.

The popularity of GPT-3 has given rise to a new profession called prompt engineering [39], which is basically to create the most effective prompts to start GPT-3 on various tasks. A partial list of possible applications for GPT-3 can be found on the OpenAI GPT-3 examples page (`https://beta.openai.com/examples/`).

XLNet

XLNet [38] is similar to GPT-3 in that it is a generalized AR model. However, it leverages both AR language modeling and **AutoEncoding** while avoiding their limitations. Instead of using only tokens from the left or right context to predict the next token, it uses all possible permutations of the tokens from the left and right contexts, thus using tokens from both the left and right contexts for prediction. Secondly, unlike AE approaches such as BERT, it does not depend on input corruption (as in masked language modeling) since it is a generalized AR language model. Empirically, under comparable experimental settings, XLNet consistently outperforms BERT on a wide spectrum of tasks.

WaveNet

WaveNet [3] is an AR generative model based on PixelCNN's architecture but operates on the raw audio waveform. As with PixelCNN, an audio sample at a particular point in time is conditioned on the samples at all previous timesteps. The conditional probability distribution is modeled as a stack of convolutional layers. The main ingredient of the WaveNet is causal convolutions. The predictions emitted by the model at a time step cannot depend on any future timesteps. When applied to text to speech, WaveNet yields state-of-the-art performance, with human listeners rating it as significantly more natural sounding for English and Mandarin than comparable text-to-speech models.

WaveRNN

WaveRNN [28] is an AR generative model that learns the joint probability of the data by factorizing the distribution into a product of conditional probabilities over each sample. The convolutional layers of the WaveNet architecture are replaced with a single-layer RNN. It also uses more efficient sampling techniques that, overall, reduce the number of operations to perform and result in approximately 4x speedup over WaveNet.

Masked generation

Masked generation models mask some random portion of themselves and pretend it is missing, and the models learn to predict the masked information using the unmasked information available to them. Unlike autoregressive models, in the case of masked generation models, there is no need for the masked information to be located before or after the unmasked information; it can be anywhere in the input.

BERT

BERT [16], or **Bidirectional Encoder Representation from Transformers**, is a transformer-based language model that was trained using text from the internet by a team from Google. It uses two objectives during the pretraining phase – **Masked Language Modeling** (**MLM**) and **Next Sentence Prediction** (**NSP**). During training, 15% of the input tokens are masked and the model learns to predict the masked token. Since the model is transformer based, it can use context from anywhere in the sentence to help with predicting the masked tokens. BERT models, once pretrained, can be fine-tuned with smaller supervised datasets for a variety of downstream tasks such as classification, sentiment analysis, textual entailment, etc. BERT is covered in more depth in *Chapter 6, Transformers*.

You can see BERT's masked generation in action using a pretrained BERT model from the Hugging Face Transformers library and the code snippet shown below. Here, we ask a pretrained BERT transformer model to predict the masked token [MASK] in the sentence "The capital of France is [MASK].":

```
from transformers import BertTokenizer, TFBertForMaskedLM
import tensorflow as tf
```

```
tokenizer = BertTokenizer.from_pretrained("bert-base-cased")
model = TFBertForMaskedLM.from_pretrained("bert-base-cased")

inputs = tokenizer("The capital of France is [MASK].", return_tensors="tf")
logits = model(**inputs).logits
mask_token_index = tf.where(inputs.input_ids == tokenizer.mask_token_id)[0][1]
predicted_token_id = tf.math.argmax(logits[:, mask token_index], axis=-1)
print(tokenizer.convert_ids_to_tokens(predicted_token_id)[0])
```

Somewhat predictably, the output of this code block is `"Paris"`.

Stacked denoising autoencoder

A stacked denoising autoencoder (AE) [29] adds random noise to images and uses them as input to a denoising AE to predict the original image. Multiple layers of denoising AEs are each individually trained and stacked. This results in the composition of several levels of non-linearity and is key to achieving better generalization performance on difficult image recognition tasks. Higher-level representations learned in this purely unsupervised manner can be used as image features to boost the performance of downstream SVM based image classifiers. Each layer functions like a regular AE, i.e., it takes an image as input and tries to reconstruct it after it passes through a "bottleneck" layer. The bottleneck layer learns a compact feature representation of the input image. Unfortunately, AEs usually end up only learning how to compress the image without learning a semantically meaningful representation. Denoising AEs address this issue by corrupting the input and requiring the network to undo the corruption and hence learn a better semantic representation of the input image.

Context autoencoder

The context autoencoder [12] masks out a region of the image and uses it to train a convolutional neural network (the context AE) to regress the missing pixel values to predict the original image. The task of a context AE is even harder than that of a denoising AE since it has to fill in larger missing areas and cannot use information from immediately neighboring pixels. This requires a much deeper semantic understanding of the image, and the ability to generate high-level features over large spatial areas. In a sense, the context AE is a more powerful generative model since it needs to fill in the missing region while maintaining coherence with the supplied context.

For that reason, the context AE is trained to reconstruct a combination of reconstruction loss and adversarial loss. This results in sharper predictions than training on reconstruction (L2) loss alone:

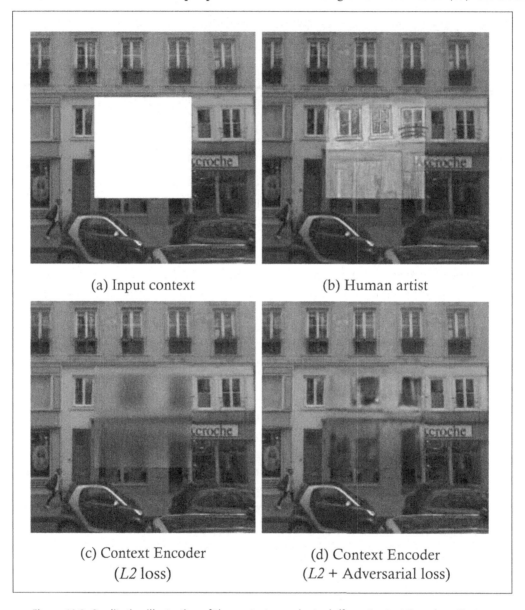

(a) Input context

(b) Human artist

(c) Context Encoder
($L2$ loss)

(d) Context Encoder
($L2$ + Adversarial loss)

Figure 10.3: Qualitative illustration of the context encoder task (from Context Encoders: Feature Learning by Inpainting [10])

Context does not have to be image features, it could also be color, as we will see in the next section.

Colorization

The paper *Colorization as a Proxy Task for Visual Understanding* [12] uses colorization as a way to learn image representations. Color images are converted to their grayscale equivalent, which is then used as input to predict the original color image. The model can be used to automatically colorize grayscale images, as well as learn a representation that can help in downstream tasks such as image classification and segmentation. In functional terms, the model predicts the *a* and *b* (color information) channels in their *Lab* encoding given their *L* (grayscale) channel. Experiments on the ImageNet dataset by the authors of this paper have resulted in models that produce state-of-the-art results against datasets for semantic segmentation and image classification for models that don't use ImageNet labels, and even surpass some earlier models that have been trained on ImageNet using supervised learning.

Innate relationship prediction

Models using this technique attempt to learn visual common-sense tasks by leveraging innate relationships between parts of an input image. Weights from these learned models could be used to generate semantic representations of images for other downstream tasks.

Relative position

The paper *Unsupervised Visual Representation Learning by Context Prediction* [8] predicts the relative position of one patch in an image with respect to another. Effectively, this approach uses spatial context as a source of self-supervision for training visual representations. Given a large unlabeled image collection, random pairs of patches are extracted from each image as shown in *Figure 10.4*. Each pair is labeled depending on the orientation of the second patch with respect to the central one. A convolutional network is trained to predict the position of the second patch relative to the first. The feature representation learned is found to capture the notion of visual similarity across images. Using this representation, it has been shown to aid in visual data mining, i.e., discovering image fragments that depict the same semantic object, against the Pascal VOC 2007 dataset:

Figure 10.4: Illustration of relative position prediction. The model must predict the configuration of the second patch relative to the (central) first patch. From the paper Unsupervised Visual Representation Learning by Context Prediction [8]

Solving jigsaw puzzles

The paper *Unsupervised Learning of Visual Representations by Solving Jigsaw Puzzles* [26] describes an approach somewhat similar to the previous approach of predicting relative position. This method attempts to learn the visual representation of images by solving jigsaw puzzles of natural images. Patches are extracted from the input image and shuffled to form a jigsaw puzzle. The network learns to reconstruct the original image from the jigsaw puzzle, i.e., to solve the jigsaw puzzle. The network used is a **Context Free Network (CFN)**, an n-way Siamese network. Each patch corresponds to a column in the n-way CFN. The shared layers in each column are implemented exactly as in AlexNet. The classification head predicts the original index of the patch (before shuffling). On the Pascal VOC dataset, it outperforms all previous self-supervised models in image classification and object detection tasks:

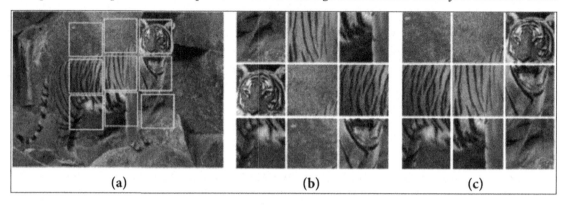

Figure 10.5: The image is split up into patches and shuffled, and the model learns to put the shuffled patches back in the correct order. From the paper Unsupervised Learning of Visual Representations [26]

Rotation

The RotNet model [34] learns an image representation by using rotation as a self-supervision signal. Input images are rotated by 0, 90, 180, and 270 degrees, and a convolutional network (RotNet) is trained to learn to predict the rotation angle as one of 4 target classes. It turns out that this apparently simple task provides a very powerful supervisory signal for semantic feature learning. RotNet features were used as input for image classification against the CIFAR-10 dataset and resulted in classification accuracy of only 1.6% less than the state-of-the-art result obtained using supervised learning. It also obtained state-of-the-art results at the time for some classification tasks against ImageNet, and some classification and object detection tasks against Pascal VOC.

Hybrid self-prediction

With hybrid self-prediction models, self-prediction is achieved using not one but multiple self-prediction strategies. For example, our first two examples, Jukebox and DALL-E, achieve self-prediction by first reducing the input data to a more manageable format using one self-supervision technique (VQ-VAE or Vector Quantized Variational AutoEncoder [35]) and then use another (AR) on the reduced image to produce the final prediction. In our third example, the predictions from the VQ-VAE component are further refined using a discriminator trained in an adversarial manner.

VQ-VAE

Since the VQ-VAE is common to all our hybrid self-prediction models, let us try to understand what it does at a high level. You have already read about autoencoders and variational autoencoders in *Chapter 8, Autoencoders*. Autoencoders try to learn to reconstruct their input by first encoding the input onto a smaller dimension and then decoding the output of the smaller dimension. However, autoencoders typically just end up compressing the input and do not learn a good semantic representation.

Variational Autoencoders (**VAEs**) can do better in this respect by enforcing a probabilistic prior, generally in the form of a standard Gaussian distribution, and by minimizing not only the reconstruction loss but also the KL divergence between the prior distribution and posterior distribution (the actual distribution in the latent space).

While the VAE learns a continuous latent distribution, the VQ-VAE learns a discrete latent distribution. This is useful because transformers are designed to take discrete data as input. VQ-VAE extends VAE by adding a discrete codebook component to the network, which is used to quantize the latent vectors output by the encoder by choosing the vector in the codebook that is closest to each latent vector by Euclidean distance. The VQ-VAE decoder is then tasked with reconstructing the input from the discretized latent vector.

Jukebox

Our first example is the Jukebox paper [32], which is a generative model for music, similar to how GPT-3 is a generative model for text and Image-GPT is a generative model for images. That is, given a musical (voice and music) prompt, Jukebox can create the music that might follow this prompt. Early attempts at generative models for audio attempted symbolic music generation in the form of a piano roll, since the problem with generating raw audio directly is the extremely large amount of information it contains and consequently, the extreme long-range dependencies that need to be modeled. The VQ-VAE addresses this problem by learning a lower-dimensional encoding of the audio with the goal of losing the least important information but retaining most of the useful information.

Jukebox uses hierarchical VQ-VAEs to discretize the input signal into different temporal resolutions, then generates a new sequence at each resolution, and finally combines the generated sequence at each level into the final prediction.

DALL-E

Our second example of hybrid prediction models is the DALL-E model [5] from OpenAI. DALL-E can also be classified as a joint learning (multimodal) model, since it attempts to learn to create images from text captions, using pairs of text and image as training input. However, we classify it here as a hybrid prediction model because, like Jukebox, it attempts to address the high dimensionality of image information (compared with the dimensionality of the associated text) using a VQ-VAE.

DALL-E receives text and images as a single stream of data. DALL-E uses a two-stage training regime. In the first stage, a VQ-VAE is trained to compress each input RGB image of size (256, 256, 3) into a grid of image tokens of size (32, 32), each element of which can assume one of 8,192 possible discrete values. This reduces the size of the image input by a factor of 192 without a corresponding loss in image quality.

In the second stage, the text is BPE-encoded and truncated to 256 tokens. **Byte Pair Encoding (BPE)** is a hybrid character/word encoding that can represent large corpora using a relatively small vocabulary by encoding common byte pairs. This encoding is then concatenated with the flattened sequence of 1,024 (32 x 32) image tokens. This combined sequence is used to train an autoregressive transformer to model the joint distribution over the text and image tokens. The first stage learns the visual codebook in the VQ-VAE and the second stage learns the prior of the discrete latent distribution over the text and image tokens. The trained DALL-E model can then be used to generate images given a text prompt.

Text-to-image generation is getting quite popular. A newer version of DALL-E, called DALL-E 2, was recently released by OpenAI. It has 35 billion parameters compared to DALL-E's 12 billion. Even though they are named similarly, DALL-E is a version of GPT-3 trained to generate images from text descriptions, and DALL-E 2 is an encoder-decoder pipeline that uses CLIP to encode the text description into a CLIP embedding, and then decode the embedding back to an image using a diffusion model that you learned about in *Chapter 9, Generative Models*. As expected, DALL-E 2 generates more realistic and accurate images than DALL-E.

Even more recently, Google Research has released Imagen, another model in this space that competes with DALL-E 2. Like DALL-E 2, Imagen uses a T5-XXL encoder to map input text into embeddings and a diffusion model to decode the embedding into an image.

VQ-GAN

The VQ-GAN [30] uses an encoder-decoder framework where the encoder uses a VQ-VAE style encoder that learns a discrete latent representation, but the decoder is a discriminator component of a **Generative Adversarial Network (GAN)**. Instead of the L2 loss used in the VQ-VAE, the VQ-GAN uses a combination of perceptual loss and discriminator loss, which helps in keeping good perceptual quality at increased compression rates. The use of a GAN architecture rather than a traditional VAE decoder helps with training efficiency.

Like VQ-VAE, the VQ-GAN learns a codebook of context-rich visual components, which are used to compose sequences for training the autoregressive component. The VQ-GAN has been found to outperform the VQ-VAE-2 model on images from ImageNet using the **Fréchet Inception Distance (FID)**, which measures the distance between feature vectors of real versus fake images) metric, even though it uses approximately 10x fewer parameters:

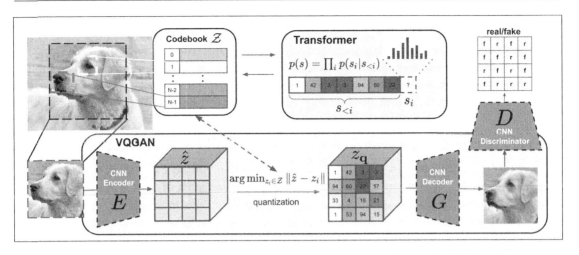

Figure 10.6: Architecture of the VQ-GAN. From the paper: Taming Transformers for High Resolution Image Synthesis [30]

Next, we will look at another popular self-supervised technique called contrastive learning.

Contrastive learning

Contrastive Learning (CL) tries to predict the relationship between a pair of input samples. The goal of CL is to learn an embedding space where pairs of similar samples are pulled close together and dissimilar samples are pushed far apart. Inputs to train CL models are in the form of *pairs of data points*. CL can be used in both supervised and unsupervised settings.

When used in an unsupervised setting, it can be a very powerful self-supervised learning approach. Similar pairs are found from existing data in a self-supervised manner, and dissimilar pairs are found from pairs of similar pairs of data. The model learns to predict if a pair of data points are similar or different.

A taxonomy of CL can be derived by considering the techniques used to generate contrastive examples. Before we do that, we will take a brief detour to explore the various training objectives that are popular in CL.

Training objectives

Early CL models used data points consisting of a single positive and a single negative example to learn from. However, the trend in more recent CL models is to learn from multiple positive and negative samples in a single batch. In this section, we will cover some training objectives (also called loss functions) that are commonly used for training CL models.

Contrastive loss

Contrastive loss [35] is one of the earliest training objectives to be used for learning using CL techniques. It tries to encode data into an embedding space such that examples from the same class have similar embeddings and examples from different classes have dissimilar embeddings. Thus, given two data pairs, (x_i, y_i) and (x_j, y_j), the contrastive loss objective is described using the following formula:

$$\mathcal{L}(x_i, x_j, \theta) = \mathbb{I}[y_i = y_j]\|f_\theta(x_i) - f_\theta(x_j)\|_2^2 + \mathbb{I}[y_i \neq y_j]max\left(0, \epsilon - \|f_\theta(x_i) - f_\theta(x_j)\|_2\right)^2$$

The first term is activated when the pairs i and j are similar, and the second term is activated when the pair is dissimilar. The objective is designed to maximize the square of the differences in the first term and minimize the square of differences in the second term (thus maximizing the second term in the case of dissimilar pairs). The ε is a hyperparameter and represents a margin of the minimum allowable distance between samples of different classes.

Triplet loss

Triplet loss [11] is an enhancement of contrastive loss in that it uses three data points instead of two – the anchor point, the positive point, and the negative point. Thus, given an anchor point x, we select a positive sample x^+ and one negative sample x^-, where x and x^+ belong to the same class and x and x^- belong to different classes. Triplet loss learns to minimize the distance between the anchor x and positive sample x^+ and maximize the distance between x and negative sample x^-. This is illustrated in *Figure 10.7*:

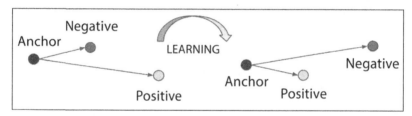

Figure 10.7: Illustration of triplet loss. Based on the paper: FaceNet: A Unified Embedding for Face Recognition and Clustering [11]

The equation for triplet loss is shown below. As with contrastive loss, the ε is a hyperparameter representing the minimum allowed difference between distances between similar and dissimilar pairs. Triplet loss-based models typically need challenging values for x^-, the so-called hard negatives, to provide good representations:

$$\mathcal{L}(x, x^+, x^-) = \sum_{x \in X} max(0, \|f(x) - f(x^+)\|_2^2 - \|f(x) - f(x^-)\|_2^2 + \epsilon)$$

N-pair loss

N-pair loss [21] generalizes triplet loss to incorporate comparison with multiple negative samples instead of just one. Thus, given an *(N+1)* tuple of training samples, $\{x, x^+, x_1^-, x_2^-, ..., x_{N+1}^-\}$, where there is one positive sample and *N-1* negative ones, the N-pair loss is defined using the following equation:

$$\mathcal{L}(x, x^+, \{x_i^-\}_{i=1}^{N-1}) = -\log\left(\frac{exp(f(x)^T f(x^+))}{exp(f(x)^T f(x^+)) + \sum_{i=1}^{N-1} exp(f(x^T)f(x_i^-))}\right)$$

Lifted structural loss

Lifted structured loss [15] is another generalization of triplet loss where it uses all pairwise edges within a training batch. This leads to better training performance. *Figure 10.8* illustrates the idea behind lifted structural loss, and how it evolved from contrastive and triplet loss. Red edges connect similar pairs and blue edges connect dissimilar pairs:

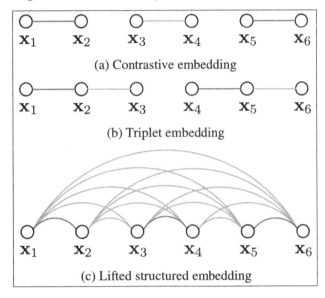

Figure 10.8: Illustration of the idea of Lifted Structured Loss. Based on the paper: Deep Metric Learning via Lifted Structured Feature Embedding [15]

NCE loss

Noise Contrastive Estimation (NCE) loss [27] uses logistic regression to distinguish positive and negative (noise) examples. The NCE loss attempts to maximize the log odds (logits) of positive examples x and minimize the log odds of negative examples $\underline{x}$. The equation for NCE loss is shown below:

$$\mathcal{L} = -\frac{1}{N}\sum_{i=1}^{N}\left[\log(sigmoid(logit(x_i))) + \log\left(1 - sigmoid(logit(\overline{x_i}))\right)\right]$$

InfoNCE loss

InfoNCE loss [2] was inspired by NCE loss (described in the previous section) and uses categorical cross-entropy loss to identify the positive sample from the set of unrelated noise samples. Given some context vector c, the positive sample should be drawn from the conditional probability distribution $p(x|c)$, while the $N-1$ negative examples can be drawn from the distribution $p(x)$ independent of the context c. The InfoNCE loss optimizes the negative log probability of classifying the positive sample correctly.

The InfoNCE loss is given by the following equation, where $f(x, c)$ estimates the density ratio $p(x|c)/p(x)$:

$$\mathcal{L} = -E\left[\log\frac{f(x,c)}{\sum_{x'\in X} f(x',c)}\right]$$

Soft nearest neighbors loss

Soft nearest neighbors loss [33] further extends the idea of contrastive loss to include multiple positive samples given known labels. Given a batch of samples, $\{(x_i, y_i)\}_{i=1}^B$ where y_i is the class label of x_i, and a similarity function f that measures similarity between two inputs, the soft nearest neighbor loss is given by the equation:

$$\mathcal{L} = -\frac{1}{B}\sum_{i=1}^B \log\left(\frac{\sum_{i\neq j, y_i=y_j, j=1,...,B} exp\left(-f\left(x_i, x_j\right)/\tau\right)}{\sum_{i\neq k, k=1,...,B} exp(f(x_i, x_k)/\tau)}\right)$$

The temperature τ is a hyperparameter and is used for tuning how concentrated the features are in the representation space. Thus, at low temperatures, the contribution of faraway points in the representation space to the soft nearest neighbors loss is also low.

Instance transformation

CL models that use instance transformation generally rely on data augmentation techniques to generate positive pairs and negative mining to generate negative pairs from pairs of positive pairs. Many such models rely on generating in-batch negative and innovative techniques for mining hard negatives.

Data augmentation techniques are used to create pairs of the original data point and its noisy version. This introduces non-essential variation into the examples without modifying semantic meaning, which the model then learns during training.

In-batch negative sampling is a technique for generating negative samples by combining information from examples within a single batch. For each positive pair (x_i, y_i) in the batch, all pairs (x_i, y_j) and (x_j, y_i) for all $i \neq j$ can be considered as negative pairs. In effect, negative pairs are created by combining elements from two random positive pairs in the same batch. This technique is practical and can be implemented efficiently on GPUs and is therefore widely used.

Some models require hard negative samples to learn how to perform their tasks well. Hard negatives are pairs that have different labels, but whose embedding features are very close to each other. You can visualize them as points that lie very close to each other in the embedding space but on opposite sides of the decision boundary. Identifying hard negatives for a given task is relatively easy for supervised learning. For unsupervised learning, one approach is to increase the batch size, which will introduce more hard negative samples. Another technique [19] is to increase the sampling probability of the candidate negative sample by its similarity with the anchor sample.

SimCLR

The SimCLR model [36] presents a simple framework for contrastive learning of visual representations. Each input image (x) is augmented in two different ways (x_i and x_j) using the same family of image augmentation strategies, resulting in *2N* positive samples.

In-batch negative sampling is used, so for each positive example, we have *(2N-1)* negative samples. A base encoder *(f)* is applied to the pair of data points in each example, and a projection head *(g)* attempts to maximize the agreement for positive pairs and minimize it for negative pairs. For good performance, SimCLR needs to use large batch sizes so as to incorporate enough negative examples in the training regime. SimCLR achieved state-of-the-art results for self-supervised and semi-supervised models on ImageNet and matches the performance of a supervised ResNet-50. *Figure 10.9* shows the architecture of the SimCLR model:

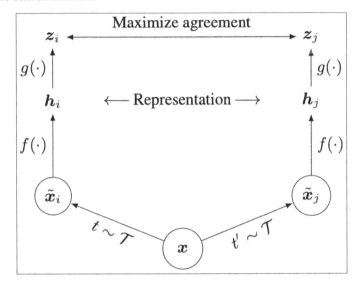

Figure 10.9: Architecture of the SimCLR model. From the paper: A Simple Framework for Contrastive Learning of Visual Representations [36]

Barlow Twins

The idea behind the Barlow Twins [20] model has its roots in neuroscience, i.e., the goal of sensory processing is to re-code highly redundant sensory inputs into a factorial code, or a code with statistically independent components. In this model, an image is distorted into two versions of itself. The distorted versions are fed into the same network to extract features and learn to make the cross-correlation matrix between these two features as close to the identity matrix as possible. In line with the neuroscience idea, the goal of this model is to reduce the redundancy between the two distorted versions of the sample by reducing the redundancy between these vectors. This is reflected in its somewhat unique loss function – in the first equation, the first term represents the difference between the identity matrix and the cross-correlation matrix, and the second term represents the redundancy reduction term. The second equation defines each element of the cross-correlation matrix C:

$$\mathcal{L} = \sum_i (1 - C_{ii})^2 + \lambda \sum_i \sum_{j \neq i} C_{ij}^2$$

$$C_{ij} = \frac{\sum_b z_{b,i}^A z_{b,j}^B}{\sqrt{\sum_b \left(z_{b,i}^A\right)^2} \sqrt{\sum_b \left(z_{b,j}^B\right)^2}}$$

Some notable differences between the Barlow Twins model and other models in this genre are that the Barlow Twins model doesn't require a large number of negative samples and can thus operate on smaller batches, and that it benefits from high-dimensional embeddings. The Barlow Twins model outperforms some previous semi-supervised models trained on ImageNet and is on par with some supervised ImageNet models.

BYOL

The **Bootstrap Your Own Latent (BYOL)** model [17] is unique in that it does not use negative samples at all. It relies on two neural networks, the online and target networks, that interact and learn from each other. The goal of BYOL is to learn a representation y_θ that can be used for downstream tasks. The online network is parameterized by a set of weights θ and comprises three stages – an encoder f_θ, a projector g_θ, and a predictor q_θ The target network has the same architecture as the online network but uses a different set of weights ξ. The target network provides the regression targets to train the online network, and its parameters ξ are an exponential moving average of the online parameters θ After every training step, the following update is performed:

$$\xi \leftarrow \tau\xi + (1 - \tau)\theta$$

BYOL produces two augmented views of each image. From the first augmented view, the online network outputs a representation y_θ and a projection z_θ. Similarly, the target network outputs a representation y_ξ and a projection z_ξ BYOL attempts to minimize the error between the L2 normalized online and target projections z_θ and z_ξ. At the end of the training, we only retain the online network (the encoder).

BYOL achieves competitive results against semi-supervised or transfer learning models on ImageNet. It is also less sensitive to changes in batch size and the type of image augmentations used compared to other models in this genre. However, later work [4] indicates that the batch normalization component in BYOL may implicitly cause a form of contrastive learning by implicitly creating negative samples as a result of data redistribution it causes.

Feature clustering

Feature clustering involves finding similar data samples by clustering them. This can be useful when data augmentation techniques are not feasible. The idea here is to use clustering algorithms to assign pseudo-labels to samples such that we can run intra-sample CL. Although similar, feature clustering differs from CL in that it relaxes the instance discrimination problem – rather than learn to distinguish between a pair of transformations on a single input image, feature clustering learns to discriminate between groups of images with similar features.

DeepCluster

The DeepCluster [24] paper is predicated on the fact that datasets for supervised learning such as ImageNet are "too small" to account for general-purpose features that go beyond image classification. For learning general-purpose features, it is necessary to train on billions of images at internet scales. However, labeling such large datasets is not feasible, so DeepCluster presents a clustering method that jointly learns the parameters of the neural network and the cluster assignments of the resulting features. DeepCluster iteratively groups these features using the K-Means clustering algorithm and uses the cluster assignments as pseudo labels to learn the parameters of the ConvNet. The end product of the training is the weights of the ConvNet. These weights have been shown to be useful general-purpose visual features and have outperformed the best published numbers on many downstream tasks regardless of the dataset.

SwAV

In the SwAV (SWapping Assignments between multiple Views) [25] model, features are learned by predicting the cluster assignment (pseudo-label) for a view from the representation of another view. SwAV uses a variant of the architecture used in CL models. The images x_1 and x_2 are transformations of the same input image x, which are sent through an encoder f_θ to produce a representation z_1 and z_2. In the case of SwAV, z_1 and z_2 are used to compute q_1 and q_2 by matching their features to a set of K prototype vectors $\{c_1, ..., c_K\}$, which are then used to predict the cluster assignment for x_2 and x_1 respectively.

Unlike DeepCluster, SwAV does online clustering (clustering of data that arrives continuously in a streaming manner and is not known before the clustering process begins) and can therefore scale to potentially unlimited amounts of data. SwAV also works well with both large and small batch sizes. The SwAV paper also proposes a new multi-crop strategy to increase the number of views of an image with no computational or memory overhead. It achieves 75% top-1 accuracy on ImageNet with ResNet50 (a supervised learning method) as well as surpassing results of supervised pretraining in all the considered transfer tasks.

InterCLR

InterCLR [18] is a hybrid model that jointly learns a visual representation by leveraging intra-image as well as inter-image invariance. It has two invariance learning branches in its pipeline, one for intra-image, and the other for inter-image. The intra-image branch constructs contrastive pairs by standard CL methods such as generating a pair of transformations from an input image. The inter-image branch constructs contrastive pairs using pseudo-labels obtained from clustering – two items within the same cluster constitute a positive pair, and two items from different clusters form a negative pair.

A variant of the InfoNCE loss function is used to compute the contrastive loss and the network is trained through back-propagation:

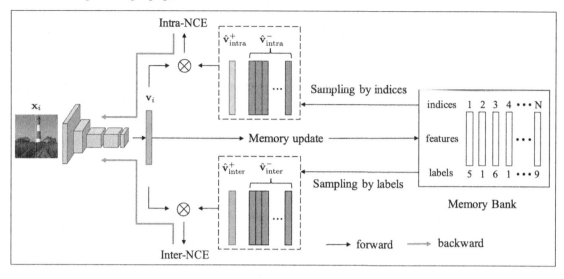

Figure 10.10: Architecture of the InterCLR model. From the paper: Delving into Inter-Image Invariance for Unsupervised Visual Representation [18]

The InterCLR paper also addresses some special considerations around pseudo label maintenance, sampling strategy, and decision boundary design for the inter-image branch, which we will skip here in the interests of space. The InterCLR model shows many improvements over state-of-the-art intra-image invariance learning methods on multiple standard benchmarks.

Multiview coding

Multiview coding has become a mainstream CL method in recent years and involves constructing positive contrastive examples using two or more views of the same object. The objective is to maximize the mutual information between the representations of the multiple views of the data for positive examples and minimize it for negative examples. This requires the model to learn higher-level features whose influence spans multiple views.

AMDIM

Augmented Multiscale Deep InfoMax (AMDIM) [31] is a model for self-supervised representational learning based on an earlier local Deep InfoMax method, which attempts to maximize the mutual information between a global summary feature that depends on the entire input, and a collection of local features that are extracted from intermediate layers in the encoder. AMDIM extends DIM by predicting features across independently augmented features of each input and simultaneously across multiple scales, as well as using a more powerful encoder.

The paper also considers other ways of producing contrastive pairs, such as instance transformation and multimodal (discussed in the next section), but it is described here because it also considers constructing contrastive pairs using multiview coding. The model beats several benchmarks for self-supervised learning objectives.

CMC

The **Contrastive Multiview Coding (CMC)** [37] model is based on the idea that when an object is represented by multiple views, each of these views is noisy and incomplete, but important factors such as the physics, geometry, and semantics of the object are usually shared across all the views. The goal of CMC is to learn a compact representation of the object that captures these important factors. CMC achieves this by using CL to learn a representation such that views of the same scene map to nearby points, whereas views of different scenes map to distant points.

Multimodal models

The class of models covered in this section includes models that use paired inputs from two or more modalities of the same data. The input to such a model could be an image and a caption, a video and text, an audio clip and its transcript, etc. These models learn a joint embedding across multiple modalities. In this class of models, we will cover the CLIP [6] and CodeSearchNet [13] models as examples.

Another class of multimodal models is frameworks that can be used to do self-supervised learning across multiple modalities. The Data2Vec [7] model is an example of such a model.

CLIP

The CLIP model [6] learns image representations by learning to predict which image goes with which caption. It is pretrained with 400 million image-text pairs from the internet. After pretraining, the model can use natural language queries to refer to learned visual concepts. CLIP can be used in zero-shot mode for downstream tasks such as image classification, text-to-image, and image-to-image image search. The model is competitive for natural images with a fully supervised baseline without the need for any additional fine-tuning. For example, CLIP can match the accuracy of the original ResNet50 on ImageNet in zero-shot mode, i.e., without additional fine-tuning. CLIP can also be fine-tuned with specialized image datasets for specific downstream tasks, such as learning visual representations for satellite imagery or tumor detection.

Figure 10.11 shows the architecture of the CLIP model for training and inference. Both image and text encoders are transformer-based encoders. The objective of pretraining is to solve the task of predicting which text as a whole is paired with which image. Thus, given a batch of N image-text pairs, CLIP learns to predict which of the $N \times N$ possible image-text pairs across the batch actually occurred. CLIP learns a multi-modal joint embedding space by maximizing the cosine similarity of the image and text embeddings of the N real pairs in the batch while minimizing the cosine similarity of the rest of the $N^2 - N$ incorrect pairs.

During inference, the input of one modality can be used to predict the output of the other, i.e., given an image, it can predict the image class as text:

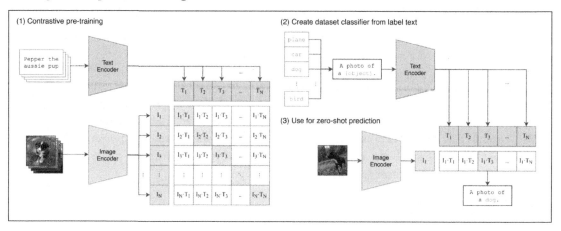

Figure 10.11: Architecture of the CLIP model. From the paper: Learning Transferable Visual Models from Natural Language Supervision [34x]

The code snippet below demonstrates the CLIP model's ability to compare images and text. Here, we take an image of two cats side by side and compare it to two text strings: "a photo of a cat" and "a photo of a dog". CLIP can compare the image with the two text strings and correctly determine that the probability that the image is similar to the string "a photo of a cat" is 0.995 as opposed to a probability of 0.005 for the image being similar to the string "a photo of a dog":

```python
import tensorflow as tf
from PIL import Image
import requests
from transformers import CLIPProcessor, TFCLIPModel

model = TFCLIPModel.from_pretrained("openai/clip-vit-base-patch32")
processor = CLIPProcessor.from_pretrained("openai/clip-vit-base-patch32")

url = "http://images.cocodataset.org/val2017/000000039769.jpg"
image = Image.open(requests.get(url, stream=True).raw)
texts = ["a photo of a cat", "a photo of a dog"]
inputs = processor(text=texts, images=image, return_tensors="tf", padding=True)

outputs = model(**inputs)
logits_per_image = outputs.logits_per_image
probs = tf.nn.softmax(logits_per_image, axis=1)
print(probs.numpy())
```

The CLIP model does this by projecting both text and image to a single embedding space. Using this common embedding approach, CLIP is also able to compute the similarity between two images and a text. It also offers the ability to extract encodings of text and images.

CodeSearchNet

The CodeSearchNet model [13] uses code snippets representing functions or methods in multiple programming languages (Go, Java, JavaScript, Python, PHP, and Ruby), and pairs them with (manually augmented) natural language comments describing the code to create positive examples. The corpus consists of approximately 2 million code-documentation pairs across all the different languages. As with CLIP, the goal of the CodeSearchNet model is to learn a joint embedding space of code and documentation, which can then be queried to return the appropriate code snippet (functions or methods) that satisfy some natural language query. The code and the natural language query are encoded using two separate encoders, and the model tries to learn a joint embedding that maximizes the inner product of the code and query encodings for positive pairs and minimizes it for negative pairs.

Data2Vec

Data2Vec [7] is a little different in that it proposes a common framework to do self-supervised learning across multiple modalities. It uses masked prediction to apply the same learning method for either speech, language, or computer vision. The core idea is to predict latent representations of the full input based on a masked view of the input. Instead of predicting modality-specific targets such as words, visual tokens, etc., it predicts contextualized latent representations that contain information for the entire input. It uses a teacher-student architecture – first, a representation of the full input data is built, which serves as the target for the learning task (teacher mode). Then a masked version of the input sample is encoded, with which the full data representation is predicted (student mode). The teacher's parameters are updated using exponentially decaying average weights of the student. At the end of the training, the teacher's weights are used as the learned embedding.

Experiments using this framework against major benchmarks in speech recognition, image classification, and natural language understanding show either state-of-the-art performance or competitive performance to popular approaches:

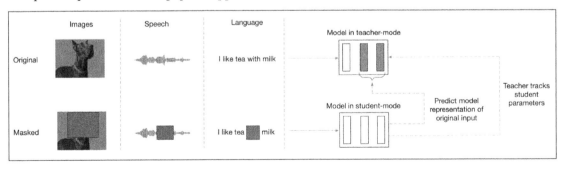

Figure 10.12: Architecture of the Data2Vec model. From the paper: data2vec: A General Framework for Self-supervised Learning in Speech, Vision and Language [7]

Pretext tasks

Pretext tasks are tasks that self-supervised learning models attempt to solve by leveraging some pattern inherent in the unlabeled data they train on. Such tasks are not necessarily useful in and of themselves, but they help the system learn a useful latent representation, or embeddings, that can then be used, either as-is or after fine-tuning, on some other downstream tasks. Training to solve pretext tasks usually happens as a precursor to building the actual model, and for that reason, it is also referred to as pretraining.

Almost all the techniques we have discussed in this chapter have been pretext tasks. While some tasks may end up being useful in and of themselves, such as colorization or super-resolution, they also result in embeddings that end up learning the semantics of the data distribution of the unlabeled data that it was trained on, in the form of learned weights. These weights can then be applied to downstream tasks.

This is not a new concept – for example, the Word2Vec algorithm, which is widely used for finding "synonyms," is based on an embedding space where words used in similar contexts cluster together. It is trained using either the skip-gram or CBOW algorithm, which attempt to predict a context word given a word, or vice versa. Neither of these objectives are useful in and of themselves, but in the process, the network ends up learning a good latent representation of the words in the input data. This representation can then be directly used to find "synonyms" for words or do word analogies, as well as being used to produce useful vector representations of words and sequences of words (such as sentences and documents) for downstream tasks, such as text classification or sentiment analysis.

The biggest advantage of pretext tasks is that the training of models for downstream tasks can be done with relatively smaller amounts of labeled data. The model learns a lot about the domain (the broad strokes) based on solving the pretext task using large quantities of readily available unlabeled data. It requires relatively smaller amounts of labeled data to learn to solve more specific downstream tasks based on what it already knows about the domain. Because labeled data is hard to come by and expensive to create, this two-step approach can often make some machine learning models possible, if not more practical.

Summary

In this chapter, we saw various self-supervised strategies for leveraging data to learn the data distribution in the form of specialized embedding spaces, which in turn can be used for solving downstream tasks. We have looked at self-prediction, contrastive learning, and pretext tasks as specific approaches for self-supervision.

In the next chapter, we will look at reinforcement learning, an approach that uses rewards as a feedback mechanism to train models for specific tasks.

References

1.   Aaron van den Oord, Nal Kalchbrenner, and Koray Kavucuoglu (2016). Pixel Recurrent Neural Networks Proceedings MLR Press: http://proceedings.mlr.press/v48/oord16.pdf

2. Aaron van den Oord, Yazhe Li, and Oriol Vinyals. *Representation Learning with Contrastive Predictive Coding*. Arxiv Preprint, arXiv 1807.03748 [cs.LG]: https://arxiv.org/pdf/1807.03748.pdf

3. Aaron van den Oord, et al. (2016). *WaveNet: A Generative Model for Raw Audio*. Arxiv Preprint, arXiv:1609.03499v2 [cs.SD]: https://arxiv.org/pdf/1609.03499.pdf

4. Abe Fetterman and Josh Albrecht. (2020). *Understanding Self-Supervised and Contrastive Learning with "Bootstrap your Own Latent" (BYOL)*. Blog post: https://generallyintelligent.ai/blog/2020-08-24-understanding-self-supervised-contrastive-learning/

5. Aditya Ramesh, et al. *Zero Shot Text to Image generation*. Arxiv Preprint, arXiv 2102.12092v2 [cs.CV]: https://arxiv.org/pdf/2102.12092.pdf

6. Alec Radford, et al. (2021). *Learning Transferable Visual Models from Natural Language Supervision*. Proceedings of Machine Learning Research (PMLR): http://proceedings.mlr.press/v139/radford21a/radford21a.pdf

7. Alexei Baevsky, et al. (2022). *data2vec: A General Framework for Self-Supervised Learning in Speech, Vision and Language*. Arxiv Preprint, arXiv 2202.03555v1 [cs.LG]: https://arxiv.org/pdf/2202.03555.pdf

8. Carl Doersch, Abhinav Gupta and Alexei Efros. (2015). *Unsupervised Visual Representation by Context Prediction*. International Conference on Computer Vision (ICCV): https://www.cv-foundation.org/openaccess/content_iccv_2015/papers/Doersch_Unsupervised_Visual_Representation_ICCV_2015_paper.pdf

9. Chuan Li. (2020). *OpenAI's GPT-3 Language Model – a Technical Overview*. LambdaLabs Blog post: https://lambdalabs.com/blog/demystifying-gpt-3/

10. Deepak Pathak, et al. (2016). *Context Encoders: Feature Learning by Inpainting*: https://openaccess.thecvf.com/content_cvpr_2016/papers/Pathak_Context_Encoders_Feature_CVPR_2016_paper.pdf

11. Florian Schroff, Dmitry Kalenichenko and James Philbin. (2025). *FaceNet: A Unified Embedding for Face Recognition and Clustering*. ArXiv Preprint, arXiv 1503.03832 [cs.CV]: https://arxiv.org/pdf/1503.03832.pdf

12. Gustav Larsson, Michael Maire and Gregory Shakhnarovich. (2017). *Colorization as a Proxy Task for Visual Understanding*: https://openaccess.thecvf.com/content_cvpr_2017/papers/Larsson_Colorization_as_a_CVPR_2017_paper.pdf

13. Hamel Husain, et al. (2020). *CodeSearchNet Challenge: Evaluating the State of Semantic Code Search*. Arxiv Preprint, arXiv: 1909.09436 [cs.LG]: https://arxiv.org/pdf/1909.09436.pdf

14. Hanting Chen, et al. (2021). *Pre-trained Image Processing Transformer*. Conference on Computer Vision and Pattern Recognition (CVPR): https://openaccess.thecvf.com/content/CVPR2021/papers/Chen_Pre-Trained_Image_Processing_Transformer_CVPR_2021_paper.pdf

15. Hyun Oh Song, Yu Xiang, Stefanie Jegelka and Silvio Savarese. (2015). *Deep Metric Learning via Lifted Structured Feature Embedding*. Arxiv Preprint, arXiv 1511.06452 [cs.CV]: https://arxiv.org/pdf/1511.06452.pdf

16. Jacob Devlin, et al. (2019). *BERT: Pre-training of Deep Bidirectional Transformers for Language Understanding.* Arxiv Preprint, arXiv: 1810.04805v2 [cs.CL]: https://arxiv.org/pdf/1810.04805.pdf

17. Jean-Bastien Grill, et al. (2020). *Bootstrap your own latent: A new approach to self-supervised learning.* Arxiv Preprint, arXiv 2006.07733 [cs.LG]: https://arxiv.org/pdf/2006.07733.pdf

18. Jiahao Xie, et al. (2021). *Delving into Inter-Image Invariance for Unsupervised Visual Representations.* Arxiv Preprint, arXiv: 2008.11702 [cs.CV]: https://arxiv.org/pdf/2008.11702.pdf

19. Joshua Robinson, Ching-Yao Chuang, Suvrit Sra and Stefanie Jegelka. (2021). *Contrastive Learning with Hard Negative Samples.* Arxiv Preprint, arXiv 2010.04592 [cs.LG]: https://arxiv.org/pdf/2010.04592.pdf

20. Jure Zobontar, et al. (2021). Barlow Twins: Self-Supervised Learning via Redundancy Reduction. Arxiv Preprint, arXiv 2103.03230 [cs.CV]: https://arxiv.org/pdf/2103.03230.pdf

21. Kihyuk Sohn. (2016). *Improved Deep Metric Learning with Multi-class N-pair Loss Objective.* Advances in Neural Information Processing Systems: https://proceedings.neurips.cc/paper/2016/file/6b180037abbebea991d8b1232f8a8ca9-Paper.pdf

22. Lilian Weng and Jong Wook Kim. (2021). *Self-supervised Learning: Self Prediction and Contrastive Learning.* NeurIPS Tutorial: https://neurips.cc/media/neurips-2021/Slides/21895.pdf

23. Lilian Weng. (Blog post 2021). Contrastive Representation Learning: https://lilianweng.github.io/posts/2021-05-31-contrastive/

24. Mathilde Caron, Piotr Bojanowsky, Armand Joulin and Matthijs Douze. (2019). *Deep Clustering for Unsupervised Learning of Visual Features.* Arxiv Preprint, arXiv: 1807.05520 [cs.CV]: https://arxiv.org/pdf/1807.05520.pdf

25. Mathilde Caron, et al. (2020). *Unsupervised Learning of Visual Features by Contrasting Cluster Assignments.* Arxiv Preprint, arXiv: 2006.099882 [cs.CV]: https://arxiv.org/pdf/2006.09882.pdf

26. Mehdi Noroozi and Paolo Favaro. (2016). *Unsupervised Learning of Visual Representations by solving Jigsaw Puzzles.* European Conference on Computer Vision: https://link.springer.com/chapter/10.1007/978-3-319-46466-4_5

27. Michael Gutmann, Aapo Hyvarinen. (2010). *Noise-contrastive estimation: A new estimation principle for unnormalized statistical models.* Proceedings of Machine Learning Research (PMLR): http://proceedings.mlr.press/v9/gutmann10a/gutmann10a.pdf

28. Nal Kalchbrenner, et al. (2018). *Efficient Neural Audio Synthesis.* Proceedings MLR Press: http://proceedings.mlr.press/v80/kalchbrenner18a/kalchbrenner18a.pdf

29. Pascal Vincent, et al. (2010). *Stacked Denoising Autoencoders: Learning Useful Representations in a Deep Network with a Local Denoising Criterion.* Journal of Machine Learning Research (JMLR): https://www.jmlr.org/papers/volume11/vincent10a/vincent10a.pdf?ref=https://githubhelp.com

30. Patrick Esser, Robin Rombach and Bjorn Ommer. (2021). Taming Transformers for High-Resolution Image Synthesis. Computer Vision and Pattern Recognition (CVPR): https://openaccess.thecvf.com/content/CVPR2021/papers/Esser_Taming_Transformers_for_High-Resolution_Image_Synthesis_CVPR_2021_paper.pdf

31. Philip Bachman, R Devon Hjelm and William Buchwalter. (2019). *Learning Representations by Maximizing Mutual Information across Views*. Advances in Neural Information Processing Systems (NeurIPS): `https://proceedings.neurips.cc/paper/2019/file/ddf354219aac374f1d40b7e760ee5bb7-Paper.pdf`

32. Prafulla Dhariwal, et al. (2020). Jukebox: *A Generative Model for Music*. Arxiv Preprint, arXiv 2005.00341v1 [eess.AS]: `https://arxiv.org/pdf/2005.00341.pdf`

33. Ruslan Salakhutdinov and Geoff Hinton. (2007). *Learning a Nonlinear Embedding by Preserving Class Neighborhood Structure*. Proceedings of Machine Learning Research (PMLR): `http://proceedings.mlr.press/v2/salakhutdinov07a/salakhutdinov07a.pdf`

34. Spyros Gidaris, Praveer Singh and Nicos Komodakis. (2018). *Unsupervised Representation Learning by Predicting Image Rotations*. Arxiv Preprint, arXiv 1803.07728v1 [cs.CV]: `https://arxiv.org/pdf/1803.07728.pdf`

35. Sumit Chopra, et al. (2005). *Learning a Similarity Metric Discriminatively, with application to Face Verification*. IEEE Computer Society: `http://www.cs.utoronto.ca/~hinton/csc2535_06/readings/chopra-05.pdf`

36. Ting Chen, Simon Kornblith, Mohammed Norouzi and Geoffrey Hinton. (2020). *A Simple Framework for Contrastive Learning*. Arxiv Preprint, arXiv 2002.05709 [cs.LG]: `https://arxiv.org/pdf/2002.05709.pdf`

37. Yonglong Tian, Dilip Krishnan and Philip Isola. (2020). *Contrastive Multiview Coding*. Arxiv Preprint, arXiv: 1906.05849 [cs.CV]: `https://arxiv.org/pdf/1906.05849.pdf?ref=https://githubhelp.com`

38. Zhilin Yang, et al. (2019). *XLNet: Generalized Autoregressive Pre-training for Language Understanding*: `https://proceedings.neurips.cc/paper/2019/file/dc6a7e655d7e5840e66733e9ee67cc69-Paper.pdf`

39. *Prompt Engineering*. (7th July 2022). Wikipedia, Wikimedia Foundation: `https://en.wikipedia.org/wiki/Prompt_engineering`

Join our book's Discord space

Join our Discord community to meet like-minded people and learn alongside more than 2000 members at: `https://packt.link/keras`

11

Reinforcement Learning

This chapter introduces **Reinforcement Learning** (**RL**)—the least explored and yet most promising learning paradigm. Reinforcement learning is very different from the supervised and unsupervised learning models we covered in earlier chapters. Starting from a clean slate (that is, having no prior information), the RL agent can go through multiple stages of trial and error, and learn to achieve a goal, all the while the only input being the feedback from the environment. The research in RL by OpenAI seems to suggest that continuous competition can be a cause for the evolution of intelligence. Many deep learning practitioners believe that RL will play an important role in the big AI dream: **Artificial General Intelligence** (**AGI**). This chapter will delve into different RL algorithms. The following topics will be covered:

- What RL is and its lingo
- Learn how to use the OpenAI Gym interface
- Applications of RL
- Deep Q-Networks
- Policy gradients

 All the code files for this chapter can be found at `https://packt.link/dltfchp11`.

An introduction to RL

What is common between a baby learning to walk, birds learning to fly, and an RL agent learning to play an Atari game? Well, all three involve:

- **Trial and error:** The child (or the bird) tries various ways, fails many times, and succeeds in some ways before it can really walk (or fly). The RL agent plays many games, winning some and losing many, before it can become reliably successful.
- **Goal:** The child has the goal to walk, the bird to fly, and the RL agent to win the game.
- **Interaction with the environment:** The only feedback they have is from their environment.

So, the first questions that arise are what is RL, and how is it different from supervised and unsupervised learning? Anyone who owns a pet knows that the best strategy to train a pet is rewarding it for desirable behavior and disciplining it for bad behavior. RL, also called **learning with a critic**, is a learning paradigm where the agent learns in the same manner. The agent here corresponds to our network (program); it can perform a set of **actions (a)**, which brings about a change in the **state (s)** of the environment, and, in turn, the agent receives a reward or punishment from the environment.

For example, consider the case of training a dog to fetch a ball: here, the dog is our agent, the voluntary muscle movements that the dog makes are the actions, and the ground (as well as the person and ball) is the environment; the dog perceives our reaction to its action in terms of giving it a treat as a reward. RL can be defined as a computational approach to goal-directed learning and decision making, from interaction with the environment, under some idealized conditions. The agent can sense the state of the environment, and the agent can perform specific well-defined actions on the environment. This causes two things: first, a change in the state of the environment, and second, a reward is generated (under ideal conditions). This cycle continues, and in theory the agent learns how to more frequently generate a reward over time:

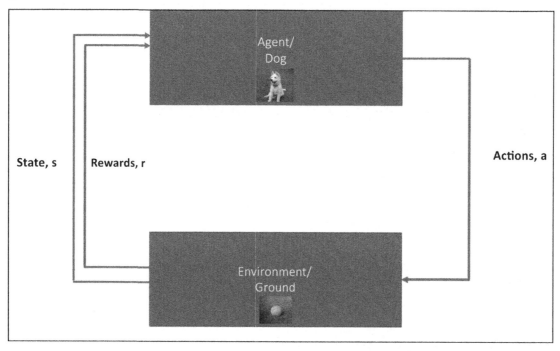

Figure 11.1: Reinforcement learning: interaction between agent and environment

Unlike supervised learning, the agent is not presented with any training examples; it does not know what the correct action is.

And unlike unsupervised learning, the agent's goal is not to find some inherent structure in the input (the learning may find some structure, but that isn't the goal); instead, its only goal is to maximize the rewards (in the long run) and reduce the punishments.

RL lingo

Before learning various RL algorithms, it is important we understand a few important terms. We will illustrate the terms with the help of two examples, first a robot in a maze, and second an agent controlling the wheels of a **Self-Driving Car** (**SDC**). The two RL agents are shown as follows:

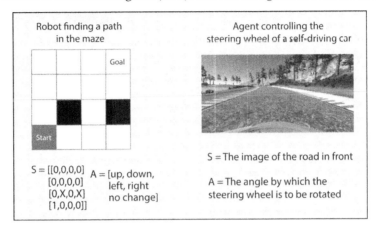

Figure 11.2: State for a robot trying to find a path in a maze (LHS). State for an agent trying to control the steering wheel of a self-driving car (RHS)

Figure 11.2 shows the two examples we will be considering. Let us start with the terms:

- **State, *S***: State is the set of tokens (or representations) that can define all of the possible states the environment can be in. It can be continuous or discrete. In the case of the robot finding its path through a maze, the state can be represented by a 4×4 matrix, with elements indicating whether that block is empty, occupied, or blocked. A block with a value of 1 means it is occupied by the robot, 0 means it is empty, and *X* represents that the block is impassable. Each element in this array, *S*, can have one of these three discrete values, so the state is discrete in nature. Next, consider the agent controlling the steering wheel of a self-driving car. The agent takes as input the front-view image. The image contains continuous valued pixels, so here the state is continuous.

- **Action, *A(S)***: Actions are the set of all possible things that the agent can do in a particular state. The set of possible actions, *A*, depends on the present state, *S*. Actions may or may not result in a change of state. Like states, they can be discrete or continuous. The robot finding a path in the maze can perform five discrete actions [**up**, **down**, **left**, **right**, **no change**]. The SDC agent, on the other hand, can rotate the steering wheel at a continuous range of angles.

- **Reward *R(S,A,S')***: Rewards are a scalar value returned by the environment based on the agent's action(s). Here *S* is the present state and *S'* is the state of the environment after action *A* is taken. It is determined by the goal; the agent gets a higher reward if the action brings it near the goal, and a low (or even negative) reward otherwise. How we define a reward is totally up to us—in the case of the maze, we can define the reward as the Euclidean distance between the agent's current position and goal. The SDC agent reward can be that the car is on the road (positive reward) or off the road (negative reward).

- **Policy** $\pi(S)$: Policy defines a mapping between each state and the action to take in that state. The policy can be *deterministic*, that is, for each state, there is a well-defined policy. In the case of the maze robot, a policy can be that if the top block is empty, move up. The policy can also be *stochastic*, that is, where an action is taken by some probability. It can be implemented as a simple look-up table, or it can be a function dependent on the present state. The policy is the core of the RL agent. In this chapter, we'll learn about different algorithms that help the agent to learn the policy.

- **Return** G_t: This is the discounted sum of all future rewards starting from the current time, mathematically defined as:

$$G_t = \sum_{k=0}^{\infty} \gamma^k R_{t+k+1}$$

- Here R_t is the reward at time t and γ is the discount factor; its value lies between 0 and 1. The discount factor determines how important future rewards are in deciding the policy. If it is near zero, the agent gives importance to the immediate rewards. A high discount factor, however, means the agent is looking far into the future. It may give up immediate reward in favor of high future rewards, just as in the game chess, you may sacrifice a pawn to later checkmate the opponent.

- **Value function** $V(S)$: This defines the "goodness" of a state in the long run. It can be thought of as the total amount of reward the agent can expect to accumulate over time, starting from the state, S. You can think of it as long-term good, as opposed to an immediate but short-lived good. What do you think is more important, maximizing the immediate reward or the value function? You probably guessed right: just as in chess, we sometimes lose a pawn to win the game a few steps later, and so the agent should try to maximize the value function.

- Normally, the value is defined either as the **state-value function** $V^\pi(S)$ or the **action-value function** $Q^\pi(S, A)$, where π is the policy followed. The state-value function is the expected return from the state S after following policy π:

$$V^\pi(S) = E_\pi[G_t | S_t = s]$$

- Here E is the expectation, and $S_t=s$ is the state at time t. The action-value function is the expected return from the state S, taking an action $A=a$ and following the policy π:

$$Q^\pi(S, A) = E_\pi[G_t | S_t = s, A_t = a]$$

- **Model of the environment:** This is an optional element. It mimics the behavior of the environment, and it contains the physics of the environment; in other words, it indicates how the environment will behave. The model of the environment is defined by the transition probability to the next state. This is an optional component; we can have **model-free** reinforcement learning as well where the transition probability is not needed to define the RL process.

In RL, we assume that the state of the environment follows the **Markov property**, that is, each state is dependent solely on the preceding state, the action taken from the action space, and the corresponding reward.

That is, if S^{t+1} is the state of the environment at time $t+1$, then it is a function of S^t state at time t, A^t is the action taken at time t, and R^t is the corresponding reward received at time t, no prior history is needed. If $P(S^{t+1}|S^t)$ is the transition probability, mathematically the Markov property can be written as:

$$P(S^{t+1}|S^t) = P(S^{t+1}|S^1, S^2, ..., S^t)$$

And thus, RL can be assumed to be a **Markov Decision Process (MDP)**.

Deep reinforcement learning algorithms

The basic idea of **Deep Reinforcement Learning (DRL)** is that we can use a deep neural network to approximate either the policy function or the value function. In this chapter, we will be studying some popular DRL algorithms. These algorithms can be classified into two classes, depending upon what they approximate:

- **Value-based methods:** In these methods, the algorithms take the action that maximizes the value function. The agent here learns to predict how good a given state or action would be. An example of the value-based method is the Deep Q-Network. Consider, for example, our robot in a maze: assuming that the value of each state is the negative of the number of steps needed to go from that box to the goal, then, at each time step, the agent will choose the action that takes it to a state with optimal value, as in the following diagram. So, starting from a value of -6, it'll move to -5, -4, -3, -2, -1, and eventually reach the goal with the value 0:

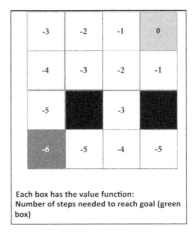

Figure 11.3: Demo value function values for the maze-finding robot

- **Policy-based methods:** In these methods, the algorithms predict the optimal policy (the one that maximizes the expected return), without maintaining the value function estimates. The aim is to find the optimal policy, instead of the optimal action. An example of the policy-based method is policy gradients. Here, we approximate the policy function, which allows us to map each state to the best corresponding action. One advantage of policy-based methods over value-based is that we can use them even for continuous action spaces.

Besides the algorithms approximating either policy or value, there are a few questions we need to answer to make reinforcement learning work.

How does the agent choose its actions, especially when untrained?

When the agent starts learning, it has no idea what the best way in which to determine an action is, or which action will provide the best Q value. So how do we go about it? We take a leaf out of nature's book. Like bees and ants, the agent makes a balance between exploring new actions and exploiting learned ones. Initially, when the agent starts, it has no idea which action among the possible actions is better, so it makes random choices, but as it learns, it starts making use of the learned policy. This is called the **exploration vs exploitation** [2] tradeoff. Using exploration, the agent gathers more information, and later exploits the gathered information to make the best decision.

How does the agent maintain a balance between exploration and exploitation?

There are various strategies; one of the most employed is the **epsilon-greedy** ($\epsilon - greedy$) policy. Here, the agent explores unceasingly, and depending upon the value of $\epsilon \in [0,1]$, at each step the agent selects a random action with probability ϵ, and with probability $1 - \epsilon$ selects an action that maximizes the value function. Normally, the value of ϵ decreases asymptotically. In Python the $\epsilon - greedy$ policy can be implemented as:

```
if np.random.rand() <= epsilon:
        a = random.randrange(action_size)
else:
        a = np.argmax(model.predict(s))
```

where `model` is the deep neural network approximating the value/policy function, `a` is the action chosen from the action space of size `action_size`, and `s` is the state. Another way to perform exploration is to use noise; researchers have experimented with both Gaussian and Ornstein-Uhlenbeck noise with success.

How to deal with the highly correlated input state space

The input to our RL model is the present state of the environment. Each action results in some change in the environment; however, the correlation between two consecutive states is very high. Now if we make our network learn based on the sequential states, the high correlation between consecutive inputs results in what is known as **catastrophic forgetting**. To mitigate the effect of catastrophic forgetting, in 2018, David Isele and Akansel Cosgun proposed the **experience replay** method.

In simplest terms, the learning algorithm first stores the MDP tuple—state, action, reward, and next state <S, A, R, S'>—in a buffer/memory. Once a significant amount of memory is built, a batch is selected randomly to train the agent. The memory is continuously refreshed with new additions and old deletions. The use of experience replay provides three benefits:

- First, it allows the same experience to be potentially used in many weight updates, hence increasing data efficiency.
- Second, the random selection of batches of experience removes the correlations between consecutive states presented to the network for training.

- Third, it stops any unwanted feedback loops that may arise and cause the network to get stuck in local minima or diverge.

A modified version of experience replay is the **Prioritized Experience Replay** (**PER**). Introduced in 2015 by Tom Schaul et al. [4], it derives from the idea that not all experiences (or, you might say, attempts) are equally important. Some attempts are better lessons than others. Thus, instead of selecting the experiences randomly, it will be much more efficient to assign higher priority to more educational experiences in selection for training. In the Schaul paper, it was proposed that experiences in which the difference between the prediction and target is high should be given priority, as the agent could learn a lot in these cases.

How to deal with the problem of moving targets

Unlike supervised learning, the target is not previously known in RL. With a moving target, the agent tries to maximize the expected return, but the maximum value goes on changing as the agent learns. In essence, this is like trying to catch a butterfly yet each time you approach it, it moves to a new location. The major reason to have a moving target is that the same networks are used to estimate the action and the target values, and this can cause oscillations in learning.

A solution to this was proposed by the DeepMind team in their 2015 paper, titled *Human-level Control through Deep Reinforcement Learning*, published in Nature. The solution is that now, instead of a moving target, the agent has short-term fixed targets. The agent now maintains two networks, both are exactly the same in architecture, one called the local network, which is used at each step to estimate the present action, and one the target network, which is used to get the target value. However, both networks have their own set of weights. At each time step, the local network learns in the direction such that its estimate and target are near to each other. After some number of time steps, the target network weights are updated. The update can be a **hard update**, where the weights of the local network are copied completely to the target network after N time steps, or it can be a **soft update**, in which the target network slowly (by a factor of Tau $\tau \epsilon [0,1]$) moves its weight toward the local network.

Reinforcement success in recent years

In the last few years, DRL has been successfully used in a variety of tasks, especially in game playing and robotics. Let us acquaint ourselves with some success stories of RL before learning its algorithms:

- **AlphaGo Zero:** Developed by Google's DeepMind team, the AlphaGo Zero paper *Mastering the game of Go without any human knowledge* starts from an absolutely blank slate (**tabula rasa**). The AlphaGo Zero uses one neural network to approximate both the move probabilities and value.
- This neural network takes as an input the raw board representation. It uses a Monte Carlo tree search guided by the neural network to select the moves. The reinforcement learning algorithm incorporates a look-ahead search inside the training loop. It was trained for 40 days using a 40-block residual CNN and, over the course of training, it played about 29 million games (a big number!). The neural network was optimized on Google Cloud using TensorFlow, with 64 GPU workers and 19 CPU parameter servers. You can access the paper here: https://www.nature.com/articles/nature24270.

- **AI-controlled sailplanes:** Microsoft has developed a controller system that can run on many different autopilot hardware platforms, such as Pixhawk and Raspberry Pi 3. It can keep the sailplane in the air without using a motor, by autonomously finding and catching rides on naturally occurring thermals. The controller helps the sailplane to operate on its own by detecting and using these thermals to travel without the aid of a motor or a person. They implemented it as a partially observable Markov decision process. They employed Bayesian reinforcement learning and used the Monte Carlo tree search to search for the best action. They've divided the whole system into level planners—a high-level planner that makes a decision based on experience and a low-level planner that uses Bayesian reinforcement learning to detect and latch onto thermals in real time. You can see the sailplane in action at Microsoft News: `https://news.microsoft.com/features/science-mimics-nature-microsoft-researchers-test-ai-controlled-soaring-machine/`.

- **Locomotion behavior:** In the paper *Emergence of Locomotion Behaviours in Rich Environments* (`https://arxiv.org/pdf/1707.02286.pdf`), DeepMind researchers provided the agents with rich and diverse environments. The environments presented a spectrum of challenges at different levels of difficulty. The agent was provided with difficulties in increasing order; this led the agent to learn sophisticated locomotion skills without performing any reward engineering (that is, designing special reward functions).

- **Data center cooling using reinforcement learning:** Data centers are workhorses of the present digital/internet revolution. With their large servers and networking devices, they facilitate data storage, data transfer, and the processing of information over the internet. Data centers account for about ~1.5% of all global energy consumption and if nothing is done about it, the consumption will only increase. DeepMind, along with Google Research in 2016, employed reinforcement learning models to reduce the energy consumption of their data centers by 40%. Using the historical data collected from the sensors within the data center, they trained a deep neural network to predict future energy efficiency and propose optimal action. You can read the details of the models and approach in the paper *Data center cooling using model-predictive control* (`https://proceedings.neurips.cc/paper/2018/file/059fdcd96baeb75112f09fa1dcc740cc-Paper.pdf`).

- **Controlling nuclear fusion plasma:** A recent (2022) and interesting application of RL is in controlling nuclear fusion plasma with the help of reinforcement learning. The results are published in a Nature paper: *Magnetic control of tokamak plasmas through reinforcement learning*.

It is really amazing to see how the DRL agent, without any implicit knowledge, learns to perform, and even beat, humans – in many specialized tasks. In the coming sections, we will explore these fabulous DRL algorithms and see them play games with almost human efficiency within a few thousand epochs.

Simulation environments for RL

As mentioned earlier, **trial and error** is an important component of any RL algorithm. Therefore, it makes sense to train our RL agent firstly in a simulated environment.

Today there exists a large number of platforms that can be used for the creation of an environment. Some popular ones are:

- **OpenAI Gym:** This contains a collection of environments that we can use to train our RL agents. In this chapter, we'll be using the OpenAI Gym interface.

- **Unity ML-Agents SDK:** It allows developers to transform games and simulations created using the Unity editor into environments where intelligent agents can be trained using DRL, evolutionary strategies, or other machine learning methods through a simple-to-use Python API. It works with TensorFlow and provides the ability to train intelligent agents for 2D/3D and VR/AR games. You can learn more about it here: `https://github.com/Unity-Technologies/ml-agents`.

- **Gazebo:** In Gazebo, we can build three-dimensional worlds with physics-based simulation. The `gym-gazebo` toolkit uses Gazebo along with the **Robot Operating System** (**ROS**) and the OpenAI Gym interface and can be used to train RL agents. To find out more about this, you can refer to the white paper: `https://arxiv.org/abs/1608.05742`.

- **Blender learning environment:** This is a Python interface for the Blender game engine, and it also works with OpenAI Gym. It has at its base Blender: a free 3D modeling software with an integrated game engine. This provides an easy-to-use, powerful set of tools for creating games. It provides an interface to the Blender game engine, and the games themselves are designed in Blender. We can then create a custom virtual environment to train an RL agent on a specific problem (`https://github.com/LouisFoucard/gym-blender`).

- **Malmo:** Built by the Microsoft team, Malmo is a platform for AI experimentation and research built on top of Minecraft. It provides a simple API for creating tasks and missions. You can learn more about Project Malmo here: `https://www.microsoft.com/en-us/research/project/project-malmo/`.

An introduction to OpenAI Gym

We will be using OpenAI Gym to provide an environment for our agent. OpenAI Gym is an open source toolkit to develop and compare RL algorithms. It contains a variety of simulated environments that can be used to train agents and develop new RL algorithms.

The first thing to do is install OpenAI Gym. The following command will install the minimal gym package:

```
pip install gym
```

If you want to install all (free) gym modules, add [all] after it:

```
pip install gym[all]
```

 The MuJoCo environment requires a purchasing license. For Atari-based games, you will need to install Atari dependencies (Box2D and ROM):

```
pip install box2d-py
```

OpenAI Gym provides a variety of environments, from simple text-based to three-dimensional games. The environments supported can be grouped as follows:

- **Algorithms:** Contains environments that involve performing computations such as addition. While we can easily perform the computations on a computer, what makes these problems interesting as RL problems is that the agent learns these tasks purely by example.
- **Atari:** This environment provides a wide variety of classic Atari/arcade games.
- **Box2D:** Contains robotics tasks in two dimensions such as a car racing agent or bipedal robot walk.
- **Classic control:** This contains the classical control theory problems, such as balancing a cart pole.
- **MuJoCo:** This is proprietary (you can get a one-month free trial). It supports various robot simulation tasks. The environment includes a physics engine; hence, it's used for training robotic tasks.
- **Robotics:** This environment also uses the physics engine of MuJoCo. It simulates goal-based tasks for fetch and shadow-hand robots.
- **Toy text:** A simple text-based environment—very good for beginners.

You can get a complete list of environments from the Gym website: `https://gym.openai.com`. To find a list of all available environments in your installation, you can use the following code:

```
from gym import envs

envall = envs.registry.all()
len(envall)
```

At the time of writing this book, it resulted in 859, that is, there are 859 different environments present in the gym module. Let us see more details of these environments. Each environment is created by using the `make` function. Associated with each environment is a unique ID, its observation space, its action space, and a default reward range. Gym allows you to access them through dot notation, as shown in the following code. We go through all the environments in the `envall` list and note down its unique ID, which is used to create the environment using the `make` method, its observation space, reward range, and the action space:

```
from tqdm import tqdm
List = []
for e in tqdm(envall):
    try:
        env = e.make()
        List.append([e.id, env.observation_space, env.action_space, env.reward_
range])
        env.close()
    except:
        continue
```

Figure 11.4 shows a random sample from the list:

	Environment	Observation Space	Action Space	Reward
418	JourneyEscape-ram-v0	Box(0, 255, (128,), uint8)	Discrete(16)	(-inf, inf)
438	KrullDeterministic-v0	Box(0, 255, (210, 160, 3), uint8)	Discrete(18)	(-inf, inf)
328	Freeway-v0	Box(0, 255, (210, 160, 3), uint8)	Discrete(3)	(-inf, inf)
113	Atlantis-v4	Box(0, 255, (210, 160, 3), uint8)	Discrete(4)	(-inf, inf)
298	ElevatorAction-ram-v0	Box(0, 255, (128,), uint8)	Discrete(18)	(-inf, inf)
571	RiverraidDeterministic-v4	Box(0, 255, (210, 160, 3), uint8)	Discrete(18)	(-inf, inf)
219	Carnival-ramNoFrameskip-v4	Box(0, 255, (128,), uint8)	Discrete(6)	(-inf, inf)
112	Atlantis-v0	Box(0, 255, (210, 160, 3), uint8)	Discrete(4)	(-inf, inf)
712	Venture-v0	Box(0, 255, (210, 160, 3), uint8)	Discrete(18)	(-inf, inf)
435	Kangaroo-ramNoFrameskip-v4	Box(0, 255, (128,), uint8)	Discrete(18)	(-inf, inf)
646	SpaceInvaders-ram-v0	Box(0, 255, (128,), uint8)	Discrete(6)	(-inf, inf)
396	IceHockey-ramDeterministic-v0	Box(0, 255, (128,), uint8)	Discrete(18)	(-inf, inf)
386	Hero-ramNoFrameskip-v0	Box(0, 255, (128,), uint8)	Discrete(18)	(-inf, inf)
674	Tennis-ramNoFrameskip-v0	Box(0, 255, (128,), uint8)	Discrete(18)	(-inf, inf)
35	Adventure-ram-v4	Box(0, 255, (128,), uint8)	Discrete(18)	(-inf, inf)
210	CarnivalDeterministic-v0	Box(0, 255, (214, 160, 3), uint8)	Discrete(6)	(-inf, inf)
460	MontezumaRevenge-v0	Box(0, 255, (210, 160, 3), uint8)	Discrete(18)	(-inf, inf)
280	DoubleDunk-v0	Box(0, 255, (210, 160, 3), uint8)	Discrete(18)	(-inf, inf)
101	Asteroids-v4	Box(0, 255, (210, 160, 3), uint8)	Discrete(14)	(-inf, inf)
107	Asteroids-ram-v4	Box(0, 255, (128,), uint8)	Discrete(14)	(-inf, inf)

Figure 11.4: Random list of environments available in OpenAI Gym

You can use these commands to find out details about any environment in Gym. For example, the following code prints details of the MountainCar environment:

```
env = gym.make('MountainCar-v0')
print(f"The Observation space is        {env.observation_space}" )

print(f"Upper Bound for Env Observation {env.observation_space.high}")
print(f"Lower Bound for Env Observation {env.observation_space.low}")
print(f"Action Space                    {env.action_space}")
```

```
env.seed(0)
obs = env.reset()
print(f"The initial observation is        {obs}")
# Take a random actionget the new observation space
new_obs, reward, done, info = env.step(env.action_space.sample())
print(f"The new observation is            {new_obs}")
env.close()
```

The core interface provided by OpenAI Gym is the unified environment interface. The agent can interact with the environment using three basic methods, that is, reset, step, and render. The reset method resets the environment and returns the observation. The step method steps the environment by one time step and returns new_obs, reward, done, and info. The render method renders one frame of the environment, like popping a window. Let us try and view some different environments and view their initial frame:

Physics Engine	Classic Control	Atari
`e = 'LunarLander-v2'`	`e = 'CartPole-v0'`	`e = 'SpaceInvaders-v0'`
`env = gym.make(e)`	`env = gym.make(e)`	`env = gym.make(e)`
`obs = env.reset()`	`env.reset()`	`env.reset()`
`img = env.`	`img = env.`	`img = env.`
`render(mode='rgb_`	`render(mode='rgb_`	`render(mode='rgb_`
`array')`	`array')`	`array')`
`env.close()`	`env.close()`	`env.close()`
`plt.imshow(img)`	`plt.imshow(img)`	`plt.imshow(img)`

Table 11.1: Different environments of OpenAI Gym and their initial state

The preceding code uses Matplotlib to display the environment; alternatively, you can directly use the render method:

```
import gym
env_name = 'Breakout-v0'
```

```
env = gym.make(env_name)
obs = env.reset()
env.render()
```

You can see the Breakout environment in *Figure 11.5*; the render function pops up the environment window:

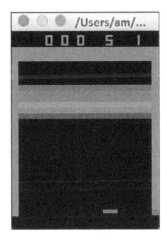

Figure 11.5: Initial state of the Breakout environment

We can use env.observation_space and env.action_space to find out more about the state space and action space for the Breakout game. The results show the state consists of a three-channel image of size 210 × 160, and the action space is discrete with four possible actions. Once you are done, do not forget to close OpenAI using:

```
env.close()
```

Random agent playing Breakout

Let's have some fun and play the Breakout game. When I first played the game, I had no idea of the rules or how to play, so I randomly chose the control buttons. Our novice agent will do the same; it will choose the actions randomly from the action space. Gym provides a function called sample(), which chooses a random action from the action space – we will be using this function. Also, we can save a replay of the game, to view it later. There are two ways to save the play, one using Matplotlib and another using an OpenAI Gym Monitor wrapper. Let us first see the Matplotlib method.

We will first import the necessary modules; we will only need gym and matplotlib for now, as the agent will be playing random moves:

```
import gym
import matplotlib.pyplot as plt
import matplotlib.animation as animation
```

We create the Gym environment:

```
env_name = 'Breakout-v0'
env = gym.make(env_name)
```

Next, we will run the game, one step at a time, choosing a random action, either for 300 steps or until the game is finished (whichever is earlier). The environment state (observation) space is saved at each step in the list `frames`:

```
frames = [] # array to store state space at each step
env.reset()
done = False
for _ in range(300):
    #print(done)
    frames.append(env.render(mode='rgb_array'))
    obs,reward,done, _ = env.step(env.action_space.sample())
    if done:
        break
```

Now comes the part of combining all the frames into a GIF image using Matplotlib Animation. We create an image object, patch, and then define a function that sets image data to a particular frame index. The function is used by the Matplotlib `Animation` class to create an animation, which we finally save in the file `random_agent.gif`:

```
patch = plt.imshow(frames[0])
plt.axis('off')
def animate(i):
    patch.set_data(frames[i])
    anim = animation.FuncAnimation(plt.gcf(), animate, \
        frames=len(frames), interval=10)
    anim.save('random_agent.gif', writer='imagemagick')
```

The code above will generate a GIF image. Below are some screen grabs from the image:

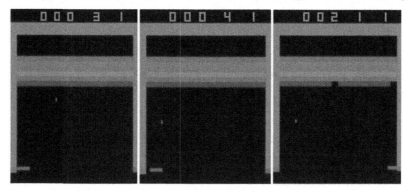

Figure 11.6: Some screenshots from the saved GIF image

Now that we are familiar with OpenAI Gym, we'll move on to wrappers—which you can use to create your own custom environments.

Wrappers in Gym

Gym provides various wrappers for us to modify the existing environment. For example, if you have image-based inputs with the RGB intensity value lying between 0 and 255, but the RL agent you use is a neural network, which works best if the input is in the range 0-1, you can use the Gym wrapper class to preprocess the state space. Below we define a wrapper that concatenates observations:

```python
from collections import deque
from gym import spaces
import numpy as np


#Class to concat observations
class ConcatObservations(gym.Wrapper):
    def __init__(self, env, n):
        gym.Wrapper.__init__(self, env)
        shape = env.observation_space.shape
        self.n = n
        self.frames = deque([], maxlen=n)
        self.observation_space = \
            spaces.Box(low=0, high=255, shape=((n,) + shape), dtype=env.
observation_space.dtype)
    def reset(self):   #reset function
        obs = self.env.reset()
        for _ in range(self.n):
            self.frames.append(obs)
        return self._get_obs()

    def step(self, action): #step function
        obs, reward, done, info = self.env.step(action)
        self.frames.append(obs)
        return self._get_obs(), reward, done, info

    def _get_obs(self):
        return np.array(self.frames)
```

You can see that we need to change the default reset function, step function, and observation function _get_obs. We also need to modify the default observation space.

Let us see how it works. If you take the `"BreakoutNoFrameskip-v4"` environment, then the initial observation space is 210 x 160 x 3:

```
env = gym.make("BreakoutNoFrameskip-v4")
print(f"The original observation space is  {env.observation_space}")
```

OUTPUT:

```
>>>The original observation space is  Box(0, 255, (210, 160, 3), uint8)
```

And now if you use the wrapper we just created:

```
env = ConcatObservations(env, 4)
print(f"The new observation space is  {env.observation_space}")
```

OUTPUT:

```
The new observation space is  Box(0, 255, (4, 210, 160, 3), uint8)
```

You can see that now a dimension is added—it has four frames, with each frame of size 210 x 160 x 3. You can use a wrapper to modify the rewards as well. In this case, you use the superclass `RewardWrapper`. Below is sample code that can clip the reward to lie within the range [-10, 10]:

```
class ClippedRewards(gym.RewardWrapper):
    def __init__(self, env):
        gym.RewardWrapper.__init__(self, env)
        self.reward_range = (-10,10)

    def reward(self, reward):
        """Clip to {+10, 0, -10} by its sign."""
        return reward if reward >= -10 and reward <= 10 else 10 *
np.sign(reward)
```

Let us try using it in the CartPole environment, which has the reward range $[-\infty, \infty]$:

```
env = ClippedRewards(gym.make("CartPole-v0"))
print(f'Clipped reward range: {env.reward_range}')
env.close()
```

OUTPUT:

```
Clipped reward range: (-10, 10)
```

Another useful application of wrappers is when you want to save the state space as an agent is learning. Normally, an RL agent requires lots of steps for proper training, and as a result, it is not feasible to store the state space at each step. Instead, we can choose to store after every 500th step (or any other number you wish) in the preceding algorithm. OpenAI Gym provides the `Wrapper  Monitor` class to save the game as a video. To do so, we need to first import wrappers, then create the environment, and finally use `Monitor`.

By default, it will store the video of 1, 8, 27, 64, (episode numbers with perfect cubes), and so on, and then every 1,000th episode; each training, by default, is saved in one folder. The code to do this is:

```python
import gym
env = gym.make("Breakout-v0")
env = gym.wrappers.Monitor(env, 'recording', force=True)
observation = env.reset()
for _ in range(1000):
    #env.render()
    action = env.action_space.sample()
    # your agent here (this takes random actions)
    observation, reward, done, info = env.step(action)
    if done:
        observation = env.reset()
env.close()
```

For Monitor to work, we require FFmpeg support. We may need to install it depending upon our OS, if it is missing.

This will save the videos in .mp4 format in the folder recording. An important thing to note here is that you have to set the force=True option if you want to use the same folder for the next training session.

If you want to train your agent on Google Colab, you will need to add the following drivers to be able to visualize the Gym output:

```
!pip install pyglet
!apt-get install -y xvfb python-opengl > /dev/null 2>&1
!pip install gym pyvirtualdisplay > /dev/null 2>&1
```

After installing the Python virtual display, you need to start it—Gym uses the virtual display to set observations. The following code can help you in starting a display of size 600 x 400:

```
from pyvirtualdisplay import Display
display = Display(visible=0, size=(600, 400))
display.start()
```

And to be able to play around with Atari games, use:

```
!wget http://www.atarimania.com/roms/Roms.rar
!mkdir /content/ROM/
!unrar e /content/Roms.rar /content/ROM/
!python -m atari_py.import_roms /content/ROM/
```

Deep Q-networks

Deep Q-Networks, DQNs for short, are deep learning neural networks designed to approximate the Q-function (value-state function). They are one of the most popular value-based reinforcement learning algorithms. The model was proposed by Google's DeepMind in NeurIPS 2013, in the paper entitled *Playing Atari with Deep Reinforcement Learning*. The most important contribution of this paper was that they used the raw state space directly as input to the network; the input features were not hand-crafted as done in earlier RL implementations. Also, they could train the agent with exactly the same architecture to play different Atari games and obtain state-of-the-art results.

This model is an extension of the simple Q-learning algorithm. In Q-learning algorithms, a Q-table is maintained as a cheat sheet. After each action, the Q-table is updated using the Bellman equation [5]:

$$Q(S_t, A_t) = (1 - \alpha)Q(S_t, A_t) + \alpha\big(R_{t+1} + \gamma \, max_A Q(S_{t+1}, A_t)\big)$$

α is the learning rate, and its value lies in the range [0,1]. The first term represents the component of the old Q value and the second term the target Q value. Q-learning is good if the number of states and the number of possible actions is small, but for large state spaces and action spaces, Q-learning is simply not scalable. A better alternative would be to use a deep neural network as a function approximator, approximating the target Q-function for each possible action. The weights of the deep neural network in this case store the Q-table information. There is a separate output unit for each possible action. The network takes the state as its input and returns the predicted target Q value for all possible actions. The question arises: how do we train this network, and what should be the loss function? Well, since our network has to predict the target Q value:

$$Q_{target} = R_{t+1} + \gamma \, max_A Q(S_{t+1}, A_t)$$

the loss function should try and reduce the difference between the Q value predicted, $Q_{predicted}$, and the target Q, Q_{target}. We can do this by defining the loss function as:

$$loss = E_\pi\big[Q_{target}(S, A) - Q_{predicted}(S, W, A)\big]$$

where W is the training parameters of our deep Q network, learned using gradient descent, such that the loss function is minimized.

The following is the general architecture of a DQN. The network takes the n-dimensional state as input and outputs the Q value of each possible action in the m-dimensional action space. Each layer (including the input) can be a convolutional layer (if we are taking the raw pixels as input, convolutional layers make more sense) or a dense layer:

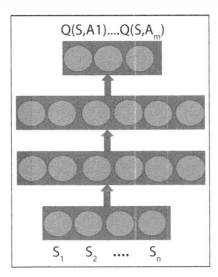

Figure 11.7: The figure shows a simple DQN network, the input layer taking State vector S, and the output predicting Q for all possible actions for the state

In the next section, we will try training a DQN. Our agent task will be to stabilize a pole on a cart. The agent can move the cart left or right to maintain balance.

DQN for CartPole

CartPole is a classic OpenAI problem with continuous state space and discrete action space. In it, a pole is attached by an un-actuated joint to a cart; the cart moves along a frictionless track. The goal is to keep the pole standing on the cart by moving the cart left or right. A reward of +1 is given for each time step the pole is standing. Once the pole is more than 15 degrees from the vertical, or the cart moves beyond 2.4 units from the center, the game is over:

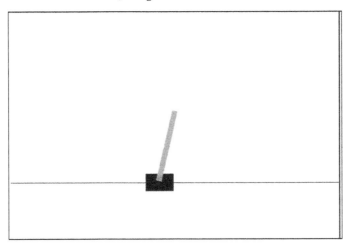

Figure 11.8: A screenshot from the CartPole Gym environment

You can check the leaderboard of OpenAI Gym for some cool entries for the CartPole environment: `https://github.com/openai/gym/wiki/Leaderboard#cartpole-v0`.

We start with importing the necessary modules. We require gym, obviously, to provide us with the CartPole environment, and `tensorflow` to build our DQN network. Besides these, we need the random and numpy modules:

```
import random
import gym
import math
import numpy as np
from collections import deque
import tensorflow as tf
from tensorflow.keras.models import Sequential
from tensorflow.keras.layers import Dense
from tensorflow.keras.optimizers import Adam
```

We set up the global values for the maximum episodes for which we will be training the agent (EPOCHS), the threshold value when we consider the environment solved (THRESHOLD), and a bool to indicate if we want to record the training or not (MONITOR). Please note that as per the official OpenAI documentation, the CartPole environment is considered solved when the agent is able to maintain the pole in the vertical position for 195 time steps (ticks). In the following code, for the sake of time, we have reduced the THRESHOLD to 45:

```
EPOCHS = 1000
THRESHOLD = 45
MONITOR = True
```

Now let us build our DQN. We declare a class DQN and in its __init__() function declare all the hyperparameters and our model. We are also creating the environment inside the DQN class. As you can see, the class is quite general, and you can use it to train any Gym environment whose state space information can be encompassed in a 1D array:

```
class DQN():
    def __init__(self, env_string, batch_size=64):
        self.memory = deque(maxlen=100000)
        self.env = gym.make(env_string)
        input_size = self.env.observation_space.shape[0]
        action_size = self.env.action_space.n
        self.batch_size = batch_size
        self.gamma = 1.0
        self.epsilon = 1.0
        self.epsilon_min = 0.01
        self.epsilon_decay = 0.995
```

```
alpha=0.01
alpha_decay=0.01
if MONITOR: self.env = gym.wrappers.Monitor(self.env,
'data/'+env_string, force=True)

# Init model
self.model = Sequential()
self.model.add(Dense(24, input_dim=input_size,
activation='tanh'))
self.model.add(Dense(48, activation='tanh'))
self.model.add(Dense(action_size, activation='linear'))
self.model.compile(loss='mse', optimizer=Adam(lr=alpha,
decay=alpha_decay))
```

The DQN that we have built is a three-layered perceptron; in the following output, you can see the model summary. We use the Adam optimizer with learning rate decay:

```
Model: "sequential"

_____
Layer (type)                 Output Shape              Param #
=================================================================
dense (Dense)                (None, 24)                120

dense_1 (Dense)              (None, 48)                1200

dense_2 (Dense)              (None, 2)                 98

=================================================================
Total params: 1,418
Trainable params: 1,418
Non-trainable params: 0
_____
```

The variable list self.memory will contain our experience replay buffer. We need to add a method for saving the <S,A,R,S'> tuple into the memory and a method to get random samples from it in batches to train the agent. We perform these two functions by defining the class methods remember and replay:

```
def remember(self, state, action, reward, next_state, done):
    self.memory.append((state, action, reward, next_state, done))

def replay(self, batch_size):
    x_batch, y_batch = [], []
    minibatch = random.sample(self.memory, min(len(self.memory),
```

```
            batch_size))
        for state, action, reward, next_state, done in minibatch:
                y_target = self.model.predict(state)
                y_target[0][action] = reward if done else reward + self.gamma *
np.max(self.model.predict(next_state)[0])
                x_batch.append(state[0])
                y_batch.append(y_target[0])

        self.model.fit(np.array(x_batch), np.array(y_batch),
        batch_size=len(x_batch), verbose=0)
```

Our agent will use the **epsilon-greedy policy** when choosing the action. This is implemented in the following method:

```
def choose_action(self, state, epsilon):
        if np.random.random() <= epsilon:
            return self.env.action_space.sample()
        else:
            return np.argmax(self.model.predict(state))
```

Next, we write a method to train the agent. We define two lists to keep track of the scores. First, we fill the experience replay buffer and then we choose some samples from it to train the agent and hope that the agent will slowly learn to do better:

```
def train(self):
    scores = deque(maxlen=100)
    avg_scores = []
    for e in range(EPOCHS):
        state = self.env.reset()
        state = self.preprocess_state(state)
        done = False
        i = 0
        while not done:
            action = self.choose_action(state,self.epsilon)
            next_state, reward, done, _ = self.env.step(action)
            next_state = self.preprocess_state(next_state)
            self.remember(state, action, reward, next_state, done)
            state = next_state
            self.epsilon = max(self.epsilon_min,
            self.epsilon_decay*self.epsilon) # decrease epsilon
```

```
        i += 1
    scores.append(i)
    mean_score = np.mean(scores)
    avg_scores.append(mean_score)
    if mean_score >= THRESHOLD and e >= 100:
        print('Ran {} episodes. Solved after {} trials ✓'.format(e, e -
100))
        return avg_scores
    if e % 100 == 0:
        print('[Episode {}] - Mean survival time over last 100 episodes was
{} ticks.'.format(e, mean_score))
    self.replay(self.batch_size)
    print('Did not solve after {} episodes :('.format(e))
    return avg_scores
```

Now that all necessary functions are done, we just need one more helper function to reshape the state of the CartPole environment so that the input to the model is in the correct shape. The state of the environment is described by four continuous variables: cart position ([-2.4-2.4]), cart velocity, pole angle ([-41.8o-41.8o]), and pole velocity :

```
def preprocess_state(self, state):
    return np.reshape(state, [1, self.input_size])
```

Let us now instantiate our agent for the CartPole environment and train it:

```
env_string = 'CartPole-v0'
agent = DQN(env_string)
scores = agent.train()
```

```
[Episode 0] - Mean survival time over last 100 episodes was 28.0 ticks.
[Episode 100] - Mean survival time over last 100 episodes was 15.71 ticks.
[Episode 200] - Mean survival time over last 100 episodes was 27.81 ticks.
Ran 259 episodes. Solved after 159 trials ✓
```

Let's plot the average reward as the agent learns:

```
import matplotlib.pyplot as plt
plt.plot(scores)
plt.show()
```

Figure 11.9 shows the agent being trained on my system. The agent was able to achieve our set threshold of 45 in 254 steps:

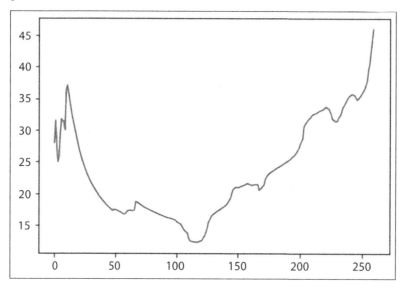

Figure 11.9: Average agent reward plot

Once the training is done, you can close the environment:

```
agent.env.close()
```

You can see that starting with no information about how to balance the pole, the agent, using a DQN, is able to balance the pole for more and more time (on average) as it learns. Starting from a blank slate, the agent is able to build information/knowledge to fulfill the required goal. Remarkable!

DQN to play a game of Atari

In the preceding section, we trained a DQN to balance a pole in CartPole. It was a simple problem, and thus we could solve it using a perceptron model. But imagine if the environment state was just the CartPole visual as we humans see it. With raw pixel values as the input state space, our previous DQN will not work. What we need is a convolutional neural network. Next, we build one based on the seminal paper on DQNs, *Playing Atari with Deep Reinforcement Learning*.

Most of the code will be similar to the DQN for CartPole, but there will be significant changes in the DQN network itself, and how we preprocess the state that we obtain from the environment.

First, let us see the change in the way state space is processed. *Figure 11.10* shows one of the Atari games, Breakout:

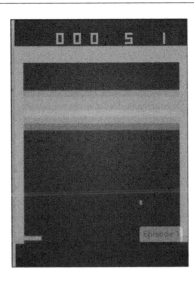

Figure 11.10: A screenshot of the Atari game, Breakout

Now, if you look at the image, not all of it contains relevant information: the top part has redundant information about the score, the bottom part has unnecessary blank space, and the image is colored. To reduce the burden on our model, it is best to remove the unnecessary information, so we crop the image, convert it to grayscale, and make it a square of size 84 × 84 (as in the paper). Here is the code to preprocess the input raw pixels:

```
def preprocess_state(self, img):
    img_temp = img[31:195]  # Choose the important area of the image
    img_temp = tf.image.rgb_to_grayscale(img_temp)
    img_temp = tf.image.resize(img_temp, [self.IM_SIZE, self.IM_SIZE],
    method=tf.image.ResizeMethod.NEAREST_NEIGHBOR)
    img_temp = tf.cast(img_temp, tf.float32)
    return img_temp[:,:,0]
```

Another important issue is that just by looking at the image at one time step, how can the agent know whether the ball is going up or down? One way could be to use LSTM along with a CNN to keep a record of the past and hence the ball movement. The paper, however, used a simple technique. Instead of a single state frame, it concatenated the state space for the past four time steps together as one input to the CNN; that is, the network sees four past frames of the environment as its input. The following is the code for combining the present and previous states:

```
def combine_images(self, img1, img2):
    if len(img1.shape) == 3 and img1.shape[0] == self.m:
        im = np.append(img1[1:,:, :],np.expand_dims(img2,0), axis=2)
        return tf.expand_dims(im, 0)
    else:
        im = np.stack([img1]*self.m, axis = 2)
        return tf.expand_dims(im, 0)
```

The model was defined in the __init__ function. We modify the function to now have a CNN with an input of (84 × 84 × 4) representing four state frames each of size 84 × 84:

```python
def __init__(self, env_string,batch_size=64, IM_SIZE = 84, m = 4):
    self.memory = deque(maxlen=5000)
    self.env = gym.make(env_string)
    input_size = self.env.observation_space.shape[0]
    action_size = self.env.action_space.n
    self.batch_size = batch_size
    self.gamma = 1.0
    self.epsilon = 1.0
    self.epsilon_min = 0.01
    self.epsilon_decay = 0.995
    self.IM_SIZE = IM_SIZE
    self.m = m


    alpha=0.01
    alpha_decay=0.01
    if MONITOR: self.env = gym.wrappers.Monitor(self.env, '../data/'+env_
string, force=True)

    # Init model
    self.model = Sequential()
    self.model.add( Conv2D(32, 8, (4,4), activation='relu',padding='valid',
input_shape=(IM_SIZE, IM_SIZE, m)))
    self.model.add( Conv2D(64, 4, (2,2), activation='relu',padding='valid'))
    self.model.add( Conv2D(64, 3, (1,1), activation='relu',padding='valid'))
    self.model.add(Flatten())
    self.model.add(Dense(512, activation='elu'))
    self.model.add(Dense(action_size, activation='linear'))
    self.model.compile(loss='mse', optimizer=Adam(lr=alpha, decay=alpha_decay))
```

Lastly, we will need to make a minor change in the train function. We will need to call the new preprocess function, along with the combine_images function to ensure that four frames are concatenated:

```python
def train(self):
    scores = deque(maxlen=100)
    avg_scores = []

    for e in range(EPOCHS):
```

```
            state = self.env.reset()
            state = self.preprocess_state(state)
            state = self.combine_images(state, state)
            done = False
            i = 0
            while not done:
                action = self.choose_action(state,self.epsilon)
                next_state, reward, done, _ = self.env.step(action)
                next_state = self.preprocess_state(next_state)
                next_state = self.combine_images(next_state, state)
                #print(next_state.shape)
                self.remember(state, action, reward, next_state, done)
                state = next_state
                self.epsilon = max(self.epsilon_min, self.epsilon_decay*self.
    epsilon) # decrease epsilon
                i += reward
            scores.append(i)
            mean_score = np.mean(scores)
            avg_scores.append(mean_score)
            if mean_score >= THRESHOLD and e >= 100:
                print('Ran {} episodes. Solved after {} trials ✓'.format(e, e -
    100))
                return avg_scores
            if e % 100 == 0:
                print('[Episode {}] - Score over last 100 episodes was
    {}.'.format(e, mean_score))
            self.replay(self.batch_size)

        print('Did not solve after {} episodes :('.format(e))
        return avg_scores
```

That's all. We can now train the agent for playing Breakout. The complete code is available on GitHub repository (`https://github.com/PacktPublishing/Deep-Learning-with-TensorFlow-and-Keras-3rd-edition/tree/main/Chapter_11`) of this chapter in the file `DQN_Atari_v2.ipynb`.

DQN variants

After the unprecedented success of DQNs, the interest in RL increased and many new RL algorithms came into being. Next, we see some of the algorithms that are based on DQNs. They all use DQNs as the base and build upon it.

Double DQN

In DQNs, the agent uses the same Q value to both select and evaluate an action. This can cause a maximization bias in learning. For example, let us consider that for a state, S, all possible actions have true Q values of zero. Now, our DQN estimates will have some values above and some values below zero, and since we are choosing the action with the maximum Q value and later evaluating the Q value of each action using the same (maximized) estimated value function, we are overestimating Q—or in other words, our agent is over-optimistic. This can lead to unstable training and a low-quality policy. To deal with this issue, Hasselt et al. from DeepMind proposed the Double DQN algorithm in their paper *Deep Reinforcement Learning with Double Q-Learning*. In Double DQN, we have two Q-networks with the same architecture but different weights. One of the Q-networks is used to determine the action using the epsilon-greedy policy and the other is used to determine its value (Q-target).

If you recall in DQNs, the Q-target was given by:

$$Q_{target} = R_{t+1} + \gamma max_A Q(S_{t+1}, A_t)$$

Here, the action A was selected using the same DQN, $Q(S,A; W)$, where W is the training parameters of the network; that is, we are writing the Q value function along with its training parameter to emphasize the difference between vanilla DQNs and Double DQN:

$$Q_{target} = R_{t+1} + \gamma max_A Q(S_{t+1}, argmax_t Q(S, A; W); W)$$

In Double DQN, the equation for the target will now change. Now, the DQN $Q(S,A;W)$ is used for determining the action and the DQN $Q(S,A;W')$ is used for calculating the target (notice the different weights). So, the preceding equation will change to:

$$Q_{target} = R_{t+1} + \gamma max_A Q(S_{t+1}, argmax_t Q(S, A; W); W')$$

This simple change reduces the overestimation and helps us to train the agent faster and more reliably.

Dueling DQN

This architecture was proposed by Wang et al. in their paper *Dueling Network Architectures for Deep Reinforcement Learning* in 2015. Like the DQN and Double DQN, it is also a model-free algorithm.

Dueling DQN decouples the Q-function into the value function and advantage function. The value function, which we discussed earlier, represents the value of the state independent of any action. The advantage function, on the other hand, provides a relative measure of the utility (advantage/goodness) of action A in the state S. The Dueling DQN uses convolutional networks in the initial layers to extract the features from raw pixels. However, in the later stages, it is separated into two different networks, one approximating the value and another approximating the advantage. This ensures that the network produces separate estimates for the value function and the advantage function:

$$Q(S, A) = A(S, A; \theta, \alpha) + V^{\pi}(S; \theta, \beta)$$

Here, θ is an array of the training parameters of the shared convolutional network (it is shared by both V and A), and α and β are the training parameters for the *Advantage* and *Value* estimator networks. Later, the two networks are recombined using an aggregating layer to estimate the Q value.

In *Figure 11.11*, you can see the architecture of Dueling DQN:

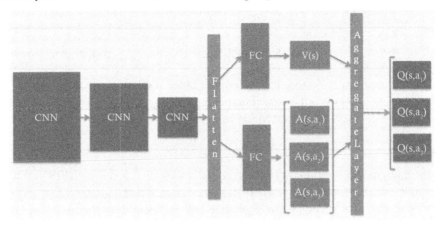

Figure 11.11: Visualizing the architecture of a Dueling DQN

You may be wondering, what is the advantage of doing all of this? Why decompose Q if we will just be putting it back together? Well, decoupling the value and advantage functions allows us to know which states are valuable, without having to take into account the effect of each action for each state. There are many states that, irrespective of the action taken, are good or bad states: for example, having breakfast with your loved ones in a good resort is always a good state, and being admitted to a hospital emergency ward is always a bad state. Thus, separating value and advantage allows one to get a more robust approximation of the value function. Next, you can see a figure from the paper highlighting how in the Atari game Enduro, the value network learns to pay attention to the road, and the advantage network learns to pay attention only when there are cars immediately in front, so as to avoid a collision:

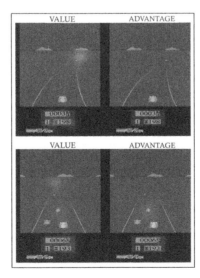

Figure 11.12: In the Atari game Enduro, the value network learns to pay attention to the road (red spot), and the advantage network focuses only when other vehicles are immediately in front. Image source: https://arxiv.org/pdf/1511.06581.pdf

The aggregate layer is implemented in a manner that allows one to recover both V and A from the given Q. This is achieved by enforcing that the advantage function estimator has zero advantage at the chosen action:

$$Q(S, A; \theta, \alpha, \beta) = A(S, A; \theta, \alpha) + V^{\pi}(S; \theta, \beta) - max_{\alpha' \epsilon |A|} A(S, A'; \theta, \alpha)$$

In the paper, Wang et al. reported that the network is more stable if the max operation is replaced by the average operation. This is so because the speed of change in advantage is now the same as the change in average, instead of the optimal (max) value.

Rainbow

Rainbow is the current state-of-the-art DQN variant. Technically, to call it a DQN variant would be wrong. In essence, it is an ensemble of many DQN variants combined together into a single algorithm. It modifies the distributional RL [6] loss to multi-step loss and combines it with Double DQN using a greedy action. Quoting from the paper:

> *The network architecture is a dueling network architecture adapted for use with return distributions. The network has a shared representation $f\xi(s)$, which is then fed into a value stream v_η with N_{atoms} outputs, and into an advantage stream $a\xi$ with $N_{atoms} \times N_{actions}$ outputs, where $a1\xi(f\xi(s), a)$ will denote the output corresponding to atom i and action a. For each atom z_i, the value and advantage streams are aggregated, as in Dueling DQN, and then passed through a softmax layer to obtain the normalised parametric distributions used to estimate the returns' distributions.*

Rainbow combines six different RL algorithms:

- N-step returns
- Distributional state-action value learning
- Dueling networks
- Noisy networks
- Double DQN
- Prioritized experience replay

Till now, we've considered value-based reinforcement learning algorithms. In the next section, we will learn about policy-based reinforcement learning algorithms.

Deep deterministic policy gradient

The DQN and its variants have been very successful in solving problems where the state space is continuous and action space is discrete. For example, in Atari games, the input space consists of raw pixels, but actions are discrete—[**up, down, left, right, no-op**]. How do we solve a problem with continuous action space? For instance, say an RL agent driving a car needs to turn its wheels: this action has a continuous action space.

One way to handle this situation is by discretizing the action space and continuing with a DQN or its variants. However, a better solution would be to use a policy gradient algorithm. In policy gradient methods, the policy $\pi(A|S)$ is approximated directly.

A neural network is used to approximate the policy; in the simplest form, the neural network learns a policy for selecting actions that maximize the rewards by adjusting its weights using the steepest gradient ascent, hence the name: policy gradients.

In this section, we will focus on the **Deep Deterministic Policy Gradient (DDPG)** algorithm, another successful RL algorithm by Google's DeepMind in 2015. DDPG is implemented using two networks; one called the actor network and the other called the critic network.

The actor network approximates the optimal policy deterministically, that is, it outputs the most preferred action for any given input state. In essence, the actor is learning. The critic on the other hand evaluates the optimal action value function using the actor's most preferred action. Before going further, let us contrast this with the DQN algorithm that we discussed in the preceding section. In *Figure 11.13*, you can see the general architecture of DDPG:

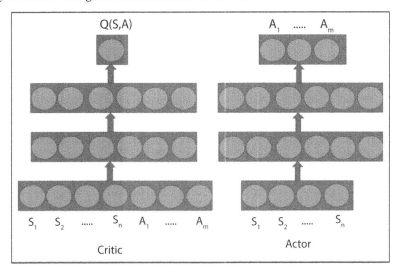

Figure 11.13: Architecture of the DDPG model

On the left-hand side of *Figure 11.13* is the critic network, it takes as input the state vector, S, and action taken, A. The output of the network is the Q value for that state and action. The right-hand figure shows the actor network. It takes as input the state vector, S, and predicts the optimum action, A, to be taken. In the figure, we have shown both the actor and critic to be of four layers. This is only for demonstration purposes.

The actor network outputs the most preferred action; the critic takes as input both the input state and action taken and evaluates its Q value. To train the critic network, we follow the same procedure as with a DQN; that is, we try to minimize the difference between the estimated Q value and the target Q value. The gradient of the Q value over actions is then propagated back to train the actor network. So, if the critic is good enough, it will force the actor to choose actions with optimal value functions.

Summary

Reinforcement learning has in recent years seen a lot of progress. To summarize all of that in a single chapter is not possible. However, in this chapter, we focused on the recent successful RL algorithms. The chapter started by introducing the important concepts in the RL field, its challenges, and the solutions to move forward. Next, we delved into two important RL algorithms: the DQN and DDPG algorithms. Toward the end of this chapter, we covered important topics in the field of deep learning.

In the next chapter, we will move on to applying what we have learned to production.

References

1. MIT Technology Review covers OpenAI experiments on reinforcement learning: `https:// www.technologyreview.com/s/614325/open-ai-algorithms-learned-tool-use-and- cooperation-after-hide-and-seek-games/`

2. Coggan, Melanie. (2014). *Exploration and Exploitation in Reinforcement Learning*. Research supervised by Prof. Doina Precup, CRA-W DMP Project at McGill University.

3. Lin, Long-Ji. (1993). *Reinforcement learning for robots using neural networks*. No. CMU-CS-93-103. Carnegie-Mellon University Pittsburgh PA School of Computer Science.

4. Schaul, Tom, John Quan, Ioannis Antonoglou, and David Silver. (2015). *Prioritized Experience Replay*. arXiv preprint arXiv:1511.05952

5. Sutton R., Barto A. *Chapter 4, Reinforcement Learning*. MIT Press: `https://web.stanford.edu/ class/psych209/Readings/SuttonBartoIPRLBook2ndEd.pdf`

6. Dabney W., Rowland M., Bellemare M G., and Munos R. (2018). *Distributional Reinforcement Learning with Quantile Regression*. In Thirty-Second AAAI Conference on Artificial Intelligence.

7. Hessel, M., Modayil, J., Van Hasselt, H., Schaul, T., Ostrovski, G., Dabney, W., Horgan, D., Piot, B., Azar, M., and Silver, D. (2018). *Rainbow: Combining improvements in Deep Reinforcement Learning*. In Thirty-Second AAAI Conference on Artificial Intelligence.

8. Details about different environments can be obtained from `https://www.gymlibrary.ml/`

9. Wiki pages are maintained for some environments at `https://github.com/openai/gym/wiki`

10. Details regarding installation instructions and dependencies can be obtained from `https:// github.com/openai/gym`

11. Link to the paper by DeepMind, *Asynchronous Methods for Deep Reinforcement Learning*: `https:// arxiv.org/pdf/1602.01783.pdf`

12. This is a blog post by Andrej Karpathy on reinforcement learning: `http://karpathy.github. io/2016/05/31/rl/`

13. Glorot X. and Bengio Y. (2010). *Understanding the difficulty of training deep feedforward neural networks*. Proceedings of the Thirteenth International Conference on Artificial Intelligence and Statistics: `http://proceedings.mlr.press/v9/glorot10a/glorot10a.pdf`

14. A good read on why RL is still hard to crack: `https://www.alexirpan.com/2018/02/14/rl- hard.html`

15. Lillicrap, T. P., Hunt, J. J., Pritzel, A., Heess, N., Erez, T., Tassa, Y., ... & Wierstra, D. (2015). *Continuous control with deep reinforcement learning. arXiv preprint arXiv:1509.02971.*

Join our book's Discord space

Join our Discord community to meet like-minded people and learn alongside more than 2000 members at: `https://packt.link/keras`

12

Probabilistic TensorFlow

Uncertainty is a fact of life; whether you are doing a classification task or a regression task, it is important to know how confident your model is in its prediction. Till now, we have covered the traditional deep learning models, and while they are great at many tasks, they are not able to handle uncertainty. Instead, they are deterministic in nature. In this chapter, you will learn how to leverage TensorFlow Probability to build models that can handle uncertainty, specifically probabilistic deep learning models and Bayesian networks. The chapter will include:

- TensorFlow Probability
- Distributions, events, and shapes in TensorFlow Probability
- Bayesian networks using TensorFlow Probability
- Understand uncertainty in machine learning models
- Model aleatory and epistemic uncertainty using TensorFlow Probability

 All the code files for this chapter can be found at `https://packt.link/dltfchp12`

Let's start with first understanding TensorFlow Probability.

TensorFlow Probability

TensorFlow Probability (**TFP**), a part of the TensorFlow ecosystem, is a library that provides tools for developing probabilistic models. It can be used to perform probabilistic reasoning and statistical analysis. It is built over TensorFlow and provides the same computational advantage.

Figure 12.1 shows the major components constituting TensorFlow Probability:

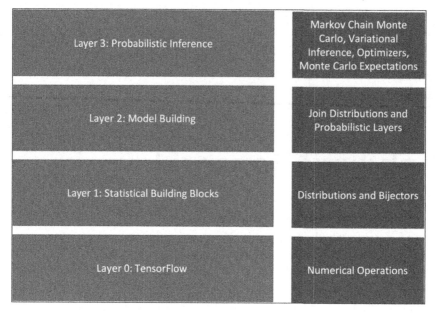

Figure 12.1: Different components of TensorFlow Probability

At the root, we have all numerical operations supported by TensorFlow, specifically the `LinearOperator` class (part of `tf.linalg`) – it contains all the methods that can be performed on a matrix, without the need to actually materialize the matrix. This provides computationally efficient matrix-free computations. TFP includes a large collection of probability distributions and their related statistical computations. It also has `tfp.bijectors`, which offers a wide range of transformed distributions.

 Bijectors encapsulate the change of variables for probability density. That is, when one transforms one variable from space A to space B, we need a way to map the probability distributions of the variables as well. Bijectors provide us with all the tools needed to do so.

TensorFlow Probability also provides `JointDistribution`, which allows the user to draw a joint sample and compute a joint log-density (log probability density function). The standard TFP distributions work on tensors, but `JointDistribution` works on the structure of tensors. `tfp.layers` provides neural network layers that can be used to extend the standard TensorFlow layers and add uncertainty to them. And finally, it provides a wide range of tools for probabilistic inference. In this chapter, we will go through some of these functions and classes; let us first start with installation. To install TFP in your working environment, just run:

```
pip install tensorflow-probability
```

Let us have some fun with TFP. To use TFP, we will need to import it. Additionally, we are going to do some plots. So, we import some additional modules:

```
import matplotlib.pyplot as plt
import tensorflow_probability as tfp
import functools, inspect, sys
```

Next, we explore the different classes of distributions available in `tfp.distributions`:

```
tfd = tfp.distributions
distribution_class =  tfp.distributions.Distribution
distributions = [name for name, obj in inspect.getmembers(tfd)
                 if inspect.isclass(obj) and issubclass(obj, distribution_
class)]
print(distributions)
```

Here is the output:

```
['Autoregressive', 'BatchBroadcast', 'BatchConcat', 'BatchReshape', 'Bates',
 'Bernoulli', 'Beta', 'BetaBinomial', 'BetaQuotient', 'Binomial', 'Blockwise',
 'Categorical', 'Cauchy', 'Chi', 'Chi2', 'CholeskyLKJ', 'ContinuousBernoulli',
 'DeterminantalPointProcess', 'Deterministic', 'Dirichlet',
 'DirichletMultinomial', 'Distribution', 'DoublesidedMaxwell', 'Empirical',
 'ExpGamma', 'ExpInverseGamma', 'ExpRelaxedOneHotCategorical', 'Exponential',
 'ExponentiallyModifiedGaussian', 'FiniteDiscrete', 'Gamma', 'GammaGamma',
 'GaussianProcess', 'GaussianProcessRegressionModel', 'GeneralizedExtremeValue',
 'GeneralizedNormal', 'GeneralizedPareto', 'Geometric', 'Gumbel', 'HalfCauchy',
 'HalfNormal', 'HalfStudentT', 'HiddenMarkovModel', 'Horseshoe', 'Independent',
 'InverseGamma', 'InverseGaussian', 'JohnsonSU', 'JointDistribution',
 'JointDistributionCoroutine', 'JointDistributionCoroutineAutoBatched',
 'JointDistributionNamed', 'JointDistributionNamedAutoBatched',
 'JointDistributionSequential', 'JointDistributionSequentialAutoBatched',
 'Kumaraswamy', 'LKJ', 'LambertWDistribution', 'LambertWNormal', 'Laplace',
 'LinearGaussianStateSpaceModel', 'LogLogistic', 'LogNormal', 'Logistic',
 'LogitNormal', 'MarkovChain', 'Masked', 'MatrixNormalLinearOperator',
 'MatrixTLinearOperator', 'Mixture', 'MixtureSameFamily', 'Moyal',
 'Multinomial', 'MultivariateNormalDiag', 'MultivariateNormalDiagPlusLowRank',
 'MultivariateNormalDiagPlusLowRankCovariance',
 'MultivariateNormalFullCovariance', 'MultivariateNormalLinearOperator',
 'MultivariateNormalTriL', 'MultivariateStudentTLinearOperator',
 'NegativeBinomial', 'Normal', 'NormalInverseGaussian', 'OneHotCategorical',
 'OrderedLogistic', 'PERT', 'Pareto', 'PixelCNN', 'PlackettLuce',
 'Poisson', 'PoissonLogNormalQuadratureCompound', 'PowerSpherical',
 'ProbitBernoulli', 'QuantizedDistribution', 'RelaxedBernoulli',
 'RelaxedOneHotCategorical', 'Sample', 'SigmoidBeta', 'SinhArcsinh', 'Skellam',
 'SphericalUniform', 'StoppingRatioLogistic', 'StudentT', 'StudentTProcess',
 'StudentTProcessRegressionModel', 'TransformedDistribution', 'Triangular',
 'TruncatedCauchy', 'TruncatedNormal', 'Uniform', 'VariationalGaussianProcess',
 'VectorDeterministic', 'VonMises', 'VonMisesFisher', 'Weibull',
 'WishartLinearOperator', 'WishartTriL', 'Zipf']
```

You can see that a rich range of distributions is available in TFP. Let us now try one of the distributions:

```
normal = tfd.Normal(loc=0., scale=1.)
```

This statement declares that we want to have a normal distribution with **mean** (loc) zero and **standard deviation** (scale) 1. We can generate random samples following this distribution using the sample method. The following code snippet generates such N samples and plots them:

```
def plot_normal(N):
    samples = normal.sample(N)
    sns.distplot(samples)
    plt.title(f"Normal Distribution with zero mean, and 1 std. dev {N} samples")
    plt.show()
```

You can see that as N increases, the plot follows a nice normal distribution:

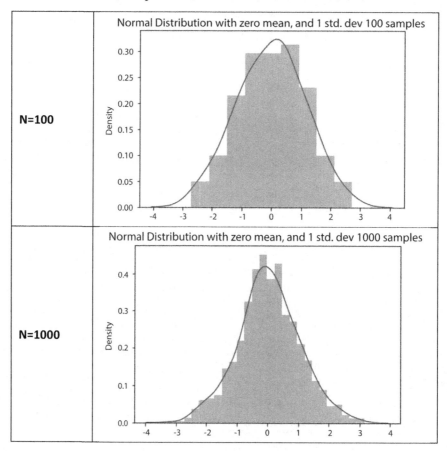

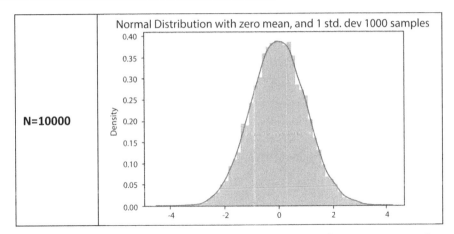

*Figure 12.2: Normal distribution from randomly generated samples of sizes 100, 1,000, and 10,000.
The distribution has a mean of zero and a standard deviation of one*

Let us now explore the different distributions available with TFP.

TensorFlow Probability distributions

Every distribution in TFP has a shape, batch, and event size associated with it. The shape is the sample size; it represents independent and identically distributed draws or observations. Consider the normal distribution that we defined in the previous section:

```
normal = tfd.Normal(loc=0., scale=1.)
```

This defines a single normal distribution, with mean zero and standard deviation one. When we use the sample function, we do a random draw from this distribution.

Notice the details regarding batch_shape and event_shape if you print the object normal:

```
print(normal)
```

```
>>> tfp.distributions.Normal("Normal", batch_shape=[], event_shape=[],
dtype=float32)
```

Let us try and define a second normal object, but this time, loc and scale are lists:

```
normal_2 = tfd.Normal(loc=[0., 0.], scale=[1., 3.])
print(normal_2)
```

```
>>> tfp.distributions.Normal("Normal", batch_shape=[2], event_shape=[],
dtype=float32)
```

Did you notice the change in batch_shape? Now, if we draw a single sample from it, we will draw from two normal distributions, one with a mean of zero and standard deviation of one, and the other with a mean of zero and standard deviation of three. Thus, the batch shape determines the number of observations from the same distribution family. The two normal distributions are independent; thus, it is a batch of distributions of the same family.

You can have batches of the same type of distribution family, like in the preceding example of having two normal distributions. You cannot create a batch of, say, a normal and a Gaussian distribution.

What if we need a single normal distribution that is dependent on two variables, each with a different mean? This is made possible using `MultivariateNormalDiag`, and this influences the event shape – it is the atomic shape of a single draw or observation from this distribution:

```
normal_3 = tfd.MultivariateNormalDiag(loc = [[1.0, 0.3]])
print(normal_3)
```

```
>>> tfp.distributions.MultivariateNormalDiag("MultivariateNormalDiag", batch_
shape=[1], event_shape=[2], dtype=float32)
```

We can see that in the above output the event_shape has changed.

Using TFP distributions

Once you have defined a distribution, you can do a lot more. TFP provides a good range of functions to perform various operations. We have already used the `Normal` distribution and `sample` method. The section above also demonstrated how we can use TFP for creating univariate, multivariate, or independent distribution/s. TFP provides many important methods to interact with the created distributions. Some of the important ones include:

- `sample(n)`: It samples n observations from the distribution.
- `prob(value)`: It provides probability (discrete) or probability density (continuous) for the value.
- `log_prob(values)`: Provides log probability or log-likelihood for the values.
- `mean()`: It gives the mean of the distribution.
- `stddev()`: It provides the standard deviation of the distribution.

Coin Flip Example

Let us now use some of the features of TFP to describe data by looking at an example: the standard coin-flipping example we are familiar with from our school days. We know that if we flip a coin, there are only two possibilities – we can have either a head or a tail. Such a distribution, where we have only two discrete values, is called a **Bernoulli** distribution. So let us consider different scenarios:

Scenario 1

A fair coin with a 0.5 probability of heads and 0.5 probability of tails.

Let us create the distribution:

```
coin_flip = tfd.Bernoulli(probs=0.5, dtype=tf.int32)
```

Now get some samples:

```
coin_flip_data = coin_flip.sample(2000)
```

Let us visualize the samples:

```
plt.hist(coin_flip_data)
```

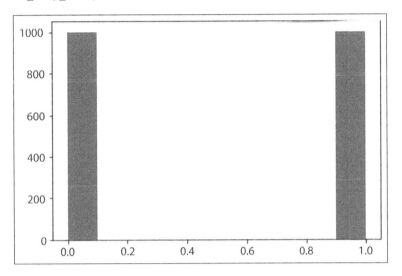

Figure 12.3: Distribution of heads and tails from 2,000 observations

You can see that we have both heads and tails in equal numbers; after all, it is a fair coin. The probability of heads and tails as 0.5:

```
coin_flip.prob(0) ## Probability of tail
```

```
>>> <tf.Tensor: shape=(), dtype=float32, numpy=0.5>
```

Scenario 2

A biased coin with a 0.8 probability of heads and 0.2 probability of tails.

Now, since the coin is biased, with the probability of heads being 0.8, the distribution would be created using:

```
bias_coin_flip = tfd.Bernoulli(probs=0.8, dtype=tf.int32)
```

Now get some samples:

```
bias_coin_flip_data = bias_coin_flip.sample(2000)
```

Let us visualize the samples:

```
plt.hist(bias_coin_flip_data)
```

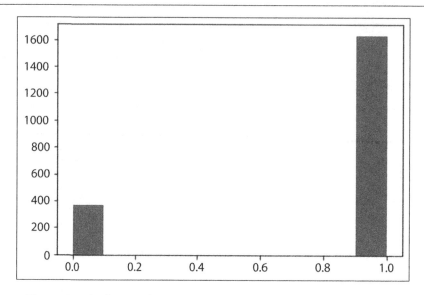

Figure 12.4: Distribution of heads and tails from 2,000 coin flips of a biased coin

We can see that now heads are much larger in number than tails. Thus, the probability of tails is no longer 0.5:

```
bias_coin_flip.prob(0) ## Probability of tail
```

```
>>> <tf.Tensor: shape=(), dtype=float32, numpy=0.19999999>
```

You will probably get a number close to 0.2.

Scenario 3

Two coins with one biased toward heads with a 0.8 probability, and the other biased toward heads with a 0.6 probability.

Now, we have two independent coins. Since the coins are biased, with the probabilities of heads being 0.8 and 0.6 respectively, we create a distribution using:

```
two_bias_coins_flip = tfd.Bernoulli(probs=[0.8, 0.6], dtype=tf.int32)
```

Now get some samples:

```
two_bias_coins_flip_data = two_bias_coins_flip.sample(2000)
```

Let us visualize the samples:

```
plt.hist(two_bias_coins_flip_data[:,0], alpha=0.8, label='Coin 1')
plt.hist(two_bias_coins_flip_data[:,1], alpha=0.5, label='Coin 2')
plt.legend(loc='center')
```

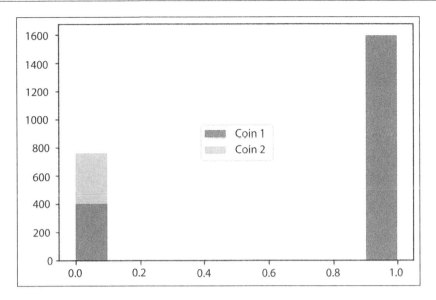

Figure 12.5: Distribution of heads and tails from 2,000 flips for two independent coins

The bar in blue corresponds to Coin 1, and the bar in orange corresponds to Coin 2. The brown part of the graphs is the area where the results of the two coins overlap. You can see that for Coin 1, the number of heads is much larger as compared to Coin 2, as expected.

Normal distribution

We can use the Bernoulli distribution where the data can have only two possible discrete values: heads and tails, good and bad, spam and ham, and so on. However, a large amount of data in our daily lives is continuous in range, with the normal distribution being very common. So let us also explore different normal distributions.

Mathematically, the probability density function of a normal distribution can be expressed as:

$$f(x; \mu, \sigma) = \frac{1}{\sigma\sqrt{2\pi}} \exp\left(-\frac{1}{2}\left(\frac{x - \mu}{\sigma}\right)^2\right)$$

where μ is the mean of the distribution, and σ is the standard deviation.

In TFP, the parameter loc represents the mean and the parameter scale represents the standard deviation. Now, to illustrate the use of how we can use distribution, let us consider that we want to represent the weather data of a location for a particular season, say summer in Delhi, India.

Univariate normal

We can think that weather depends only on temperature. So, by having a sample of temperature in the summer months over many years, we can get a good representation of data. That is, we can have a univariate normal distribution.

Now, based on weather data, the average high temperature in the month of June in Delhi is 35 degrees Celsius, with a standard deviation of 4 degrees Celsius. So, we can create a normal distribution using:

```
temperature = tfd.Normal(loc=35, scale = 4)
```

Get some observation samples from it:

```
temperature_data = temperature.sample(1000)
```

And let us now visualize it:

```
sns.displot(temperature_data, kde= True)
```

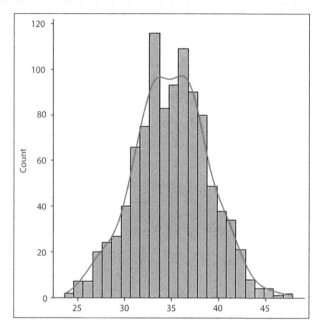

Figure 12.6: Probability density function for the temperature of Delhi in the month of June

It would be good to verify if the mean and standard deviation of our sample data is close to the values we described.

Using the distribution, we can find the mean and standard deviation using:

```
temperature.mean()
```

```
# output
>>> <tf.Tensor: shape=(), dtype=float32, numpy=35.0>
```

```
temperature.stddev()
```

```
# output
>>> <tf.Tensor: shape=(), dtype=float32, numpy=4.0>
```

And from the sampled data, we can verify using:

```
tf.math.reduce_mean(temperature_data)
```

```
# output
>>> <tf.Tensor: shape=(), dtype=float32, numpy=35.00873>
```

```
tf.math.reduce_std(temperature_data)
```

```
# output
>>> <tf.Tensor: shape=(), dtype=float32, numpy=3.9290223>
```

Thus, the sampled data is following the same mean and standard deviation.

Multivariate distribution

All is good so far. I show my distribution to a friend working in meteorology, and he says that using only temperature is not sufficient; the humidity is also important. So now, each weather point depends on two parameters – the temperature of the day and the humidity of the day. This type of data distribution can be obtained using the MultivariateNormalDiag distribution class, as defined in TFP:

```
weather = tfd.MultivariateNormalDiag(loc = [35, 56], scale_diag=[4, 15])
weather_data = weather.sample(1000)
plt.scatter(weather_data[:, 0], weather_data[:, 1], color='blue', alpha=0.4)
plt.xlabel("Temperature Degree Celsius")
plt.ylabel("Humidity %")
```

Figure 12.7, shows the multivariate normal distribution of two variables, temperature and humidity, generated using TFP:

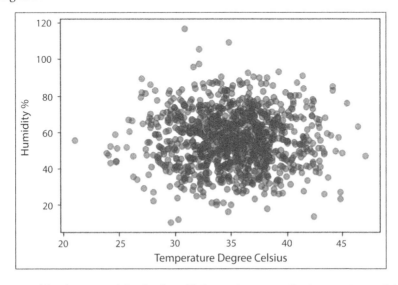

Figure 12.7: Multivariate normal distribution with the x-axis representing temperature and the y-axis humidity

Using the different distributions and bijectors available in TFP, we can generate synthetic data that follows the same joint distribution as real data to train the model.

Bayesian networks

Bayesian Networks (BNs) make use of the concepts from graph theory, probability, and statistics to encapsulate complex causal relationships. Here, we build a **Directed Acyclic Graph (DAG)**, where nodes, called factors (random variables), are connected by the arrows representing cause-effect relationships. Each node represents a variable with an associated probability (also called a **Conditional Probability Table (CPT)**). The links tell us about the dependence of one node over another. Though they were first proposed by Pearl in 1988, they have regained attention in recent years. The main cause of this renowned interest in BNs is that standard deep learning models are not able to represent the cause-effect relationship.

Their strength lies in the fact that they can be used to model uncertainties combined with expert knowledge and data. They have been employed in diverse fields for their power to do probabilistic and causal reasoning. At the heart of the Bayesian network is Bayes' rule:

$$P(A|B) = \frac{P(B|A)P(A)}{P(B)}$$

Bayes' rule is used to determine the joint probability of an event given certain conditions. The simplest way to understand the BN is that the BN can determine the causal relationship between the hypothesis and evidence. There is some unknown hypothesis H, about which we want to assess the uncertainty and make some decisions. We start with some prior belief about hypothesis H, and then based on evidence E, we update our belief about H.

Let us try to understand it by example. We consider a very standard example: a garden with grass and a sprinkler. Now, using common sense, we know that if the sprinkler is on, the grass is wet. Let us now reverse the logic: what if you come back home and find that the grass is wet, what is the probability that the sprinkler is on, and what is the probability that it actually rained? Interesting, right? Let us add further evidence – you find that the sky is cloudy. Now, what do you think is the reason for the grass being wet?

This sort of reasoning based on evidence is encompassed by BNs in the form of DAGs, also called causal graphs – because they provide an insight into the cause-effect relationship.

To model the problem, we make use of the `JointDistributionCoroutine` distribution class. This distribution allows both the sampling of data and computation of the joint probability from a single model specification. Let us make some assumptions to build the model:

- The probability that it is cloudy is 0.2
- The probability that it is cloudy and it rains is 0.8, and the probability that it is not cloudy but it rains is 0.1
- The probability that it is cloudy and the sprinkler is on is 0.1, and the probability that it is not cloudy and the sprinkler is on is 0.5

• Now, for the grass, we have four possibilities:

Sprinkler	Rain	Grass Wet
F	F	0
F	T	0.8
T	F	0.9
T	T	0.99

Table 12.1: The conditional probability table for the Sprinkler-Rain-Grass scenario

Figure 12.8 shows the corresponding BN DAG:

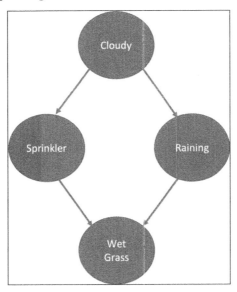

Figure 12.8: Bayesian Network for our toy problem

This information can be represented by the following model:

```
Root = tfd.JointDistributionCoroutine.Root
def model():
  # generate the distribution for cloudy weather
  cloudy = yield Root(tfd.Bernoulli(probs=0.2, dtype=tf.int32))
  # define sprinkler probability table
  sprinkler_prob = [0.5, 0.1]
  sprinkler_prob = tf.gather(sprinkler_prob, cloudy)
  sprinkler = yield tfd.Bernoulli(probs=sprinkler_prob, dtype=tf.int32)
  # define rain probability table
  raining_prob = [0.1, 0.8]
  raining_prob = tf.gather(raining_prob, cloudy)
  raining = yield tfd.Bernoulli(probs=raining_prob, dtype=tf.int32)
```

```
#Conditional Probability table for wet grass
grass_wet_prob = [[0.0, 0.8],
                  [0.9, 0.99]]
grass_wet_prob = tf.gather_nd(grass_wet_prob, _stack(sprinkler, raining))
grass_wet = yield tfd.Bernoulli(probs=grass_wet_prob, dtype=tf.int32)
```

The above model will function like a data generator. The Root function is used to tell the node in the graph without any parent. We define a few utility functions, broadcast and stack:

```
def _conform(ts):
  """Broadcast all arguments to a common shape."""

  shape = functools.reduce(
      tf.broadcast_static_shape, [a.shape for a in ts])
  return [tf.broadcast_to(a, shape) for a in ts]

def _stack(*ts):
  return tf.stack(_conform(ts), axis=-1)
```

To do inferences, we make use of the `MarginalizableJointDistributionCoroutine` class, as this allows us to compute marginalized probabilities:

```
d = marginalize.MarginalizableJointDistributionCoroutine(model)
```

Now, based on our observations, we can obtain the probability of other factors.

Case 1:

We observe that the grass is wet (the observation corresponding to this is 1 – if the grass was dry, we would set it to 0), we have no idea about the state of the clouds or the state of the sprinkler (the observation corresponding to an unknown state is set to "marginalize"), and we want to know the probability of rain (the observation corresponding to the probability we want to find is set to "tabulate"). Converting this into observations:

```
observations = ['marginalize', # We don't know the cloudy state
                'tabulate', # We want to know the probability of rain
                'marginalize', # We don't know the sprinkler state.
                1]              # We observed a wet lawn.
```

Now we get the probability of rain using:

```
p = tf.exp(d.marginalized_log_prob(observations))
p = p / tf.reduce_sum(p)
```

The result is array([0.27761015, 0.72238994], dtype=float32), that is, there is a 0.722 probability that it rained.

Case 2:

We observe that the grass is wet, we have no idea about the state of the clouds or rain, and we want to know the probability of whether the sprinkler is on. Converting this into observations:

```
observations = ['marginalize',
                'marginalize',
                'tabulate',
                1]
```

This results in probabilities `array([0.61783344, 0.38216656], dtype=float32)`, that is, there is a `0.382` probability that the sprinkler is on.

Case 3:

What if we observe that there is no rain, and the sprinkler is off? What do you think is the state of the grass? Logic says the grass should not be wet. Let us confirm this from the model by sending it the observations:

```
observations = ['marginalize',
                0,
                0,
                'tabulate']
```

This results in the probabilities `array([1., 0], dtype=float32)`, that is, there is a 100% probability that the grass is dry, just the way we expected.

As you can see, once we know the state of the parents, we do not need to know the state of the parent's parents – that is, the BN follows the local Markov property. In the example that we covered here, we started with the structure, and we had the conditional probabilities available to us. We demonstrate how we can do inference based on the model, and how despite the same model and CPDs, the evidence changes the **posterior probabilities**.

 In Bayesian networks, the structure (the nodes and how they are interconnected) and the parameters (the conditional probabilities of each node) are learned from the data. They are referred to as structured learning and parameter learning respectively. Covering the algorithms for structured learning and parameter learning are beyond the scope of this chapter.

Handling uncertainty in predictions using TensorFlow Probability

At the beginning of this chapter, we talked about the uncertainties in prediction by deep learning models and how the existing deep learning architectures are not able to account for those uncertainties. In this chapter, we will use the layers provided by TFP to model uncertainty.

Before adding the TFP layers, let us first understand the uncertainties a bit. There are two classes of uncertainty.

Aleatory uncertainty

This exists because of the random nature of the natural processes. It is inherent uncertainty, present due to the probabilistic variability. For example, when tossing a coin, there will always be a certain degree of uncertainty in predicting whether the next toss will be heads or tails. There is no way to remove this uncertainty. In essence, every time you repeat the experiment, the results will have certain variations.

Epistemic uncertainty

This uncertainty comes from a lack of knowledge. There can be various reasons for this lack of knowledge, for example, an inadequate understanding of the underlying processes, an incomplete knowledge of the phenomena, and so on. This type of uncertainty can be reduced by understanding the reason, for example, to get more data, we conduct more experiments.

The presence of these uncertainties increases risk. We require a way to quantify these uncertainties and, hence, quantify the risk.

Creating a synthetic dataset

In this section, we will learn how to modify the standard deep neural networks to quantify uncertainties. Let us start with creating a synthetic dataset. To create the dataset, we consider that output prediction y depends on input x linearly, as given by the following expression:

$$y_i = 2.7x_i + 3 + 0.74\varepsilon$$

Here, $\varepsilon \sim N(0,1)$ follows a normal distribution with mean zero and standard deviation 1 around x. The function below will generate this synthetic data for us. Do observe that to generate this data, we made use of the Uniform distribution and Normal distributions available as part of TFP distributions:

```
def create_dataset(n, x_range):
    x_uniform_dist = tfd.Uniform(low=x_range[0], high=x_range[1])
    x = x_uniform_dist.sample(n).numpy() [:, np.newaxis]
    y_true = 2.7*x+3
    eps_uniform_dist = tfd.Normal(loc=0, scale=1)
    eps = eps_uniform_dist.sample(n).numpy() [:, np.newaxis] *0.74*x
    y = y_true + eps
    return x, y, y_true
```

y_true is the value without including the normal distributed noise ε.

Now we use it to create a training dataset and a validation dataset:

```
x_train, y_train, y_true = create_dataset(2000, [-10, 10])
x_val, y_val, _ = create_dataset(500, [-10, 10])
```

This will give us 2,000 datapoints for training and 500 datapoints for validation. *Figure 12.9* shows the plots of the two datasets, with ground truth (the value of y in the absence of any noise) in the background:

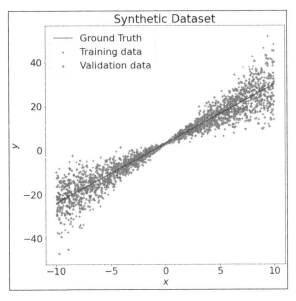

Figure 12.9: Plot of the synthetic dataset

Building a regression model using TensorFlow

We can build a simple Keras model to perform the task of regression on the synthetic dataset created in the preceding section:

```
# Model Architecture
model = Sequential([Dense(1, input_shape=(1,))])


# Compile
model.compile(loss='mse', optimizer='adam')


# Fit
model.fit(x_train, y_train, epochs=100, verbose=1)
```

Let us see how good the fitted model works on the test dataset:

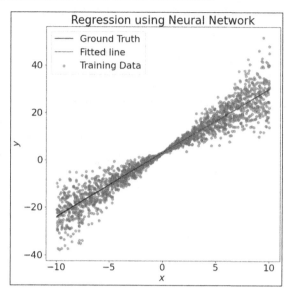

Figure 12.10: Ground truth and fitted regression line

It was a simple problem, and we can see that the fitted regression line almost overlaps the ground truth. However, there is no way to tell the uncertainty of predictions.

Probabilistic neural networks for aleatory uncertainty

What if instead of linear regression, we build a model that can fit the distribution? In our synthetic dataset, the source of aleatory uncertainty is the noise, and we know that our noise follows a normal distribution, which is characterized by two parameters: the mean and standard deviation. So, we can modify our model to predict the mean and standard deviation distributions instead of actual y values. We can accomplish this using either the `IndependentNormal` TFP layer or the `DistributionLambda` TFP layer. The following code defines the modified model architecture:

```
model = Sequential([Dense(2, input_shape = (1,)),
    tfp.layers.DistributionLambda(lambda t: tfd.Normal(loc=t[..., :1],
scale=0.3+tf.math.abs(t[...,1:])))
])
```

We will need to make one more change. Earlier, we predicted the *y* value; therefore, the mean square error loss was a good choice. Now, we are predicting the distribution; therefore, a better choice is the negative log-likelihood as the loss function:

```
# Define negative loglikelihood loss function
def neg_loglik(y_true, y_pred):
    return -y_pred.log_prob(y_true)
```

Let us now train this new model:

```
model.compile(loss=neg_loglik, optimizer='adam')


# Fit
model.fit(x_train, y_train, epochs=500, verbose=1)
```

Since now our model returns a distribution, we require the statistics mean and standard deviation for the test dataset:

```
# Summary Statistics
y_mean = model(x_test).mean()
y_std = model(x_test).stddev()
```

Note that the predicted mean now corresponds to the fitted line in the first case. Let us now see the plots:

```
fig = plt.figure(figsize = (20, 10))
plt.scatter(x_train, y_train, marker='+', label='Training Data', alpha=0.5)
plt.plot(x_train, y_true, color='k', label='Ground Truth')
plt.plot(x_test, y_mean, color='r', label='Predicted Mean')
plt.fill_between(np.squeeze(x_test), np.squeeze(y_mean+1*y_std), np.squeeze(y_
mean-1*y_std), alpha=0.6, label='Aleatory Uncertainty (1SD)')
plt.fill_between(np.squeeze(x_test), np.squeeze(y_mean+2*y_std), np.squeeze(y_
mean-2*y_std), alpha=0.4, label='Aleatory Uncertainty (2SD)')
plt.title('Aleatory Uncertainty')
plt.xlabel('$x$')
plt.ylabel('$y$')
plt.legend()
plt.show()
```

The following curve shows the fitted line, along with the aleatory uncertainty:

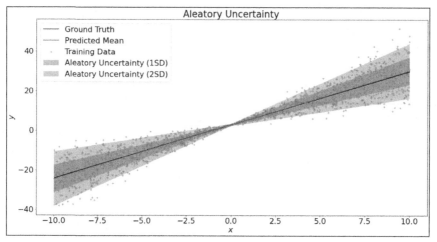

Figure 12.11: Modelling aleatory uncertainty using TFP layers

You can see that our model shows less uncertainty near the origin, but as we move further away, the uncertainty increases.

Accounting for the epistemic uncertainty

In conventional neural networks, each weight is represented by a single number, and it is updated such that the loss of the model with respect to its weight is minimized. We assume that weights so learned are the optimum weights. But are they? To answer this question, we replace each weight with a distribution, and instead of learning a single value, we will now make our model learn a set of parameters for each weight distribution. This is accomplished by replacing the Keras Dense layer with the DenseVariational layer. The DenseVariational layer uses a variational posterior over the weights to represent the uncertainty in their values. It tries to regularize the posterior to be close to the prior distribution. Hence, to use the DenseVariational layer, we will need to define two functions, one prior generating function and another posterior generating function. We use the posterior and prior functions defined at https://www.tensorflow.org/probability/examples/Probabilistic_Layers_Regression.

Our model now has two layers, a DenseVariational layer followed by a DistributionLambda layer:

```
model = Sequential([
  tfp.layers.DenseVariational(1, posterior_mean_field, prior_trainable, kl_
weight=1/x_train.shape[0]),
  tfp.layers.DistributionLambda(lambda t: tfd.Normal(loc=t, scale=1)),
])
```

Again, as we are looking for distributions, the loss function that we use is the negative log-likelihood function:

```
model.compile(optimizer=tf.optimizers.Adam(learning_rate=0.01), loss=negloglik)
```

We continue with the same synthetic data that we created earlier and train the model:

```
model.fit(x_train, y_train, epochs=100, verbose=1)
```

Now that the model has been trained, we make the prediction, and to understand the concept of uncertainty, we make multiple predictions for the same input ranges. We can see the difference in variance in the result in the following graphs:

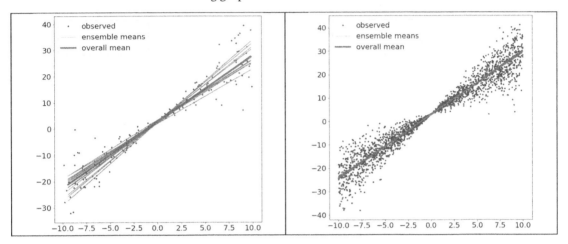

Figure 12.12: Epistemic uncertainty

Figure 12.12 shows two graphs, one when only 200 training data points were used to build the model, and the second when 2,000 data points were used to train the model. We can see that when there is more data, the variance and, hence, the epistemic uncertainty reduces. Here, *overall mean* refers to the mean of all the predictions (100 in number), and in the case of *ensemble mean*, we considered only the first 15 predictions. All machine learning models suffer from some level of uncertainty in predicting outcomes. Getting an estimate or quantifiable range of uncertainty in the prediction will help AI users build more confidence in their AI predictions and will boost overall AI adoption.

Summary

This chapter introduced TensorFlow Probability, the library built over TensorFlow to perform probabilistic reasoning and statistical analysis. The chapter started with the need for probabilistic reasoning – the uncertainties both due to the inherent nature of data and due to a lack of knowledge. We demonstrated how to use TensorFlow Probability distributions to generate different data distributions. We learned how to build a Bayesian network and perform inference. Then, we built Bayesian neural networks using TFP layers to take into account aleatory uncertainty. Finally, we learned how to account for epistemic uncertainty with the help of the DenseVariational TFP layer.

In the next chapter, we will learn about TensorFlow AutoML frameworks.

References

1. Dillon, J. V., Langmore, I., Tran, D., Brevdo, E., Vasudevan, S., Moore, D., Patton, B., Alemi, A., Hoffman, M., and Saurous, R. A. (2017). *TensorFlow distributions*. arXiv preprint arXiv:1711.10604.

2. Piponi, D., Moore, D., and Dillon, J. V. (2020). *Joint distributions for TensorFlow probability*. arXiv preprint arXiv:2001.11819.

3. Fox, C. R. and Ülkümen, G. (2011). *Distinguishing Two Dimensions of Uncertainty*, in Essays in Judgment and Decision Making, Brun, W., Kirkebøen, G. and Montgomery, H., eds. Oslo: Universitetsforlaget.

4. Hüllermeier, E. and Waegeman, W. (2021). *Aleatoric and epistemic uncertainty in machine learning: An introduction to concepts and methods*. Machine Learning 110, no. 3: 457–506.

Join our book's Discord space

Join our Discord community to meet like-minded people and learn alongside more than 2000 members at: `https://packt.link/keras`

13

An Introduction to AutoML

The goal of AutoML is to enable domain experts who are unfamiliar with machine learning technologies to use ML techniques easily.

In this chapter, we will go through a practical exercise using Google Cloud Platform and do quite a bit of hands-on work after briefly discussing the fundamentals.

We will cover:

- Automatic data preparation
- Automatic feature engineering
- Automatic model generation
- AutoKeras
- Google Cloud AutoML with its multiple solutions for table, vision, text, translation, and video processing

Let's begin with an introduction to AutoML.

What is AutoML?

During the previous chapters, we introduced several models used in modern machine learning and deep learning. For instance, we have seen architectures such as dense networks, CNNs, RNNs, autoencoders, and GANs.

Two observations are in order. First, these architectures are manually designed by deep learning experts and are not necessarily easy to explain to non-experts. Second, the composition of these architectures themselves was a manual process, which involved a lot of human intuition and trial and error.

Today, one primary goal of artificial intelligence research is to achieve **Artificial General Intelligence** (**AGI**) – the intelligence of a machine that can understand and automatically learn any type of work or activity that a human being can do. It should be noted that many researchers do not believe that AGI is achievable because there is not only one form of intelligence but many forms.

Personally, I tend to agree with this view. See `https://twitter.com/ylecun/status/1526672565233758213` for Yann LeCun's position on this subject. However, the reality was very different before AutoML research and industrial applications started. Indeed, before AutoML, designing deep learning architectures was very similar to crafting – the activity or hobby of making decorative articles by hand.

Take, for instance, the task of recognizing breast cancer from X-rays. After reading the previous chapters, you will probably think that a deep learning pipeline created by composing several CNNs may be an appropriate tool for this purpose. That is probably a good intuition to start with. The problem is that it is not easy to explain to the users of your model why a *particular* composition of CNN works well within the breast cancer detection domain. Ideally, you want to provide easily accessible deep learning tools to the domain experts (in this case, medical professionals) without such a tool requiring a strong machine learning background.

The other problem is that it is not easy to understand whether or not there are variants (for example, different compositions) of the original manually crafted model that can achieve better results. Ideally, you want to provide deep learning tools for exploring the space of variants (for example, different compositions) in a more principled and automatic way.

So, the central idea of AutoML is to reduce the steep learning curve and the huge costs of handcrafting machine learning solutions by making the whole end-to-end machine learning pipeline more automated. To this end, we assume that the AutoML pipeline consists of three macro-steps: data preparation, feature engineering, and automatic model generation, as shown in *Figure 13.1*:

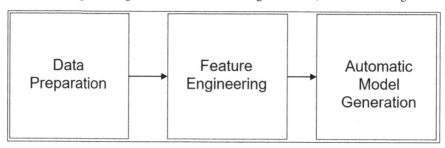

Figure 13.1: Three steps of an AutoML pipeline

Throughout the initial part of this chapter, we are going to discuss these three steps in detail. Then, we will focus on Google Cloud AutoML.

Achieving AutoML

How can AutoML achieve the goal of end-to-end automatization? Well, you have probably already guessed that a natural choice is to use machine learning – that's very cool. AutoML uses ML for automating ML pipelines.

What are the benefits? Automating the creation and tuning of machine learning end to end offers simpler solutions, reduces the time to produce them, and ultimately might produce architectures that could potentially outperform models that were crafted by hand.

Is this a closed research area? Quite the opposite. At the beginning of 2022, AutoML is a very open research field, which is not surprising, as the initial paper drawing attention to AutoML was published at the end of 2016.

Automatic data preparation

The first stage of a typical machine learning pipeline deals with data preparation (recall the pipeline in *Figure 13.1*). There are two main aspects that should be taken into account: data cleansing and data synthesis:

Data cleansing is about improving the quality of data by checking for wrong data types, missing values, and errors, and by applying data normalization, bucketization, scaling, and encoding. A robust AutoML pipeline should automate all of these mundane but extremely important steps as much as possible.

Data synthesis is about generating synthetic data via augmentation for training, evaluation, and validation. Normally, this step is domain-specific. For instance, we have seen how to generate synthetic CIFAR10-like images (*Chapter 4*) by using cropping, rotation, resizing, and flipping operations. One can also think about generating additional images or video via GANs (see *Chapter 9*) and using the augmented synthetic dataset for training. A different approach should be taken for text, where it is possible to train RNNs (*Chapter 5*) to generate synthetic text or to adopt more NLP techniques such as BERT, Seq2Seq, or Transformers (see *Chapter 6*) to annotate or translate text across languages and then translate it back to the original one – another domain-specific form of augmentation.

A different approach is to generate synthetic environments where machine learning can occur. This became very popular in reinforcement learning and gaming, especially with toolkits such as OpenAI Gym, which aims to provide an easy-to-set-up simulation environment with a variety of different (gaming) scenarios.

Put simply, we can say that synthetic data generation is another option that should be provided by AutoML engines. Frequently, the tools used are very domain-specific and what works for image or video would not necessarily work in other domains such as text. Therefore, we need a (quite) large set of tools for performing synthetic data generation across domains.

Automatic feature engineering

Feature engineering is the second step of a typical machine learning pipeline (see *Figure 13.1*). It consists of three major steps: feature selection, feature construction, and feature mapping. Let's look at each of them in turn:

Feature selection aims at selecting a subset of *meaningful* features by discarding those that are making little contribution to the learning task. In this context, "meaningful" truly depends on the application and the domain of your specific problem.

Feature construction has the goal of building new derived features, starting from the basic ones. Frequently, this technique is used to allow better generalization and to have a richer representation of the data.

Feature mapping aims at altering the original feature space by means of a mapping function. This can be implemented in multiple ways; for instance, it can use autoencoders (see *Chapter 8*), PCA (see *Chapter 7*), or clustering (see *Chapter 7*).

In short, feature engineering is an art based on intuition, trial and error, and a lot of human experience. Modern AutoML engines aim to make the entire process more automated, requiring less human intervention.

Automatic model generation

Model generation and hyperparameter tuning is the typical third macro-step of a machine learning pipeline (see *Figure 13.1*).

Model generation consists of creating a suitable model for solving specific tasks. For instance, you will probably use CNNs for visual recognition, and you will use RNNs for either time series analysis or for sequences. Of course, many variants are possible, each of which is manually crafted through a process of trial and error and works for very specific domains.

Hyperparameter tuning happens once the model is manually crafted. This process is generally very computationally expensive and can significantly change the quality of the results in a positive way. That's because tuning the hyperparameters can help to optimize our model further.

Automatic model generation is the ultimate goal of any AutoML pipeline. How can this be achieved? One approach consists of generating the model by combining a set of primitive operations including convolution, pooling, concatenation, skip connections, recurrent neural networks, autoencoders, and pretty much all the deep learning models we have encountered throughout this book. These operations constitute a (typically very large) search space to be explored, and the goal is to make this exploration as efficient as possible. In AutoML jargon, the exploration is called **NAS**, or **Neural Architecture Search**. The seminal paper on AutoML [1] was produced in November 2016. The key idea (see *Figure 13.2*) is to use reinforcement learning (RL, see *Chapter 11*). An RNN acts as the controller, and it generates the model descriptions of candidate neural networks. RL is used to maximize the expected accuracy of the generated architectures on a validation set.

On the CIFAR-10 dataset, this method, starting from scratch, designed a novel network architecture that rivals the best human-invented architecture in terms of test set accuracy. The CIFAR-10 model achieves a test error rate of 3.65, which is 0.09 percent better and 1.05x faster than the previous state-of-the-art model that used a similar architectural scheme. On the Penn Treebank dataset, the model can compose a novel recurrent cell that outperforms the widely used LSTM cell (see *Chapter 9*) and other state-of-the-art baselines. The cell achieves a test set perplexity of 62.4 on the Penn Treebank, which is 3.6 better than the previous state-of-the-art model.

The key outcome of the paper is shown in *Figure 13.2*. A controller network based on RNNs produces a sample architecture A with probability p. This candidate architecture A is trained by a child network to get a candidate accuracy R. Then a gradient of p is computed and scaled by R to update the controller. This reinforcement learning operation is computed in a cycle a number of times. The process of generating an architecture stops if the number of layers exceeds a certain value.

The details of how an RL-based policy gradient method is used by the controller RNN to generate better architectures are in [1]. Here we emphasize the fact that NAS uses a meta-modeling algorithm based on Q-learning with an ϵ-greedy exploration strategy and with experience replay (see *Chapter 11*) to explore the model search space:

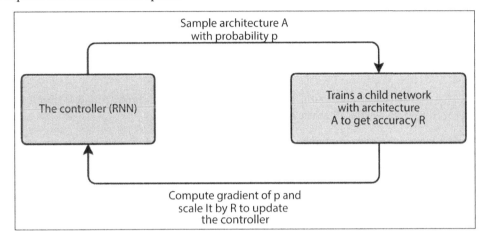

Figure 13.2: NAS with recurrent neural networks

Since the original paper in late 2016, a Cambrian explosion of model generation techniques has been observed. Initially, the goal was to generate the entire model in one single step. Later, a *cell-based* approach was proposed where the generation is divided into two macro-steps: first, a cell structure is automatically built, and then a predefined number of discovered cells are stacked together to generate an entire end-to-end architecture [2]. This **Efficient Neural Architecture Search (ENAS)** delivers strong empirical performance using significantly fewer GPU hours compared with all existing automatic model design approaches, and notably, is 1,000x less computationally expensive than standard neural architecture search (in 2018). Here, the primary ENAS goal is to reduce the search space via hierarchical composition. Variants of the cell-based approach have been proposed including pure hierarchical methods where higher-level cells are generated by incorporating lower-level cells iteratively.

A completely different approach to NAS is to use transfer learning (see *Chapter 5*) to transfer the learning of an existing neural network into a new neural network in order to speed up the design [3]. In other words, we want to use transfer learning in AutoML.

Another approach is based on **Genetic Programming (GP)** and **Evolutionary Algorithms (EAs)**, where the basic operations constituting the model search space are encoded into a suitable representation, and then this encoding is gradually mutated to progressively better models in a way that resembles the genetic evolution of living beings [4].

Hyperparameter tuning consists of finding the optimal combination of hyperparameters both related to learning optimization (batch size, learning rate, and so on) and model-specific ones (kernel size; number of feature maps and so on for CNNs; or number of neurons for dense or autoencoder networks, and so on). Again, the search space can be extremely large. There are three approaches generally used: Bayesian optimization, grid search, and random search.

Bayesian optimization builds a probability model of the objective function and uses it to select the most promising hyperparameters to evaluate in the true objective function.

Grid search divides the search space into a discrete grid of values and tests all the possible combinations in the grid. For instance, if there are three hyperparameters and a grid with only two candidate values for each of them, then a total of 2 x 3 = 6 combinations must be checked. There are also hierarchical variants of grid search, which progressively refine the grid for regions of the search space and provide better results. The key idea is to use a coarse grid first, and after finding a better grid region, implement a finer grid search on that region.

Random search performs a random sampling of the parameter search space, and this simple approach has been proven to work very well in many situations [5].

Now that we have briefly discussed the fundamentals, we will do quite a bit of hands-on work on Google Cloud. Let's start.

AutoKeras

AutoKeras [6] provides functions to automatically search for architecture and hyperparameters of deep learning models. The framework uses Bayesian optimization for efficient neural architecture search. You can install the alpha version by using `pip`:

```
pip3 install autokeras # for 1.19 version
```

The architecture is explained in *Figure 13.3* [6]:

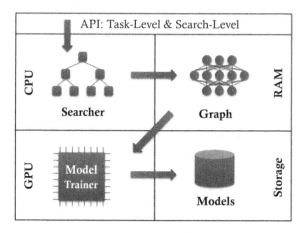

Figure 13.3: AutoKeras system overview

The architecture follows these steps:

1. The user calls the API.
2. The searcher generates neural architectures on the CPU.
3. Real neural networks with parameters are built on RAM from the neural architectures.

4. The neural network is copied to the GPU for training.
5. The trained neural networks are saved on storage devices.
6. The searcher is updated based on the training results.

Steps 2 to 6 will repeat until a time limit is reached.

Google Cloud AutoML and Vertex AI

Google Cloud AutoML (https://cloud.google.com/automl/) is a full suite of products for image, video, and text processing. AutoML can be used to train high-quality custom machine learning models with minimal effort and machine learning expertise.

Vertex AI brings together the Google Cloud services for building ML under one, unified UI and API. In Vertex AI, you can now easily train, compare, test, and deploy models. Then you can serve a model with sophisticated ways to monitor and run experiments (see https://cloud.google.com/vertex-ai).

As of 2022, the suite consists of the following components, which do not require you to know how the deep learning networks are shaped internally:

Vertex AI

- Unified platform to help you build, deploy, and scale more AI models

Structured data

- AutoML Tables: Automatically build and deploy state-of-the-art machine learning models on structured data

Sight

- AutoML Image: Derive insights from object detection and image classification, in the cloud or at the edge
- AutoML Video: Enable powerful content discovery and engaging video experiences

Language

- AutoML Text: Reveal the structure and meaning of text through machine learning
- AutoML Translation: Dynamically detect and translate between languages

In the remainder of this chapter, we will review three AutoML solutions: AutoML Tables, AutoML Text, and AutoML Video.

Using the Google Cloud AutoML Tables solution

Let's see an example of using Google Cloud AutoML Tables. We'll aim to import some tabular data and train a classifier on that data; we'll use some marketing data from a bank. Note that this and the following examples might be charged by Google according to different usage criteria (please check online for the latest cost estimation – see https://cloud.google.com/products/calculator/).

The first step required is to enable the Vertex AI API:

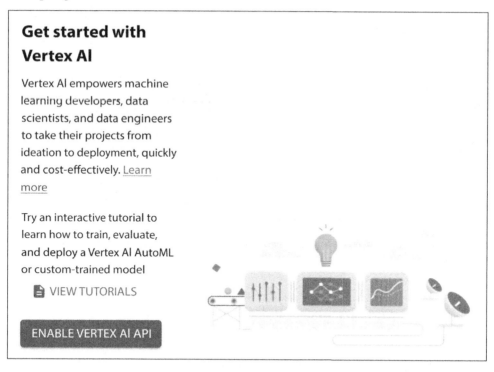

Figure 13.4: Enable the Vertex AI API

We can then select the **TABULAR** dataset from the console (see *Figure 13.5*). The name of the dataset is bank-marketing.csv:

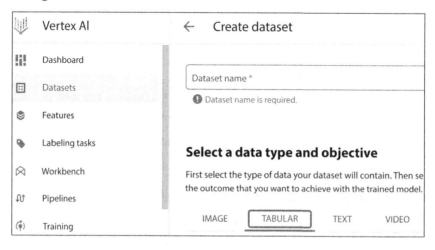

Figure 13.5: Selecting TABULAR datasets

On the next screen, we indicate that we want to load the data from CSV:

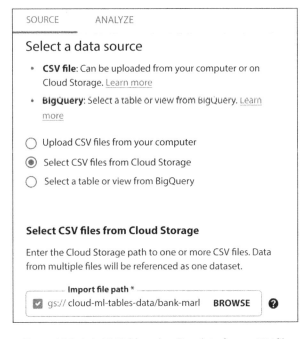

Figure 13.6: AutoML Tables – loading data from a CSV file

Next, we can train a new model, as shown in *Figure 13.7*:

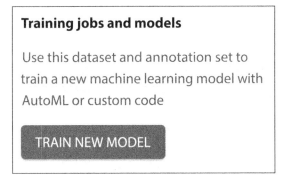

Figure 13.7: Training a new model

Several options for training are offered for **Classification** and **Regression:**

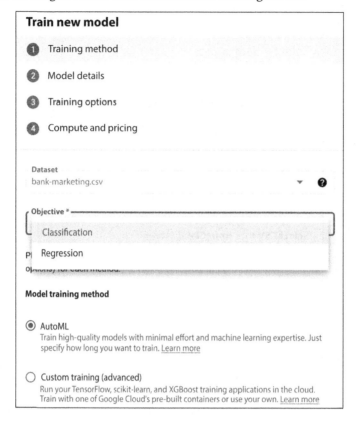

Figure 13.8: Options offered for Classification and Regression

Let's select the target as the **Deposit** column. The dataset is described at https://archive.ics.uci. edu/ml/datasets/bank+marketing. The data is related to direct marketing campaigns (phone calls) of a Portuguese banking institution. The classification goal is to predict if the client will subscribe to a term deposit.

Since the selected column is categorical data, AutoML Tables will build a classification model. This will predict the target from the classes in the selected column. The classification is binary: *1* represents a negative outcome, meaning that a deposit is not made at the bank; *2* represents a positive outcome, meaning that a deposit is made at the bank, as shown in *Figure 13.9*:

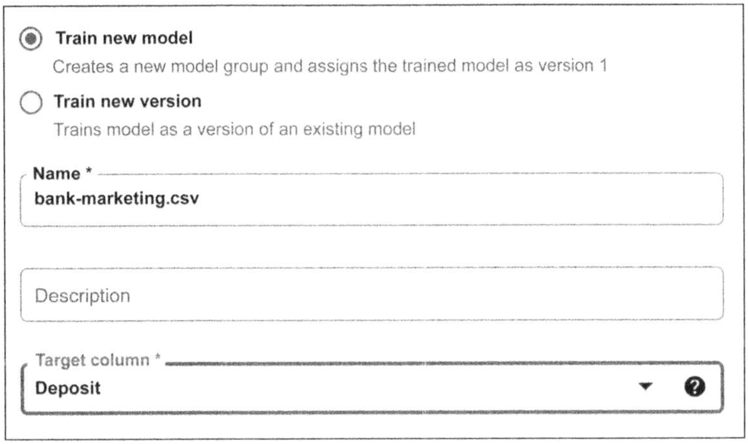

Figure 13.9: Training a new model with Target column set to Deposit

We can then inspect the dataset (see *Figure 13.10*), which gives us the opportunity to inspect the dataset with several features, such as *names, type, missing values, distinct values, invalid values, correlation with the target, mean,* and *standard deviation*:

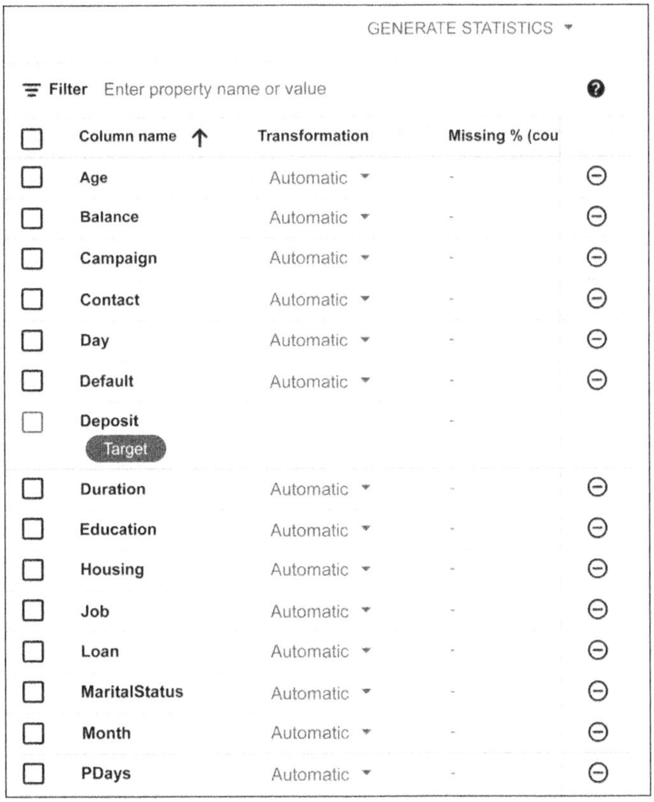

Figure 13.10: AutoML Tables – inspecting the dataset

It is now time to train the model by using the **Train** tab. First let's give a budget for training, as shown in *Figure 13.11*:

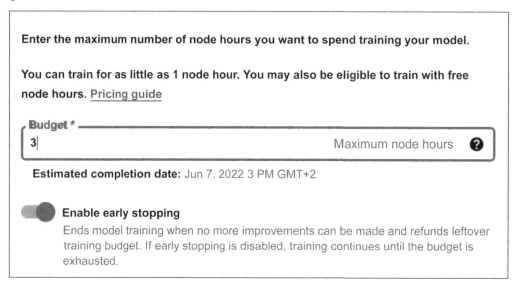

Figure 13.11: Setting up the budget for training

In this example, we accept **3** hours as our training budget. During this time, you can go and take a coffee whilst AutoML works on your behalf (see *Figure 13.12*). The training budget is a number between 1 and 72 for the maximum number of node hours to spend training your model. If your model stops improving before then, AutoML Tables will stop training and you'll only be charged the money corresponding to the actual node budget used:

Figure 13.12: AutoML Tables training process

While training, we can check the progress, as shown in *Figure 13.13*:

Figure 13.13: Checking the training progress

After less than one hour, Google AutoML should send an email to our inbox:

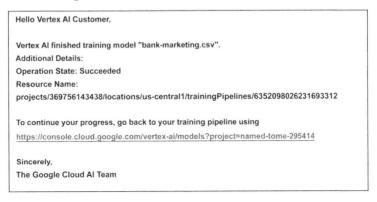

Figure 13.14: AutoML Tables: training is concluded, and an email is sent to my account

Clicking on the suggested URL, it is possible to see the results of our training. The AutoML-generated model reached an accuracy of 94% (see *Figure 13.15*). Remember that accuracy is the fraction of classification predictions produced by the model that were correct on a test, set which is held automatically. The log-loss (for example, the cross-entropy between the model predictions and the label values) is also provided. In the case of log-loss, a lower value indicates a higher-quality model:

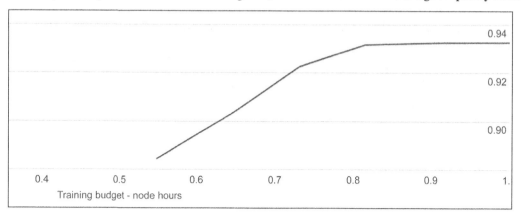

Figure 13.15: AutoML Tables – analyzing the results of our training

In addition, the **Area Under the Receiver Operating Characteristic Curve (AUC ROC)** is represented. This ranges from zero to one, and a higher value indicates a higher-quality model. This statistic summarizes an AUC ROC curve, which is a graph showing the performance of a classification model at all classification thresholds. The **True Positive Rate (TPR)** (also known as "recall") is:

$$TPR = \frac{TP}{TP + FN}$$

where *TP* is the number of true positives and *FN* is the number of false negatives. The **False Positive Rate (FPR)** is:

$$FPR = \frac{FP}{FP + TN}$$

where *FP* is the number of false positives and *TN* is the number of true negatives.

A ROC curve plots TPR vs. FPR at different classification thresholds. In *Figure 13.16* you will see the **Area Under the Curve (AUC)** for one threshold of a ROC curve:

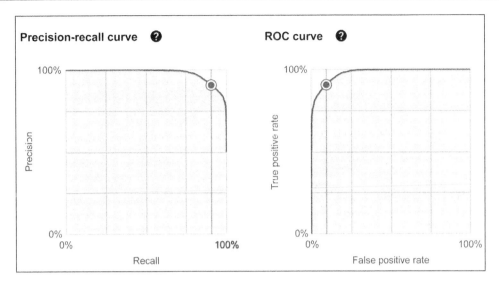

Figure 13.16: AutoML Tables – deep dive on the results of our training

It is possible to deep dive into the evaluation and access the confusion matrix (see *Figure 13.17*):

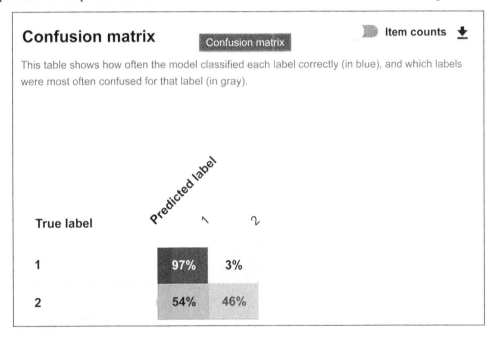

Figure 13.17: AutoML Tables – additional deep dive on the results of our training

Note that manually crafted models available in https://www.kaggle.com/uciml/adult-census-income/kernels get to an accuracy of ~86-90%. Therefore, our model generated with AutoML is definitively a very good result!

We can also have a look at the importance of each feature in isolation, as shown in *Figure 13.18*:

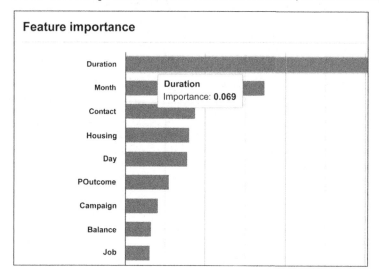

Figure 13.18: Specific importance of each feature considered in isolation

If we are happy with our results, we can then deploy the model in production via **DEPLOY & TEST** (see *Figure 13.19*). We can decide to create a Docker container deployable at the edge or we can simply use an endpoint. Let's go for this option and just use the default setting for each available choice:

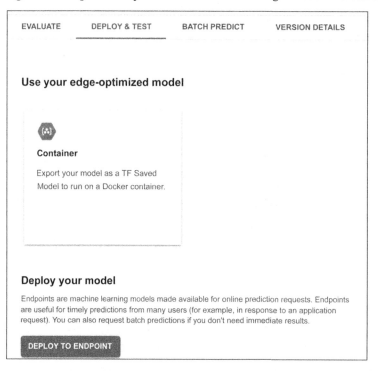

Figure 13.19: AutoML Tables – deploying in production

Then it is possible to make online predictions of income by using a REST API (see https://en.wikipedia.org/wiki/Representational_state_transfer), using this command for the example we're looking at in this chapter, as shown in *Figure 13.20*:

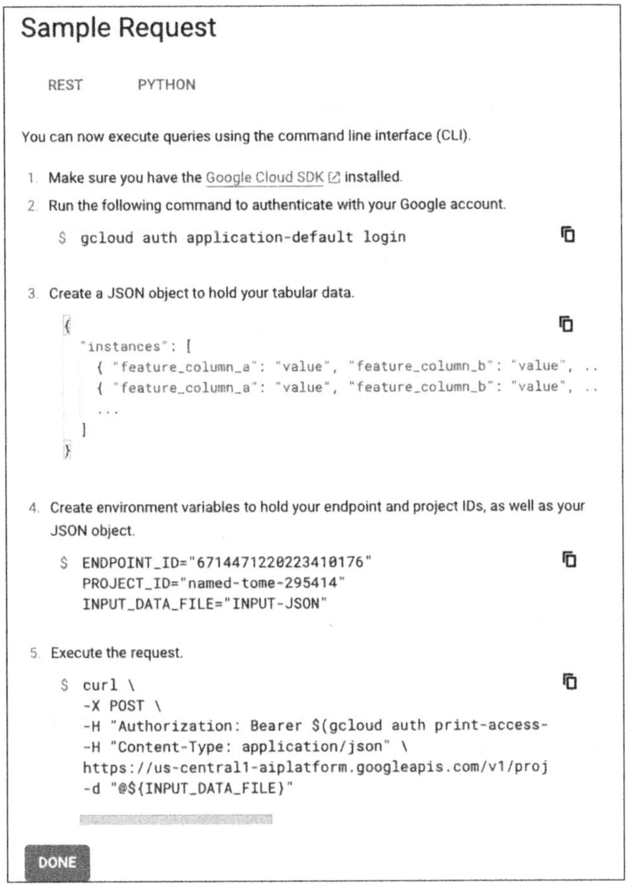

Sample Request

REST   PYTHON

You can now execute queries using the command line interface (CLI).

1. Make sure you have the Google Cloud SDK ↗ installed.
2. Run the following command to authenticate with your Google account.

```
$ gcloud auth application-default login
```

3. Create a JSON object to hold your tabular data.

```
{
  "instances": [
    { "feature_column_a": "value", "feature_column_b": "value", ..
    { "feature_column_a": "value", "feature_column_b": "value", ..
    ...
  ]
}
```

4. Create environment variables to hold your endpoint and project IDs, as well as your JSON object.

```
$ ENDPOINT_ID="6714471220223410176"
  PROJECT_ID="named-tome-295414"
  INPUT_DATA_FILE="INPUT-JSON"
```

5. Execute the request.

```
$ curl \
  -X POST \
  -H "Authorization: Bearer $(gcloud auth print-access-
  -H "Content-Type: application/json" \
  https://us-central1-aiplatform.googleapis.com/v1/proj
  -d "@${INPUT_DATA_FILE}"
```

DONE

Figure 13.20: AutoML Tables – querying the deployed model in production

Put simply, we can say that Google Cloud ML is very focused on simplicity of use and efficiency for AutoML. Let's summarize the main steps required (see *Figure 13.21*):

1. The dataset is imported.
2. Your dataset schema and labels are defined.
3. The input features are automatically recognized.
4. AutoML performs magic by automatically doing feature engineering, creating a model, and tuning the hyperparameters.
5. The automatically built model can then be evaluated.
6. The model is then deployed in production.

Of course, it is possible to repeat the steps 2-6 by changing the schema and the definition of the labels.

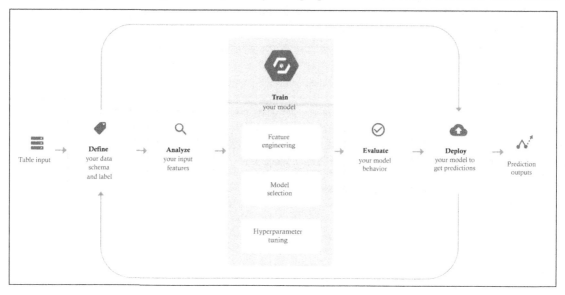

Figure 13.21: AutoML Tables – the main steps required

In this section, we have seen an example of AutoML focused on ease of use and efficiency. The progress made is shown in Faes et al. [7], quoting the paper:

> *"We show, to our knowledge, a first of its kind automated design and implementation of deep learning models for health-care application by non-AI experts, namely physicians. Although comparable performance to expert-tuned medical image classification algorithms was obtained in internal validations of binary and multiple classification tasks, more complex challenges, such as multilabel classification, and external validation of these models was insufficient. We believe that AI might advance medical care by improving efficiency of triage to subspecialists and the personalisation of medicine through tailored prediction models. The automated approach to prediction model design improves access to this technology, thus facilitating engagement by the medical community and providing a medium through which clinicians can enhance their understanding of the advantages and potential pitfalls of AI integration."*

In this case, Cloud AutoML Tables has been used. So, let's look at another example.

Using the Google Cloud AutoML Text solution

In this section, we are going to build a classifier using AutoML. Let's create a dataset for text from the Vertex AI console. We want to focus on the task of single-label classification:

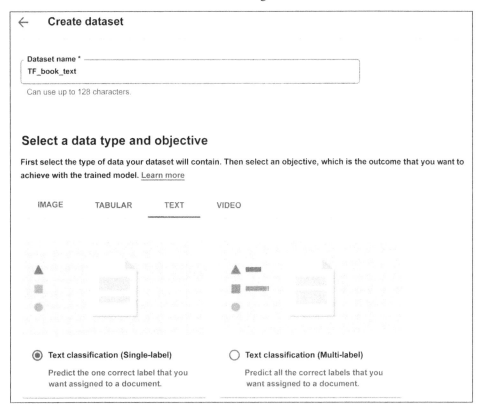

Figure 13.22: AutoML Text classification – creating a dataset

We are going to use a dataset already available online (the happy moments dataset is stored in `cloud-ml-data/NL-classification/happiness.csv`), load it into a dataset named **happiness**, and perform single-label classification (as shown in *Figure 13.23*). This can take several minutes or more.

We will be emailed once processing completes:

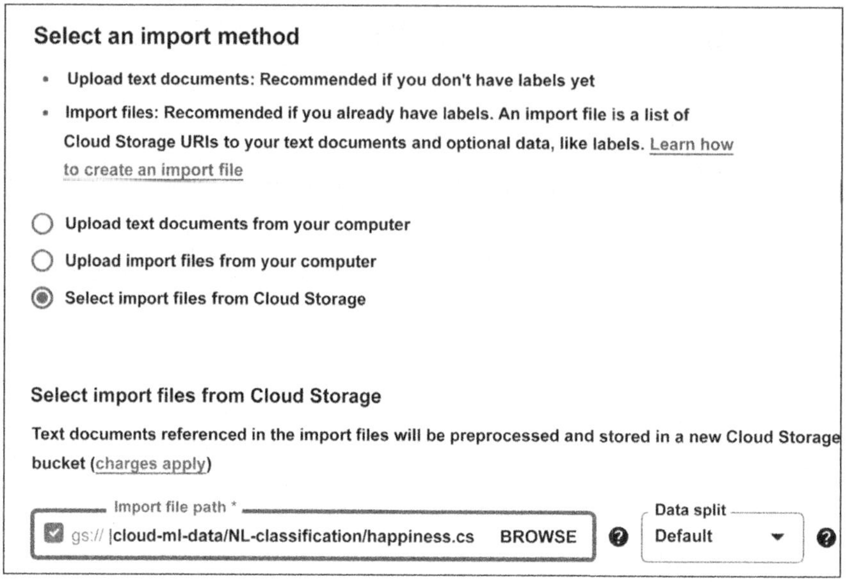

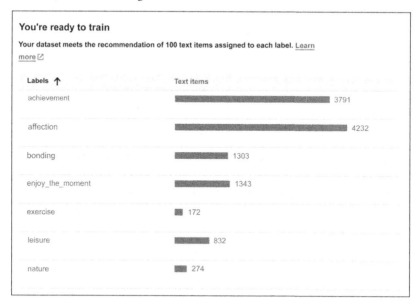

Figure 13.23: AutoML Text classification – creating the dataset

Once the dataset is loaded, you should be able to see that each text fragment is annotated with one category out of seven, as shown in *Figure 13.24*:

You're ready to train

Your dataset meets the recommendation of 100 text items assigned to each label. Learn more 🗗

Labels ↑	Text items
achievement	3791
affection	4232
bonding	1303
enjoy_the_moment	1343
exercise	172
leisure	832
nature	274

Figure 13.24: AutoML Text classification – a sample of categories

It is now time to start training the model:

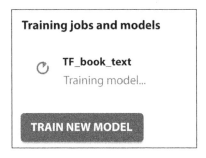

Figure 13.25: AutoML Text classification – start training

By the end, the model is built, and it achieves a good precision of 90.2% and recall of 86.7%:

Average precision ❓	0.959
Precision ❓	90.2%
Recall ❓	86.7%
Created	Jun 9, 2022, 3:05:42 PM
Total items	11,947
Training items	9,555
Validation items	1,207
Test items	1,185

Figure 13.26: AutoML Text classification – precision and recall

We can also have a look at the precision-recall curve and precision-recall by threshold (see *Figure 13.27*). These curves can be used to calibrate the classifier, calibrating on the threshold (based on the prediction probabilities that are greater than the threshold):

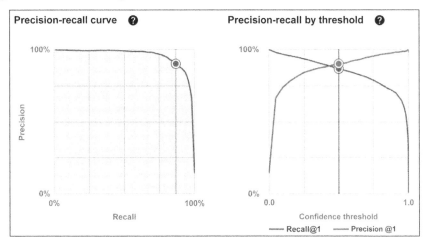

Figure 13.27: Precision-recall and Precision-recall by threshold

The confusion matrix is shown in *Figure 13.28*:

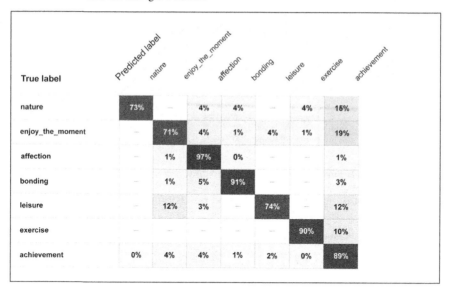

Figure 13.28: Confusion matrix for the text classification problem

Using the Google Cloud AutoML Video solution

In this solution, we are going to automatically build a new model for video classification. The intent is to be able to sort different video segments into various categories (or classes) based on their content. The first step is to create the dataset, as shown in *Figure 13.29*:

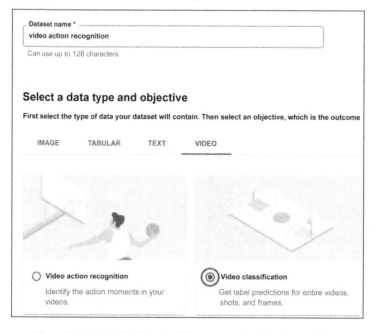

Figure 13.29: AutoML Video intelligence – a classification problem

We are going to use a collection of about 5,000 videos available in a demo already stored in a GCP bucket on `automl-video-demo-data/hmdb_split1_5classes_all.csv`, as shown in *Figure 13.30*:

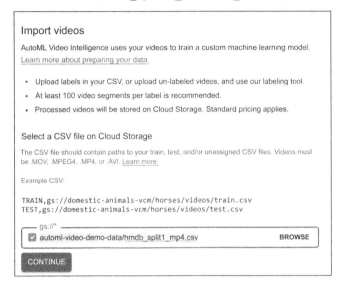

Figure 13.30. Importing the demo dataset

As usual, importing will take a while and we will be notified when it is done with an email. Once the videos are imported, we can preview them with their associated categories:

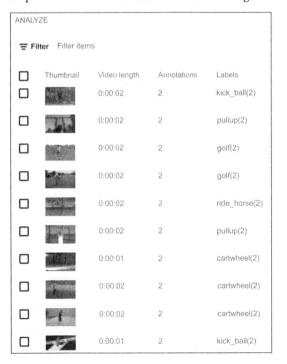

Figure 13.31: AutoML Video intelligence – imported video preview

We can now start to build a model. There are a number of options including training with AutoML, using AutoML at the edge for models to be exported at the edge, and custom models built on TensorFlow. Let's use the default, as shown in *Figure 13.32*:

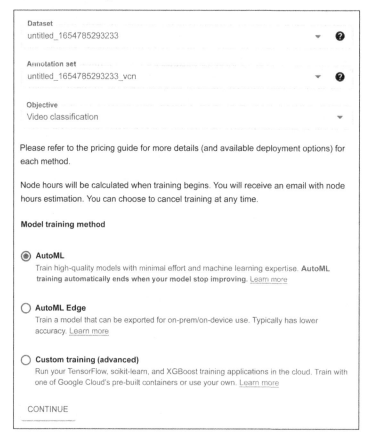

Figure 13.32: AutoML Video intelligence – warning to get more videos

In this case, we decide to run an experiment training with a few labels and divide the dataset into 20% training and 80% testing:

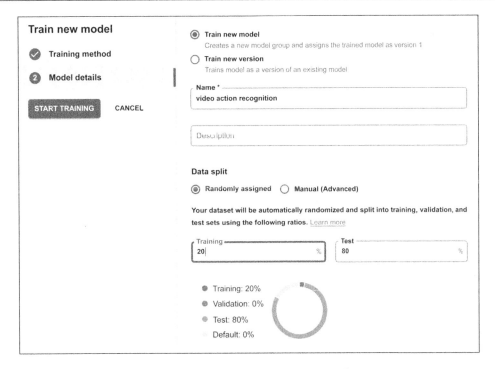

Figure 13.33: Test and Training dataset split

Once the model is trained, you can access the results from the console (*Figure 13.34*). In this case, we achieved a precision of 99.5% and a recall of 99.5% even though we were using only 20% of the labels for training in our experiment. We wanted to keep the training short and still achieve awesome results. You can play with the model, for instance, increasing the number of labeled videos available, to see how the performance will change:

All labels

Average precision ❓	1
Precision ❓	99.5%
Recall ❓	99.5%
Created	Jun 10, 2022, 11:24:44 AM
Training videos	100
Test videos	400

Figure 13.34: AutoML Video intelligence – evaluating the results

Let's have a detailed look at the results. For instance, we can analyze the precision/recall graph for different levels of threshold:

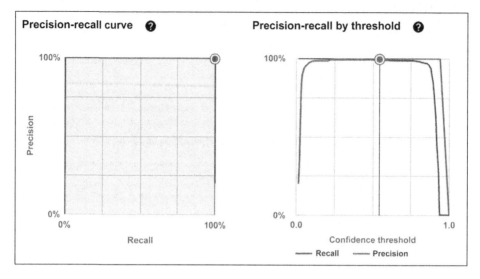

Figure 13.35: AutoML Video intelligence – precision and recall

The confusion matrix shows examples of the wrong classification of shots:

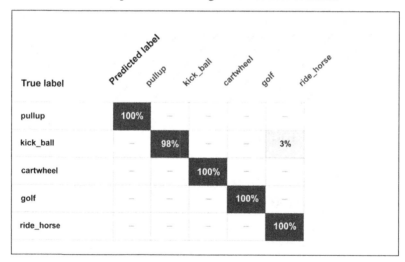

Figure 13.36: AutoML Video intelligence – confusion matrix

Cost

Training on GCP has different costs depending on the type of AutoML adopted; for example, training all the solutions presented in this chapter and serving models for testing had a cost of less than $10 in 2022. This is, however, not including the initial six hours of free discount that were available for the account (around $150 were available at the time of writing). Depending on your organizational needs, this is likely to work out significantly less than the cost of buying expensive on-premises hardware.

Summary

The goal of AutoML is to enable domain experts who are not familiar with machine learning technologies to use ML techniques easily. The primary goal is to reduce the steep learning curve and the huge costs of handcrafting machine learning solutions by making the whole end-to-end machine learning pipeline (data preparation, feature engineering, and automatic model generation) more automated.

After reviewing the state-of-the-art solution available at the end of 2022, we discussed how to use Google Cloud AutoML both for text, videos, and images, achieving results comparable to the ones achieved with handcrafted models. AutoML is probably the fastest-growing research topic and interested readers can find the latest results at `https://www.automl.org/`.

The next chapter discusses the math behind deep learning, a rather advanced topic that is recommended if you are interested in understanding what is going on "under the hood" when you play with neural networks.

References

1. Zoph, B., Le, Q. V. (2016). *Neural Architecture Search with Reinforcement Learning.* `http://arxiv.org/abs/1611.01578`

2. Pham, H., Guan, M. Y., Zoph, B., Le, Q. V., Dean, J. (2018). *Efficient Neural Architecture Search via Parameter Sharing.* `https://arxiv.org/abs/1802.03268`

3. Borsos, Z., Khorlin, A., Gesmundo, A. (2019). *Transfer NAS: Knowledge Transfer between Search Spaces with Transformer Agents.* `https://arxiv.org/abs/1906.08102`

4. Lu, Z., Whalen, I., Boddeti V., Dhebar, Y., Deb, K., Goodman, E., and Banzhaf, W. (2018). *NSGA-Net: Neural Architecture Search using Multi-Objective Genetic Algorithm.* `https://arxiv.org/abs/1810.03522`

5. Bergstra, J., Bengio, Y. (2012). *Random search for hyper-parameter optimization.* `http://www.jmlr.org/papers/v13/bergstra12a.html`

6. Jin, H., Song, Q., and Hu, X. (2019). *Auto-Keras: An Efficient Neural Architecture Search System.* `https://arxiv.org/abs/1806.10282`

7. Faes, L., et al. (2019). *Automated deep learning design for medical image classification by healthcare professionals with no coding experience: a feasibility study.* The Lancet Digital Health Volume 1, Issue 5, September 2019. Pages e232-e242. `https://www.sciencedirect.com/science/article/pii/S2589750019301086`

Join our book's Discord space

Join our Discord community to meet like-minded people and learn alongside more than 2000 members at: https://packt.link/keras

14

The Math Behind Deep Learning

In this chapter, we discuss the math behind deep learning. This topic is quite advanced and not necessarily required for practitioners. However, it is recommended reading if you are interested in understanding what is going on *under the hood* when you play with neural networks.

Here is what you will learn:

- A historical introduction
- The concepts of derivatives and gradients
- Gradient descent and backpropagation algorithms commonly used to optimize deep learning networks

Let's begin!

History

The basics of continuous backpropagation were proposed by Henry J. Kelley [1] in 1960 using dynamic programming. Stuart Dreyfus proposed using the chain rule in 1962 [2]. Paul Werbos was the first to use backpropagation (backprop for short) for neural nets in his 1974 PhD thesis [3]. However, it wasn't until 1986 that backpropagation gained success with the work of David E. Rumelhart, Geoffrey E. Hinton, and Ronald J. Williams published in Nature [4]. In 1987, Yann LeCun described the modern version of backprop currently used for training neural networks [5].

The basic intuition of **Stochastic Gradient Descent (SGD)** was introduced by Robbins and Monro in 1951 in a context different from neural networks [6]. In 2012 – or 52 years after the first time backprop was first introduced – AlexNet [7] achieved a top-5 error of 15.3% in the ImageNet 2012 Challenge using GPUs. According to The Economist [8], *Suddenly people started to pay attention, not just within the AI community but across the technology industry as a whole.* Innovation in this field was not something that happened overnight. Instead, it was a long walk lasting more than 50 years!

Some mathematical tools

Before introducing backpropagation, we need to review some mathematical tools from calculus. Don't worry too much; we'll briefly review a few areas, all of which are commonly covered in high school-level mathematics.

Vectors

We will review two basic concepts of geometry and algebra that are quite useful for machine learning: vectors and the cosine of angles. We start by giving an explanation of vectors. Fundamentally, a vector is a list of numbers. Given a vector, we can interpret it as a direction in space. Mathematicians most often write vectors as either a column x or row vector x^T. Given two column vectors u and v, we can form their dot product by computing $u.v = u^T v = \sum_i u_i v_i$. It can be easily proven that $u.v = ||u||.||v||cos(\theta)$ where θ is the angle between the two vectors.

Here are two easy questions for you. What is the result when the two vectors are very close? And what is the result when the two vectors are the same?

Derivatives and gradients everywhere

Derivatives are a powerful mathematical tool. We are going to use derivatives and gradients to optimize our network. Let's look at the definition. The derivative of a function $y = f(x)$ of a variable x is a measure of the rate at which the value y of the function changes with respect to the change of the variable x.

If x and y are real numbers, and if the graph of f is plotted against x, the derivative is the "slope" of this graph at each point.

If the function is linear $y = f(x) = ax + b$, the slope is $a = \frac{\Delta y}{\Delta x}$. This is a simple result of calculus, which can be derived by considering that:

$$y + \Delta(y) = f(x + \Delta x) = a(x + \Delta x) + b = ax + a\Delta x + b = y + a\Delta x$$

$$\Delta(y) = a\Delta(x)$$

$$a = \frac{\Delta y}{\Delta x}$$

In *Figure 14.1*, we show the geometrical meaning of Δx, Δy, and the angle θ between the linear function and the x-cartesian axis:

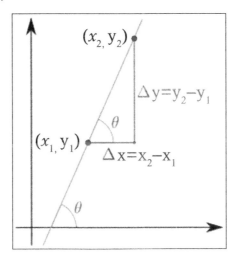

Figure 14.1: An example of a linear function and rate of change

If the function is not linear, then computing the rate of change as the mathematical limit value of the ratio of the differences $\frac{\Delta y}{\Delta x}$ as $\Delta(x)$ becomes infinitely small. Geometrically, this is the tangent line at $(x, y = f(x))$ as shown in *Figure 14.2*:

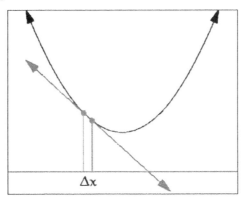

Figure 14.2: Rate of change for $f(x) = x^2$ and the tangential line as $\Delta x \to 0$

For instance, considering $f(x) = x^2$ and the derivative $f'(x) = 2x$ in a given point, say $x = 2$, we can see that the derivative is positive $f'(2) = 4$, as shown in *Figure 14.3*:

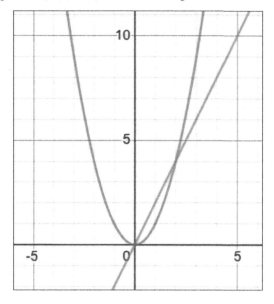

Figure 14.3: $f(x) = x^2$ and $f'(x) = 2x$

A gradient is a generalization of the derivative for multiple variables. Note that the derivative of a function of a single variable is a scalar-valued function, whereas the gradient of a function of several variables is a vector-valued function. The gradient is denoted with an upside-down delta ∇, and called "del" or *nabla* from the Greek alphabet. This makes sense as delta indicates the change in one variable, and the gradient is the change in all variables. Suppose $x \in \mathbb{R}^m$ (e.g. the space of real numbers with m dimensions) and f maps from $\mathbb{R}^n$ to $\mathbb{R}$; the gradient is defined as follows:

$$\nabla(f) = \left(\frac{\partial f}{\partial x_1}, \dots, \frac{\partial f}{\partial x_m}\right)$$

In math, a partial derivative $\frac{\partial f}{\partial x_i}$ of a function of several variables is its derivative with respect to one of those variables, with the others held constant.

Note that it is possible to show that the gradient is a vector (a direction to move) that:

- Points in the direction of the greatest increase of a function.
- Is 0 at a local maximum or local minimum. This is because if it is 0, it cannot increase or decrease further.

The proof is left as an exercise to the interested reader. (Hint: consider *Figure 14.2* and *Figure 14.3*.)

Gradient descent

If the gradient points in the direction of the greatest increase for a function, then it is possible to move toward a local minimum for the function by simply moving in a direction opposite to the gradient. That's the key observation used for gradient descent algorithms, which will be used shortly.

An example is provided in *Figure 14.4*:

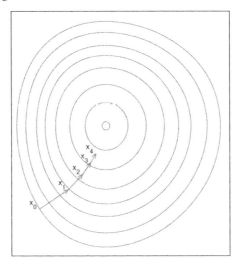

Fig.14.4: Gradient descent for a function in 3 variables

Chain rule

The chain rule says that if we have a function $y = g(x)$ and $z = f\big(g(x)\big) = f(y)$, then the derivative is defined as follows:

$$\frac{dz}{dx} = \frac{dz}{dy}\frac{dy}{dx}$$

This chaining can be generalized beyond the scalar case. Suppose $x \in \mathbb{R}^m$ and $y \in \mathbb{R}^n$ with g, which maps from $\mathbb{R}^m$ to $\mathbb{R}^n$, and f, which maps from $\mathbb{R}^n$ to $\mathbb{R}$. With $y = g(x)$ and $z = f(y)$, we can deduce:

$$\frac{\partial z}{\partial x_i} = \sum_j \frac{\partial z}{\partial y_j}\frac{\partial y_j}{\partial x_i}$$

The generalized chain rule using partial derivatives will be used as a basic tool for the backpropagation algorithm when dealing with functions in multiple variables. Stop for a second and make sure that you fully understand it.

A few differentiation rules

It might be useful to remind ourselves of a few additional differentiation rules that will be used later:

- Constant differentiation: $c' = 0$, where c is a constant.
- Variable differentiation: $\frac{dz}{dz}z = 1$, when deriving the differentiation of a variable.
- Linear differentiation: $[af(x) + bg(x)]' = af'(x) + bg'(x)$
- Reciprocal differentiation: $\left[\frac{1}{f(x)}\right]' = -\frac{f'(x)}{f(x)^2}$
- Exponential differentiation: $[f(x)^n]' = n * f(x)^{n-1}$

Matrix operations

There are many books about matrix calculus. Here we focus only on only a few basic operations used for neural networks. Recall that a matrix $m \times n$ can be used to represent the weights w_{ij}, with $0 \leq i \leq m, 0 \leq j \leq n$ associated with the arcs between two adjacent layers. Note that by adjusting the weights we can control the "behavior" of the network and that a small change in a specific w_{ij} will be propagated through the network following its topology (see *Figure 14.5*, where the edges in bold are the ones impacted by the small change in a specific w_{ij}):

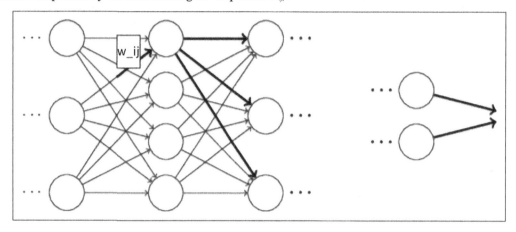

Figure 14.5: Propagating w_{ij} changes through the network via the edges in bold

Now that we have reviewed some basic concepts of calculus, let's start applying them to deep learning. The first question is how to optimize activation functions. Well, I am pretty sure that you are thinking about computing the derivative, so let's do it!

Activation functions

In *Chapter 1, Neural Network Foundations with TF*, we saw a few activation functions including sigmoid, tanh, and ReLU. In the section below, we compute the derivative of these activation functions.

Derivative of the sigmoid

Remember that the sigmoid is defined as $\sigma(z) = \frac{1}{1+e^{-z}}$ (see *Figure 14.6*):

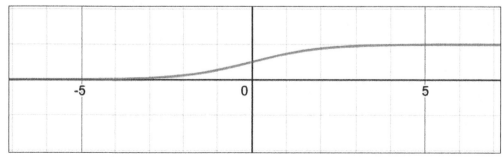

Figure 14.6: Sigmoid activation function

The derivative can be computed as follows:

$$\sigma'(z) = \frac{d}{dz}\left(\frac{1}{1+e^{-z}}\right) = \frac{1}{(1+e^{-z})^{-2}}\frac{d}{dz}\left(e^{-z}\right) = \frac{e^{-z}}{(1+e^{-z})}\frac{1}{(1+e^{-z})} = \frac{e^{-z}+1-1}{(1+e^{-z})}$$

$$= \frac{e^{-z}+1-1}{(1+e^{-z})}\frac{1}{(1+e^{-z})} = \left(\frac{(1+e^{-z})}{(1+e^{-z})} - \frac{1}{(1+e^{-z})}\right)\frac{1}{(1+e^{-z})}$$

$$= \left(1 - \frac{1}{(1+e^{-z})}\right)\left(\frac{1}{(1+e^{-z})}\right)\left(1-\sigma(z)\right)\sigma(z)$$

Therefore the derivative of $\sigma(z)$ can be computed as a very simple form: $\sigma'(z) = \left(1 - \sigma(z)\right)\sigma(z)$.

Derivative of tanh

Remember that the arctan function is defined as $\tanh(z) = \frac{e^z - e^{-z}}{e^z + e^{-z}}$ as seen in *Figure 14.7*:

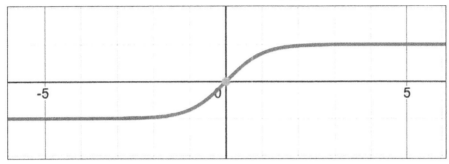

Figure 14.7: Tanh activation function

If you remember that $\frac{d}{dz}e^z = e^z$ and $\frac{d}{dz}e^{-z} = -e^{-z}$, then the derivative is computed as:

$$\frac{d}{dz}\tanh(x) = \frac{(e^z + e^{-z})(e^z + e^{-z}) - (e^z - e^{-z})(e^z - e^{-z})}{(e^z + e^{-z})^2} = 1 - \frac{(e^z - e^{-z})^2}{(e^z + e^{-z})^2} = 1 - \tanh^2(z)$$

Therefore the derivative of $\tanh(z)$ can be computed as a very simple form: $\tanh'(z) = 1 - \tanh^2(z)$.

Derivative of ReLU

The ReLU function is defined as $f(x) = \max(0, x)$ (see *Figure 14.8*). The derivative of ReLU is:

$$f'(x) = \begin{cases} 1, & if\ x > 0 \\ 0, & otherwise \end{cases}$$

Note that ReLU is non-differentiable at zero. However, it is differentiable anywhere else, and the value of the derivative at zero can be arbitrarily chosen to be a 0 or 1, as demonstrated in *Figure 14.8*:

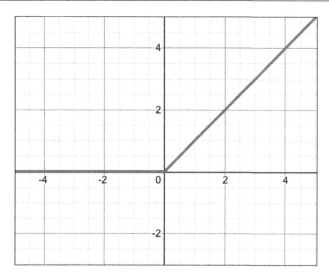

Figure 14.8: ReLU activation function

Backpropagation

Now that we have computed the derivative of the activation functions, we can describe the backpropagation algorithm — the mathematical core of deep learning. Sometimes, backpropagation is called *backprop* for short.

Remember that a neural network can have multiple hidden layers, as well as one input layer and one output layer.

In addition to that, recall from *Chapter 1, Neural Network Foundations with TF,* that backpropagation can be described as a way of progressively correcting mistakes as soon as they are detected. In order to reduce the errors made by a neural network, we must train the network. The training needs a dataset including input values and the corresponding true output value. We want to use the network for predicting output as close as possible to the true output value. The key intuition of the backpropagation algorithm is to update the weights of the connections based on the measured error at the output neuron(s). In the remainder of this section, we will explain how to formalize this intuition.

When backpropagation starts, all the weights have some random assignment. Then the net is activated for each input in the training set; values are propagated forward from the input stage through the hidden stages to the output stage where a prediction is made (note that we keep the figure below simple by only representing a few values with green dotted lines, but in reality, all the values are propagated forward through the network):

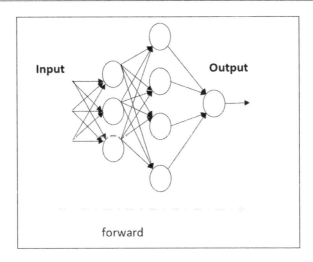

Figure 14.9: Forward step in backpropagation

Since we know the true observed value in the training set, it is possible to calculate the error made in the prediction. The easiest way to think about backtracking is to propagate the error back (see *Figure 14.10*), using an appropriate optimizer algorithm such as gradient descent to adjust the neural network weights, with the goal of reducing the error (again, for the sake of simplicity only a few error values are represented here):

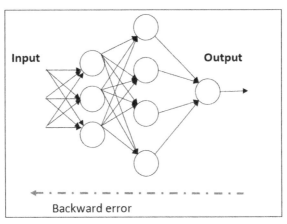

Figure 14.10: Backward step in backpropagation

The process of forward propagation from input to output and backward propagation of errors is repeated several times until the error goes below a predefined threshold. The whole process is represented in *Figure 14.11*. A set of features is selected as input to a machine learning model that produces predictions.

The predictions are compared with the (true) label, and the resulting loss function is minimized by the optimizer, which updates the weights of the model:

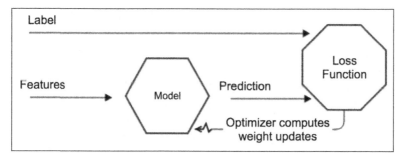

Figure 14.11: Forward propagation and backward propagation

Let's see in detail how the forward and backward steps are realized. It might be useful to have a look back at *Figure 14.5* and recall that a small change in a specific w_{ij} will be propagated through the network following its topology (see *Figure 14.5*, where the edges in bold are the ones impacted by the small change in specific weights).

Forward step

During the forward steps, the inputs are multiplied with the weights and then all summed together. Then the activation function is applied (see *Figure 14.12*). This step is repeated for each layer, one after another. The first layer takes the input features as input and it produces its output. Then, each subsequent layer takes as input the output of the previous layer:

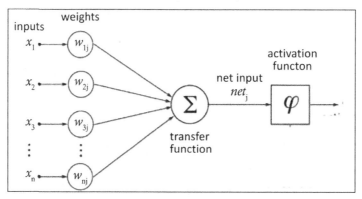

Figure 14.12: Forward propagation

If we look at one single layer, mathematically we have two equations:

- The transfer equation $z = \sum_i w_i x_i + b$, where x_i are the input values, w_i are the weights, and b is the bias. In vector notation $z = w^T x$. Note that b can be *absorbed* in the summatory by setting $w_0 = b$ and $x_0 = 1$.

- The activation function: $y = \sigma(z)$, where σ is the chosen activation function.

An artificial neural network consists of an input layer I, an output layer O, and any number of hidden layers H_i situated between the input and the output layers. For the sake of simplicity, let's assume that there is only one hidden layer, since the results can be easily generalized.

As shown in *Figure 14.12*, the features x_i from the input layer are multiplied by a set of fully connected weights w_{ij} connecting the input layer to the hidden layer (see the left side of *Figure 14.12*). The weighted signals are summed together and with the bias to calculate the result $z_j = \sum_i w_i x_i + b_j$ (see the center of *Figure 14.12*). The result is passed through the activation function $y_j = \sigma_j(z_j)$, which leaves the hidden layer to the output layer (see the right side of *Figure 14.12*).

In summary, during the forward step we need to run the following operations:

1. For each neuron in a layer, multiply each input by its corresponding weight.
2. Then for each neuron in the layer, sum all input weights together.
3. Finally, for each neuron, apply the activation function on the result to compute the new output.

At the end of the forward step, we get a predicted vector y_o from the output layer o given the input vector x presented at the input layer. Now the question is: how close is the predicted vector y_o to the true value vector t?

That's where the backstep comes in.

Backstep

To understand how close the predicted vector y_o is to the true value vector t, we need a function that measures the error at the output layer o. That is the *loss function* defined earlier in the book. There are many choices for loss function. For instance, we can define the mean squared error defined as follows:

$$E = \frac{1}{2}\sum_o (y_o - t_o)^2$$

Note that E is a quadratic function and, therefore, the difference is quadratically larger when t is far away from y_o, and the sign is not important. Note that this quadratic error (loss) function is not the only one that we can use. Later in this chapter, we will see how to deal with cross-entropy.

Now, remember that the key point is that during the training, we want to adjust the weights of the network to minimize the final error. As discussed, we can move toward a local minimum by moving in the opposite direction to the gradient $-\nabla w$. Moving in the opposite direction to the gradient is the reason why this algorithm is called *gradient descent*. Therefore, it is reasonable to define the equation for updating the weight w_{ij} as follows:

$$w_{ij} \leftarrow w_{ij} - \nabla w_{ij}$$

For a function in multiple variables, the gradient is computed using partial derivatives. We introduce the hyperparameter η – or, in ML lingo, the learning rate – to account for how large a step should be in the direction opposite to the gradient.

Considering the error, E, we have the equation:

$$\nabla w = -\eta \frac{\partial E}{\partial w_{ij}}$$

The preceding equation is simply capturing the fact that a slight change will impact the final error, as seen in *Figure 14.13*:

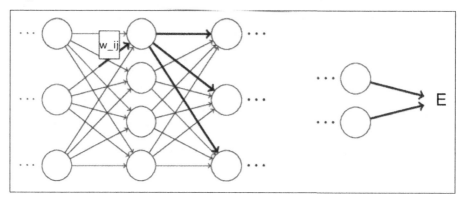

Figure 14.13: A small change in w_{ij} will impact the final error E

Let's define the notation used throughout our equations in the remaining section:

- z_j is the input to node j for layer l.
- δ_j is the activation function for node j in layer l (applied to z_j).
- $y_j = \delta_j(z_j)$ is the output of the activation of node j in layer l.
- w_{ij} is the matrix of weights connecting the neuron i in layer $l - 1$ to the neuron j in layer l.
- b_j is the bias for unit j in layer l.
- t_o is the target value for node o in the output layer.

Now we need to compute the partial derivative for the error at the output layer ∂E when the weights change by ∂w_{ij}. There are two different cases:

- **Case 1:** Weight update equation for a neuron from hidden (or input) layer to output layer.
- **Case 2:** Weight update equation for a neuron from hidden (or input) layer to hidden layer.

We'll begin with Case 1.

Case 1: From hidden layer to output layer

In this case, we need to consider the equation for a neuron from hidden layer j to output layer o. Applying the definition of E and differentiating we have:

$$\frac{\partial E}{\partial w_{jo}} = \frac{\partial \frac{1}{2} \Sigma_o (y_o - t_o)^2}{\partial w_{jo}} = (y_o - t_o) \frac{\partial (y_o - t_o)}{\partial w_{jo}}$$

Here the summation disappears because when we take the partial derivative with respect to the j-th dimension, the only term that is not zero in the error is the j-th. Considering that differentiation is a linear operation and that $\frac{\partial t_o}{\partial w_{jo}} = 0$ – because the true t_0 value does not depend on w_{jo} – we have:

$$\frac{\partial(y_o - t_o)}{\partial w_{jo}} = \frac{\partial y_o}{\partial w_{jo}} - 0$$

Applying the chain rule again and remembering that $y_o = \delta_o(z_o)$, we have:

$$\frac{\partial E}{\partial w_{jo}} = (y_o - t_o)\frac{\partial y_o}{\partial w_{jo}} = (y_o - t_o)\frac{\partial \delta_o(z_o)}{\partial w_{jo}} = (y_o - t_o)\delta'_o(z_o)\frac{\partial z_o}{\partial w_{jo}}$$

Remembering that $z_o = \sum_j w_{jo}\delta_j(z_j) + b_o$, we have $\frac{\partial z_o}{\partial w_{jo}} = \delta_j(z_j)$ again because when we take the partial derivative with respect to the j-th dimension the only term that is not zero in the error is the j-th. By definition $\delta_j(z_j) = y_j$, so putting everything together we have:

$$\frac{\partial E}{\partial w_{jo}} = (y_o - t_o)\delta'_o(z_o)y_j$$

The gradient of the error E with respect to the weights w_j from the hidden layer j to the output layer o is therefore simply the product of three terms: the difference between the prediction y_o and the true value t_o, the derivative $\delta'_o(z_o)$ of the output layer activation function, and the activation output y_j of node j in the hidden layer. For simplicity we can also define $v_o = (y_o - t_o)\delta'_o(z_o)$ and get:

$$\frac{\partial E}{\partial w_{jo}} = v_o y_j$$

In short, for Case 1, the weight update equation for each of the hidden-output connections is:

$$w_{jo} \leftarrow w_{jo} - \eta\frac{\partial E}{\partial w_{jo}}$$

Note: if we want to explicitly compute the gradient with respect to the output layer biases, the steps to follow are similar to the ones above with only one difference:

$$\frac{\partial z_o}{\partial b_o} = \frac{\partial \sum_j w_{jo}\delta_j(z_j) + b_o}{\partial b_o} = 1$$

so in this case $\frac{\partial E}{\partial b_o} = v_o$.

Next, we'll look at Case 2.

Case 2: From hidden layer to hidden layer

In this case, we need to consider the equation for a neuron from a hidden layer (or the input layer) to a hidden layer. *Figure 14.13* showed that there is an indirect relationship between the hidden layer weight change and the output error. This makes the computation of the gradient a bit more challenging. In this case, we need to consider the equation for a neuron from hidden layer i to hidden layer j.

Applying the definition of E and differentiating we have:

$$\frac{\partial E}{\partial w_{ij}} = \frac{\partial \frac{1}{2}\Sigma_o(y_o - t_o)^2}{\partial w_{ij}} = \sum_o (y_o - t_o)\frac{\partial(y_o - t_o)}{\partial w_{ij}} = \sum_o (y_o - t_o)\frac{\partial y_o}{\partial w_{ij}}$$

In this case, the sum will not disappear because the change of weights in the hidden layer is directly affecting the output. Substituting $y_o = \delta_o(z_o)$ and applying the chain rule we have:

$$\frac{\partial E}{\partial w_{ij}} = \sum_o (y_o - t_o)\frac{\partial \delta_o(z_o)}{\partial w_{ij}} = \sum_o (y_o - t_o)\delta'_o(z_o)\frac{\partial z_o}{\partial w_{ij}}$$

The indirect relation between z_0 and the internal weights w_{ij} (*Figure 14.13*) is mathematically expressed by the expansion:

$$z_o = \sum_j w_{jo}\delta_j(z_j) + b_o = \sum_j w_{jo}\delta_j\left(\sum_i w_{ij}z_i + b_i\right) + b_o$$

since $z_j = \Sigma_i w_{ij}z_i + b_i$.

This suggests applying the chain rule again:

$$\frac{\partial z_o}{\partial w_{ij}} =$$

Applying the chain rule:

$$= \frac{\partial z_o}{\partial y_j}\frac{\partial y_j}{\partial w_{ij}} =$$

Substituting z_0:

$$= \frac{\partial y_j w_{jo}}{\partial y_j}\frac{\partial y_j}{\partial w_{ij}} =$$

Deriving:

$$= w_{jo}\frac{\partial y_j}{\partial w_{ij}} =$$

Substituting $y_j = \delta_j(z_j)$:

$$= w_{jo}\frac{\partial \delta_j(z_j)}{\partial w_{ij}} =$$

Applying the chain rule:

$$= w_{jo} \delta'_j(z_j) \frac{\partial z_j}{\partial w_{ij}} =$$

Substituting $z_j = \sum_i y_i w_{ij} + b_i$:

$$= w_{jo} \delta'_j(z_j) \frac{\partial \left(\sum_i y_i w_{ij} + b_i \right)}{\partial w_{ij}} =$$

Deriving:

$$w_{jo} \delta'_j(z_j) y_i$$

Now we can combine the above two results:

$$\frac{\partial E}{\partial w_{ij}} = \sum_o (y_o - t_o) \delta'_o(z_o) \frac{\partial z_o}{\partial w_{ij}}$$

$$\frac{\partial z_o}{\partial w_{ij}} = w_{jo} \delta'_j(z_j) y_i$$

and get:

$$\frac{\partial E}{\partial w_{ij}} = \sum_o (y_o - t_o) \delta'_o(z_o) w_{jo} \delta'_j(z_j) y_i = y_i \delta'_j(z_j) \sum_o (y_o - t_o) \delta'_o(z_o) w_{jo}$$

Remembering the definition: $v_o = (y_o - t_o) \delta'_o(z_o)$, we get:

$$\frac{\partial E}{\partial w_{ij}} = \sum_o (y_o - t_o) \delta'_o(z_o) w_{jo} \delta'_j(z_j) y_i = y_i \delta'_j(z_j) \sum_o v_o w_{jo}$$

This last substitution with v_o is particularly interesting because it backpropagates the signal v_o computed in the subsequent layer. The rate of change ∂E with respect to the rate of change of the weights w_{ij} is therefore the multiplication of three factors: the output activations y_i from the layer below, the derivative of hidden layer activation function δ'_j, and the sum of the backpropagated signal v_o previously computed in the subsequent layer weighted by w_{jo}. We can use this idea of backpropagating the error signal by defining $v_j = \delta'_j(z_j) \sum_o v_o w_{jo}$ and therefore $\frac{\partial E}{\partial w_{ij}} = y_i v_j$. This suggests that in order to calculate the gradients at any layer l in a deep neural network, we can simply multiply the backpropagated error signal v_j and multiply it by the feed-forward signal y_{l-1}, arriving at the layer l. Note that the math is a bit complex but the result is indeed very very simple! The intuition is given in *Figure 14.14*. Given a function $z = f(x, y)$, computed locally to a neuron with the input x, and y, the gradients $\frac{\partial L}{\partial z}$ are backpropagated. Then, they are combined via the chain rule with the local gradients $\frac{\partial z}{\partial x}$ and $\frac{\partial z}{\partial y}$ for further backpropagation.

Here, L denotes the error from the generic previous layer:

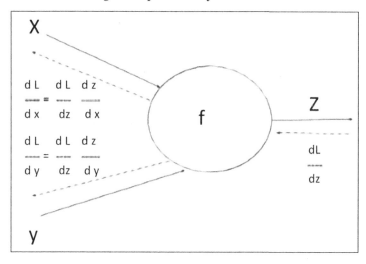

Figure 14.14: An example of the math behind backpropagation

Note: if we want to explicitly compute the gradient with respect to the output layer biases, it can be proven that $\frac{\partial E}{\partial b_i} = v_j$. We leave this as an exercise for you.

In short, for Case 2 (hidden-to-hidden connection) the weight delta is $\Delta w = \eta v_j y_i$ and the weight update equation for each of the hidden-hidden connections is simply:

$$w_{ij} \leftarrow w_{ij} - \eta \frac{\partial E}{\partial w_{ij}}$$

We have arrived at the end of this section and all the mathematical tools are defined to make our final statement. The essence of the backstep is nothing more than applying the weight update rule one layer after another, starting from the last output layer and moving back toward the first input layer. Difficult to derive, to be sure, but extremely easy to apply once defined. The whole forward-backward algorithm at the core of deep learning is then the following:

1. Compute the feedforward signals from the input to the output.
2. Compute the output error E based on the predictions y_o and the true value t_o.
3. Backpropagate the error signals; multiply them with the weights in previous layers and with the gradients of the associated activation functions.
4. Compute the gradients $\frac{\partial E}{\partial \theta}$ for all of the parameters θ based on the backpropagated error signal and the feedforward signals from the inputs.
5. Update the parameters using the computed gradients $\theta \leftarrow \theta - \eta \frac{\partial E}{\partial \theta}$.

Note that the above algorithm will work for any choice of differentiable error function E and for any choice of differentiable activation δ_l function. The only requirement is that both must be differentiable.

Gradient descent with backpropagation is not guaranteed to find the global minimum of the loss function, but only a local minimum. However, this is not necessarily a problem observed in practical application.

Cross entropy and its derivative

Gradient descent can be used when cross-entropy is adopted as the loss function. As discussed in *Chapter 1, Neural Network Foundations with TF*, the logistic loss function is defined as:

$$E = L(c, p) = -\sum_i [c_i \ln(p_i) + (1 - c_i) \ln(1 - p_i)]$$

Where c refers to one-hot-encoded classes (or labels) whereas p refers to softmax-applied probabilities. Since cross-entropy is applied to softmax-applied probabilities and to one-hot-encoded classes, we need to take into account the chain rule for computing the gradient with respect to the final weights $score_i$. Mathematically, we have:

$$\frac{\partial E}{\partial score_i} = \frac{\partial E}{\partial p_i} \frac{\partial p_i}{\partial score_i}$$

Computing each part separately, let's start from $\frac{\partial E}{\partial p_i}$:

$$\frac{\partial E}{\partial p_i} = \frac{\partial(-\sum[c_i \ln(p_i) + (1 - c_i)\ln(i - p_i)])}{\partial p_i} = \frac{\partial(-[c_i \ln(p_i) + (1 - c_i)\ln(i - p_i)])}{\partial p_i}$$

(noting that for a fixed ∂p_i all the terms in the sum are constant except the chosen one).

Therefore, we have:

$$-\frac{\partial c_i \ln p_i}{\partial p_i} - \frac{\partial(1 - c_i)\ln(1 - p_i)}{\partial p_i} = -\frac{c_i}{p_i} - \frac{(1 - c_i)}{(1 - p_i)} \frac{\partial(1 - p_i)}{\partial p_i}$$

(applying the partial derivative to the sum and considering that $\ln'(x) = \frac{1}{x}$)

Therefore, we have:

$$\frac{\partial E}{\partial p_i} = -\frac{c_i}{p_i} + \frac{(1 - c_i)}{(1 - p_i)}$$

Now let's compute the other part $\frac{\partial p_i}{\partial score_i}$ where p_i is the softmax function defined as:

$$\sigma(x_j) = \frac{e^{x_j}}{\sum_i e^{x_i}}$$

The derivative is:

$$\frac{\partial \sigma(x_j)}{\partial x_k} = \sigma(x_j)\left(1 - \sigma(x_j)\right), \qquad if\ j = k$$

and

$$\frac{\partial \sigma(x_j)}{\partial x_k} = -\sigma(e^{x_j})\sigma(e^{x_k}), \qquad if\ j \neq k$$

Using the Kronecker delta $\delta_{ij} = \begin{cases} 1, & for\ j = k, \\ 0, & otherwise \end{cases}$ we have:

$$\frac{\partial \sigma(x_j)}{\partial x_k} = \sigma(x_j)\left(\delta_{ij} - \sigma(x_j)\right)$$

Therefore, considering that we are computing the partial derivative, all the components are zeroed with the exception of only one, and we have:

$$\frac{\partial p_i}{\partial score_i} = p_i(1 - p_i)$$

Combining the results, we have:

$$\frac{\partial E}{\partial score_i} = \frac{\partial E}{\partial p_i}\frac{\partial p_i}{\partial score_i} = \left[-\frac{c_i}{p_i} + \frac{(1-c_i)}{(1-p_i)}\right][p_i(1 - p_i)]$$

$$= -\frac{c_i[p_i(1-p_i)]}{p_i} + \frac{(1-c_i)p_i(1-p_i)}{(1-p_i)} = -c_i(1 - p_i) + (1 - c_i)p_i$$

$$= -c_i + c_ip_i + p_i - c_ip_i = p_i - c_i$$

Where c_i denotes the one-hot-encoded classes and p_i refers to the softmax probabilities. In short, the derivative is both elegant and easy to compute:

$$\frac{\partial E}{\partial score_i} = p_i - c_i$$

Batch gradient descent, stochastic gradient descent, and mini-batch

If we generalize the previous discussion, then we can state that the problem of optimizing a neural network consists of adjusting the weights w of the network in such a way that the loss function is minimized. Conveniently, we can think about the loss function in the form of a sum, as in this form it's indeed representing all the loss functions commonly used:

$$Q(w) = \frac{1}{n}\sum_{i=1}^{n} Q_i(w)$$

In this case, we can perform a derivation using steps very similar to those discussed previously, following the update rule, where η is the learning rate and ∇ is the gradient:

$$w = w - \eta\nabla Q(w) = w - \eta\sum_{i-1}^{n} \nabla Q_i(w)$$

In many cases, evaluating the above gradient might require an expensive evaluation of the gradients from all summand functions. When the training set is very large, this can be extremely expensive. If we have three million samples, we have to loop through three million times or use the dot product. That's a lot! How can we simplify this? There are three types of gradient descent, each different in the way they handle the training dataset.

Batch gradient descent

Batch Gradient Descent (**BGD**) computes the change of error but updates the whole model only once the entire dataset has been evaluated. Computationally it is very efficient, but it requires that the results for the whole dataset be held in the memory.

Stochastic gradient descent

Instead of updating the model once the dataset has been evaluated, **Stochastic Gradient Descent** (**SGD**) does so after every single training example. The key idea is very simple: SGD samples a subset of summand functions at every step.

Mini-batch gradient descent

Mini-Batch Gradient Descent (**MBGD**) is very frequently used in deep learning. MBGD (or mini-batch) combines BGD and SGD in one single heuristic. The dataset is divided into small batches of about size *bs*, generally 64 to 256. Then each of the batches is evaluated separately.

Note that *bs* is another hyperparameter to fine-tune during training. MBGD lies between the extremes of BGD and SGD – by adjusting the batch size and the learning rate parameters, we sometimes find a solution that descends closer to the global minimum than what can be achieved by either of the extremes.

In contrast with gradient descent, where the cost function is minimized more smoothly, the mini-batch gradient has a bit more of a noisy and bumpy descent, but the cost function still trends downhill. The reason for the noise is that mini-batches are a sample of all the examples and this sampling can cause the loss function to oscillate.

Thinking about backpropagation and ConvNets

In this section, we will examine backprop and ConvNets. For the sake of simplicity, we will focus on an example of convolution with input X of size 3x3, one single filter W of size 2x2 with no padding, stride 1, and no dilation (see *Chapter 3, Convolutional Neural Networks*). The generalization is left as an exercise.

The standard convolution operation is represented in *Figure 14.15*. Simply put, the convolutional operation is the forward pass:

Input	Weights	Convolution
X11	W11	W11X11+W12X12+W21X21+W22X22
X12	W12	W11X12+W12X13+W21X21+W22X23
X13		
	W21	W11X21+W12X22+W21X31+W22X32
X21	W22	W11X22+W12X23+W21X32+W22X33
X22		
X23		
X31		
X32		
X33		

Figure 14.15: Forward pass for our ConvNet toy example

Following the examination of *Figure 14.15*, we can now focus our attention on the backward pass for the current layer. The key assumption is that we receive a backpropagated signal $\frac{\partial L}{\partial h_{ij}}$ as input, and we need to compute $\frac{\partial L}{\partial w_{ij}}$ and $\frac{\partial L}{\partial x_{ij}}$. This computation is left as an exercise, but please note that each weight in the filter contributes to each pixel in the output map or, in other words, any change in a weight of a filter affects all the output pixels.

Thinking about backpropagation and RNNs

Remember from *Chapter 5, Recurrent Neural Networks*, the basic equation for an RNN is $s_t = \tanh\left(U_{x_t} + W_{s_{t-1}}\right)$, the final prediction is $\hat{y}_t = softmax(Vs_t)$ at step t, the correct value is y_t, and the error E is the cross-entropy. Here U, V, and W are learning parameters used for the RNN's equations. These equations can be visualized as shown in *Figure 14.16*, where we unroll the recurrency. The core idea is that total error is just the sum of the errors at each time step.

If we used SGD, we need to sum the errors and the gradients at each time step for one given training example:

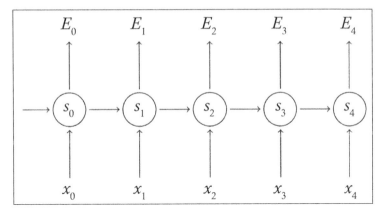

Figure 14.16: RNN unrolled with equations

We are not going to write all the tedious math behind all the gradients but rather focus only on a few peculiar cases. For instance, with math computations similar to the ones made in the previous sections, it can be proven by using the chain rule that the gradient for V depends only on the value at the current time step s_3, y_3 and $\hat{y}_3$:

$$\frac{\partial E_3}{\partial V} = \frac{\partial E_3}{\partial \hat{y}_3}\frac{\partial \hat{y}_3}{\partial V} = \frac{\partial E_3}{\partial \hat{y}_3}\frac{\partial \hat{y}_3}{\partial z_3}\frac{\partial z_3}{\partial V} = (\hat{y}_3 - y_3)s_3$$

However, $\frac{\partial E_3}{\partial W}$ has dependencies carried across time steps because, for instance, $s_3 = \tanh\left(U_{x_t} + W_{s_2}\right)$ depends on s_2, which depends on W_2 and s_1. As a consequence, the gradient is a bit more complicated because we need to sum up the contributions of each time step:

$$\frac{\partial E_3}{\partial W} = \sum_{k=0}^{3} \frac{\partial E_3}{\partial \hat{y}_3}\frac{\partial \hat{y}_3}{\partial s_3}\frac{\partial s_3}{\partial s_k}\frac{\partial s_k}{\partial W}$$

To understand the preceding equation, imagine that we are using the standard backpropagation algorithm used for traditional feedforward neural networks but for RNNs. We need to additionally add the gradients of W across time steps. That's because we can effectively make the dependencies across time explicit by unrolling the RNN. This is the reason why backprop for RNNs is frequently called **Backpropagation Through Time (BPTT)**.

The intuition is shown in *Figure 14.17*, where the backpropagated signals are represented:

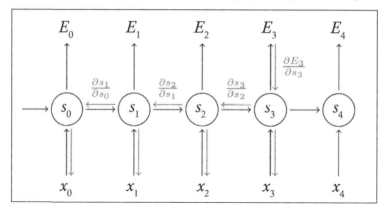

Figure 14.17: RNN equations and backpropagated signals

I hope that you have been following up to this point because now the discussion will be slightly more difficult. If we consider:

$$\frac{\partial E_3}{\partial W} = \sum_{k=0}^{3} \frac{\partial E_3}{\partial \hat{y}_3} \frac{\partial \hat{y}_3}{\partial s_3} \frac{\partial s_3}{\partial s_k} \frac{\partial s_k}{\partial W}$$

then we notice that $\frac{\partial s_3}{\partial s_k}$ should be again computed with the chain rule, producing a number of multiplications. In this case, we take the derivative of a vector function with respect to a vector, so we need a matrix whose elements are all the pointwise derivatives (in math, this matrix is called a Jacobian). Mathematically, it can be proven that:

$$\frac{\partial s_3}{\partial s_k} = \prod_{j=k+1}^{3} \frac{\partial s_j}{\partial s_{j-1}}$$

Therefore, we have:

$$\frac{\partial E_3}{\partial W} = \sum_{k=0}^{3} \frac{\partial E_3}{\partial \hat{y}_3} \frac{\partial \hat{y}_3}{\partial s_3} \left(\prod_{j=k+1}^{3} \frac{\partial s_j}{\partial s_{j-1}} \right) \frac{\partial s_k}{\partial W}$$

The multiplication in the above equation is particularly problematic since both the sigmoid and tanh get saturated at both ends and their derivative goes to 0. When this happens, they drive other gradients in previous layers toward 0. This makes the gradient vanish completely after a few time steps and the network stops learning from "far away."

Chapter 5, Recurrent Neural Networks, discussed how to use **Long Short-Term Memory (LSTM)** and **Gated Recurrent Units (GRUs)** to deal with the problem of vanishing gradients and efficiently learn long-range dependencies. In a similar way, the gradient can explode when one single term in the multiplication of the Jacobian matrix becomes large. *Chapter 5* discussed how to use gradient clipping to deal with this problem.

We have now concluded this journey, and you should now understand how backpropagation works and how it is applied in neural networks for dense networks, CNNs, and RNNs. In the next section, we will discuss how TensorFlow computes gradients, and why this is useful for backpropagation.

A note on TensorFlow and automatic differentiation

TensorFlow can automatically calculate derivatives, a feature called automatic differentiation. This is achieved by using the chain rule. Every node in the computational graph has an attached gradient operation for calculating the derivatives of input with respect to output. After that, the gradients with respect to parameters are automatically computed during backpropagation.

Automatic differentiation is a very important feature because you do not need to hand-code new variations of backpropagation for each new model of a neural network. This allows for quick iteration and running many experiments faster.

Summary

In this chapter, we discussed the math behind deep learning. Put simply, a deep learning model computes a function given an input vector to produce the output. The interesting part is that it can literally have billions of parameters (weights) to be tuned. Backpropagation is a core mathematical algorithm used by deep learning for efficiently training artificial neural networks, following a gradient descent approach that exploits the chain rule. The algorithm is based on two steps repeated alternatively: the forward step and the backstep.

During the forward step, inputs are propagated through the network to predict the outputs. These predictions might be different from the true values given to assess the quality of the network. In other words, there is an error and our goal is to minimize it. This is where the backstep plays a role, by adjusting the weights of the network to minimize the error. The error is computed via loss functions such as **Mean Squared Error** (**MSE**), or cross-entropy for non-continuous values such as Boolean (*Chapter 1, Neural Network Foundations with TF*). A gradient-descent-optimization algorithm is used to adjust the weight of neurons by calculating the gradient of the loss function. Backpropagation computes the gradient, and gradient descent uses the gradients for training the model. A reduction in the error rate of predictions increases accuracy, allowing machine learning models to improve. SGD is the simplest thing you could possibly do by taking one step in the direction of the gradient. This chapter does not cover the math behind other optimizers such as Adam and RMSProp (*Chapter 1*). However, they involve using the first and the second moments of the gradients. The first moment involves the exponentially decaying average of the previous gradients, and the second moment involves the exponentially decaying average of the previous squared gradients.

There are three big properties of our data that justify using deep learning; otherwise, we might as well use regular machine learning:

- Very-high-dimensional input (text, images, audio signals, videos, and temporal series are frequently a good example).

- Dealing with complex decision surfaces that cannot be approximated with a low-order polynomial function.
- Having a large amount of training data available.

Deep learning models can be thought of as a computational graph made up of stacking together several basic components such as dense networks (*Chapter 1*), CNNs (*Chapter 3*), embeddings (*Chapter 4*), RNNs (*Chapter 5*), GANs (*Chapter 9*), autoencoders (*Chapter 8*) and, sometimes, adopting shortcut connections such as "peephole," "skip," and "residual" because they help data flow a bit more smoothly. Each node in the graph takes tensors as input and produces tensors as output. As discussed, training happens by adjusting the weights in each node with backprop, where the key idea is to reduce the error in the final output node(s) via gradient descent. GPUs and TPUs (*Chapter 15*) can significantly accelerate the optimization process since it is essentially based on (hundreds of) millions of matrix computations.

There are a few other mathematical tools that might be helpful to improve your learning process. Regularization (L1, L2, and Lasso (*Chapter 1*)) can significantly improve learning by keeping weights normalized. Batch normalization (*Chapter 1*) helps to basically keep track of the mean and the standard deviation of your dataset across multiple deep layers. The key idea is to have data resembling a normal distribution while it flows through the computational graph. Dropout (Chapters *1*, *3*, *5*, *6*, *9*, and *20*) helps by introducing some elements of redundancy in your computation; this prevents overfitting and allows better generalization.

This chapter has presented the mathematical foundation behind intuition. As discussed, this topic is quite advanced and not necessarily required for practitioners. However, it is recommended reading if you are interested in understanding what is going on "under the hood" when you play with neural networks.

The next chapter will introduce the **Tensor Processing Unit** (**TPU**), a special chip developed at Google for ultra-fast execution of many mathematical operations described in this chapter.

References

1. Kelley, Henry J. (1960). *Gradient theory of optimal flight paths*. ARS Journal. 30 (10): 947–954. Bibcode:1960ARSJ...30.1127B. doi:10.2514/8.5282.

2. Dreyfus, Stuart. (1962). *The numerical solution of variational problems*. Journal of Mathematical Analysis and Applications. 5 (1): 30–45. doi:10.1016/0022-247x(62)90004-5.

3. Werbos, P. (1974). *Beyond Regression: New Tools for Prediction and Analysis in the Behavioral Sciences*. PhD thesis, Harvard University.

4. Rumelhart, David E.; Hinton, Geoffrey E.; Williams, Ronald J. (1986-10-09). *Learning representations by back-propagating errors*. Nature. 323 (6088): 533–536. Bibcode:1986Natur.323..533R. doi:10.1038/323533a0.

5. LeCun, Y. (1987). *Modèles Connexionnistes de l'apprentissage (Connectionist Learning Models)*, Ph.D. thesis, Université P. et M. Curie.

6. Herbert Robbins and Sutton Monro. (1951). *A Stochastic Approximation Method. The Annals of Mathematical Statistics, Vol. 22, No. 3.* pp. 400–407.

7. Krizhevsky, Alex; Sutskever, Ilya; Hinton, Geoffrey E. (June 2017). *ImageNet classification with deep convolutional neural networks* (PDF). Communications of the ACM. 60 (6): 84–90. doi:10.1145/3065386. ISSN 0001-0782.

8. *From not working to neural networking.* The Economist. (25 June 2016)

Join our book's Discord space

Join our Discord community to meet like-minded people and learn alongside more than 2000 members at: `https://packt.link/keras`

15

Tensor Processing Unit

This chapter introduces the **Tensor Processing Unit** (TPU), a special chip developed at Google for ultra-fast execution of neural network mathematical operations. As with **Graphics Processing Units** (**GPUs**), the idea here is to have a special processor focusing only on very fast matrix operations, with no support for all the other operations normally supported by **Central Processing Units** (CPUs). However, the additional improvement with TPUs is to remove from the chip any hardware support for graphics operations normally present in GPUs (rasterization, texture mapping, frame buffer operations, and so on). Think of a TPU as a special purpose co-processor specialized for deep learning, being focused on matrix or tensor operations. In this chapter, we will compare CPUs and GPUs with the four generations of TPUs and with Edge TPUs. All these accelerators are available as of April 2022. The chapter will include code examples of using TPUs.

In this chapter, you will learn the following:

- C/G/T processing units
- Four generations of TPUs and Edge TPUs
- TPU performance
- How to use TPUs with Colab

So with that, let's begin.

C/G/T processing units

In this section we discuss CPUs, GPUs, and TPUs. Before discussing TPUs, it will be useful for us to review CPUs and GPUs.

CPUs and GPUs

You are probably somewhat familiar with the concept of a CPU, a general-purpose chip sitting in each computer, tablet, and smartphone. CPUs are in charge of all of the computations: from logical controls, to arithmetic, to register operations, to operations with memory, and many others. CPUs are subject to the well-known Moore's law [1], which states that the number of transistors in a dense integrated circuit doubles about every two years.

Many people believe that we are currently in an era where this trend cannot be sustained for long, and indeed it has already declined during the past decade. Therefore, we need some additional technology if we want to support the demand for faster and faster computation to process the ever-growing amount of data that is available out there.

One improvement came from GPUs, special-purpose chips that are perfect for fast graphics operations such as matrix multiplication, rasterization, frame-buffer manipulation, texture mapping, and many others. In addition to computer graphics where matrix multiplications are applied to pixels of images, GPUs turned out to be a great match for deep learning. This is a funny story of serendipity (serendipity is the occurrence and development of events by chance in a happy or beneficial way) – a great example of technology created for one goal and then being met with staggering success in a domain completely unrelated to the one it was originally envisioned for.

TPUs

One problem encountered in using GPUs for deep learning is that these chips are made for graphics and gaming, not only for fast matrix computations. This would of course be the case, given that the G in GPU stands for Graphics! GPUs led to unbelievable improvements in deep learning but, in the case of tensor operations for neural networks, large parts of the chip are not used at all. For deep learning, there is no need for rasterization, no need for frame-buffer manipulation, and no need for texture mapping. The only thing that is necessary is a very efficient way to compute matrix and tensor operations. It should be no surprise that GPUs are not necessarily the ideal solution for deep learning, since CPUs and GPUs were designed long before deep learning became successful.

Before going into technical details, let's first discuss the fascinating genesis of Tensor Processing Unit version 1, or TPU v1. In 2013, Jeff Dean, the Chief of the Brain Division at Google, estimated (see *Figure 15.1*) that if all the people owning a mobile phone were talking in calls for only 3 minutes more per day, then Google would have needed two or three times more servers to process this data. This would have been an unaffordable case of success-disaster, i.e., where great success has led to problems that cannot be properly managed. It was clear that neither CPUs nor GPUs were a suitable solution. So, Google decided that they needed something completely new – something that would allow a 10x growth in performance with no significant cost increase. That's how TPU v1 was born! What is impressive is that it took only 15 months from initial design to production. You can find more details about this story in Jouppi et al., 2014 [3], where a detailed report about different inference workloads seen at Google in 2013 is also reported:

Name	LOC	Layers					Nonlinear Function	Weights	TPUv1 Ops / Weight Byte	TPUv1 Batch Size	% Deployed
		FC	Conv	Vector	Pool	Total					
MLP0	0.1k	5				5	ReLU	20M	200	200	61%
MLP1	1k	4				4	ReLU	5M	168	168	
LSTM0	1k	24		34		58	sigmoid, tanh	52M	64	64	29%
LSTM1	1.5k	37		19		56	sigmoid, tanh	34M	96	96	
CNN0	1k		16			16	ReLU	8M	2888	8	5%
CNN1	1k	4	72		13	89	ReLU	100M	1750	32	

Figure 15.1: Different inference workloads seen at Google in 2013 (source [3])

Let's talk a bit about the technical details. A TPU v1 is a special device (or an **Application-Specific Integrated Circuit**, or **ASIC** for short) designed for super-efficient tensor operations. TPUs follow the philosophy *less is more*. This philosophy has an important consequence: TPUs do not have all the graphic components that are needed for GPUs. Because of this, they are both very efficient from an energy consumption perspective, and frequently much faster than GPUs. So far, there have been four generations of TPUs. Let's review them.

Four generations of TPUs, plus Edge TPU

As discussed, TPUs are domain-specific processors expressly optimized for matrix operations. Now, you might remember that the basic operation of matrix multiplication is a dot product between a line from one matrix and a column from the other matrix. For instance, given a matrix multiplication $Y = X * W$, computing $Y[i, 0]$ is:

$$Y[i, 0] = X[i, 0] * W[0,0] + X[i, 1] * W[1,0] + X[i, 2] * W[2,0] + \ldots + X[i, n] * W[n, 0]$$

The sequential implementation of this operation is time-consuming for large matrices. A brute-force computation has a time complexity of $O(n^3)$ for n x n matrices so it's not feasible for running large computations.

First generation TPU

The first generation TPU (TPU v1) was announced in May 2016 at Google I/O. TPU v1 [1] supports matrix multiplication using 8-bit arithmetic. TPU v1 is specialized for deep learning inference but it does not work for training. For training there is a need to perform floating-point operations, as discussed in the following paragraphs.

A key function of TPU is the "systolic" matrix multiplication. Let's see what this means. Remember that the core of deep learning is a core product $Y = X * W$, where, for instance, the basic operation to compute $Y[i, 0]$ is:

$$Y[i, 0] = X[i, 0] * W[0,0] + X[i, 1] * W[1,0] + \ldots + X[i, n] * W[n, 0]$$

"Systolic" matrix multiplication allows multiple $Y[i, j]$ values to be computed in parallel. Data flows in a coordinated manner and, indeed, in medicine the term "systolic" refers to heart contractions and how blood flows rhythmically in our veins. Here systolic refers to the data flow that pulses inside the TPU. It can be proven that a systolic multiplication algorithm is less expensive than the brute-force one [2]. A TPU v1 has a **Matrix Multiply Unit** (**MMU**) running systolic multiplications on 256 x 256 cores so that 65,536 multiplications can be computed in parallel in one single shot. In addition, a TPU v1 sits in a rack and it is not directly accessible. Instead, a CPU acts as the host controlling data transfer and sending commands to the TPU for performing tensor multiplications, for computing convolutions, and for applying activation functions. The CPU ↔ TPU v1 communication happens via a standard PCIe 3.0 bus. From this perspective, a TPU v1 is closer in spirit to a **Floating-Point Unit** (**FPU**) coprocessor than it is to a GPU. However, a TPU v1 has the ability to run whole inference models to reduce dependence on the host CPU. *Figure 15.2* represents TPU v1, as shown in [3]. As you see in the figure, the processing unit is connected via a PCI port, and it fetches weights via a standard DDR4 DRAM chip. Multiplication happens within the MMU with systolic processing. Activation functions are then applied to the results. The MMU and the unified buffer for activations take up a lot of space. There is an area where the activation functions are computed.

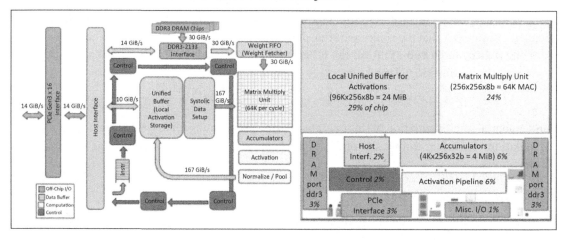

Figure 15.2: TPU v1 design schema (source [3])

TPU v1s are manufactured on a 28 nm process node with a die size of ≤ 331 mm2, a clock speed of 700 MHz, 28 MiB of on-chip memory, 4 MiB of 32-bit accumulators, and a 256 x 256 systolic array of 8-bit multipliers. For this reason, we can get 700 MHz*65,536 (multipliers) → 92 Tera operations/sec. This is an amazing performance for matrix multiplications; *Figure 15.3* shows the TPU circuit board and flow of data for the systolic matrix multiplication performed by the MMU. In addition, TPU v1 has an 8 GiB of dual-channel 2133 MHz DDR3 SDRAM offering 34 GB/s of bandwidth. The external memory is standard, and it is used to store and fetch the weights used during the inference. Notice also that TPU v1 has a thermal design power of 28–40 watts, which is certainly low consumption compared to GPUs and CPUs. Moreover, TPU v1s are normally mounted in a PCI slot used for SATA disks so they do not require any modification in the host server [3]. Up to four cards can be mounted on each server. *Figure 15.3* shows a TPU v1 card and the process of systolic computation:

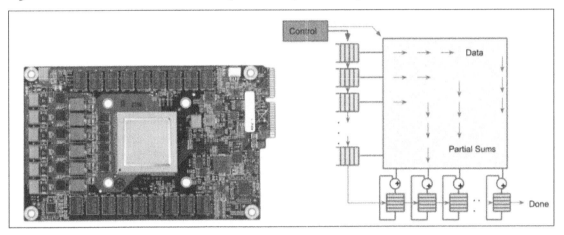

Figure 15.3: On the left you can see a TPU v1 board, and on the right an example of how the data is processed during the systolic computation

If you want to have a look at TPU performance compared to GPUs and CPUs, you can refer to [3] and see (in a log-log scale graph) that the performance is two orders of magnitude higher than a Tesla K80 GPU. The graph shows a "rooftop" performance, which is growing until the point where it reaches the peak and then it is constant.

The higher the roof, the better performance is:

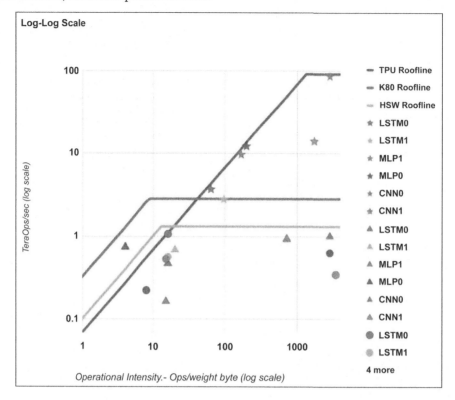

Figure 15.4: TPU v1 peak performance can be up to 3x higher than a Tesla K80

Second generation TPU

The second generation TPUs (TPU2s) were announced in 2017. In this case, the memory bandwidth is increased to 600 GB/s and performance reaches 45 TFLOPS. Four TPU2s are arranged in a module with 180 TFLOPS of performance. Then 64 modules are grouped into a pod with 11.5 PFLOPS of performance. TPU2s adopt floating-point arithmetic and therefore they are suitable for both training and inference.

A TPU2 has an MNU for matrix multiplications of 128*128 cores and a **Vector Processing Unit** (**VPU**) for all other tasks such as applying activations etc. The VPU handles float32 and int32 computations. The MXU on the other hand operates in a mixed precision 16–32 bit floating-point format.

Each TPU v2 chip has two cores, and up to four chips are mounted on each board. In TPU v2, Google adopted a new floating-point model called bfloat16 The idea is to sacrifice some resolution but still be very good for deep learning. This reduction in resolution allows us to improve the performance of the TPU2s, which are more power-efficient than the v1s. Indeed, It can be proven that a smaller mantissa helps reduce the physical silicon area and multiplier power. Therefore, the bfloat16 uses the same standard IEEE 754 single-precision floating-point format, but it truncates the mantissa field from 23 bits to just 7 bits.

Preserving the exponent bits allows the format to keep the same range as the 32-bit single precision. This allows for relatively simpler conversion between the two data types:

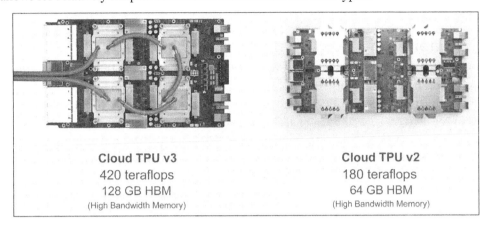

Figure 15.5: Cloud TPU v2 and Cloud TPU v3

Google offers access to these TPU v2 and TPU v3 via **Google Compute Engine** (GCE), and via **Google Kubernetes Engine** (GKE). Plus, it is possible to use them for free via Colab.

Third generation TPU

The third generation TPUs (TPU3) were announced in 2018 [4]. TPU3s are 2x faster than TPU2 and they are grouped in 4x larger pods. In total, this is an 8x performance increase. Cloud TPU v3 Pods can deliver more than 100 petaflops of computing power. On the other hand, Cloud TPU v2 Pods released in alpha in 2018 can achieve 11.5 petaflops – another impressive improvement. As of 2019, both TPU2 and TPU3 are in production at different prices:

Figure 15.6: Google announced TPU v2 and v3 Pods in beta at the Google I/O 2019

A TPU v3 board has four TPU chips, eight cores, and liquid cooling. Google has adopted ultra-high-speed interconnect hardware derived from supercomputer technology for connecting thousands of TPUs with very low latency.

Each time a parameter is updated on a single TPU, all the others are informed via a reduce-all algorithm typically adopted for parallel computation. So, you can think about a TPU v3 as one of the fastest supercomputers available today for matrix and tensor operations, with thousands of TPUs inside it.

Fourth generation TPUs

Google's fourth generation TPU ASIC has more than double the matrix multiplication TFLOPs of TPU v3, a considerable boost in memory bandwidth, and more advances in interconnect technology. Each TPU v4 chip provides more than 2x the compute power of a TPU v3 chip – up to 275 peak TFLOPS. Each TPU v4 Pod delivers 1.1 exaflops/s of peak performance. Google claims that TPU v4 Pods are used extensively to develop research breakthroughs such as MUM and LaMDA, and improve core products such as Search, Assistant, and Translate (see `https://blog.google/technology/developers/io21-helpful-google/`). As of April 2022, TPU v4s are only available in preview (*Figure 15.7*):

Figure 15.7: A TPU v4 chip and a portion of a TPU v4 Pod – source: https://twitter.com/google/status/1394785686683783170

In this section, we have introduced four generations of TPUs. Before concluding, I wanted to mention that it is possible to save money by using preemptible Cloud TPUs for fault-tolerant machine learning workloads. These workloads include but are not limited to long training runs with checkpointing or batch prediction on large datasets.

Edge TPU

In addition to the three generations of TPUs already discussed, in 2018 Google announced a special generation of TPUs running on the edge. This TPU is particularly appropriate for the **Internet of Things** (**IoT**) and for supporting TensorFlow Lite on mobile and IoT. An individual Edge TPU can perform 4 trillion (fixed-point) operations per second (4 TOPS), using only 2 watts of power. An Edge TPU is designed for small, low-power devices and is ideal for on-device ML, with it being fast and power-efficient. Edge TPUs support the TensorFlow Lite development framework (see *Figure 15.8*). At the end of 2019, Google announced the Pixel 4 smartphone containing an Edge TPU called the Pixel Neural Core:

Figure 15.8: Two Edge TPUs on one penny – source: https://coral.ai/docs/edgetpu/faq/#what-is-the-edge-tpu

With this we conclude the introduction to TPU v1, v2, v3, v4, and Edge TPU. In the next section we will briefly discuss performance.

TPU performance

Discussing performance is always difficult because it is important to first define the metrics that we are going to measure, and the set of workloads that we are going to use as benchmarks. For instance, Google reported an impressive linear scaling for TPU v2 used with ResNet-50 [4] (see *Figure 15.9* and *Figure 15.10*):

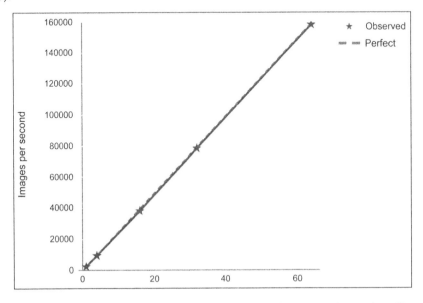

Figure 15.9: Linear scalability in the number of TPUs v2 when increasing the number of images

In addition, you can find online a comparison of ResNet-50 [4] where a full Cloud TPU v2 Pod is >200x faster than a V100 NVIDIA Tesla GPU for ResNet-50 training:

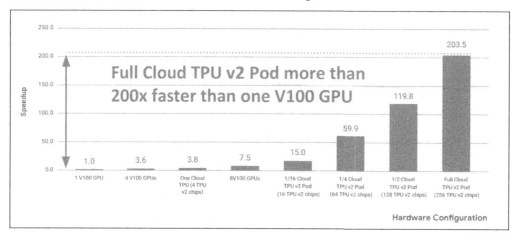

Figure 15.10: A full Cloud TPU v2 Pod is >200x faster than a V100 NVIDIA Tesla GPU for training a ResNet-50 model

According to Google, TPU v4 givse top-line results for MLPerf1.0 [5] when compared with NVIDIA A100 GPUs (see *Figure 15.11*). Indeed, these accelerators are designed by keeping in mind the latest large models encompassing billions and sometimes trillions of parameters (think about GPT-3, T5, and the Switch Transformer):

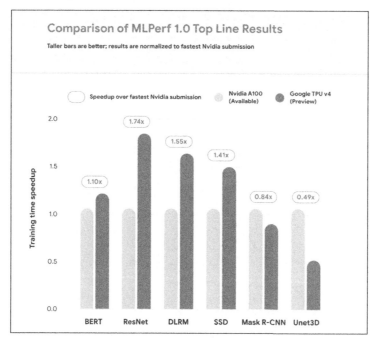

Figure 15.11: MLPerf 1.0 TPU v4 Pod performance – source: https://cloud.google.com/blog/products/ ai-machine-learning/google-wins-mlperf-benchmarks-with-tpu-v4

How to use TPUs with Colab

In this section, we show how to use TPUs with Colab. Just point your browser to `https://colab.research.google.com/` and change the runtime from the **Runtime** menu as shown in *Figure 15.12*. First, you'll need to enable TPUs for the notebook, then navigate to **Edit→Notebook settings** and select **TPU** from the **Hardware accelerator** drop-down box:

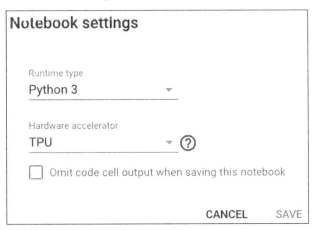

Figure 15.12: Setting TPU as the hardware accelerator

Checking whether TPUs are available

First of all, let's check if there is a TPU available, by using this simple code fragment that returns the IP address assigned to the TPU. Communication between the CPU and TPU happens via **gRPC (gRPC Remote Procedure Call)**, which is a modern, open-source, high-performance **Remote Procedure Call (RPC)** framework that can run in any environment:

```
%tensorflow_version 2.x
import tensorflow as tf
print("Tensorflow version " + tf.__version__)

try:
  tpu = tf.distribute.cluster_resolver.TPUClusterResolver()  # TPU detection
  print('Running on TPU ', tpu.cluster_spec().as_dict()['worker'])
except ValueError:
  raise BaseException('ERROR: Not connected to a TPU runtime; please see the
previous cell in this notebook for instructions!')

tf.config.experimental_connect_to_cluster(tpu)
tf.tpu.experimental.initialize_tpu_system(tpu)
tpu_strategy = tf.distribute.experimental.TPUStrategy(tpu)
```

You should see something like the following:

```
Tensorflow version 2.8.0
Running on TPU  ['10.36.66.50:8470']
INFO:tensorflow:Deallocate tpu buffers before initializing tpu system.
INFO:tensorflow:Deallocate tpu buffers before initializing tpu system.
INFO:tensorflow:Initializing the TPU system: grpc://10.36.66.50:8470
INFO:tensorflow:Initializing the TPU system: grpc://10.36.66.50:8470
INFO:tensorflow:Finished initializing TPU system.
INFO:tensorflow:Finished initializing TPU system.
WARNING:absl:'tf.distribute.experimental.TPUStrategy' is deprecated, please use
the non experimental symbol 'tf.distribute.TPUStrategy' instead.
INFO:tensorflow:Found TPU system:
INFO:tensorflow:Found TPU system:
INFO:tensorflow:*** Num TPU Cores: 8
INFO:tensorflow:*** Num TPU Cores: 8
INFO:tensorflow:*** Num TPU Workers: 1
INFO:tensorflow:*** Num TPU Workers: 1
INFO:tensorflow:*** Num TPU Cores Per Worker: 8
INFO:tensorflow:*** Num TPU Cores Per Worker: 8
```

We've confirmed that a TPU is available!

Keras MNIST TPU end-to-end training

Referring to the notebook available on Google Research Colab (see https://colab.research.google.
com/github/GoogleCloudPlatform/training-data-analyst/blob/master/courses/fast-and-lean-
data-science/01_MNIST_TPU_Keras.ipynb#scrollTo=Hd5zB1G7Y9-7), we can check how TPUs or
GPUs are detected with this code snippet, which uses either TPUs or GPUs as a fallback:

```
try: # detect TPUs
    tpu = tf.distribute.cluster_resolver.TPUClusterResolver.connect() # TPU
detection
    strategy = tf.distribute.TPUStrategy(tpu)
except ValueError: # detect GPUs
    strategy = tf.distribute.MirroredStrategy() # for GPU or multi-GPU machines
    #strategy = tf.distribute.get_strategy() # default strategy that works on
CPU and single GPU
    #strategy = tf.distribute.experimental.MultiWorkerMirroredStrategy() # for
clusters of multi-GPU machines
print("Number of accelerators: ", strategy.num_replicas_in_sync)
```

Note that the strategy tf.distribute.TPUStrategy(tpu) is the only change you need in code for
synchronous training on TPUs and TPU Pods. Then, to run TF2 programs on TPUs, you can either use
.compile or .fit APIs in tf.keras with TPUStrategy.

If you want you can write your own customized training loop by calling `strategy.run` directly (see `https://www.tensorflow.org/api_docs/python/tf/distribute/TPUStrategy`).

Using pretrained TPU models

Google offers a collection of models pretrained with TPUs available in the GitHub `tensorflow/tpu` repository (`https://github.com/tensorflow/tpu`). Models include image recognition, object detection, low-resource models, machine translation and language models, speech recognition, and image generation. Whenever it is possible, my suggestion is to start with a pretrained model [6], and then fine-tune it or apply some form of transfer learning. As of April 2022, the following models are available:

Image Recognition, Segmentation, and More	Machine Translation and Language Models	Speech Recognition	Image Generation
Image Recognition AmoebaNet-D ResNet-50/101/152/2000 Inception v2/v3/v4	**Machine Translation** (transformer based)	ASR Transformer	Image Transformer
Object Detection RetinaNet Mask R-CNN	**Sentiment Analysis** (transformer based) **Question Answer**		DCGAN GAN
Image Segmentation Mask R-CNN DeepLab RetinaNet	BERT		
Low-Resource Models MnasNet MobileNet SqueezeNet			

Table 15.1: State-of-the-art collection of models pretrained with TPUs available on GitHub

The best way to play with the repository is to clone it on the Google Cloud console and use the environment available at `https://github.com/tensorflow/tpu/blob/master/README.md`. You should be able to browse what is shown in *Figure 15.13*:

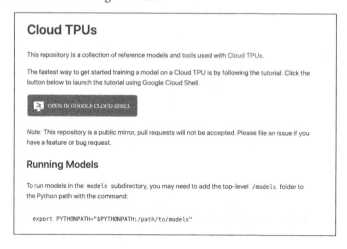

Figure 15.13: Cloud TPUs

If you click the button **OPEN IN GOOGLE CLOUD SHELL**, then the system will clone the Git repository into your cloud shell and then open the shell (see *Figure 15.14*):

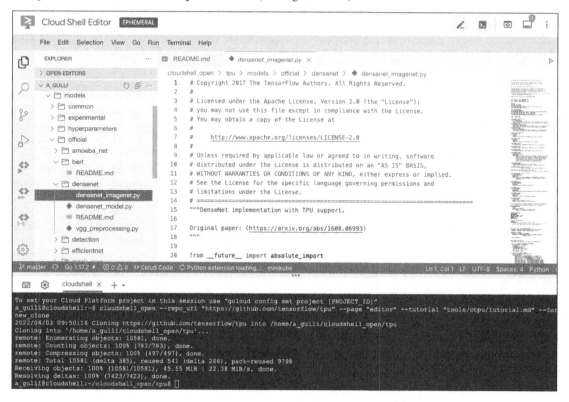

Figure 15.14: Google Cloud Shell with the TPU Git repository cloned on your behalf

From there, you can play with a nice Google Cloud TPU demo for training a ResNet-50 on MNIST with a TPU flock – a Compute Engine VM and Cloud TPU pair (see *Figure 15.15*):

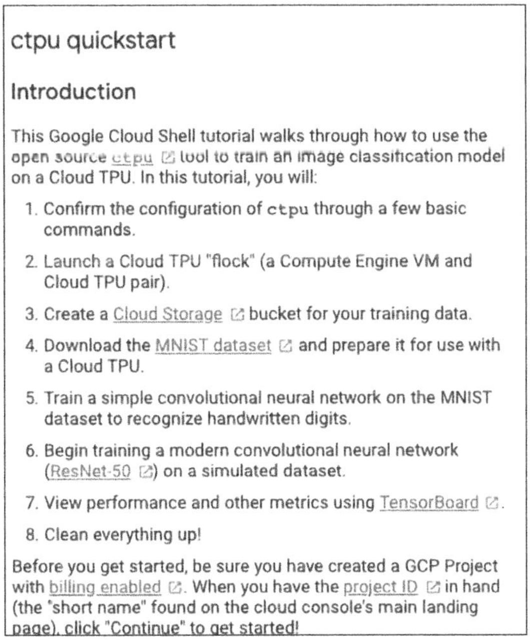

---

ctpu quickstart

Introduction

This Google Cloud Shell tutorial walks through how to use the open source ctpu ☑ tool to train an image classification model on a Cloud TPU. In this tutorial, you will:

1. Confirm the configuration of ctpu through a few basic commands.

2. Launch a Cloud TPU "flock" (a Compute Engine VM and Cloud TPU pair).

3. Create a Cloud Storage ☑ bucket for your training data.

4. Download the MNIST dataset ☑ and prepare it for use with a Cloud TPU.

5. Train a simple convolutional neural network on the MNIST dataset to recognize handwritten digits.

6. Begin training a modern convolutional neural network (ResNet-50 ☑) on a simulated dataset.

7. View performance and other metrics using TensorBoard ☑.

8. Clean everything up!

Before you get started, be sure you have created a GCP Project with billing enabled ☑. When you have the project ID ☑ in hand (the "short name" found on the cloud console's main landing page), click "Continue" to get started!

Figure 15.15: Google Cloud TPU demo for training a ResNet-50 on MNIST with a TPU flock

I will leave this training demo for you if you are interested in looking it up.

Summary

TPUs are very special ASIC chips developed at Google for executing neural network mathematical operations in an ultra-fast manner. The core of the computation is a systolic multiplier that computes multiple dot products (row * column) in parallel, thus accelerating the computation of basic deep learning operations. Think of a TPU as a special-purpose co-processor for deep learning that is focused on matrix or tensor operations. Google has announced four generations of TPUs so far, plus an additional Edge TPU for IoT. Cloud TPU v1 is a PCI-based specialized co-processor, with 92 teraops and inference only. Cloud TPU v2 achieves 180 teraflops and it supports training and inference. Cloud TPU v2 Pods released in alpha in 2018 can achieve 11.5 petaflops. Cloud TPU v3 achieves 420 teraflops with both training and inference support. Cloud TPU v3 Pods can deliver more than 100 petaflops of computing power. Each TPU v4 chip provides more than 2x the compute power of a TPU v3 chip – up to 275 peak TFLOPS. Each TPU v4 Pod delivers 1.1 exaflops/s of peak performance.

That's a world-class supercomputer for tensor operations!

In the next chapter, we will see some other useful deep learning libraries.

References

1. Moore's law: https://en.wikipedia.org/wiki/Moore%27s_law

2. Milovanović, I. Ž. et al. (May 2010). *Forty-three ways of systolic matrix multiplication.* Article in International Journal of Computer Mathematics 87(6):1264–1276.

3. Jouppi, N. P. et al. (June 2014). *In-Datacenter Performance Analysis of a Tensor Processing Unit.* 44th International Symposium on Computer Architecture (ISCA).

4. Google TPU v2 performance: https://storage.googleapis.com/nexttpu/index.html

5. MLPerf site: https://mlperf.org/

6. A collection of models pretrained with TPU: https://cloud.google.com/tpu

Join our book's Discord space

Join our Discord community to meet like-minded people and learn alongside more than 2000 members at: https://packt.link/keras

16

Other Useful Deep Learning Libraries

TensorFlow from Google is not the only framework available for deep learning tasks. There is a good range of libraries and frameworks available, each with its special features, capabilities, and use cases. In this chapter, we will explore some of the popular deep learning libraries and compare their features.

The chapter will include:

- Hugging Face
- H2O
- PyTorch
- ONNX
- Open AI

 All the code files for this chapter can be found at `https://packt.link/dltfchp16`.

Let's begin!

Hugging Face

Hugging Face is not new for us; *Chapter 6, Transformers,* introduced us to the library. Hugging Face is an NLP-centered startup, founded by Delangue and Chaumond in 2016. It has, in a short time, established itself as one of the best tools for all NLP-related tasks. The AutoNLP and accelerated inference API are available for a price. However, its core NLP libraries datasets, tokenizers, Accelerate, and transformers (*Figure 16.1*) are available for free. It has built a cool community-driven open-source platform.

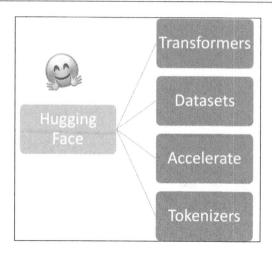

Figure 16.1: NLP libraries from Hugging Face

The core of the Hugging Face ecosystem is its transformers library. The Tokenizers and Datasets libraries support the Transformers library. To use these libraries, we need to install them first. Transformers can be installed using a simple `pip install` command:

```
pip install transformers
```

Some of the out-of-the-box models available with Hugging Face are text summarization, question answering, text classification, audio classification, automatic speech recognition, feature extraction, image classification, and translation. In *Figure 16.2*, we can see the result of the out-of-the-box summarization model available with Hugging Face.

A causal model makes predictions about the behavior of a system. In particular, a causal model entails the truth value, or the probability, of counterfactual claims about the system; it predicts the effects of interventions; and it entails the probabilistic dependence or independence of variables included in the model. Causal models also facilitate the inverse of these inferences: if we have observed probabilistic correlations among variables, or the outcomes of experimental interventions, we can determine which causal models are consistent with these observations. The discussion will focus on what it is possible to do in "in principle". For example, we will consider the extent to which we can infer the correct causal structure of a system, given perfect information about the probability distribution over the variables in the system. This ignores the very real problem of inferring the true probabilities from finite sample data. In addition, the entry will discuss the application of causal models to the logic of counterfactuals, the analysis of causation, and decision theory.

A causal model makes predictions about the behavior of a system . It entails the truth value, or the probability, of counterfactual claims about the system . Causal models also facilitate the inverse of these inferences . Discussion will focus on what it is possible to do in principle . For example, we will consider the extent to which we can infer the correct causal structure . This ignores the very real problem of inferring the true probabilities from finite sample data .

Figure 16.2: Out-of-the-box text summarization using Hugging Face

Besides these out-of-the-box models, we can use the large number of models and datasets available at Hugging Face Hub and can use them with PyTorch, TensorFlow, and JAX to build customized models.

OpenAI

OpenAI is another well-known name for people working in the field of reinforcement learning. Their Gym module is a standard toolkit used by developers across the globe for developing and comparing reinforcement learning algorithms. In *Chapter 11, Reinforcement Learning*, we have already covered the Gym module in detail. In this chapter, we will explore two more offerings by OpenAI.

OpenAI GPT-3 API

"OpenAI GPT3 is a machine learning platform that allows developers to build custom algorithms for deep learning. This platform was released in December of 2017 and has been widely used by businesses and individuals in the field of artificial intelligence. One of the primary reasons that GPT3 has been so successful is because it is easy to use and has a wide range of features. This platform is able to learn from data and can be used for a variety of tasks, including deep learning, natural language processing, and image recognition. GPT3 is also popular because it is open source and can be used by anyone. This makes it an ideal platform for anyone who wants to learn about deep learning and the various ways that it can be used. Overall, GPT3 is a powerful and easy-to-use machine learning platform that has been widely used by businesses and individuals in the field of artificial intelligence."

This is the text generated by the OpenAI GPT-3 API, when asked to write on GPT-3 itself (`https://beta.openai.com/playground`):

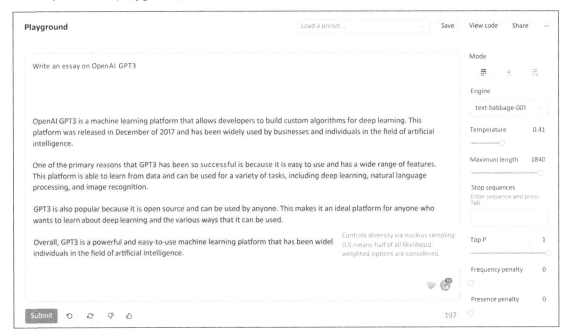

Figure 16.3: Text generation using OpenAI GPT-3 API

The OpenAI GPT-3 API offers the following tasks:

- **Text Completion:** Here, the GPT-3 API is used to generate or manipulate text and even code. You can use it to write a tagline, an introduction, or an essay, or you can leave a sentence half-written and ask it to complete it. People have used it to generate stories and advertisement leads.

- **Semantic Search:** This allows you to do a semantic search over a set of documents. For example, you can upload documents using the API; it can handle up to 200 documents, where each file can be a maximum of 150 MB in size, and the total limited to 1 GB at any given time. The API will take your query and rank the documents based on the semantic similarity score (ranges normally between 0-300).

- **Question Answering:** This API uses the documents uploaded as the source of truth; the API first searches the documents for relevance to the question. Then it ranks them based on the semantic relevance and finally, answers the question.

- **Text Classification:** The text classification endpoint of OpenAI GPT-3 takes as input a labeled set of examples and then uses the labels in it to label the query text. There are a lot of examples where this feature has been used to perform sentiment analysis.

Initially, the OpenAI GPT-3 was available only after applying for it, but now, anyone can use the API; there is no longer a waitlist.

OpenAI DALL-E 2

The GPT-3 API by OpenAI deals with all things related to NLP; DALL-E 2 goes a step further. DALL-E was originally released by OpenAI in January 2021. It claims to produce photorealistic images based on the textual description provided to the model. It can also make realistic edits to existing images; you can use it to add or remove objects and elements from the image, and when it does so, it considers the effect on shadows, reflections, and texture. *Figure 16.4* shows some of the remarkable feats by DALL-E 2. In the figures on the top row, I gave DALL-E 2 a text describing what I want: "Albert Einstein flying on dinosaur over the Amazon Forest." It generated a cartoon-like image. The images in the lower row are generated using the image-editor feature of DALL-E 2. I added the image on the left, and it generated four variations. The variations look very realistic if you ignore that the faces are blurred:

Figure 16.4: On top is the image generated by DALL-E 2, and below are the images edited by DALL-E 2

At the time of writing this book (August 2022), DALL-E 2 is not available for public use. But imagine the possibilities for artists and professionals working in creating digital media once the model is available as an API.

OpenAI Codex

When a student starts with their first lessons of programming, as a teacher, I often recommend that they think of a program as a set of instructions – the only important thing to master is writing those instructions as clearly as possible in whatever language you know.

Well, Codex makes it happen, you just need to give it the instructions of what you want to achieve, and it will generate the respective code for you.

OpenAI launches it as a general-purpose programming model, and it has been trained on publicly available GitHub codes.

Below are a few snippets of the task and corresponding code generated by Codex:

```python
""" Ask the user for their name and say "Hello" in Python """
print("Hello, world!")
name = input("Please type your name: ")
print("Hello, " + name + "!")



""" Write a program in Python to find sum of n fibonacci sequences """
def Fibonacci(n):
    if n < 0:
        print("Incorrect input")
    elif n == 1:
        return 0
    elif n == 2:
        return 1
    else:
        return Fibonacci(n - 1) + Fibonacci(n - 2)
n = int(input("Enter the number of terms: "))
```

```
# check if the number of terms is valid
if n <= 0:
    print("Please enter a positive integer")
else:
    print("Fibonacci sequence: ")
    for I in range(1, n + 1):
        print(Fibonacci(n), end=' ')
```

The first task, as you can see, is done flawlessly. In the second task, we asked it to find the sum of the Fibonacci sequence; instead, it generated the Fibonacci sequence, which is a more common problem. This tells us that while it is great at doing run-of-the-mill jobs, the need for real programmers is still there.

PyTorch

Like TensorFlow, PyTorch is a full-fledged deep learning framework. In AI-based social groups, you will often find die-hard fans of PyTorch and TensorFlow arguing that theirs is best. PyTorch, developed by Facebook (Meta now), is an open-source deep learning framework. Many researchers prefer it for its flexible and modular approach. PyTorch also has stable support for production deployment. Like TF, the core of PyTorch is its tensor processing library and its automatic differentiation engine. In a C++ runtime environment, it leverages TorchScript for an easy transition between graph and eager mode. The major feature that makes PyTorch popular is its ability to use dynamic computation, i.e., its ability to dynamically build the computational graph – this gives the programmer flexibility to modify and inspect the computational graphs anytime.

The PyTorch library consists of many modules, which are used as building blocks to make complex models. Additionally, PyTorch also provides convenient functions to transfer variables and models between different devices viz CPU, GPU, or TPU. Of special mention are the following three powerful modules:

- **NN Module:** This is the base class where all layers and functions to build a deep learning network are. Below, you can see the code snippet where the NN module is used to build a network. The network can then be instantiated using the statement net = My_Net(1,10,5); this creates a network with one input channel, 10 output neurons, and a kernel of size 5x5:

```
import torch.nn as nn
import torch.nn.functional as F

class My_Net(nn.Module):

    def __init__(self, input_channel, output_neurons, kernel_size):
        super(My_Net, self).__init__()
        self.conv1 = nn.Conv2d(input_channel, 6, kernel_size)
        self.conv2 = nn.Conv2d(6, 16, 5)
```

```
        self.fc1 = nn.Linear(16 * 5 * 5, 120)
        self.fc2 = nn.Linear(120, 84)
        self.fc3 = nn.Linear(84,output_neurons)

    def forward(self, x):
        x = F.max_pool2d(F.relu(self.conv1(x)), (2, 2))
        x = F.max_pool2d(F.relu(self.conv2(x)), 2)
        x = x.view(-1, self.num_flat_features(x))
        x = F.relu(self.fc1(x))
        x = F.relu(self.fc2(x))
        x = self.fc3(x)
        return x

    def num_flat_features(self, x):
        size = x.size()[1:]
        num_features = 1
        for s in size:
            num_features *= s
        return num_features
```

Here is a summary of the network:

```
My_Net(
    (conv1): Conv2d(1, 6, kernel_size=(5, 5), stride=(1, 1))
    (conv2): Conv2d(6, 16, kernel_size=(5, 5), stride=(1,
    1))
    (fc1): Linear(in_features=400, out_features=120,
    bias=True)
    (fc2): Linear(in_features=120, out_features=84,
    bias=True)
    (fc3): Linear(in_features=84, out_features=10,
    bias=True)
)
```

- **Autograd Module:** This is the heart of PyTorch. The module provides classes and functions that are used for implementing automatic differentiation. The module creates an acyclic graph called the dynamic computational graph; the leaves of this graph are the input tensors, and the root is the output tensors. It calculates a gradient by tracing the root to the leaf and multiplying every gradient in the path using the chain rule. The following code snippet shows how to use the Autograd module for calculating gradients. The backward() function computes the gradient of the loss with respect to all the tensors whose requires_grad is set to True. So suppose you have a variable w, then after the call to backward(), the tensor w.grad will give us the gradient of the loss with respect to w.

We can then use this to update the variable w as per the learning rule:

```
loss = (y_true - y_pred).pow(2).sum()


loss.backward()
# Here the autograd is used to compute the backward pass.


With torch.no_grad():
    W = w - lr_rate * w.grad
    w.grad = None # Manually set to zero after updating
```

- **Optim Module:** The Optim module implements various optimization algorithms. Some of the optimizer algorithms available in Optim are SGD, AdaDelta, Adam, SparseAdam, AdaGrad, and LBFGS. One can also use the Optim module to create complex optimizers. To use the Optim module, one just needs to construct an optimizer object that will hold the current state and will update the parameters based on gradients.

PyTorch is used by many companies for their AI solutions. **Tesla** uses PyTorch for **AutoPilot**. The Tesla Autopilot, which uses the footage from eight cameras around the vehicle, passes that footage through 48 neural networks for object detection, semantic segmentation, and monocular depth estimation. The system provides level 2 vehicle automation. They take video from all eight cameras to generate road layout, any static infrastructure (e.g., buildings and traffic/electricity poles), and 3D objects (other vehicles, persons on the road, and so on). The networks are trained iteratively in real time. While a little technical, this 2019 talk by Andrej Karpathy, Director of AI at Tesla, gives a bird's-eye view of Autopilot and its capabilities: `https://www.youtube.com/watch?v=oBklltKXtDE&t=670s`. Uber's Pyro, a probabilistic deep learning library, and OpenAI are other examples of big AI companies using PyTorch for research and development.

ONNX

Open Neural Network Exchange (ONNX) provides an open-source format for AI models. It supports both deep learning models and traditional machine learning models. It is a format designed to represent any type of model, and it achieves this by using an intermediate representation of the computational graph created by different frameworks. It supports PyTorch, TensorFlow, MATLAB, and many more deep learning frameworks. Thus, using ONNX, we can easily convert models from one framework to another. This helps in reducing the time from research to deployment. For example, you can use ONNX to convert a PyTorch model to ONNX.js form, which can then be directly deployed on the web.

H2O.ai

H2O is a fast, scalable machine learning and deep learning framework developed by H2O.ai, released under the open-source Apache license. According to the company website, as of the time of writing this book, more than 20,000 organizations use H2O for their ML/deep learning needs. The company offers many products like H2O AI cloud, H2O Driverless AI, H2O wave, and Sparkling Water. In this section, we will explore its open-source product, H2O.

It works on big data infrastructure on Hadoop, Spark, or Kubernetes clusters and it can also work in standalone mode. It makes use of distributed systems and in-memory computing, which allows it to handle a large amount of data in memory, even with a small cluster of machines. It has an interface for R, Python, Java, Scala, and JavaScript, and even has a built-in web interface.

H2O includes a large number of statistical-based ML algorithms such as generalized linear modeling, Naive Bayes, random forest, gradient boosting, and all major deep learning algorithms. The best part of H2O is that one can build thousands of models, compare the results, and even do hyperparameter tuning with only a few lines of code. H2O also has better data pre-processing tools.

H2O requires Java, therefore, ensure that Java is installed on your system. You can install H2O to work in Python using PyPi, as shown in the following code:

```
pip install h2o
```

H2O AutoML

One of the most exciting features of H2O is **AutoML**, the automatic ML. It is an attempt to develop a user-friendly ML interface that can be used by beginners and non-experts. H2O AutoML automates the process of training and tuning a large selection of candidate models. Its interface is designed so that users just need to specify their dataset, input and output features, and any constraints they want on the number of total models trained, or time constraints. The rest of the work is done by the AutoML itself, in the specified time constraint; it identifies the best performing models and provides a **leaderboard**. It has been observed that usually, the Stacked Ensemble model, the ensemble of all the previously trained models, occupies the top position on the leaderboard. There is a large number of options that advanced users can use; details of these options and their various features are available at http://docs.h2o.ai/h2o/latest-stable/h2o-docs/automl.html.

To learn more about H2O, visit their website: http://h2o.ai.

AutoML using H2O

Let us try H2O AutoML on a synthetically created dataset. We use the scikit-learn make_circles method to create the data and save it as a CSV file:

```
from sklearn.datasets import make_circles
import pandas as pd

X, y = make_circles(n_samples=1000, noise=0.2, factor=0.5, random_state=9)
df = pd.DataFrame(X, columns=['x1','x2'])
df['y'] = y
df.head()
df.to_csv('circle.csv', index=False, header=True)
```

Before we can use H2O, we need to initiate its server, which is done using the init() function:

```
import h2o
h2o.init()
```

The following shows the output we will receive after initializing the H2O server:

```
Checking whether there is an H2O instance running at http://localhost:54321
..... not found.
Attempting to start a local H2O server...
  Java Version: openjdk version "11.0.15" 2022-04-19; OpenJDK Runtime
Environment (build 11.0.15+10-Ubuntu-0ubuntu0.18.04.1); OpenJDK 64-Bit Server
VM (build 11.0.15+10-Ubuntu-0ubuntu0.18.04.1, mixed mode, sharing)
  Starting server from /usr/local/lib/python3.7/dist-packages/h2o/backend/bin/
h2o.jar
  Ice root: /tmp/tmpm2fsae68
  JVM stdout: /tmp/tmpm2fsae68/h2o_unknownUser_started_from_python.out
  JVM stderr: /tmp/tmpm2fsae68/h2o_unknownUser_started_from_python.err
  Server is running at http://127.0.0.1:54321
Connecting to H2O server at http://127.0.0.1:54321 ... successful.
H2O_cluster_uptime:      05 secs
H2O_cluster_timezone:      Etc/UTC
H2O_data_parsing_timezone:      UTC
H2O_cluster_version:      3.36.1.1
H2O_cluster_version_age:      27 days
H2O_cluster_name:      H2O_from_python_unknownUser_45enk6
H2O_cluster_total_nodes:      1
H2O_cluster_free_memory:      3.172 Gb
H2O_cluster_total_cores:      2
H2O_cluster_allowed_cores:      2
H2O_cluster_status:      locked, healthy
H2O_connection_url:      http://127.0.0.1:54321
H2O_connection_proxy:      {"http": null, "https": null}

H2O_internal_security:      False
Python_version:      3.7.13 final
```

We read the file containing the synthetic data that we created earlier. Since we want to treat the problem as a classification problem, whether the points lie in a circle or not, we redefine our label 'y' as asfactor() – this will tell the H2O AutoML module to treat the variable y as categorical, and thus the problem as classification. The dataset is split into training, validation, and test datasets in a ratio of 60:20:20:

```
class_df = h2o.import_file("circle.csv",\
                          destination_frame="circle_df")
class_df['y'] = class_df['y'].asfactor()

train_df,valid_df,test_df = class_df.split_frame(ratios=[0.6, 0.2],\
                                        seed=133)
```

And now we invoke the AutoML module from H2O and train on our training dataset. AutoML will search a maximum of 10 models, but you can change the parameter `max_models` to increase or decrease the number of models to test:

```
from h2o.automl import H2OAutoML as AutoML
aml = AutoML(max_models = 10, max_runtime_secs=100, seed=2)
aml.train(training_frame= train_df, \
          validation_frame=valid_df, \
          y = 'y', x=['x1','x2'])
```

For each of the models, it gives a performance summary, for example, in *Figure 16.5*, you can see the evaluation summary for a binomial GLM:

```
ModelMetricsBinomialGLM: stackedensemble
** Reported on validation data. **

MSE: 0.07563334941320102
RMSE: 0.2750151803322882
LogLoss: 0.251286872739174
Null degrees of freedom: 180
Residual degrees of freedom: 176
Null deviance: 250.97578384206275
Residual deviance: 90.96584793158101
AIC: 100.96584793158101
AUC: 0.9610741561961074
AUCPR: 0.972166745366916
Gini: 0.9221483123922147

Confusion Matrix (Act/Pred) for max f1 @ threshold = 0.33317394055922517:
```

		0	1	Error	Rate
0	0	70.0	12.0	0.1463	(12.0/82.0)
1	1	6.0	93.0	0.0606	(6.0/99.0)
2	Total	76.0	105.0	0.0994	(18.0/181.0)

Figure 16.5: Performance summary of one of the models by H2O AutoML

You can check the performance of all the models evaluated by H2O AutoML on a leaderboard:

```
lb = aml.leaderboard
lb.head()
```

Here is the snippet of the leaderboard:

```
model_id        auc      logloss     aucpr      mean_per_class_error      rmse       mse
StackedEnsemble_BestOfFamily_1_AutoML_2_20220511_61356          0.937598      0.315269
0.940757      0.117037      0.309796      0.0959735
StackedEnsemble_AllModels_1_AutoML_2_20220511_61356          0.934905      0.323695
0.932648      0.120348      0.312413      0.0976021
XGBoost_2_AutoML_2_20220511_61356          0.93281      0.322668      0.938299
0.122004      0.313339      0.0981811
```

```
XGBoost_3_AutoML_2_20220511_61356        0.932392     0.330866     0.929846
0.130168      0.319367      0.101995
GBM_2_AutoML_2_20220511_61356        0.926839     0.353181     0.923751     0.141713
0.331589      0.109951
XRT_1_AutoML_2_20220511_61356        0.925743     0.546718     0.932139     0.154774
0.331096      0.109625
GBM_3_AutoML_2_20220511_61356        0.923935     0.358691     0.917018     0.143374
0.334959      0.112197
DRF_1_AutoML_2_20220511_61356        0.922535     0.705418     0.921029     0.146669
0.333494      0.111218
GBM_4_AutoML_2_20220511_61356        0.921954     0.36403      0.911036     0.151582
0.336908      0.113507
XGBoost_1_AutoML_2_20220511_61356        0.919142     0.365454     0.928126
0.130227      0.336754      0.113403
```

H2O model explainability

H2O provides a convenient wrapper for a number of explainability methods and their visualizations using a single function explain() with a dataset and model. To get explainability on our test data for the models tested by AutoML, we will use aml.explain(). Below, we use the explain module for the StackedEnsemble_BestOfFamily model – the topmost in the leaderboard (we are continuing with the same data that we created in the previous section):

```
exa = aml.leader.explain(test_df)
```

The results are:

StackedEnsemble_BestOfFamily_1_AutoML_2_20220511_61356

```
Confusion Matrix (Act/Pred) for max f1 @ threshold = 0.3938662902106022:
              0      1   Error       Rate   ✐
0     0   104.0  10.0  0.0877   (10.0/114.0)

1     1    10.0  88.0   0.102   (10.0/98.0)

2  Total  114.0  98.0  0.0943   (20.0/212.0)
```

Figure 16.6: A confusion matrix on test dataset generated by H2O explain module

The ground truth is displayed in rows and the prediction by the model in columns. For our data, 0 was predicted correctly 104 times, and 1 was predicted correctly 88 times.

Partial dependence plots

Partial Dependence Plots (PDP) provide a graphical depiction of the marginal effect of a variable on the response of the model. It can tell us about the relationship between the output label and the input feature. *Figure 16.7* shows the PDP plots as obtained from the H2O explain module on our synthetic dataset:

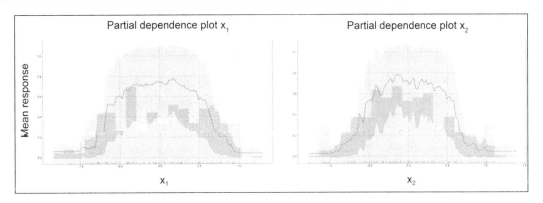

Figure 16.7: PDP for input features x_1 and x_2

For building PDP plots for each feature, H2O considers the rest of the features as constant. So, in the PDP plot for x_1 (x_2), the feature x_2 (x_1) is kept constant and the mean response is measured, as x_1 (x_2) is varied. The graph shows that both features play an important role in determining if the point is a circle or not, especially for values lying between [-0.5, 0.5].

Variable importance heatmap

We can also check the importance of variables across different models:

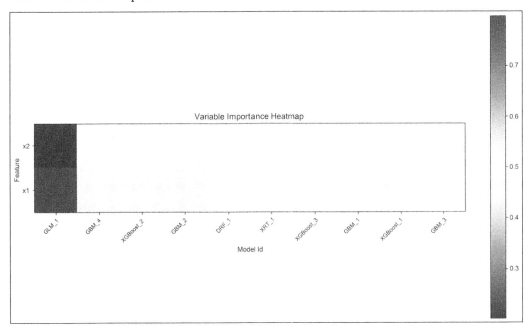

Figure 16.8: Variable importance heatmap for input features x_1 and x_2

Figure 16.8 shows how much importance was given to the two input features by different algorithms. We can see that the models that gave almost equal importance to the two features are doing well on the leaderboard, while **GLM_1**, which treated both features quite differently, has only about 41% accuracy.

Model correlation

The prediction between different models is correlated; we can check this correlation:

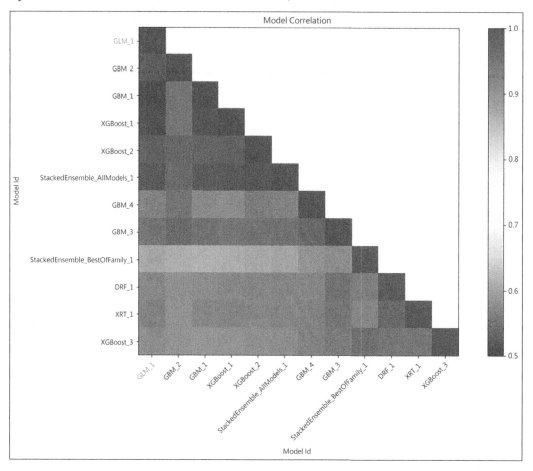

Figure 16.9: Model correlation

Figure 16.9 shows the model correlation; it shows the correlation between the predictions on the test dataset for different models. It measures the frequency of identical predictions to calculate correlations. Again, we can see that except for **GLM_1**, most other models perform almost equally, with accuracy ranging from 84-93% on the leaderboard.

What we have discussed here is just the tip of the iceberg; each of the frameworks listed here has entire books on their features and applications. Depending upon your use case, you should choose the respective framework. If you are building a model for production, TensorFlow is a better choice for both web-based and Edge applications. If you are building a model where you need better control of training and how the gradients are updated, then PyTorch is better suited. If you need to work cross-platform very often, ONNX can be useful. And finally, H2O and platforms like OpenAI GPT-3 and DALL-E 2 provide a low-threshold entry into the field of artificial intelligence and deep learning.

Summary

In this chapter, we briefly covered the features and capabilities of some other popular deep learning frameworks, libraries, and platforms. We started with Hugging Face, a popular framework for NLP. Then we explored OpenAI's GPT-3 and DALL-E 2, both very powerful frameworks. The GPT-3 API can be used for a variety of NLP-related tasks, and DALL-E 2 uses GPT-3 to generate images from textual descriptions. Next, we touched on the PyTorch framework. According to many people, PyTorch and TensorFlow are equal competitors, and PyTorch indeed has many features comparable to TensorFlow. In this chapter, we briefly talked about some important features like the NN module, Optim module, and Autograd module of PyTorch. We also discussed ONNX, the open-source format for deep learning models, and how we can use it to convert the model from one framework to another. Lastly, the chapter introduced H2O and its AutoML and `explain` modules.

In the next chapter, we will learn about graph neural networks.

Join our book's Discord space

Join our Discord community to meet like-minded people and learn alongside more than 2000 members at: `https://packt.link/keras`

17

Graph Neural Networks

In this chapter, we will look at a relatively new class of neural networks, the **Graph Neural Network (GNN)**, which is ideally suited for processing graph data. Many real-life problems in areas such as social media, biochemistry, academic literature, and many others are inherently "graph-shaped," meaning that their inputs are composed of data that can best be represented as graphs. We will cover what graphs are from a mathematical point of view, then explain the intuition behind "graph convolutions," the main idea behind GNNs. We will then describe a few popular GNN layers that are based on variations of the basic graph convolution technique. We will describe three major applications of GNNs, covering node classification, graph classification, and edge prediction, with examples using TensorFlow and the **Deep Graph Library (DGL)**. DGL provides the GNN layers we have just mentioned plus many more. In addition, it also provides some standard graph datasets, which we will use in the examples. Following on, we will show how you could build a DGL-compatible dataset from your own data, as well as your own layer using DGL's low-level message-passing API. Finally, we will look at some extensions of graphs, such as heterogeneous graphs and temporal graphs.

We will cover the following topics in this chapter:

- Graph basics
- Graph machine learning
- Graph convolutions
- Common graph layers
- Common graph applications
- Graph customizations
- Future directions

 All the code files for this chapter can be found at https://packt.link/dltfchp17

Let's begin with the basics.

Graph basics

Mathematically speaking, a graph G is a data structure consisting of a set of vertices (also called nodes) V, connected to each other by a set of edges E, i.e:

$$G = (V, E)$$

A graph can be equivalently represented as an adjacency matrix A of size (n, n) where n is the number of vertices in the set V. The element $A[I, j]$ of this adjacency matrix represents the edge between vertex i and vertex j. Thus the element $A[I, j] = 1$ if there is an edge between vertex i and vertex j, and 0 otherwise. In the case of weighted graphs, the edges might have their own weights, and the adjacency matrix will reflect that by setting the edge weight to the element $A[i, j]$. Edges may be directed or undirected. For example, an edge representing the friendship between a pair of nodes x and y is undirected, since x is friends with y implies that y is friends with x. Conversely, a directed edge can be one in a follower network (social media), where x following y does not imply that y follows x. For undirected graphs, $A[I, j] = A[j, i]$.

Another interesting property of the adjacency matrix A is that A^n, i.e., the product of A taken n times, exposes n-hop connections between nodes.

The graph-to-matrix equivalence is bi-directional, meaning the adjacency matrix can be converted back to the graph representation without any loss of information. Since **Machine Learning** (**ML**) methods, including **Deep Learning** (**DL**) methods, consume input data in the form of tensors, this equivalence means that graphs can be efficiently represented as inputs to all kinds of machine learning algorithms.

Each node can also be associated with its own feature vector, much like records in tabular input. Assuming a feature vector of size f, the set of nodes X can be represented as (n, f). It is also possible for edges to have their own feature vectors. Because of the equivalence between graphs and matrices, graphs are usually represented by libraries as efficient tensor-based structures. We will examine this in more detail later in this chapter.

Graph machine learning

The goal of any ML exercise is to learn a mapping F from an input space X to an output space y. Early machine learning methods required feature engineering to define the appropriate features, whereas DL methods can infer the features from the training data itself. DL works by hypothesizing a model M with random weights θ, formulating the task as an optimization problem over the parameters θ:

$$\min_{\theta} \mathcal{L}(y, F(x))$$

and using gradient descent to update the model weights over multiple iterations until the parameters converge:

$$\theta \leftarrow \theta - \eta \nabla_{\theta} \mathcal{L}$$

Not surprisingly, GNNs follow this basic model as well.

However, as you have seen in previous chapters, ML and DL are often optimized for specific structures. For example, you might instinctively choose a simple **FeedForward Network** (**FFN**) or "dense" network when working with tabular data, a **Convolutional Neural Network** (**CNN**) when dealing with image data, and a **Recurrent Neural Network** (**RNN**) when dealing with sequence data like text or time series. Some inputs may reduce to simpler structures such as pixel lattices or token sequences, but not necessarily so. In their natural form, graphs are topologically complex structures of indeterminate size and are not permutation invariant (i.e., instances are not independent of each other).

For these reasons, we need special tooling to deal with graph data. We will introduce in this chapter the DGL, a cross-platform graph library that supports users of MX-Net, PyTorch, and TensorFlow through the use of a configurable backend and is widely considered one of the most powerful and easy-to-use graph libraries available.

Graph convolutions – the intuition behind GNNs

The convolution operator, which effectively allows values of neighboring pixels on a 2D plane to be aggregated in a specific way, has been successful in deep neural networks for computer vision. The 1-dimensional variant has seen similar success in natural language processing and audio processing as well. As you will recall from *Chapter 3, Convolutional Neural Networks*, a network applies convolution and pooling operations across successive layers and manages to learn enough global features across a sufficiently large number of input pixels to succeed at the task it is trained for.

Examining the analogy from the other end, an image (or each channel of an image) can be thought of as a lattice-shaped graph where neighboring pixels link to each other in a specific way. Similarly, a sequence of words or audio signals can be thought of as another linear graph where neighboring tokens are linked to each other. In both cases, the deep learning architecture progressively applies convolutions and pooling operations across neighboring vertices of the input graph until it learns to perform the task, which is generally classification. Each convolution step encompasses an additional level of neighbors. For example, the first convolution merges signals from distance 1 (immediate) neighbors of a node, the second merges signals from distance 2 neighbors, and so on.

Figure 17.1 shows the equivalence between a 3 x 3 convolution in a CNN and the corresponding "graph convolution" operation. The convolution operator applies the filter, essentially a set of nine learnable model parameters, to the input and combines them via a weighted sum. You can achieve the same effect by treating the pixel neighborhood as a graph of nine nodes centered around the middle pixel.

A graph convolution on such a structure would just be a weighted sum of the node features, the same as the convolution operator in the CNN:

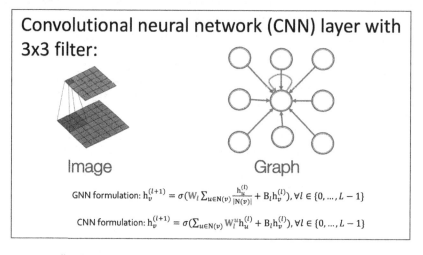

Figure 17.1: Parallels between convolutions in images and convolutions in graphs. Image source: CS-224W machine learning with Graphs, Stanford Univ.

The corresponding equations for the convolution operation on the CNN and the graph convolution are shown below. As you can see, on CNN, the convolution can be considered as a weighted linear combination of the input pixel and each of its neighbors. Each pixel brings its own weight in the form of the filter being applied. On the other hand, the graph convolution is also a weighted linear combination of the input pixel and an aggregate of all its neighbors. The aggregate effect of all neighbors is averaged into the convolution output:

$$h_v^{(l+1)} = \sigma\left(\sum_{u \in N(v)} W_l^u h_u^{(l)} + B_l h_v^{(l)}\right) \quad \dots (CNN)$$

$$h_v^{(l+1)} = \sigma\left(W_l \sum_{u \in N(v)} \frac{h_u^{(l)}}{|N(v)|} + B_l h_v^{(l)}\right) \quad \dots (Graph)$$

Graph convolutions are thus a variation of convolutions that we are already familiar with. In the following section, we will see how these convolutions can be composed to build different kinds of GCN layers.

Common graph layers

All the graph layers that we discuss in this section use some variation of the graph convolution operation described above. Contributors to graph libraries such as DGL provide prebuilt versions of many of these layers within a short time of it being proposed in an academic paper, so you will realistically never have to implement one of these. The information here is mainly for understanding how things work under the hood.

Graph convolution network

The **Graph Convolution Network (GCN)** is the graph convolution layer proposed by Kipf and Welling [1]. It was originally presented as a scalable approach for semi-supervised learning on graph-structured data. They describe the GCN as an operation over the node feature vectors X and the adjacency matrix A of the underlying graph and point out that this can be exceptionally powerful when the information in A is not present in the data X, such as citation links between documents in a citation network, or relations in a knowledge graph.

GCNs combine the value of each node's feature vector with those of its neighbors using some weights (initialized to random values). Thus, for every node, the sum of the neighboring node's features is added. This operation can be represented as follows:

$$X_i' = update(X_i, aggregate([X_j, j \in N(i)]))$$

Here the *update* and *aggregate* are different kinds of summation functions. This sort of projection on node features is called a message-passing mechanism. A single iteration of this message passing is equivalent to a graph convolution over each node's immediate neighbors. If we wish to incorporate information from more distant nodes, we can repeat this operation several times.

The following equation describes the output of the GCN at layer $(l+1)$ at node i. Here, $N(i)$ is the set of neighbors of node I (including itself), c_{ij} is the product of the square root of node degrees, and sigma is an activation function. The $b(l)$ term is an optional bias term:

$$h_i^{(l+1)} = \sigma(b^{(l)} + \sum_{j \in N(i)} \frac{1}{c_{ij}} h_j^{(l)} W^{(l)})$$

Next up, we will look at the graph attention network, a variant of the GCN where the coefficients are learned via an attentional mechanism instead of being explicitly defined.

Graph attention network

The **Graph Attention Network (GAT)** layer was proposed by Velickovic, et al. [2]. Like the GCN, the GAT performs local averaging of its neighbors' features. The difference is instead of explicitly specifying the normalization term c_{ij}, the GAT allows it to be learned using self-attention over the node features to do so. The corresponding normalization term is written as α for the GAT, which is computed based on the hidden features of the neighboring nodes and the learned attention vector. Essentially, the idea behind the GAT is to prioritize feature signals from similar neighbor nodes compared to dissimilar ones.

Every neighbor $j \in$ neighborhood $N(i)$ of node i sends its own vector of attentional coefficients α_{ij}. The following set of equations describes the output of the GAT at layer $(i+1)$ for node i. The attention α is computed using Bahdanau's attention model using a feedforward network:

$$h_i^{(l+1)} = \sum_{j \in N(i)} \alpha_{ij} W^{(l)} h_j^{(l)}$$

$$\alpha_{ij}^l = softmax(e_{ij}^l)$$

$$e_{ij}^l = LeakyReLU(\vec{a}^T[Wh_i || Wh_j])$$

GCN and GAT architectures are suitable for small to medium-sized networks. The GraphSAGE architecture, described in the next section, is more suitable for larger networks.

GraphSAGE (sample and aggregate)

So far, the convolutions we have considered require that all nodes in the graph be present during the training, and are therefore transductive and do not naturally generalize to unseen nodes. Hamilton, Ying, and Leskovec [3] proposed GraphSAGE, a general, inductive framework that can generate embeddings for previously unseen nodes. It does so by sampling and aggregating from a node's local neighborhood. GraphSAGE has proved successful at node classification on temporally evolving networks such as citation graphs and Reddit post data.

GraphSAGE samples a subset of neighbors instead of using them all. It can define a node neighborhood using random walks and sum up importance scores to determine the optimum sample. An aggregate function can be one of MEAN, GCN, POOL, and LSTM. Mean aggregation simply takes the element-wise mean of the neighbor vectors. The LSTM aggregation is more expressive but is inherently sequential and not symmetric; it is applied on an unordered set derived from a random permutation of the node's neighbors. The POOL aggregation is both symmetric and trainable; here, each neighbor vector is independently fed through a fully connected neural network and max pooling is applied across the aggregate information across the neighbor set.

This set of equations shows how the output for node i at layer $(l+1)$ is generated from node i and its neighbors $N(i)$ at layer l:

$$h_{N(i)}^{(l+1)} = aggregate([h_j^l \forall j \in N(i)])$$

$$h_i^{(l+1)} = \sigma(W . concat(h_i^l, h_{N(i)}^{(l+1)}))$$

$$h_i^{(l+1)} = norm(h_i^{(l+1)})$$

Now that we have seen strategies for handling large networks using GNNs, we will look at strategies for maximizing the representational (and therefore the discriminative) power of GNNs, using the graph isomorphism network.

Graph isomorphism network

Xu, et al. [4] proposed the **Graph Isomorphism Network (GIN)** as a graph layer with more expressive power compared to the ones available. Graph layers with high expressive power should be able to distinguish between a pair of graphs that are topologically similar but not identical. They showed that GCNs and GraphSAGE are unable to distinguish certain graph structures. They also showed that SUM aggregation is better than MEAN and MAX aggregation in terms of distinguishing graph structures. The GIN layer thus provides a better way to represent neighbor's aggregation compared to GCNs and GraphSAGE.

The following equation shows the output at node i and layer $(l+1)$. Here, the function f_θ is a callable activation function, *aggregate* is an aggregation function such as SUM, MAX, or MEAN, and ε is a learnable parameter that will be learned over the course of the training:

$$h_i^{(l+1)} = f_\theta((1 + \epsilon)h_i^l + aggregate(h_j^l, j \in N(i)))$$

Having been introduced to several popular GNN architectures, let us now direct our attention to the kind of tasks we can do with GNNs.

Common graph applications

We will now look at some common applications of GNNs. Typically, applications fall into one of the three major classes listed below. In this section, we will see code examples on how to build and train GNNs for each of these tasks, using TensorFlow and DGL:

- Node classification
- Graph classification
- Edge classification (or link prediction)

There are other applications of GNNs as well, such as graph clustering or generative graph models, but they are less common and we will not consider them here.

Node classification

Node classification is a popular task on graph data. Here, a model is trained to predict the node category. Non-graph classification methods can use the node feature vectors alone to do so, and some pre-GNN methods such as DeepWalk and node2vec can use the adjacency matrix alone, but GNNs are the first class of techniques that can use both the node feature vectors and the connectivity information together to do node classification.

Essentially, the idea is to apply one or more graph convolutions (as described in the previous section) to all nodes of a graph, to project the feature vector of the node to a corresponding output category vector that can be used to predict the node category. Our node classification example will use the CORA dataset, a collection of 2,708 scientific papers classified into one of seven categories. The papers are organized into a citation network, which contains 5,429 links. Each paper is described by a word vector of size 1,433.

We first set up our imports. If you have not already done so, you will need to install the DGL library into your environment with pip install dgl. You will also need to set the environment variable DGLBACKEND to TensorFlow. On the command line, this is achieved by the command export DGLBACKEND=tensorflow, and in a notebook environment, you can try using the magic %env DGLBACKEND=tensorflow:

```
import dgl
import dgl.data
import matplotlib.pyplot as plt
import numpy as np
```

```
import os
import tensorflow as tf
import tensorflow_addons as tfa


from dgl.nn.tensorflow import GraphConv
```

The CORA dataset is pre-packaged as a DGL dataset, so we load the dataset into memory using the following call:

```
dataset = dgl.data.CoraGraphDataset()
```

The first time this is called, it will log that it is downloading and extracting to a local file. Once done, it will print out some useful statistics about the CORA dataset. As you can see, there are 2,708 nodes and 10,566 edges in the graph. Each node has a feature vector of size 1,433 and a node is categorized as being in one of seven classes. In addition, we see that it has 140 training samples, 500 validation samples, and 1,000 test samples:

```
    NumNodes: 2708
    NumEdges: 10556
    NumFeats: 1433
    NumClasses: 7
    NumTrainingSamples: 140
    NumValidationSamples: 500
    NumTestSamples: 1000
Done saving data into cached files.
```

Since this is a graph dataset, it is expected to contain data pertaining to a set of graphs. However, CORA is a single citation graph. You can verify this by len(dataset), which will give you 1. This also means that downstream code will work on the graph given by dataset[0] rather than on the complete dataset. The node features will be contained in the dictionary dataset[0].ndata as key-value pairs, and the edge features in dataset[0].edata. The ndata contains the keys train_mask, val_mask, and test_mask, which are Boolean masks signifying which nodes are part of the train, validation, and test splits, respectively, and a feat key, which contains the feature vector for each node in the graph.

We will build a NodeClassifier network with two GraphConv layers. Each layer will compute a new node representation by aggregating neighbor information. GraphConv layers are just simple tf.keras.layers.Layer objects and can therefore be stacked. The first GraphConv layer projects the incoming feature size (1,433) to a hidden feature vector of size 16, and the second GraphConv layer projects the hidden feature vector to an output category vector of size 2, from which the category is read.

Note that GraphConv is just one of many graph layers that we can drop into the NodeClassifier model. DGL makes available a variety of graph convolution layers that can be used to replace GraphConv if needed:

```
class NodeClassifier(tf.keras.Model):
  def __init__(self, g, in_feats, h_feats, num_classes):
```

```
      super(NodeClassifier, self).__init__()
      self.g = g
      self.conv1 = GraphConv(in_feats, h_feats, activation=tf.nn.relu)
      self.conv2 = GraphConv(h_feats, num_classes)

   def call(self, in_feat):
     h = self.conv1(self.g, in_feat)
     h = self.conv2(self.g, h)
     return h


 g = dataset[0]
 model = NodeClassifier(
   g, g.ndata["feat"].shape[1], 16, dataset.num_classes)
```

We will train this model with the CORA dataset using the code shown below. We will use the AdamW optimizer (a variation of the more popular Adam optimizer that results in models with better generalization capabilities), with a learning rate of *1e-2* and weight decay of *5e-4*. We will train for 200 epochs. Let us also detect if we have a GPU available, and if so, assign the graph to the GPU.

TensorFlow will automatically move the model to the GPU if the GPU is detected:

```
 def set_gpu_if_available():
   device = "/cpu:0"
   gpus = tf.config.list_physical_devices("GPU")
   if len(gpus) > 0:
     device = gpus[0]
   return device


 device = set_gpu_if_available()
 g = g.to(device)
```

We also define a do_eval() method that computes the accuracy given the features and the Boolean mask for the split being evaluated:

```
 def do_eval(model, features, labels, mask):
   logits = model(features, training=False)
   logits = logits[mask]
   labels = labels[mask]
   preds = tf.math.argmax(logits, axis=1)
   acc = tf.reduce_mean(tf.cast(preds == labels, dtype=tf.float32))
   return acc.numpy().item()
```

Finally, we are ready to set up and run our training loop as follows:

```python
NUM_HIDDEN = 16
LEARNING_RATE = 1e-2
WEIGHT_DECAY = 5e-4
NUM_EPOCHS = 200

with tf.device(device):
  feats = g.ndata["feat"]
  labels = g.ndata["label"]
  train_mask = g.ndata["train_mask"]
  val_mask = g.ndata["val_mask"]
  test_mask = g.ndata["test_mask"]
  in_feats = feats.shape[1]
  n_classes = dataset.num_classes
  n_edges = dataset[0].number_of_edges()

  model = NodeClassifier(g, in_feats, NUM_HIDDEN, n_classes)
  loss_fcn = tf.keras.losses.SparseCategoricalCrossentropy(from_logits=True)
  optimizer = tfa.optimizers.AdamW(
    learning_rate=LEARNING_RATE, weight_decay=WEIGHT_DECAY)

  best_val_acc, best_test_acc = 0, 0
  history = []
  for epoch in range(NUM_EPOCHS):
    with tf.GradientTape() as tape:
      logits = model(feats)
      loss = loss_fcn(labels[train_mask], logits[train_mask])
      grads = tape.gradient(loss, model.trainable_weights)
      optimizer.apply_gradients(zip(grads, model.trainable_weights))

    val_acc = do_eval(model, feats, labels, val_mask)
    history.append((epoch + 1, loss.numpy().item(), val_acc))

    if epoch % 10 == 0:
      print("Epoch {:3d} | train loss: {:.3f} | val acc: {:.3f}".format(
        epoch, loss.numpy().item(), val_acc))
```

The output of the training run shows the training loss decreasing from 1.9 to 0.02 and the validation accuracy increasing from 0.13 to 0.78:

```
Epoch   0 | train loss: 1.946 | val acc: 0.134
Epoch  10 | train loss: 1.836 | val acc: 0.544
Epoch  20 | train loss: 1.631 | val acc: 0.610
Epoch  30 | train loss: 1.348 | val acc: 0.688
Epoch  40 | train loss: 1.032 | val acc: 0.732
Epoch  50 | train loss: 0.738 | val acc: 0.760
Epoch  60 | train loss: 0.504 | val acc: 0.774
Epoch  70 | train loss: 0.340 | val acc: 0.776
Epoch  80 | train loss: 0.233 | val acc: 0.780
Epoch  90 | train loss: 0.164 | val acc: 0.780
Epoch 100 | train loss: 0.121 | val acc: 0.784
Epoch 110 | train loss: 0.092 | val acc: 0.784
Epoch 120 | train loss: 0.073 | val acc: 0.784
Epoch 130 | train loss: 0.059 | val acc: 0.784
Epoch 140 | train loss: 0.050 | val acc: 0.786
Epoch 150 | train loss: 0.042 | val acc: 0.786
Epoch 160 | train loss: 0.037 | val acc: 0.786
Epoch 170 | train loss: 0.032 | val acc: 0.784
Epoch 180 | train loss: 0.029 | val acc: 0.784
Epoch 190 | train loss: 0.026 | val acc: 0.784
```

We can now evaluate our trained node classifier against the hold-out test split:

```
test_acc = do_eval(model, feats, labels, test_mask)
print("Test acc: {:.3f}".format(test_acc))
```

This prints out the overall accuracy of the model against the hold-out test split:

```
Test acc: 0.779
```

Graph classification

Graph classification is done by predicting some attribute of the entire graph by aggregating all node features and applying one or more graph convolutions to it. This could be useful, for example, when trying to classify molecules during drug discovery as having a particular therapeutic property. In this section, we will showcase graph classification using an example.

In order to run the example, please make sure DGL is installed and set to use the TensorFlow backend; refer to the previous section on node classification for information on how to do this. To begin the example, let us import the necessary libraries:

```
import dgl.data
import tensorflow as tf
```

```
import tensorflow_addons as tfa

from dgl.nn import GraphConv
from sklearn.model_selection import train_test_split
```

We will use the protein dataset from DGL. The dataset is a set of graphs, each with node features and a single label. Each graph represents a protein molecule and each node in the graph represents an atom in the molecule. Node features list the chemical properties of the atom. The label indicates if the protein molecule is an enzyme:

```
dataset = dgl.data.GINDataset("PROTEINS", self_loop=True)

print("node feature dimensionality:", dataset.dim_nfeats)
print("number of graph categories:", dataset.gclasses)
print("number of graphs in dataset:", len(dataset))
```

The call above downloads the protein dataset locally and prints out some information about the dataset. As you can see, each node has a feature vector of size 3, the number of graph categories is 2 (enzyme or not), and the number of graphs in the dataset is 1113:

```
node feature dimensionality: 3
number of graph categories: 2
number of graphs in dataset: 1113
```

We will first split the dataset into training, validation, and test. We will use the training dataset to train our GNN, validate using the validation dataset, and publish the results of our final model against the test dataset:

```
tv_dataset, test_dataset = train_test_split(
    dataset, shuffle=True, test_size=0.2)
train_dataset, val_dataset = train_test_split(
    tv_dataset, test_size=0.1)
print(len(train_dataset), len(val_dataset), len(test_dataset))
```

This splits the dataset into a training, validation, and test split of 801, 89, and 223 graphs, respectively. Since our datasets are large, we need to train our network using mini-batches so as not to overwhelm GPU memory. So, this example will also demonstrate mini-batch processing using our data.

Next, we define our GNN for graph classification. This consists of two `GraphConv` layers stacked together that will encode the nodes into their hidden representations. Since the objective is to predict a single category for each graph, we need to aggregate all the node representations into a graph-level representation, which we do by averaging the node representations using `dgl.mean_nodes()`:

```
class GraphClassifier(tf.keras.Model):
    def __init__(self, in_feats, h_feats, num_classes):
        super(GraphClassifier, self).__init__()
```

```
    self.conv1 = GraphConv(in_feats, h_feats, activation=tf.nn.relu)
    self.conv2 = GraphConv(h_feats, num_classes)

  def call(self, g, in_feat):
    h = self.conv1(g, in_feat)
    h = self.conv2(g, h)
    g.ndata["h"] = h
    return dgl.mean_nodes(g, "h")
```

For the training, we set the training parameters and the do_eval() function:

```
HIDDEN_SIZE = 16
BATCH_SIZE = 16
LEARNING_RATE = 1e-2
NUM_EPOCHS = 20


device = set_gpu_if_available()

def do_eval(model, dataset):
  total_acc, total_recs = 0, 0
  indexes = tf.data.Dataset.from_tensor_slices(range(len(dataset)))
  indexes = indexes.batch(batch_size=BATCH_SIZE)

  for batched_indexes in indexes:
    graphs, labels = zip(*[dataset[i] for i in batched_indexes])
    batched_graphs = dgl.batch(graphs)
    batched_labels = tf.convert_to_tensor(labels, dtype=tf.int64)
    batched_graphs = batched_graphs.to(device)
    logits = model(batched_graphs, batched_graphs.ndata["attr"])
    batched_preds = tf.math.argmax(logits, axis=1)
    acc = tf.reduce_sum(tf.cast(batched_preds == batched_labels,
                                dtype=tf.float32))
    total_acc += acc.numpy().item()
    total_recs += len(batched_labels)


  return total_acc / total_recs
```

Finally, we define and run our training loop to train our GraphClassifier model. We use the Adam optimizer with a learning rate of 1e-2 and the SparseCategoricalCrossentropy as the loss function, training, or 20 epochs:

```
with tf.device(device):
  model = GraphClassifier(
```

```
      dataset.dim_nfeats, HIDDEN_SIZE, dataset.gclasses)
  optimizer = tf.keras.optimizers.Adam(learning_rate=LEARNING_RATE)
  loss_fcn = tf.keras.losses.SparseCategoricalCrossentropy(
    from_logits=True)

  train_indexes = tf.data.Dataset.from_tensor_slices(
    range(len(train_dataset)))
  train_indexes = train_indexes.batch(batch_size=BATCH_SIZE)

  for epoch in range(NUM_EPOCHS):
    total_loss = 0
    for batched_indexes in train_indexes:
      with tf.GradientTape() as tape:
        graphs, labels = zip(*[train_dataset[i] for i in batched_indexes])
        batched_graphs = dgl.batch(graphs)
        batched_labels = tf.convert_to_tensor(labels, dtype=tf.int32)
        batched_graphs = batched_graphs.to(device)
        logits = model(batched_graphs, batched_graphs.ndata["attr"])
        loss = loss_fcn(batched_labels, logits)
        grads = tape.gradient(loss, model.trainable_weights)
        optimizer.apply_gradients(zip(grads, model.trainable_weights))
        total_loss += loss.numpy().item()

    val_acc = do_eval(model, val_dataset)
    print("Epoch {:3d} | train_loss: {:.3f} | val_acc: {:.3f}".format(
        epoch, total_loss, val_acc))
```

The output shows that the loss decreases and validation accuracy increases as the `GraphClassifier`
model is trained over 20 epochs:

```
Epoch    0 | train_loss: 34.401 | val_acc: 0.629
Epoch    1 | train_loss: 33.868 | val_acc: 0.629
Epoch    2 | train_loss: 33.554 | val_acc: 0.618
Epoch    3 | train_loss: 33.184 | val_acc: 0.640
Epoch    4 | train_loss: 32.822 | val_acc: 0.652
Epoch    5 | train_loss: 32.499 | val_acc: 0.663
Epoch    6 | train_loss: 32.227 | val_acc: 0.663
Epoch    7 | train_loss: 32.009 | val_acc: 0.697
Epoch    8 | train_loss: 31.830 | val_acc: 0.685
Epoch    9 | train_loss: 31.675 | val_acc: 0.685
Epoch   10 | train_loss: 31.580 | val_acc: 0.685
Epoch   11 | train_loss: 31.525 | val_acc: 0.708
```

```
Epoch  12 | train_loss: 31.485 | val_acc: 0.708
Epoch  13 | train_loss: 31.464 | val_acc: 0.708
Epoch  14 | train_loss: 31.449 | val_acc: 0.708
Epoch  15 | train_loss: 31.431 | val_acc: 0.708
Epoch  16 | train_loss: 31.421 | val_acc: 0.708
Epoch  17 | train_loss: 31.411 | val_acc: 0.708
Epoch  18 | train_loss: 31.404 | val_acc: 0.719
Epoch  19 | train_loss: 31.398 | val_acc: 0.719
```

Finally, we evaluate the trained model against our hold-out test dataset:

```
test_acc = do_eval(model, test_dataset)
print("test accuracy: {:.3f}".format(test_acc))
```

This prints out the accuracy of the trained `GraphClassifier` model against the held-out test split:

```
test accuracy: 0.677
```

The accuracy shows that the model can successfully identify a molecule as an enzyme or non-enzyme slightly less than 70% of the time.

Link prediction

Link prediction is a type of edge classification problem, where the task is to predict if an edge exists between two given nodes in the graph.

Many applications, such as social recommendation, knowledge graph completion, etc., can be formulated as link prediction, which predicts whether an edge exists between a pair of nodes. In this example, we will predict if a citation relationship, either citing or cited, exists between two papers in a citation network.

The general approach would be to treat all edges in the graph as positive examples and sample a number of non-existent edges as negative examples and train the link prediction classifier for binary classification (edge exists or not) on these positive and negative examples.

Before running the example, please make sure DGL is installed and set to use the TensorFlow backend; refer to the *Node classification* section for information on how to do this. Let us start by importing the necessary libraries:

```
import dgl
import dgl.data
import dgl.function as fn
import tensorflow as tf
import itertools
import numpy as np
import scipy.sparse as sp
```

```
from dgl.nn import SAGEConv
from sklearn.metrics import roc_auc_score
```

For our data, we will reuse the CORA citation graph from the DGL datasets that we had used for our node classification example earlier. We already know what the dataset looks like, so we won't dissect it again here. If you would like to refresh your memory, please refer to the node classification example for the relevant details:

```
dataset = dgl.data.CoraGraphDataset()
g = dataset[0]
```

Now, let us prepare our data. For training our link prediction model, we need a set of positive edges and a set of negative edges. Positive edges are one of the 10,556 edges that already exist in the CORA citation graph, and negative edges are going to be 10,556 node pairs without connecting edges sampled from the rest of the graph. In addition, we need to split both the positive and negative edges into training, validation, and test splits:

```
u, v = g.edges()

# positive edges
eids = np.arange(g.number_of_edges())
eids = np.random.permutation(eids)

test_size = int(len(eids) * 0.2)
val_size = int((len(eids) - test_size) * 0.1)
train_size = g.number_of_edges() - test_size - val_size

u = u.numpy()
v = v.numpy()

test_pos_u = u[eids[0:test_size]]
test_pos_v = v[eids[0:test_size]]
val_pos_u = u[eids[test_size:test_size + val_size]]
val_pos_v = v[eids[test_size:test_size + val_size]]
train_pos_u = u[eids[test_size + val_size:]]
train_pos_v = v[eids[test_size + val_size:]]

# negative edges
adj = sp.coo_matrix((np.ones(len(u)), (u, v)))
adj_neg = 1 - adj.todense() - np.eye(g.number_of_nodes())
neg_u, neg_v = np.where(adj_neg != 0)

neg_eids = np.random.choice(len(neg_u), g.number_of_edges())
test_neg_u = neg_u[neg_eids[:test_size]]
```

```
test_neg_v = neg_v[neg_eids[:test_size]]
val_neg_u = neg_u[neg_eids[test_size:test_size + val_size]]
val_neg_v = neg_v[neg_eids[test_size:test_size + val_size]]
train_neg_u = neg_u[neg_eids[test_size + val_size:]]
train_neg_v = neg_v[neg_eids[test_size + val_size:]]

# remove edges from training graph
test_edges = eids[:test_size]
val_edges = eids[test_size:test_size + val_size]
train_edges = eids[test_size + val_size:]
train_g = dgl.remove_edges(g, np.concatenate([test_edges, val_edges]))
```

We now construct a GNN that will compute the node representation using two GraphSAGE layers, each layer computing the node representation by averaging its neighbor information:

```
class LinkPredictor(tf.keras.Model):
  def __init__(self, g, in_feats, h_feats):
    super(LinkPredictor, self).__init__()
    self.g = g
    self.conv1 = SAGEConv(in_feats, h_feats, 'mean')
    self.relu1 = tf.keras.layers.Activation(tf.nn.relu)
    self.conv2 = SAGEConv(h_feats, h_feats, 'mean')

  def call(self, in_feat):
    h = self.conv1(self.g, in_feat)
    h = self.relu1(h)
    h = self.conv2(self.g, h)
    return h
```

However, link prediction requires us to compute representations of pairs of nodes, DGL recommends that you treat the pairs of nodes as another graph since you can define a pair of nodes as an edge. For link prediction, we will have a positive graph containing all the positive examples as edges, and a negative graph containing all the negative examples as edges. Both positive and negative graphs contain the same set of nodes as the original graph:

```
train_pos_g = dgl.graph((train_pos_u, train_pos_v),
  num_nodes=g.number_of_nodes())
train_neg_g = dgl.graph((train_neg_u, train_neg_v),
  num_nodes=g.number_of_nodes())

val_pos_g = dgl.graph((val_pos_u, val_pos_v),
  num_nodes=g.number_of_nodes())
val_neg_g = dgl.graph((val_neg_u, val_neg_v),
```

```
        num_nodes=g.number_of_nodes())

    test_pos_g = dgl.graph((test_pos_u, test_pos_v),
        num_nodes=g.number_of_nodes())
    test_neg_g = dgl.graph((test_neg_u, test_neg_v),
        num_nodes=g.number_of_nodes())
```

Next, we will define a predictor class that will take the set of node representations from the LinkPredictor class and use the DGLGraph.apply_edges method to compute edge feature scores, which are the dot product of the source node features and the destination node features (both output together from the LinkPredictor in this case):

```
class DotProductPredictor(tf.keras.Model):
    def call(self, g, h):
        with g.local_scope():
            g.ndata['h'] = h
            # Compute a new edge feature named 'score' by a dot-product
            # between the source node feature 'h' and destination node
            # feature 'h'.
            g.apply_edges(fn.u_dot_v('h', 'h', 'score'))
            # u_dot_v returns a 1-element vector for each edge so you
            # need to squeeze it.
            return g.edata['score'][:, 0]
```

You can also build a custom predictor such as a multi-layer perceptron with two dense layers, as the following code shows. Note that the apply_edges method describes how the edge score is calculated:

```
class MLPPredictor(tf.keras.Model):
    def __init__(self, h_feats):
        super().__init__()
        self.W1 = tf.keras.layers.Dense(h_feats, activation=tf.nn.relu)
        self.W2 = tf.keras.layers.Dense(1)

    def apply_edges(self, edges):
        h = tf.concat([edges.src["h"], edges.dst["h"]], axis=1)
        return {
            "score": self.W2(self.W1(h))[:, 0]
        }

    def call(self, g, h):
        with g.local_scope():
            g.ndata['h'] = h
            g.apply_edges(self.apply_edges)
            return g.edata['score']
```

We instantiate the LinkPredictor model we defined earlier, select the Adam optimizer, and declare our loss function to be BinaryCrossEntropy (since our task is binary classification). The predictor head that we will use in our example is the DotProductPredictor. However, the MLPPredictor can be used as a drop-in replacement instead; just replace the pred variable below to point to the MLPPredictor instead of the DotProductPredictor:

```
HIDDEN_SIZE = 16
LEARNING_RATE = 1e-2
NUM_EPOCHS = 100

model = LinkPredictor(train_g, train_g.ndata['feat'].shape[1],
    HIDDEN_SIZE)
optimizer = tf.keras.optimizers.Adam(learning_rate=LEARNING_RATE)
loss_fcn = tf.keras.losses.BinaryCrossentropy(from_logits=True)

pred = DotProductPredictor()
```

We also define a couple of convenience functions for our training loop. The first one computes the loss between the scores returned from the positive graph and the negative graphs, and the second computes the **Area Under the Curve (AUC)** from the two scores. AUC is a popular metric to evaluate binary classification models:

```
def compute_loss(pos_score, neg_score):
    scores = tf.concat([pos_score, neg_score], axis=0)
    labels = tf.concat([
      tf.ones(pos_score.shape[0]),
      tf.zeros(neg_score.shape[0])
    ], axis=0
)
    return loss_fcn(labels, scores)


def compute_auc(pos_score, neg_score):
    scores = tf.concat([pos_score, neg_score], axis=0).numpy()
    labels = tf.concat([
      tf.ones(pos_score.shape[0]),
      tf.zeros(neg_score.shape[0])
    ], axis=0).numpy()
    return roc_auc_score(labels, scores)
```

We now train our LinkPredictor GNN for 100 epochs of training, using the following training loop:

```
for epoch in range(NUM_EPOCHS):
  in_feat = train_g.ndata["feat"]
```

```
with tf.GradientTape() as tape:
  h = model(in_feat)
  pos_score = pred(train_pos_g, h)
  neg_score = pred(train_neg_g, h)
  loss = compute_loss(pos_score, neg_score)
  grads = tape.gradient(loss, model.trainable_weights)
  optimizer.apply_gradients(zip(grads, model.trainable_weights))

val_pos_score = pred(val_pos_g, h)
val_neg_score = pred(val_neg_g, h)
val_auc = compute_auc(val_pos_score, val_neg_score)

if epoch % 5 == 0:
  print("Epoch {:3d} | train_loss: {:.3f}, val_auc: {:.3f}".format(
    epoch, loss, val_auc))
```

This returns the following training logs:

```
Epoch   0 | train_loss: 0.693, val_auc: 0.566
Epoch   5 | train_loss: 0.681, val_auc: 0.633
Epoch  10 | train_loss: 0.626, val_auc: 0.746
Epoch  15 | train_loss: 0.569, val_auc: 0.776
Epoch  20 | train_loss: 0.532, val_auc: 0.805
Epoch  25 | train_loss: 0.509, val_auc: 0.820
Epoch  30 | train_loss: 0.492, val_auc: 0.824
Epoch  35 | train_loss: 0.470, val_auc: 0.833
Epoch  40 | train_loss: 0.453, val_auc: 0.835
Epoch  45 | train_loss: 0.431, val_auc: 0.842
Epoch  50 | train_loss: 0.410, val_auc: 0.851
Epoch  55 | train_loss: 0.391, val_auc: 0.859
Epoch  60 | train_loss: 0.371, val_auc: 0.861
Epoch  65 | train_loss: 0.350, val_auc: 0.861
Epoch  70 | train_loss: 0.330, val_auc: 0.861
Epoch  75 | train_loss: 0.310, val_auc: 0.862
Epoch  80 | train_loss: 0.290, val_auc: 0.860
Epoch  85 | train_loss: 0.269, val_auc: 0.856
Epoch  90 | train_loss: 0.249, val_auc: 0.852
Epoch  95 | train_loss: 0.228, val_auc: 0.848
```

We can now evaluate the trained model against the hold-out test set:

```
pos_score = tf.stop_gradient(pred(test_pos_g, h))
neg_score = tf.stop_gradient(pred(test_neg_g, h))
print('Test AUC', compute_auc(pos_score, neg_score))
```

This returns the following test AUC for our `LinkPredictor` GNN:

```
Test AUC 0.8266960571287392
```

This is quite impressive as it implies that the link predictor can correctly predict 82% of the links presented as ground truths in the test set.

Graph customizations

We have seen how to build and train GNNs for common graph ML tasks. However, for convenience, we have chosen to use prebuilt DGL graph convolution layers in our models. While unlikely, it is possible that you might need a layer that is not provided with the DGL package. DGL provides a message passing API to allow you to build custom graph layers easily. In the first part of this section, we will look at an example where we use the message-passing API to build a custom graph convolution layer.

We have also loaded datasets from the DGL data package for our examples. It is far more likely that we will need to use our own data instead. So, in the second part of this section, we will see how to convert our own data into a DGL dataset.

Custom layers and message passing

Although DGL provides many graph layers out of the box, there may be cases where the ones provided don't meet our needs exactly and we need to build your own.

Fortunately, all these graph layers are based on a common underlying concept of message passing between nodes in the graph. So, in order to build a custom GNN layer, you need to understand how the message-passing paradigm works. This paradigm is also known as the **Message Passing Neural Network (MPNN)** framework [5]:

$$m_{u \to v}^{(l)} = M^{(l)}(h_v^{(l-1)}, h_u^{(l-1)}, e_{u \to v}^{(l-1)})$$

$$m_v^{(l)} = \sum_{u \in N(v)} m_{u \to v}^{(l)}$$

$$h_v^{(l)} = U^{(l)}(h_v^{(l-1)}, m_v^{(l)})$$

Each node u in the graph has a hidden state (initially its feature vector) represented by h_u. For each node u and v, where nodes u and v are neighbors, i.e., connected by an edge $e_{u \to v}$, we apply some function M called the *message function*. The message function M is applied to every node on the graph. We then aggregate the output of M for all nodes with the output of all their neighboring nodes to produce the message m. Here $\sum$ is called the *reduce function*. Note that even though we represent the reduce function by the summation symbol $\sum$, it can be any aggregation function. Finally, we update the hidden state of node v using the obtained message and the previous state of the node. The function U applied at this step is called the *update function*.

The message-passing algorithm is repeated a specific number of times. After that, we reach the *readout phase* where we extract the feature vector from each node that represents the entire graph. For example, the final feature vector for a node might represent the node category in the case of node classification.

In this section, we will use the MPNN framework to implement a GraphSAGE layer. Even though DGL provides the `dgl.nn.SAGEConv`, which implements this already, this is an example to illustrate the creation of custom graph layers using MPNN. The message-passing steps of a GraphSAGE layer are given by:

$$h_{N(v)}^k \leftarrow AVG(h_u^{k-1}, \forall u \in N(v))$$

$$h_v^k \leftarrow ReLU(W^k . CONCAT(h_v^{k-1}, h_{N(v)}^k))$$

The code to implement our custom GraphSAGE layer using MPNN is shown below. The DGL function `update_all` call allows you to specify a `message_fn` and a `reduce_fn`, which are also DGL built-in functions, and the `tf.concat` and `Dense` layers represent the final update function:

```python
import dgl
import dgl.data
import dgl.function as fn
import tensorflow as tf


class CustomGraphSAGE(tf.keras.layers.Layer):
  def __init__(self, in_feat, out_feat):
    super(CustomGraphSAGE, self).__init__()
    # A Linear submodule for projecting the input and neighbor
    # feature to the output.
    self.linear = tf.keras.layers.Dense(out_feat, activation=tf.nn.relu)

  def call(self, g, h):
    with g.local_scope():
        g.ndata["h"] = h
        # update_all is a message passing API.
        g.update_all(message_func=fn.copy_u('h', 'm'),
                     reduce_func=fn.mean('m', 'h_N'))
        h_N = g.ndata['h_N']
        h_total = tf.concat([h, h_N], axis=1)
        return self.linear(h_total)
```

Here, we see that the `update_all` function specifies a `message_func`, which just copies the node's current feature vector to a message vector m, and then averages all the message vectors in the neighborhood of each node. As you can see, this faithfully follows the first GraphSAGE equation above. DGL provides many such built-in functions (`https://docs.dgl.ai/api/python/dgl.function.html`).

Once the neighborhood vector h_N is computed in the first step, it is concatenated with the input feature vector h, and then passed through a `Dense` layer with a ReLU activation, as described by the second equation for GraphSAGE above. We have thus implemented the GraphSAGE layer with our `CustomGraphSAGE` object.

The next step is to put it into a GNN to see how it works. The following code shows a `CustomGNN` model that uses two layers of our custom `SAGEConv` implementation:

```
class CustomGNN(tf.keras.Model):
  def __init__(self, g, in_feats, h_feats, num_classes):
    super(CustomGNN, self).__init__()
    self.g = g
    self.conv1 = CustomGraphSAGE(in_feats, h_feats)
    self.relu1 = tf.keras.layers.Activation(tf.nn.relu)
    self.conv2 = CustomGraphSAGE(h_feats, num_classes)

  def call(self, in_feat):
    h = self.conv1(self.g, in_feat)
    h = self.relu1(h)
    h = self.conv2(self.g, h)
    return h
```

We will run it to do node classification against the CORA dataset, details of which should be familiar from previous examples.

The above code assumes an unweighted graph, i.e., edges between nodes have the same weight. This condition is true for the CORA dataset, where each edge represents a citation from one paper to another.

However, we can imagine scenarios where edges may be weighted based on how many times some edge has been invoked, for example, an edge that connects a product and a user for user recommendations.

The only change we need to make to handle weighted edges is to allow the weight to play a part in our message function. That is, if an edge between our node u and a neighbor node v occurs k times, we should consider that edge k times. The code below shows our custom GraphSAGE layer with the ability to handle weighted edges:

```
class CustomWeightedGraphSAGE(tf.keras.layers.Layer):
  def __init__(self, in_feat, out_feat):
    super(CustomWeightedGraphSAGE, self).__init__()
    # A linear submodule for projecting the input and neighbor
    # feature to the output.
    self.linear = tf.keras.layers.Dense(out_feat, activation=tf.nn.relu)

  def call(self, g, h, w):
    with g.local_scope():
      g.ndata['h'] = h
      g.edata['w'] = w
      g.update_all(message_func=fn.u_mul_e('h', 'w', 'm'),
                   reduce_func=fn.mean('m', 'h_N'))
      h_N = g.ndata['h_N']
```

```
    h_total = tf.concat([h, h_N], axis=1)
    return self.linear(h_total)
```

This code expects an additional edge property w, which contains the edge weights, which you can simulate on the CORA dataset by:

```
g.edata["w"] = tf.cast(
    tf.random.uniform((g.num_edges(), 1), minval=3, maxval=10,
                        dtype=tf.int32),
    dtype=tf.float32)
```

The message_func in CustomWeightedGraphSAGE has changed from simply copying the feature vector h to the message vector m, to multiplying h and w to produce the message vector m. Everything else is the same as in CustomGraphSAGE. The new CustomWeightedGraphSAGE layer can now be simply dropped into the calling class CustomGNN where CustomGraphSAGE was originally being called.

Custom graph dataset

A more common use case that you are likely to face is to use your own data to train a GNN model. Obviously, in such cases, you cannot use a DGL-provided dataset (as we have been using in all our examples so far) and you must wrap your data into a custom graph dataset.

Your custom graph dataset should inherit from the dgl.data.DGLDataset object provided by DGL and implement the following methods:

*   __getitem__(self, i) – retrieve the i-th example from the dataset. The retrieved example contains a single DGL graph and its label if applicable.
*   __len__(self) – the number of examples in the dataset.
*   process(self) – defines how to load and process raw data from the disk.

As we have seen before, node classification and link prediction operate on a single graph, and graph classification operates on a set of graphs. While the approach is largely identical for both cases, there are some concerns specific to either case, so we will provide an example to do each of these below.

Single graphs in datasets

For our example, we will choose Zachary's Karate Club graph, which represents the members of a Karate Club observed over three years. Over time, there was a disagreement between an administrator (Officer) and the instructor (Mr. Hi), and the club members split and reformed under the Officer and Mr. Hi (shown below as blue and red nodes, respectively). The Zachary Karate Club network is available for download from the NetworkX library:

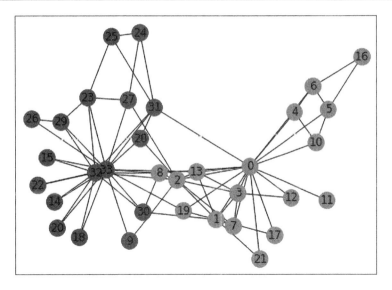

Figure 17.2: Graph representation of the Karate Club Network

The graph contains 34 nodes labeled with one of "Officer" or "Mr. Hi" depending on which group they ended up in after the split. It contains 78 edges, which are undirected and unweighted. An edge between a pair of members indicates that they interact with each other outside the club. To make this dataset more realistic for GNN usage, we will attach a 10-dimensional random feature vector to each node, and an edge weight as an edge feature. Here is the code to convert the Karate Club graph into a DGL dataset that you can then use for downstream node or edge classification tasks:

```
class KarateClubDataset(DGLDataset):
  def __init__(self):
    super().__init__(name="karate_club")

  def __getitem__(self, i):
    return self.graph

  def __len__(self):
    return 1

  def process(self):
    G = nx.karate_club_graph()
    nodes = [node for node in G.nodes]
    edges = [edge for edge in G.edges]
    node_features = tf.random.uniform(
        (len(nodes), 10), minval=0, maxval=1, dtype=tf.dtypes.float32)
    label2int = {"Mr. Hi": 0, "Officer": 1}
```

```
node_labels = tf.convert_to_tensor(
    [label2int[G.nodes[node]["club"]] for node in nodes])
edge_features = tf.random.uniform(
    (len(edges), 1), minval=3, maxval=10, dtype=tf.dtypes.int32)
edges_src = tf.convert_to_tensor([u for u, v in edges])
edges_dst = tf.convert_to_tensor([v for u, v in edges])

self.graph = dgl.graph((edges_src, edges_dst), num_nodes=len(nodes))
self.graph.ndata["feat"] = node_features
self.graph.ndata["label"] = node_labels
self.graph.edata["weight"] = edge_features

# assign masks indicating the split (training, validation, test)
n_nodes = len(nodes)
n_train = int(n_nodes * 0.6)
n_val = int(n_nodes * 0.2)
train_mask = tf.convert_to_tensor(
  np.hstack([np.ones(n_train), np.zeros(n_nodes - n_train)]),
  dtype=tf.bool)
val_mask = tf.convert_to_tensor(
  np.hstack([np.zeros(n_train), np.ones(n_val),
             np.zeros(n_nodes - n_train - n_val)]),
  dtype=tf.bool)
test_mask = tf.convert_to_tensor(
  np.hstack([np.zeros(n_train + n_val),
             np.ones(n_nodes - n_train - n_val)]),
  dtype=tf.bool)
self.graph.ndata["train_mask"] = train_mask
self.graph.ndata["val_mask"] = val_mask
self.graph.ndata["test_mask"] = test_mask
```

Most of the logic is in the process method. We call the NetworkX method to get the Karate Club as a NetworkX graph, then convert it to a DGL graph object with node features and labels. Even though the Karate Club graph does not have node and edge features defined, we manufacture some random numbers and set them to these properties. Note that this is only for purposes of this example, to show where these features would need to be updated if your graph had node and edge features. Note that the dataset contains a single graph.

In addition, we also want to split the graph into training, validation, and test splits for node classification purposes. For that, we assign masks indicating whether a node belongs to one of these splits. We do this rather simply by splitting the nodes in the graph 60/20/20 and assigning Boolean masks for each split.

In order to instantiate this dataset from our code, we can say:

```
dataset = KarateClubDataset()
g = dataset[0]
print(g)
```

This will give us the following output (reformatted a little for readability). The two main structures are the ndata_schemas and edata_schemas, accessible as g.ndata and g.edata, respectively. Within ndata_schemas, we have keys that point to the node features (feats), node labels (label), and the masks to indicate the training, validation, and test splits (train_mask, val_mask, and test_mask), respectively. Under edata_schemas, there is the weight attribute that indicates the edge weights:

```
Graph(num_nodes=34,
      num_edges=78,
      ndata_schemes={
          'feat': Scheme(shape=(10,), dtype=tf.float32),
          'label': Scheme(shape=(), dtype=tf.int32),
          'train_mask': Scheme(shape=(), dtype=tf.bool),
          'val_mask': Scheme(shape=(), dtype=tf.bool),
          'test_mask': Scheme(shape=(), dtype=tf.bool)
      }
      edata_schemes={
          'weight': Scheme(shape=(1,), dtype=tf.int32)
      }
)
```

Please refer to the examples on node classification and link prediction for information on how to use this kind of custom dataset.

Set of multiple graphs in datasets

Datasets that support the graph classification task will contain multiple graphs and their associated labels, one per graph. For our example, we will consider a hypothetical dataset of molecules represented as graphs, and the task would be to predict if the molecule is toxic or not (a binary prediction).

We will use the NetworkX method random_regular_graph() to generate synthetic graphs with a random number of nodes and node degree. To each node of each graph, we will attach a random 10-dimensional feature vector. Each node will have a label (0 or 1) indicating if the graph is toxic. Note that this is just a simulation of what real data might look like. With real data, the structure of each graph and the values of the node vectors, which are random in our case, will have a real impact on the target variable, i.e., the toxicity of the molecule.

The figure below shows some examples of what the synthetic "molecules" might look like:

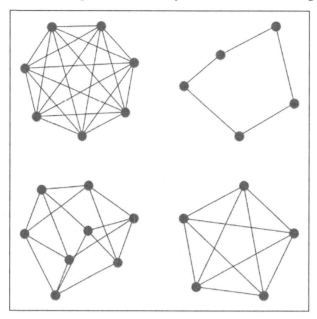

Figure 17.3: Some examples of random regular graphs generated using NetworkX

Here is the code to convert a set of random NetworkX graphs into a DGL graph dataset for graph classification. We will generate 100 such graphs and store them in a list in the form of a DGL dataset:

```python
from networkx.exception import NetworkXError

class SyntheticDataset(DGLDataset):
    def __init__(self):
        super().__init__(name="synthetic")

    def __getitem__(self, i):
        return self.graphs[i], self.labels[i]

    def __len__(self):
        return len(self.graphs)

    def process(self):
        self.graphs, self.labels = [], []
        num_graphs = 0
        while(True):
            d = np.random.randint(3, 10)
            n = np.random.randint(5, 10)
            if ((n * d) % 2) != 0:
```

```
            continue
        if n < d:
          continue
        try:
          g = nx.random_regular_graph(d, n)
        except NetworkXError:
          continue
        g_edges = [edge for edge in g.edges]
        g_src = [u for u, v in g_edges]
        g_dst = [v for u, v in g_edges]
        g_num_nodes = len(g.nodes)
        label = np.random.randint(0, 2)
        # create graph and add to list of graphs and labels
        dgl_graph = dgl.graph((g_src, g_dst), num_nodes=g_num_nodes)
        dgl_graph.ndata["feats"] = tf.random.uniform(
            (g_num_nodes, 10), minval=0, maxval=1, dtype=tf.dtypes.float32)
        self.graphs.append(dgl_graph)
        self.labels.append(label)

        num_graphs += 1
        if num_graphs > 100:
          break

    self.labels = tf.convert_to_tensor(self.labels, dtype=tf.dtypes.int64)
```

Once created, we can then call it from our code as follows:

```
dataset = SyntheticDataset()
graph, label = dataset[0]
print(graph)
print("label:", label)
```

This produces the following output for the first graph in the DGL dataset (reformatted slightly for readability). As you can see, the first graph in the dataset has 6 nodes and 15 edges and contains a feature vector (accessible using the feats key) of size 10. The label is a 0-dimensional tensor (i.e., a scalar) of type long (int64):

```
Graph(num_nodes=6, num_edges=15,
      ndata_schemes={
        'feats': Scheme(shape=(10,), dtype=tf.float32)}
      edata_schemes={})
label: tf.Tensor(0, shape=(), dtype=int64)
```

As before, in order to see how you would use this custom dataset for some task such as graph classification, please refer to the example on graph classification earlier in this chapter.

Future directions

Graph neural networks are a rapidly evolving discipline. We have covered working with static homogeneous graphs on various popular graph tasks so far, which covers many real-world use cases. However, it is likely that some graphs are neither homogeneous nor static, and neither can they be easily reduced to this form. In this section, we will look at our options for dealing with heterogenous and temporal graphs.

Heterogeneous graphs

Heterogeneous graphs [7], also called heterographs, differ from the graphs we have seen so far in that they may contain different kinds of nodes and edges. These different types of nodes and edges might also contain different types of attributes, including possible representations with different dimensions. Popular examples of heterogeneous graphs are citation graphs that contain authors and papers, recommendation graphs that contain users and products, and knowledge graphs that can contain many different types of entities.

You can use the MPNN framework on heterogeneous graphs by manually implementing message and update functions individually for each edge type. Each edge type is defined by the triple (source node type, edge type, and destination node type). However, DGL provides support for heterogeneous graphs using the dgl.heterograph() API, where a graph is specified as a series of graphs, one per edge type.

Typical learning tasks associated with heterogeneous graphs are similar to their homogeneous counterparts, namely node classification and regression, graph classification, and edge classification/ link prediction. A popular graph layer for working with heterogeneous graphs is the **Relational GCN** or **R-GCN**, available as a built-in layer in DGL.

Temporal Graphs

Temporal Graphs [8] is a framework developed at Twitter to handle dynamic graphs that change over time. While GNN models have primarily focused on static graphs that do not change over time, adding the time dimension allows us to model many interesting phenomena in social networks, financial transactions, and recommender systems, all of which are inherently dynamic. In such systems, it is the dynamic behavior that conveys the important insights.

A dynamic graph can be represented as a stream of timed events, such as additions and deletions of nodes and edges. This stream of events is fed into an encoder network that learns a time-dependent encoding for each node in the graph. A decoder is trained on this encoding to support some specific task such as link prediction at a future point in time. There is currently no support in the DGL library for Temporal Graphs, mainly because it is a very rapidly evolving research area.

At a high level, a **Temporal Graph Network** (**TGN**) encoder works by creating a compressed representation of the nodes based on their interaction and updates over time. The current state of each node is stored in TGN memory and acts as the hidden state s_t of an RNN; however, we have a separate state vector $s_i(t)$ for each node i and time point t.

A message function similar to what we have seen in the MPNN framework computes two messages m_i and m_j for a pair of nodes i and j using the state vectors and their interaction as input. The message and state vectors are then combined using a memory updater, which is usually implemented as an RNN. TGNs have been found to outperform their static counterparts on the tasks of future edge prediction and dynamic node classification both in terms of accuracy and speed.

Summary

In this chapter, we have covered graph neural networks, an exciting set of techniques to learn not only from node features but also from the interaction between nodes. We have covered the intuition behind why graph convolutions work and the parallels between them and convolutions in computer vision. We have described some common graph convolutions, which are provided as layers by DGL. We have demonstrated how to use the DGL for popular graph tasks of node classification, graph classification, and link prediction. In addition, in the unlikely event that our needs are not met by standard DGL graph layers, we have learned how to implement our own graph convolution layer using DGL's message-passing framework. We have also seen how to build DGL datasets for our own graph data. Finally, we look at some emerging directions of graph neural networks, namely heterogeneous graphs and temporal graphs. This should equip you with skills to use GNNs to solve interesting problems in this area.

In the next chapter, we will turn our attention to learning about some best ML practices associated with deep learning projects.

References

1. Kipf, T. and Welling, M. (2017). *Semi-supervised Classification with Graph Convolutional Networks*. Arxiv Preprint, arXiv: 1609.02907 [cs.LG]. Retrieved from `https://arxiv.org/abs/1609.02907`

2. Velickovic, P., et al. (2018). *Graph Attention Networks*. Arxiv Preprint, arXiv 1710.10903 [stat.ML]. Retrieved from `https://arxiv.org/abs/1710.10903`

3. Hamilton, W. L., Ying, R., and Leskovec, J. (2017). *Inductive Representation Learning on Large Graphs*. Arxiv Preprint, arXiv: 1706.02216 [cs.SI]. Retrieved from `https://arxiv.org/abs/1706.02216`

4. Xu, K., et al. (2018). *How Powerful are Graph Neural Networks?*. Arxiv Preprint, arXiv: 1810.00826 [cs.LG]. Retrieved from `https://arxiv.org/abs/1810.00826`

5. Gilmer, J., et al. (2017). *Neural Message Passing for Quantum Chemistry*. Arxiv Preprint, arXiv: 1704.01212 [cs.LG]. Retrieved from `https://arxiv.org/abs/1704.01212`

6. Zachary, W. W. (1977). *An Information Flow Model for Conflict and Fission in Small Groups*. Journal of Anthropological Research. Retrieved from `https://www.journals.uchicago.edu/doi/abs/10.1086/jar.33.4.3629752`

7. Pengfei, W. (2020). *Working with Heterogeneous Graphs in DGL*. Blog post. Retrieved from `https://www.jianshu.com/p/767950b560c4`

8. Bronstein, M. (2020). *Temporal Graph Networks*. Blog post. Retrieved from `https://towardsdatascience.com/temporal-graph-networks-ab8f327f2efe`

Join our book's Discord space

Join our Discord community to meet like-minded people and learn alongside more than 2000 members at: https://packt.link/keras

18

Machine Learning Best Practices

Machine learning is much more than building and training models. Till now in this book, we focused on different deep learning algorithms and introduced the latest algorithms, their power, and their limitations. In this chapter, we change our focus, from the ML/DL algorithms to the practices that can make us better machine learning engineers and scientists.

The chapter will include:

- The need for best practices for AI/ML
- Data best practices
- Model best practices

The need for best practices

Today, deep learning algorithms are not just an active research area but part and parcel of many commercial systems and products. *Figure 18.1* shows the investment in AI start-ups in the last five years. You can see that the interest in AI start-ups is continuously increasing. From healthcare to virtual assistants, from room cleaning robots to self-driving cars, AI today is the driving force behind many of the recent important technological advances. AI is deciding whether a person should be hired, or should be given a loan. AI is creating the feeds you see on social media. There are **Natural Language Processing (NLP)** bots generating content, images, faces – anything you can think of – there is someone trying to put AI into it. Since most teams consist of multiple team members working cross-domain, it is important to build best practices. What should be the best practices? Well, there is no definitive answer to this question as best practices in ML depend on the specific problem domain and dataset.

However, in this chapter we will provide some general tips for best practices in machine learning:

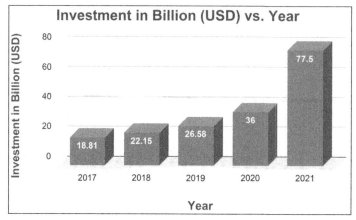

Figure 18.1: Investment in AI start-ups in the last five years (2017–2022)

Below are a few reasons why having best practices in machine learning is important:

- It can ensure that models are built in a way that is both effective and efficient.
- It can help to avoid issues such as overfitting, which can lead to poor performance on unseen data.
- It can ensure that the models are interpretable and can be easily explained to non-technical audiences.
- It can help to promote reproducibility in machine learning research.

In the coming sections, you will be introduced to some best practices as advocated by the **FAANG** (**Facebook, Amazon, Apple, Netflix,** and **Google**) companies and AI influencers. Following this advice can help you avoid common mistakes that can lead to inaccurate or poor results. These best practices will help ensure that your AI services are accurate and reliable. And finally, best practices can help you optimize your AI services for performance and efficiency.

Data best practices

Data is becoming increasingly important in today's world. Not just people in the field of AI but various world leaders are calling data "the new gold" or "the new oil" – basically the commodity that will drive the economy around the world. Data is helping in decision making processes, managing transport, dealing with supply chain issues, supporting healthcare, and so on. The insights derived from data can help businesses improve their efficiency and performance.

Most importantly, data can be used to create new knowledge. In business, for example, data can be used to identify new trends. In medicine, data can be used to uncover new relationships between diseases and to develop new treatments. However, our models are only as good as the data they are trained on. And therefore, the importance of data is likely to continue to increase in the future. As data becomes more accessible and easier to use, it will become increasingly important in a variety of fields. Let us now see some common bottlenecks and the best way to deal with them.

Feature selection

The first step when we start with any AI/ML problem is to propose a hypothesis: what are the input features that can help us in classifying or predicting our output? Choosing the right features is essential for any machine learning model, but it can be difficult to know which ones to choose. If you include too many irrelevant features in your model, your results will be inaccurate. If you include too few features, your model may not be able to learn from your data. Thus, feature selection is a critical step in machine learning that helps you reduce noise and improve the accuracy of your models:

- As a rule, before using any feature engineering, one should start with directly observed and reported features instead of learned features. Learned features are the features generated either by an external system (like a clustering algorithm) or by employing a deep model itself. Simplifying can help you achieve a solid baseline performance, after which you can experiment with more esoteric strategies.

- Remove the features that you are not using. Unused features create technical debt. They make your code more difficult to read and maintain and can also lead to unexpected bugs and security vulnerabilities. Of course, it can be difficult to keep track of which features are being used and which are not. However, do not drop the features arbitrarily; perform data analysis and exploration carefully – understand the features. A good way to do this would be to assign an owner to each feature. The feature owner would be responsible for maintaining the feature and documenting its rationale so that the knowledge can be shared across teams. This also means that whenever a feature owner leaves the team, ownership is transferred to other members. By taking the time to understand and remove unused features, you can keep your code clean and avoid accumulating technical debt.

- Often, we think more features equal a better model, but that is far from true. Instead of using millions of features you do not understand, it is better to work with specific features; you can use the method of regularization to remove the features that apply to too few examples.

- You can also combine and modify the features to create new features. There are a variety of ways you can combine and modify. For example, you can discretize continuously valued features into many discrete features. You can also create synthetic new features by crossing (multiplying) two or more existing features. For example, if you have the features "height" and "weight," you can create a new feature called "BMI" by combining those two features. Feature crossing can provide predictive abilities beyond what those features can provide individually. Two features that are each somewhat predictive of the desired outcome may be much more predictive when combined. This is because the combined feature captures information that is not captured by either individual feature. Feature crossing is a powerful tool that can help to improve the accuracy of predictive models.

Features and data

One of the problems when we move from learning data science to solving real problems is the lack of data. Despite the internet, mobile, and IoT devices generating loads of data, getting good-quality labeled data is a big hurdle. The cost of annotation is normally as high as it is time-consuming and requires subject matter expertise.

Thus, we need to ensure we have sufficient data to train the model. As a rule of thumb, the number of input features (n) that a model can learn is roughly proportional to the amount of data (N) you have ($n << N$). A few tips that can be followed in such a situation are:

- Scale model learning to the size of the data. For example, if we have only 1,000 labeled samples, then use highly human-engineered features. A good number would be to have a dozen well-selected features for 1,000 labeled samples. But if we have millions of examples, then we can afford to have about a hundred thousand features. And assuming we have billions of data samples, we can build a model with millions of features.

- If we have too much data, we do not arbitrarily drop it; instead, we can use **Importance Weight Sampling** (https://web.stanford.edu/class/archive/cs/cs224n/cs224n.1214/reports/final_reports/report247.pdf). The idea is to assign a weight of importance to each sample based on some distributional feature that captures similarity to the specialized domain data.

- Another way to deal with a lack of sufficient data is using data augmentation. Initially proposed for image data by H. S. Baird in his article, *Document image analysis* [7], it has proven to be a good way to increase image data by making use of simple image transformations, like horizontal flips, vertical flips, rotation, translation, etc. Most deep learning frameworks have data generators, which you can use to perform this augmentation on the go, as shown in *Figure 18.2*:

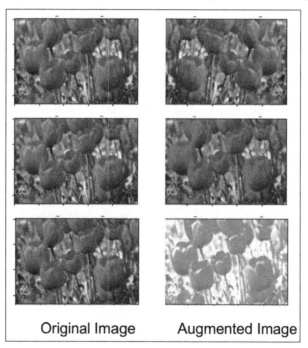

Original Image   Augmented Image

Figure 18.2: Original and augmented images

While augmenting image data is readily available in all the major deep learning frameworks, augmenting textual data and audio data is not that straightforward. Next, we present some of the techniques you can use to augment textual and speech data.

Augmenting textual data

Some of the simple ways that we can use to augment textual data are:

- **Synonym replacement:** In this, random words from the sentence are chosen and replaced by their synonyms using WordNet. For example, if we have the sentence "This book **focuses** on deep learning using TensorFlow and Keras and is meant for both **novices** and experts," we can choose the two words in bold for synonym replacement, resulting in this sentence: "This book **centers** on deep learning using TensorFlow and Keras and is meant for both **beginners** and experts."

- **Back translation:** The method was proposed by Sennrich et al. in 2016. The basic idea is that a sentence is translated into another language and then translated back to the original language. We can use language translation APIs or Python modules like googletrans. The following code snippet translates a sentence from English to German and back. For the code to work, we need to have googletrans installed:

```
from googletrans import Translator
translator = Translator()
text = 'I am going to the market for a walk'
translated = translator.translate(text, src='en', dest='de')
synthetic_text = translator.translate(translated.text, src='de', dest='en')
print(f'text: {text}\nTranslated: {translated.text}\nSynthetic Text:
{synthetic_text.text}')
```

Now we have two sentences "I am going to the market" and "I walk to the market" belonging to the same class. *Figure 18.3* details the process of data augmentation using back translation:

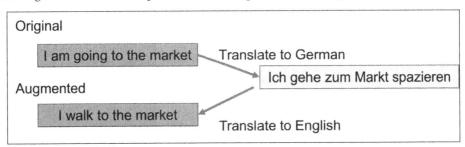

Figure 18.3: Data augmentation using back translation

In the review paper *A survey of Data Augmentation Approaches for NLP*, the authors provide an extensive list of many other augmentation methods. This paper provides an in-depth analysis of data augmentation for NLP.

In recent years, with the success of large language models and transformers, people have experimented with using them for the task of data augmentation. In the paper entitled *Data augmentation using pretrained transformers*, by the Amazon Alexa AI team, the authors demonstrate how by using only 10 training samples per class they can generate synthetic data using the pretrained transformers.

They experimented with three different pretrained models: an autoencoder LM BERT, an autoregressive LM GPT2, and the pretrained `seq2seq` model BART. *Figure 18.4* shows their algorithm for generating synthetic data using pretrained models:

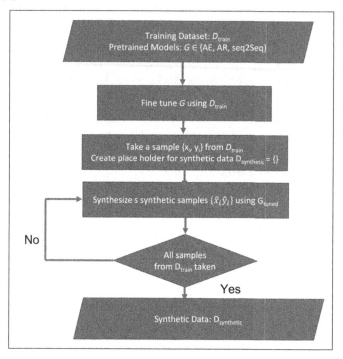

Figure 18.4: Algorithm for generating synthetic textual data using pretrained transformers

Speech data can also be augmented using techniques like:

- **Time warping:** Here a random point is selected and data is warped to either left or right with a distance w. The distance w is not fixed, and instead is chosen from a uniform distribution $[0, W]$.

- **Frequency Masking:** Here a range of frequency channels $[f_0, f_0+f)]$ are masked; the choice of frequency f_0 and f depends upon the number of frequency channels and frequency mask parameter F.

- **Time Masking:** In this case, the consecutive time steps are masked.

These techniques were proposed by the Google Team in 2019, in their paper *SpecAugment: A simple data augmentation method for Automatic Speech Recognition*.

Model best practices

Model accuracy and performance are critical to success for any machine learning and deep learning project. If a model is not accurate enough, the associated business use case will not be successful. Therefore, it is important to focus on model accuracy and performance to increase the chances of success. There are a number of factors that impact model accuracy and performance, so it is important to understand all of them in order to optimize accuracy and performance. Below we list some of the model best practices that can help us leverage best from our model development workflow.

Baseline models

A baseline model is a tool used in machine learning to evaluate other models. It is usually the simplest possible model, and acts as a comparison point for more complex models. The goal is to see if the more complex models are actually providing any improvements over the baseline model. If not, then there is no point in using the more complex model. Baseline models can also be used to help detect data leakage. Data leakage occurs when information from the test set bleeds into the training set, resulting in overfitting. By comparing the performance of the baseline model to other models, it is possible to detect when data leakage has occurred. Baseline models are an essential part of machine learning and provide a valuable perspective on the performance of more complex models. Thus, whenever we start working on a new problem, it is good to think of the simplest model that can fit the data and get a baseline.

Once we have built a satisfactory baseline model, we need to carefully review it.

Review the initial hypothesis about the dataset and the choice of our initial algorithms. For example, maybe when we first began working with the data, we hypothesized that the patterns we are observing would be best explained by a **Gaussian Mixture Model (GMM)**. However, after further exploration, we may find that the GMM is not able to capture the underlying structure of the data accurately. In that case we will need to rethink our strategy. Ultimately, our choice of algorithms is dictated by the nature of the data itself.

Confirm if the model is overfitting or underfitting. If the model is overfitting, try more data, reduce model complexity, increase batch size, or include regularization methods like **ridge**, **lasso**, or **dropout**. If the model is underfitting, try increasing model complexity, adding more features, and training for more epochs.

Analyze the model based on its performance metrics. For example, if we have made a classification model, analyze its confusion metrics and its precision/recall as per the business use case. Identify which class model is not predicting correctly; this should give us an insight into the data for those classes.

Perform hyperparameter tuning to get a strong baseline model. It is important that we establish a strong baseline model because it serves as a benchmark for future model improvements. The baseline should incorporate all the business and technical requirements, and test the data engineering and model deployment pipelines. By taking the time to develop a strong baseline, we can ensure that our machine learning project is on the right track from the start. Furthermore, a good baseline can help us identify potential areas of improvement as we iterate on our models. As such, it is well worth investing the time and effort to create a robust baseline model.

Pretrained models, model APIs, and AutoML

When we want to launch a commercial product, time and energy are often two of the most important factors. When working on a new project, it can be very time-consuming to train a baseline model from scratch. However, there are now a number of sources where we can find pretrained models that can save us a lot of time and effort. These include GitHub, Kaggle, and various cloud-based APIs from companies like Amazon, Google, OpenAI, and Microsoft.

In addition, there are specialized start-ups like Scale AI and Hugging Face that offer pretrained models for a variety of different tasks. By taking advantage of these resources, we can quickly get our machine learning projects up and running without having to spend a lot of time training a model from scratch. So, if our problem is a standard classification or regression problem, or we have structured tabular data available, we can make use of either pretrained models, or APIs provided by companies like Amazon, Google, and Microsoft. Using these approaches can save us valuable time and energy and allow us to get started with our project quickly.

Another solution that is evolving is using **AutoML**, or **Automatic Machine Learning**. Using AutoML, we can create custom models that are more tailored to a company's specific needs. If you are limited in terms of organizational knowledge and resources, we can still take advantage of machine learning at scale by utilizing AutoML. This solution has already been helping companies large and small to meet their business goals in a more efficient and accurate manner. In the future, it is likely that AutoML will only become more prevalent and popular as awareness of its capabilities grows.

Model evaluation and validation

In this section, we talk about ways of evaluating our model. Here we are not talking about conventional machine learning metrics, but instead focusing on the experience of the end user:

- **User experience techniques:** When our model is near production, we should test it further. Crowdsourcing is a great way to get feedback from our audience before we release the product. We can either pay people or use live experiments on real users in order for them to give valuable opinions about what works best. We can create user personas early in a process, that is, create hypothetical users – for example, if we are a team with an age group lying between 19–40 and we build a recommender system, we can create a user persona for someone in their sixties. Later, we can perform usability testing by bringing in actual people and watching their reactions to our site.

- **Use model deltas:** When we're releasing a new model, one of the best ways to measure its success is by calculating how different it is from the one in production. For example, if our ranking algorithm has been giving better results than expected but not as much so that people would notice, or care, then we should run both models on samples through the entire system with weights given by position rank. If we find that the difference between the two queries is very small, then we know that there will be little change. However, if the difference is large, we should ensure that the change is good. In this case we should explore the queries where symmetric differences are high; this will enable you to understand the change qualitatively.

- **Utilitarian power is more important than predictive power:** We may have a model with the highest accuracy and best prediction. But that is not the end; the question is what we do with that prediction. For example, if we build a model to semantically rank the documents, then the quality of the final ranking matters more than the prediction. Let us consider another example: let us say you built a spam filter, and our model predicts the probability whether the given message is spam or ham; we follow it with a cut-off on what text is blocked. In such a situation, what we allow to pass through matters most. So, it is possible that we get a model with better log loss, but still no improvement in overall performance. In such a case, we should look for other features to improve the performance.

- **Look for patterns in measured errors**: In training samples, check the ones the model is not able to predict correctly. Explore features that we have not yet considered yet; can they improve the prediction for the incorrect samples? Do not be very specific with features; we can add a dozen of them, and let the model decide what can be done with them. To visualize errors in classification problems, we can use a confusion matrix, and in regression tasks, we can look for cases where the loss is high.

- **Test on unseen data**: To measure the performance of our model, test it on the data that is gathered after the model has been trained; this way we will get an estimate of the performance in production. This may result in reduced performance, but the reduction should not be severe.

Performance monitoring is a crucial part of model development. The performance between training and production data can vary drastically, which means that we must continuously monitor the behavior of deployed models to make sure they're not doing anything unexpected in our system. We should build a monitoring pipeline that continuously monitors performance, quality and skew metrics, fairness metrics, model explanations, and user interactions.

Model improvements

Once a reliable model is built and deployed, the work is far from over. The model may need to be changed for various reasons, such as data drift or concept drift. Data drift occurs when the distribution of data changes over time, and concept drift occurs when the properties of dependent (labeled) variables change over time. To account for these changes, the model must be retrained on new data and updated accordingly. This process can be time-consuming and expensive, but it is essential to maintaining a high-performing machine learning model. However, before we jump into model improvement, it is important to identify and measure the reasons for low performance – **"measure first, optimize second"**:

Data drift: The performance of a machine learning model can vary depending on when it is trained and when it is deployed. This is because the data used during training and serving can be different. To avoid this problem, it is important to log the features at the time of deployment. This can allow us to monitor the variation in serving data (data in production). Once the data drift (the difference between training data and serving data) crosses a threshold, we should retrain the model with new data. This will ensure that the model is trained on the same data that it will be deployed on, and thus improve its performance.

Training-serving skew: Training-serving skew can be a major problem for machine learning models. If there is a discrepancy between how the model is trained and how it is used in the real world, this can lead to poor performance and inaccuracies. There are three main causes of training-serving skew: a discrepancy between the data used in training and serving, a change in the data between training and serving, and a feedback loop between the model and the algorithm. For example, if we have built a recommender system to recommend movies, we can then retrain the recommender later based on the movies users saw from the recommended list. The first two causes can be addressed by careful data management, while the third cause requires special attention when designing machine learning models.

It is possible that even after sufficient experimentation, we find that with the present features we cannot improve the model performance any further. However, to stay in business, continuous growth is necessary. Thus, when we find that our model performance has plateaued, it is time to look for new sources for improvements, instead of working with the existing features.

The software development process is never really "done." Even after a product is launched, there are always going to be new features that could be added or existing features that could be improved. The same is true for machine learning models. Even after a model is "finished" and deployed to production, there will always be new data that can be used to train a better model. And as data changes over time, the model will need to be retrained on new data to remain accurate. Therefore, it's important to think of machine learning models as being in a constant state of flux. It's never really "done" until you stop working on it.

As we build our model, it is important to think about how easy it is to add or remove features. Can we easily create a fresh copy of the pipeline and verify its correctness? Is it possible to have two or three copies of the model running in parallel? These are all important considerations when building our model. By thinking about these things upfront, we can save ourselves a lot of time and effort down the line.

Summary

In this chapter, we focused on the strategies and rules to follow to get the best performance from your models. The list here is not exhaustive, and since AI technology is still maturing, in the years to come we may see more rules and heuristics emerge. Still, if you follow the advice in the chapter, you will be able to move from the alchemical nature of AI models to more reliable, robust, and reproducible behavior.

In the next chapter, we will explore the TensorFlow ecosystem and see how we can integrate all that is covered in this book into practical business applications.

References

1. Soni, N., Sharma, E. K., Singh, N., and Kapoor, A. (2020). *Artificial intelligence in business: from research and innovation to market deployment.* Procedia Computer Science, *167*, 2200–2210.

2. Feng, S. Y., Gangal, V., Wei, J., Chandar, S., Vosoughi, S., Mitamura, T., and Hovy, E. (2021). *A survey of data augmentation approaches for NLP.* arXiv preprint arXiv:2105.03075.

3. Sennrich, R., Haddow, B., and Birch, A. (2016). *Improving Neural Machine Translation Models with Monolingual Data.* In Proceedings of the 54th Annual Meeting of the Association for Computational Linguistics (Volume 1: Long Papers), pages 86–96, Berlin, Germany. Association for Computational Linguistics.

4. Kumar, V., Choudhary, A., and Cho, E. (2020). *Data augmentation using pre-trained transformer models.* arXiv preprint arXiv:2003.02245.

5. Park, D. S., Chan, W., Zhang, Y., Chiu, C. C., Zoph, B., Cubuk, E. D., and Le, Q. V. (2019). *SpecAugment: A Simple Data Augmentation Method for Automatic Speech Recognition.* arXiv preprint arXiv:1904.08779.

6. Rules of Machine Learning: Best practices for ML engineering. Martin Zinkewich. `https://developers.google.com/machine-learning/guides/rules-of-ml`

7. Baird, H. S. (1995). *Document image analysis*. Chapter: Document Image Defect Models, pages 315–325. IEEE Computer Society Press, Los Alamitos, CA, USA.

Join our book's Discord space

Join our Discord community to meet like-minded people and learn alongside more than 2000 members at: `https://packt.link/keras`

19

TensorFlow 2 Ecosystem

In this chapter, we will learn about the different components of the TensorFlow ecosystem. The chapter will elaborate upon TensorFlow Hub – a repository for pretrained deep learning models – and TensorFlow Datasets – a collection of ready-to-use datasets for ML tasks. TensorFlow JS, the solution for training and deploying ML models on the web, will be introduced. We will also learn about TensorFlow Lite, an open-source deep learning framework for mobile and edge devices. Some examples of Android, iOS, and Raspberry Pi applications will be discussed, together with examples of deploying pretrained models such as MobileNet v1, v2, v3 (image classification models designed for mobile and embedded vision applications), PoseNet for pose estimation (a vision model that estimates the poses of people in image or video), DeepLab segmentation (an image segmentation model that assigns semantic labels (for example, dog, cat, and car) to every pixel in the input image), and MobileNet SSD object detection (an image classification model that detects multiple objects with bounding boxes). The chapter will conclude with an example of federated learning, a decentralized machine learning framework that is thought to respect user privacy. The chapter includes:

- TensorFlow Hub
- TensorFlow Datasets
- TensorFlow Lite and using it for mobile and edge applications
- Federated learning at edge
- TensorFlow JS
- Using Node.js with TensorFlow models

 All the code files for this chapter can be found at https://packt.link/dltfchp19

Let's begin with TensorFlow Hub.

TensorFlow Hub

Even if you have a powerful computer, training a machine learning model can take days or weeks. And once you've trained the model, deploying it to different devices can be difficult and time-consuming. Depending upon the platform you want to deploy, you might need it in different formats.

You can think of TensorFlow Hub as a library with many pretrained models. It contains hundreds of trained, ready-to-deploy deep learning models. TensorFlow Hub provides pretrained models for image classification, image segmentation, object detection, text embedding, text classification, video classification and generation, and much more. The models in TF Hub are available in SavedModel, TFLite, and TF.js formats. We can use these pretrained models directly for inference or fine-tune them. With its growing community of users and developers, TensorFlow Hub is the go-to place for finding and sharing machine learning models. To use TensorFlow Hub, we first need to install it:

```
pip install tensorflow_hub
```

Once installed, we can import it simply using:

```
import tensorflow_hub as hub
```

and load the model using the load function:

```
model = hub.load(handle)
```

Here handle is a string, which contains the link of the model we wants to use. If we want to use it as part of our existing model, we can wrap it as a Keras layer:

```
hub.KerasLayer(
    handle,
    trainable=False,
    arguments=None,
    _sentinel=None,
    tags=None,
    signature=None,
    signature_outputs_as_dict=None,
    output_key=None,
    output_shape=None,
    load_options=None,
    **kwargs
)
```

By changing the parameter trainable to True, we can fine-tune the model for our specific data.

Figure 19.1 shows the easy-to-use web interface to select different models at the tfhub.dev site. Using the filters, we can easily find a model to solve our problem.

We can choose which type and format we need, as well as who published it!

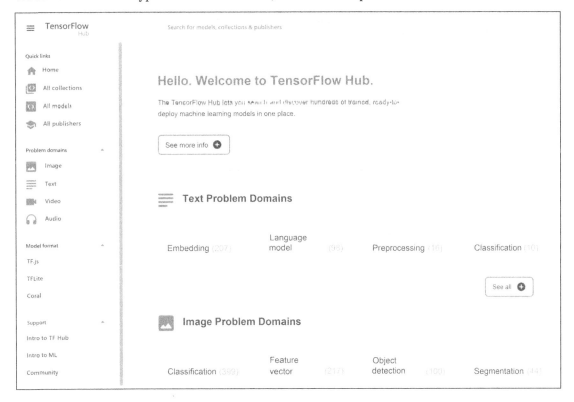

Figure 19.1: The tfhub.dev site showing different filters

Using pretrained models for inference

Let us see how you can leverage pretrained models from TensorFlow Hub. We will consider an example of image classification:

1.   Let us import the necessary modules:

```
import tensorflow as tf
import tensorflow_hub as hub

import requests
from PIL import Image
from io import BytesIO

import matplotlib.pyplot as plt
import numpy as np
```

2. We define a function for loading an image from a URL. The functions get the image from the web, and we reshape it by adding batch indexes for inference. Also, the image is normalized and resized according to the pretrained model chosen:

```
def load_image_from_url(img_url, image_size):
  """Get the image from url. The image return has shape [1, height,
width, num_channels]."""
  response = requests.get(img_url, headers={'User-agent': 'Colab Sample
(https://tensorflow.org)'})
  image = Image.open(BytesIO(response.content))
  image = np.array(image)
  # reshape image
  img_reshaped = tf.reshape(image, [1, image.shape[0], image.shape[1],
image.shape[2]])
  # Normalize by convert to float between [0,1]
  image = tf.image.convert_image_dtype(img_reshaped, tf.float32)
  image_padded = tf.image.resize_with_pad(image, image_size, image_size)
  return image_padded, image
```

3. Another helper function to show the image:

```
def show_image(image, title=''):
  image_size = image.shape[1]
  w = (image_size * 6) // 320
  plt.figure(figsize=(w, w))
  plt.imshow(image[0], aspect='equal')
  plt.axis('off')
  plt.title(title)
  plt.show()
```

4. The model we are using is EfficientNet-B2 (https://arxiv.org/abs/1905.11946) trained on the ImageNet dataset. It gives better accuracy, is smaller in size, and gives faster inference. For convenience, we choose images to be resized to 330 x 330 pixels. We use the helper function defined in step 2 to download the image from Wikimedia:

```
image_size = 330
print(f"Images will be converted to {image_size}x{image_size}")
img_url = "https://upload.wikimedia.org/wikipedia/commons/c/c6/Okonjima_
Lioness.jpg"
image, original_image = load_image_from_url(img_url, image_size)
show_image(image, 'Scaled image')
```

Figure 19.2: The image taken from the web for classification, scaled to size 330 x 330 pixels

5. For completeness, we also get all the labels of ImageNet data so that we can infer the label from the model prediction; we download it from a public repository of TensorFlow:

```
labels_file = "https://storage.googleapis.com/download.tensorflow.org/
data/ImageNetLabels.txt"

#download labels and creates a maps
downloaded_file = tf.keras.utils.get_file("labels.txt", origin=labels_
file)

classes = []

with open(downloaded_file) as f:
  labels = f.readlines()
  classes = [l.strip() for l in labels]
```

6. Now that all the ingredients are ready, we download the model from tfhub.dev:

```
classifier = hub.load("https://tfhub.dev/tensorflow/efficientnet/b2/
classification/1")
```

7. We get the softmax probabilities for all the classes for the image downloaded in step 5:

    ```
    probabilities = tf.nn.softmax(classifier(image)).numpy()
    ```

8. Let us see the top prediction:

    ```
    top_5 = tf.argsort(probabilities, axis=-1, direction="DESCENDING")[0]
    [:5].numpy()

    show_image(image, f'{classes[top_5[0]+1]}: {probabilities[0][top_5]
    [0]:.4f}')
    ```

Figure 19.3: The image with the label prediction of lion

So, as we can see, in a few lines of code we get a perfect inference – the image is of a lioness, and the closest label for it in the ImageNet dataset is that of a lion, which the model has correctly predicted. By using the pretrained models of TF Hub, we can focus on our product workflow, and get better models and faster production.

TensorFlow Datasets

TensorFlow Datasets (TFDS) is a powerful tool for anyone working with machine learning. It provides a collection of ready-to-use datasets that can be easily used with TensorFlow or any other Python ML framework. All datasets are exposed as `tf.data.Datasets`, making it easy to use them in your input pipeline.

With TFDS, you can quickly get started with your machine learning projects and save time by not having to collect and prepare your own data. The library currently contains a wide variety of datasets, including image classification, object detection, text classification, and more. In addition, the library provides tools for creating new datasets from scratch, which can be useful for researchers or developers who need to create custom datasets for their own projects. TFDS is open source and released under the Apache 2.0 license. To be able to use TFDS, you will need to install it:

```
pip install tensorflow-datasets
```

Once installed, you can import it as:

```
import tensorflow_datasets as tfds
```

At the time of writing this book, TFDS contained 224 public datasets for a large range of tasks:

```
datasets = tfds.list_builders()
print(f"TFDS contains {len(datasets)} datasets")
```

```
### Output
TFDS contains 224 datasets
```

In this section, we will introduce you to TFDS and show how it can simplify your training process by exploring its underlying structure as well as providing some best practices for loading large amounts into machine learning models efficiently.

Load a TFDS dataset

Each dataset in TFDS is identified by its unique name, and associated with each dataset is also a publisher and dataset version. To get the data, you can use the TFDS load function (it is a powerful function with a lot of flexibility; you can read more about the function at https://www.tensorflow. org/datasets/api_docs/python/tfds/load):

```
tfds.load(
    name: str,
    *,
    split: Optional[Tree[splits_lib.SplitArg]] = None,
    data_dir: Optional[str] = None,
    batch_size: tfds.typing.Dim = None,
    shuffle_files: bool = False,
    download: bool = True,
    as_supervised: bool = False,
    decoders: Optional[TreeDict[decode.partial_decode.DecoderArg]] =
None,
    read_config: Optional[tfds.ReadConfig] = None,
    with_info: bool = False,
    builder_kwargs: Optional[Dict[str, Any]] = None,
    download_and_prepare_kwargs: Optional[Dict[str, Any]] = None,
```

```
    as_dataset_kwargs: Optional[Dict[str, Any]] = None,
    try_gcs: bool = False
)
```

You only need to specify the dataset name; the rest of the parameters are optional. You can read more about the optional arguments from TFDS docs. For example, below, we are downloading the famous MNIST dataset:

```
data, info = tfds.load(name="mnist", as_supervised=True, split=['train',
'test'], with_info=True)
```

The preceding statement downloads both the training and test dataset of MNIST into the variable data. Since the as_supervised flag is set to True, the labels are downloaded with the data, and the detailed information about the dataset is downloaded in info.

Let us first check the info:

```
print(info)
```

```
### output
tfds.core.DatasetInfo(
    name='mnist',
    version=3.0.1,
    description='The MNIST database of handwritten digits.',
    homepage='http://yann.lecun.com/exdb/mnist/',
    features=FeaturesDict({
        'image': Image(shape=(28, 28, 1), dtype=tf.uint8),
        'label': ClassLabel(shape=(), dtype=tf.int64, num_classes=10),
    }),
    total_num_examples=70000,
    splits={
        'test': 10000,
        'train': 60000,
    },
    supervised_keys=('image', 'label'),
    citation="""@article{lecun2010mnist,
      title={MNIST handwritten digit database},
      author={LeCun, Yann and Cortes, Corinna and Burges, CJ},
      journal={ATT Labs [Online]. Available: http://yann.lecun.com/exdb/mnist},
      volume={2},
      year={2010}
    }""",
    redistribution_info=,
)
```

So, we can see that the information is quite extensive. It tells us about the splits and the total number of samples in each split, the keys available if used for supervised learning, the citation details, and so on. The variable data here is a list of two TFDS dataset objects – the first one corresponding to the test dataset and the second one corresponding to the train dataset. TFDS dataset objects are dict by default. Let us take one single sample from the train dataset and explore:

```
data_train = data[1].take(1)
for sample, label in data_train:
  print(sample.shape)
  print(label)
```

```
### output
(28, 28, 1)
tf.Tensor(2, shape=(), dtype=int64)
```

You can see that the sample is an image of handwritten digits of the shape 28 x 28 x 1 and its label is 2. For image data, TFDS also has a method show_examples, which you can use to view the sample images from the dataset:

```
fig = tfds.show_examples(data[0], info)
```

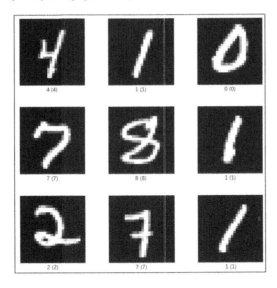

Figure 19.4: Sample from test dataset of MNIST dataset

Building data pipelines using TFDS

Let us build a complete end-to-end example using the TFDS data pipeline:

1. As always, we start with importing the necessary modules. Since we will be using TensorFlow to build the model, and TFDS for getting the dataset, we are including only these two for now:

```
import tensorflow as tf
import tensorflow_datasets as tfds
```

2. Using the Keras Sequential API, we build a simple convolutional neural network with three convolutional layers and two dense layers:

```
model = tf.keras.models.Sequential([
    tf.keras.layers.Conv2D(16, (3,3), activation='relu', input_shape=(300,
300, 3)),
    tf.keras.layers.MaxPooling2D(2, 2),
    tf.keras.layers.Conv2D(32, (3,3), activation='relu'),
    tf.keras.layers.MaxPooling2D(2,2),
    tf.keras.layers.Conv2D(64, (3,3), activation='relu'),
    tf.keras.layers.MaxPooling2D(2,2),
    tf.keras.layers.Flatten(),
    tf.keras.layers.Dense(256, activation='relu'),
    tf.keras.layers.Dense(1, activation='sigmoid')
])
```

3. We will be building a binary classifier, so we choose binary cross entropy as the loss function, and Adam as the optimizer:

```
model.compile(optimizer='Adam', loss='binary_
crossentropy',metrics=['accuracy'])
```

4. Next, we come to the dataset. We are using the horses_or_humans dataset, so we use the tfds. load function to get the training and validation data:

```
data = tfds.load('horses_or_humans', split='train', as_supervised=True)
val_data = tfds.load('horses_or_humans', split='test', as_
supervised=True)
```

5. The images need to be normalized; additionally, for better performance, we will augment the images while training:

```
def normalize_img(image, label):
    """Normalizes images: 'uint8' -> 'float32'."""
    return tf.cast(image, tf.float32) / 255., label

def augment_img(image, label):
    image, label = normalize_img(image, label)
    image = tf.image.random_flip_left_right(image)
    return image, label
```

6. So now we build the pipeline; we start with cache for better memory efficiency, apply the pre-processing steps (normalization and augmentation), ensure that data is shuffled while training, define the batch size, and use prefetch so that the next batch is brought in as the present batch is being trained on. We repeat the same steps for the validation data. The difference is that validation data need not be augmented or shuffled:

```
data = data.cache()
data = data.map(augment_img, num_parallel_calls=tf.data.AUTOTUNE)
train_data = data.shuffle(1024).batch(32)
train_data = train_data.prefetch(tf.data.AUTOTUNE)
val_data = val_data.map(normalize_img, num_parallel_calls=tf.data.
AUTOTUNE)
val_data = val data.batch(32)
val_data = val_data.cache()
val_data = val_data.prefetch(tf.data.AUTOTUNE)
```

7. And finally, we train the model:

```
%time history = model.fit(train_data, epochs=10, validation_data=val_
data, validation_steps=1)
```

Play around with different parameters of the data pipeline and see how it affects the training time. For example, try removing `prefetch` and `cache` and not specifying `num_parallel_calls`.

TensorFlow Lite

TensorFlow Lite is a lightweight platform designed by TensorFlow. This platform is focused on mobile and embedded devices such as Android, iOS, and Raspberry Pi. The main goal is to enable machine learning inference directly on the device by putting a lot of effort into three main characteristics: (1) a small binary and model size to save on memory, (2) low energy consumption to save on the battery, and (3) low latency for efficiency. It goes without saying that battery and memory are two important resources for mobile and embedded devices. To achieve these goals, Lite uses a number of techniques such as quantization, FlatBuffers, mobile interpreter, and mobile converter, which we are going to review briefly in the following sections.

Quantization

Quantization refers to a set of techniques that constrains an input made of continuous values (such as real numbers) into a discrete set (such as integers). The key idea is to reduce the space occupancy of **Deep Learning (DL)** models by representing the internal weight with integers instead of real numbers. Of course, this implies trading space gains for some amount of performance of the model. However, it has been empirically shown in many situations that a quantized model does not suffer from a significant decay in performance. TensorFlow Lite is internally built around a set of core operators supporting both quantized and floating-point operations.

Model quantization is a toolkit for applying quantization. This operation is applied to the representations of weights and, optionally, to the activations for both storage and computation. There are two types of quantization available:

*   Post-training quantization quantizes weights and the result of activations post-training.

- Quantization-aware training allows for the training of networks that can be quantized with minimal accuracy drop (only available for specific CNNs). Since this is a relatively experimental technique, we are not going to discuss it in this chapter, but the interested reader can find more information in [1].

TensorFlow Lite supports reducing the precision of values from full floats to half-precision floats (`float16`) or 8-bit integers. TensorFlow reports multiple trade-offs in terms of accuracy, latency, and space for selected CNN models (see *Figure 19.5*, source: `https://www.tensorflow.org/lite/performance/model_optimization`):

Model	Top-1 Accuracy (Original)	Top-1 Accuracy (Post-Training Quantized)	Top-1 Accuracy (Quantization-Aware Training)	Latency (Original) (ms)	Latency (Post-Training Quantized) (ms)	Latency (Quantization-Aware Training) (ms)	Size (Original) (MB)	Size (Optimized) (MB)
Mobilenet-v1-1-224	0.709	0.657	0.70	124	112	64	16.9	4.3
Mobilenet-v2-1-224	0.719	0.637	0.709	89	98	54	14	3.6
Inception_v3	0.78	0.772	0.775	1130	845	543	95.7	23.9
Resnet_v2_101	0.770	0.768	N/A	3973	2868	N/A	178.3	44.9

Figure 19.5: Trade-offs for various quantized CNN models

FlatBuffers

FlatBuffers (`https://google.github.io/flatbuffers/`) is an open-source format optimized to serialize data on mobile and embedded devices. The format was originally created at Google for game development and other performance-critical applications. FlatBuffers supports access to serialized data without parsing/unpacking for fast processing. The format is designed for memory efficiency and speed by avoiding unnecessary multiple copies in memory. FlatBuffers works across multiple platforms and languages such as C++, C#, C, Go, Java, JavaScript, Lobster, Lua, TypeScript, PHP, Python, and Rust.

Mobile converter

A model generated with TensorFlow needs to be converted into a TensorFlow Lite model. The converter can introduce optimizations for improving the binary size and performance. For instance, the converter can trim away all the nodes in a computational graph that are not directly related to inference but instead are needed for training.

Mobile optimized interpreter

TensorFlow Lite runs on a highly optimized interpreter that is used to optimize the underlying computational graphs, which in turn are used to describe the machine learning models. Internally, the interpreter uses multiple techniques to optimize the computational graph by inducing a static graph order and by ensuring better memory allocation. The interpreter core takes ~100 kb alone or ~300 kb with all supported kernels.

Computational graphs are the graphical representation of the learning algorithm; here, nodes describe the operations to be performed and edges connecting the nodes represent the flow of data. These graphs provide the deep learning frameworks with performance efficiency, which we are not able to achieve if we construct a neural network in pure NumPy.

Supported platforms

On Android, the TensorFlow Lite inference can be performed using either Java or C++. On iOS, TensorFlow Lite inference can run in Swift and Objective-C. On Linux platforms (such as Raspberry Pi), inferences run in C++ and Python. TensorFlow Lite for microcontrollers is an experimental port of TensorFlow Lite designed to run machine learning models on microcontrollers based on Arm Cortex-M (https://developer.arm.com/ip-products/processors/cortex-m) and series processors, including Arduino Nano 33 BLE Sense (https://store.arduino.cc/nano-33-ble-sense-with-headers), SparkFun Edge (https://www.sparkfun.com/products/15170), and the STM32F746 Discovery kit (https://www.st.com/en/evaluation-tools/32f746gdiscovery.html). These microcontrollers are frequently used for IoT applications.

Architecture

The architecture of TensorFlow Lite is described in *Figure 19.6* (from https://www.tensorflow.org/lite/convert/index). As you can see, both **tf.keras** (for example, TensorFlow 2.x) and **low-Level APIs** are supported. A standard TensorFlow 2.x model can be converted by using **TFLite Converter** and then saved in a **TFLite FlatBuffer** format (named .tflite), which is then executed by the **TFLite interpreter** on available devices (GPUs and CPUs) and on native device APIs. The concrete function in *Figure 19.6* defines a graph that can be converted to a TensorFlow Lite model or be exported to a **SavedModel**:

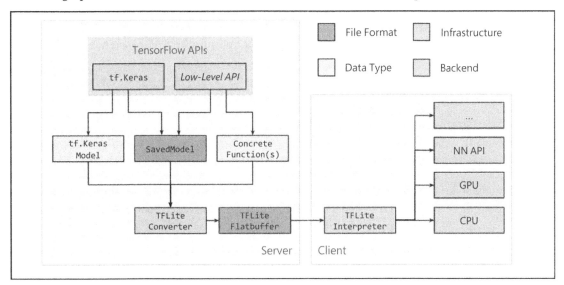

Figure 19.6: TensorFlow Lite internal architecture

Using TensorFlow Lite

Using TensorFlow Lite involves the following steps:

1. **Model selection:** A standard TensorFlow 2.x model is selected for solving a specific task. This can be either a custom-built model or a pretrained model.

2. **Model conversion:** The selected model is converted with the TensorFlow Lite converter, generally invoked with a few lines of Python code.

3. **Model deployment:** The converted model is deployed on the chosen device, either a phone or an IoT device, and then run by using the TensorFlow Lite interpreter. As discussed, APIs are available for multiple languages.

4. **Model optimization:** The model can be optionally optimized by using the TensorFlow Lite optimization framework.

A generic example of an application

In this section, we are going to see how to convert a model to TensorFlow Lite and then run it. Note that training can still be performed by TensorFlow in the environment that best fits your needs. However, inference runs on the mobile device. Let's see how with the following code fragment in Python:

```python
import tensorflow as tf
converter = tf.lite.TFLiteConverter.from_saved_model(saved_model_dir)
tflite_model = converter.convert()
open("converted_model.tflite", "wb").write(tflite_model)
```

The code is self-explanatory. A standard TensorFlow 2.x model is opened and converted by using `tf.lite.TFLiteConverter.from_saved_model(saved_model_dir)`. Pretty simple! Note that no specific installation is required. We simply use the `tf.lite` API (https://www.tensorflow.org/api_docs/python/tf/lite). It is also possible to apply a number of optimizations. For instance, post-training quantization can be applied by default:

```python
import tensorflow as tf
converter = tf.lite.TFLiteConverter.from_saved_model(saved_model_dir)
converter.optimizations = [tf.lite.Optimize.DEFAULT]
tflite_quant_model = converter.convert()
open("converted_model.tflite", "wb").write(tflite_quant_model)
```

Once the model is converted, it can be copied onto the specific device. Of course, this step is different for each different device. Then the model can run by using the language you prefer. For instance, in Java the invocation happens with the following code snippet:

```java
try (Interpreter interpreter = new Interpreter(tensorflow_lite_model_file)) {
  interpreter.run(input, output);
}
```

Again, pretty simple! What is very useful is that the same steps can be followed for a heterogeneous collection of mobile and IoT devices.

Using GPUs and accelerators

Modern phones frequently have accelerators on board that allow floating-point matrix operations to be performed faster. In this case, the interpreter can use the concept of Delegate, and specifically, GpuDelegate(), to use GPUs. Let's look at an example in Java:

```java
GpuDelegate delegate = new GpuDelegate();
Interpreter.Options options = (new Interpreter.Options()).
addDelegate(delegate);
Interpreter interpreter = new Interpreter(tensorflow_lite_model_file, options);
try {
  interpreter.run(input, output);
}
```

Again, the code is self-commenting. A new GpuDelegate() is created and then it is used by the interpreter to run the model on a GPU.

An example of an application

In this section, we are going to use TensorFlow Lite for building an example application that is later deployed on Android. We will use Android Studio (https://developer.android.com/studio/) to compile the code. The first step is to clone the repo with:

```
git clone https://github.com/tensorflow/examples
```

Then we open an existing project (see *Figure 19.7*) with the path examples/lite/examples/image_classification/android.

Then you need to install Android Studio from https://developer.android.com/studio/install and an appropriate distribution of Java. In my case, I selected the Android Studio macOS distribution and installed Java via brew with the following command:

```
brew tap adoptopenjdk/openjdk
brew cask install  homebrew/cask-versions/adoptopenjdk8
```

After that, you can launch the sdkmanager and install the required packages. In my case, I decided to use the internal emulator and deploy the application on a virtual device emulating a Google Pixel 3 XL. The required packages are reported in *Figure 19.7*:

```
From—4590-back-to-2018-to-observe-the-world-before-the-big-fall:~ antonio$ sdkmanager —list
Warning: File /Users/antonio/.android/repositories.cfg could not be loaded.
Installed packages:=====================] 100% Computing updates...
  Path                                              | Version | Description
  --------                                          | ------- | -------
  add-ons;addon-google_apis-google-24               | 1       | Google APIs
  build-tools;28.0.3                                | 28.0.3  | Android SDK Build-Tools 28.0.3
  build-tools;29.0.2                                | 29.0.2  | Android SDK Build-Tools 29.0.2
  emulator                                          | 29.2.1  | Android Emulator
  patcher;v4                                        | 1       | SDK Patch Applier v4
  platforms;android-28                              | 6       | Android SDK Platform 28
  platforms;android-29                              | 3       | Android SDK Platform 29
  system-images;android-29;google_apis_playstore;x86 | 8     | Google Play Intel x86 Atom System Image
  tools                                             | 26.1.1  | Android SDK Tools 26.1.1
```

Figure 19.7: Required packages to use a Google Pixel 3 XL emulator

Then, start Android Studio and select **Open an existing Android Studio project,** as shown in *Figure 19.8*:

Figure 19.8: Opening a new Android project

Open **Adv Manager** (under the **Tool** menu) and follow the instructions for how to create a virtual device, like the one shown in *Figure 19.9*:

Figure 19.9: Creating a virtual device

Now that you have the virtual device ready, let us dive into the TensorFlow Lite models and see how we can use them.

Pretrained models in TensorFlow Lite

For many interesting use cases, it is possible to use a pretrained model that is already suitable for mobile computation. This is a field of active research with new proposals coming pretty much every month. Pretrained TensorFlow Lite models are available on TensorFlow Hub; these models are ready to use (https://www.tensorflow.org/lite/models/). As of August 2022, these include:

- **Image classification:** Used to identify multiple classes of objects such as places, plants, animals, activities, and people.
- **Object detection:** Used to detect multiple objects with bounding boxes.
- **Audio speech synthesis:** Used to generate speech from text.
- **Text embedding:** Used to embed textual data.
- **Segmentations:** Identifies the shape of objects together with semantic labels for people, places, animals, and many additional classes.
- **Style transfers:** Used to apply artistic styles to any given image.
- **Text classification:** Used to assign different categories to textual content.
- **Question and answer:** Used to provide answers to questions provided by users.

In this section, we will discuss some of the optimized pretrained models available in TensorFlow Lite out of the box as of August 2022. These models can be used for a large number of mobile and edge computing use cases. Compiling the example code is pretty simple.

You just import a new project from each example directory and Android Studio will use Gradle (https://gradle.org/) for synching the code with the latest version in the repo and for compiling.

If you compile all the examples, you should be able to see them in the emulator (see *Figure 19.10*). Remember to select **Build | Make Project**, and Android Studio will do the rest:

Figure 19.10: Emulated Google Pixel 3 XL with TensorFlow Lite example applications

 Edge computing is a distributed computing model that brings computation and data closer to the location where it is needed.

Image classification

As of August 2022, the list of available models for pretrained classification is rather large, and it offers the opportunity to trade space, accuracy, and performance as shown in *Figure 19.11* (source: https://www.tensorflow.org/lite/models/trained):

Model name	Model size	Top-1 accuracy	Top-5 accuracy	TF Lite performance
Mobilenet_V1_0.25_128_quant	0.5 Mb	39.5%	64.4%	3.7 ms
Mobilenet_V1_0.25_160_quant	0.5 Mb	42.8%	68.1%	5.5 ms
Mobilenet_V1_0.25_192_quant	0.5 Mb	45.7%	70.8%	7.9 ms
Mobilenet_V1_0.25_224_quant	0.5 Mb	48.2%	72.8%	10.4 ms
Mobilenet_V1_0.50_128_quant	1.4 Mb	54.9%	78.1%	8.8 ms
Mobilenet_V1_0.50_160_quant	1.4 Mb	57.2%	80.5%	13.0 ms
Mobilenet_V1_0.50_192_quant	1.4 Mb	59.9%	82.1%	18.3 ms
Mobilenet_V1_0.50_224_quant	1.4 Mb	61.2%	83.2%	24.7 ms
Mobilenet_V1_0.75_128_quant	2.6 Mb	55.9%	79.1%	16.2 ms
Mobilenet_V1_0.75_160_quant	2.6 Mb	62.4%	83.7%	24.3 ms
Mobilenet_V1_0.75_192_quant	2.6 Mb	66.1%	86.2%	33.8 ms
Mobilenet_V1_0.75_224_quant	2.6 Mb	66.9%	86.9%	45.4 ms
Mobilenet_V1_1.0_128_quant	4.3 Mb	63.3%	84.1%	24.9 ms
Mobilenet_V1_1.0_160_quant	4.3 Mb	66.9%	86.7%	37.4 ms
Mobilenet_V1_1.0_192_quant	4.3 Mb	69.1%	88.1%	51.9 ms
Mobilenet_V1_1.0_224_quant	4.3 Mb	70.0%	89.0%	70.2 ms
Mobilenet_V2_1.0_224_quant	3.4 Mb	70.8%	89.9%	53.4 ms
Inception_V1_quant	6.4 Mb	70.1%	89.8%	154.5 ms
Inception_V2_quant	11 Mb	73.5%	91.4%	235.0 ms
Inception_V3_quant	23 Mb	77.5%	93.7%	637 ms
Inception_V4_quant	41 Mb	79.5%	93.9%	1250.8 ms

Figure 19.11: Space, accuracy, and performance trade-offs for various mobile models

MobileNet V1 is a quantized CNN model described in Benoit Jacob [2]. MobileNet V2 is an advanced model proposed by Google [3]. Online, you can also find floating-point models, which offer the best balance between model size and performance. Note that GPU acceleration requires the use of floating-point models. Note that recently, AutoML models for mobile have been proposed based on an automated **mobile neural architecture search** (**MNAS**) approach [4], beating the models handcrafted by humans.

We discussed AutoML in *Chapter 13, An Introduction to AutoML*, and the interested reader can refer to MNAS documentation in the references [4] for applications to mobile devices.

Object detection

TensorFlow Lite format models are included in TF Hub. There is a large number of pretrained models that can detect multiple objects within an image, with bounding boxes. Eighty different classes of objects are recognized. The network is based on a pretrained quantized COCO SSD MobileNet V1 model. For each object, the model provides the class, the confidence of detection, and the vertices of the bounding boxes (`https://tfhub.dev/s?deployment-format=lite&module-type=image-object-detection`).

Pose estimation

TF Hub has a TensorFlow Lite format pretrained model for detecting parts of human bodies in an image or a video. For instance, it is possible to detect noses, left/right eyes, hips, ankles, and many other parts. Each detection comes with an associated confidence score (`https://tfhub.dev/s?deployment-format=lite&module-type=image-pose-detection`).

Smart reply

TF Hub also has a TensorFlow Lite format pretrained model for generating replies to chat messages. These replies are contextualized and similar to what is available on Gmail (`https://tfhub.dev/tensorflow/lite-model/smartreply/1/default/1`).

Segmentation

There are pretrained models (`https://tfhub.dev/s?deployment-format=lite&module-type=image-segmentation`) for image segmentation, where the goal is to decide what the semantic labels (for example, person, dog, and cat) assigned to every pixel in the input image are. Segmentation is based on the DeepLab algorithm [5].

Style transfer

TensorFlow Lite also supports artistic style transfer (see *Chapter 20, Advanced Convolutional Neural Networks*) via a combination of a MobileNet V2-based neural network, which reduces the input style image to a 100-dimension style vector, and a style transform model, which applies the style vector to a content image to create the stylized image (`https://tfhub.dev/s?deployment-format=lite&module-type=image-style-transfer`).

Text classification

There are models for text classification and sentiment analysis (https://tfhub.dev/s?deployment-format=lite&module-type=text-classification) trained on the Large Movie Review Dataset v1.0 (http://ai.stanford.edu/~amaas/data/sentiment/) with IMDb movie reviews that are positive or negative. An example of text classification is given in *Figure 19.12*:

Figure 19.12: An example of text classification on Android with TensorFlow Lite

Large language models

There are pretrained large language models based on transformer architecture (`https://tfhub.dev/s?deployment-format=lite&q=bert`). The models are based on a compressed variant of BERT [6] (see *Chapter 6, Transformers*) called MobileBERT [7], which runs 4x faster and has a 4x smaller size. An example of Q&A is given in *Figure 19.13*:

Figure 19.13: An example of Q&A on Android with TensorFlow Lite and BERT

A note about using mobile GPUs

This section concludes the overview of pretrained models for mobile devices and IoT. Note that modern phones are equipped with internal GPUs. For instance, on Pixel 3, TensorFlow Lite GPU inference accelerates inference to 2–7x faster than CPUs for many models (see *Figure 19.14*, source: `https://blog.tensorflow.org/2019/01/tensorflow-lite-now-faster-with-mobile.html`):

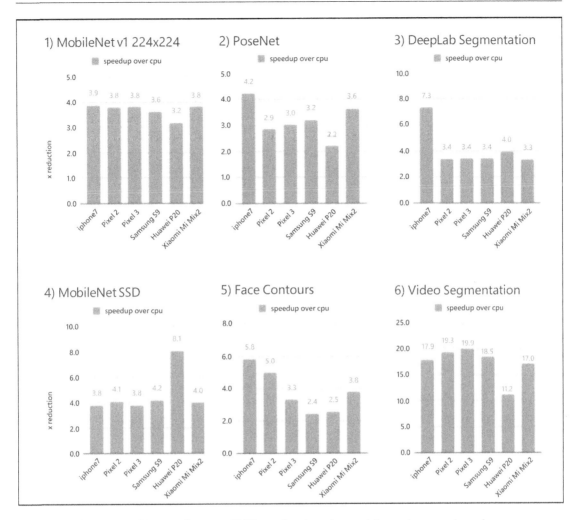

Figure 19.14: GPU speed-up over CPU for various learning models running on various phones

An overview of federated learning at the edge

As discussed, edge computing is a distributed computing model that brings computation and data closer to the location where it is needed.

Now, let's introduce **Federated Learning (FL)** [8] at the edge, starting with two use cases.

Suppose you built an app for playing music on mobile devices and then you want to add recommendation features aimed at helping users to discover new songs they might like. Is there a way to build a distributed model that leverages each user's experience without disclosing any private data?

Suppose you are a car manufacturer producing millions of cars connected via 5G networks, and then you want to build a distributed model for optimizing each car's fuel consumption. Is there a way to build such a model without disclosing the driving behavior of each user?

Traditional machine learning requires you to have a centralized repository for training data either on your desktop, in your data center, or in the cloud. Federated learning pushes the training phase at the edge by distributing the computation among millions of mobile devices. These devices are ephemeral in that they are not always available for the learning process, and they can disappear silently (for instance, a mobile phone can be switched off all of a sudden). The key idea is to leverage the CPUs and the GPU of each mobile phone that is made available for an FL computation. Each mobile device that is part of the distributed FL training downloads a (pretrained) model from a central server, and it performs local optimization based on the local training data collected on each specific mobile device. This process is similar to the transfer learning process (see *Chapter 20, Advanced Convolutional Neural Networks*), but it is distributed at the edge. Each locally updated model is then sent back by millions of edge devices to a central server to build an averaged shared model.

Of course, there are many issues to be considered. Let's review them:

- **Battery usage:** Each mobile device that is part of an FL computation should save as much as possible on local battery usage.
- **Encrypted communication:** Each mobile device belonging to an FL computation has to use encrypted communication with the central server to update the locally built model.
- **Efficient communication:** Typically, deep learning models are optimized with optimization algorithms such as SGD (see *Chapter 1, Neural Network Foundations with TF*, and *Chapter 14, The Math Behind Deep Learning*). However, FL works with millions of devices and there is, therefore, a strong need to minimize the communication patterns. Google introduced a Federated Averaging algorithm [8], which is reported to reduce the amount of communication 10x–100x when compared with vanilla SGD. Plus, compression techniques [9] reduce communication costs by an additional 100x with random rotations and quantization.
- **Ensure user privacy:** This is probably the most important point. All local training data acquired at the edge must stay at the edge. This means that the training data acquired on a mobile device cannot be sent to a central server. Equally important, any user behavior learned in locally trained models must be anonymized so that it is not possible to understand any specific action performed by specific individuals.

Figure 19.15 shows a typical FL architecture [10]. An FL server sends a model and a training plan to millions of devices. The training plan includes information on how frequently updates are expected and other metadata.

Each device runs the local training and sends a model update back to the global services. Note that each device has an FL runtime providing federated learning services to an app process that stores data in a local example store. The FL runtime fetches the training examples from the example store:

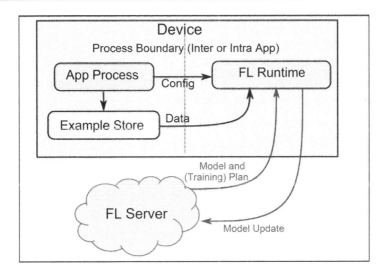

Figure 19.15: An example of federated learning architecture

TensorFlow FL APIs

The TensorFlow Federated (TTF) platform has two layers:

- **Federated learning (FL)**, as discussed earlier, is a high-level interface that works well with tf.keras and non-tf.keras models. In the majority of situations, we will use this API for distributed training that is privacy-preserving.

- **Federated core (FC)**, a low-level interface that is highly customizable and allows you to interact with low-level communications and with federated algorithms. You will need this API only if you intend to implement new and sophisticated distributed learning algorithms. This topic is rather advanced, and we are not going to cover it in this book. If you wish to learn more, you can find more information online (https://www.tensorflow.org/federated/federated_core).

The FL API has three key parts:

1. **Models**: Used to wrap existing models for enabling federating learning. This can be achieved via the tff.learning.from_keras_model(), or via the subclassing of tff.learning.Model(). For instance, you can have the following code fragment:

```
keras_model = …
keras_model.compile(...)
keras_federated_model = tff.learning.from_compiled_keras_model(keras_
model, ..)
```

2. **Builders:** This is the layer where the federated computation happens. There are two phases: compilation, where the learning algorithm is serialized into an abstract representation of the computation, and execution, where the represented computation is run.

3. **Datasets:** This is a large collection of data that can be used to simulate federated learning locally – a useful step for initial fine-tuning.

We conclude this overview by mentioning that you can find a detailed description of the APIs online and also a number of coding examples (`https://www.tensorflow.org/federated/federated_learning`). Start by using the Colab notebook made available by Google (`https://colab.research.google.com/github/tensorflow/federated/blob/v0.10.1/docs/tutorials/federated_learning_for_image_classification.ipynb`). The framework allows us to simulate the distributed training before running it in a real environment. The library in charge of FL learning is `tensorflow_federated`. *Figure 19.16* discusses all the steps used in federated learning with multiple nodes, and it might be useful to better understand what has been discussed in this section:

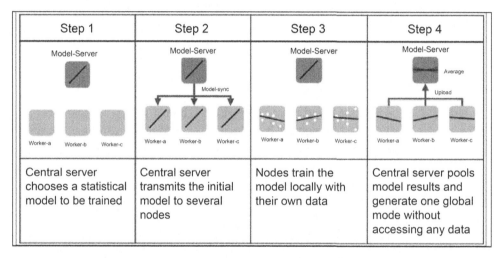

Figure 19.16: An example of federated learning with multiple nodes (source: https://upload.wikimedia. org/wikipedia/commons/e/e2/Federated_learning_process_central_case.png)

The next section will introduce TensorFlow.js, a variant of TensorFlow that can be used natively in JavaScript.

TensorFlow.js

TensorFlow.js is a JavaScript library for machine learning models that can work either in vanilla mode or via Node.js. In this section, we are going to review both of them.

Vanilla TensorFlow.js

TensorFlow.js is a JavaScript library for training and using machine learning models in a browser. It is derived from deeplearn.js, an open-source, hardware-accelerated library for doing deep learning in JavaScript, and is now a companion library to TensorFlow.

The most common use of TensorFlow.js is to make pretrained ML/DL models available on the browser. This can help in situations where it may not be feasible to send client data back to the server due to network bandwidth or security concerns. However, TensorFlow.js is a full-stack ML platform, and it is possible to build and train an ML/DL model from scratch, as well as fine-tune an existing pretrained model with new client data.

An example of a TensorFlow.js application is the TensorFlow Projector (https://projector.tensorflow.org), which allows a client to visualize their own data (as word vectors) in 3-dimensional space, using one of several dimensionality reduction algorithms provided. There are a few other examples of TensorFlow.js applications listed on the TensorFlow.js demo page (https://www.tensorflow.org/js/demos).

Similar to TensorFlow, TensorFlow.js also provides two main APIs – the Ops API, which exposes low-level tensor operations such as matrix multiplication, and the Layers API, which exposes Keras-style high-level building blocks for neural networks.

At the time of writing, TensorFlow.js runs on three different backends. The fastest (and also the most complex) is the WebGL backend, which provides access to WebGL's low-level 3D graphics APIs and can take advantage of GPU hardware acceleration. The other popular backend is the Node.js backend, which allows the use of TensorFlow.js in server-side applications. Finally, as a fallback, there is the CPU-based implementation in plain JavaScript that will run in any browser.

In order to gain a better understanding of how to write a TensorFlow.js application, we will walk through an example of classifying MNIST digits using a CNN provided by the TensorFlow.js team (https://storage.googleapis.com/tfjs-examples/mnist/dist/index.html).

The steps here are similar to a normal supervised model development pipeline – load the data, define, train, and evaluate the model.

JavaScript works inside a browser environment, within an HTML page. The HTML file (named index.html) below represents this HTML page. Notice the two imports for TensorFlow.js (tf.min.js) and the TensorFlow.js visualization library (tfjs-vis.umd.min.js) – these provide library functions that we will use in our application. The JavaScript code for our application comes from data.js and script.js files, located in the same directory as our index.html file:

```
<!DOCTYPE html>
<html>
<head>
  <meta charset="utf-8">
  <meta http-equiv="X-UA-Compatible" content="IE=edge">
  <meta name="viewport" content="width=device-width, initial-scale=1.0">
  <!-- Import TensorFlow.js -->
  <script src="https://cdn.jsdelivr.net/npm/@tensorflow/tfjs@1.0.0/dist/tf.min.js"></script>
  <!-- Import tfjs-vis -->
```

```
<script src="https://cdn.jsdelivr.net/npm/@tensorflow/tfjs-vis@1.0.2/dist/
tfjs-vis.umd.min.js"></script>
  <!-- Import the data file -->
  <script src="data.js" type="module"></script>
  <!-- Import the main script file -->
  <script src="script.js" type="module"></script>
</head>
<body>
</body>
</html>
```

For deployment, we will deploy these three files (index.html, data.js, and script.js) on a web server, but for development, we can start a web server up by calling a simple one bundled with the Python distribution. This will start up a web server on port 8000 on localhost, and the index.html file can be rendered on the browser at http://localhost:8000:

```
python -m http.server
```

The next step is to load the data. Fortunately, Google provides a JavaScript script that we have called directly from our index.html file. It downloads the images and labels from GCP storage and returns shuffled and normalized batches of image and label pairs for training and testing. We can download this to the same folder as the index.html file using the following command:

```
wget -cO - https://storage.googleapis.com/tfjs-tutorials/mnist_data.js > data.
js
```

For Windows users, you will need to first download Wget: https://eternallybored.org/misc/wget/

Model definition, training, and evaluation code is all specified inside the script.js file. The function to define and build the network is shown in the following code block. As you can see, it is very similar to the way you would build a sequential model with tf.keras. The only difference is the way you specify the arguments, as a dictionary of name-value pairs instead of a list of parameters. The model is a sequential model, that is, a list of layers. Finally, the model is compiled with the Adam optimizer:

```
function getModel() {
  const IMAGE_WIDTH = 28;
  const IMAGE_HEIGHT = 28;
  const IMAGE_CHANNELS = 1;
  const NUM_OUTPUT_CLASSES = 10;

  const model = tf.sequential();
  model.add(tf.layers.conv2d({
```

```
    inputShape: [IMAGE_WIDTH, IMAGE_HEIGHT, IMAGE_CHANNELS],
    kernelSize: 5,
    filters: 8,
    strides: 1,
    activation: 'relu',
    kernelInitializer: 'varianceScaling'
  }));
  model.add(tf.layers.maxPooling2d({
    poolSize: [2, 2], strides: [2, 2]
  }));
  model.add(tf.layers.conv2d({
    kernelSize: 5,
    filters: 16,
    strides: 1,
    activation: 'relu',
    kernelInitializer: 'varianceScaling'
  }));
  model.add(tf.layers.maxPooling2d({
    poolSize: [2, 2], strides: [2, 2]
  }));
  model.add(tf.layers.flatten());
  model.add(tf.layers.dense({
    units: NUM_OUTPUT_CLASSES,
    kernelInitializer: 'varianceScaling',
    activation: 'softmax'
  }));
  const optimizer = tf.train.adam();
  model.compile({
    optimizer: optimizer,
    loss: 'categoricalCrossentropy',
    metrics: ['accuracy'],
  });
  return model;
}
```

The model is then trained for 10 epochs with batches from the training dataset and validated inline using batches from the test dataset. A best practice is to create a separate validation dataset from the training set. However, to keep our focus on the more important aspect of showing how to use TensorFlow.js to design an end-to-end DL pipeline, we are using the external data.js file provided by Google, which provides functions to return only a training and test batch. In our example, we will use the test dataset for validation as well as evaluation later.

This is likely to give us better accuracies compared to what we would have achieved with an unseen (during training) test set, but that is unimportant for an illustrative example such as this one:

```
async function train(model, data) {
  const metrics = ['loss', 'val_loss', 'acc', 'val_acc'];
  const container = {
    name: 'Model Training', tab: 'Model', styles: { height: '1000px' }
  };
  const fitCallbacks = tfvis.show.fitCallbacks(container, metrics);

  const BATCH_SIZE = 512;
  const TRAIN_DATA_SIZE = 5500;
  const TEST_DATA_SIZE = 1000;
  const [trainXs, trainYs] = tf.tidy(() => {
    const d = data.nextTrainBatch(TRAIN_DATA_SIZE);
    return [
      d.xs.reshape([TRAIN_DATA_SIZE, 28, 28, 1]),
      d.labels
    ];
  });
  const [testXs, testYs] = tf.tidy(() => {
    const d = data.nextTestBatch(TEST_DATA_SIZE);
    return [
      d.xs.reshape([TEST_DATA_SIZE, 28, 28, 1]),
      d.labels
    ];
  });
  return model.fit(trainXs, trainYs, {
    batchSize: BATCH_SIZE,
    validationData: [testXs, testYs],
    epochs: 10,
    shuffle: true,
    callbacks: fitCallbacks
  });
}
```

Once the model finishes training, we want to make predictions and evaluate the model on its predictions. The following functions will do the predictions and compute the overall accuracy for each of the classes over all the test set examples, as well as produce a confusion matrix across all the test set samples:

```
const classNames = [
  'Zero', 'One', 'Two', 'Three', 'Four',
  'Five', 'Six', 'Seven', 'Eight', 'Nine'];
```

```
function doPrediction(model, data, testDataSize = 500) {
  const IMAGE_WIDTH = 28;
  const IMAGE_HEIGHT = 28;
  const testData = data.nextTestBatch(testDataSize);
  const testxs = testData.xs.reshape(
    [testDataSize, IMAGE_WIDTH, IMAGE_HEIGHT, 1]);
  const labels = testData.labels.argMax([-1]);
  const preds = model.predict(testxs).argMax([-1]);
  testxs.dispose();
  return [preds, labels];
}
async function showAccuracy(model, data) {
  const [preds, labels] = doPrediction(model, data);
  const classAccuracy = await tfvis.metrics.perClassAccuracy(
    labels, preds);
  const container = {name: 'Accuracy', tab: 'Evaluation'};
  tfvis.show.perClassAccuracy(container, classAccuracy, classNames);
  labels.dispose();
}
async function showConfusion(model, data) {
  const [preds, labels] = doPrediction(model, data);
  const confusionMatrix = await tfvis.metrics.confusionMatrix(
    labels, preds);
  const container = {name: 'Confusion Matrix', tab: 'Evaluation'};
  tfvis.render.confusionMatrix(
      container, {values: confusionMatrix}, classNames);
  labels.dispose();
}
```

Finally, the run() function will call all these functions in sequence to build an end-to-end ML pipeline:

```
import {MnistData} from './data.js';
async function run() {
  const data = new MnistData();
  await data.load();
  await showExamples(data);
  const model = getModel();
  tfvis.show.modelSummary({name: 'Model Architecture', tab: 'Model'}, model);
  await train(model, data);
  await showAccuracy(model, data);
  await showConfusion(model, data);
}
```

```
document.addEventListener('DOMContentLoaded', run);
```

Refreshing the browser location, `http://localhost:8000/index.html`, will invoke the `run()` method above. *Figure 19.17* shows the model architecture and the plots of the progress of the training.

On the left are the loss and accuracy values on the validation dataset observed at the end of each batch, and on the right are the same loss and accuracy values observed on the training dataset (blue) and validation dataset (red) at the end of each epoch:

Model Architecture			
Layer Name	**Output Shape**	**# Of Params**	**Trainable**
conv2d_Conv2D1	[batch,24,24,8]	208	true
max_pooling2d_MaxPooling2D1	[batch,12,12,8]	0	true
conv2d_Conv2D2	[batch,8,8,16]	3,216	true
max_pooling2d_MaxPooling2D2	[batch,4,4,16]	0	true
flatten_Flatten1	[batch,256]	0	true
dense_Dense1	[batch,10]	2,570	true

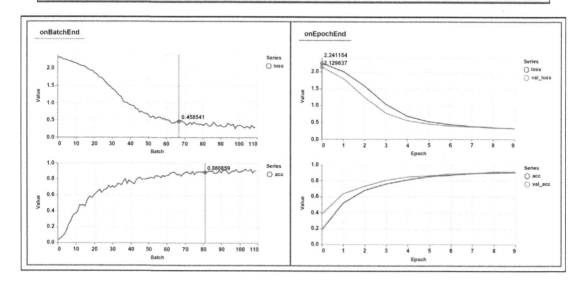

Figure 19.17: Model loss and accuracy as it is being trained

In addition, the following figure shows the accuracies across different classes for predictions from our trained model on the test dataset, as well as the confusion matrix of predicted versus actual classes for test dataset samples:

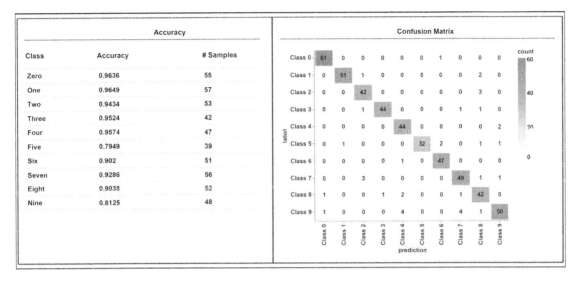

Figure 19.18: Confusion metrics and accuracy for each class as obtained by the trained model

Readers might enjoy seeing this live example from the TensorFlow team training a TFJS model on the MNIST dataset: https://storage.googleapis.com/tfjs-examples/mnist/dist/index.html.

We have seen how to use TensorFlow.js within the browser. The next section will explain how to convert a model from Keras into TensorFlow.js.

Converting models

Sometimes it is convenient to convert a model that has already been created with tf.keras. This is very easy and can be done offline with the following command, which takes a Keras model from /tmp/model.h5 and outputs a JavaScript model into /tmp/tfjs_model:

```
tensorflowjs_converter --input_format=keras /tmp/model.h5 /tmp/tfjs_model
```

To be able to use this command, you will need a Python environment with TensorFlow JS installed using:

```
pip install tensorflowjs
```

This will install the above converter. The next section will explain how to use pretrained models in TensorFlow.js.

Pretrained models

TensorFlow.js comes with a significant number of pretrained models for deep learning with image, video, and text. The models are hosted on npm, so it's very simple to use them if you are familiar with Node.js development.

Table 19.1 summarizes some of the pretrained models available as of August 2022 (source: `https://github.com/tensorflow/tfjs-models`):

Images		
Model	**Details**	**Install**
MobileNet (`https://github.com/tensorflow/tfjs-models/tree/master/mobilenet`)	Classify images with labels from the ImageNet database.	`npm i @tensorflow-models/mobilenet`
PoseNet (`https://github.com/tensorflow/tfjs-models/tree/master/posenet`)	A machine learning model that allows for real-time human pose estimation in the browser; see a detailed description here: `https://medium.com/tensorflow/real-time-human-pose-estimation-in-the-browser-with-tensorflow-js-7dd0bc881cd5`.	`npm i @tensorflow-models/posenet`
Coco SSD (`https://github.com/tensorflow/tfjs-models/tree/master/coco-ssd`)	Object detection model that aims to localize and identify multiple objects in a single image; based on the TensorFlow object detection API (`https://github.com/tensorflow/models/blob/master/research/object_detection/README.md`).	`npm i @tensorflow-models/coco-ssd`
BodyPix (`https://github.com/tensorflow/tfjs-models/tree/master/body-pix`)	Real-time person and body-part segmentation in the browser using TensorFlow.js.	`npm i @tensorflow-models/body-pix`
DeepLab v3(`https://github.com/tensorflow/tfjs-models/tree/master/deeplab`)	Semantic segmentation.	`npm i @tensorflow-models/deeplab`
Audio		
Model	**Details**	**Install**
Speech Commands (`https://github.com/tensorflow/tfjs-models/tree/master/speech-commands`)	Classify 1-second audio snippets from the speech commands dataset (`https://github.com/tensorflow/docs/blob/master/site/en/r1/tutorials/sequences/audio_recognition.md`).	`npm i @tensorflow-models/speech-commands`

Text		
Model	**Details**	**Install**
Universal Sentence Encoder (`https://github.com/ tensorflow/tfjs-models/ tree/master/universal- sentence-encoder`)	Encode text into a 512-dimensional embedding to be used as inputs to natural language processing tasks such as sentiment classification and textual similarity.	`npm i @tensorflow- models/universal- sentence-encoder`
Text Toxicity (`https:// github.com/tensorflow/ tfjs-models/tree/master/ toxicity`)	Score the perceived impact a comment might have on a conversation, from "Very toxic" to "Very healthy".	`npm i @tensorflow- models/toxicity`
General Utilities		
Model	**Details**	**Install**
KNN Classifier (`https:// github.com/tensorflow/ tfjs-models/tree/master/ knn-classifier`)	This package provides a utility for creating a classifier using the K-nearest neighbors algorithm; it can be used for transfer learning.	`npm i @tensorflow- models/knn- classifier`

Table 19.1: A list of some of the pretrained models on TensorFlow.js

Each pretrained model can be directly used from HTML. For instance, this is an example with the KNN classifier:

```
<html>
  <head>
    <!-- Load TensorFlow.js -->
    <script src="https://cdn.jsdelivr.net/npm/@tensorflow/tfjs"></script>
    <!-- Load MobileNet -->
    <script src="https://cdn.jsdelivr.net/npm/@tensorflow-models/mobilenet"></
script>
    <!-- Load KNN Classifier -->
    <script src="https://cdn.jsdelivr.net/npm/@tensorflow-models/knn-
classifier"></script>
  </head>
```

The next section will explain how to use pretrained models in Node.js.

Node.js

In this section, we will give an overview of how to use TensorFlow with Node.js. Let's start.

The CPU package is imported with the following line of code, which will work for all macOS, Linux, and Windows platforms:

```
import * as tf from '@tensorflow/tfjs-node'
```

The GPU package is imported with the following line of code (as of November 2019, this will work only on a GPU in a CUDA environment):

```
import * as tf from '@tensorflow/tfjs-node-gpu'
```

An example of Node.js code for defining and compiling a simple dense model is reported below. The code is self-explanatory:

```
const model = tf.sequential();
model.add(tf.layers.dense({ units: 1, inputShape: [400] }));
model.compile({
  loss: 'meanSquaredError',
  optimizer: 'sgd',
  metrics: ['MAE']
});
```

Training can then start with the typical Node.js asynchronous invocation:

```
const xs = tf.randomUniform([10000, 400]);
const ys = tf.randomUniform([10000, 1]);
const valXs = tf.randomUniform([1000, 400]);
const valYs = tf.randomUniform([1000, 1]);
async function train() {
  await model.fit(xs, ys, {
    epochs: 100,
    validationData: [valXs, valYs],
  });
}
train();
```

In this section, we have discussed how to use TensorFlow.js with both vanilla JavaScript and Node.js using sample applications for both the browser and backend computation.

Summary

In this chapter, we have discussed different components of the TensorFlow ecosystem. We started with TensorFlow Hub, the place where many pretrained models are available. Next, we talked about the TensorFlow Datasets and learned how to build a data pipeline using TFDS. We learned how to use TensorFlow Lite for mobile devices and IoT and deployed real applications on Android devices. Then, we also talked about federated learning for distributed learning across thousands (millions) of mobile devices, taking into account privacy concerns. The last section of the chapter was devoted to TensorFlow.js for using TensorFlow with vanilla JavaScript or with Node.js.

The next chapter is about advanced CNNs, where you will learn some advanced CNN architectures and their applications.

References

1. Quantization-aware training: `https://github.com/tensorflow/tensorflow/tree/r1.13/tensorflow/contrib/quantize`

2. Jacob, B., Kligys, S., Chen, B., Zhu, M., Tang, M., Howard, A., Adam, H., and Kalenichenko, D. (Submitted on 15 Dec 2017). *Quantization and Training of Neural Networks for Efficient Integer-Arithmetic-Only Inference.* `https://arxiv.org/abs/1712.05877`

3. Sandler, M., Howard, A., Zhu, M., Zhmoginov, A., Chen, L-C. (Submitted on 13 Jan 2018 (v1), last revised 21 Mar 2019 (v4)). *MobileNetV2: Inverted Residuals and Linear Bottlenecks.* `https://arxiv.org/abs/1806.08342`

4. Tan, M., Chen, B., Pang, R., Vasudevan, V., Sandler, M., Howard, A., and Le, Q. V. *MnasNet: Platform-Aware Neural Architecture Search for Mobile.* `https://arxiv.org/abs/1807.11626`

5. Chen, L-C., Papandreou, G., Kokkinos, I., Murphy, K., and Yuille, A. L. (May 2017). *DeepLab: Semantic Image Segmentation with Deep Convolutional Nets, Atrous Convolution, and Fully Connected CRFs.* `https://arxiv.org/pdf/1606.00915.pdf`

6. Devlin, J., Chang, M-W., Lee, K., and Toutanova, K. (Submitted on 11 Oct 2018 (v1), last revised 24 May 2019 v2). *BERT: Pre-training of Deep Bidirectional Transformers for Language Understanding.* `https://arxiv.org/abs/1810.04805`

7. Anonymous authors, Paper under double-blind review. (modified: 25 Sep 2019). *MOBILEBERT: TASK-AGNOSTIC COMPRESSION OF BERT BY PROGRESSIVE KNOWLEDGE TRANSFER.* ICLR 2020 Conference Blind Submission Readers: Everyone. `https://openreview.net/pdf?id=SJxjVaNKwB`

8. McMahan, H. B., Moore, E., Ramage, D., Hampson, and S., Arcas, B. A. y. (Submitted on 17 Feb 2016 (v1), last revised 28 Feb 2017 (this version, v3)). *Communication-Efficient Learning of Deep Networks from Decentralized Data.* `https://arxiv.org/abs/1602.05629`

9. Konečný, J., McMahan, H. B., Yu, F. X., Richtárik, P., Suresh, A. T., and Bacon, D. (Submitted on 18 Oct 2016 (v1), last revised 30 Oct 2017 (this version, v2)). *Federated Learning: Strategies for Improving Communication Efficiency.* `https://arxiv.org/abs/1610.05492`

10. Bonawitz, K. et al. (22 March 2019). *TOWARDS FEDERATED LEARNING AT SCALE: SYSTEM DESIGN.* `https://arxiv.org/pdf/1902.01046.pdf`

Join our book's Discord space

Join our Discord community to meet like-minded people and learn alongside more than 2000 members at: https://packt.link/keras

20

Advanced Convolutional Neural Networks

In this chapter, we will see some more advanced uses for **Convolutional Neural Networks (CNNs)**. We will explore:

- How CNNs can be applied within the areas of computer vision, video, textual documents, audio, and music
- How to use CNNs for text processing
- What capsule networks are
- Computer vision

 All the code files for this chapter can be found at https://packt.link/dltfchp20.

Let's start by using CNNs for complex tasks.

Composing CNNs for complex tasks

We have discussed CNNs quite extensively in *Chapter 3, Convolutional Neural Networks*, and at this point, you are probably convinced about the effectiveness of the CNN architecture for image classification tasks. What you may find surprising, however, is that the basic CNN architecture can be composed and extended in various ways to solve a variety of more complex tasks. In this section, we will look at the computer vision tasks mentioned in *Figure 20.1* and show how they can be solved by turning CNNs into larger and more complex architectures.

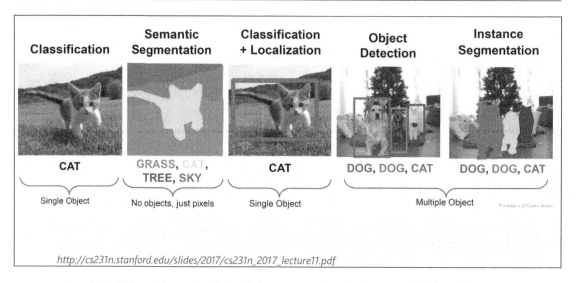

Figure 20.1: Different Computer Vision Tasks – source: Introduction to Artificial Intelligence and Computer Vision Revolution (https://www.slideshare.net/darian_f/introduction-to-the-artificial-intelligence-and-computer-vision-revolution)

Classification and localization

In the classification and localization task, not only do you have to report the class of object found in the image, but also the coordinates of the bounding box where the object appears in the image. This type of task assumes that there is only one instance of the object in an image.

This can be achieved by attaching a "regression head" in addition to the "classification head" in a typical classification network. Recall that in a classification network, the final output of convolution and pooling operations, called the feature map, is fed into a fully connected network that produces a vector of class probabilities. This fully connected network is called the classification head, and it is tuned using a categorical loss function (L_c) such as categorical cross-entropy.

Similarly, a regression head is another fully connected network that takes the feature map and produces a vector (x, y, w, h) representing the top left x and y coordinates, and the width and height of the bounding box. It is tuned using a continuous loss function (L_R) such as mean squared error. The entire network is tuned using a linear combination of the two losses, i.e.,

$$L = \alpha L_c + (1 - \alpha)L_r$$

Here, α is a hyperparameter and can take a value between 0 and 1. Unless the value is determined by some domain knowledge about the problem, it can be set to 0.5.

Figure 20.2 shows a typical classification and localization network architecture:

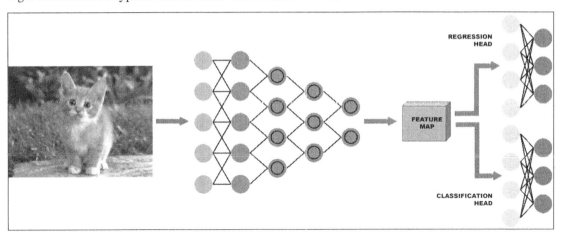

Figure 20.2: Network architecture for image classification and localization

As you can see, the only difference with respect to a typical CNN classification network is the additional regression head at the top right-hand side.

Semantic segmentation

Another class of problem that builds on the basic classification idea is "semantic segmentation." Here the aim is to classify every single pixel on the image as belonging to a single class.

An initial method of implementation could be to build a classifier network for each pixel, where the input is a small neighborhood around each pixel. In practice, this approach is not very performant, so an improvement over this implementation might be to run the image through convolutions that will increase the feature depth, while keeping the image width and height constant. Each pixel then has a feature map that can be sent through a fully connected network that predicts the class of the pixel. However, in practice, this is also quite expensive and is not normally used.

A third approach is to use a CNN encoder-decoder network, where the encoder decreases the width and height of the image but increases its depth (number of features), while the decoder uses transposed convolution operations to increase its size and decrease its depth. Transposed convolution (or upsampling) is the process of going in the opposite direction of a normal convolution. Input to this network is the image and the output is the segmentation map. A popular implementation of this encoder-decoder architecture is the U-Net (a good implementation is available at https://github. com/jakeret/tf_unet), originally developed for biomedical image segmentation, which has additional skip connections between corresponding layers of the encoder and decoder.

Figure 20.3 shows the U-Net architecture:

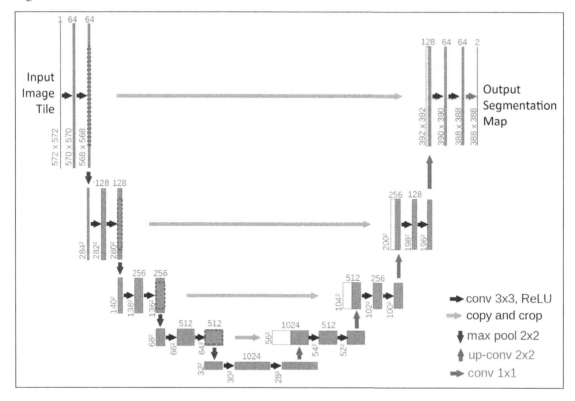

Figure 20.3: U-Net architecture

Object detection

The object detection task is similar to the classification and localization task. The big difference is that now there are multiple objects in the image, and for each one of them, we need to find the class and the bounding box coordinates. In addition, neither the number of objects nor their size is known in advance. As you can imagine, this is a difficult problem, and a fair amount of research has gone into it.

A first approach to the problem might be to create many random crops of the input image and, for each crop, apply the classification and localization network we described earlier. However, such an approach is very wasteful in terms of computing and unlikely to be very successful.

A more practical approach would be to use a tool such as Selective Search (*Selective Search for Object Recognition*, by Uijlings et al., `http://www.huppelen.nl/publications/selectiveSearchDraft.pdf`), which uses traditional computer vision techniques to find areas in the image that might contain objects. These regions are called "region proposals," and the network to detect them is called **Region-based CNN**, or **R-CNN**. In the original R-CNN, the regions were resized and fed into a network to yield image vectors. These vectors were then classified with an SVM-based classifier (see `https://en.wikipedia.org/wiki/Support-vector_machine`), and the bounding boxes proposed by the external tool were corrected using a linear regression network over the image vectors. An R-CNN network can be represented conceptually as shown in *Figure 20.4*:

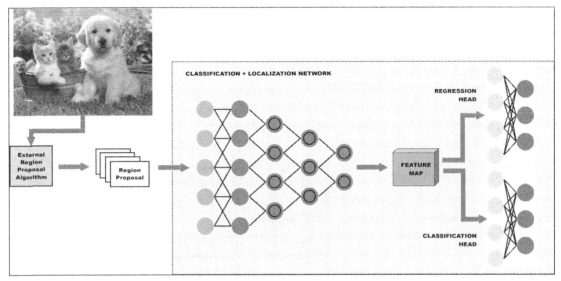

Figure 20.4: R-CNN network

The next iteration of the R-CNN network is called the Fast R-CNN. The Fast R-CNN still gets its region proposals from an external tool, but instead of feeding each region proposal through the CNN, the entire image is fed through the CNN and the region proposals are projected onto the resulting feature map. Each region of interest is fed through a **Region Of Interest** (**ROI**) pooling layer and then to a fully connected network, which produces a feature vector for the ROI.

ROI pooling is a widely used operation in object detection tasks using CNNs. The ROI pooling layer uses max pooling to convert the features inside any valid region of interest into a small feature map with a fixed spatial extent of H x W (where H and W are two hyperparameters). The feature vector is then fed into two fully connected networks, one to predict the class of the ROI and the other to correct the bounding box coordinates for the proposal. This is illustrated in *Figure 20.5*:

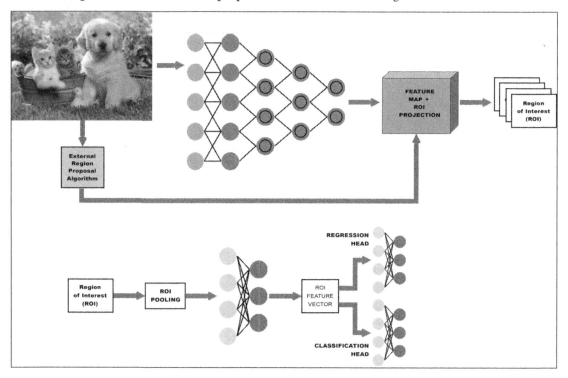

Figure 20.5: Fast R-CNN network architecture

The Fast R-CNN is about 25x faster than the R-CNN. The next improvement, called the Faster R-CNN (an implementation is at `https://github.com/tensorpack/tensorpack/tree/master/examples/FasterRCNN`), removes the external region proposal mechanism and replaces it with a trainable component, called the **Region Proposal Network** (**RPN**), within the network itself. The output of this network is combined with the feature map and passed in through a similar pipeline to the Fast R-CNN network, as shown in *Figure 20.6*.

The Faster R-CNN network is about 10x faster than the Fast R-CNN network, making it approximately 250x faster than an R-CNN network:

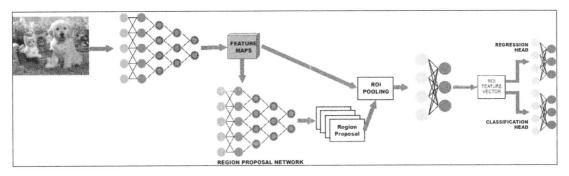

Figure 20.6: Faster R-CNN network architecture

Another somewhat different class of object detection networks are **Single Shot Detectors** (**SSD**) such as **YOLO** (**You Only Look Once**). In these cases, each image is split into a predefined number of parts using a grid. In the case of YOLO, a 7 x 7 grid is used, resulting in 49 sub-images. A predetermined set of crops with different aspect ratios are applied to each sub-image. Given B bounding boxes and C object classes, the output for each image is a vector of size $(7 * 7 * (5B + C))$. Each bounding box has a confidence and coordinates (x, y, w, h), and each grid has prediction probabilities for the different objects detected within them.

The YOLO network is a CNN, which does this transformation. The final predictions and bounding boxes are found by aggregating the findings from this vector. In YOLO, a single convolutional network predicts the bounding boxes and the related class probabilities. YOLO is the faster solution for object detection. An implementation is at `https://www.kaggle.com/aruchomu/yolo-v3-object-detection-in-tensorflow`.

Instance segmentation

Instance segmentation is similar to semantic segmentation – the process of associating each pixel of an image with a class label – with a few important distinctions. First, it needs to distinguish between different instances of the same class in an image. Second, it is not required to label every single pixel in the image. In some respects, instance segmentation is also similar to object detection, except that instead of bounding boxes, we want to find a binary mask that covers each object.

The second definition leads to the intuition behind the Mask R-CNN network. The Mask R-CNN is a Faster R-CNN with an additional CNN in front of its regression head, which takes as input the bounding box coordinates reported for each ROI and converts it to a binary mask [11]:

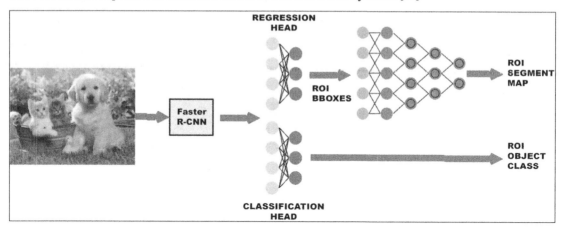

Figure 20.7: Mask R-CNN architecture

In April 2019, Google released Mask R-CNN in open source, pretrained with TPUs. This is available at

`https://colab.research.google.com/github/tensorflow/tpu/blob/master/models/official/`
`mask_rcnn/mask_rcnn_demo.ipynb`.

I suggest playing with the Colab notebook to see what the results are. In *Figure 20.8*, we see an example of image segmentation:

Figure 20.8: An example of image segmentation

Google also released another model trained on TPUs called DeepLab, and you can see an image (*Figure 20.9*) from the demo. This is available at

`https://colab.research.google.com/github/tensorflow/models/blob/master/research/deeplab/deeplab_demo.ipynb#scrollTo=edGukUHXyymr:`

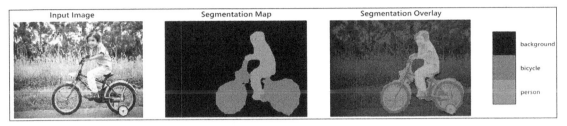

Figure 20.9: An example of image segmentation

In this section, we have covered, at a somewhat high level, various network architectures that are popular in computer vision. Note that all of them are composed by the same basic CNN and fully connected architectures. This composability is one of the most powerful features of deep learning. Hopefully, this has given you some ideas for networks that could be adapted for your own computer vision use cases.

Application zoos with tf.Keras and TensorFlow Hub

One of the nice things about transfer learning is that it is possible to reuse pretrained networks to save time and resources. There are many collections of ready-to-use networks out there, but the following two are the most used.

Keras Applications

Keras Applications (Keras Applications are available at `https://www.tensorflow.org/api_docs/python/tf/keras/applications`) includes models for image classification with weights trained on ImageNet (Xception, VGG16, VGG19, ResNet, ResNetV2, ResNeXt, InceptionV3, InceptionResNetV2, MobileNet, MobileNetV2, DenseNet, and NASNet). In addition, there are a few other reference implementations from the community for object detection and segmentation, sequence learning, reinforcement learning (see *Chapter 11*), and GANs (see *Chapter 9*).

TensorFlow Hub

TensorFlow Hub (available at `https://www.tensorflow.org/hub`) is an alternative collection of pretrained models. TensorFlow Hub includes modules for text classification, sentence encoding (see *Chapter 4*), image classification, feature extraction, image generation with GANs, and video classification. Currently, both Google and DeepMind contribute to TensorFlow Hub.

Let's look at an example of using `TF.Hub`. In this case, we have a simple image classifier using MobileNetv2:

```python
import matplotlib.pylab as plt
import tensorflow as tf
import tensorflow_hub as hub
import numpy as np
import PIL.Image as Image


classifier_url ="https://tfhub.dev/google/tf2-preview/mobilenet_v2/
classification/2" #@param {type:"string"}
IMAGE_SHAPE = (224, 224)
# wrap the hub to work with tf.keras
classifier = tf.keras.Sequential([
    hub.KerasLayer(classifier_url, input_shape=IMAGE_SHAPE+(3,))
])
grace_hopper = tf.keras.utils.get_file('image.jpg','https://storage.googleapis.
com/download.tensorflow.org/example_images/grace_hopper.jpg')
grace_hopper = Image.open(grace_hopper).resize(IMAGE_SHAPE)
grace_hopper = np.array(grace_hopper)/255.0
result = classifier.predict(grace_hopper[np.newaxis, ...])
predicted_class = np.argmax(result[0], axis=-1)
print (predicted_class)
```

Pretty simple indeed. Just remember to use `hub.KerasLayer()` for wrapping any Hub layer. In this section, we have discussed how to use TensorFlow Hub.

Next, we will focus on other CNN architectures.

Answering questions about images (visual Q&A)

One of the nice things about neural networks is that different media types can be combined together to provide a unified interpretation. For instance, **Visual Question Answering** (**VQA**) combines image recognition and text natural language processing. Training can use VQA (VQA is available at https://visualqa.org/), a dataset containing open-ended questions about images. These questions require an understanding of vision, language, and common knowledge to be answered. The following images are taken from a demo available at https://visualqa.org/.

Note the question at the top of the image, and the subsequent answers:

Figure 20.10: Examples of visual question and answers

If you want to start playing with VQA, the first thing is to get appropriate training datasets such as the VQA dataset, the CLEVR dataset (available at `https://cs.stanford.edu/people/jcjohns/clevr/`), or the FigureQA dataset (available at `https://datasets.maluuba.com/FigureQA`); alternatively, you can participate in a Kaggle VQA challenge (available at `https://www.kaggle.com/c/visual-question-answering`). Then you can build a model that is the combination of a CNN and an RNN and start experimenting. For instance, a CNN can be something like this code fragment, which takes an image with three channels (224 x 224) as input and produces a feature vector for the image:

```python
import tensorflow as tf
from tensorflow.keras import layers, models
# IMAGE
#
# Define CNN for visual processing
cnn_model = models.Sequential()
cnn_model.add(layers.Conv2D(64, (3, 3), activation='relu', padding='same',
        input_shape=(224, 224, 3)))
cnn_model.add(layers.Conv2D(64, (3, 3), activation='relu'))
cnn_model.add(layers.MaxPooling2D(2, 2))
cnn_model.add(layers.Conv2D(128, (3, 3), activation='relu', padding='same'))
cnn_model.add(layers.Conv2D(128, (3, 3), activation='relu'))
cnn_model.add(layers.MaxPooling2D(2, 2))
cnn_model.add(layers.Conv2D(256, (3, 3), activation='relu', padding='same'))
cnn_model.add(layers.Conv2D(256, (3, 3), activation='relu'))
cnn_model.add(layers.Conv2D(256, (3, 3), activation='relu'))
cnn_model.add(layers.MaxPooling2D(2, 2))
cnn_model.add(layers.Flatten())
cnn_model.summary()

#define the visual_model with proper input
image_input = layers.Input(shape=(224, 224, 3))
visual_model = cnn_model(image_input)
```

Text can be encoded with an RNN; for now, think of it as a black box taking a text fragment (the question) in input and producing a feature vector for the text:

```python
# TEXT
#
#define the RNN model for text processing
```

```
question_input = layers.Input(shape=(100,), dtype='int32')
emdedding = layers.Embedding(input_dim=10000, output_dim=256,
    input_length=100)(question_input)
encoded_question = layers.LSTM(256)(emdedding)
```

Then the two feature vectors (one for the image, and one for the text) are combined into one joint vector, which is provided as input to a dense network to produce the combined network:

```
# combine the encoded question and visual model
merged = layers.concatenate([encoded_question, visual_model])
#attach a dense network at the end
output = layers.Dense(1000, activation='softmax')(merged)

#get the combined model
vqa_model = models.Model(inputs=[image_input, question_input], outputs=output)
vqa_model.summary()
```

For instance, if we have a set of labeled images, then we can learn what the best questions and answers are for describing an image. The number of options is enormous! If you want to know more, I suggest that you investigate Maluuba, a start-up providing the FigureQA dataset with 100,000 figure images and 1,327,368 question-answer pairs in the training set. Maluuba has been recently acquired by Microsoft, and the lab is advised by Yoshua Bengio, one of the fathers of deep learning.

In this section, we have discussed how to implement visual Q&A. The next section is about style transfer, a deep learning technique used for training neural networks to create art.

Creating a DeepDream network

Another interesting application of CNNs is DeepDream, a computer vision program created by Google [8] that uses a CNN to find and enhance patterns in images. The result is a dream-like hallucinogenic effect. Similar to the previous example, we are going to use a pretrained network to extract features. However, in this case, we want to "enhance" patterns in images, meaning that we need to maximize some functions. This tells us that we need to use a gradient ascent and not a descent. First, let's see an example from Google gallery (available at https://colab.research.google.com/github/tensorflow/docs/blob/master/site/en/tutorials/generative/deepdream.ipynb) where the classic Seattle landscape is "incepted" with hallucinogenic dreams such as birds, cards, and strange flying objects.

Google released the DeepDream code as open source (available at `https://github.com/google/deepdream`), but we will use a simplified example made by a random forest (available at `https://www.tensorflow.org/tutorials/generative/deepdream`):

Figure 20.11: DeepDreaming Seattle

Let's start with some image preprocessing:

```
# Download an image and read it into a NumPy array,
def download(url):
    name = url.split("/")[-1]
    image_path = tf.keras.utils.get_file(name, origin=url)
    img = image.load_img(image_path)
    return image.img_to_array(img)


# Scale pixels to between (-1.0 and 1.0)
def preprocess(img):
    return (img / 127.5) - 1


# Undo the preprocessing above
def deprocess(img):
    img = img.copy()
    img /= 2.
    img += 0.5
    img *= 255.
```

```
    return np.clip(img, 0, 255).astype('uint8')

# Display an image
def show(img):
  plt.figure(figsize=(12,12))
  plt.grid(False)
  plt.axis('off')
  plt.imshow(img)

# https://commons.wikimedia.org/wiki/File:Flickr_-_Nicholas_T_-_Big_Sky_(1).jpg
url = 'https://upload.wikimedia.org/wikipedia/commons/thumb/d/d0/Flickr_-_
Nicholas_T_-_Big_Sky_%281%29.jpg/747px-Flickr_-_Nicholas_T_-_Big_Sky_%281%29.
jpg'
img = preprocess(download(url))
show(deprocess(img))
```

Now let's use the Inception pretrained network to extract features. We use several layers, and the goal is to maximize their activations. The `tf.keras` functional API is our friend here:

```
# We'll maximize the activations of these layers
names = ['mixed2', 'mixed3', 'mixed4', 'mixed5']
layers = [inception_v3.get_layer(name).output for name in names]

# Create our feature extraction model
feat_extraction_model = tf.keras.Model(inputs=inception_v3.input,
outputs=layers)

def forward(img):

  # Create a batch
  img_batch = tf.expand_dims(img, axis=0)

  # Forward the image through Inception, extract activations
  # for the layers we selected above
  return feat_extraction_model(img_batch)
```

The loss function is the mean of all the activation layers considered, normalized by the number of units in the layer itself:

```
def calc_loss(layer_activations):

  total_loss = 0

  for act in layer_activations:
```

```python
    # In gradient ascent, we'll want to maximize this value
    # so our image increasingly "excites" the layer
    loss = tf.math.reduce_mean(act)

    # Normalize by the number of units in the layer
    loss /= np.prod(act.shape)
    total_loss += loss

  return total_loss
```

Now let's run the gradient ascent:

```python
img = tf.Variable(img)
steps = 400

for step in range(steps):

  with tf.GradientTape() as tape:
    activations = forward(img)
    loss = calc_loss(activations)

  gradients = tape.gradient(loss, img)
  # Normalize the gradients
  gradients /= gradients.numpy().std() + 1e-8

  # Update our image by directly adding the gradients
  img.assign_add(gradients)

  if step % 50 == 0:
    clear_output()
    print ("Step %d, loss %f" % (step, loss))
    show(deprocess(img.numpy()))
    plt.show()

# Let's see the result
clear_output()
show(deprocess(img.numpy()))
```

This transforms the image on the left into the psychedelic image on the right:

Figure 20.12: DeepDreaming of a green field with clouds

Inspecting what a network has learned

A particularly interesting research effort is being devoted to understand what neural networks are actually learning in order to be able to recognize images so well. This is called neural network "interpretability." Activation atlases is a promising recent technique that aims to show the feature visualizations of averaged activation functions. In this way, activation atlases produce a global map seen through the eyes of the network. Let's look at a demo available at `https://distill.pub/2019/activation-atlas/`:

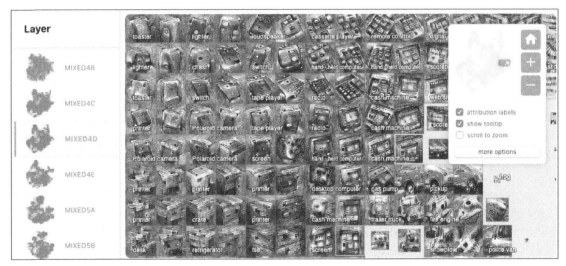

Figure 20.13: Examples of inspections

In this image, an InceptionV1 network used for vision classification reveals many fully realized features, such as electronics, screens, a Polaroid camera, buildings, food, animal ears, plants, and watery backgrounds. Note that grid cells are labeled with the classification they give the most support for. Grid cells are also sized according to the number of activations that are averaged within. This representation is very powerful because it allows us to inspect the different layers of a network and how the activation functions fire in response to the input.

In this section, we have seen many techniques to process images with CNNs. Next, we'll move on to video processing.

Video

In this section, we are going to discuss how to use CNNs with videos and the different techniques that we can use.

Classifying videos with pretrained nets in six different ways

Classifying videos is an area of active research because of the large amount of data needed for processing this type of media. Memory requirements are frequently reaching the limits of modern GPUs and a distributed form of training on multiple machines might be required. Researchers are currently exploring different directions of investigation, with increasing levels of complexity from the first approach to the sixth, as described below. Let's review them:

- The **first approach** consists of classifying one video frame at a time by considering each one of them as a separate image processed with a 2D CNN. This approach simply reduces the video classification problem to an image classification problem. Each video frame "emits" a classification output, and the video is classified by taking into account the more frequently chosen category for each frame.

- The **second approach** consists of creating one single network where a 2D CNN is combined with an RNN (see *Chapter 9*, *Generative Models*). The idea is that the CNN will take into account the image components and the RNN will take into account the sequence information for each video. This type of network can be very difficult to train because of the very high number of parameters to optimize.

- The **third approach** is to use a 3D ConvNet, where 3D ConvNets are an extension of 2D ConvNets operating on a 3D tensor (time, image width, and image height). This approach is another natural extension of image classification. Again, 3D ConvNets can be hard to train.

- The **fourth approach** is based on a clever idea: instead of using CNNs directly for classification, they can be used for storing offline features for each frame in the video. The idea is that feature extraction can be made very efficient with transfer learning, as shown in a previous recipe. After all the features are extracted, they can be passed as a set of inputs into an RNN, which will learn sequences across multiple frames and emit the final classification.

- The **fifth approach** is a simple variant of the fourth, where the final layer is an MLP instead of an RNN. In certain situations, this approach can be simpler and less expensive in terms of computational requirements.

- The **sixth approach** is a variant of the fourth, where the phase of feature extraction is realized with a 3D CNN that extracts spatial and visual features. These features are then passed into either an RNN or an MLP.

Deciding upon the best approach is strictly dependent on your specific application, and there is no definitive answer. The first three approaches are generally more computationally expensive and less clever, while the last three approaches are less expensive, and they frequently achieve better performance.

So far, we have explored how CNNs can be used for image and video applications. In the next section, we will apply these ideas within a text-based context.

Text documents

What do text and images have in common? At first glance, very little. However, if we represent a sentence or a document as a matrix, then this matrix is not much different from an image matrix where each cell is a pixel. So, the next question is, how can we represent a piece of text as a matrix?

Well, it is pretty simple: each row of a matrix is a vector that represents a basic unit for the text. Of course, now we need to define what a basic unit is. A simple choice could be to say that the basic unit is a character. Another choice would be to say that a basic unit is a word; yet another choice is to aggregate similar words together and then denote each aggregation (sometimes called cluster or embedding) with a representative symbol.

Note that regardless of the specific choice adopted for our basic units, we need to have a 1:1 mapping from basic units into integer IDs so that the text can be seen as a matrix. For instance, if we have a document with 10 lines of text and each line is a 100-dimensional embedding, then we will represent our text with a matrix of 10 x 100. In this very particular "image," a "pixel" is turned on if that sentence, X, contains the embedding, represented by position Y. You might also notice that a text is not really a matrix but more a vector because two words located in adjacent rows of text have very little in common. Indeed, this is a major difference when compared with images, where two pixels located in adjacent columns are likely to have some degree of correlation.

Now you might wonder: *I understand that we represent the text as a vector but, in doing so, we lose the position of the words. This position should be important, shouldn't it?* Well, it turns out that in many real applications, knowing whether a sentence contains a particular basic unit (a char, a word, or an aggregate) or not is pretty useful information even if we don't keep track of where exactly in the sentence this basic unit is located.

For instance, CNNs achieve pretty good results for **sentiment analysis**, where we need to understand if a piece of text has a positive or a negative sentiment; for **spam detection**, where we need to understand if a piece of text is useful information or spam; and for **topic categorization**, where we need to understand what a piece of text is all about. However, CNNs are not well suited for a **Part of Speech** (**POS**) analysis, where the goal is to understand what the logical role of every single word is (for example, a verb, an adverb, a subject, and so on). CNNs are also not well suited for **entity extraction**, where we need to understand where relevant entities are located in sentences.

Indeed, it turns out that a position is pretty useful information for the last two use cases. 1D ConvNets are very similar to 2D ConvNets. However, the former operates on a single vector, while the latter operates on matrices.

Using a CNN for sentiment analysis

Let's have a look at the code. First of all, we load the dataset with `tensorflow_datasets`. In this case we use IMDB, a collection of movie reviews:

```
import tensorflow as tf
from tensorflow.keras import datasets, layers, models, preprocessing
import tensorflow_datasets as tfds

max_len = 200
n_words = 10000
dim_embedding = 256
EPOCHS = 20
BATCH_SIZE =500

def load_data():
    #load data
    (X_train, y_train), (X_test, y_test) = datasets.imdb.load_data(num_words=n_
words)
    # Pad sequences with max_len
    X_train = preprocessing.sequence.pad_sequences(X_train, maxlen=max_len)
    X_test = preprocessing.sequence.pad_sequences(X_test, maxlen=max_len)
    return (X_train, y_train), (X_test, y_test)
```

Then we build a suitable CNN model. We use embeddings (see *Chapter 4, Word Embeddings*) to map the sparse vocabulary typically observed in documents into a dense feature space of dimensions `dim_embedding`. Then we use `Conv1D`, followed by a `GlobalMaxPooling1D` for averaging, and two `Dense` layers – the last one has only one neuron firing binary choices (positive or negative reviews):

```
def build_model():
    model = models.Sequential()
    #Input - Embedding Layer
    # the model will take as input an integer matrix of size (batch, input_
length)
    # the model will output dimension (input_length, dim_embedding)
    # the largest integer in the input should be no larger
    # than n_words (vocabulary size).
    model.add(layers.Embedding(n_words,
        dim_embedding, input_length=max_len))
```

```
    model.add(layers.Dropout(0.3))
    model.add(layers.Conv1D(256, 3, padding='valid',
        activation='relu'))

    #takes the maximum value of either feature vector from each of the n_words
features
    model.add(layers.GlobalMaxPooling1D())
    model.add(layers.Dense(128, activation='relu'))
    model.add(layers.Dropout(0.5))
    model.add(layers.Dense(1, activation='sigmoid'))

    return model

(X_train, y_train), (X_test, y_test) = load_data()
model=build_model()
model.summary()
```

The model has more than 2,700,000 parameters, and it is summarized as follows:

Layer (type)	Output Shape	Param #
embedding (Embedding)	(None, 200, 256)	2560000
dropout (Dropout)	(None, 200, 256)	0
conv1d (Conv1D)	(None, 198, 256)	196864
global_max_pooling1d (Globa lMaxPooling1D)	(None, 256)	0
dense (Dense)	(None, 128)	32896
dropout_1 (Dropout)	(None, 128)	0
dense_1 (Dense)	(None, 1)	129

```
Total params: 2,789,889
Trainable params: 2,789,889
Non-trainable params: 0
```

Then we compile and fit the model with the Adam optimizer and binary cross-entropy loss:

```
model.compile(optimizer = "adam", loss = "binary_crossentropy",
    metrics = ["accuracy"]
)


score = model.fit(X_train, y_train,
    epochs= EPOCHS,
    batch_size = BATCH_SIZE,
    validation_data = (X_test, y_test)
)


score = model.evaluate(X_test, y_test, batch_size=BATCH_SIZE)
print("\nTest score:", score[0])
print('Test accuracy:', score[1])
```

The final accuracy is 88.21%, showing that it is possible to successfully use CNNs for textual processing:

```
Epoch 19/20
25000/25000 [==============================] - 135s 5ms/sample - loss: 7.5276e-
04 - accuracy: 1.0000 - val_loss: 0.5753 - val_accuracy: 0.8818
Epoch 20/20
25000/25000 [==============================] - 129s 5ms/sample - loss: 6.7755e-
04 - accuracy: 0.9999 - val_loss: 0.5802 - val_accuracy: 0.8821
25000/25000 [==============================] - 23s 916us/sample - loss: 0.5802
- accuracy: 0.8821

Test score: 0.5801781857013703
Test accuracy: 0.88212
```

Note that many other non-image applications can also be converted to an image and classified using CNNs (see, for instance, https://becominghuman.ai/sound-classification-using-images-68d4770df426).

Audio and music

We have used CNNs for images, videos, and texts. Now let's have a look at how variants of CNNs can be used for audio.

So, you might wonder why learning to synthesize audio is so difficult. Well, each digital sound we hear is based on 16,000 samples per second (sometimes 48K or more), and building a predictive model where we learn to reproduce a sample based on all the previous ones is a very difficult challenge.

Dilated ConvNets, WaveNet, and NSynth

WaveNet is a deep generative model for producing raw audio waveforms. This breakthrough technology was introduced (available at https://deepmind.com/blog/wavenet-a-generative-model-for-raw-audio/) by Google DeepMind for teaching computers how to speak. The results are truly impressive, and online you can find examples of synthetic voices where the computer learns how to talk with the voice of celebrities such as Matt Damon. There are experiments showing that WaveNet improved the current state-of-the-art **Text-to-Speech** (**TTS**) systems, reducing the difference with respect to human voices by 50% for both US English and Mandarin Chinese. The metric used for comparison is called **Mean Opinion Score** (**MOS**), a subjective paired comparison test. In the MOS tests, after listening to each sound stimulus, the subjects were asked to rate the naturalness of the stimulus on a five-point scale from "Bad" (1) to "Excellent" (5).

What is even cooler is that DeepMind demonstrated that WaveNet can be also used to teach computers how to generate the sound of musical instruments such as piano music.

Now some definitions. TTS systems are typically divided into two different classes: concatenative and parametric.

Concatenative TTS is where single speech voice fragments are first memorized and then recombined when the voice has to be reproduced. However, this approach does not scale because it is possible to reproduce only the memorized voice fragments, and it is not possible to reproduce new speakers or different types of audio without memorizing the fragments from the beginning.

Parametric TTS is where a model is created to store all the characteristic features of the audio to be synthesized. Before WaveNet, the audio generated with parametric TTS was less natural than concatenative TTS. WaveNet enabled significant improvement by modeling directly the production of audio sounds, instead of using intermediate signal processing algorithms as in the past.

In principle, WaveNet can be seen as a stack of 1D convolutional layers with a constant stride of one and with no pooling layers. Note that the input and the output have by construction the same dimension, so ConvNets are well suited to modeling sequential data such as audio sounds. However, it has been shown that in order to reach a large size for the receptive field in the output neuron, it is necessary to either use a massive number of large filters or increase the network depth prohibitively. Remember that the receptive field of a neuron in a layer is the cross-section of the previous layer from which neurons provide inputs. For this reason, pure ConvNets are not so effective in learning how to synthesize audio.

The key intuition behind WaveNet is the so-called **Dilated Causal Convolutions** [5] (sometimes called **atrous convolution**), which simply means that some input values are skipped when the filter of a convolutional layer is applied. "Atrous" is a "bastardization" of the French expression "à trous," meaning "with holes." So an atrous convolution is a convolution with holes. As an example, in one dimension, a filter w of size 3 with a dilation of 1 would compute the following sum: $w[0]\, x[0] + w[1]\, x[2] + w[3]\, x[4]$.

In short, in D-dilated convolution, usually the stride is 1, but nothing prevents you from using other strides. An example is given in *Figure 20.14* with increased dilatation (hole) sizes = 0, 1, 2:

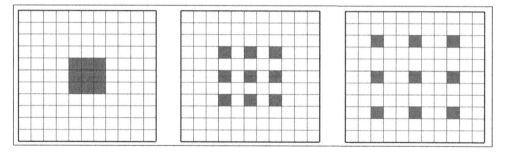

Figure 20.14: Dilatation with increased sizes

Thanks to this simple idea of introducing *holes*, it is possible to stack multiple dilated convolutional layers with exponentially increasing filters and learn long-range input dependencies without having an excessively deep network.

A WaveNet is therefore a ConvNet where the convolutional layers have various dilation factors, allowing the receptive field to grow exponentially with depth and therefore efficiently cover thousands of audio timesteps.

When we train, the inputs are sounds recorded from human speakers. The waveforms are quantized to a fixed integer range. A WaveNet defines an initial convolutional layer accessing only the current and previous input. Then, there is a stack of dilated ConvNet layers, still accessing only current and previous inputs. At the end, there is a series of dense layers combining previous results, followed by a softmax activation function for categorical outputs.

At each step, a value is predicted from the network and fed back into the input. At the same time, a new prediction for the next step is computed. The loss function is the cross-entropy between the output for the current step and the input at the next step. *Figure 20.15* shows the visualization of a WaveNet stack and its receptive field as introduced in Aaron van den Oord [9]. Note that generation can be slow because the waveform has to be synthesized in a sequential fashion, as x_t must be sampled first in order to obtain $x_{>t}$ where x is the input:

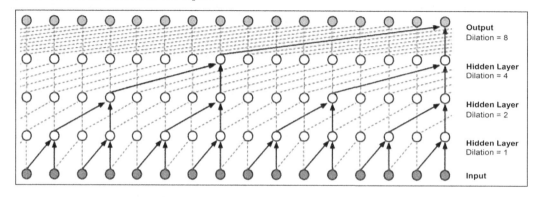

Figure 20.15: WaveNet internal connections

A method for performing a sampling in parallel has been proposed in Parallel WaveNet [10], which achieves a three orders-of-magnitude speedup. This uses two networks as a WaveNet teacher network, which is slow but ensures a correct result, and a WaveNet student network, which tries to mimic the behavior of the teacher; this can prove to be less accurate but is faster. This approach is similar to the one used for GANs (see *Chapter 9, Generative Models*) but the student does not try to fool the teacher, as typically happens in GANs. In fact, the model is not just quicker but also of higher fidelity, capable of creating waveforms with 24,000 samples per second:

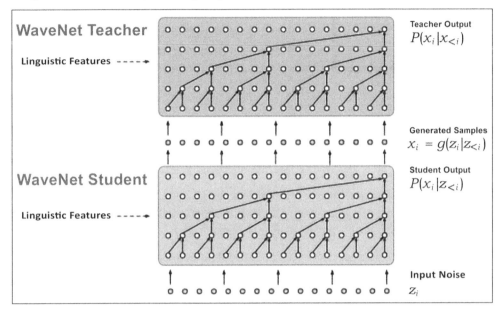

Figure 20.16: Examples of WaveNet Student and Teacher

This model has been deployed in production at Google, and is currently being used to serve Google Assistant queries in real time to millions of users. At the annual I/O developer conference in May 2018, it was announced that new Google Assistant voices were available thanks to WaveNet.

Two implementations of WaveNet models for TensorFlow are currently available. One is the original implementation of DeepMind's WaveNet, and the other is called Magenta NSynth. The original WaveNet version is available at `https://github.com/ibab/tensorflow-wavenet`. NSynth is an evolution of WaveNet recently released by the Google Brain group, which, instead of being causal, aims at seeing the entire context of the input chunk. Magenta is available at `https://magenta.tensorflow.org/nsynth`.

The neural network is truly complex, as depicted in the image below, but for the sake of this introductory discussion, it is sufficient to know that the network learns how to reproduce its input by using an approach based on reducing the error during the encoding/decoding phases:

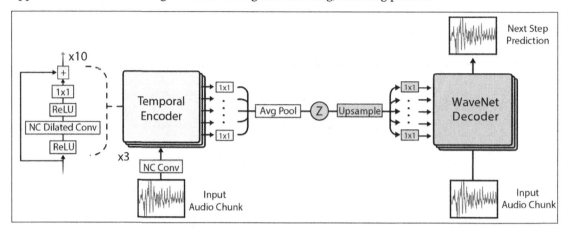

Figure 20.17: Magenta internal architecture

If you are interested in understanding more, I would suggest having a look at the online Colab notebook where you can play with models generated with NSynth. NSynth Colab is available at `https://colab. research.google.com/notebooks/magenta/nsynth/nsynth.ipynb`.

MuseNet is a very recent and impressive cool audio generation tool developed by OpenAI. MuseNet uses a sparse transformer to train a 72-layer network with 24 attention heads. MuseNet is available at `https://openai.com/blog/musenet/`. Transformers, discussed in *Chapter 6*, are very good at predicting what comes next in a sequence – whether text, images, or sound.

In transformers, every output element is connected to every input element, and the weightings between them are dynamically calculated according to a process called attention. MuseNet can produce up to 4-minute musical compositions with 10 different instruments, and can combine styles from country, to Mozart, to the Beatles. For instance, I generated a remake of Beethoven's "Für Elise" in the style of Lady Gaga with piano, drums, guitar, and bass. You can try this for yourself at the link provided under the section **Try MuseNet**:

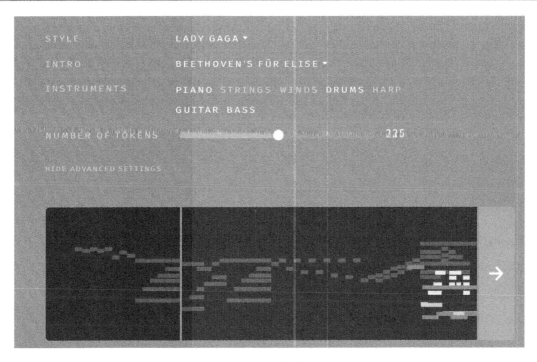

Figure 20.18: An example of using MuseNet

A summary of convolution operations

In this section, we present a summary of different convolution operations. A convolutional layer has I input channels and produces O output channels. I x O x K parameters are used, where K is the number of values in the kernel.

Basic CNNs

Let's remind ourselves briefly what a CNN is. CNNs take in an input image (two dimensions), text (two dimensions), or video (three dimensions) and apply multiple filters to the input. Each filter is like a flashlight sliding across the areas of the input, and the areas that it is shining over are called the receptive field. Each filter is a tensor of the same depth of the input (for instance, if the image has a depth of three, then the filter must also have a depth of three).

When the filter is sliding, or convolving, around the input image, the values in the filter are multiplied by the values of the input. The multiplications are then summarized into one single value. This process is repeated for each location, producing an activation map (a.k.a. a feature map). Of course, it is possible to use multiple filters where each filter will act as a feature identifier. For instance, for images, the filter can identify edges, colors, lines, and curves. The key intuition is to treat the filter values as weights and fine-tune them during training via backpropagation.

A convolution layer can be configured by using the following config parameters:

- **Kernel size:** This is the field of view of the convolution.
- **Stride:** This is the step size of the kernel when we traverse the image.
- **Padding:** Defines how the border of our sample is handled.

Dilated convolution

Dilated convolutions (or atrous convolutions) introduce another config parameter:

- **Dilation rate:** This is the spacing between the values in a kernel.

Dilated convolutions are used in many contexts including audio processing with WaveNet.

Transposed convolution

Transposed convolution is a transformation going in the opposite direction of a normal convolution. For instance, this can be useful to project feature maps into a higher dimensional space or for building convolutional autoencoders (see *Chapter 8, Autoencoders*). One way to think about transposed convolution is to compute the output shape of a normal CNN for a given input shape first. Then we invert input and output shapes with the transposed convolution. TensorFlow 2.0 supports transposed convolutions with Conv2DTranspose layers, which can be used, for instance, in GANs (see *Chapter 9, Generative Models*) for generating images.

Separable convolution

Separable convolution aims at separating the kernel in multiple steps. Let the convolution be $y = conv(x, k)$ where y is the output, x is the input, and k is the kernel. Let's assume the kernel is separable, $k = k1.k2$ where . is the dot product – in this case, instead of doing a 2-dimension convolution with k, we can get to the same result by doing two 1-dimension convolutions with $k1$ and $k2$. Separable convolutions are frequently used to save on computation resources.

Depthwise convolution

Let's consider an image with multiple channels. In the normal 2D convolution, the filter is as deep as the input, and it allows us to mix channels for generating each element of the output. In depthwise convolutions, each channel is kept separate, the filter is split into channels, each convolution is applied separately, and the results are stacked back together into one tensor.

Depthwise separable convolution

This convolution should not be confused with the separable convolution. After completing the depthwise convolution, an additional step is performed: a 1x1 convolution across channels. Depthwise separable convolutions are used in Xception. They are also used in MobileNet, a model particularly useful for mobile and embedded vision applications because of its reduced model size and complexity.

In this section, we have discussed all the major forms of convolution. The next section will discuss capsule networks, a new form of learning introduced in 2017.

Capsule networks

Capsule networks (or CapsNets) are a very recent and innovative type of deep learning network. This technique was introduced at the end of October 2017 in a seminal paper titled *Dynamic Routing Between Capsules* by Sara Sabour, Nicholas Frost, and Geoffrey Hinton (https://arxiv.org/abs/1710.09829) [14]. Hinton is the father of deep learning and, therefore, the whole deep learning community is excited to see the progress made with Capsules. Indeed, CapsNets are already beating the best CNN on MNIST classification, which is... well, impressive!!

What is the problem with CNNs?

In CNNs, each layer "understands" an image at a progressive level of granularity. As we discussed in multiple sections, the first layer will most likely recognize straight lines or simple curves and edges, while subsequent layers will start to understand more complex shapes such as rectangles up to complex forms such as human faces.

Now, one critical operation used for CNNs is pooling. Pooling aims at creating positional invariance and it is used after each CNN layer to make any problem computationally tractable. However, pooling introduces a significant problem because it forces us to lose all the positional data. This is not good. Think about a face: it consists of two eyes, a mouth, and a nose, and what is important is that there is a spatial relationship between these parts (for example, the mouth is below the nose, which is typically below the eyes). Indeed, Hinton said: *The pooling operation used in convolutional neural networks is a big mistake and the fact that it works so well is a disaster*. Technically, we do not need positional invariance but instead we need equivariance. Equivariance is a fancy term for indicating that we want to understand the rotation or proportion change in an image, and we want to adapt the network accordingly. In this way, the spatial positioning among the different components in an image is not lost.

What is new with capsule networks?

According to Hinton et al., our brain has modules called "capsules," and each capsule is specialized in handling a particular type of information. In particular, there are capsules that work well for "understanding" the concept of position, the concept of size, the concept of orientation, the concept of deformation, textures, and so on. In addition to that, the authors suggest that our brain has particularly efficient mechanisms for dynamically routing each piece of information to the capsule that is considered best suited for handling a particular type of information.

So, the main difference between CNN and CapsNets is that with a CNN, we keep adding layers for creating a deep network, while with CapsNet, we nest a neural layer inside another. A capsule is a group of neurons that introduces more structure to a network, and it produces a vector to signal the existence of an entity in an image. In particular, Hinton uses the length of the activity vector to represent the probability that the entity exists and its orientation to represent the instantiation parameters. When multiple predictions agree, a higher-level capsule becomes active. For each possible parent, the capsule produces an additional prediction vector.

Now a second innovation comes in place: we will use dynamic routing across capsules and will no longer use the raw idea of pooling. A lower-level capsule prefers to send its output to higher-level capsules for which the activity vectors have a big scalar product, with the prediction coming from the lower-level capsule. The parent with the largest scalar prediction vector product increases the capsule bond. All the other parents decrease their bond. In other words, the idea is that if a higher-level capsule agrees with a lower-level one, then it will ask to send more information of that type. If there is no agreement, it will ask to send fewer of them. This dynamic routing by the agreement method is superior to the current mechanism like max pooling and, according to Hinton, routing is ultimately a way to parse the image. Indeed, max pooling is ignoring anything but the largest value, while dynamic routing selectively propagates information according to the agreement between lower layers and upper layers.

A third difference is that a new nonlinear activation function has been introduced. Instead of adding a squashing function to each layer as in CNN, CapsNet adds a squashing function to a nested set of layers. The nonlinear activation function is represented in *Equation 1*, and it is called the squashing function:

$$v_j = \frac{\|s_j\|^2}{1 + \|s_j\|^2} \frac{s_j}{\|s_j\|} \tag{1}$$

where v_j is the vector output of capsule j and s_j is its total input.

Moreover, Hinton and others show that a discriminatively trained, multi-layer capsule system achieves state-of-the-art performances on MNIST and is considerably better than a convolutional net at recognizing highly overlapping digits.

Based on the paper *Dynamic Routing Between Capsules*, a simple CapsNet architecture looks as follows:

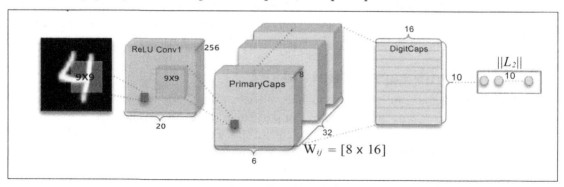

Figure 20.19: An example of CapsNet

The architecture is shallow with only two convolutional layers and one fully connected layer. Conv1 has 256 9 x 9 convolution kernels with a stride of 1 and ReLU activation. The role of this layer is to convert pixel intensities to the activities of local feature detectors that are then used as inputs to the PrimaryCapsules layer. PrimaryCapsules is a convolutional capsule layer with 32 channels; each primary capsule contains 8 convolutional units with a 9 x 9 kernel and a stride of 2. In total, PrimaryCapsules has [32, 6, 6] capsule outputs (each output is an 8D vector) and each capsule in the [6, 6] grid shares its weights with each other. The final layer (DigitCaps) has one 16D capsule per digit class and each one of these capsules receives input from all the other capsules in the layer below. Routing happens only between two consecutive capsule layers (for example, PrimaryCapsules and DigitCaps).

Summary

In this chapter, we have seen many applications of CNNs across very different domains, from traditional image processing and computer vision to close-enough video processing, not-so-close audio processing, and text processing. In just a few years, CNNs have taken machine learning by storm.

Nowadays, it is not uncommon to see multimodal processing, where text, images, audio, and videos are considered together to achieve better performance, frequently by means of combining CNNs together with a bunch of other techniques such as RNNs and reinforcement learning. Of course, there is much more to consider, and CNNs have recently been applied to many other domains such as genetic inference [13], which are, at least at first glance, far away from the original scope of their design.

References

1. Yosinski, J. and Clune, Y. B. J. *How transferable are features in deep neural networks*. Advances in Neural Information Processing Systems 27, pp. 3320–3328.

2. Szegedy, C., Vanhoucke, V., Ioffe, S., Shlens, J., and Wojna, Z. (2016). *Rethinking the Inception Architecture for Computer Vision*. 2016 IEEE Conference on Computer Vision and Pattern Recognition (CVPR), pp. 2818–2826.

3. Sandler, M., Howard, A., Zhu, M., Zhmonginov, A., and Chen, L. C. (2019). *MobileNetV2: Inverted Residuals and Linear Bottlenecks*. Google Inc.

4. Krizhevsky, A., Sutskever, I., Hinton, G. E., (2012). *ImageNet classification with deep convolutional neural networks*.

5. Huang, G., Liu, Z., van der Maaten, L., and Weinberger, K. Q. (28 Jan 2018). *Densely Connected Convolutional Networks*. http://arxiv.org/abs/1608.06993

6. Chollet, F. (2017). *Xception: Deep Learning with Depthwise Separable Convolutions*. https://arxiv.org/abs/1610.02357

7. Gatys, L. A., Ecker, A. S., and Bethge, M. (2016). *A Neural Algorithm of Artistic Style*. https://arxiv.org/abs/1508.06576

8. Mordvintsev, A., Olah, C., and Tyka, M. (2015). *DeepDream - a code example for visualizing Neural Networks*. Google Research.

9. van den Oord, A., Dieleman, S., Zen, H., Simonyan, K., Vinyals, O., Graves, A., Kalchbrenner, N., Senior, A., and Kavukcuoglu, K. (2016). *WaveNet: A generative model for raw audio*. arXiv preprint.

10. van den Oord, A., Li, Y., Babuschkin, I., Simonyan, K., Vinyals, O., Kavukcuoglu, K., van den Driessche, G., Lockhart, E., Cobo, L. C., Stimberg, F., Casagrande, N., Grewe, D., Noury, S., Dieleman, S., Elsen, E., Kalchbrenner, N., Zen, H., Graves, A., King, H., Walters, T., Belov, D., and Hassabis, D. (2017). *Parallel WaveNet: Fast High-Fidelity Speech Synthesis.*

11. He, K., Gkioxari, G., Dollár, P., and Girshick, R. (2018). *Mask R-CNN.*

12. Chen, L-C., Zhu, Y., Papandreou, G., Schroff, F., and Adam, H. (2018). *Encoder-Decoder with Atrous Separable Convolution for Semantic Image Segmentation.*

13. Flagel, L., Brandvain, Y., and Schrider, D.R. (2018). *The Unreasonable Effectiveness of Convolutional Neural Networks in Population Genetic Inference.*

14. Sabour, S., Frosst, N., and Hinton, G. E. (2017). *Dynamic Routing Between Capsules* https://arxiv.org/abs/1710.09829

Join our book's Discord space

Join our Discord community to meet like-minded people and learn alongside more than 2000 members at: https://packt.link/keras

packt.com

Subscribe to our online digital library for full access to over 7,000 books and videos, as well as industry leading tools to help you plan your personal development and advance your career. For more information, please visit our website.

Why subscribe?

- Spend less time learning and more time coding with practical eBooks and Videos from over 4,000 industry professionals
- Improve your learning with Skill Plans built especially for you
- Get a free eBook or video every month
- Fully searchable for easy access to vital information
- Copy and paste, print, and bookmark content

At www.packt.com, you can also read a collection of free technical articles, sign up for a range of free newsletters, and receive exclusive discounts and offers on Packt books and eBooks.

Other Books
You May Enjoy

If you enjoyed this book, you may be interested in these other books by Packt:

Machine Learning with PyTorch and Scikit-Learn

Sebastian Raschka

Yuxi (Hayden) Liu

Vahid Mirjalili

ISBN: 9781801819312

- Explore frameworks, models, and techniques for machines to 'learn' from data
- Use scikit-learn for machine learning and PyTorch for deep learning
- Train machine learning classifiers on images, text, and more
- Build and train neural networks, transformers, and boosting algorithms
- Discover best practices for evaluating and tuning models
- Predict continuous target outcomes using regression analysis
- Dig deeper into textual and social media data using sentiment analysis

Transformers for Natural Language Processing, Second Edition

Denis Rothman

ISBN: 9781803247335

- Find out how ViT and CLIP label images (including blurry ones!) and create images from a sentence using DALL-E
- Discover new techniques to investigate complex language problems
- Compare and contrast the results of GPT-3 against T5, GPT-2, and BERT-based transformers
- Carry out sentiment analysis, text summarization, casual speech analysis, machine translations, and more using TensorFlow, PyTorch, and GPT-3
- Measure the productivity of key transformers to define their scope, potential, and limits in production

Natural Language Processing with TensorFlow, Second Edition

Thushan Ganegedara

ISBN: 9781838641351

- Learn core concepts of NLP and techniques with TensorFlow
- Use state-of-the-art Transformers and how they are used to solve NLP tasks
- Perform sentence classification and text generation using CNNs and RNNs
- Utilize advanced models for machine translation and image caption generation
- Build end-to-end data pipelines in TensorFlow
- Learn interesting facts and practices related to the task at hand
- Create word representations of large amounts of data for deep learning

Packt is searching for authors like you

If you're interested in becoming an author for Packt, please visit authors.packtpub.com and apply today. We have worked with thousands of developers and tech professionals, just like you, to help them share their insight with the global tech community. You can make a general application, apply for a specific hot topic that we are recruiting an author for, or submit your own idea.

Share your thoughts

Now you've finished *Deep Learning with TensorFlow and Keras, Third Edition*, we'd love to hear your thoughts! Scan the QR code below to go straight to the Amazon review page for this book and share your feedback or leave a review on the site that you purchased it from.

https://packt.link/r/1803232919

Your review is important to us and the tech community and will help us make sure we're delivering excellent quality content.

Index

Made in the USA
Las Vegas, NV
10 November 2022

59172762R00385